W9-BGI-349

The Sports Event Management and Marketing Playbook

Second Edition

Frank Supovitz
Robert Goldwater

WILEY

This book is printed on acid-free paper. ♾

Published by John Wiley & Sons, Inc., Hoboken, New Jersey.
Published simultaneously in Canada.

Library of Congress Cataloging-in-Publication Data

Supovitz, Frank.
The sports event management and marketing playbook / Frank Supovitz, Robert Goldwater.— Second edition.
1 online resource.
Includes index.
Description based on print version record and CIP data provided by publisher; resource not viewed.
ISBN 978-1-118-24411-1 (cloth)
1. Sports—Marketing—Handbooks, manuals, etc. 2. Sports—Economic aspects—Handbooks, manuals, etc. 3. Sports administration—Handbooks, manuals, etc. I. Title.
GV716
796.0688—dc23

2013006400

Printed in the United States of America
10 9 8 7 6 5 4 3 2

The Sports Event Management and Marketing Playbook

Second Edition

The Wiley Event Management Series

Series Editor: Dr. Joe Goldblatt, Ed.D., FRSA

Special Events: Creating and Sustaining a New World for Celebration Seventh Edition
by Dr. Joe Goldblatt, FRSA

The Sports Event Management and Marketing Playbook, Second Edition
by Frank Supovitz and Robert Goldwater

Ethics and Corporate Responsibility in the Meetings and Events Industry
by Elizabeth Henderson, CMP, CMM, M.E. Des., and Mariela McIlwraith, CMP, CMM, MBA

The Complete Guide to Greener Meetings and Events
by Samuel deBlanc Goldblatt

The Complete Guide to Careers in Special Events
by Gene Columbus

Event Marketing: How to Successfully Promote Events, Festivals, Conventions, and Expositions
by C. A. Preston

Professional Event Coordination, Second Edition
by Julia Rutherford Silvers, CSEP

Dictionary of Event Management, Second Edition
by Dr. Joe Goldblatt, CSEP, and Kathleen S. Nelson, CSEP

Corporate Event Project Management
by William O'Toole and Phyllis Mikolaitis

Event Risk Management and Safety
by Peter E. Tarlow, Ph.D.

Event Sponsorship
by Bruce E. Skinner and Vladimir Rukavina

The Complete Guide to Event Entertainment and Production
by Mark Sonder, MM, CSEP

The Guide to Successful Destination Management
by Pat Schaumann, CMP, CSEP

Art of the Event: Complete Guide to Designing and Decorating Special Events
by James C. Monroe, CMP, CSEP

Global Meetings and Exhibitions
by Carol Krugman, CMP, CMM, and Rudy R. Wright, CMP

DEDICATION

This book is dedicated to
Edwin and Shirley Supovitz,
who encouraged their son to chase his dreams,
and to Catherine, Matt, Ethan, and Jake, who live within them;
and to Bob Goldwater,
who introduced the magic of sports events to his ever-grateful son,
and to Colleen Callahan,
who introduced the gift of sharing magical events with her ever-grateful husband.

CONTENTS

FOREWORD

There is nothing more exciting than attending a football game.

Growing up in Washington, D.C., in the 1960s, I was fortunate to attend a few Colts and Redskins games at Memorial Stadium and RFK Stadium and fell in love with football from those seats. I often hear from fans that attending NFL games with their family and friends is how they, too, fell in love with football. Nothing beats being surrounded by passionate reactions—smiles, shouts, high fives—in response to each and every play. And when that big play happens—the 80-yard run, the one-handed touchdown catch, the pick-six—nothing replaces being there.

Nearly half a century after my first football game, I am still fortunate to attend NFL games around the country. During a time when distractions are numerous and constant, we firmly believe that the live event experience is more important than ever. We strive to do everything possible to make sure our stadiums stay full, because that's where the excitement is created. When you turn on a football game on TV, you want to see a full stadium.

We continue to push ourselves to make it more attractive for fans to come to our stadiums by investing in our stadiums, implementing new technologies to enhance the fan experience, and with our teams, instituting a Fan Code of Conduct to promote good fan behavior. The home viewing experience has become so outstanding that we have to compete with that in some fashion by making sure that we create an exciting environment in our stadiums.

The in-stadium experience directly affects the television viewing experience. A live event with an excited and lively audience is the building block to good television. While the enhancements implemented in-stadium may only be experienced directly by 70,000 fans, there is a ripple effect felt by millions of fans watching at home—when the live event is produced correctly.

Live games are the essence of the National Football League—from preseason, to 256 regular season games, to the playoffs and Super Bowl—but it does not stop there. Over the past three decades we have seen the incredible growth of the NFL Draft and built the NFL Scouting Combine into a national event. In 2012, we executed our 10th NFL Kickoff celebration to rally the country around the start of our 93rd season.

When Frank Supovitz joined our team in 2005, I knew we had the right man to take NFL events to the next level. Frank's original title was head of the NFL Special Events Department, but shortly after he joined us, we changed it to the "NFL Events Department" because I felt strongly that everything we do as a league should be "special."

And Frank ensures that is the case.

Frank and his team have led the NFL and our fans through many successful and memorable events, including Super Bowl XLVI, the most-watched television show in US history. I have always been impressed with Frank's ability to understand everyone's needs and priorities and plan and execute an event that satisfies all parties—from the players and teams, the fans, the broadcasters and the viewers. With his vast experience and industry knowledge, I cannot think of a better author for this book. And in true form, as Frank always pulls in others' voices and insight to shape plans and strategy, for this edition he's joined as co-author by another respected sports event veteran, Bobby Goldwater.

As I am reminded with every game and every production, the most incredible part of planning NFL events is that we never know how they will end. For all the organization, logistics, time, and effort that Frank and his team invest in our events, planning for the unexpected has to be part of any plan. The NFL is the ultimate reality show, and there is nothing that can prepare any of us for the outcome.

While a lot has changed since the 1960s when I attended my first football game, one thing stays the same: There is nothing more exciting than being in those seats, part of one collective gasp, when that special moment happens.

—Roger S. Goodell
Commissioner of the National Football League

SERIES EDITOR FOREWORD

Have you ever dreamed of having a friendly security guard open the back gate of a major stadium at the National Football League Super Bowl, the Major League Baseball World Series, the Olympic Games, the World Cup, Wimbledon, the Ryder Cup, the Stanley Cup Finals, or another major sports event and say, "Come on in!" This book provides you with this rare and exclusive opportunity to step behind the scenes at sports events, both large and small, with tour guides who are two of the world's leading figures in sports event management.

In this new book, you will meet many sports event management and marketing heroes. Two of my personal heroes are the authors themselves. The American mythologist, writer, and lecturer Joseph Campbell (1904–1987) defined a hero as someone who has given his or her life to something bigger than oneself. Indeed, the authors of this new book have given you their lifetime experiences in sports management and marketing to help advance this rapidly growing field of study and practice.

Frank Supovitz and Bobby Goldwater have over 60 years of combined professional experience in the world of staging professional sports events. Frank and Bobby have brought their rich experience, skills, and contacts to provide you with a fast lane for entering the field of sports event management or improving your current practice. Frank rose from serving as an usher at Radio City Music Hall in New York City to serving as Senior Vice President for Events for one of the world's most famous sports brands, the United States' National Football League (NFL). Along the way he amassed such credits as the opening and closing ceremonies of the US Olympic Festival and the NFL Super Bowl XXII halftime show that featured 88 grand pianos, and for many years was in charge of events for the National Hockey League. Bobby's career includes serving as a leading light in the world of sports administration through his transformational leadership of major sports stadiums and arenas in the United States.

Both Frank and Bobby have spent time in college and university classrooms sharing their vast expertise with the next generation of sports event promoters and producers. Therefore, they are skilled teachers as well as experienced practioners. This new and improved ***Second Edition*** of ***The Sports Events Management and Marketing Playbook*** includes the sum and substance of their combined experience as both practioners as well as educators. By opening this book, you are walking into a dynamic and lively classroom filled with dozens of exciting and relevant case studies told by those individuals who were there on the sidelines closely examining all of the action.

This new edition features new important and valuable information that, to my knowledge, has not appeared before in other sports events books. The authors have included examples of how to best utilize the growing technological presence in sports to create greater efficiencies and reach more and more fans in the future. In addition, they have described in detail how you may take charge of your career to help achieve your dreams in this highly competitive industry. Finally, and most importantly, they provide many new examples of how corporate social responsibility (CSR) may be incorporated through sports events to help you create a sustainable future for your sports organization as well as yourself.

Many years ago, Frank Supovitz invited me to shadow him while he produced the National Hockey League All-Star Game in New York City's famed Madison Square Garden. I took copious notes while Frank walked through the world-famous arena inspecting the pressroom setup, greeting the officials and players, and finally settling into his command center next to the penalty box. Shortly after the game began, hockey pucks began flying near our heads and I noticed how Frank remained calm and focused on the details of the sports event. He was not distracted by other aspects that he could not control. During a break between periods, a friendly and handsome athlete skated up to the penalty box and graciously signed the hockey pucks that had landed practically in our laps. I asked Frank who this player was, and he smiled and said, "Wayne Gretzky."

For the one or two people in the world who do not know the name Wayne Gretzky, he was and is one of the universe's most honored athletes who, when he was asked to describe the secret of his success, famously said, "A good hockey player plays where the puck is. A *great* hockey player plays where the puck is going to be."

Frank Supovitz and Bobby Goldwater have expertly skated to the future of sports event management and marketing to provide you with a great opportunity for future success. Joseph Campbell is also well known for his philosophy that is encapsulated in the phrase "Follow your bliss." Therefore, I invite you to follow your bliss, as have the authors, in sports event management and marketing and create a future that is truly boundless. Indeed, this book is your behind-the-scenes guide to becoming a future hero in one of the world's most exciting and fastest-growing industries.

—Dr. Joe Goldblatt, Ed.D., FRSA
Wiley Event Management Series Editor
Executive Director
International Centre for the Study of Planned Events
Queen Margaret University
Edinburgh, Scotland

PREFACE

Sports Events Are Something Special

Dr. Joe Goldblatt, Ed.D., FRSA, tells the story of how the late Disneyland executive Robert F. Jani developed the Main Street Electrical Parade. On opening day, as Walt Disney noticed his guests leaving his new park in the late afternoon, he turned to Jani, then his director of public relations, and asked him to create an attraction to keep people in the park into the night. Jani used the term "special event" to describe his new attraction, and, when asked to define this new term of art, he replied: "I guess it is something that is different from a normal day of living."

Applying Jani's definition, every sports competition could be considered a special event. Competitors vary from race to race; opponents change from game to game; and the outcome of any meet, match, or competition will remain unpredictable whether the event is one of 82 in a season, or a contest held just once a year. The underlying principles of planning, promotion, management, marketing, budgeting, and presentation are similar for organizations that play a full schedule of games and for event organizers who present a single-day event. Although the ***Second Edition*** of ***The Sports Event Management and Marketing Playbook*** provides the best practices applicable for managing everything from one-time annual events and season-long schedules, it is also devoted to the creation, development, management, marketing, production, and execution of sports events that stand out from the weekly team calendar.

Building a foundation to support and execute unique special events is like building an entirely new company or introducing a new brand. It starts with creating a product (an event) to meet the wants and needs of potential customers (the participants, audience, and sponsors). The costs of designing, fabricating, and bringing the product to market must be identified; the expected revenue projected; and the final financial results forecasted. Human resources must be organized and applied to create and sell the product, and modifications to the product must be considered after consumers provide feedback.

Although the management and marketing of sports events require a thorough grounding in traditional business disciplines, they are much more complex than a typical product introduction. To ensure success, event organizers must build alliances in their host community with local government and businesses, the event facility, sponsors and other business partners, media writers and broadcasters, and a variety of others with a vested interest in the successful outcome of the event.

About This Book

Welcome to Your Playbook

Exacting, strategic planning and the effective marketing of sports events are unquestionably integral ingredients for success; by themselves, however, they will not ensure victory or provide a finished product. Flawless execution of these events is equally essential to keep audiences excited, viewers tuned in, participants engaged, and sponsors fulfilled. After all, other than the event's business partners, no one leaves a sports event comparing statistics about how well the marketing plan performed.

Hours and days, weeks and months must be spent attending to the hundreds of management, operations, and production details that are required to execute a seamless event. Although the preparatory process for one sports event can be essentially different from that of another, most of the details on the planning checklist can be applied to a broad range of programs, regardless of size or budget. The ***Second Edition*** of ***The Sports Event Management and Marketing Playbook*** helps event organizers to apply the latest and best industry practices to methodically plan, monitor, manage, and evaluate their progress during the entire event-planning process. It offers an organic view of sports event planning and, as a result, is the only book to truly combine the disciplines of sports marketing and event management—as defined by their practitioners—into a single, integrated approach.

New to This Edition

English poet and essayist Samuel Johnson (1709–1784) once wrote: "Knowledge is of two kinds. We know a subject ourselves, or we know where we can find information upon it." The ***Second Edition*** of ***The Sports Event Management and Marketing Playbook*** serves as a practical reference handbook that is as relevant and current for grassroots sports organizers as it is for professional event managers, marketers, and promoters. Every step of the planning process for developing, planning, managing, and executing flawless sports events is explored and discussed with the following updated features:

- New, helpful **charts** and **figures** ensure that every detail is considered before the gates open and the scoreclock begins its inexorable countdown.
- Illustrative **Sideline Stories** include more current real-life anecdotes from the field that were a favorite feature of the previous edition. These stories provide vivid examples of best practices, as well as plays that were proven best to avoid.
- Revised **Post-Play Analysis** summary sections and **Coach's Clipboard** review exercises reflect new content per chapter.
- An expanded section of useful **forms**, **sample documents**, and **checklists** can be accessed in the appendices at the end of the text and on a companion website (www.wiley.com/college/supovitz), a new tool that will be periodically refreshed as information is updated and innovations are introduced.

Organization and Theme

Eventually, like a concert pianist's fingers gliding effortlessly across the keyboard at speeds unfathomable and seemingly as reflex, experienced sports event organizers and marketers will come to know much of what it takes to produce spectacular results intuitively. But until you do, keep this volume close. It is as important to recognize what the questions are as it is to know where and how to derive the answers. The ***Second Edition*** of ***The Sports Event Management and Marketing Playbook*** has been organized so you can easily access specific areas of importance, as outlined at the start of each chapter, or "play."

We selected a playbook theme for this book because of the striking parallels between the activities presented on the playing field and the efforts invested behind the scenes. Some earn a livelihood by competing in or managing sports events; others are involved for pure enjoyment and the satisfaction of achieving success for their team or community. The team—whether its members are wearing jerseys, golf shirts, or staff credentials—is made up of specialists and role players who each contribute what they do best to the overall performance of the event.

Not every play is applicable in every game or in every situation. Proven fail-safe plays are not always executed in the same order or in the same combinations. Their effective use depends on the progress of the event; some make more sense early in the game, while others at the end. At the stadium, arena, ball field, track, rink, recreation center, parking lot, or street course, victory is achieved by building the right team. Coaches must provide insightful training, instruction, and even cheerleading in order to familiarize the participants with the plays to be run, and then turn them loose. Event organizers, those who operate events, promoters, and those who market them also build and coach a team of planners, managers, and role players on the event's objectives, provide guidance on what actions need to be undertaken to achieve them, and then, yes, turn them loose as well. You know you have the right team when the most common trait becomes apparent on the emotional level: losing is not an option, whether leaving the locker room or managing a budget.

Time to Start Planning

"Does thou love life? Then, do not squander time; for that's the stuff life is made of," said American statesman and philosopher Benjamin Franklin. Time and again, the most common reason we encounter for the cancellation or postponement of a sports event is a lack of sufficient planning time. For the audience, sports events seem to unfold spontaneously, primarily because the nature of sports contests themselves is so spontaneous. But for anyone who has ever tried to organize a sports event, it is no news that these programs—again depending on their size and complexity—can take anywhere from a few months to a few years or more to plan, promote, and execute. Anyone who has planned a wedding can probably relate—it always seems to take a whole lot more time to plan than originally anticipated.

Some events are fixed on the calendar because they depend on existing league schedules, academic semesters, playing seasons, weather, or analogous factors beyond the control of the organizer. Other events are more flexible. Either way, start with the most desirable date for your event and work backward. Read Play 1 to determine what you want your event to achieve, and Plays 2 and 3 to understand the costs and financial benefits. Finally, apply the lessons learned in Play 5 about the event planning process to map out all the details that will have to be considered and how long each will take to complete. It is likely that you will find that no matter how distant the event date, the latest advisable time to start planning is now. So let's get going.

Supplemental Offerings

For those of you using this book in a classroom setting, an online **Instructor's Manual** with **Test Bank** accompanies this book and is available to instructors to help them effectively manage their time and to enhance student learning opportunities.

The **Test Bank** has been specifically formatted for **Respondus**, an easy-to-use software program for creating and managing exams that can be printed to paper or published directly to Blackboard, WebCT, Desire2Learn, eCollege, ANGEL, and other eLearning systems. Instructors who adopt this book can download the test bank for free.

A password-protected Wiley Instructor Book Companion website devoted entirely to this book (www.wiley.com/college/supovitz) provides access to the online **Instructor's Manual, select appendices,** and the text-specific teaching resources. The **Respondus Test Bank** and the **PowerPoint** lecture slides are also available on the website for download.

ACKNOWLEDGMENTS

The ***Second Edition*** of ***The Sports Event Management and Marketing Playbook*** would not have been possible without the hundreds of people who helped me to grow as a person and professional while contributing to and producing sports, entertainment, civic, and corporate events over more than 25 years. Many have helped us directly in the preparation of this book, and countless more have been teachers, counselors, coaches, mentors, collaborators, critics, employers, clients, colleagues, and friends without whom I could not have learned the lessons that Robert and I have tried to share.

First, I would like to thank Robert Goldwater, my co-author on the second edition, for his collegial friendship over the years. From our first collaboration at the 1994 NHL All-Star Weekend at Madison Square Garden to Bobby's broad expertise in running venues and delivering world-class customer experiences, his tenure as a sports commission executive, and his academic leadership at Georgetown University made him a natural partner to work with me on the preparation of this revised and expanded volume.

NHL Commissioner Gary Bettman and then-COO Jon Litner enabled me to write the First Edition of ***The Sports Event Management and Marketing Playbook*** during my 13th season at the National Hockey League. Working for them to passionately promote the great frozen game in the United States, Canada, and internationally was a great honor and incredible fun. Special thanks to former NHL Enterprises executives Steve Ryan and Steve Flatow, who originally persuaded me to transfer my entertainment event experience into the world of professional sports more than two decades ago, and, as a result, set me on the path to the best jobs I have ever had.

I knew from our first meeting that NFL Commissioner Roger Goodell would make an outstanding mentor and a professional who challenges himself and those around him to constantly grow, excel, and do everything better than before. He may not know it, but I always look forward to his last words before a major event begins: "Don't mess this up." I recognize how lucky I have been to work for him, Executive Vice President of NFL Business Ventures Eric Grubman, and an organization as admired and successful as the National Football League. It has provided me with the opportunity to test myself on a daily basis while producing events that I hope help define the best that sports events can offer. It is truly a privilege to work for the leaders in American sports.

The NFL events department staff helps to make my days truly spectacular. They toil endlessly to make the league shine without expecting any notoriety for themselves and have become my second family. My thanks to: Mary Pat Augenthaler, Sunday Billings, Sherri Caraccia, Erin Casey, Sammy Choi, Catherine Danielowich, Allison deGroot, Brett Diamond, Nicki Ewell, Eric Finkelstein, Tisha Ford, Deanna Forgione, Maria Franklin, Dave Houghton, Katie Keenan, Mimi MacKinnon, Bill McConnell, Erin Merrell, Heather Nanberg, Fred Otto, Brendan Raughter, Joan Ryan-Canu, Carly Slivinski, Gregg Strasser, Dave Wintergrass, and Daphne Wood.

My family has selflessly loaned me to sports events, leagues, and celebrations over my entire career, and has provided the balance and lasting value in my life. My wife, Catherine, and sons, Matt, Ethan, and Jake, have tolerated the long absences from home, and anchor me when the pressure seems insurmountable. Thank you, all, for lovingly granting me some of the little precious time we have together to write the first and second editions of this book.

—*Frank Supovitz*

The invitation from my friend Frank to co-author the ***Second Edition*** of ***The Sports Event Management and Marketing Playbook*** was a direct result of my being a faculty member in Georgetown University's Sports Industry Management graduate program. I had come to Frank with a few thoughts based on my using the book as required course reading, and he floored me with the flattering offer to collaborate on updating the book. There is nothing more satisfying than the interaction I am able to have with the enthusiastic students, outstanding sports industry faculty colleagues, and supportive SIM and School of Continuing Studies staff while teaching at Georgetown.

No one was more fortunate than I to be able to serve 24 years at The World's Most Famous Arena, Madison Square Garden. There are so many indelible memories and priceless lessons from those years and so many extraordinary people who remain with me wherever I go. Collectively, they provided the foundation for what I have been able to contribute to this book. My affection for and my gratitude to everyone and every event at the Garden are boundless.

Tim Leiweke convinced me to leave the Garden to help him, Phil Anschutz, and Ed Roski develop and open STAPLES Center. I would not have the benefit of the professional and personal experiences I continue to draw on from my time in Los Angeles without Tim's personal salesmanship and encouragement.

While I was the chief executive of the DC Sports and Entertainment Commission, the two board chairmen, John Richardson and Jack Mahoney, were leaders who sought excellence in sports event and venue management, an attribute we hope is stimulated in those who read and use this book.

My consulting firm, The Goldwater Group, has afforded me opportunities to contribute to a gratifying array of clients and projects, sometimes with accomplished partners. While it is not possible here to mention all of them, I must acknowledge Soccer United Marketing, CONCACAF, and everyone with whom I have had the pleasure of working on the Gold Cup international soccer tournament for being tremendous sources of applied knowledge and information.

As a long-time member of the International Association of Venue Managers, I have been inspired by many profoundly dedicated executives and special friends in the venue management industry. It is my hope that our book contributes positively to the IAVM, as well as to the current and future members of the Event and Arena Marketing Conference, the assembly of energetic and creative marketers on whom sports and entertainment events and venues rely, and to the Sport Leadership and Management majors at my alma mater, Miami University.

Finally, there are four people to whom I wish to express the deepest appreciation.

My dad, Bob. My overflowing passion for sports events and venues and for having a career in our industry was a natural result of the support of and experiences provided by my father, who also was the best journalism teacher and copy editor a young sports writer could possibly have had.

I am very proud to be the husband of an exceptional college educator, a devoted sports fan, a thoughtful editor, a remarkably patient and giving individual, and the person with the most extraordinary spirit in the universe, Colleen Callahan.

Alex Greer was the valedictorian of the inaugural graduating class of Georgetown's Sports Industry Management program. He took a course I taught during his first semester and later became a valued teaching assistant, then an able co-instructor for a course. Alex enthusiastically, articulately, and tirelessly contributed to this book as our very capable and meticulous assistant. We cannot thank him enough for all he did.

And, Frank Supovitz. I haven't met and can't imagine there is a more talented and genuinely caring person in the sports event industry than Frank. As I have come to know over close to 20 years and as the world is reminded every first Sunday in February with the Super Bowl, Frank has literally and figuratively written the book on sports event management and marketing. He is, in a word, spectacular. My sincere thanks to him for this opportunity.

—*Robert Goldwater*

Our collective thanks to Dr. Joe Goldblatt, the Event Series editor for John Wiley & Sons, and our source of inspiration and encouragement to update and expand this book for the new generation of sports event management and marketing professionals and students, and to Christine McKnight, Mary Cassells, Julie Kerr, Cheryl Ferguson, Wendy Lai, and Anna Melhorn, our editors and associates at Wiley, who have been wonderful partners throughout our preparations.

A special thanks to the host of colleagues whose insights, expertise, and advice were freely provided to us both and which can be found throughout this book: Ken Aagaard (CBS Sports), Glenn Adamo (NFL Films), Bill Bannon (BWD Group LLC), Jim Brown (JBC International), Chris Browne (formerly Greater Washington Sports Alliance), Mary Davis (formerly Washington Sports & Entertainment), Helene Elliott (*Los Angeles Times*), Buffy Filippell (TeamWork Online), Chris Folk (2010 *Living OUR Legacy Game* class president), Jill Fracisco (CONCACAF), Fred Gaudelli (NBC Sports), Ben Goss (Missouri State University), David Grant (Velocity Sports & Entertainment), Tara Green (American Airlines Center), Shana Gritsavage (Under Armour), Carl Hirsh and Rich Oriolo (Stafford Sports), Paul Hogan (New Hampshire Technical Institute), Glenn Horine (Iona College), Chris Hutson (Turnstyles Ticketing), Court Jeske (Soccer United Marketing), David Job (Media Concepts), Stephen Keener (Little League Baseball), Allan Kreda (Bloomberg News), Allison Melangton (2012 Indianapolis Super Bowl Host Committee), Thom Meredith (Thom Meredith, Inc.), Marisabel Munoz (Major League Soccer/Soccer United Marketing), Sherali Najak (Canadian Broadcasting Corporation), Dr. Christie L. Nordhielm (J.L. Kellogg Graduate School of Management, Northwestern University), Lon Rosenberg (Washington Redskins), Alan Rothenberg (Los Angeles Sports Council), Bob Russo (formerly Madison Square Garden), Susan Sherer (Detroit Super Bowl Host Committee), Linda Shetina Logan (Greater Columbus Sports Commission), John Shumate (Gatorade), Jon Tatum (Genesco Sports Enterprises), John Urban (formerly Madison Square Garden), Mike Whalen (Morale Entertainment), Sheri Wish (formerly *Los Angeles Times*), and Mary Wittenberg (New York Road Runners Club).

Thanks also to the reviewers of the ***Second Edition*** manuscript: Dr. Albert F. Bolognese, Winthrop University; Brett M. Burchette, Drexel University; Dr. Andrew Gillentine, University of South Carolina; Derek Hillestad, University of Minnesota; Dr. Pam L. Young, Johnson & Wales University.

We hope to see you at the game!

—*Frank Supovitz and Robert Goldwater*

INTRODUCTION

"Good luck is a residue of preparation."

—*Jack Youngblood, Hall of Fame defensive end, Los Angeles Rams*

This section will . . .

- Explore the size, scope, and excitement of the sports event management and marketing industry.
- Get you started with your first play—"Supovitz's Flying Wedge of Sports Event Success."
- Explore the philosophy that sports event management is based on the development of successful partnerships, as demonstrated by the USO (Understanding Stakeholders' Objectives) Principle.
- Discuss the latest trends in sports event management and marketing.

The Power of Sports Event Marketing

To the more than one billion sports fans worldwide who leap out of their seats when the home team scores with under a minute to go on the clock, who sacrifice sleep for the thrills of sudden-death overtime, who check their mobile devices for game updates seemingly every minute, and who can't read, hear and watch enough about sports from countless media sources, the grand strategists of sports are the coaches, trainers, and general managers who guide their favorite team or athletes. The objectives of these leaders are uncompromising and clear—the pursuit of unequaled excellence in the form of a winning score, a championship season, or a record-beating performance. They embrace a philosophy, system, and playbook that put them in the best possible competitive position. They consider the interpersonal chemistry on the roster, past performance, and the best practices of champions, all while taking into account the time and money available to invest in winning. During the game, they act quickly and decisively to capitalize on rapidly unfolding developments and to stave off looming disaster. They change the plan when the plan needs changing. And, after the crowds have gone and the locker rooms have cleared, they study the game footage, uncovering unforeseen weaknesses and learning from the successes of their opponents as well as noting what worked well.

The most successful sports event managers and directors—from professional league executives to community Little League volunteers—approach their mission in much the same way. They identify an event's objectives; develop the plan and raise the revenues to achieve them; assemble the best team of dedicated role players; monitor costs; and continually assess the progress they are making. They adjust to changing conditions by reading the field for signs of trouble or triumph. And finally, when it's all over, they conduct postmortems to evaluate how to build on their successes and learn from their mistakes.

Sports event marketing is big business, by some estimates a $500 billion+ industry and growing. Its roots can be seen sprouting in every schoolyard and gymnasium, in parks, on corners, and in cul-de-sacs across the globe. What makes sports events the world's most compelling entertainment form is the emotional capital the audience invests in the outcome of the contest. Unlike the ending of a motion picture, with a more or less formulaic structure, the ultimate result of a sports event is a perfect mystery at the outset and, at its most sublime, up to its final moments. Sports events are the original reality entertainment experiences—unpredictable and involving dramas for which the resolution defies prediction. News and sports websites, blogs, Internet services, and social networks have exploited this hunger for instant results on the grassroots, college, and professional levels. Sports fans are now able to access scores, statistics, replays, and real-time broadcast coverage via wireless and broadband connections when they can neither attend nor view the excitement on television. Social networks such as Twitter, Facebook, and successors, and proprietary sports sites, provide not only instant bulletins on the course of an event but also enhanced, behind-the-scenes content, fan and media reactions to developments on the field, and information that until recently were accessible only to the most well-connected sports and event insiders.

The power of sports events is as personal as it is cultural. It is this emotional investment in sports that attracts live audiences as well as media, sponsors, a variety of stakeholders, and, of course, the athletes themselves. The allure of sports across a wide diversity of cultures is so pervasive that it occupies multiple pages in every daily general-interest news outlet every day of the week, and is often featured in stand-alone sections at least once a week. News-oriented radio stations offer updates at :15 and :45 each hour and sports talk radio draws rabid listeners in markets around the country. Programs on television and other media feature highlights and insights, provocative opinions, and up-close-and-personal stories throughout the day, every day. Those dozens of pages, hours of broadcast airtime, and vast array of online content peddle newspapers and magazines, pull in viewers and listeners, and sell advertising space to hundreds of companies that recognize how habit-forming sports really are.

Savvy marketers—from the corner drugstore to multinational corporations—know how audiences react to the action, excitement, grace, and fan interactivity of sports and sports events, and they use this knowledge to great advantage. They appreciate how their potential customers are already categorized and delivered in ready-made, easy-to-classify demographic bundles, because every sport has its distinctive "average fan," every event its target audience. Education, affluence, socioeconomics, technological literacy, geographic distribution, politics, and consumer spending patterns are among the many variables that can be readily identified among the fans or audience of a particular sport or sports event.

Corporations invest heavily in sports and sports events because their customers, in record numbers, likewise devote their dollars and emotions in record numbers. Marketers understand that establishing an association between a consumer's loyalties and passions and a company's product can pay enormous dividends in terms of sales. In addition, the marketplace is unquestionably immense. In 2011, total attendance of just the top 11 professional sports leagues around the globe was estimated at 221 million fans, and attendance for the seven largest college, semi-professional and amateur leagues in the United States was estimated at an additional 79 million, according to industry compilations.

Add to these impressive numbers the attending fans of organized sports not accounted for in the above figures, such as minor league professional sports, auto racing, horse racing, rodeo and bull riding, golf, tennis, bowling, skating, skiing, curling, lacrosse, volleyball, boxing, mixed martial arts, and the broad range of action sports, to name just a few, and the number of participants and spectators of organized sports competition for youth, including Little League Baseball, Pop Warner Football, and others. Then, consider the friends, family, and businesses that support a community's young athletes by attending and sponsoring their events, and it is easy to imagine that perhaps as many as one billion people worldwide attend a live sporting event in any given year. Factor in those who watch sports on television or a mobile device or listen on radio, and the financial impact of the industry and its influence in our daily lives becomes all the more impressive.

Marketers recognize sports as a powerful and influential platform to sell their products and services because of both the emotional involvement of the consumer and the great size of the marketplace. The growing collective financial investment they make has become a cornerstone of the event planning and budgeting process and has revolutionized how organizers conceive, prepare, and execute their events.

The Evolution of Sports Event Marketing

Not so long ago, captive audiences numbering in the tens of thousands faithfully filled ballparks game after game, leaping to their feet as their hometown's star left fielder went diving for line drives hit in the gap. Over the course of a few afternoon hours, fans sat in full view of dozens of billboards that wallpapered the area above and beside the outfield fence. One of these advertisements might have offered a new suit to the batter lucky enough to hit a bull's eye with a towering home run. The most common sports marketing activities in organized sports' early years were stadium sign advertising, commercials during game broadcasts, and player product endorsements.

Today's more sophisticated and complex sports event marketplace is a rapidly changing environment. While the sale of advertising and promotion of production endorsements remain staples of the industry, the costs of doing business have increased dramatically for all concerned, causing sponsors to demand more and obligating sports event organizers to respond and deliver. Previously unknown economic pressures, changing consumer demographics and spending behavior, time-shifting and on-demand media viewing habits, increased competition from a host of new entertainment options, and the influence of increasingly fast, portable, and reliable access via handheld devices and tablets, among many factors, have significantly changed the way we consume sports and the way marketers reach us through events. Ticket prices have soared to all-time highs, even as fans were feeling uncertainty about the state of the economy. A finite universe of television viewers is getting sliced into ever-diminishing shares of the market as new channels and new ways of receiving content compete for broadcast, cable, and satellite audience. Fans can interact with their favorite sports, teams and athletes on a year-round, 24/7 basis, gaining instant, up-to-the-second information and a growing number of live game broadcasts over their mobile devices. Television channels such as NFL RedZone now offer fans the ability to watch potentially pivotal plays in real time, switching its coverage between all National Football League games in progress to ensure that viewers don't miss a single scoring opportunity anywhere in the league.

Changes in the sports event marketplace are particularly evident in the area of event marketing. As the global economy treads new territory daily, corporate partners are increasingly sensitive to the costs of doing business in the sports arena. They are more vigilant than ever about identifying clear business objectives to guide their participation—and increasingly aggressive about achieving them. Sports marketers have to read signals from the marketplace to remain in the batter's box. Sports event organizers have to keep a finger on the pulse of the ticket buying public, evaluate economic pressures on corporate sponsors, and keep abreast of merchandising innovations. They must stay current on television viewing habits and trends, new technologies and content delivery systems, the day-to-day profit and loss forecasts for associated sports properties or events, the ongoing effectiveness of an event's marketing plan, and a host of other continually evolving factors that constitute the sports business environment. A sports event organizer must simultaneously be an administrator, marketer, and promoter, a financial planner and prognosticator, equally at ease interacting with a facility manager and a local government official. (For this reason, the terms *organizer* and *promoter* will often be used interchangeably in this book.) He or she must remain creative and cost conscious, free thinking yet focused.

Your Introductory Play—Supovitz's Flying Wedge

More than a century ago, an infamous and irresistibly powerful football play called the "flying wedge" made its debut during a second half kickoff return at a historic contest between Harvard and Yale in 1892. With the momentum of a full-speed run, the entire receiving Harvard team rushed from two sides of the field, coalescing to form a tightly packed human spearhead in front of their ball carrier, halfback Charlie Brewer. The speed and sheer force of 11 players pushing each other forward, single-mindedly focusing their energy toward the leading tip of the triangle, ripped through the stunned Yale line before being stopped 20 yards from a touchdown.

It was a play never before seen in football history and one that, for a time, revolutionized on-field strategy. Early football historian and coach of the 1893 Wisconsin Badgers, Parke Davis, wrote: "Sensation runs through the stands at the novel play, which is the most organized and beautiful one ever seen upon a football field." This crowd-pleasing demonstration of brutal efficiency and focused human energy caused the flying wedge to quickly sweep into coaching playbooks as a fan-favorite opening play.

Ultimately, in those early days of college football, with protective gear virtually unknown, serious and even fatal injuries resulted from the use of the awesome flying wedge. It turned out that the play was too powerful, too efficient for its day, and so it was outlawed within two seasons to protect the health and lives of opposing players. It simply worked too well too much of the time, and at a horrendous human cost.

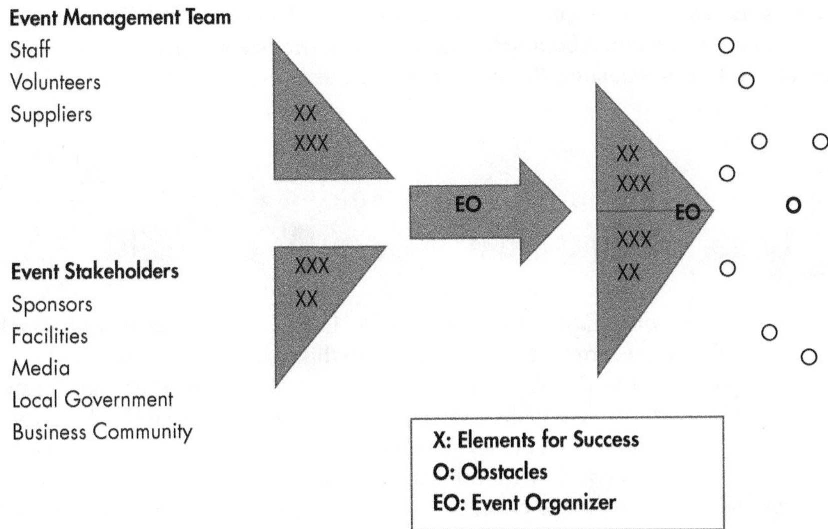

Figure I.1 Supovitz's "Flying Wedge" of Sports Event Success

Coaches' playbooks often include diagrams of successful plays, with Xs and Os indicating the field positions and movements of a team's players and their opponents. Figure I.1 illustrates one such play, "Supovitz's Flying Wedge of Sports Event Success," inspired by Harvard's landmark strategy. In this figure, the Xs symbolize your event team, and all of the partners, sponsors, and other involved parties that will work together with you to achieve success. The Os denote the many obstacles, large and small, that are prepared to stand in the way of your event's progress. The EO in between the two wedges on the left, and at the leading edge of the flying wedge on the right, is the event organizer, the individual or group providing the leadership to pull all stakeholders and staff together. Unlike Harvard's play, in which the ball carrier was at the rear protected at all costs by his team, the sports event organizer must pilot the wedge from the front, applying the force of his or her expertise and experience to determine whether to meet a particular obstacle head on or to sweep around its flank.

There is no question that the strength and appeal of a sports event begins at the venue, with the athletes and participants whom the fans will come to see. But beyond where the action takes place, the execution of a successful sports event is the result of intelligent planning and well-integrated teamwork. The team is composed of a staff of individuals—professional, volunteer, or a combination of both—working as a single unit, dedicated to the achievement of the event's objectives. Coached/led by the event director or organizer, the staff is joined by a second unit composed of stakeholders that include the event facility, sponsors, local government and business, broadcasters, and others from the media. To achieve greatness for the event, the two units combine to form an irresistible wedge, sweeping obstacles aside or navigating around them.

As illustrated by Figure I.1, the event staff makes up only one side of the flying wedge. It was the coming together of squads from two sides of the field that made Harvard's wedge so stunningly effective. The event's staff members will similarly need to join with a second squad, a combination of outside stakeholders united to create the unstoppable flying wedge. If event organizers can harness and focus the energy of their team of staff and stakeholders to work as one to execute their events, they will surely execute Davis's "most organized and beautiful play ever seen." The glue we use to attract and bind both halves of the wedge irresistibly together is our own Sports Event Golden Rule: *Understanding Stakeholders' Objectives* (USO).

The Sports Event Golden Rule— Understanding Stakeholders' Objectives (USO)

As you explore the ***Second Edition*** of ***The Sports Event Management and Marketing Playbook***, you will note a recurrent theme, starting with this introduction. To succeed in the long term in today's sports event marketplace, you must embrace a USO philosophy and attitude and truly desire to understand the stakeholders' objectives. In most cases, the days of sports organizers seemingly marching into town and dictating how, when, and where a sports event will take place are over, if they ever really existed. With the increased sophistication and pragmatism of event sponsors, broadcasters, facilities, and communities, event organizers are obligated to demonstrate the great advantages of hosting a particular event and the essential contribution their participation will make. A successful sports event is born of a partnership between all of these parties, as well as athletes who will compete and the fans who will attend. Understanding what each of these entities want and need from an event is paramount in building consensus to moving this partnership forward, forming a virtually indestructible, diamond-hard point to your own flying wedge.

Application of the USO philosophy finds its way into nearly every major play—or chapter—in this book. Although the importance of this golden rule in building partnerships and reinforcing the leading tip of the flying wedge is evident throughout this playbook, the core concept of USO is perhaps most noticeable in the plays devoted to host cities and venues, sponsors, media, broadcasters, and community involvement. Keeping these stakeholders engaged and focused on the success of your event requires regular dialogue and ongoing negotiation and collaboration. As any good negotiator will tell you, reaching agreement is far easier when both sides understand what the other wants from the relationship.

Facilities, such as arenas, stadiums, recreation centers, ice rinks, training centers, racetracks, convention centers, natatoriums, velodromes, marinas, golf courses, hotels, recreation and amusement centers, and a range of others, exist to host events. As you begin planning your program, you will have to recognize that most of these venues look at sports events as means of producing revenues and exposure for themselves. Play 4 will help you to develop an understanding of what sports event facilities want from you and what you can expect from them.

Play 4 will also help you to gain insights into the complex and multidimensional reasons why cities, counties, and states compete fiercely for the honor of hosting sports events. Municipal governments know that sports events generate sales tax dollars, hotel occupancy, expenditures on food and beverages, and income taxes, among many other economic benefits. They also appreciate that advertising, broadcasts of the event, media coverage, and postings on blogs and social media before and after the fact can generate positive exposure and interest from other sports and entertainment properties, as well as from business entities and pleasure travelers. There are a multitude of other reasons why cities spend time, money, and human energy bidding for sports events through their local sports commissions and convention and visitors bureaus. Even small, grassroots sports events generate some form of economic and lifestyle impact. Understanding how cities evaluate this impact will help you solicit the support of the community in your efforts to stage the best and most cost-efficient event possible.

SIDELINE STORY

The Costs and Benefits of Hosting Major Sports Events

Cities competing to host sports events are often questioned by local media and politicians who question the benefits of applying resources such as city services and facilities in pursuit of a winning bid. The economics and value of every event differ greatly, of course, and economists use different methodologies to ascertain the real benefits of hosting sports events. Some conclude that there is no real direct economic advantage to staging sports events, while others point to multiple millions of dollars in local tax revenues, job creation, and promotional positives that will generate future revenues from tourism and other events. What is clear, however, is that many cities bid time after time to host major sports events, and invest heavily in their success. Few cities that have successfully hosted sports events later determine that their support did not contribute sufficiently to their economies or public image, at least enough so to re-enter the market to compete for future host opportunities.

In 2012, the city of London, England, was projected to spend £9.3 billion (US$14.6 billion) in public-sector funding in support of the Summer Olympic Games, and estimated that hosting the event would provide £1 billion in advertising value alone. This extraordinary level of public support, combined with ticket revenues, sponsorship, and other local revenue streams, would help the Games generate a profit. London hosted the Olympics at the right time in its history, as well. Although the region won the bid to host the event seven years before the date of the opening ceremonies, the Olympics also provided an important, timely, and highly visible promotional tool to counteract the damage done to the image of London and the United Kingdom in the wake of widely publicized civil riots that wracked the country less than one year prior to the Games.

Notwithstanding the broad disagreement among economists on the real benefits of sports events to a regional economy, additional anecdotal evidence of their perceived value is presented by considering the history of cities that have successfully competed to host the NFL's Super Bowl. In the Super Bowl's first half century, Miami and New Orleans alone represented 20 of the NFL's championship games, each having captured the right to host the event 10 times. If there was a question about the value of hosting this major North American sports event, one would think it would have been answered long before bidding on a 10th Super Bowl.

Broadcasters are at the same time beneficiaries and risk-taking partners. Unlike corporate sponsors, their investment is not a marketing or brand positioning expense. Their financial outlay, in the form of production expenses and rights fees paid to the sports organization, is generally at risk. Their product is the event broadcast itself and they have to generate interest at a minimum of two levels. First, broadcasters have to sell advertising to offset their rights fees and production costs and, ultimately, to generate profits. A broadcaster also has to promote the event to viewers or listeners, whose very act of consuming the sports event via television or radio will justify the advertising rates it will charge for commercials. If it fails to generate sufficient viewership, the broadcaster may have to "make good" on its promises to sponsors by offering bonus advertising free or at a reduced cost. Knowing the great benefits they can bring to an event organizer and recognizing that their investments can be so high and their ability to generate profits so risky, broadcasters can be very demanding. Play 13 will help you to better understand their point of view, the issues that inevitably arise during the broadcast planning process, and the best ways to work with these essential partners.

The beneficiaries of sports events who are most frequently taken for granted and overlooked are the athletes, participants, and fans. Events sometimes succeed in generating expected revenues, providing significant economic impact to the community, and meeting the needs of corporate sponsors, yet fail to survive in subsequent years because the organizers forgot the essential, basic requirement of providing the athletes and the audience with an enjoyable and rewarding experience during every phase of the event. The excitement should begin from the time they first hear of the event and be appreciated well after they return home. Losing sight of the needs and expectations of the athletes and fans will endanger the long-term success of your events. Don't forget to identify and deliver what they deserve and expect: an outstanding entertainment and performance environment.

Understand what other sports and other leisure-time options the contenders and the audience attend and why. Is your event designed to attract only the sport's loyal, most avid fan base, those with a vested interest in the outcome of the event? Is there an opportunity to expand the event's appeal to casual fans or even curious nonfans? Design your marketing plan to communicate how your sports event will deliver value and unforgettable experiences to the audiences you would most like to attract. Remember that sports events are generally at their most exciting when presented before an emotionally charged, capacity audience.

Current Trends in Sports Event Management and Marketing

Hockey Hall of Fame great Wayne Gretzky once explained that the key to his scoring success was not based on where the puck was at any given moment. "I skate to where the puck is going to be," he said. The key to an event's long-term success is dependent on the organizer's ability to understand his or her market and where it is heading. During recent periods of economic uncertainty, sports event organizers have come under increasing pressure to achieve more with less and provide even greater value for their partners. Sponsors continue to seek ways to increase sales and market share while trying to reduce costs. Some have cut their sports marketing expenditures while others have redirected where and how their sports marketing budgets are used. Many are exploring how the sports events they support can best leverage their company's expertise, products, and services, perhaps combined with a smaller amount of cash, to meet their requirements. A more detailed exploration of what sponsors want and need from today's sports events partnerships is included in Plays 6 and 7.

At one time, media partners such as newspapers, radio stations, television broadcasters, and online services participated as sponsors of events by offering advertising space or commercial time in exchange for sponsor benefits. In more challenging marketing environments, media are less willing to offer space or time in exchange for "official sponsor" designations and their associated benefits. In fact, many frequently make their participation contingent on some purchase of advertising by the event organizer. Some may offer to provide extra space or time to the event, perhaps one or two times as many free ads for every one purchased. They value the extra space/time as the "value in kind" that will buy them a sponsorship position. Play 8 will help you to understand the key media wants and needs in today's sports event marketplace. This chapter will also help you to understand what the editorial side of the media world—those providing reporting coverage before, during, and after the event—needs from organizers. It is incumbent upon organizers to understand what journalists need in order to report fairly and comprehensively on the event.

Recognizing current market sensitivities and ensuring that your sports events are being managed and marketed with the application of sound and current business practices are essential to achieving the objectives of your program. The more complex the event, the longer the timeframe for planning. The longer the planning process, the more likely and more often event organizers will have to change planning details midstream—such as ticket prices, participant accommodations, ancillary grassroots events, and facilities—to meet the constantly shifting pressures of the business environment. Anyone who has ever managed any form of budgeting, at home or in business, knows that it is impossible to determine exactly how much money is going to be spent on precisely every product or service six months, one year, or three years in advance. Yet, many large events require two- to four-year planning windows, and almost all events need more than six months. After you have developed your sports event, continuous evaluation and flexibility in planning and financial reforecasting are vital. This book is peppered with the insights, tips, and options that can help you anticipate areas where such changes might be necessary and how to deal with them.

Having an understanding of the economic environment can help sports event organizers project changes in revenue and anticipate expenses for the following year's program. Against the turbulent backdrop of a global economic downturn and frequent temperamental swings in financial markets, however, prudent organizers planning sports events more than one year in advance often embrace the philosophy of zero-growth budgeting. This enables sports event organizers to remain nimble over the long term, providing the opportunity to adjust ticketing pricing policies, shift strategies for generating sponsor participation, exploit emerging content distribution technologies, and even change the structures of the events themselves to remain economically competitive and grow. The combination of a rapidly changing technological environment and unpredictable economic times has necessitated this flexibility. Sports event organizers, perhaps now more than at any time in the past, need to listen to their customers and stakeholders—their fans, sponsors, broadcasters, and other business partners—to understand what they want from their experience and partnership and to serve them better. Their needs are often evolving faster than the events they support and organizers who react or, better yet, correctly predict these trends will prosper. Those who do not will lose their relevance to the people and organizations that support them with their presence and money.

Understanding the economy and its effect on partners and fans has increasingly been joined by another consideration—the impact on the host region's physical environment. Spectators inevitably leave behind mountains of trash and tons of paper and raw construction materials are often expended in preparation for an event. The consumption of fuel from added motor traffic, air conditioning, and power generation increases the carbon impact on the host region and hundreds of pounds of prepared, unserved food are wasted to no benefit of fans or participants or to the bottom line of the organizer. Sustainability policies, previously infrequently and inconsistently employed in the sports event industry, have become more than just the right thing to do. They help build the relationship between a sports event and its host community and, if properly implemented, can leave the region better than if the event had not been held. This relationship can be further enhanced with a strategic community relations plan, leaving lasting impacts on the causes that best resonate with the region. Play 10 will explore how identifying the causes that appeal to the local community and investing time and a portion of the sports event budget can invest the host region in the sports event's success.

Providing a comfortable, safe and secure environment for athletes and fans has taken on an increasingly visible role in the design, planning, and operation of sports events. Although safety has always been of paramount importance at sports events for organizers and venue managers both on the playing field and in the stands, planning for and dealing with conditions beyond the scope of your control—the essence of risk management—have emerged as issues to be considered early and often in the sports event management process. Best practices for crowd control, severe weather planning, disruptive fans, and other potentially threatening conditions are discussed in Play 14 and illustrated with several pertinent Sideline Story case studies.

The advancement and proliferation of new technologies and software for budgeting, event planning, ticketing, marketing and promotion, event production, and guest management functions, among others, have raised the professionalism of special events and increased the productivity of event personnel. But, the impact of technology is no longer simply manifested in the systems the sports event organizer applies to better manage or present an event. Today, fans and participants bring technology with them to sports events at such an accelerating rate that most venues are required to keep up with the capabilities and services that audiences demand to stay connected to the information and interactions they want during the event. Audiences enjoy sports events on more levels and in more ways than at any time in history. Fans at a sports event now often replace or supplement the mass media, updating their friends and family over social media networks and their own blogs in real time. Followers of professional sports want quick access to statistics to play fantasy sports while the real events are unfolding. Spectators want to review plays on their own mobile devices to relive the magic of a just-experienced athletic moment and to evaluate the referee's call to formulate their own opinion of a ruling. The power and interaction of a fan with the live sports event is beginning to rival broadcast and digital media, which have been the organizer's valued collaborators for raising event exposure and biggest competitors for live audience attention.

Providing customer service is no longer just about hiring and deploying friendly and knowledgeable staff, the lynchpin of any well-designed service program. It now extends to all interactions with the athlete and fan. Convenient ticket purchasing and reselling options, advance printing of parking passes, and instant access to complete event schedule and venue information including what to do, where to go, and what to expect are just a few examples of services that are now imperatives. Building the relationship with the fan attending a sports event is a 365-days-a-year, 24-hours-a-day job, and never more deeply than on the day of the event.

PLAY 1

Defining and Developing Objectives, Strategies, and Tactics

"All winning teams are goal-oriented. Teams like these win consistently because everyone connected with them concentrates on specific objectives. . . nothing will distract them from achieving their aims."

—*Lou Holtz, Former Notre Dame football coach*

This play will help you to:

- Set the primary objectives for your sports event.
- Develop your event's full potential using the P-A-P-E-R Test (promotion, audience, partnerships, environment, and revenue) to identify the many secondary objectives that can be achieved.
- Set strategies to achieve your primary and secondary objectives in the pursuit of greater sports event success.
- Develop the tactics that will effectively apply your strategies to achieve the greatest results.

Introduction

The best place to begin the event management process is at the end.

Know what you want the event to do for your organization once the audience has gone home and all the bills have been paid. Define whether the event is charged with the responsibility of generating a profit, raising funds for a cause-related charity, or promoting a particular lifestyle or sport. Determine the best date and time to stage the event that best meets these objectives. Know what you want both the audience and the athletes or participants to experience. Start with a single primary objective, the essential reason for going to all the trouble to organize your sports event, and dedicate all of your planning to achieve—at a minimum—this one objective, the one that, if met, would qualify the event as a success if all else failed.

It would be naïve to suggest that any singular event should exist for one pure reason. As will shortly be evident, the potential for any sports event can be broadened to achieve a wide range of positive outcomes with a little additional effort. But, it is essential to first identify one key objective, the attainment of which is the highest priority. Ensure that every member of your event team understands the primary objective, and, no matter what other bells and whistles you add later, never lose sight of the purest reason beneath. This will help to keep the highest priority in focus for all members of the event organization team; there should be no confusion about the priority and goals for the event.

Figure 1.1 illustrates examples of the primary objectives for three fictional sports events: an amateur community baseball event, a not-for-profit participatory athletic event, and a professional sports fan festival. Each of the events' organizers has defined a singular goal that is easy to communicate to their respective staffs and stakeholders. They can also achieve great secondary benefits for their respective communities, sports, and organizations.

Example 1: Community Youth League All-Star Game

Primary Objective: Give our town's best youth league players a great end-of-season competition that will recognize them for their great performance during the regular season.

Example 2: Road Runners Club Downtown 10K Road Race

Primary Objective: Promote our sport and healthy lifestyles by giving our city's runners a safe, unobstructed downtown road course, and reinforce the excitement of recreational running by encouraging the community to cheer them on from the sidewalks.

Example 3: Playoffs Pregame Fan Festival

Primary Objective: Reward and excite loyal fans with a street festival preceding the team's first playoff game in three years.

Figure 1.1 Primary Objectives of Three Types of Events

The P-A-P-E-R Test

The primary objective for each of the events in Figure 1.1 is clear, simple, and easily communicated. But, if these were the only identified objectives, the organizers would forsake a large number of opportunities that could leverage their events to achieve a wider range of goals. Although some of these opportunities might seem obvious and might intuitively surface on their own, a method of more comprehensive analysis is available to ensure that few possible benefits are overlooked. Organizers can maximize their event's value by considering all of the other positive things it can do for their community and organization, and then putting them on P-A-P-E-R.

The *P-A-P-E-R Test* (which stands for *promotion, audience, partnerships, environment, and revenue*) is a useful framework against which organizers can create a more comprehensive list of additional, or secondary, objectives. Consider each of the P-A-P-E-R elements and key questions to develop additional aspirations for your event (see Figure 1.2). The authors, of course, recognize that sound and sustainable environmental practices should be applied to every level of sports event planning and production, a subject we will more fully demonstrate in Play 10. So, lest there be any confusion, we encourage you to avoid adding to the waste stream by committing to electronic form the many drafts you will create, revise, and circulate of your event's P-A-P-E-R Test.

First, brainstorm strategically about all of the things that your event can do without regard to the tactics you would have to use to achieve these ends. As you let your imagination go wild during this phase of analysis, it doesn't hurt to get others in your organization involved in the P-A-P-E-R Test. The more ideas on what your event can achieve, the better. Staff members focused on different areas of your operation will often have different perspectives on how the event can drive better results. Don't be concerned if there is some amount of duplication in the answers—duplication only strengthens the validity of the responses.

By considering the answers to these questions, you will quickly see that some outcomes will be more valuable and important to you and your organization than others. Some will also be more complicated and difficult, and others far easier to achieve. Know up front that by expanding your list to include desirable secondary objectives, more time, work, people, and other resources will inevitably be needed to achieve them. Prioritize, selecting the secondary objectives that are most important to your organization, and determine whether it will be more feasible, efficient, and desirable for you to pursue one or two of the more difficult, time-consuming objectives, or a greater number of the easier, less work-intensive goals. Consider your time and financial resources. For example, is long-term growth of an event's profit potential more important than a short-term monetary gain? Go for the goals with the greatest payoffs in whatever time frame is the most relevant, but with the least possible drain on your organization.

To illustrate how this framework can work for you, let's apply the P-A-P-E-R Test to the three sample events in Figure 1.1. The first is a prototypical grassroots community sports event with little or no budget, and a staff comprised totally of volunteers. (Throughout this book, a grassroots event will often be used to describe an amateur, not-for-profit community sports program.) Notwithstanding the minimal resources available, the event has the potential to generate excitement and advance the growth and aims of this community organization. Figure 1.3 illustrates by applying the P-A-P-E-R Test a youth league all-star game.

Developing Tactics

To begin the actual process of planning an event, your objectives have to be supported by the *tactics* you will employ to achieve them. It is against the backdrop of these tactics that you can

Promotion: The marketing and communication strategies and tactics to inform targeted audiences about your event.

- What essential message or important information do I want to communicate to the public about the event, my sport, or my organization?
- Can I build interest in my sport or organization before, during, or after the event? By what measure can this increased interest be demonstrated?
- How do I want the event to position our sport in the community, and what kind of legacy should it leave?

Audience: The group(s) potentially interested in attending or participating in your event.

- Who is our target audience for the event, the people who are most likely to participate, attend, or purchase a ticket?
- Beyond the most likely target, what audiences with similar interests can be attracted or invited to increase attendance, interest, and relevance for our event and further our organization's overall objectives?
- Is there an opportunity to win entirely new fans or enthusiasts to our sport by encouraging their attendance?

Partnerships: The strategic, beneficial relationships and associations established to enhance the event experience and/or to provide needed resources for your event.

- Can we use the event to develop, maintain, or strengthen the relationship with our organization's partners and supporters (e.g., our fans, athletes, members, donors, sponsors, community leaders, local government)?
- What kind of experience do we want to leave our athletes and other partners with? How do we want them to feel before, during, and after the event?

Environment: The factors that can directly and indirectly affect the successful planning and execution of your event.

- Who are our competitors, and what do we want to communicate to differentiate our sports organization from theirs, and our event from the programs they stage?
- Do we need to set ourselves apart from other similar organizations operating in our community or business environment that compete for a share of available dollars, time, or attention?
- What do we need to communicate about the positive attributes of our sports event that sets it apart from other leisure activities similarly competing for the public's or a potential sponsor's attention?
- Do we need to address a perceived time and economic inconvenience that attendees, participants, or partners may encounter when deciding to attend?
- Do we need to address a preconceived notion about our sport or organization that makes it more difficult to generate attendance or participation?

Figure 1.2 Key Elements of the P-A-P-E-R Test

Revenue: The positive financial returns of your event before expenses.

- How much revenue do we need to generate for the event and/or for the organization?
- Do we want or need to generate revenues in excess of expenses? Is this potential profit essential to growing the event in the future?
- How much money can we invest beyond expected revenues to achieve our objectives?
- Is our event, or should our event be, associated with a community cause or charity? How much money do we need to generate for them?

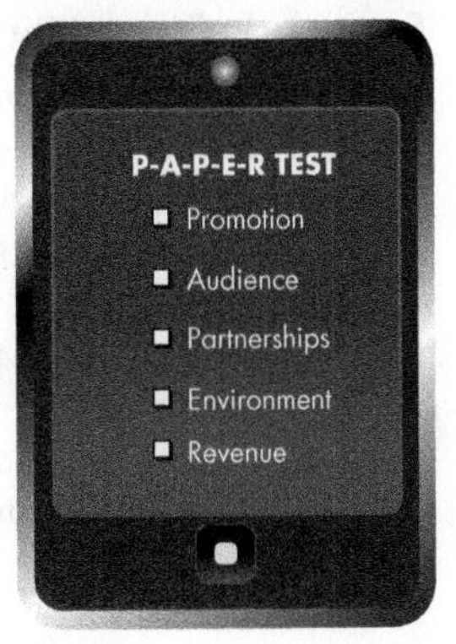

P-A-P-E-R TEST
Promotion
Audience
Partnerships
Environment
Revenue

Figure 1.2 *(Continued)*

begin to identify costs and revenue opportunities and, ultimately, formulate a budget. Often, event budgets are developed considering only the cost of staging the competitive event or main program, with insufficient thought and resources devoted to maximizing its marketing and promotional value or, in some cases, even toward attracting and accommodating spectators. Be sure your budget can accommodate the efforts and expenses—the tactics—of addressing your desired objectives.

The volunteer chairman of the youth league in Figure 1.3 realizes that a children's all-star game can do so much more for its participants and teams, the community, and its own organization than staging the game simply for competition's sake. As a volunteer with limited time and resources, the chairman knows that the game can exist without any of these additional considerations, and achieve its primary objective with a minimum amount of time investment. All he needs is a permit for the ball field and to hire an umpire. To achieve even a small number of these added secondary objectives, the chairman will have to appoint a committee or task force to prioritize which objectives should be considered necessary, which ones would be nice, and which are just not worth the effort. Clearly, even the most basic grassroots sports event can achieve a multitude of previously unconsidered aims.

Secondary objectives are frequently interrelated and mutually supportive. Sometimes a seemingly less important, but more easily achieved, secondary objective will be pursued to reinforce the success of more pertinent agenda items. In the case of the Youth League All-Star Game, getting community leaders (audience) to the event will help to impress businesses from the Chamber of Commerce (partnerships) and encourage coverage by the local media (promotion). A full set of bleachers (audience) watching a well-run, spirited youth activity (environment) will also position future league events as worthy of sponsorship by local businesses and grants sponsored by local politicians (revenue).

It is also helpful to develop secondary objectives against the host organization's overall mission and challenges. The event chairman in this hypothetical case wants to keep registration fees as low as possible, but knows that money is going to be required the following season to replace equipment and level a field that tends to flood after even a brief, moderate shower. The all-star game is a perfect opportunity to raise the money required, whether dollar-by-dollar through the sales of cold soda or raffle tickets to family members in the bleachers, a few hundred dollars at a

Example 1: Community Youth League All-Star Game

- **Primary Objective:** Give our town's best youth league players a great end-of-season competition that will recognize them for their great performance during the regular season.
- **Additional Objectives:**
  - Promotion
    1. Encourage the local media to position our youth league as an important component of our community's quality-of-life, providing our children with a safe, supervised activity that will "keep them off the streets."
    2. Generate advance publicity to bring more kids and families to the event to cheer on their friends and relatives.
    3. Use the event to get more kids to register to play in the league next season.
  - Audience
    1. Fill the bleachers and standing areas with at least 200 spectators. (The more people who attend, the more importance the all-stars and the media will place on the game.)
    2. Get new kids from the community to the game to encourage registration at the ball field for next season.
    3. Attract more parents in the community as volunteer coaches and assistants.
    4. Get town and civic leaders (e.g., mayor, city manager, councilmember, state senator, chamber of commerce representative) to attend to validate the importance of the game to both the players and fans. Demonstrate to these leaders the important place our league occupies in our community.
  - Partnerships
    1. Strengthen our ties to the local chamber of commerce and its member businesses to encourage current team sponsors to renew their relationships, and to identify new prospective team sponsors for next season.
    2. Use these strengthened ties to local businesses and town government to solicit grants to improve the antiquated dugout area and improve overall field maintenance.
  - Environment
    1. Demonstrate that our league is highly organized, motivated, and dedicated to coaching our kids to improve their skills and to promote good sportsmanship.
    2. Demonstrate that our organization emphasizes kids having a good time and is the best alternative to the highly competitive leagues in which winning is more important.
  - Revenue
    1. Generate $500 to replace old equipment (e.g., new batting helmets, bases, batting tees) and to help pay for All-Star trophies.
    2. Increase player preregistration for next season by 10 percent.

Figure 1.3 Expanded Community Youth League All-Star Game Objectives

time through an expanded group of sponsors, through grants from the county, or all three. Staging the all-star game without engaging in all of the extra work may have provided just as wonderful an experience for the children participating. But, with some extra aforethought, planning and effort, the game could also provide an outstanding opportunity to improve the experience for the players this year, as well as in seasons to come.

The second fictional event presented in Figure 1.1 is staged by a local running club. This organization has a handful of permanent administrative staff supplemented by a large body of volunteers, event marshals, and municipal employees assigned by the city. The primary objective for the event is consistent with the overall goals for the organization, but could also pertain to any of the nearly 30 other running events the club stages each year, or to any races staged by similar organizations. Figure 1.4 illustrates how the P-A-P-E-R Test can be applied to allow the Downtown 10K Road Race to stand out uniquely from the rest of the club's calendar.

The executive director of the Downtown Road Runners Club knows that she can use the scenic attractiveness and excitement of running through the downtown area to revitalize one of the organization's annual 10K races, and has set realistic goals to increase membership and race registration. She also recognizes that she can use the event to establish a working relationship with local businesses in the downtown area to achieve mutual objectives—the repositioning of a business district that is exciting in daylight hours five days a week, but sleepy during nonworking hours. Working with the local chamber of commerce, the race can create unique opportunities for area business owners, and, in turn, present new sponsorship and official supplier possibilities. Area restaurants and retailers can engage in promotions that will convert work-week customers into weekend event spectators, and may also support efforts to increase participation as places for recreational runners to pick up registration materials, application forms, and information. The expansion of the list of secondary objectives also reveals another possible opportunity: the potential for future short-distance road race events during evening hours to further promote the vitality of the city after regular business hours.

Amassing and evaluating secondary objectives provides event organizers with a framework upon which to develop tactics and strategies that will transform an event-for-its-own-sake into a dynamic, multifaceted event marketing tool for its organizers, sponsors, the local community, and a host of other stakeholders. For example, the Road Runners' desire to increase the number of recreational runners in the community might lead the organization to consider configuring the event to have two starting lines. The second, located near the midpoint of the original route, and following in parallel lanes so as not to interfere with competitive runners, might be offered to the public at a reduced registration fee to families with young children so an upcoming generation of runners can feel the thrill of passing the finish line. The inaugural effort to add a family component to the race could also serve as a market test to determine whether the club might subsequently consider "family" or "junior" membership tiers to increase membership and annual dues revenues.

To strengthen the club's relationship with the city agencies whose participation is integral to the successful execution of the event, organizers might consider offering the police, fire, streets, and sanitation departments a limited number of free race registrations. These agencies can, in turn, donate these free spots to their widows and orphans organizations, Big Brothers/Big Sisters, or another worthy group, thereby reaping some of the public relations benefits of supporting those in need. The club would be well served by monitoring how these free spots will be used so that it can encourage the media to generate human interest stories on the beneficiaries, further increasing publicity for the event.

It is rarely possible to achieve all of the secondary objectives an organization might desire from a particular event. Organizers need to prioritize which are most valuable, timely, relevant, and cost-effective to achieve with the financial and human resources available. However, in this fictional case, the P-A-P-E-R Test identified several areas of opportunity the organization may

Example 2: Road Runners Club Downtown 10K Road Race

- **Primary Objective:** To promote our sport and healthy lifestyles by giving our city's runners a safe, unobstructed downtown road course, and to reinforce the excitement of recreational running by encouraging the community to cheer them on from the sidewalks.
- **Secondary Objectives:**
  - Promotion
    1. Demonstrate that our sport is a great lifestyle choice for the entire community, providing health and social benefits to all participants regardless of age or income.
    2. Promote our organization as one of the region's top associations of recreational runners.
    3. Encourage spectators to gather at the finish line and at designated locations along the route to cheer on the runners.
    4. Designate an official radio station in our market that will appeal to our target market, and promote both the registration drive prior to the race and spectator attendance on race day.
  - Audience
    1. Capitalize on advance promotion to increase race registration by 33 percent over last year.
    2. Encourage families and friends to "sample" recreational running together for the first time, and reactivate interest among former runners.
    3. Convert those sampling the event into regular recreational runners.
    4. Use advance promotion and the on-site excitement of spectators to increase club membership by 15 percent.
    5. Demonstrate the popularity and vitality of running and the benefits of our association to potential sponsors of future races and events.
  - Partnerships
    1. Strengthen our ties to the city's parks and recreation, police, street, and sanitation departments, upon whose active cooperation we depend to run races year round.
    2. Establish a working relationship with the downtown business improvement district, among whose objectives include bringing visitors and entertainment seekers to the downtown core during low-traffic weekends and summer evenings.
  - Environment
    1. Demonstrate that, as compared to other ways of spending an hour or two, running is fun, healthy, mentally and emotionally refreshing, accessible, and inexpensive.
    2. Demonstrate that as compared to other sports, running requires little economic investment and is easy to learn because it has few rules.
  - Revenue
    1. Generate net proceeds of $50,000 to pay for operational expenses.
    2. Increase club membership and member revenues by 15 percent.

Figure 1.4 Expanded Downtown 10K Road Race Objectives

wish to pursue at the next or future events. To further illustrate how this might be achieved, we turn from the hypothetical organization illustrated in Figure 1.4 to a real-life analogue, one of the premier running clubs in the world (see the accompanying Sideline Story).

The P-A-P-E-R Test is as useful for event managers and marketers in professional sports organizations as it is in the realms of community grassroots and world-class amateur events, and

SIDELINE STORY

New York Road Runners

In 1958, a small group of passionate New Yorkers took to the streets with a simple goal: bring running to the people. Fifty years later their local running club would become a global champion of the running movement. Today, New York Road Runners (NYRR) transcends the primary mission of its founders and continues to grow by encouraging people the world over to get up, get out, and "Run For Life." "Today, we are the world's premier community running organization, and our efforts and events serve all runners and active individuals, from beginners to professional athletes, the young, the elderly, and the underserved of all abilities," says NYRR CEO Mary Wittenberg.

NYRR is widely known for its world-class race properties—including the famed ING New York City Marathon and more than 55 other events—which attract and inspire more than 300,000 runners globally, including 60,000 NYRR members. The organization's long-term commitment to the runners of tomorrow by providing youth programs that educate and motivate more than 100,000 New York City kids each week will help to continue to drive interest in the sport, the club and its events. According to Wittenberg, "It is NYRR's unique nonprofit model that teams contributions from corporate, foundation, and individual donors with earned income from its best-in-class events that enables its mission to give everyone on the planet both a reason to run and the means and opportunity to keep running and never stop." NYRR believes that signing up for a race is just the push someone needs to get out the door and start moving.

The ING New York City Marathon has become a year-round platform with associated events and activities extending well beyond race day. The scope of the event is enormous, annually generating more than $340 million of economic impact for New York City and raising more than $34 million for charity. In 2012, NYRR introduced the immensely popular NYC Half and Brooklyn Half Marathons. In the NYC Half, more than 15,000 runners traverse the rolling hills of Central Park, run through the heart of Times Square, and finish at the South Street Seaport. The week before Memorial Day, NYRR helps to kick off summer with the Brooklyn Half Marathon, where more than 15,000 runners start by the Brooklyn Museum, experience Prospect Park, and sprint to the finish on the world-famous Coney Island boardwalk.

NYRR's diverse portfolio of training opportunities, classes, and annual events include road, track, cross-country, and triathlon races—and in perhaps the most New York of idioms, stair-climbing competitions—ranging from very small with a grassroots feel to nationally televised premium events with large fields featuring the world's best professional runners. In what other sport can the casual participant compete in the same venue at the same time as the very best in the world? That's what NYRR is all about—combining community roots with global ambitions to provide platforms and means to motivate and serve runners of all skill levels and abilities.

is perhaps even more essential to their businesses. With budgets and human resources stretched to the limit, it is a matter of survival for sports events to wring every possible benefit from their staging. To fully realize the potential of a multidisciplinary approach to the development of professional sports events, the entire organization—not just the department charged with managing the event—must be mobilized. Because more staff members with divergent skills, contacts, specialties, and reporting relationships are frequently applied to the management and execution of a professional sports event, it is even more critical to develop clearly defined primary and secondary objectives and priorities.

The third hypothetical sports event in Figure 1.1 is a playoff pregame fan festival to be held on the street outside a team's home arena. There is great demand and excitement in the community because the team has failed to reach the playoffs over the past two seasons, and tickets for the first postseason game have sold out in a single day. Capturing and savoring the buzz in the marketplace, in itself, can be a great reason to stage a fan celebration. But, as Figure 1.5 illustrates, the P-A-P-E-R Test can reveal many more potential prospects.

The organizers of the Fan Festival in Figure 1.5 have been presented with the kind of opportunity every team dreams of—the ability to take advantage of an appearance in the playoffs to achieve the overall marketing, revenue, and organizational goals of the club. With a program of free festivities outside the arena, ticket holders for the game can arrive early and celebrate with their fellow fans. The team and the sponsors of the festival would be happiest if they could fill the plaza in front of their arena with thousands of people incremental to those who will already be arriving to attend the playoff game in order to achieve their merchandise and concessions revenue objectives. But they also realize that the resulting traffic and competition for parking could upset their most loyal ticket holders.

If the team has sufficient space, a "season ticket holder only" area could be created with expanded, premium food menu items, exclusive activities, and meet-and-greet sessions with former team members, giving the most loyal customers a unique and valuable level of access to the event to compensate for any inconveniences they might otherwise experience. Working with the city to add buses to the mass transportation schedule prior to and after game time could also help to reduce congestion and demonstrate how convenient it can be to get to and from the arena. From the city's point of view, providing extra shuttles would give fans the ability to sample the ease of access the mass transit system can provide.

The team will not want its loyal fans who could not get tickets to the game, but want to enjoy the match on television or via the Internet, to decide not to attend the pregame celebration because they are afraid of missing parts of the broadcast. It makes strategic sense to extend the festivities during the game by installing large video screens on the event site so they can savor every second, provided appropriate measures are taken to ensure orderly behavior and fan safety and the broadcaster provides permission for public viewing. Additional WiFi access points can be added inside and outside of the arena to accommodate the higher-than-normal concentration of devices uploading and downloading content to social networks and to friends via text. The crowds excitedly watching the game outside the arena will also provide outstanding opportunities for incremental sales of merchandise and concessions, as well as compelling news footage and remote broadcast locations for local television and radio outlets not permitted in the building during the game.

The inclusion of civic leaders and elected officials is not a political decision, although to suggest that politics and sports are strangers would be naïve. Rather, their presence also demonstrates to a wider audience the importance of the team and the event to the community. These are not the type of guests who shy away from cameras and microphones, so just their presence can help expand the media coverage of the event beyond sports to news and feature reporting.

Example 3: Playoffs Pregame Fan Festival

- **Primary Objective:** Reward loyal fans with a street festival preceding the team's first playoff game in three years.
- **Secondary Objectives:**
  - **P**romotion
    1. Generate added publicity for the team beyond the sports page, and off of our customary game coverage.
    2. Provide the media with attractive, camera-friendly opportunities to capture the excitement of our team's appearance in the playoffs as a lead story, or as a lead-in to the local news.
    3. Demonstrate how the excitement surrounding the team contributes to the community's quality of life for both residents and local businesses.
    4. Increase the level of fan conversation about our team on social networks.
  - **A**udience
    1. Encourage the early arrival of playoff ticket holders to the arena.
    2. Bring fans who are not ticket holders to the arena to add to the excitement of game day.
    3. Attract casual sports fans to the arena to build their level of interest in our team and sport.
    4. Enable members of the community with limited economic resources the ability to enjoy the playoff celebration to the fullest extent possible.
  - **P**artnerships
    1. Provide our sponsors with an opportunity to market to, and communicate with, both loyal fans and casual fans at a time of heightened interest in the team.
    2. Provide civic leaders with an opportunity to appear before the widest range of their constituents.
    3. Provide our radio and television partners with opportunities to enhance the ratings of their pregame coverage, and attract additional viewers and listeners to the game broadcasts.
    4. Provide our online partners with unique content that drives increased page views.
  - **E**nvironment
    1. Present a celebration at least as highly regarded by the fans, media, and community at large as the one staged by our local baseball franchise before its last appearance in a playoff game three years ago.
    2. Demonstrate to those who are unfamiliar with the arena that it is in a safe and easy-to-reach location.
    3. Demonstrate to the community that our fans are passionate, loyal, and excited, but also well-behaved and good-natured.
  - **R**evenue
    1. Sell standing-room tickets to the game.
    2. Increase season ticket sales and sell multigame plans for next season while excitement for the team is at its zenith.
    3. Renew existing and expired season ticket accounts.
    4. Generate $200,000+ in sponsor sales to cover expenses.
    5. Increase playoff and team merchandise sales by 15 percent over average regular season in-arena sales.
    6. Increase concessions revenues by 10 percent over average regular season in-arena sales.

Figure 1.5 Expanded Playoffs Pregame Fan Festival

Chances are the team will never have a more exciting opportunity to speak directly to an audience broader than its season ticket holders, unless the team goes on to win a championship. This is the time to present celebrants with the ability to take advantage of special ticket promotions to help sell new season tickets or multigame packages for the following season. Capitalizing on the "got to be there" nature of events of this type, the club could offer purchasers free event-related merchandise with a deposit for a multigame package for the coming year.

Progress from Strategies to Tactics

After the discussion of each of the sample sports events presented in this chapter, a number of strategies and tactics have been described to illustrate how to develop various programs that can meet a wide variety of event objectives. Objectives state only what event organizers are hoping to achieve, not how they will set about achieving them. Identifying objectives and developing strategies cost your event budget nothing but time, creativity, and analytical thought. The tactics that are selected and employed are the things that cost and potentially make you money. To illustrate, when you take a road trip, you know where you want to go (objective), and by consulting a map or GPS device, you identify what roads you will need to take to get there (strategy). You start spending money once you decide to get in your car and begin paying for gas and tolls to drive there (tactic).

So, before a budget can be drafted, you have to develop your list of objectives and determine the best, most realistic, and most cost-effective strategies that will achieve as many of these goals as possible at the lowest cost of capital and labor. Only then can you design the tactics—the event itself—you will employ that fit your strategies. It is at this stage that you will evaluate whether the tactics you embrace will be too complex, too expensive, or too labor-intense to achieve. Perhaps even the most simple and inexpensive tactics to attain a particular objective are still beyond your reach, given your budget, available time, and all else you wish to accomplish. Here, you may determine that your event is trying to do too much, and that some lower-priority objectives

SIDELINE STORY

The Labatt/NHL Pick-Up Hockey Marathon

The 50th NHL All-Star Game was held in Toronto, the site of the first NHL All-Star Game in 1947. As is the case with many such exhibitions, the game is the centerpiece of a week of NHL All-Star Weekend activities, ranging from arena events featuring the stars to grassroots activities and fan festivals. The Labatt Brewing Company, a Toronto-based sponsor, requested that organizers create an event surrounding the weekend that would capture the attention of the national public, and would embrace two key attributes of their Labatt Blue brand of beer, those of genuineness and being "uniquely Canadian."

may need to be sacrificed to benefit some of the more important ones. This evaluation process can continue throughout the budgeting process, as the affordability of pursuing a given tactic may not become completely apparent until the numbers start falling into place.

Although there are countless strategies that sports event organizers can consider in their pursuit of identifying the proper tactics to employ, using the P-A-P-E-R Test framework can help add direction and focus to the evaluation process. As you review Figure 1.6, a brief checklist of some general questions you can apply to event objectives, as identified by the P-A-P-E-R Test, you will note how the answers to many of these questions can serve multiple purposes and achieve multiple aims.

Sports Events as Business Solutions

The sample events traced through this chapter are presented as responses to specific challenges or desires on the part of the organizer or promoter. With the growth in popularity of sports event marketing as a powerful addition to the traditional marketing mix for corporations of nearly every size, events are frequently not simply born as a whim or fancy of a sports event organizer; often they are also a response to a business partner company's marketing objectives. Leading sports event managers are often approached by marketers and their agencies to develop a program that achieves the objectives of their partners, such as launching new products, relaunching existing products, increasing sales, and marketing lifestyle programs.

The preceding Sideline Story demonstrates that a sports event organizer can apply the needs of a sponsor, as well as its own organization, to the creation of a completely new and compelling event concept. It is even more important to apply the P-A-P-E-R Test to these events to expand the relevance and impact of the program beyond the primary objective of positioning the sponsor's product. The development of additional secondary objectives ensures that the event can be used to achieve multiple benefits for the sponsor and the sports organization, as well as other stakeholders.

In response, the NHL created the Labatt Blue/NHL All-Star Pick-Up Hockey Marathon. Labatt and the NHL solicited the heartiest amateur adult hockey players throughout Canada to qualify to play on one of two teams that would compete on a frozen rink in front of Toronto City Hall continuously, 24 hours per day, until one side no longer possessed the ability to put a sufficient number of players on the ice. The puck dropped on Monday at 8:00 A.M., and play continued through four days and three nights until approximately 7:30 A.M. on Thursday morning, attracting thousands of curiosity seekers, generating hours of national television and radio coverage, and earning a place in the Guinness Book of World Records (which has since been eclipsed). Though the event clearly met many objectives for the NHL, this memorable program would never have been developed without the inspiration, challenge, and support of the Labatt Brewing Company.

Promotion

- What key messages do I want my promotional plans to communicate? How will I encourage the media to help me achieve the outcomes I want before the event (e.g., advance ticket sales, walk-up attendance, increased tune-in), as well as afterward (e.g., positive press coverage, increased membership, financial contributions)?
- How can I use publicity, promotion, and advertising to get my message out to the people that I want to hear it? What traditional media outlets—daily, weekly, and monthly newspapers and magazines, radio stations, television stations, Internet websites—would be right in which to try to place stories?
- How can I use social media networks to provide content and increase engagement directly with our fans?
- How can I use the event as a publicity and promotional engine for my sports organization before, during, and after the event? What compelling stories can I tell? What can I develop or add to the program to make my event more newsworthy?
- Can I work with local school districts to deliver educational programs, school visits, or field trips to students that also promote my message?
- What long-term legacies or benefits can the event leave behind? Is there a possibility of staging the event again in this same marketplace? If there is the opportunity for the growth of the event in future years, how will we achieve it?
- How will we clarify, correct, or debunk any misconceptions about my sport or organization?
- How will I develop and pursue my promotion strategies? Can I expect to achieve my objectives with existing staff and resources, or do I need to get more help from the outside?

Audience

- How can I stage this sports event to keep it fast-paced, involving, and exciting for the attendees?
- How can I make the event easy to buy tickets to, easy to get to, and comfortable for spectators?
- What can I do to add value to the event for our existing fans?
- How can I get new people to my event? How can I turn them into fans, boosters, members, or supporters?
- What events attract an audience that is similar to mine with which I can create cross-promotions to build awareness and attendance?
- How can I educate the public about my sport, organization, or event?
- How can I bring more people into the event through live or recorded media? Is the event worthy of a live broadcast on television or radio, or by streaming to mobile devices? Alternatively, can a broadcast be packaged into a compressed, tape-delayed, or highlights-only form? How can I present the opportunity to make live radio updates or reports from the event site ("remotes") attractive to a partner station?
- Are there ways that digital resources such as our website and social media platforms can engage more deeply and more often with our fans who are at the event and beyond?

Partnerships

- How can I use this sports event to strengthen our organization's ties to current sponsors by entertaining their guests and providing them with superior service? Are there opportunities to provide sponsors with unique access to the event, special hospitality opportunities, exclusive mementos, or other perquisites that go beyond the terms of our contracts and that demonstrate their value to our organization?

Figure 1.6 Strategy-to-Tactics Development Checklist

- How can I use this event as a showcase for potential future sponsors by exposing them to existing satisfied partners? Are there opportunities to provide prospective future partners with one or more of the perquisites of a current sponsor that will demonstrate the value of joining our family?
- Are there exposure opportunities I can offer a partner through pre- and postevent advertising, on-site signage, participant awards and trophy ceremonies, special entertainment segments and audience promotions, giveaways, sweepstakes, recognition on athlete uniforms and staff attire, or printed and digital materials (e.g., tickets, e-mail, invitations, websites, flyers, posters, rack brochures, information guides, programs, scorecards, apps)?

Environment

- Is there another event or organization with which I am competing with for audience, attention, sponsors, or athletes? How can I set my event apart from my competition? Will a cross-promotional partnership with the competitor be in our mutual best interest?
- Can the event solve or draw positive attention to a pressing issue in the host community?
- How is the local community trying to portray itself, and how can our event support those efforts? How can that portrayal benefit my organization, sport, or event?
- What dates and times for the event might fill an entertainment void in the marketplace?

Revenue

- Can or should I sell admission tickets? How many and for how much? If we are interested in having children attend should there be a reduced children's price? A family package price? Discounted prices available only through sponsor promotions? A special price for friends and family of staff and athletes?
- Can I sell merchandise? How much? Will I be selling existing inventory and/or event-specific merchandise? What kind of merchandise—low price points for kids, high price points for premium adult merchandise? Is there a market for high-priced collectibles and memorabilia?
- Can I sell food and/or beverages? What kind and how much? Hot foods and drinks for open, cold weather venues; cold foods and drinks for open, hot-weather events? Are there special regional foods that should be among the offerings? Is it appropriate to serve beer at the event and, if so, what will local ordinances permit?
- Can I sell sponsorships? How many, for how much, and to whom? Can I package this sponsorship with similar opportunities at upcoming events? Should I make low-cost packages available for new sponsors who want to test their association with my event or organization? Can I offer multievent or multiyear sponsorship packages? Do I need outside help to design and sell these packages?
- Can I create a printed commemorative program and sell it, or sell advertisements and give it away for free? Who will sell the ads and to whom will they sell them? Is there revenue potential in developing and providing digital content?
- How can I use the event to encourage sales of tickets to other upcoming events? Can I sell those tickets at the event? Should I distribute discount coupons for these or other events?

Figure 1.6 *(Continued)*

SIDELINE STORY

Putting the P-A-P-E-R Test into Action

Students under the direction of Dr. Benjamin Goss, associate professor at Missouri State University's (MSU) College of Business Administration, used the chapter you are reading, and the P-A-P-E-R Test, to develop the potential of the *Living OUR Legacy Game* (visit the MSU Legacy Game website). Approached with the concept by head men's soccer coach Jon Leamy, Dr. Goss's 2009 event management class created the framework for the game's festivities, the sole MSU Athletics event designed, developed, and operated exclusively by undergraduate students.

To begin the process, the class of 19 students identified their primary objective: "To create a marquee event for the Missouri State men's soccer team that will provide an exceptional experience for attendees, drive revenue for the team, and contribute to the public affairs mission of the university [which are (a) ethical leadership; (b) cultural competence; and (c) community engagement] through a positive impact on the Springfield (Mo.) community."

The class then broke out secondary objectives, strategies, and tactics using the P-A-P-E-R Test to fully develop its community engagement theme for the first year's event. As a result, the first *Living OUR Legacy Game* generated enough revenue to help Ozarks Food Harvest provide more than 750 meals to neighbors in need, as well as funding other local endeavors.

Goss's class embraced a "Soccer Salutes Service" theme for the third *Living OUR Legacy Game* in 2011. "We realized the wonderful opportunity we had during the year of the tenth anniversary of September 11, 2001, to honor the men and women protecting our streets, caring for injuries, and preventing and responding to disasters," said Coach Leamy in the press release that announced the event. "Shortly after those initial discussions, a major portion of the nearby city of Joplin was devastated by a powerful tornado, and in the aftermath, we were reminded once again of the highly important service roles played by men and women who selflessly dedicate their lives to our communities every day." Local first responders, law enforcement, and firefighters were honored during the ceremonies preceding the game.

Post-Play Analysis

To realize the full potential of a sports event, it is essential for organizers to develop a comprehensive list of event objectives before creating a budget and devising a business plan. Identify the primary objective first—the goal the organization feels is essential above all else to reach. Use the P-A-P-E-R Test (promotion, audience, partnerships, environment, and revenue) as a framework to develop the host of secondary objectives that will offer additional benefits for the organizer, sponsors, and other stakeholders.

Defining your objectives sets up the targets you want to hit. Developing strategies defines how you will achieve your objectives (e.g., I will hit the target with my bow and arrow). Identifying tactics helps you to define in detail how those strategies will be actualized (e.g., I will buy a quality bow and the right kind of arrows, learn how to use them, practice my marksmanship, and fire from a reasonable distance). Developing the skills you will need to accurately hit a bull's-eye is the focus of the rest of this book.

Coach's Clipboard

1. Your school's football team is in the top third in the standings. As a result, the campus may host a regional championship game in three weeks. Use the P-A-P-E-R Test to outline what the game can achieve for the school, the athletic department, and the team. Prioritize these objectives based on their importance to these three entities, and how feasible they are to achieve given the time remaining before a possible event. What are the implications if the event must be canceled the week before it is to be staged if the team does not make the playoffs?
2. You are the brand manager of a line of lifestyle clothing with a modest budget for sports marketing. How can you use the P-A-P-E-R Test to identify the best sports events to fit the marketing aims for your product?
3. What tactics can you employ to make the 10K road race in Figure 1.4 more attractive to a potential B2B sponsor (i.e., business-to-business, a company that has customers that are primarily other companies, rather than individual consumers)?
4. An energy bar sponsor approaches a minor league sports organization, seeking a new event or promotion that will help to fight the perception that the product is candy, rather than a viable and nutritionally valid meal replacement bar. The potential sponsor wants the event to portray an active lifestyle, and be something it can "own" (i.e., be instantly and ever recognized as a program associated with its product). Design an event that achieves these aims, and expand this primary objective to serve the needs of the sports organization.

PLAY 2

Identifying Costs

"The lack of money is the root of all evil."

—*George Bernard Shaw, Irish dramatist (1856–1950)*

This play will help you to:

- Develop and manage the expense side of your event's budget.
- Become familiar with the types of costs most common to sports events.
- Understand the dynamics of fixed and variable event expenses.

Introduction

Now that you know what you are trying to achieve, and hopefully have a reasonable concept of what kind of event you would like to stage as your plan to get there, it is time to begin constructing an event budget. Your budget will identify areas of revenue opportunities and expense items. Although revenue generally appears first on most budgets, it is often more practical to start developing a budget from the expense side, so an event organizer can know how much revenue will be needed to support your event and fulfill the event's objectives. If there are not enough obvious revenue opportunities to cover these expenses, try to develop new ones. If there is still insufficient funding, it's time to go back to your objectives, tactics, and expenses to determine what cost categories can be reduced or sacrificed.

Fledgling sports events most frequently fail to take wing for the same reasons new businesses often fail—undercapitalization and an underestimation of expenses, the root of Mr. Shaw's evil. Simply put, it will take money to plan, develop, manage, and execute an event, and a fair amount of it will have to be spent before the very first ticket, T-shirt, or sponsorship is sold. Therefore, some investment is almost always required to get a project moving forward. The larger the event, the greater the initial cash outlay is likely to be needed.

A thorough examination of all of the expected and potential costs will be required to ensure that your event's budget is realistic and that your revenue goals will meet or exceed the costs of doing business. You will find that there are seemingly limitless ways to spend your money when planning an event, and it is essential to know exactly on what, and have some idea of how much, you will have to spend before the invoices start piling up. Use any of the widely available spreadsheet software programs to chart your expenses, and make it a point to use the formula functions that automatically add columns and perform other mathematical tasks so you can easily calculate the effect on the bottom line as you adjust individual budget categories.

A worksheet of typical event budget expenses appears in Appendix 1. It provides a comprehensive list of major expense categories suitable for many sports events, though it is by no means complete. Use this table as a guideline while preparing the expense budget of your event, but it should be your goal to think of every possible detail, such as equipment and other specifics to your sport and event, to ensure that all of your anticipated costs are fully considered.

The definitions of many of the expenses in Appendix 1 will be obvious and familiar. The rest of this chapter provides you with more details, as well as some vagaries, peculiarities, tricks of the trade, hints, and warning signs for expenses that are more particular to sports events.

Expenses fall into two broad categories—*fixed costs* and *variable costs*. Fixed costs, as the name implies, remain immutable regardless of how successful the event is in attracting spectators or selling sponsorships. On the one hand, examples of fixed costs include player and equipment costs and operational expenses, marketing costs, and flat-rate facility rentals. Variable costs, on the other hand, are those that increase or decrease as attendance or sales grow or fail to develop. Examples of variable costs include facility rentals based on a percentage of ticket sales, sales taxes, commissions paid on sponsorship sales, and, expenses for venue staffing (i.e., more guest services, custodial, and security personnel are required as attendance grows).

Facility Costs

Because a significant portion of a sports event's costs may be spent on leasing and preparing a site to host the event, it is wise to begin constructing your budget by selecting the venues most suited and affordable for holding your event. If you are restricted to a particular city or community, your choices will likely be limited to one, or perhaps just a few, event-appropriate facilities. Yet, if you have some flexibility as to the community that can host your event, you will, of course, have a wider range of venue options and your bargaining power during the selection process can potentially save thousands of dollars in venue costs. Play 4 provides more details on how to apply the economic benefits of an event to drive down venue and host city expenses for organizers who can make their program available to competitive bidders.

Rent

In most cases, the facility you will use to host your sports event is in the business of making money, or must at least cover its operating costs. That you may have to pay some form of rent or permit fee is probably obvious, but, if you have never leased an arena, stadium, convention center, or other similar facility, you will be amazed at the unexpected additional costs that can burden a budget. Request a *pro forma* copy of the lease agreement for any facility you are thinking of using while you prepare your expense budget. A pro forma is essentially a "fill in the blanks" standard lease form that outlines the major points of an organizer's relationship with the facility. The facility may request some amount of information about the event to help it prepare the most appropriate first-draft lease. The agreement should also contain the rules and regulations of hosting events in the venue, as well as the rates for additional charges such as labor, equipment rentals, and value-added event services provided by the facility. The more potentially profitable your event is for a prospective host venue, the more negotiable its management may be with respect to adjusting the terms and prices in the lease agreement.

The biggest, most prestigious events can provide sufficient noncash incentives for a city or venue manager to consider hosting an event at a reduced rate or, in some cases, on a rent-free basis. Some incentives that often tip the scale toward reduced-rate rentals include an unusually large number of hotel room-nights the event could generate for a city, unusually strong promotional benefits for a local team or positive publicity for the host city, and national or international media exposure, among others.

Most sports events fall into the realm of potentially profitable prospects for an arena, stadium, or other public assembly venue, but the rental rate formula is frequently negotiable. It may be paid as a flat sum, a percentage of gross ticket sales, or some combination of a reduced flat fee plus a percentage of sales. If you are relatively confident in your organization's ability to sell tickets or your ticket prices are premium priced, your budget will go further if you can secure the lowest possible flat rate. If, however, your ticket prices are low or you are less confident in your ticket selling prospects due to the event's past history, its status as a first-time event, or as a result of external factors such as the effects of the economy or political instability on attendance, consider negotiating a variable rental fee that is more heavily weighted toward a percentage of sales. This strategy can also help you better manage a tight budget, inasmuch as the effective rental rate will rise only as the success of your event increases. In most cases, you will probably have to pay some minimum guarantee if the rent will be calculated in some measure on a percentage of sales. Remember that facility managers are smart, experienced businesspeople, and they will be vigilant and conscientious about finding ways to maximize their revenue while you are attempting to reduce your event's financial exposure. Work honestly and candidly with the facility representatives during negotiations. Your mutual interests are best served when both sides have realistic expectations and benefit from each other's success.

The rental rate, as well as other facilities costs, will be covered in the lease agreement for the venue. The lease should be negotiated early in the budgeting process, because building costs can make up a sizable portion of your event budget. When you receive your first copy of the lease agreement, expect that most terms will be written to benefit and protect the facility. Work with an experienced attorney and, if possible, a seasoned industry professional to review all terms of the agreement before signing.

Ticket Sales Deductions
Taxes and Facility Usage Fees

Although the deductions from ticket sales revenues are technically costs, they are not listed on our sports event budget worksheet under expenses. They are classified as "negative revenues," because that money is never really received from the box office or ticket sellers. Every dollar of each ticket sold may carry with it payment obligations, probably in the form of taxes, levies, usage charges, or commissions. Thus, although these costs are discussed here, they will appear on the revenue side of the budget worksheet, but as deductions. They are, nonetheless, costs of doing business that need to be properly accounted when constructing your financial model for the event.

Make sure your lease agreement covers all expected areas in which the event will incur costs that will be charged by the facility, or through the venue, its contractors, labor unions, and public agencies. For example, be sure that all deductions from ticket revenues are unambiguously defined in your contract. Many facilities charge a small per-ticket fee variously known as a "capital replacement fee" or "facility usage fee." This deduction usually ranges from one to several dollars per ticket or as a percentage of the ticket price, and may represent an obligation the building must collect on behalf of the local government to cover the financing costs on the facility's construction. As a result, these fees are often nonnegotiable. Be sure to determine whether this fee is traditionally charged to the organizer, or whether it is most often passed along to the ticket buyer as a cost added to the face ticket price. The total impact of this expense on the overall budget will, as a variable cost, increase or decrease with the tickets actually sold. Events are not charged a usage fee for seats that go unsold, and such a fee may or may not be payable on tickets that are issued on a complimentary basis, depending on the facility.

There are several other costs that will vary with ticket sales. In most cases, payment will be the responsibility of the event organizer, and is not usually added to the consumer's ticket price. As they are variable costs and not payable before a ticket is sold, these charges are usually deducted from your ticket revenues by the venue before you receive them. The most common deductions are sales and amusement taxes, which are commonly levied by local, state, or provincial governments. As acts of legislation, their rates are normally not negotiable. They will differ widely between municipalities, so analyze the effect of local taxes on your bottom line before you award an event to a host city or facility. Current, applicable tax rates can often be found on the host government's website.

It is not safe to simply assume that the prevailing local sales tax rate will be the ultimate rate you will be charged on ticket sales. In some cases, the rates may be higher because of an added "amusement" or "entertainment" tax levy or lower because a separate amusement tax will apply, but the sales tax will not. Be sure to check with the finance managers of your selected event venue to determine the actual rate for which you will be liable on ticket sales in that locality.

SIDELINE STORY

A Major League Tax Waiver

There have been instances in which state or local legislators consider and agree to pass a bill that waives tax liabilities for specific sports events. Such a waiver was granted to Major League Baseball and the National Football League in the State of Florida that specifically excludes MLB All-Star Games, the World Series, and the Super Bowl from being obligated to pay taxes on the sale of event tickets. This waiver extends only to these organizations for the purpose of providing additional incentive for the leagues to stage these drivers of high economic impact in their state, and as of this writing are only applicable for those specific events. Such considerations can become politically sensitive and matters of public debate, and have the potential to result in serious public relations fallout for both the host city and event organizer.

In many states, provinces, and cities, sales and/or admissions taxes may be payable on the value of at least some tickets that are issued on a complimentary basis. Generally, if the tickets are exchanged for some form of valuable consideration, they are subject to taxation. For example, an organizer may be required to provide complimentary tickets as a benefit to companies that provide an event with either cash or with products and services as part of their sponsorship agreements. Even if tickets make up only a small portion of what the sponsor is entitled to as part of the deal, the value of those tickets may be taxable as though you accepted cash for their face value. In most instances, where complimentary tickets are issued as a courtesy to VIP guests, player families, charities, and to the general fan population as a gesture of goodwill, for which no recompense in any form is received or expected, they are usually free of tax obligations. Event organizers should seek professional advice on whether and how sales or amusement taxes may apply to complimentary tickets issued in the locality where the event is being held. If the host venue has been the site of a number of similar events, its chief financial officer can usually provide this information.

Ticket Sales Deductions—Commissions

There are a number of other deductions from ticket sales revenues that usually apply, and these are often overlooked during the budgeting process by first-time sports event organizers. Credit card commissions, for example, can erode ticket revenues by as much as 3 percent. When tickets are purchased by credit card, it is the responsibility of the event organizer to pay a fixed percentage of the transaction to the credit card company. If you are working with an established sports or entertainment venue, you will probably be asked to pay credit card commissions to the facility at a blended rate; that is, as a flat fixed percentage of the transaction. This amount is deducted from ticket revenues by the box office to cover the commissions to the card issuer, plus a nominal handling fee for the facility. It is usually best to utilize the existing box office and its relationship with the credit card companies to save you the hassle of installing data lines, establishing an account, and employing your own staff of ticket sellers.

Not all of your tickets will be purchased with a credit card, such as those paid by check on behalf of groups and corporations. If you expect to be accepting credit cards and you forecast that at least some sizable portion of your ticket buyers will be using that method of payment, it is recommended your budget presume that *all* patrons will take advantage of this option. This will protect your budget with a small, hidden contingency fund should other expenses rise beyond expectations.

Many larger sports events, particularly those held in existing sports and entertainment facilities, make use of a digital ticketing system. Using the best available technology to provide fans with the most convenient access to purchase tickets—via the Internet, by phone, or in person at the box office—must be a priority. Anyone who has ever purchased an event ticket knows that the ticket service will collect some "per ticket" and "per order" service fee from the purchaser. What many novice sports event organizers may not realize is that they may be liable for certain transaction fees as well.

The contracts between event venues and their ticket sales provider will vary, but in many cases you will not be liable for any appreciable fees for tickets sold through the system at the venue's box office—that is, at the stadium, arena, or other facility in which the event will occur. Usually, you will get the best deal by being included under the existing contract between the venue and the digital ticket seller. If your event is very large, or if you are not staging your event in a facility with existing ticketing options, and you wish to avail yourself of the additional sales opportunities a ticket service can provide, you will have to negotiate your own best deal with the ticket service.

Many stadiums and arenas maintain a database of tour and school groups, bus companies, youth organizations, booster clubs, and other avid ticket buyers that make purchases in block quantities, either through an in-house group sales department or an outside agency. Group sales can be a very effective supplemental means to fill your event venue, but the old maxim that "there is no such thing as a free lunch" applies here, too. You will have to pay the group sales agency and any in-house group sales function provided by the arena a pre-agreed commission rate in the form of discounted prices (e.g., the agency charges the group the full price and retains the difference), a service fee per ticket, and/or a flat fee for handling and processing. Using today's various communication technologies, getting group sales information directly to likely buyers is quicker and more cost-efficient than ever. Because of the large multiples of tickets that can sold through group sales efforts, they are, in most cases, an effective, revenue-generating option for event organizers that is generally worth the expense of commissions.

Facility Labor

It takes dozens, and sometimes hundreds, of facility employees to staff a sports event, and you can expect to have to pay for all of them. The most obvious are the *front-of-house staff*—the ushers, ticket takers, security officers, guest services or crowd management force, and box office personnel the public most often encounters, along with their supervisors and managers. These facility employees are usually paid by the hour, with a predetermined minimum number of hours per event, plus an overtime differential before and after certain times of the day (e.g., after midnight or before 7:00 A.M.), on certain days (e.g., Sundays and holidays), or after a specified number of working hours per day. The venue will most often charge you an hourly rate that is marked up from the employee's actual pay rate, "plus benefits" (e.g., the cost of health insurance premiums and/or vacation accruals). You may also be charged an "administrative fee," which is the facility's way of offsetting the costs of scheduling employees, keeping track of their hours, and servicing their payroll. Once you have provided the facility with enough detail to give a good understanding of your event, the management can provide you with an estimate of what to expect in the way of front-of-house labor costs. Make sure the estimate includes all administrative, payroll, and benefits charges as well.

Your labor costs will surely also include some *back-of-house* building staff, such as electricians, carpenters, riggers, maintenance workers and event presentation personnel such as stagehands, stage managers, spotlight operators, audio technicians, production crews, and operators to support video boards, scoreboards, and other electronic displays. Many facilities are bound by labor union agreements for at least some of those job functions, which will also obligate any lessee. The venue will provide you with the hourly rates for each of these labor categories, from which you can calculate costs based on your load-in (installation), rehearsal/practice, event, and load-out (dismantle) schedule.

The event organizer's obligation to pay for back-of-house staff may also include a "conversion" charge. The facility may have to reconfigure itself from the form or condition it was in the day before loading in your event, and then back again after your event has vacated. For example, if an arena was being leased to host a martial arts competition following an ice hockey game, a number of operations personnel will be required for the conversion, or changeover. In order to be in a condition conducive to host the martial arts event, the boards, glass, and netting around the rink would need to be removed and the ice would need to be covered with an insulating surface such as homosote (a paper-based insulating board), plywood, and/or carpeting. Additional items such as floor seating, tables, and equipment for scoring might be added, and the center scoreboard adjusted to the appropriate height (also known as its *trim*). After the event, these materials would need to be removed and stored and the venue returned to its original condition. In this case, the cost of the labor required to convert to and from the ice hockey configuration could be charged to the event organizer.

Additional facility expenses worth mentioning are restoration costs, the amount of money required after the event to repair damage and replace broken equipment. Ideally, you want to encounter no such costs, but you should be prepared for the possibility that the venue or its assets might be damaged during your event and that some recompense might be required. It is wise to examine the host facility before beginning work on your event and make a record of visible damage already in place. If your organization or your vendors, participants, or spectators subsequently damage the facility while preparing for, staging, viewing, participating in, or dismantling the event, you may be liable for the cost of restoration. Determine to what extent your insurance coverage will protect you from this potential liability.

Facility costs are not limited only to those just described, and are dependent on both the nature of your event and the type of venue in which it is held. The expenses for some items will be charged to the organizer directly by the facility; others will be purchased or rented directly by the event organizer to help prepare the venue to properly host the event. The checklist in Figure 2.1 will assist you in the process of identifying these types of costs.

Rent

- ☐ Event day(s)
- ☐ Installation, practice/rehearsal, and dismantle days

Venue Labor*

- ☐ Front-of-house staff (e.g., ushers, ticket takers, security/crowd management, box office, guest services)
- ☐ Back-of-house staff (e.g., stagehands, electricians, carpenters, riggers, maintenance workers)
- ☐ Public safety personnel (e.g., police, fire, EMS)
- ☐ Overnight security
- ☐ Event presentation production crews/operators
- ☐ Medical and first aid staff
- ☐ Conversion crew
- ☐ Taxes and/or facility usage fees*
- ☐ Credit card commissions*
- ☐ Group sales and other sales commissions*
- ☐ Event equipment (e.g., scoreboards, goals, nets, benches, communications)
- ☐ Crowd control equipment (e.g., barricades, ropes, stanchions)
- ☐ Catering and hospitality*
- ☐ Merchandise operations
- ☐ Chair and table rentals
- ☐ Pipe and drape dividers
- ☐ Power and utilities*
- ☐ Postevent cleaning
- ☐ Restoration

*Variable costs

Figure 2.1 Typical Sports Event Facility Costs

Player- and Game-Related Expenses

There are few instances in the sports event world in which the participants or players are not recognized for their achievement in some fashion. In grassroots and amateur athletics, this recognition might take the simple form of medals or trophies. For team and individual championships, from professional and collegiate to scholastic and club, banners and wall plaques are hung to visibly serve as permanent reminders of great accomplishment. In professional sports, trophies, if awarded at all, are increasingly supplemented with more valuable considerations, including expensive championship rings, cars, and/or other gifts, as well as cash awards that might take the form of appearance fees, prizes for outstanding performance, bonuses for achieving certain benchmarks, and a winner's prize pool, among others.

In addition to setting aside funds for prizes, appearance fees and winner pools, consider whether you will require the services of athletes beyond the actual competition and whether you can include incremental appearances in the compensation or recognition structure for professional or semiprofessional players. Including a meet-and-greet opportunity with athletes for fans, or for a sponsor's guests, can go a long way toward generating new ticket buyers and corporate partners, so it is strongly recommended that event organizers either seek to include an appearance or two within an athlete's understanding of his/her obligations, or put some cash aside to pay for some number of appearances. (This is not something to be offered in most amateur and grassroots sports organizations, where payment in cash, products, or services could violate league or collegiate rules or those of another governing body.)

Some organizations combine the participation of marquee athletes with amateur competitors to add star power to an event and pique spectator interest. The New York Road Runners, for instance, invite a roster of elite runners who are paid appearance fees to participate in the New York City Marathon, running side-by-side—at least for the first mile or so—with accountants, lawyers, clerks, businesspeople, and other purely recreational runners. Many pro-am golf tournaments operate under a similar model, where amateur duffers get to play the sport they love alongside the greats of the links.

Appearance fees	$100,000
Winner's prize pool	$100,000
MVP award	$10,000
Supplementary appearance fees	$40,000
Total Player Prize Pool	**$250,000**

Figure 2.2 Sample Prize Pool

For organizers who must offer cash incentives to participating athletes, there is no one right way to design a compensation scenario. Figure 2.2 illustrates how a sample prize pool can be constructed for a two-team sports event that ensures that every player has an incentive to participate and compete. In this example, the event organizer has budgeted a $250,000 prize pool. The organizer can decide to award the entire sum to the winning team, or split the funds available to ensure that everyone goes home rewarded, at least to some degree.

For the purposes of this example, let's assume there are 15 players on each of two teams, for a total of 30 players. The organizer wants to reward each player with a guaranteed minimum fee for participating. Dividing the $100,000 appearance fee pool by all 30 participants provides a $3,333.33 guarantee for every player. In this compensation scheme, a player can triple his or her award to $10,000.00 by playing on the winning squad. This figure is derived by dividing the winner's prize pool of an additional $100,000 among the 15 winning players, adding $6,666.67 to the guaranteed appearance fee. The event's Most Valuable Player (MVP) is awarded an additional prize of $10,000. Presuming the MVP is on the winning team, that player would be paid a grand total of $20,000. Exclusive of additional fees available for supplementary appearances, the total player prize pool has been divided into $3,333 for players on the losing team, $10,000 for players on the winning team, and $20,000 for the MVP (if on the winning squad, or $13,333 if on the losing side).

The prize pool includes funds for supplementary appearance fees, allowing occasions for the players to meet and greet sponsors, guests, or fans. For illustrative purposes, let us assume there are 20 such opportunities during this event, each opportunity representing one hour of time beyond participating in the competition itself. Players can earn $2,000 for each hour they agree to participate, and may increase their earnings by appearing for more than a single hour. A player on the losing team, then, can increase his/her earnings to more than $5,300 with one additional supplemental appearance.

If you are organizing a tournament, determine how you will recognize the winners. Consider into how many age and gender brackets your players will be divided among and to what level in each bracket you will recognize with trophies, medals, or other prizes (e.g., first place only, first through third place, etc.). Determine those to whom you expect to award the trophies or medals. Will you recognize only a select few top achievers or all of the athletes, the coaches, staff, or the organizations they represent? Identify all of these expenses and capture them in your game- and player-related expense budget. See Figure 2.3 for a checklist of game- and player-related line items to include in your budget, where applicable.

- ☐ Accommodations
- ☐ Appearance fees
- ☐ Beverages (water/sports drinks) and snacks for locker rooms/benches
- ☐ Equipment
- ☐ Equipment managers and trainers
- ☐ Gifts
- ☐ Ice
- ☐ Laundry
- ☐ Locker room supplies
- ☐ Meals and per diems
- ☐ Medical staff, EMTs, ambulance
- ☐ Officiating fees and expenses
- ☐ Player guest expenses
- ☐ Playing surface preparation and maintenance
- ☐ Playing surface lighting
- ☐ Prize money and recognition (e.g., trophies, medals, plaques)
- ☐ Scoreboards and timing equipment
- ☐ Temporary construction
- ☐ Towels
- ☐ Trainers fees, equipment, and supplies
- ☐ Transportation, in-bound/out-bound (to/from home airport, airfares)
- ☐ Transportation, local (to/from airport, hotels, and event sites)
- ☐ Uniforms, including numbering and lettering

Figure 2.3 Typical Game- and Player-Related Costs

Event Operations Expenses

The event operations expenses category contains all the costs classified as "overhead," the items that are essential to run the event but have little direct visible impact on the experiences of the audience or the athletes. They would include the costs for staff hired specifically for the event, and all of the support equipment, systems, and supplies required by the staff members to execute their responsibilities. See Figure 2.4 to help you account for the most common event operations expenses.

Most of the expenses listed in Figure 2.4 are relatively straightforward, and may be estimated by simply contacting prospective vendors and requesting price quotes. The area of most financial exposure and business concern, however, is the issue of insurance. How much and what type(s) of insurance should be purchased vary with the type of event you are staging, where you are holding it, and the kinds of athletes participating (e.g., amateur or professional, their age and training). In today's litigious society and world political climate, recommended coverage and the cost of insurance is climbing at an increasing, almost prohibitive, rate. You cannot afford not to have

- ☐ Accounting services
- ☐ Accreditation (e.g., credential badges, ID cards, lanyards)
- ☐ Communications services (e.g., phones, data lines or WiFi connections)
- ☐ Computers and printers
- ☐ Copiers/scanners/fax
- ☐ Gratuities
- ☐ Insurance
- ☐ Legal services
- ☐ Mobile communications equipment (e.g., walkie-talkies, mobile devices)
- ☐ Office space, hotel meeting rooms, and/or office trailers
- ☐ Office supplies
- ☐ Payroll services
- ☐ Postage
- ☐ Power and generators (to the extent not provided by the facility)
- ☐ Power distribution (the labor to bring power to where it is needed)
- ☐ Recycling and material recovery
- ☐ Shipping, trucking, and overnight couriers
- ☐ Software (existing applications and custom programming)
- ☐ Staff and volunteer expenses (refreshments, meals or per diems, transportation, parking)
- ☐ Staff attire
- ☐ Storage and warehousing
- ☐ Temporary staff salaries and fees, including event specialists, freelancers, and interns
- ☐ Ticket design and printing (if not electronic)
- ☐ Vehicle and equipment rentals (e.g., cars, vans, trucks, golf carts, Segways, lifts)
- ☐ Volunteer program expenses (e.g., recognition, food and beverage, parking)

Figure 2.4 Typical Sports Event Operations Expenses

adequate insurance coverage for your sports event and its organizing entities, and it is essential to the financial well-being of your program to get preliminary quotes before you complete the budgeting process. At minimum, some form of liability coverage is required to protect the event, its parent organization, and its executives, employees, and sponsors. Proof of liability insurance coverage, often in the millions to tens-of-millions of dollars per occurrence, is a requirement that appears in the leases of most event facilities. Organizers should consult with their legal counsel and insurance broker to determine what additional insurance coverage would be advisable, particularly in regard to audience and athlete safety, the potential for injury, and other risks associated with the event.

Outdoor events may consider acquiring "weather insurance," coverage that will pay benefits to the organizer if the program must be canceled because of adverse weather conditions. Premiums for this type of coverage are often expensive, and the conditions that are required to trigger the payment of benefits are often extreme. An organizer should carefully analyze the financial exposure of an uninsured weather cancellation or postponement against the expense of purchasing insurance. The greater the potential loss to the organizer, the more attractive weather cancellation insurance may become. Unless an organizer is able to self-finance unrecoverable expenses and refunds to sponsors and ticket holders, coverage merits serious consideration.

Another expensive variation of cancellation insurance is terrorism insurance. This type of policy protects organizers from the financial calamity that might be faced due to a terrorist activity directed at the event, or a similar action occurring within a prescribed geographic radius that makes holding the event inadvisable. In uncertain times, insurance companies are charging premiums for this type of coverage that are, unfortunately, out of reach for most event organizers. A more comprehensive discussion of this and other types of insurance coverage, as well as risk management issues, can be found in Play 14.

Marketing and Promotion Expenses

You may be planning the best and most compelling sports event ever staged, but unless you have a plan that will get the word out to both participants and the potential audience, you could be faced with a sparsely attended tournament or empty bleachers. You may not have designed a complete marketing plan at this point, but you will need to set aside funds for advertising, publicity, promotions, website and social media platforms, as well as for the entities that will help you create and manage these marketing vehicles. Preevent publicity will help generate public awareness and ticket sales, but a well-conceived advertising plan is strongly recommended to supplement such efforts.

The marketing of your event does not end once the program is underway. Postevent coverage is particularly useful in demonstrating the vitality and relevance of your event to community leaders, potential sponsors, future ticket buyers, and other key stakeholders. If your event is particularly newsworthy, you may have to provide facilities and services that will enable the media to cover your event. Relevant items of importance include a comfortable and unobstructed vantage point from which to view the event, as well as media working space with access to power, high-speed data lines or sufficient wireless capability, and other communication services to facilitate the filing of stories directly from the event site. In addition, a press conference area for interviewing athletes, coaches, and other key officials is also often prepared for major events. Media representatives are accustomed to the periodic receipt of official statistics during an event, and, in the case of televised sports events, monitors with which to view replays and live broadcast coverage. Many organizers will also provide the media with access to food or snacks, either complimentary

- ☐ Advertising agency billable expenses
- ☐ Advertising agency fees (hourly charges for staff time and creative charges)
- ☐ Branding and logo development
- ☐ Information services (telephone information center, text response service, or live chat capability)
- ☐ Kick-off or announcement news conference or event
- ☐ Media accreditation
- ☐ Media center/workroom expenses (rental of furnishings, draping, Internet access, phone, copier, fax, monitors)
- ☐ Media hospitality (meals, refreshments, snacks, gifts)
- ☐ Outdoor advertising (creative, production, and rental of billboards and street banners)
- ☐ Preevent promotional giveaway items
- ☐ Press conference area
- ☐ Print advertising creative (design)
- ☐ Print advertising space
- ☐ Public relations agency expenses
- ☐ Public relations agency fees (see "advertising agency fees")
- ☐ Radio advertising production (i.e., costs of creating the commercial)
- ☐ Radio advertising time
- ☐ Social media content production and management
- ☐ Staff photographer and videographer
- ☐ Statistician(s)
- ☐ Television advertising production
- ☐ Television advertising time
- ☐ Website development and management

Figure 2.5 Typical Sports Event Marketing and Promotion Expenses

or for a small fee, appropriate to the time of day, along with soft drinks, water, and coffee (happy media write happier stories). Draw applicable expense categories from Figure 2.5 as you develop your marketing budget, and refer to Play 8 for more details on how to work with and service the media.

Sponsor Fulfillment Expenses

Sponsors expect, and are entitled to, a host of contractual benefits and, in many cases, noncontractual perquisites that are attendant to their support of your event. Expenses undertaken to service sponsor needs, whether dictated by the contract or provided as added bonuses by the organizer, are called *fulfillment expenses*.

Almost every event sponsorship agreement will include a minimum quantity of site-specific signage positions that display the sponsor's logo, company name, and/or product identification to the public. Unless otherwise defined by the sponsor's contract, the expense of designing, fabricating,

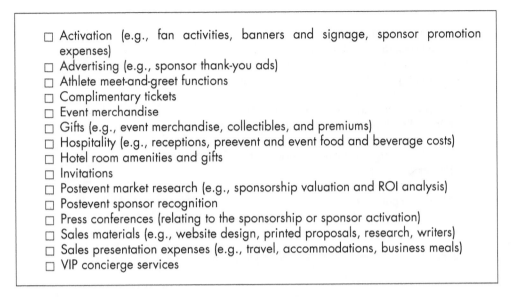

- ☐ Activation (e.g., fan activities, banners and signage, sponsor promotion expenses)
- ☐ Advertising (e.g., sponsor thank-you ads)
- ☐ Athlete meet-and-greet functions
- ☐ Complimentary tickets
- ☐ Event merchandise
- ☐ Gifts (e.g., event merchandise, collectibles, and premiums)
- ☐ Hospitality (e.g., receptions, preevent and event food and beverage costs)
- ☐ Hotel room amenities and gifts
- ☐ Invitations
- ☐ Postevent market research (e.g., sponsorship valuation and ROI analysis)
- ☐ Postevent sponsor recognition
- ☐ Press conferences (relating to the sponsorship or sponsor activation)
- ☐ Sales materials (e.g., website design, printed proposals, research, writers)
- ☐ Sales presentation expenses (e.g., travel, accommodations, business meals)
- ☐ VIP concierge services

Figure 2.6 Typical Sponsorship Expenses

installing, and dismantling this signage is a cost to the event budget. Event organizers will usually be obligated to provide a specified number of complimentary tickets, the cost of which (i.e., the lost revenue represented by these complimentary tickets) should also be accounted for in the budget.

Because the content of sponsor packages varies so widely among different types of events and across the industry, there is no rule of thumb governing what percentage of an organizer's sponsor revenues should be set aside to cover fulfillment costs. The revenue-to-expense ratio will differ even among the family of sponsors for a single event. Any expense that results from an obligation made to a sponsor, and that would not have been incurred if that sponsor was not involved, should be included in this budget line. Extra perquisites that you intend to add that are not contractually required should also be included. Such expenses may include hosting private VIP receptions, advertisements acknowledging the sponsors' support, special gifts, premiums, and presentations, supplemental athlete appearances, custom-made staff attire displaying the sponsor's logo, labor for product sampling—the list and variety of these costs are can seem endless. Refer to Figure 2.6 for a summary of sponsorship expenses.

By budgeting for sponsor fulfillment costs before a package of benefits is offered to potential sponsors, event organizers will avoid one of the most basic mistakes in event marketing—offering a sponsor package that will cost too much to manage and fulfill compared to the revenue it will generate. Creating sponsorship packages of value to both the organizer and the business partner will be more fully discussed in Plays 6 and 7.

Guest Management and Hospitality Expenses

Sports events have become a major hospitality opportunity, not only for the sponsors that support them but also for the organizations that stage them. From tournaments to touring events, championship matches to all-star games, and fan festivals to skills exhibitions, organizers take

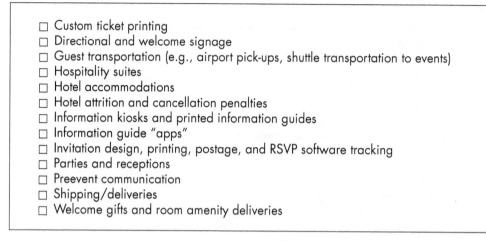

- ☐ Custom ticket printing
- ☐ Directional and welcome signage
- ☐ Guest transportation (e.g., airport pick-ups, shuttle transportation to events)
- ☐ Hospitality suites
- ☐ Hotel accommodations
- ☐ Hotel attrition and cancellation penalties
- ☐ Information kiosks and printed information guides
- ☐ Information guide "apps"
- ☐ Invitation design, printing, postage, and RSVP software tracking
- ☐ Parties and receptions
- ☐ Preevent communication
- ☐ Shipping/deliveries
- ☐ Welcome gifts and room amenity deliveries

Figure 2.7 Typical Sports Event Guest Management and Hospitality Expenses

advantage of the cachet generated by their programs to invite, excite, and attract VIP guests, sponsors, potential future business partners, celebrities, and other influential individuals to their events. Determine early in the planning process how many guests you will be able to accommodate on a complimentary basis including to what degree you will entertain and service them. Although Play 11 explores this area in greater detail, organizers can use the checklist in Figure 2.7 to identify the most common guest management and hospitality expenses.

Event Presentation Expenses

Many sports events include opening and/or closing ceremonies, pregame festivities, player introductions, and intermission or halftime entertainment programs—ranging from the most simple to the visually spectacular—that require some level of creative, technical, and production support. Stadium and arena keyboard instruments have been providing entertainment atmosphere during stoppages in play—and, in some sports, during play—for decades. Today, the playback of recorded music is programmed for specific game situations (and in sports such as figure skating, is essential to the competition itself), and video boards and other electronic displays entertain and inform fans with visual and audio features including replays and highlights, statistics and scores, participatory promotions and interactive engagement. Specialized lighting and effects are frequently used to excite the crowd, and to celebrate game-turning plays, goals, and home runs. Live talent may perform during pregame, deliver anthems, and entertain during halftimes and intermissions. Some sports events are pure entertainment, celebrating a sport with production, entertainment, pageantry, and noncompetitive athlete appearances, such as an opening ceremony, awards dinner, or fan festival. All of the traditional elements of entertainment event production may be applied to sports events, including those enumerated in the checklist in Figure 2.8, and discussed in more detail in Play 12.

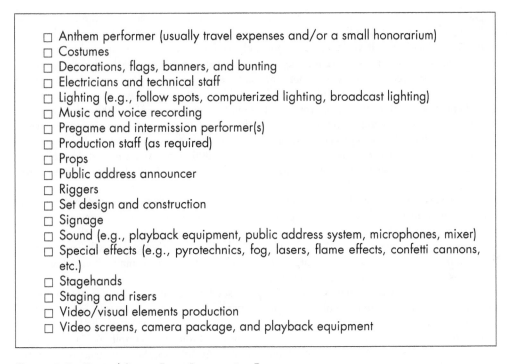

- ☐ Anthem performer (usually travel expenses and/or a small honorarium)
- ☐ Costumes
- ☐ Decorations, flags, banners, and bunting
- ☐ Electricians and technical staff
- ☐ Lighting (e.g., follow spots, computerized lighting, broadcast lighting)
- ☐ Music and voice recording
- ☐ Pregame and intermission performer(s)
- ☐ Production staff (as required)
- ☐ Props
- ☐ Public address announcer
- ☐ Riggers
- ☐ Set design and construction
- ☐ Signage
- ☐ Sound (e.g., playback equipment, public address system, microphones, mixer)
- ☐ Special effects (e.g., pyrotechnics, fog, lasers, flame effects, confetti cannons, etc.)
- ☐ Stagehands
- ☐ Staging and risers
- ☐ Video/visual elements production
- ☐ Video screens, camera package, and playback equipment

Figure 2.8 Typical Sports Event Presentation Expenses

Depending on the nature and scale of the sports event, a team of production specialists may be required to properly plan and stage the entertainment portions of the program. This team might include event producers, stage managers, technical directors, lighting designers, sound engineers, and script writers, to name a few. The right team of experts and the right presentation tools can elevate a simple athletic contest into a sports entertainment vehicle that makes a lasting and positive impression on the fan, the viewer, and the public at large.

Capital Investment and Amortization

Your sports event budget may require the acquisition of physical assets that are included among many of the identified expense categories, but can be stored and reused in future years, or applied to other events your organization stages during the same year. These assets might include equipment for the field of play, signage and display hardware, timing equipment, reusable banners, props, costumes, staging, video and sound equipment, video monitors, computer and digital equipment, tools, road cases, and more. If you purchase these items for an event you expect to stage annually, or for a series of events during a single year, the expense may be amortized, or spread out for bookkeeping purposes, over the course of their expected useful lives.

It is often preferable to rent what is needed when possible, because capital assets that are purchased, but not used all the time, can create additional annual expenses such as the leasing of storage space, trucking, and refurbishment. But some custom-designed and custom-built elements might still be required for a particular event. If you have the storage space, and are certain these assets can be used again, you can amortize their costs. Of course, all the cash will have to be spent at the time of purchase. But, the event expenses charged against the first year can be reduced as long as you are prepared to carry that same amortized expense forward until the full cost has been completely accounted for. For example, let's say you have to acquire 25 video monitors at $400 and 10 mobile devices at $200 each, and that you have sufficient storage space available to accommodate them after the purchase. While you have to spend the entire sum of $12,000 immediately to take possession of these assets, you expect to use these same monitors and devices for three years before they will need to be replaced. By dividing the total expense by the number of years you will use these assets, and you can charge only one-third, or $4,000, to this year's budget. However, you must remember that you will have also "already spent" the same sum in the budgets for events over the next two years.

There is nothing to say that you cannot amortize your assets over a series of events during the same year, or that you have to charge the same percentage to each. Let's say you have to build three interactive information kiosks that cost $5,000 each. You will use all three kiosks at your biggest annual event, and only one at three smaller events. Although you will have to spend $15,000 in cash right now, you can charge each of your event budgets a smaller figure. Figure 2.9 illustrates the calculations for this hypothetical example.

There will be occasions when assets, the expenses for which you have already amortized, do not reach their projected useful life due to accidental damage, wear and tear, or simple malfunction. If the asset must be replaced, you will need to liquidate, or *write off,* the balance of its value—that is, the portion not yet used by future events. From the example in Figure 2.9, if a kiosk becomes unusable after two years (two-thirds of its useful life), the value charged to events in the third year (the remaining third of the total value, or $5,000), may be reallocated among the budgets of the events at which the asset already provided benefit. If the kiosk is replaced, the ability to amortize that new individual asset over a new three-year period begins again. Similarly, if an event is canceled, or the need for a particular asset in future events is no longer required, the remaining value will have to be liquidated by reallocating the remaining value over one or more of the budgets for events at which the asset was utilized.

Obviously, if you are acquiring assets for a sports event that will likely occur only once, and that will have no further use at any future events, you will not be able to enjoy the financial advantages of capital amortization. Renting assets is the most advisable and cost-effective approach for such singular sports events. However, there may the need for unique capital items that must be designed, built, or acquired that cannot be rented. The total cost of such assets should be charged

Total expense to build kiosks: $15,000
Annual championships: 3 units used × 1 time per year × 3 years useful life = 9 usages
Fundraising events: 1 unit used × 3 times per year × 3 years useful life = 9 usages
Total usages = 18
Amortized value per kiosk per use = $833.33
Charge to each annual championship = $833.33 × 3 kiosks = $2,500.00
Charge to each fundraising event = $833.33 × 1 kiosk = $833.33

Figure 2.9 Sample Capital Amortization Calculation

to the event budget, even if you have a plan to later sell or otherwise derive some value from salvaging the items. Any value received on the postevent sale of the asset can later be booked as miscellaneous revenue.

Miscellaneous Expenses and Contingency Allowances

Wise drivers always fasten their seatbelts before leaving the driveway because they know that accidents can happen without warning, whether in front of their home or miles away. They also know that there is an 80 percent or greater chance they will survive a mishap by simply taking this precaution before leaving the driveway. The unforeseen can also befall a sports event organizer from the moment the budget is drafted, throughout the planning process, and even after an event is long concluded. For this reason, a wise organizer includes a contingency allowance line for unexpected expenses. By buckling this financial seatbelt before work on an event begins, the organizer will vastly improve the budget's, the event's, and his or her own career's probability of survival.

The contingency line in your budget should not be confused or co-mingled with a line for miscellaneous expenses. The miscellaneous expense line is where individual expenditures that are too small to warrant their own budget categories, or odds and ends that do not easily fit a specific budgeted expense line, should be charged. A contingency line exists as an additional safety net, with fervent hopes that it will not be needed in large part, or at all. It is there to be used in an emergency, to cover cost overruns, restoration or replacement costs, or, if all goes according to plan, to contribute to net profits if it ultimately goes unused.

If possible, set aside a contingency allowance representing an average of 10 percent of the total event budget. Contingencies of 10 percent, or as much as 15 percent, are most important for sports events with relatively modest expense budgets of under $50,000 to ensure sufficient funds are set aside in case of emergency. For larger budgets ($50,000 to $250,000 in expenses), it may be safe to lower the contingency to 7.5 percent if it helps close a budget gap. It is recommended that for the largest budgets ($250,000 and higher), the safety belt not be permitted to slip below 5 percent, but set higher if possible.

A miscellaneous event expense line is a catchall for anticipated small-cost items, but is not for the payment of unforeseen expenses—that is the purpose of the contingency allowance. The miscellaneous amount is comparatively small, as individual large expenses deserve their own budget lines. A large allotment for miscellaneous expenses in a sports event budget is often viewed by management with suspicion, a warning signal that the organizer may not have a clear and firm understanding of the expenses the event will ultimately encounter.

Reforecasts

Experienced sports event organizers periodically reforecast their expense estimates after the budget has been finalized, throughout the planning, production, and execution phases leading to event day, and even up until the books close after the event. The worksheet in Appendix 1 provides a partial illustration of the form for a simple sports event reforecast. The original budget spreadsheet is extended to include several additional columns of figures. Immediately beside the approved budget is a column of forecast expenses, the final amount the organizer expects on each budget line at the end of the event. Once finalized, the numbers in the "Budget" on each line are never adjusted. It is the forecast column where expectations on the final disposition of each budget line will be periodically updated. Next is the column for actual expenses, those costs for which invoices have been received, or contracts have been signed. The actual expense column will help validate the accuracy of the forecast column to its left, showing the money already spent, and, by extension, indicating the amount remaining. Finally, a variance column shows the difference between the original budget and the forecast, line by line.

The reforecasting process enables the organizer to reallocate budgeted funds originally overestimated in one area to another budget line that may be suffering from cost overages. Throughout the planning and production process, the combined value of forecasted budget overestimates must be matched or exceeded by the subtotal of underestimates for the budget to balance. If it does not, the event organizer must undergo the painful process of cutting expenses. To be effective, forecasting, like the budgeting process itself, must be grounded in realistic expectations. Make sure when you reduce a budget line to make up for a cost overrun in another area that you will be able to reduce the expense in fact, and not simply on paper.

Post-Play Analysis

Sports event expenses may be many and varied. The major categories of expenses include facilities costs, game and player-related expenses, event operations, marketing and promotion, sponsor fulfillment, guest management and hospitality, event presentation, miscellaneous expenses, and contingency allowances. Certain costs for the acquisition of assets that may be used over several events and/or several years may be written off, or amortized, over the useful life of those items, allowing event organizers to spread the cost of an asset over several event budgets. Throughout the planning and execution process, event organizers reforecast the financial performance of their budgets to better manage costs, and apply cost savings in some areas to offset cost overruns in others.

Coach's Clipboard

1. Create an expense budget for a new college tournament in the sport of your choice featuring teams from five universities in your region and five from outside the area.
2. A children's hospital asks you to manage a pro-am golf tournament (foursomes composed of both professionals and amateurs) to raise awareness of, and generate revenues for, its facility. How much will you advise the hospital it must invest in order to stage the tournament before revenues begin to be received? How can this initial investment be covered if the hospital is unable to contribute any capital in advance?
3. An annual street hockey tournament for amateur adult teams requires the acquisition of two portable rink board and flooring systems costing \$15,000 each. If the rinks have a useful life of three years, what amount should be allocated to each year's event? If you can use the rink systems more often by organizing similar annual tournaments in two nearby communities, what amount should be allocated to each event per year?

PLAY 3

Identifying Revenue Streams

"Never spend your money before you have it."

—*Thomas Jefferson, third president of the United States, 1743–1826*

This play will help you to:

- Develop and manage the revenue side of your event's budget.
- Become familiar with the types of revenues that sports events can generate.
- Set realistic revenue expectations.

Introduction

Few sports events can exist without some form of funding. Successful sports event organizers are not in the habit of investing capital without great confidence that they will be able to recoup it by the time the event has concluded. But expenses begin to accumulate the moment an event budget is approved, if not before. Be sure you have developed your event's *revenue streams*—the various sources and times of arrival for incoming cash—to ensure you will have money on hand to satisfy your financial obligations.

Naturally, the larger and more complex an event is, the greater the costs will be and the more urgent the need for revenues to offset expenses. By defining your event's objectives in detail, you already have an idea of how you want your bottom line to turn out; that is, whether you aim to make money, break even, or spend a predetermined sum as a promotional or fan development investment. You next compile a detailed analysis of the resources that will be required to stage

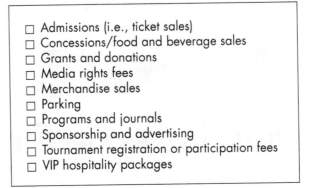

- ☐ Admissions (i.e., ticket sales)
- ☐ Concessions/food and beverage sales
- ☐ Grants and donations
- ☐ Media rights fees
- ☐ Merchandise sales
- ☐ Parking
- ☐ Programs and journals
- ☐ Sponsorship and advertising
- ☐ Tournament registration or participation fees
- ☐ VIP hospitality packages

Figure 3.1 Typical Sports Event Revenue Streams

your event, and project the level of expenses you expect to encounter. Then, by comparing your desired bottom line against anticipated expenses, you know how much total revenue you need to generate. The question now is how to go about generating it.

The revenue streams available to a sports event organizer depend on the type of event, the venue in which it will be held, and its net income objectives (i.e., the amount of profit or loss). Is the event the beneficiary of a charitable endeavor, a break-even not-for-profit effort, or a profit-generating enterprise? The reality is that there are far more ways of spending money than making it. Although revenue streams will vary from event to event, Figure 3.1 provides a list of the most typical from which to choose when creating your event budget.

Ticket Sales

Admission tickets are probably the oldest and most common income generator for sports events. Today, they remain the lifeblood of most top amateur and professional sports events, commanding prices that range from just a few dollars to more than a thousand for premium seating and events. Although ticket revenue can account for 50 percent or more of total revenues for a sports event, the financial value provided by the ticket holder goes far deeper. A full stadium, arena, or other venue adds value to sponsorships and to an organizer's other business partnerships by exposing an event's corporate partners' products and promotional messages to the eyes of more potential customers. For televised programs, a standing-room-only (SRO) crowd adds prestige and excitement to the event for the viewing audience and demonstrates that there is a market for your event large enough to fill the venue, and, by extension, to reach into the viewers' living rooms.

There is, of course, a more practical, immediate reason why struggling to fill your inventory of seats or spectator space is of paramount importance. The more people at your event, the more revenue you can generate beyond ticket sales from the sales of merchandise, food and beverage, and, for those who operate their own facilities, parking.

There are many sports events where it is either impractical or even undesirable to sell tickets to spectators. For example, running events such as 5Ks, 10Ks, and mini-marathons derive much of their revenue from registration fees and sponsorships. A finish line seating or standing area might be created to accommodate financial contributors, city officials, and partner corporations, but access to such areas is usually a benefit of some form of association with the event, such as sponsorship, or provided as a form of VIP hospitality and is not usually sold to a ticket-buying public. (However, it is no less important to the perception of an event's success to ensure these areas are filled.) Grassroots sports events, such as those staged by community youth leagues and other not-for-profit organizations, often do not charge for tickets. In their world, it is frequently more important to draw the greatest number of family members and spectators possible and to cover their expenses in merchandise resale, refreshments, journal advertising, and low-cost sponsorships purchased by local businesses.

Calculating the Gross Potential

For events that rely on admission income, the first step in projecting ticket revenues is to assess your inventory. If your sports event is being held in a stadium or arena, chances are good that there is already a seating plan for a similar program held previously, with a section-by-section accounting of the precise number of seats available. As the playing surface configuration of various sports differs in shape and size, the same facility's seating plan may vary widely by sport. New York's Madison Square Garden, for example, will seat 18,200 for ice hockey, 19,763 for basketball, and even more for boxing. The seating plans for most permanent sports and entertainment facilities feature natural and obvious divisions of desirability, most often defined by the relative height of the seating levels, the distance and orientation radiating from the center of playing action (e.g., red line, 50-yard line, home plate, behind the basket), the physical size and comfort of the seats themselves, and accompanying perquisites such as access to adjoining club lounge areas or other exclusive spaces. These divisions, also known as price breaks, provide convenient ways to offer the ticket-buying audience different economic options. Generally, the closer a seat is to the action and the more exclusive the environment, the higher the price you can charge for a ticket.

If you have to provide a seating area where none normally exists—for example, in a convention center, on a field, in a parking lot, or along a city street—you should contact a reputable bleacher or seat rental company during the budgeting process. The rental company can measure the proposed site to determine the number of seating locations that can be installed so your audience can enjoy the event in safety and comfort. If you must install temporary seating for which tickets will be sold, it is essential that a reliable seating plan be created before sales begin. The rental company can assist with a key element in developing the plan by being familiar with and handling the permit, inspection, and approval process required by a local jurisdiction. As it is not usually practical to wait until the bleachers or chairs have been physically installed to first begin selling tickets, the organizer must depend on the expertise of a vendor, or one's own experienced resources, to accurately define the seating plan. This is absolutely essential if tickets are sold on a reserved seat basis, as opposed to general admission. Reserved seat tickets entitle the purchaser to a specific location defined by a seat number. General admission ticket plans, sometimes known as festival seating, allow the purchaser to sit in any location on a first-come, first-served basis.

Temporary seating areas can also be designed to have natural price breaks. Whether in permanent or temporary locations, it is always a good idea to ensure that price breaks are separated by some obvious landmark or barrier—a different level, sections separated by aisles or rows separated by some concourse or transverse aisle. Otherwise, ticket buyers at the outer edge of the price breaks may be upset that someone sitting just a few feet immediately behind or next to them paid less for those tickets than they did.

Before entering a sum in the budget for ticket revenue, the organizer must first calculate the event's gross potential. To derive the gross potential, multiply the number of tickets within each price break by the price you wish to set for each. Figure 3.2 depicts a fictional event with 2,350 seats configured into six price breaks. In this case, because the promoter believes that front row

Seating Area	Inventory	Ticket Price	Potential
Front row	150	$50.00	$7,500
Lower seating, mid-arena	750	$35.00	$26,250
Lower seating, end zone	500	$25.00	$12,500
Upper level, mid-arena	500	$25.00	$12,500
Upper level, end zone	350	$17.50	$6,125
Standing room	100	$10.00	$1,000
GROSS POTENTIAL	**2,350**		**$65,875**

Figure 3.2 Calculation of Gross Revenue Potential

seats will sell well at a premium price, he has created a special category for just this small number of seats. Promoters who embrace this philosophy should ensure that front-row seats—even without a visible break—actually offer a prestigious, unobstructed view of the event. The sidelines between the audience and the playing surface in some sports, such as football and soccer, can be crammed with officials, trainers, cameramen, photographers, and unengaged players, so unless the seating in the front row is elevated above the shoulders of those individuals, patrons purchasing front-row seats are actually enjoying less of the event than those farther away. Professional basketball teams offer courtside seats at which fans pay for the privilege of sitting immediately adjacent to team benches and having their feet literally on the sidelines. In many cases, front-row seating for a live sports event can be so exciting that a price premium of 50 to 100 percent, or more, can be commanded.

Unless your event is a proven property that enjoys a consistent track record of selling out year after year, it is not recommended that the gross potential be the final number placed in the budget as ticket revenue. Project the percentage of your inventory you can expect to sell with a great degree of confidence. A good rule of thumb is 75 to 85 percent. If you are uncertain of selling at least 75 percent of your gross potential, you may have selected a facility that is too large for your event's audience. If you feel you can safely sell 80 percent of the gross potential, use that number on the ticket revenue line of your event budget. Referring to Figure 3.2, this would mean selling a minimum of 1,880 tickets (2,350 × 0.80) for a projected $52,700 ($65,875 × 0.80). In budgeting for your event, a good rule to follow is be as conservative as practical in your estimates; if your calculations can work at the lowest end of this range and still cover your expenses, the chances for greater financial upside increase.

Do not forget to deduct any applicable sales and amusement taxes and facility use fees from the gross potential. As the organizer will never see any of those revenues, which are kept by the municipality and/or venue, they are best deducted here. (There are no taxes or fees payable in this example.)

You will likely be issuing complimentary tickets to special guests, sponsors, and other business partners. If desired, you may also deduct "comps" from your ticket revenue line. We prefer to categorize complimentary tickets as expenses, so we deduct them like any other expense on the opposite side of the income statement. Our philosophy is that issuing of comps is a cost of doing business, as opposed to a missed revenue opportunity. A comp seat is really sold, but instead of accepting cash, the event is deriving some other benefit. Comp tickets are usually provided to sponsors as a benefit of their association, and the event has accepted a sponsor's cash, product, or service somewhere else in the budget. Part of the cost in fulfilling the sponsorship agreement is providing the ticket and, therefore, it is categorized as an expense. Other comps, for special guests and celebrities, may lend an event more prestige, legitimacy, or even increased cooperation from local businesses, suppliers, and municipalities. They may help develop new business opportunities or future fans. Therefore, you will find "Complimentary Tickets" listed as an expense item in our event budgets, as opposed to having their value deducted from the "Ticket Revenue" line.

Setting Ticket Prices

Figure 3.2 also suggests that seats located in the middle, or along the long axis, of the arena are more desirable than those in the end zone for this event. As a result, there is a price break between mid-arena and end zone seating. This price break is also emulated in the upper level of the arena, where upper-end-zone seats are the second-lowest priced ticket. The promoter of this fictional event feels that tickets for the lower end zone and the upper mid-arena are of similar desirability and has priced both sections equally so fans can select a mid-priced ticket in either section, according to their own preferences. Finally, the facility, with permission from the local fire marshal, has determined that a small number of patrons can be safely accommodated in standing-room locations. The promoter has scaled these tickets at the lowest possible price to encourage the attendance of die-hard fans who cannot otherwise afford tickets, or who purchase tickets after all seating sections are sold out. As a general rule, event organizers should not offer standing-room options unless approved by the facility and/or local fire marshal.

The next step is to determine how much should you charge for tickets. Setting ticket prices can be very tricky, and mistakes can prove disastrous. If you set prices too high, it might prove difficult to sell your entire inventory of tickets. If you charge too little, you may have insufficient funds with which to pay your expenses, or you will generate a smaller than otherwise possible net profit. The checklist in Figure 3.3 provides some useful questions, tips, and philosophies to be considered when pondering the level to set for ticket prices.

Event organizers carefully and thoughtfully consider the checklist questions offered in Figure 3.3 in order to identify the answers that are appropriate for their specific circumstances. For

SIDELINE STORY

Is Ticket Scaling Ancient History?

Historians tell us that admission to one of the oldest and most famous icons of sports facilities—the Roman Colosseum—was totally free. The emperor staged all manner of sporting events, including those infamous gladiator death matches, for free to maintain his popularity and the political support of the citizenry. Where you sat, however, was a function of class or office, with the commoners occupying the highest, most distant locations, and government officials and visiting dignitaries enjoying the best views. As many as 50,000 spectators could enjoy each day of competition at the Colosseum, courtesy of the caesars. Perhaps the original multiuse arena, the Roman Colosseum, which could also be flooded for reenactments of heroic naval battles, remained a dominant sports and entertainment venue for more than 400 years. It was also ahead of its time in terms of one element of fan service—the Colosseum was designed to be able to empty the entire capacity of the building after an event in a spectator-friendly five minutes.

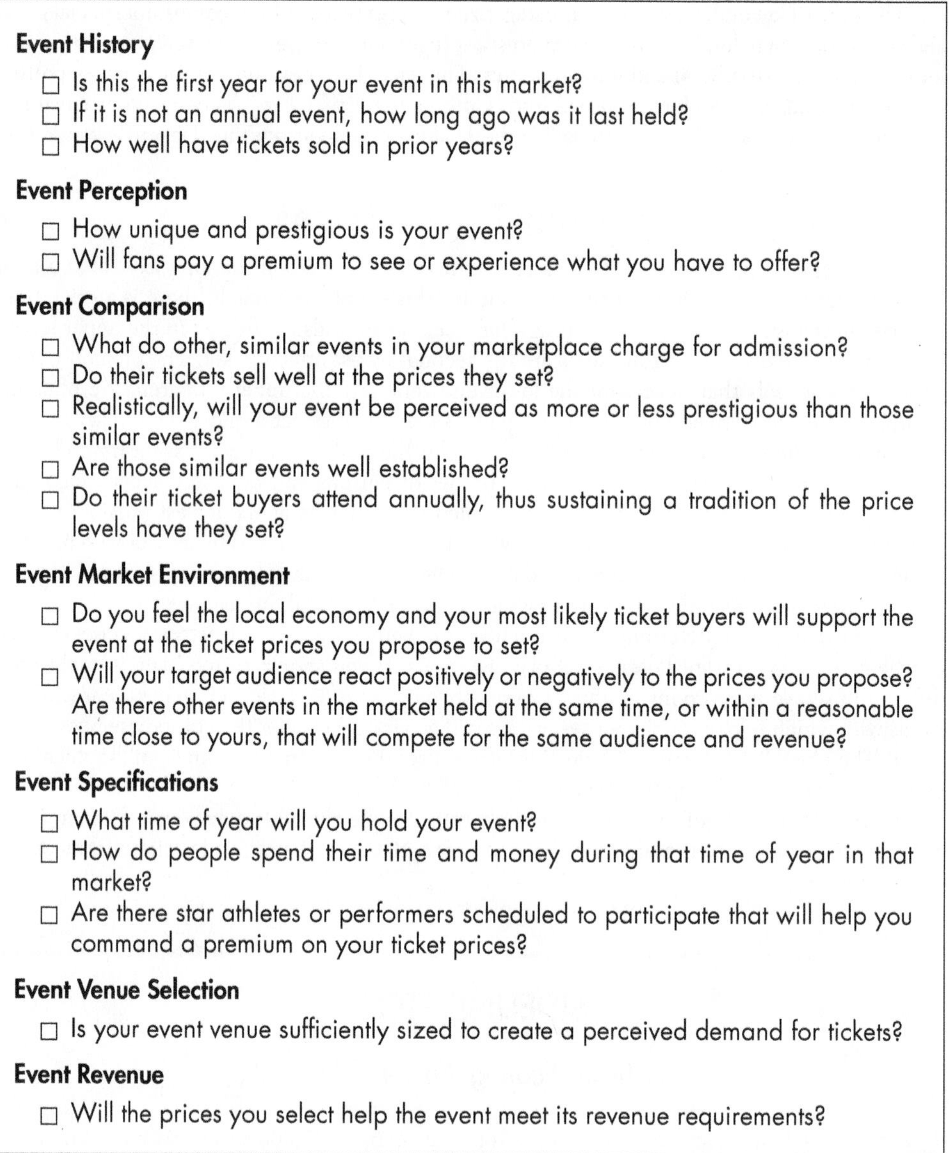

Event History

- ☐ Is this the first year for your event in this market?
- ☐ If it is not an annual event, how long ago was it last held?
- ☐ How well have tickets sold in prior years?

Event Perception

- ☐ How unique and prestigious is your event?
- ☐ Will fans pay a premium to see or experience what you have to offer?

Event Comparison

- ☐ What do other, similar events in your marketplace charge for admission?
- ☐ Do their tickets sell well at the prices they set?
- ☐ Realistically, will your event be perceived as more or less prestigious than those similar events?
- ☐ Are those similar events well established?
- ☐ Do their ticket buyers attend annually, thus sustaining a tradition of the price levels have they set?

Event Market Environment

- ☐ Do you feel the local economy and your most likely ticket buyers will support the event at the ticket prices you propose to set?
- ☐ Will your target audience react positively or negatively to the prices you propose? Are there other events in the market held at the same time, or within a reasonable time close to yours, that will compete for the same audience and revenue?

Event Specifications

- ☐ What time of year will you hold your event?
- ☐ How do people spend their time and money during that time of year in that market?
- ☐ Are there star athletes or performers scheduled to participate that will help you command a premium on your ticket prices?

Event Venue Selection

- ☐ Is your event venue sufficiently sized to create a perceived demand for tickets?

Event Revenue

- ☐ Will the prices you select help the event meet its revenue requirements?

Figure 3.3 Sports Event Ticket Pricing: A Checklist for Decision-Making

example, in asking how tickets have sold in prior years as part of an event's history, a modest increase in prices may be considered if tickets have previously sold well and sold quickly.

As part of the event comparison, unless your event is significantly more prestigious (i.e., includes more and better activities, features more marquee athletes, is a championship event, etc.), it is unlikely you will be able to charge more than a less premium event. On the one hand, if your event is breaking into the market, you may want to encourage sales by setting prices a little lower until your program becomes better known and more highly regarded. On the other hand, setting prices too low can also create the impression of the event as a vastly inferior experience compared to similar programs.

The event venue selection process requires similar attention to strategic thinking. The larger the venue you have chosen, the more of a perception could exist that buying tickets will be easy and that an immediate or timely purchase is not a matter of urgency. One strategy involves ensuring a sellout in the early years of your event by selecting a venue that offers fewer seats than you expect will be in demand. If you are able, let the perception build over the course of two or three years that those who wait until the day of the event to try to purchase tickets might be out of luck. Then, in subsequent years, you can either select a venue of greater size to accommodate more people, or increase prices while demand is still outpacing supply. There is a secondary reason to limit the number of seats available. It may be preferable for your event to appear sold out at 5,000 seats in a smaller venue, than appear two-thirds full with 6,000 fans in a 9,000-seat venue (assuming you can afford to look the other way on the revenue that can be derived from the extra 1,000 seats). Of course, if you are confident that your event can fill the larger venue, by all means go for it.

Finally, in considering event revenue, you may have to adjust your thinking on prices—or expenses—after plugging all your numbers into your budget. Resist the urge to increase prices to cover expenses unless you are certain that the market will as easily tolerate a higher cost for tickets. By taking the necessary time and consulting the appropriate resources to conduct the due diligence to fully evaluate the answers in the checklist, you should discover the decision-making process for the all-important subject of sports event ticket pricing will be simplified.

Pricing for Multiday Events

If your event spans the course of more than a single day, your revenue opportunities and expense liabilities will increase accordingly. Many events, particularly tournaments, are composed of "preliminaries," or early-round matches, or may, in some cases, include events that are in some way subsidiary to the main event. Events that run for several days, resulting in quarterfinals, semifinals, and final matches, frequently increase their ticket prices with each succeeding round, presuming that the later rounds are more exciting and attractive to the audience. The premium as competition progresses can be anywhere from 10 to 100 percent of the initial, preliminary rounds. Event organizers will frequently sell tickets as a package deal that includes all rounds, also known as a "strip," "series" or "subscription," before individual tickets go on sale to the general public. With this arrangement, the best seats are made available to your best customers, those who will attend the most matches. As a side benefit, it also creates a sense of urgency in the market among those interested only in one or two rounds. It is not unusual for a number of friends to decide to purchase a package together, and then split the individual tickets to ensure they get the best seats before the field is opened to the single-date ticket buyers. Usually, there is no discount for buying a strip of tickets. To the ticket buyer, the benefit derived is often simply receiving the best possible seating locations. But if your event is new, and you want to sell tickets more quickly, you can certainly consider a discounted package price, if only to reduce the ticket inventory.

Packaging tickets also helps to fill seats to the "weaker" events, those that might be perceived as less desirable to the public due to any number of factors, such as the day of the week (in almost all cases, weekends naturally and routinely sell better than weekdays), time of day, location, familiarity of the event in the local market, marquee value of the athletes involved, relevance of a particular match or event, and so forth.

As discussed in Play 2, do not forget to consider the costs of local, state, and federal taxes, facility fees, credit card commissions, group sales commissions, and box office/ticketing services when determining your ticket prices. The higher your ticket prices, the greater the expenses organizers will encounter in many of these variable cost categories.

SIDELINE STORY

Baseball All-Star Game Packages Drive Attendance

When Major League Baseball's (MLB's) All-Star Game was first played at Comiskey Park as part of the mid-summer festivities for the 1933 Chicago World's Fair, few could have foreseen the long-term commercial success of *Chicago Tribune* sports editor Arch Ward's original idea. Watching the likes of Babe Ruth hit the first home run in All-Star Game history, Lou Gehrig protecting first base, and other future Hall of Famers with names like Pie, Lefty, and Gabby at bat and on the same field was novel enough to command enormous attention. More recently, however, MLB's annual showcase of its stars includes far more than just the game, and at varying price points that appeal to a wide range of audiences. In 2012, Taco Bell All-Star Sunday featured a doubleheader including the SiriusXM All-Star Futures Game and Taco Bell All-Star Legends & Celebrity Softball Game, concluding with fireworks. The MLB All-Star FanFest, a convention center–based interactive baseball theme park, also catered to a family audience demographic. Recognizing that families would be most likely to attend FanFest on the weekend, the All-Star Sunday ticket was offered in a Monday- or Tuesday-only package to further bolster attendance on days that might be more difficult to sell to their target market.

Sponsorship and Advertising

Sponsorship is a pervasive, persuasive, and necessary source of funding for sports events at all levels. If organizers had to rely only on ticket sales and the other revenue sources discussed in this chapter, the cost of most event tickets, which continue to rise steadily, would need to be astronomically higher to cover the rapidly increasing costs of staging sports events. The support of sponsors, and the overt, sometimes obtrusive, manifestations of their participation, is generally accepted by ticket buyers as a natural component of today's event experience. Sidelines, playing surfaces, scoreboards, and time clocks the world over are covered with sponsor advertising messages. In North American professional sports, games are periodically halted for longer stoppages of play after whistles to allow broadcasters to air commercials. Video boards showcase replays, features and activities designed both to increase entertainment value and sponsorship revenue. Uniforms worn by players from Little League baseball to professional soccer teams are emblazoned with the name of the team's primary sponsor. Plays 6 and 7 will explore in detail how sports event organizers can partner with sponsors to stage better and more engaging events to their mutual benefit. For now, the event organizer has to assess the degree of relevance and interest a program will have in the corporate community, and the dollars the event might generate. While sponsors evaluate sports events against their own set of objectives and criteria, sponsorship revenue potential for each event will vary depending on factors such as each event's size, scope, audience demographics, visibility, and cultural relevance, to name a few. From grassroots handshake deals of a few hundred dollars to the multimillion dollar contracts negotiated with the Olympic Games and professional major league sports, the guiding principle is generally the same—the event must deliver sales opportunities both on site and at their regular retail locations, exposure at the event, online, and in the media, and goodwill for the sponsor.

How much should your budget project for sponsorship revenue? Corporate support for mature sports events can be among the most lucrative sources of revenue for event organizers, but also the most elusive and potentially the most labor intense to capture. Success usually lies in a combination of the personal business contacts of the event promoter or agency, past event history, and the ability to design, communicate and deliver clear, obvious, risk-free opportunities for the companies writing the checks. Set reasonable expectations and attainable revenue goals for your event, and get out into the sponsorship marketplace as early as possible, long before you have gone to market with ticket sales (because, among other reasons, top-level sponsors will want recognition in the title or as a presenter of the event, on the ticket, and on all associated marketing collateral).

Many first-time sports events overestimate their appeal and price their sponsorship packages beyond what a sensible company would spend. Because sponsorship revenues can provide a major source of funding for event planning and operations, overpricing can cause the entire program to fall apart before the first ticket is even sold. It is also far less risky to have the option of altering the size and budget of your event after it is determined sponsorship revenue appears to be failing to meet expectations, before advertising has begun and tickets have been sold. In the broadest general terms, if you have other sources of revenue, try not to weight your event budget to be significantly dependent on corporate support for a first-year sports event. If your objective is to generate a net profit, it is safest to plan to have sponsorship support provide all or most of the profit margin, assuming you are confident that ticket sales and other revenue streams can get you to at least a breakeven position. As your event becomes more established, and its sponsorship track record becomes more predictable, you can start thinking about using more sponsor money to pay for expenses.

Established events, especially those with multiyear sponsorship deals, however, can rely on past history to project sponsorship income. It is a good idea for event organizers with multiyear sponsors to keep a close eye on when those deals expire, and take these expirations into account when preparing their revenue projections. It is also wise to offer sponsorships of differing expiration dates to ensure that not all deals will end on the same year. If sponsors must be renewed or replaced when deals end, it is advantageous not to have all of that marketing opportunity at risk at the same time.

In many cases, sports events require some amount of sponsorship capital to provide the cash needed to cover expenses that will be incurred before any other revenues are received. As you prepare the expense side of your budget, identify the costs you will incur early in the planning process, before tickets are sold. Unless you have other sources of capital to invest in planning and staging the event, the total of those costs may form your minimum sponsorship revenue requirement. (*Caution*: Remember that using ticket revenues to pay for all of your pre-event expenses is also inherently risky, as the cancellation or postponement of an event may require you to have cash on hand to issue immediate refunds to ticket holders, and, eventually, to sponsors. Event cancellation insurance can protect against some part of this risk, although it is usually the case that payment will not be immediate enough to satisfy ticket holders. See Play 14 for a more complete discussion of event insurance.)

Remember to include a line in your expense budget for "sponsorship fulfillment" whenever you expect to generate sponsor revenues. You should not expect simply to cash a check without providing service to or value expected by your sponsor, and it will surely take some amount of money to do so. You may have accounted for some of your costs in your "complimentary tickets" line, but there will certainly be more expenses to consider, such as banners and signage, gifts, hospitality and advertising, among many others.

Budgeting Value-In-Kind (Barter)

Sponsors and other business partners are increasingly asking sports event organizers to accept their products and services in lieu of, or in addition to, cash. This makes good sense to sponsors because it costs them far less to compensate your organization with their products or services, even when calculated at a wholesale value, than to pay you in cash. It can also move excess inventory out of their warehouses and, in cases where the products are used in view of the public, provide them with additional promotional value. This practice is variously known as accepting *value-in-kind* (VIK), barter, or contra, and, in tight economic times, becomes an increasingly attractive option for business partners.

Accepting VIK is most advantageous to sports event organizers when it offsets an anticipated expense that would have otherwise been paid in cash. The partner company provides the required product in partial or total payment for receiving sponsor benefits, and the event organizer accepts these necessary items without expending cash. VIK can also be attractive when the products or services add value to an event without adding expenses to the budget.

Although no cash changes hands in pure VIK deals, it is wise to account for them as though cash was accepted, and the cash was then used to purchase the products. In other words, if you estimate that your event will encounter $10,000 in gasoline expenses, and a sponsor oil company offers to provide you with $10,000 VIK, forecast the same $10,000 in gasoline expenses and $10,000 in sponsor revenue. In cases where a VIK deal adds value to an event without offsetting costs, you will ultimately "gross up" your budget, adding the retail cost of the product as a new, unbudgeted expense on one side of the ledger, and an unanticipated extra source of revenue on the other side. Even though these "value added" deals may improve the event experience or deliver better operational solutions to the organizer, they do not in such cases help you reduce anticipated expenses, nor do they help you reach your revenue goals. They may, in fact, create additional tax liabilities, as the value of a barter deal is often treated the same way as income from cash in many localities. Accepting VIK for products or services for which your event has not already planned could actually end up costing your budget some unanticipated amount of cash in taxes.

Finally, be selective about agreeing to accept VIK deals. If a potential VIK deal would provide you with products or services that neither offset cash expenses nor add value to the event experience, it is probably not a worthwhile deal. To encourage companies seeking VIK deals to spend a little cash alongside providing their product, you can create a sponsor category for purely VIK partners with fewer or reduced benefits, such as an "official supplier" designation, and offer full benefits and "sponsor" status in return for an added amount of cash.

Prospective sponsors also occasionally offer "activation only" deals in lieu of providing cash or product. As will be further explored in Plays 6 and 7, activation can be loosely defined as those activities a partner company undertakes to support its sponsorship beyond the fees and expenses spent directly with the organizer. A pure activation deal may offer attractive advertising and promotional benefits to the event without payment of cash or VIK. A soft-drink distributor, for example, might create a bottle-cap promotion or a quick-service restaurant a tray liner offer, each with a corresponding advertising campaign that would add significant exposure benefits that will help to build attendance or ticket sales for the event. To some extent, these activities could reduce the amount of money originally set aside by the organizer for advertising, and may be incredibly attractive from a promotional point of view. However, organizers must weigh these benefits against the fulfillment costs that will still be incurred, recognizing that an activation-only deal does not generally reduce the revenues required to meet the sponsorship goal in any way (although ideally, the savings realized by reducing forecast advertising expenses could cover these costs). Such a deal will also exclude the organizer from making a cash or VIK deal with any competitor of the activation partner. Cash will still be required for most events to remain viable, so an activation-only deal should represent only a portion of the value provided by the event's family of sponsors.

In sum, there are important truths and practicalities in considering VIK opportunities. Whether or not you receive cash or reduce or eliminate an expense, there can be helpful financial opportunities for your event's bottom line and an increased nimbleness to your sponsorship strategy by considering appropriate and beneficial VIK sponsor relationships.

Advertising

Although advertising and on-site marketing rights are usually a perquisite of sports event sponsorship deals, smaller sports events may offer nonsponsor companies limited advertising benefits that do not require the larger investments that define more comprehensive sponsor relationships. The ability to sell a limited amount of advertising that does not conflict with the rights of existing event sponsors can provide sports event organizers with an added revenue stream from the corporate community. Assuming you will reserve the best signage positions for sponsors who are paying top dollar, additional scoreboard and venue signage, video board commercials, entrance/exit sampling areas, and other venue-dependent advertising positions may be offered on a limited basis to corporate advertisers.

Before committing to specific advertising benefits, be sure to consult your facility lease and venue manager. Your agreement with the event venue may preclude certain forms of added advertising, such as sponsor signage that competes with a venue sponsor, or you may be charged a fee for its display. In most cases, existing advertising sold by the facility may not be covered or obstructed for event-specific signage, so organizers may have to create new positions for advertising, with the advance approval of the venue.

Advertising on an event's website can provide another possible revenue source. Inventory such as sponsored banners on a home page, interactive media ads and information features and other commercially driven content are both affordable to sponsors and reasonably low in cost to produce, a potentially popular and profitable combination.

Event organizers should take care not to offer advertising benefits to a company from an industry category where a larger sponsor relationship might later be available. Closing a sponsorship deal with a soft drink company after selling an advertising package to its competitor could be difficult to impossible. For this reason, most organizers sell nonsponsor advertising packages only late in the process, after it appears that sponsorship prospects in those categories have largely dried up.

Merchandise

The process of budgeting revenue for merchandise sales at sports events must blend realistic expectations, a familiarity with your audience, and, frankly, your gut instincts. Merchandise first must be designed and purchased by the event organizer, incurring costs to develop and create inventory, and then (it is hoped) resold to consumers with sufficient profit margin to cover all other expenses that might be involved in the transaction (e.g., shipping, labor/commissions, fixtures, supplies [such as shopping bags], taxes, credit card fees, etc.). Thus, the net revenues projected for merchandise sales will be a compound number that subtracts the "cost of goods sold" from the gross revenues the event organizer expects to realize. It is also important to plan for the significant lead-time, often six to nine months or longer, and related expenses required to produce and to ship merchandise to meet your event date, particularly if it must be imported from a foreign supplier.

Most professional sports stadium and arena facilities either provide in-house retail merchandising services or have entered into an exclusive partnership with a retail merchandise concessionaire to provide this capability. The terms of what the in-house retailer will be paid to sell your merchandise must be negotiated at the same time as the facility lease. Most often, the facility retailer will expect to sell event merchandise on a "consignment" basis; that is, they will sell your items without purchasing them from you first. At the end of the event, the retailer will return the unsold inventory to you, along with payment for the items sold on a previously negotiated price schedule (e.g., 75 percent of the retail price), less agreed-upon deductions (e.g., taxes and credit card commissions). Facilities insist on this type of arrangement because it presents the least amount of risk to them. Creating event-related merchandise is risky for the same reason it is attractive to the ultimate purchaser, the fan—it is a souvenir of a specific time, place, and event, and once the event is over, its value drops precipitously. Therefore, not having to purchase event-related merchandise in advance is usually essential to third-party retailers. Make sure your estimate of revenues accounts for some amount of "spoilage," the merchandise that will not successfully be resold. Not only will revenues not be received on whatever is left over after the event ends, the expense to have had items made in the first place will further reduce your net merchandise revenues.

If a sports event is well-established, with a proven track-record of high merchandise sales results, the organizer has more leverage in negotiating a better deal with the retailer, or one that shifts more of the risk to the merchandiser. In such cases, the organizer can designate "licensees," or exclusive suppliers, from whom the retailer must purchase approved event merchandise, and receive royalties on sales from the licensee, the merchandiser, or to some degree, both. Organizers of proven, major events with a history of high merchandise volume may be able to negotiate a 10 to 25 percent share of sales in cases where the in-house retailer purchases event-specific merchandise directly from a licensee, usually net of taxes and credit card commissions. Event organizers prefer this arrangement because now they incur no risk of unsold inventory remaining after the audience has departed.

Local amateur grassroots sports events in community-owned facilities usually have the luxury of assigning their own volunteers and boosters to sell merchandise themselves, accepting only cash, and offering some combination of event-specific and organization-generic items. To minimize the likelihood of being stuck with excess, unsalable merchandise, volunteer organizers would be well advised to limit their acquisition of event-specific items (such as T-shirts with a date like "the 2014 Columbus Softball Association's July 4th All-Star Game), and weight their inventory with a greater proportion of organization-generic merchandise (e.g., Columbus Softball Association caps). To reduce or eliminate any possibility of financial risk, grassroots organizations may want to consider attempting to have their merchandise donated by a local supplier in return for name or logo recognition on the item, or sponsored in part by a local business for similar recognition.

Regardless of how items are acquired or sold, the most common method of deriving a budget number for merchandise revenue is based on a per capita estimate of sales (also known as a *per cap*). The per cap is the amount of money the event organizer expects to realize in merchandise sales, on average, from each person at the event site. In professional sports events, the number of audience members is usually used, while grassroots events may include both audience and the participating athletes who would also be likely to buy remembrances of the day. The projected per cap for the event will depend on the product mix being offered and price ranges, as well as a judgment on the part of the organizer as to how desirable the merchandise will be to the attendees. Remember, it is not generally realistic to expect that every spectator will purchase an item, so organizers are advised to think conservatively when projecting the per cap for their event. To derive a merchandise revenue number for your event budget, simply multiply the per cap by the number of spectators and/or participants expected to attend. Figure 3.4 illustrates an example of how to derive a merchandise revenue projection utilizing a per cap estimation.

REVENUE CALCULATION	
A. "Per Cap" Estimation	$ 0.75
B. Number of Spectators Expected	2,500
C. Projected Gross Revenue (A × B)	$1,875.00
D. Cost of Merchandise Sold	$950.00
E. Budgeted Net Merchandise Revenue (C–D)	$ 925.00

Figure 3.4 Sample Sports Event Merchandise Revenue Calculation

The example in Figure 3.4 shows a very conservative per cap. Established sports events can enjoy merchandise per caps in the range of $4.00 to $10.00 and even more. Per caps are also dependent on the product mix and the price points of the various items for sale. In order to make a realistic per cap determination, you must have an understanding of your audience. Will you have an upscale audience that will pay $50.00 to $70.00 for a sweatshirt, or is it comprised of families who are more likely to buy a $20.00 T-shirt, a $15.00 cap, an $8.00 plush ball, or a $4.00 key chain? Alternatively, does the audience have a significant representation of kids, whose parents have sent them off to the merchandise stand by themselves with a $10.00 bill for souvenirs? Consider who is likely to be in the stands before determining what kind of merchandise you will offer, how much you need to acquire, and how large a per cap you want to work toward. Think, too, about whether the merchandiser can accept credit cards. Will attendees have expected to purchase high-priced items and have brought enough cash?

While there are events and teams that are reducing or even eliminating them in favor of online content, programs, journals, and other publications remain a special merchandise item from which you may derive revenue from more than one source. Most printed programs include advertising, the revenues from which ideally should offset or exceed the cost of their design and printing. If the organizer can completely cover the cost of the program or journal with advertising revenues, the publication may be distributed the program free to all attendees with any further financial risk while providing attractive exposure for advertisers. Alternatively, the item may be sold to produce an additional revenue stream, presuming the quality and content are attractive enough to potential purchasers.

Here are some more tips that can help to increase your merchandise sales potential. Consider negotiating a deal with one or more local retailers who will help promote your event by selling your products on consignment (they will only pay you for what they sell and then return the balance for full credit), or on another basis in advance of game day away from the event venue. If your event will be staged in a public space where no retail merchandiser has exclusive rights, you may be able keep costs down by recruiting a body of volunteers or using your own hourly staff to sell your merchandise. For a more professional presentation without the headaches of managing inventory and labor, you may want to consider contracting the merchandiser from a nearby arena or stadium, or a large reputable sporting goods store. These vendors may have an interest in servicing your event on a mutually agreeable fee schedule and may also be able to provide points-of-sale kiosks, stands, tables, chairs, and other fixtures if they are not being used by their home facility or store during the same time period.

Concessions and Food and Beverage Sales

Concession revenues comprise the net income from food and beverage items sold to spectators on the event site. As in the case of merchandise sales, virtually all professional event sports stadiums and arenas provide concession services or have entered into an exclusive partnership with a food and beverage concessionaire to provide this capability. In these venues, it is most common that event organizers will not be able to negotiate to receive any share of food and beverage sales, nor will they be able to vend any of their own products.

If you are hosting your event in a facility or public space where no such exclusivities exist, you will have the opportunity to benefit from concession revenue and may be able to engage a volunteer staff and provide your own products for sale. For grassroots, not-for-profit, and charitable organizations, this may present an even greater opportunity to generate significant revenues by vending products donated by a retailer, distributor, or manufacturer. Event organizers can negotiate deals with food vendors just as festivals and carnivals do, in which events are guaranteed either a flat fee for each vendor authorized to be at the event site, or some mutually agreeable share of sales. Try to negotiate a 20 to 40 percent share of sales after expenses (such as labor and provisions), keeping in mind that the higher your percentage, the more expensive food prices will likely be for the fans. Think carefully about whether you will achieve greater net sales by taking a 20 percent share on a $4.00 hamburger or a 40 percent share on the same item at $6.00, but selling fewer of them.

If your event is in the position to either vend or arrange for others to sell food and beverage products, the same evaluation process with respect to product mix, price points, and per caps applies as with merchandise. Know your audience, and provide the kinds of refreshments they would enjoy, appropriate to the time of day, the time of year, and the age groups expected to be present. Sports events that promote healthy lifestyles should ensure that healthful refreshment options are also available and should always offer a selection of beverages.

Broadcasting

A small percentage of sports events are desirable enough to broadcasting programmers to devote time to covering them on television and/or on radio and an even smaller percentage so attractive that a broadcaster will agree to pay for the right to cover them. The growth of cable and digital programming services presents more options for event organizers on national sports networks, regional sports networks, local cable affiliates, public access channels, and online streaming for home and mobile devices. Here is the simple challenge: It costs broadcasters significant money in labor, equipment, talent, and airtime to cover an event, so they have to be confident they will be able to sell sufficient advertising, or resell the program to another broadcasting entity, for far more money than it will cost them to cover it. The value of their programming time is also a consideration. In other words, can they spend less and make more money by airing alternative programming? And that's before they start thinking about paying any fees to the organizer for broadcasting rights.

Even though relatively few sports events out of the thousands being staged generate broadcast opportunities, not to mention rights fees, the budget line for broadcasting rights is mentioned here so you do not forget to include it if your event is fortunate enough to realize such potential. As in considering sponsor revenues, be sure to check your broadcasting agreement to determine what expenses, if any, you are expected to cover out of your side of the fee. Also, check your facility lease to identify any costs, such as "broadcast origination fees," labor and utilities that might be payable to the venue, and determine whether the event or the broadcaster will be responsible for them.

There is another option available to sports event organizers seeking to get their program on the air, most commonly known as a time-buy. Time-buys are generally risky for organizers who undertake them without having corporate sponsors ready to pay the bill. In a time-buy arrangement, an event organizer obtains an agreement with a broadcaster to actually purchase the time required to cover the event on a channel or network, generally costing in the range of tens, or even hundreds, of thousands of dollars often calculated on a per-hour basis. The event organizer is then responsible to sell the advertising time to generate the revenues that will cover the cost of the time-buy.

The organizer is also likely to be responsible for all of the costs of actually producing the television program. If you pursue a time-buy, be sure to identify all of the expenses you will be expected to cover, and all of the advertising revenues that will be required to cover these costs before finalizing an agreement. More details on time-buys and other broadcasting issues may be found in Play 13.

When rights fees and time-buys are not practical or available, event organizers interested in reaching larger, out-of-venue audiences in real-time have an increasing range of options to do so. A growing number of programmers have established an incredibly powerful presence on the web using proprietary or public services, starting with YouTube, that has the potential to attract hundreds of millions of viewers monthly and hundreds of billions of playbacks annually from their web-based, video-sharing platforms. The programming covers the gamut of events, from youth and high school sports to food-eating contests and one-of-a-kind stunts. Major sports leagues and associations and intercollegiate athletic conferences have significant online presences with their own websites and content properties. All of these web-based programming sources are generating impressive, even worldwide, exposure possibilities and ever-increasing revenue opportunities.

Tournament and Participation Fees

Grassroots tournaments most often do not charge admission for spectators, but may derive their income from registration or entry fees on a per-player or per-team basis. Similarly, non-team sports events such as marathons, races and other individual athletic meets often use participation fees to cover expenses. The process of establishing a fee for tournament or race participants is similar to determining ticket prices for a spectator event. Consider what similar tournaments and races charge participants, the prestige or rewards attached to your event compared to others, and how many and what other events you are competing against in the marketplace; there may be other relevant factors as well. Adapt the ticket-pricing checklist in this chapter to help structure your thinking. Tournaments also have an inventory limit. Organizers will need to structure their tournament brackets in advance of finalizing their revenue budget to determine how many teams or participants may be accommodated given the time and facilities available, and, therefore, their gross potential for registration or entry fees. Marathons and races have a limited capacity for individual participants that should similarly be set in advance to control costs and overcrowding. (More than 100,000 runners apply annually to participate in the New York City Marathon, but only 47,000 can be accommodated.)

Most organized amateur competitors are familiar with the concept of paying fees to participate in tournaments. They know that it takes money to rent facilities, provide trophies and recognition, and manage a tournament or race. Although the cost of participant fees can vary from just a few dollars for individuals to hundreds of dollars for teams, the organizer should also survey the pricing structure of similar meets to be sure to include similar features. For example, do other tournaments in which the same athletes compete offer dormitory housing, meals or refreshments, merchandise, ground transportation, recognition premiums, and other considerations included in the registration fee? Can you provide the same level of experience—or even greater?

Grants and Donations

Sports events staged by a not-for-profit organization or that aim to provide a community with significant "quality of life" benefits can further pursue their objectives by applying for and receiving grants in the form of cash or services from governmental, quasi-public, corporate foundations, or other charitable entities. Many state, county, and city sports foundations and commissions maintain budgets to assist events that bring economic impact or other benefits to the community, local businesses, or its citizens. Generally, a lengthy application and review process is required, during which the grantor evaluates an event and its organizer according to formalized criteria, and after which the organization determines whether the event will qualify. If an event does indeed meet these criteria, the grantor can determine how much funding it is willing to offer and specifically how the funds may be used to benefit the program. If you have sufficient lead time, which could be as much as a year or more, investigate what organizations exist in your area and/or in your sport whose mission involves supporting and promoting events such as the one you are planning. Do not overlook charitable foundations managed by major corporations. They can make funds available to qualifying events from budgets that are totally separate from the sponsorships that are managed by the company's marketing department.

For events that travel or tour from year to year, it is best to apply for grants before the event is awarded to a particular community. Most sports commissions and foundations are charged with the responsibility of attracting events to their area and occasionally offer grants to successfully compete against other candidate communities.

Tickets to some sports events are sold in the form of a donation. That is, the proceeds of ticket sales are used to fund a not-for-profit group's operations or generate income for an important humanitarian cause. E-mailed invitations or direct-mail pieces are often used to sell tickets to a qualified list of people the organizer believes are most likely to support the cause. Organizers of events of this type can increase their charitable bottom line, with respect to donations, by including a line on the response card that enables recipients who cannot attend to send a donation in lieu of a ticket purchase (e.g., "No, I cannot attend. Please accept my donation of $_____ to help support programs for para-athletes.").

Miscellaneous Revenues

In addition to the most common and important sources of revenue for sports events already described, the additional possible opportunities available are as diverse as the types of events organizers can develop and where they may be staged. Areas of revenue potential may include site-specific benefits like parking and valet services, coat and bag checking, the sale of passes to VIP hospitality receptions, purchased admissions to postgame parties or other exclusive-access events, on-site fundraising activities, and raffles and lotteries, to name just a few.

Balancing the Books

Total up your projected revenues and subtract your estimated expenses (including the ever-important contingency allowance line). Have you met your net income goal? If the first pass at constructing your event's budget falls short of your expectations, welcome to a very large, very nonexclusive club. It is now time to go back into your expense budget and adjust the numbers so the bottom line meets the event's financial goals. Or, reexamine your ticket prices and other revenue assumptions. Have you been too conservative in projecting revenue or too liberal in projecting expenses? Sharpen your pencil and take another pass at balancing the budget.

SIDELINE STORY

The Super Bowl Tailgate Party

The Super Bowl Tailgate Party, held near the host stadium on the afternoon of the National Football League's championship game, is one of corporate America's most prestigious parties. The widely viewed pregame show on the game's host broadcast network often features live broadcasts of top-name musical entertainment and celebrity interviews staged from the Tailgate Party. Because of space and budget constraints, there are a limited number of invited guests, who are composed primarily of league sponsors and business partners, licensees, broadcasters, alumni, and other partners of the teams and league. The event is the largest social event on the NFL's calendar and is considered a key networking opportunity for businesses and executives who are closely affiliated with the sport of American football. Corporate business partners are each allotted a specific number of tickets, as defined by their respective sponsor, broadcasting, or licensing agreements.

The popularity of the event has grown over the years to the extent that partners regularly desire significantly more tickets than they are allotted. Although tickets for this exclusive event are not sold publicly, a per-person price for additional party tickets has been derived *for partners only* to accommodate the demand and enable the organizer to cover the additional food and beverage costs, table and chair rentals, and décor expenses involved in expanding the invitation list, while remaining on-budget for the party.

For sports event budgeting, a working knowledge of spreadsheet software programs is absolutely essential. Remember to set up your spreadsheet with formulas that automatically recalculate totals and subtotals as you make adjustments to the budget so you can see the immediate effect of any single decision on the bottom line.

Figure 3.5 illustrates a small portion of an event budget, specifically the event ticket revenue section, prepared on a spreadsheet. The "Budget" column includes a formula that instantly multiplies the number of tickets in the section by the price per ticket. The subtotal row contains a formula that automatically adds the columns containing the number of tickets per section, and the budget line for each ticket section, respectively. The number in the sales tax cell is a formula that multiplies the budget subtotal by 0.03 (representing 3 percent sales tax), and the number on the facilities usage fee line is derived from a formula multiplying the sum of the ticket inventory lines by $1.00 for each ticket.

Figure 3.6 shows the same spreadsheet segment, with three adjustments subsequently made by the organizer. In this example, 25 lower seating section locations have been eliminated from inventory (commonly known as "killed" seats) because of obstructed views. The upper-level end zone was increased in price to $19.50, and 10 additional standing-room ticket locations have been approved by the facility. The only changes made by the organizer to the spreadsheet are noted in the three shaded cells. The formulas inserted into each of the cells, as noted in the description of Figure 3.5, have simultaneously adjusted each cell, line, and column affected by these three revisions without the necessity of manually changing each line in the budget and reducing the inherent possibility of arithmetic errors on the part of the organizer. It is also a good idea to include a footnote with the date and time the budget was last revised, which can also be automatically stamped by the spreadsheet program.

XYZ SPORTS EVENT
PROJECTED TICKET REVENUES
(Preliminary draft—subject to change)

TICKET REVENUE	#	Price	Budget
Front row	150	$50.00	$7,500.00
Lower seating, mid-arena	750	$35.00	$26,250.00
Lower seating, end zone	500	$25.00	$12,500.00
Upper level, mid-arena	500	$25.00	$12,500.00
Upper level, end zone	350	$17.50	$6,125.00
Standing room	100	$10.00	$1,000.00
Subtotals	**2,350**		**$65,875.00**
Ticket Revenue Deductions			
Sales tax (3%)			($1,976.25)
Facility use fee ($1.00/ticket)			($2,350.00)
Net Ticket Revenues			**$61,548.75**

Figure 3.5 Sports Event Budget Worksheet Sample: Ticket Revenues

XYZ SPORTS EVENT
PROJECTED TICKET REVENUES
(Revised—January 6, 2013, 8:30 A.M.)

TICKET REVENUE	#	Price	Budget
Front row	150	$50.00	$7,500.00
Lower seating, mid-arena	725	$35.00	$25,375.00
Lower seating end zone	500	$25.00	$12,500.00
Upper level, mid-arena	500	$25.00	$12,500.00
Upper level, end zone	350	$19.50	$6,825.00
Standing room	110	$10.00	$1,100.00
Subtotals	**2,335**		**$65,800.00**
Ticket Revenue Deductions			
Sales tax (3%)			($1,974.00)
Facility use fee ($1.00/ticket)			($2,335.00)
Net Ticket Revenues		**$61,491.00**	

Figure 3.6 Sports Event Budget Worksheet Sample: Revised Ticket Revenues

The process of revising the budget must be pursued with the greatest forethought and most realistic expectations. Increasing or decreasing budget lines or forecasts do not necessarily cause the actual expenses you will incur to go up or down. Make sure that revising the budget is not simply just the action of moving numbers around to make the budget look better to you, as tempting as that may be. Make sure that you will actually be able to reduce or avoid costs that you remove from early drafts of the budget, and that you will really be able to generate the additional revenues you will need before you finalize your spreadsheet. Once you set these numbers in stone, you will have to live with them.

Reforecasts

Once the budget has been finalized, new information will invariably show your budget to be less than a totally accurate prediction of actual revenues and expenses. As discussed in Play 2, you will discover that some budget lines will be inadequate to cover both the actual expenses already incurred plus those still expected, others may suggest lower than expected revenues, and still others may point to probable areas of cost avoidance or extra cash. You will be better able to manage the finances of your event by reforecasting each budget line regularly. Rather than altering your finalized budget during this process, extend your spreadsheet to include more columns, as illustrated in Figure 3.7.

In this depiction of a partial budget spreadsheet, the organizer has inserted an "Actual" column next to the finalized budget figures, showing the total of invoices received to date that are applicable to these expense lines. This will help her estimate the values in the next column, the "Forecast" for each line. The organizer feels that most areas appear to be on target, but sees that

Expenses	Budget	Actual	Forecast	Variance	Notes
Event Operations					
Temporary staff	15,000	7,500	15,000	0	
Temporary staff expenses	4,500	2,238	4,500	0	
Volunteer staff expenses	3,500	0	3,500	0	
Staff travel expenses	1,000	985	1,500	(500)	
Staff meals or per diem	2,000	540	1,500	500	
Staff wardrobe/uniforms	2,500	1,200	2,500	0	
Site surveys/planning trips	1,500	450	1,000	500	
Pre-event planning meetings	500	200	500	0	
Event location office rent	5,000	2,500	5,000	0	
Event location office equipment	1,000	1,400	3,000	(2,000)	Higher copier costs
Event location office supplies	750	500	750	0	
SUBTOTAL	**37,250**	**17,513**	**38,750**	**(1,500)**	

Figure 3.7 Sample Budget Reforecast (Note: Budget codes should be added to every budget and reforecast for ease of bookkeeping and analysis. See Appendices 1 and 2.)

$985, almost all of her original estimate of $1,000 in staff travel expenses, has already been paid. Knowing that she still has a few weeks until the event, she can safely assume that she will be over budget on this line and has forecast an overage of 50 percent, or $500. She similarly sees several areas of potential savings, in staff meals and site surveys, where less money than expected has been spent to date. She can see this immediately because the software program she has used to set up her expense budget worksheet displays the values in the "Variance" column that are automatically calculated based on the difference between the budget and the forecast.

As shown in Figure 3.7, her biggest problem area is in location office equipment, where a significant overage is predicted. To make her postevent analysis easier, she has inserted a note as to why there was such a large difference between budgeted and forecasted expenses. Her automatic subtotals tell her exactly where she is: $1,500 short of expectations. To stay on track financially, she will have to enact cost-savings measures that must reduce her forecast in other areas. Again, it is important that she does not simply adjust the numbers, but instead take actions that will result in the numbers as adjusted.

The use of a spreadsheet program provides event organizers with maximum flexibility in designing a form that works best for their projects. Because many of the events the authors produce are held annually, we place some additional columns between the budget item descriptions and the current budget that show final line-item figures from one or more of the previous years' events. That way, we can compare exactly what we spent in each budget line the year before, and the year before that. This is a very useful tool for events that take place in a different city each year, allowing organizers to predict expense increases or decreases from city-to-city, where such items as taxes, labor rates, hotel room rates, airfares, and many others can be expected to vary widely. For example, we would be able to predict intuitively that hotel room rates for an event in Florida in January would be expected to be significantly higher, at the height of their winter tourist season, than an event held at about the same time a year before in St. Louis.

Use a budget form with column headings that work best for you and your event. But, reforecast your budget and analyze your variances as regularly and frequently as you can. Expect surprises, but manage their effects by staying on top of your budget at all times and taking the actions necessary to stay on track.

Post-Play Analysis

Although there are many ways to generate the revenue needed to fund a sports event, there are not nearly as many as there are ways to spend it (see Appendix 2). Examine your objectives to determine what you must target for your bottom line (a cost of doing business, an investment, break-even results, or profit), and find ways to maximize your revenue to get there. Major revenue streams include ticket sales, sponsorship, merchandise, and concessions, among others. Grassroots tournaments and races frequently charge a registration or entry fee to generate revenues instead of ticket sales. Broadcasting fees are generally available only to events of major importance to the viewing public, or to organizers who are willing and able to take on the financial exposure and labor-intensive effort of buying airtime and selling the advertising themselves.

Compare your projected revenues to expenses on a spreadsheet program. Design a spreadsheet that works for your event, and be sure to include automatic formulas that maximize accuracy and efficiency. Above all, monitor all costs and revenues, and reforecast the financial performance of your events on as regular and frequent a basis as possible.

Coach's Clipboard

1. You would like to improve the food and beverage *per cap* at your basketball tournament from a historical $4.00 to $5.00, a 25 percent increase. How can you achieve this by raising or lowering the prices on existing items at your concessions stands? Are there other ways of increasing the per cap?
2. You are organizing an adult recreational softball tournament for employees of businesses in your area. You want to generate at least $1,000 for a local children's hospital. What revenue streams can you create to meet this objective? What kinds of expenses will reduce your net revenues? Set up a budget for this event on a spreadsheet.
3. Your college alumni association wants to stage a series of games and contests at the campus's recreation facilities on the weekend before classes resume, featuring returning athletes from the school's 10th and 20th reunion classes. Create a financial model for an event that will identify costs and the revenue streams that will be needed, and when, to cover event costs at no risk to the association.
4. You have been asked to organize a youth football skills competition, and have been given $2,000 in starting capital to develop the event and recruit participants. How will you use your seed money to generate enough revenue for an event you estimate will ultimately cost $10,000?

PLAY 4

Soliciting and Selecting Host Cities and Venues

"If you don't try to win, you might as well hold the Olympics in somebody's backyard."

—*Jesse Owens, American Olympian, 1931–1980*

This play will help you to:

- Understand how cities and facilities evaluate the desirability of hosting a sports event and determine how to compete for the opportunity.
- Develop the support and partnership of the host community.
- Negotiate the best deal possible for the facility selected to host your event.

Introduction

Winning sports events begin their path to glory by selecting markets and venues that will actively support and promote the program. A collaborative, enthusiastic host community and a cooperative, engaged host facility can dramatically increase a sports event's chances for success. Approximately seven weeks before the NHL Entry Draft was to be held in Winnipeg, Manitoba, the host team Winnipeg Jets announced its intention to move the franchise to another city. Suddenly, the event needed a new home—and fast. Within days, the city of Edmonton, Alberta, its storied Edmonton Oilers, and Northlands Coliseum offered to serve as last-minute substitute hosts. With little more than 45 days to plan and promote an event that normally requires a year of preparation, the city, team, and arena mobilized to fill the arena with 12,000 fervent fans. (The Jets' exit from Winnipeg in favor of Phoenix, Arizona, was devastating to the community. Although the city lost the draft, local business and government officials with a keen understanding of the benefits of being the home of a major league team worked tirelessly to find ways to lure the NHL back to the city. Happily for Winnipeggers and in recognition of the community's aggressive drive to return professional hockey to the city, when the Atlanta Thrashers relocated to Manitoba, the team resumed the tradition of having the NHL team in Winnipeg called the Jets.)

In December 2011, "America's Game"—the annual Army–Navy football contest—came to the Washington, D.C., area for the first time in the storied rivalry between the two great military academies. As is often the case with events that come to the nation's capital, cooperative efforts and collaborative strengths among stakeholders in three jurisdictions—the District of Columbia, Maryland, and Virginia—were aligned to create a memorable and successful event. From the bid process that was coordinated by the Greater Washington Sports Alliance, a regional sports commission, to the hospitable lodging and restaurants, primarily in the District and Northern Virginia, to the attentive venue operations and event coordination at FedEx Field, located in Landover, Maryland, the Army–Navy Game was considered an outstanding success in every way. The nation's capital region also positioned itself for future Army–Navy games as well as showcased itself for other high-profile, revenue-generating sports events.

Working with motivated hosts can indeed produce winning results. Sports event managers who take their properties to different cities, either annually or as part of a multistop seasonal tour, know well that organizing successful events is in large part dependent on developing, cultivating, and maintaining a series of strategic and functional partnerships in each market they visit. In order to forge an effective partnership, all parties involved—both hosts and organizers—must acquire an intimate understanding of the wants, needs, and interests of each other. When savvy sports event organizers set out to find a home for their event, they are careful to evaluate how much they can count on the active support of the local government and various segments of the indigenous business community. Regional business groups essential to the success of sports events commonly include the hotel and restaurant industries, area newspapers, radio and television stations, and the membership of local chambers of commerce and other business groups. Experienced organizers know that except for having to acquire necessary permits and observing community ordinances, managing an event without the active participation of local businesses and city government is far from impossible. There is no question, however, that one is virtually assured of better results by engaging top regional officials and obtaining at least their philosophical investment in the event's success. Soliciting and obtaining their more active involvement can help to achieve even greater success.

Generally, every city or region that seeks to host sports events will sing its own praises and offer glowing platitudes on how uniquely successful an event will be if awarded to its community. It is essential that event organizers get a clear and true sense ahead of time of how a prospective host will embrace a program once the event has been awarded. All too often, ambivalence, attitudes of reduced importance and even laziness begin to emerge after the deal is finalized. Some sports commissions, for example, are charged only with the responsibility of promoting and selling a city to event organizers. With all respect to the exceptions to the rule, the service provided by many sports commissions disappears once the event is awarded. As their mission is fulfilled, the commissions are already applying their limited resources to promoting their destination to other potential future business prospects. Sports commissions that remain involved to help identify and mobilize local resources are of great value to visiting event organizers and the business community, as their assistance can result in an even greater share of the budget being spent locally.

Although there is no way to guarantee how a community will eventually respond, the best way to engage its leaders' interest and support is to understand what they want to gain by hosting a sports event and then to demonstrate a sensitivity to their needs. Ask community leaders what they envision the event will achieve for their city, and respond with a plan that addresses what the event can reasonably deliver and how. Open a dialogue to determine how the community defines success and to provide it with insights on how you do, too. If you want the community to invest in the success of your event, demonstrate your organization's commitment to invest in the success of the community.

What Host Cities Really Want from Sports Events

Sports events may be exciting, involving programs that improve a city's quality of life, but just like most organizers, the local governments, business communities, and facilities that host the events are most interested in generating revenue. Cities often undertake financial responsibility for many hidden costs when hosting events, including paying for the extra police, fire, ambulance, and sanitation department members that may be assigned to provide for traffic flow, public safety, and the protection and maintenance of community assets. The local government may have helped to finance the community's sports facilities and may be paying interest on the debt that was incurred on construction or renovation of its arena, stadium, or convention center.

Visiting sports events can help the local government offset these costs in both direct and indirect ways. Events that increase hotel occupancies generate revenue in sales taxes and, in many cities, special hotel taxes. These special taxes are usually acts of local legislation, earmarking the revenue visiting guests generate for specific purposes, such as paying the debt service on airport improvements, a convention center, or other public buildings that attract business to a city or region. Additionally, any event that brings visitors to area hotels also generates sales taxes on the additional meals consumed in restaurants, on rental cars and taxis, and on significant direct spending in the local market on the part of the organizer. The more hotel rooms your event can fill with athletes, staff, guests, and visitors—whether the event budget is paying for them or the guests are reaching into their own pockets is immaterial—the more a city will embrace you and the event you are organizing.

To gauge the interest of a potential host community, the first group to contact is the city's convention and visitors bureau (CVB), an organization dedicated to drawing business meetings, sports and entertainment events, and tourists to its hotel, resort, convention, meeting, and event facilities. The CVB will often share office space with the executive director of a sports commission, or have an account representative on staff who specializes in attracting sports events. These individuals will be able to guide you to the best facilities, hotels, and hospitality sites to accommodate your sports event's needs.

The two factors that most frequently determine the degree to which a city will strive to attract an event, although there are others, are economic impact and its close cousin, hotel room occupancy generated by inbound visitors. CVBs use *room nights* as their unit of measure for hotel occupancy, defined as one room occupied for one night.

Economic Impact

As is their mandate, CVBs and sports commissions will analyze the potential economic impact an event can be expected to generate based on information from the organizer, the results of which will determine how aggressively they will pursue and invest in a sports property. Economic impact is a measure of the dollars that will flow into, or out of, a region solely and specifically because of the presence of a particular event, be it a sports event, a convention, a political action, an act of legislation, or virtually any activity that generates new revenues or losses for the local economy.

Economic impact and consumer spending figures provided or circulated by event organizers have come under increasing media scrutiny for years, owing to their seemingly fantastic numbers. On its website, the New Orleans Host Committee for Super Bowl XLVII stated, "The average economic impact of the Super Bowl on a host city is $300–400 million. Most recent studies estimated a $375M impact for Super Bowl XLII in Tampa Bay in 2009." A report released by Visa Europe predicted an $8.2 billion boost to the economy of the United Kingdom from consumer spending related to the 2012 Summer Olympic and Paralympic Games in London. The Ministry of Sport in Brazil issued a study stating that hosting the 2014 World Cup soccer tournament should add $10.5 billion to the country's economy.

Although some quotes of economic impact and other financial projections may seem difficult to conceive, it is inarguable that the positive effect of sports events on the local economy can be nevertheless impressive. Published estimates for Major League Baseball's All-Star Game have been pegged at approximately $60 million to $70 million. In 2009, the NBA All-Star Game brought an estimated $67 million to Phoenix, and the NHL Winter Classic is thought to have injected $22 million into the Pittsburgh economy. But, your event doesn't have to be from one of North America's major professional sports to provide the kind of value and economic impact to a city that makes a sports event a highly prized and hotly contested property. The estimated impact for the Cincinnati area from the three-division 2010 AAU Girls 13U Basketball National Tournament was $2 million, and the 2012 Ohio Senior Olympics State Games was projected to generate $500,000 in economic impact for Northeast Ohio. The 2009 John Hunter Regatta at Lake Lanier in Georgia generated approximately $100,000 in direct spending, as reported by the local convention and visitors bureau.

In 2007 alone, the sporting events industry in Southern California generated an all-time high of more than $5 billion in total economic impact, according to a study released by the Los Angeles Sports Council and the Los Angeles Area Chamber of Commerce, with nearly 25 million people attending area sporting events that year. "Sports is not just a section in the newspaper, it's also a sector of the economy, and an underrated one at that," said Alan Rothenberg, chairman of the Sports Council. "Anything that contributes a $5 billion impact each year is substantial."

Since that report, Southern California has drawn a range of other events and their accompanying economic impact, such as ESPN's X Games, which in 2010 added a reported $50 million in identifiable benefits to the Los Angeles economy, and the 2011 NBA All-Star Game, which produced an estimated $85 million in increased economic activity in Los Angeles County. Financial benefits generated by sports events have continued to increase in Southern California and throughout the country and can be expected to do so for the foreseeable future.

The Canadian Sports Tourism Alliance (CSTA), recognizing the value of being able to evaluate a credible and reliable measure of an event's economic impact, developed a Sport Tourism Economic Assessment Model (STEAM). The online model is accessible to CSTA members by visiting the CSTA home page and clicking on the Canadian Sport Tourism link. By entering estimated values in a series of pull-down questionnaires, local and provincial governments can calculate and compare the impact of various potential events on their region based on a consistent set of criteria, including gross domestic product (the net value added by industries), wages, employment, taxes (e.g., income, sales, payroll, etc.), and a total gross economic impact figure. All events analyzed by the STEAM model generate results according to uniform guidelines, enabling member sports commissions and CVBs to make sound business decisions on the comparative desirability of hosting specific sports events in their communities.

The Hawaii Tourism Authority (HTA) develops timely economic impact data from a mandatory state form that is distributed to passengers on every airline flight arriving to the Islands. The collected forms provide information on how long arriving visitors will stay, what islands they will visit, and what types of activities they will enjoy while in Hawaii. The survey also asks for the primary reason for visiting Hawaii, and "to attend a sports event" is one of the choices offered. By comparing the data from the travelers indicating they are coming to Hawaii for "a sports event" with the calendar of sports activities scheduled, HTA can extrapolate the incremental number of visitors generated by a specific event, as well as the economic impact by multiplying each traveler by the number of days the visitor will stay.

Estimating your event's economic impact can make it more salable and attractive to a city actively seeking to host sports events. Your organization may be best served by retaining an independent consultant with relevant experience who can be found through searching trade publications, websites, and other industry sources, particularly if the objectivity and reliability of your figures is of particular political importance. If the limited resources of your organization require devising a more do-it-yourself estimate of economic impact, you can prepare one using the formula in Figure 4.1 and the instructions that follow.

Instructions for Figure 4.1:

- **Line A:** Examine the event's expense budget and determine, line by line, what portion of each category might be spent in the local market. Exclude expenses that are paid to vendors outside of the region where the event will be held, as well as any overhead costs and payroll for event offices and staff if they are not located in the community hosting the event. If your organization will spend additional funds in the community that are accounted for in areas outside of the event budget, or by other departments within your organization, be sure to include an estimate of their spending as well, and enter the sum of all such expenses on line A.
- **Line B:** Then, calculate the number of hotel rooms that will be occupied by event participants or spectators, but are not already accounted for on line A (i.e., those not paid for by the event budget). Multiply the number of rooms by the average number of nights they will be in use to determine the number of room nights your event will generate. Enter this amount on line B.
- **Line C:** Rooms not paid for by the organizer should include estimates for in-bound athletes, spectators, fans, sponsors, vendors, and others whose presence in the community is directly attributable to the event. The local sports commission or CVB will be most interested in the

A. Direct spending by organizer in market		______
B. Participant/audience room nights	______	
C. Participant/audience hotel room rate	______	
D. Participant/audience hotel spending (B × C)		______
E. # Participants/audience	______	
F. # Days in market	______	
G. Per-diem spending estimate per participant/audience	______	
H. Participant/audience per diem spending (E × F × G)		______
I. Direct spending by sponsors/partners in market		______
J. Other estimated spending		______
K. SUBTOTAL (A + D + H + I + J)		______
L. Economic multiplier		2.25
M. Total Estimated Economic Impact (K × L)		______

Figure 4.1 Preparation of an Economic Impact Analysis for Sports Events

number of room nights generated by the event, whether paid for by the event budget or by other visitors arriving specifically to attend or participate in the event. Enter the average hotel room rate per night, plus occupancy and sales taxes, gratuities, and any other fees on line C.

- **Line D:** Multiply line B by line C and enter the result on line D.
- **Line E:** Estimate the number of participants and spectators coming from outside the community and enter this figure on line E. As this number refers to individuals, rather than traveling parties, this number should be greater than the number of hotel rooms you expect the event to fill.
- **Line F:** Spectators from within the community are excluded from this number because most economists feel that the dollars they spend on an event in their own market represents money they would have spent on other activities in the area anyway, and, therefore, they generate no additional economic impact. Estimate the average number of days, and fractions thereof, that you expect them to be in town for the events and enter on line F.
- **Line G:** Then, enter an estimated "per diem" number on line G. A per diem is the amount of money you expect the participants and spectators to spend in the area on meals, refreshments, entertainment, and personal items such as laundry and other services. This amount will vary widely based on the demographics of your participating athletes, target audience, and the cost of living in the city in which the event is held. To get an idea of reasonable per-diem rates in various communities in the United States and beyond, several government websites maintain information used for recompensing their employees and vendors, including the General Services Administration website for domestic rates, and the US State Department website for rates in cities outside of the United States. Although these figures should be considered minimums if your guests are paying for all of their meals and expenses, the actual per-diem rates for participants may be lower if the event provides a number of meals or receptions that have already been included in line A. You may also add to or subtract from the per-diem rate if you feel it does not adequately reflect the actual expenses you expect your inbound participants or spectators to encounter (e.g., a more upscale audience is very likely to spend more than an average federal employee on meals and entertainment).
- **Line H:** Multiply lines E, F, and G and enter the result on line H.
- **Line I:** An event's sponsors, licensees, merchandisers, broadcast rights holders, vendors, and other stakeholders may host meals or receptions, purchase gifts, or stage events for their own guests during your event. Even though the event organizer does not manage these events or purchases, they are a direct result of the event being staged in that market, and, therefore, may be included in the economic impact analysis. Estimate the direct spending within the community of your various partners in each expense area, including staff who may need to be housed, the additional guests they may attract to hotels, and the direct spending on the ancillary events they may host, and enter your best judgment on line I.
- **Line J:** There may be any number of other spending categories specific to your audience, the marketplace, or event. For example, sports events held in resort or vacation destinations often result in extended hotel stays by attendees, greens and/or activities fees, skiing and other recreational expenses, attraction admission fees, and non-event-specific souvenir purchases, to name a few. These, plus other estimated expenses for participants and spectators such as local ground transportation (e.g., taxi and mass transportation, car rentals, gasoline, tolls, parking), local retail purchases, and any other reasonably conceivable spending, should be inserted on line J.
- **Line K:** Add the expenses estimated on lines A, D, H, I, and J and enter the sum on line K. This subtotal yields an estimate of the direct economic impact generated by your event.
- **Line L:** Interestingly, many economists consider the overall economic impact of an event to be greater than the sum of direct spending. It is believed that every dollar spent as described above stimulates the local economy and causes each new dollar to be spent

again within the community, and more than once, so the final impact can actually be between 2.25 and 2.50 times greater than the direct spending total.

- **Line M:** Applying the more conservative economic multiplier number, multiply the subtotal on line K by 2.25 and enter the result on line M. This quantity is the gross economic impact of your program, a key figure sought after by host cities when considering whether or not to host a sports event.

Room Nights and Other Factors

The importance of the hotel room nights generated by sports events has already been discussed as a component of the event's overall economic impact. For CVBs, this is often the key determinant, as room nights are the life-blood of their most influential and vocal constituent of their membership, the hotel industry. In the accommodations business, the quantity of room nights generated by an event is like a fossil record left behind by an organizer. Past host hotels and CVBs share intelligence with potential future event hosts, so the truthfulness of an organizer's estimates will affect how the community will judge the reliability of every assertion that follows. Event organizers should, therefore, be candid—and careful—with the numbers they project during the bidding process.

Potential host cities may also combine their thirst for room nights and economic impact with other business, political, quality-of-life, and/or promotional motivations in the pursuit of certain sports events. An event's timeframe may fit what convention and visitors bureaus call an "opportunity period," times of the year when hotel occupancy is otherwise low. A market may also wish to demonstrate to organizers of larger events its ability to host and handle smaller, but relevant, visible, and well-regarded sports events. City leaders may believe that media coverage of the event will help promote their city as a tourist destination, or invest in the event with extra city services to attract future corporate meetings, incentives, and conventions held by companies associated with the program. A particular sport may be very strong on the grassroots level in a region, and its ubiquity in the marketplace perceived as a portent for an event's likely success (thus generating a greater economic impact and publicity for the region).

Every community evaluates its interest in bidding on an event based on different criteria and the needs of the marketplace. When Tara Green, now Chief Revenue Officer of American Airlines Center in Dallas, Texas, led sports tourism marketing for the city's convention and visitors bureau, her city targeted at least one "major" sports event per year, and attempted to fill the rest of the calendar with as many head in bed events (high room-night generators) as possible. "A major event is one that brings national or international media exposure to the city as well as significant economic impact," says Green. "The 'head in bed' events are your amateur youth events. They fill up the hotels but don't bring any kind of media exposure. Those have as much importance to the hotel community as the major ones. They become a city's 'bread and butter,' so to speak."

Linda Shetina Logan, the executive director of the Greater Columbus (Ohio) Sports Commission, analyzes more than just an event's projected economic impact, hotel occupancy potential, exposure opportunities, and contributions to the region's quality of life. She researches the history of an event with past hosts, analyzes the availability of appropriate event facilities in the market, and tries to match the grassroots interest of the community with events up for bid. "The Ohio Valley Region of USA Volleyball has the largest membership in the country, thus we pursue many volleyball events," says Logan. "Not only to 'grow the game,' but to provide Ohio Valley members more opportunities to participate in marquee events, and for bragging rights. Because of our strong membership, we can host a first-class event."

For Chris Browne, a vice president with the Greater Washington Sports Alliance (GWSA), there is one overarching priority to consider when the regional sports commission evaluates whether or not to bid to bring an event to the nation's capital: how does the community benefit?

"Whether it's for the Army–Navy Game, the Frozen Four, or the World Police and Fire Games, we have a series of questions that we ask before bidding on an event," says Browne. "Is the event profitable? Can there be a return on investment? Is there corporate and political support for the event? Is there local interest in the event? There are a number of other questions that are part of our research and analysis, a process that is designed to identify how the community will benefit by the investment in and hosting of a specific event."

The USO Principle—understanding stakeholders' objectives—is hard at work uniting event organizers and host cities. Organizers are best served when they understand what a host city wants and expects from its involvement in a sports event. Do not be shy about trading a demonstrated willingness to assist a community in achieving its objectives in return for the city's understanding and support of your own. Ask the sports commission, CVB, the office of the mayor, and other governmental officials what they would want your event to do for their community and constituents. Talk to local chambers of commerce and business associations to learn what the area's leaders of industry might hope to gain from the event. And, consult with one or more public relations agencies on what past events have proved successful, and why. Gain insights on why others might have gone wrong. By hearing the community's side of the story, you will at minimum make them feel invested and listened to, like an event insider. At best, you will be able to design the event and its supporting promotions to help them achieve objectives they would be less likely to accomplish without your coming to town, gaining their support in return.

Figure 4.2 summarizes some of the most common reasons communities seek to host sports events, many of which have already been discussed. As the figure demonstrates, there are many motivations, ranging from the altruistic to the political, and their relative importance may differ from city to city, based on local priorities. Remember that any number may be operating at the same time.

What Sports Events Really Want from Host Cities

Successful sports event organizers know that achieving their objectives is far easier with the support of local government and their constituent businesses, trade organizations, and citizens than without them. It is certainly possible to stage an event in an ambivalent or even antagonistic

- To generate hotel room occupancy
- To stimulate the local economy (i.e., generate economic impact)
- To generate tax revenues
- To showcase new sports, athletic or other public assembly facilities to the community, media, potential corporate sponsors, and organizers of other potential events
- To attract larger, or more newsworthy, events to their facilities or community
- To showcase the community or region to potential future visitors
- To attract professional teams and athletes to their premier facilities
- To position themselves as leaders among neighboring (sometimes rival) communities
- To revitalize an economically disadvantaged or newly developed part of the community
- To present a positive quality-of-life program to the community
- To present a high-profile event in a critical election year
- To demonstrate the need for improved sports/public assembly facilities

Figure 4.2 Common Reasons Why Communities Host Sports Events

marketplace, although doing so foreshadows the possibility of great tribulations and rough roads ahead. For this reason, it is strongly suggested that event organizers get a clear understanding of the degree and nature of a community's support, and to have as many relationships formalized in writing with letters of agreement and contracts as possible during the romance period before an event is awarded. While it is usually counterproductive and detrimental to an organizer's reputation to pursue legal remedies should a city government or business group renege on promises made during early discussions, it is less likely that they will, knowing that their assertions are in writing and their own reputations are on the line. Having these assurances in writing greatly reduces the potential of later misunderstandings.

Naturally, event organizers will, and should, attempt to manage their budgets by avoiding, or at least reducing, whatever costs they can. Sometimes, the community can provide services, equipment, or other forms of support on either a governmental or business level that will help organizers spend their budget money more efficiently, and enable them to expand and improve their event without avoidable or debilitating drains on expenses.

Soliciting Bids with a Request for Proposal

Sports event organizers owe to themselves and prospective hosts a clear description of an event's needs, specific requirements, and expectations from the start. This allows organizers to eliminate less-serious contenders and permits the most interested communities to make the best impression. If a community knows how an organizer will make a decision, it can communicate the salient benefits of awarding the event to its city, and can incorporate relevant commitments into the strongest possible expression of interest. The most effective way for organizers to begin the process of identifying the ideal host for a sports event is to generate a thoughtful and comprehensive bid document, or *request for proposal* (RFP). RFPs are also frequently used to qualify vendors who wish to bid on supplying or contributing products or services.

An effective RFP is not just an outline of the organizer's expectations. It is also a sales and marketing document. Through this important document, the event organizer is formally asking the prospective host community to participate in ensuring the success of the program. The preparation of a winning bid will require significant time and energy investments on the part of the community, so it is wise to present to an event in the most thorough and enthusiastic, but genuine, terms. To illustrate, a sample RFP for a fictional event titled the "Big Street Sports Tournament" may be found in Appendix 3. The components of this hypothetical RFP are based on the generalized format illustrated in Figure 4.3, and followed with additional description.

I. Introduction
II. Event Description (including history and impacts)
III. Event Schedule
IV. Role of the Event Organizer
V. Role of the Host City
VI. Definition of the Ideal Event Site (including requirements of the event)
VII. Benefits to the Host City
VIII. Sponsors and Marketing Rights
IX. Response Format

Figure 4.3 Sports Event Request for Proposal Components

SIDELINE STORY

Indianapolis and Detroit Join the Super Bowl Club

If there is any single indicator that host cities do indeed benefit greatly from the public exposure and economic impact generated by major events, one has only to look at the first 48 years of Super Bowl history. Just two cities—Miami and New Orleans—account for 20 Super Bowls between them, more than 40 percent of every AFC-NFC championship game ever played. If events of this magnitude were not enormously beneficial to their host communities, it is difficult to conceive why these two perennial hosts haven't yet stopped bidding on Super Bowls.

The competition to even these traditional Super Bowl regions has grown dramatically, and new entrants bidding on the event have resulted in cities like Indianapolis earning a Super Bowl in 2012 and New York/New Jersey hosting the metropolitan area's first Super Bowl in 2014. Allison Melangton, president and CEO of the 2012 Indianapolis Super Bowl Host Committee, points to a number of factors that led Indianapolis and the NFL Colts to pursue hosting the Super Bowl: "As the City was growing and expanding, strategic plans for new venues were being developed that would provide the opportunity for Indianapolis to qualify as a potential Super Bowl host city," said Melangton. "This included a new 70,000-seat stadium, a significant expansion of the Indiana Convention Center to 600,000 square feet, a new JW Marriott Hotel complex with over 1,000 rooms, and a new, largely expanded airport complex. The unique urban setting of [all these venues in] downtown Indianapolis was a deliberate plan with the hope of attracting conventions and events whose participants would enjoy the atmosphere and environment an urban, convenient setting."

"The opportunities that hosting the Super Bowl would bring to Indianapolis included economic impact, youth programs and activities, community engagement at multiple levels, catalyst for infrastructure expansions, legacy initiatives, and so on. Indianapolis had invested three decades in building a sports product, gaining valuable experience and gaining loyal and trusted volunteers. Hosting a Super Bowl would bring all of those components together for what would be an amazing stage for the world to see. It's an affirmation more than a culmination of the progress that has truly been made."

The event RFP should begin with an "Introduction" that describes the event in general terms, and communicates some of the advantages of hosting the event to the interested community. In the case of the "Big Street Sports Tournament," the organizer points out that the event will attract fans and a family audience from the surrounding region, as well as athletes who will travel to the area from across North America. The RFP further describes the most exciting elements of the event and notes that the program has been completely updated to capitalize on the growth of extreme action sports.

The next section, the "Event Description," should describe the event in more detail, providing estimates for the number of in-bound athletes, guests, and fans, based on historical performance, if available. Define whether the event will be ticketed or free and open to the public. In the case of this fictional event, the fact that the event is free to all was included in the first section because the organizer felt it was a significant enough sales point to be worthy of particular emphasis. If the event has a history of being held in other communities, their identities

Another nontraditional market, Detroit, Michigan, has hosted the Super Bowl twice, once in 1982 and again for the 40th game in 2006. "The genesis of hosting a game was the enormous commitment of one of the NFL's original team owners, William Clay Ford, to move the team from Pontiac, Michigan, to downtown Detroit. This move and investment into the league was pivotal in securing the region's second Super Bowl," recalls Detroit Super Bowl Host Committee president Susan Sherer. "The vision for both the bid and the host team was to '*change the conversation about Detroit.*' So while the host committee was faithful to the obligations of the bid, we took great care to be sure everything we invested in would tie into this vision." Billionaire industrialist Roger Penske, well-known in the world of auto racing, chaired the host committee and provided much of the vision along with Sherer of how Super Bowl could transform the public's perception of Detroit. As a result of the Super Bowl being awarded to the city, $150 million was raised by the city from a wide range of sources to improve the city's downtown infrastructure in time for the massive influx of media and business leaders for the event. A massive weeklong outdoor winter festival called "Motown Winter Blast" in the downtown area was created to accommodate Michiganders and inbound fans alike. And, the host committee, like Indianapolis several years later, provided outstanding hospitality to all who visited to enjoy the Super Bowl.

Did all that hard work change the conversation about Detroit? Consider these quotes from national media reports: "I have to admit it, I was dreading going to Detroit. I thought it would be too cold and be a miserable place to host a Super Bowl. Man, was I wrong, Detroit freaking ROCKS!" (*Sports Illustrated*). "I come in praise of Detroit. That's right. I like Detroit, I love Detroit. I could live here. Really" (*The Boston Globe*).

By the time Indianapolis joined the Super Bowl club of host cities, praise in print and on broadcast media was joined by reporters and visitors in social network media in short bursts no less warm and glowing for this traditionally cold winter city: "Indy you get an 11 out of 10. Best collective effort by any city hosting any sporting event I've attended" (*Mike Tirico, ESPN*). "Adios Indy. You crushed it. Congratulations" (*Rich Eisen, NFL Network*). Yes, hosting a major event like Super Bowl can, indeed, change the conversation about a city or region.

should be disclosed. The prospective host will almost certainly want to research the experiences of, and impact on, past host cities. This research can be conducted via the Internet, media accounts, and other third parties without several interested cities inundating a single contact individual with requests for information. It is best to provide individual contacts for past references only upon request for two reasons—first, so that only serious contenders, those who take the time to call you to seek this information, will disturb your past contacts, and, second, so you know which cities are doing their due diligence and will most likely submit a bid. Resist the urge to overdramatize, embellish, or exaggerate past history in your RFP, as cities commonly share intelligence on events and you will want to protect the reputation of your organization, as well as your own, by providing truthful, candid, and accurate information. Include a paragraph at the end of the Event Description section that describes how the prospective host should respond, the deadline for submissions, and a personal contact at your organization to whom questions may be directed.

SIDELINE STORY

Hometown Hosts—World-Class Event

The partnership between host cities and sports events can run so deep that it is hard to conceive of them ever moving elsewhere. The city of Williamsport, Pennsylvania (29,381 population 2010 census), is the birthplace of Little League Baseball and arguably the most popular grassroots sports event in the United States. What started as a statewide tournament in 1947 has grown to the 16-team Little League World Series, drawing an attendance of close to 400,000 live spectators as well as millions of viewers on ESPN, ESPN2, ESPN3, and ABC. Tickets to the event are free.

Spectators eight-times outnumber the combined local population of Williamsport and the neighboring host borough of South Williamsport. "Both communities roll out the red carpet for the Little League World Series," says Little League Baseball president Stephen Keener. "We are very fortunate to conduct a premier sports championship event in a small-town atmosphere. It really is what gives this event its charm." The entire region mobilizes in preparation for event day. Fire, police, security, and media emergency personnel of both communities assist with the operation of the event. The Chamber of Commerce's Tourism Department assists with housing, transportation, and the other needs of inbound visitors, and hosts a hospitality day for corporate partners at the Williamsport Country Club. In the case of the Little League Baseball World Series, the hometown values of the organizer and community are truly as one—their objectives are simply well-deserved pride and service to America's youth.

The "Event Schedule" section that follows may contain as many details as the organizer feels comfortable providing, but, at a minimum should define a target date for the event, and when athletes, guests, and fans can be expected to arrive in and depart from the community. Operating hours, ancillary social and hospitality events (parties, receptions, fan events), and other details, if available, should also be included in this section.

The next section, the "Role of the Event Organizer," should list all of the responsibilities, both operational and financial, of the organization requesting proposals. Try to be as comprehensive as possible, as inadvertent omissions may be perceived as areas of responsibility that will fall to the community. It is also a good idea to provide background information and qualifications of the event organizer within this section to reinforce the legitimacy of the program and the experience and reliability of its management.

If the event is supported by sponsors that have already secured exclusive rights to the program, it is essential that the organizer provides their identities in the RFP. This will let the prospective host city know that these sponsor categories are already occupied, and may not be offered to competitors in the marketplace. As sponsors can be continually added, you may list these in a separate or an accompanying attachment (as an addendum) to the RFP and specifically note that this list may be updated periodically.

Host communities should play a prominent and meaningful role in ensuring the success of sports events. The section entitled "Role of the Host City" should provide the details those preparing proposals will need in order to determine their community's ability to accommodate and successfully compete for the event. It is likely that the individual or group formally applying for the event will know its community far better than the event organizer. The familiarity with facilities, past history of similar events, city ordinances, and other market-specific data can provide the essential information that can help to make the selection process faster, more efficient, and less expensive for everyone involved.

As this is the section that will outline the minimum requirements for a successful bid, the organizer should provide and request as much detailed information as possible. Although the response to an RFP can take any form, a helpful tool to include is a questionnaire at the end of the document that can be used by the reviewer as a uniform executive summary to make it easier to review and compare the first round of submissions. The majority of the bid requirements will often be found in the host city section, and may include requests for detailed information including event site commitments or recommendations, venue floor plans and seating diagrams, hotel and local office space recommendations, proposed local newspaper, radio, and television promotional partners and other community marketing assets, signage requirements, equipment and services available from the host city, sources of volunteer staffing, and other topics of interest.

It is not uncommon for sports event organizers to request letters of support from various governmental officials, such as a mayor, governor, senators, congresspeople, or county commissioners, as well as representatives of the local sports commission, convention and visitors bureau, chamber of commerce, and other essential city partners and civic leaders. These letters will ensure that the highest offices and prominent stakeholders in the region are aware of their constituents' interest and are committed to a successful event in their jurisdiction.

Another important inclusion is background information about the key individuals with whom the event organizer can expect to interact during the planning and presentation of the event. These important contacts may be part of a local organizing committee (LOC), the management staff of the venue or another entity that will have responsibilities for the event. The relevant experience these people have in staging events can be a key factor in evaluating a candidate city's response to an RFP.

Since the availability of an appropriate event site is one of the most important factors when evaluating a bid submission, it is recommended that a section be included in the RFP that defines "The Ideal Event Site." This section should outline the minimum requirements and dimensions of the event site, seating configurations, locker room and other support areas, and the dates that are required by the organizer for loading in, setting up, conducting the event, and loading out. Any other requirement, definition, or disclosure specific to the event site, such as requests for information regarding signage restrictions, sponsor exclusivities, merchandise sales, availability and costs of power, lights, water or other necessities, or maximum rental fees or associated costs, should also be included here.

Now that you have outlined what the community must do for you, it is time to let the community know what you can do for the community in the "Benefits to the Host City" section. Your ability to deliver benefits to the city in exchange for the city's interest and participation in hosting your event is the first indication that you will approach your relationship in a spirit of partnership. Outline all of the rights the community will enjoy as your partner, including the use of event marks, pre-event promotional exposure, on-site exposure, and special, exclusive opportunities, events, access, and marketing rights available only to the host city. If the host has the ability to sell local sponsorships, all of the specifics including categories available for sale, pricing (if available), and the formula for revenue sharing between the organizer and the city, should be outlined in this section.

Distributing Your RFP

One copy of the RFP should be sent to the senior decision maker in the communities under consideration, most often the top official at the local convention and visitors bureau or sports commission. Additional copies may also be sent to other stakeholders in the community upon that decision-maker's request. If information about your event is best disseminated to a wide range of communities the National Association of Sports Commissions (NASC) is an outstanding resource of target organizations in more than 225 cities across the United States. The NASC's website offers a comprehensive roster of member organizations and key contacts. Organizers who wish to make events available to NASC members for bidding may become a "rights holder" member for an annual fee. Rights holder members are entitled to post detailed information about their event on the NASC website, and may include a brief version of their event's RFP. Members are also entitled to receive the NASC newsletter containing valuable intelligence on the North American marketplace, as well as member-only rates on the organization's popular Sports Event Symposium held each April, among other networking and professional development benefits. The National Association of Sports Commissions may be contacted at 9916 Carver Road, Suite 100, Cincinnati, OH 45242 (phone: 513-281-3888; fax: 513-281-1765; e-mail: NASC@sportscommissions.org) and information may be found at its website.

Another excellent resource for intelligence on potential host cities, as well as posting information on events seeking proposals, is *SportsTravel Magazine* (www.sportstravelmagazine.com). This publication also hosts an annual networking, conference, and expo event called TEAMS (Travel, Events, and Management in Sports). *SportsTravel* magazine is available through the website or by contacting Schneider Publishing Company, Inc., 11835 West Olympic Boulevard, 12th Floor, Los Angeles, CA 90064 (phone: 310-577-3700; fax: 310-577-3715).

Every RFP should contain a realistic deadline date for the submission and acceptance of proposals. Depending on the amount of information requested by the organizer, giving interested cities 60 to 90 days after receipt of the RFP is generally reasonable for small to medium-sized events. The more work that is required of prospective cities (e.g., soliciting and holding hotel rooms and event venues, and confirming points of agreement that may require acts of legislation), the more time should be allowed for their responses. Some major events may require six months to a year of proposal preparation. As part of the RFP response process, many event organizers often choose to schedule a required or optional conference call, video conference, or meeting to answer questions from or to highlight key information to interested parties. A summary of the topics discussed may be distributed to all participants on the call or to everyone who received the RFP.

Seeking the right home for your event is like finding the right home for your family. It is a process best not rushed. Permit sufficient time for the community preparing the bid, as well as for analysis and evaluation after submission. Be sure to be as specific as possible in your request for all of the information you will require so that you are equipped to make the best decision for your event.

Evaluating Responses to RFPs

Once the deadline has passed, it is time to begin evaluating and comparing the proposals you have received. Read and analyze each submission carefully and list salient points of comparison, the pros and cons offered by each city. You can set up another spreadsheet to help compare responses to the questionnaire at a glance (see the example in Appendix 4). Contrast the opportunities of each market, such as the size of the population, the size of the business base (the most likely universe of potential sponsors), and the degree of interest in your sport that might be expected of residents in the local community. Compare the event facilities that are available, and the costs of doing business in each market. Consider the convenience and accessibility of each city to the athletes or participants who will travel to compete there. Review the letters of commitment included in each response, and evaluate the depth of support that each community will apply to your event in the form of facilities, services, labor, and equipment. Study the event management experience of the key contacts with whom you might be working. If your event will be located outdoors, examine weather records for the targeted event dates in each region. If you are selling tickets, compare household income levels, amusement and sales tax rates, and other factors that might detract from gross revenues. Remember that the prices of tickets that would be deemed reasonable could vary greatly between the bidding cities. Analyze the gross potential in each city based on the venue being proposed, expected tickets sales, and the ticket prices likely to be set market by market. Don't forget to deduct applicable taxes and payable facility usage fees.

The most important question included on your RFP response form is: "We agree to the bid specifications outlined in this request for proposal: Yes or no." If the answer is yes, you can generally bank on an interested city following through. If the answer is no, be sure to ask respondents to provide a complete and detailed list of any exceptions they wish to make to the bid specifications. Sometimes, these exceptions are minor, or are legally required by local ordinances, and might be worth overlooking if the rest of the bid is particularly strong. Other times, they are so significant that no further consideration of the bid is required and the city may be eliminated from contention. Agreeing to bid specifications, presuming they are reasonable, is certainly a major factor in a positive response to a host city proposal, but it is by no means the sole determinant. Figure 4.4 lists some of the most common reasons why cities are chosen by organizers to host sports events, the relative importance of each being dependent on the event's objectives and business model.

Some RFPs issued by event organizers require a bid fee that must accompany the submission of a proposal, or a host fee upon being awarded the event. Bid fees are relatively rare, and more commonly required for large, prestigious, and high-exposure events. They are sometimes necessary to offset the organizer's costs of having one or more event managers travel into the market to survey the proposed event sites, and to meet with prospective hosts, officials, and sponsors. Bid fees are not recommended for smaller or less-known events, as sports commissions and CVBs are reluctant to invest their money chasing after an unknown quantity or a program that does not generate significant impact or exposure. Few events are awarded without a physical inspection of event facilities and other important resources such as hotels, convention centers, and other city infrastructure. If your event has not required a bid fee, select only the top two or three most attractive proposals and consider visiting only those communities for a full evaluation. It is not unusual, nor unseemly, to request that the host city cover the cost of hotels and ground transportation

- Availability of best facilities to stage the event
- Favorable rates on facility rentals, labor, and services in the local market
- Active support of the organizer's objectives by local government, businesses, and media
- Services and support beyond the minimum requirements of the RFP
- Demonstrable community experience in hosting successful sports events of similar size, scope, and structure
- Financial incentives or cost savings offered by local government, the facility, and local businesses beyond those required by the RFP
- No, or affordable, taxes on event revenues
- A natural local affinity, or fan base, for the sport

Figure 4.4 Common Reasons Why Communities Are Chosen to Host Sports Events

during the site visit. Chances are the CVB will be able to secure complimentary accommodations on behalf of the city to defray the costs of your survey.

If you represent an event with a successful track record, or a totally new event that offers exceptionally good value for a prospective host city, you may encounter two or more responses that meet your minimum bid specifications exactly and are equally attractive on every other level. All other things being equal, it is both acceptable and common practice to re-approach the two "finalists" with the response that their proposals are being viewed favorably and that an opportunity exists for them to offer additional incentives that further strengthen their respective bids. Rather than being forced to make an arbitrary decision between two or more equally competitive cities, the organizer can encourage prospective hosts to contribute more creativity and benefits to the event as a demonstration of their interest and commitment, and to find a point of differentiation between them.

Despite the best of intentions on the part of prospective event sites, only one is typically selected to play host to an event. Cities and venues failing to be chosen have every right to inquire as to where their proposal fell short. Figure 4.5 lists some of the most common factors contributing to a city's elimination from the bidding process. Surprisingly, the most often encountered is an inability or unwillingness to meet the minimum requirements of the RFP. This does not mean that cities must adhere with blind obedience to the minimum requirements. Some RFPs may be more demanding than their prestige, economic impact, exposure potential, or other attendant benefits might warrant. Host cities should certainly evaluate the bid specifications of an RFP before simply agreeing to everything an event organizer requests. Prestigious, high-profile events can demand and receive more from a bidding city, and prospective hosts risk losing the opportunity to win the award by falling short of the minimum requirements. Newer and less-prestigious events or event organizations may issue RFPs that are perfectly reasonable and well-scaled for the benefits they offer prospective hosts, but reasonability is always in the eyes of the beholder. Organizers may simply be testing the marketplace to see what cities will offer the best deal, even if the "minimum" requirements are not met by any that ultimately submit responses. Event organizers might still consider prospective host cities submitting proposals that do not meet the minimum specifications, particularly if no other community offers a superior deal. But, cities that do not submit proposals at all can be assured that they will be passed over. As hockey great Wayne Gretzky once said, "You will miss 100 percent of the shots you never take."

This is an appropriate point to offer some advice to prospective host cities—take your best shot, and offer the deal that fits both the economic reality of your community and the importance of the event to your civic objectives. If the opportunity to stage a highly desirable event presents itself and the bid specifications are appropriate to its attractiveness (and, therefore, will be equally attractive to other cities), by all means submit your best effort. However, if an event of lesser importance to the community comes knocking with unreasonable expectations but still offers great opportunities (and does not charge a bid fee), you lose nothing but time by putting your best foot forward, even if it means falling a little short of the minimum bid specifications.

Once a host city has been selected, there may be great interest on the part of both parties to announce the award. It is wise to resist the temptation to circulate this information to both the media and the public until some form of formal agreement is reached between the organizer and the host entity, as well as with any essential stakeholder whose participation is considered vital. These may include the actual event venue, hotels, or other local resources without which the deal would fall apart. A letter agreement or contract as detailed as possible should be drafted to confirm what the host has agreed to provide, as well as any important deadline dates covering the disposition of any areas not yet confirmed. Failure to meet certain deadline dates might force unfavorable or unacceptable changes to the program, or risk its viability in that market. Therefore, the organizer should include a stipulation allowing cancellation or postponement if the host parties fail to meet their obligations as outlined in the agreement. Frequently, the initial

SIDELINE STORY

A Trip Back to the Drawing Board Yields Success

Indianapolis's highly successful turn at hosting Super Bowl XLVI in 2012 was a result of the city's second attempt to win the bid, after competing for the 2011 game. "Participating in the NFL bid application process for the 2011 Super Bowl was an opportunity to learn the process and understand the bid requirements and host city qualifications," says Allison Melangton, president and CEO of the 2012 Indianapolis Super Bowl Host Committee, and now president of the Indiana Sports Corporation. "The Super Bowl bid process has many aspects that are similar to other rights owners' bid processes, but it also had many aspects that are unique to the NFL and its franchise owners'. The unsuccessful 2011 bid application process was a learning experience, so when the team regrouped to work on the bid for the 2012 Super Bowl, more time was available to work on the concepts and guarantees of the bid versus answering the technical questions of the bid. The significant difference in the XLV and the XLVI bids was the addition of a unique and very impactful local partnership."

"Over the past few decades, whenever Indianapolis has hosted a major sporting event, we've tried to ensure that we used the event as a catalyst for the greater good—leaving a lasting benefit or legacy from the event. For the 2012 bid, the Host Committee proposed an aggressive Legacy initiative that would partner the Host Committee with organizations and residents of a near downtown neighborhood to help the residents achieve their own vision for the redevelopment of their neighborhood. The neighborhood is known locally as the Near Eastside and it is located adjacent to downtown. Historically, it was a vibrant, working-class neighborhood; however, over the past 40 years it has seen unprecedented decline and disinvestment and has been challenged by pervasive issues related to poverty.

"This partnership resulted in more than $150 million of investment in the effort to turnaround this area. These investments have impacted more than 400 housing units with new builds or rehab, spurned the redevelopment of the neighborhood's traditional business corridor, and led to the building of 27,000 square foot wellness, fitness, and education facility. This facility is on the campus of a public high school strategically located within the Near Eastside neighborhood as a part of the NFL's Youth Education Town program. The Near Eastside is an area with 40,000 residents without a YMCA or a Boys & Girls Club so the new facility on the campus of Arsenal Technical High School was desperately needed. We believe that the presentation of this Legacy Initiative resonated with the NFL ownership and they were anxious to be a partner in a program that would significantly and positively change generations to come in that neighborhood."

letter agreement with the host entity is relatively brief, and attaches the RFP and the proposal response form as appendices. In these cases, the letter usually states that each requirement of the RFP is material to the agreement, unless modified by the contract. Any additional points not addressed by the RFP, but agreed to between the parties during the evaluation process, should also be included. Without completing this important extra step, entities that were essential to the success of the bid can subsequently back away from promises they might have made before the announcement, and any leverage the organizer once had would vaporize as soon as the award became a matter of public record.

- Failure to meet the minimum requirements of the RFP when bids from other competing cities agree to them
- Superior incentives offered by competing cities beyond the minimum requirements of the RFP
- Inadequate or poorly located event facilities
- Inadequate, inappropriate, or high-priced accommodations
- Excessive facility rental fees
- Comparatively high tax rates on ticket sales
- Comparatively high costs of doing business (e.g., hotel room rates, labor rates, etc.)
- Restrictions placed on the organizer regarding event sponsor recognition
- Lack of sufficient event management experience

Figure 4.5 Most Common Reasons Communities Are Eliminated from the Bidding Process

What Event Facilities Really Want from Sports Events

Like event organizers and the cities that pursue them, event facilities are most frequently interested in generating revenue. How they generate revenue, and how much they must generate, varies from one venue to the next, and is also dependent upon the ownership and management of the facility.

Event venues are of two general types—those that are privately owned and those that are public facilities. Privately owned event sites are generally in the business of making money. They aggressively pursue sports events that can contribute to their profitability, and try to fill every available date on their schedule. The busier the facility, the more potentially lucrative to the event site an organizer must be to schedule its dates there. However, event facilities lose money every day they are empty, so sometimes an event with low profit potential looks better to a facility manager than no event at all (although a manager could be more likely to confirm dates for less profitable events late in the process, when it appears nothing more profitable is likely to be scheduled).

Some recreation facilities that operate for public participation allocate time and space to special events for additional revenues and promotional exposure. One ski resort event coordinator notes: "If someone comes to our department proposing holding an event at the mountain first thing we do is crunch the numbers. Will we make a profit, break even, or lose money?" How an event will affect other regularly scheduled facility operations is another key consideration. "We never want to disrupt or take away a highly used area, or an area that would disturb lodging guests and on-hill skiers or riders," the coordinator.

A special subset of privately owned sports facilities is composed of those run by colleges and universities. Some of these venues forgo the opportunity to host outside events completely in compliance with the stipulations of their charter or the directives of their board. Others may have criteria other than financial gain that they use in considering whether to host outside events. Although generating revenues is often mentioned as a reason why collegiate facilities consider hosting outside sports events, Paul Hogan, director of athletics, men's basketball coach, and professor of sports management at New Hampshire Technical Institute in Concord, New Hampshire, cites "exposure . . . getting potential people on our campus and having a chance to converse about our facilities, programs, departments, and majors" as another key incentive.

Public event facilities operate in a totally different and frequently more flexible marketplace. These venues may include convention centers, fairgrounds, municipal arenas and stadiums, outdoor playing fields, armories, parking lots, streets, or any other event site that is owned by the local community, state, or provincial authority. In some cases, and particularly commonplace in the arena or stadium business, facilities are owned by a local government entity, and a management company is charged with the responsibility to rent space, sell event tickets, and manage its overall business. The contract with the government may charge the management company with the responsibility of generating a minimum amount of revenue or profit. The company's own corporate profitability is often tied to achieving or exceeding this minimum. Facility management companies can be wonderful partners that enthusiastically embrace the philosophy of keeping their venues utilized and filled with spectators, realizing revenues on some combination of rent, ticket sales participation, concessions, merchandise, and parking. They are not obligated to accept a deal with an event organizer that does not meet their corporate objectives, although the government/owner may occasionally exert some pressure to accept an event that may serve the community better than the management company's profit and loss profile, at a slightly less attractive financial deal. Although event facility managers are not generally in the business of sponsoring the programs staged in their buildings, a contract may obligate them to accept a fixed number of "civic" events per year at the government's direction at no, or at a reduced, rental cost.

Public facilities without an outside management entity may also be motivated by the need to generate revenue to pay down the debt of their construction or to fund day-to-day operations. Alternatively, their mission may simply be to serve their community and may be satisfied with a nominal fee for the usage of space. Others, as is often the case with many convention centers, may be operated by the local CVB, and exist primarily to attract the booking of events that generate those "heads in beds." These facilities will trade hotel room night guarantees in the local market for a reduced, or even a waived, rental fee. Still others, including nontraditional event sites such as streets, parking lots, abandoned runways, and other unorthodox venues, may be made available by the host city at no cost simply to contribute to the success of the event and the enjoyment of the community.

Negotiating with Sports Event Facilities

If you are a sports event organizer, maintain a realistic image of the prestige your event carries as you negotiate with potential host facilities. A venue's history of presenting previous high-prestige events can have a significant impact on its ability to attract future events of equal or greater impact and magnitude. Therefore, the more prestigious an event, the more negotiating power accrues to the benefit of the organizer. Remember that the number of events that facilities would consider high-profile or high-prestige lessees is but a small fraction of the marketplace that such venues serve. As Dallas's Tara Green reminds us, there are countless other tournaments, meets, matches, and other contests and exhibitions that also have great earning potential, but are not globally significant events. There are as many events with earning potential that are questionable, speculative, or risky, and against which facility managers must remain ever vigilant.

It will come as no surprise to facility managers that sports event organizers want to get as much as they can for as little as they can spend. They will always seek the best possible rental rates, the highest possible percentage of the gross potential, and the greatest freedom in hiring third-party vendors and labor. Of course, event facilities are best served when they seek precisely the opposite—the highest possible rental rates, the highest percentage of the gross potential for themselves, and the ability to charge for as many additional items, services, and labor as they are equipped to provide or arrange.

With the objectives of event organizers and the facilities in which they hold events often at such polar extremes, negotiations for mutually agreeable terms can be long and arduous. The more prestigious, attractive, and potentially profitable an event appears, the more likely a venue will concede some portion of the rent or share of ticket revenues in favor of concluding a deal with the event organizer. The more speculative the event, or the less familiar the promoter is to the venue, the more likely the facility will demand substantial guarantees against ticket sales and/or other revenues.

Lon Rosenberg, the senior vice president, operations, of the National Football League's Washington Redskins who oversees the management of the team's 85,000-seat stadium, FedEx Field, knows that the performance of an event organizer reflects directly on his facility. "We always want to know what we're going to get so reputation and past performance are very important to us," says Rosenberg. "Given the size and location of FedEx Field, most of the events that come here and the people who run them are familiar to us. Building and maintaining relationships are keys to success."

But, less familiar, sometimes less-sophisticated promoters, who may be local businesspeople with little or no sports event experience but have a vested interest in a particular event, approach venues for dates. In these cases, the process of booking a venue to inexperienced promoters tends to be a lengthy one. Facility managers will take an opportunity to get to know the promoter and assess his or her capabilities and resources and will follow up on references and do credit checks. Sometimes the posting of a nonrefundable deposit helps establish an event organizer's credibility and, in some cases, letters of credit or other forms of security are required. A nonrefundable deposit may represent 50 percent of the rental fee, plus 50 percent of the additional estimated costs for labor, equipment, and other in-house charges. Payment of these obligations in advance provides some degree of proof to the facility that the promoter is sufficiently capitalized and will not run out of money before event day.

"In most cases, our license agreement with a promoter requires that we control our box office," Rosenberg adds. "The money on deposit through ticket sales serves as financial security for the stadium against expenses and we ensure our fans are going to be treated as they expect."

Aside from cash deposits, another key determinant that event facilities use to evaluate the bona fides of an unfamiliar event promoter is the latter's ability to secure an acceptable liability insurance policy. Proof of insurance is also proof of insurability. That is, the facility can enjoy some sense of confidence if an event promoter is sufficiently capitalized to be able to purchase coverage, usually for between $2 million and $5 million in liability protection, under which the venue will be named as an additional insured. To facility managers, sports event organizers who are able to secure an underwriter confident enough to write a sizable liability policy may be sufficiently good risks with whom to enter into a lease.

What Sports Event Organizers Want from Event Facilities

Just as facilities seek to host profitable events managed by reputable, reliable organizers, so do most organizers search for venues that will be interested, involved, and service-oriented partners in achieving success. Promoters want to work with venues that actively participate in ensuring their clients' events achieve their objectives, and hit their attendance and profitability goals. "The management and staff of any venue know their facility, its capabilities and, ultimately, how to work together to help us achieve our goals," says Soccer United Marketing senior director, international business Court Jeske. "No matter the size of the stadium, our best events are always the ones where we get great support from the venue and a local host committee. We count on the local expertise and commitment of the management and staff and we value those relationships."

Smart facility managers know that an established event organizer will stage more events in the future and will want the organizer to consider their house in subsequent years, or for other programs. A venue with a staff that is pleasant, professional, competent, helpful, and involved will earn the loyalty of event organizers, and establish a reputation within their circle of influence and opinion. For example, event directors want to know what to expect with respect to a facility's billable costs with a reasonable degree of accuracy. Hidden or undisclosed charges don't remain hidden for long after an event has concluded, and frequently become subjects of contention during the settlement process.

Presuming the physical characteristics and costs are equal between two facilities, event organizers will look for flexibility in their ability to fulfill sponsorships and in the hiring of vendors and labor. In the facilities business, being forced to work with vendors and labor providers that have exclusive contracts with the venue generally means higher costs to the promoter. Facing no meaningful competition, there is little incentive for contractors enjoying exclusive rights in a facility to negotiate with organizers over rates or prices. Organizers will also look at what labor and equipment is included in the rental rate, and the costs they will have to incur to procure the people and equipment that are not included in the overall deal. They will also favor venues that can help them promote their event through the range of a facility's available resources—including website and media platforms, e-mail, database lists of individual and group sales customers, broadcast programming, marketing and advertising programs, interior and exterior signage and marquees, and publicity channels. These services may be provided by the venue at a cost, but being able to reach a prequalified group of potential ticket buyers is of great value to sports event promoters.

Evaluating Sports Event Facilities

Many factors contribute to an organizer's final decision on facility selection. Some sports events, such as competitive diving, enjoy few options with respect to the types of facilities that can host a particular event. Venues with a diving pool are the only feasible choices. Other sports event organizers need only file for a permit with their community's parks and recreation department to reserve a pool, ball field, rink, or court. For those in search of a professionally operated events facility, whether a stadium, arena, exhibition hall, hotel ballroom, theatre, or gymnasium, prepare a Facility Selection Survey Form such as the one found in Appendix 6. This document can help you to organize your most pertinent requirements before examining facilities, ensure that no important detail is neglected during your inspection, and assist in the comparison and final evaluation of venues afterwards. Event facilities and how they do business may differ greatly from city to city, or even within the same municipality. Once completed, the form will allow you to compare venues along uniform guidelines. The following paragraphs will describe the process of completing the survey form in detail.

Every event will have some time requirement for loading in (the process of delivering, installing, and setting up the equipment and configuration you need to conduct the event) and loading out (the process of dismantling and removing the organizer's property and rented equipment from the facility). Load-ins can range from a few hours to set up tables, chairs, and decorations for a simple sports awards dinner to a week or more to build sets and tents, install playing surfaces, and decorate an event site for a major fan festival. Even a community ball field hosting a schedule of Little League games needs some turnaround time to remove the banners and equipment belonging to the previous team (load-out), and to install the banners, bats, and bases for the next one (load-in). You will need some understanding of what your event will require in terms of set-up and dismantle time when checking on available dates with a potential host facility to ensure that sufficient time will be available. This is also important because your rental terms may increase as you hold the space for more load-in or load-out time than is necessary. It is not uncommon for the rental rates on these nonevent days to be offered at a cheaper per-day cost.

Determine whether your load-in and load-out can be accomplished during normal working hours, which can avoid overtime labor costs. Will it be more cost effective to pay for one day less in rent and absorb the overtime to move in and set up overnight? Regardless of cost, an organizer can ill afford to have too little time to set up an event and risk not being ready on event day. Neither can it delay the organizers of the next event from moving in by booking too little time or labor to vacate the premises as scheduled in the lease. It is essential that these requirements be carefully evaluated and accurately projected before booking the venue.

Next, it is important to consider the number of tickets that may be sold at various levels of the facility. If the seating plan will define a single price for every ticket or a general admission policy (i.e., nonreserved seats offered on a first-to-arrive, first-to-enjoy basis), your planning will be made easy; your gross potential is calculated simply by multiplying the ticket price by the number of available tickets. Event facilities, however, usually offer the ability to create "price breaks" based on a particular section's distance from the playing surface, or height off the event floor. While it is not necessary to finalize a ticket price in each price break during the initial site selection survey, the facility manager can provide you with sample price breaks, with the number of available seats per break, even by section and row, for your budget planning purposes. The Facility Site Selection Survey Form provides you with a place to record the name of the section (e.g., lower end zone, lower sidelines, mezzanine end zone, mezzanine sidelines, etc.) and the number of tickets available for sale in each area. It also offers planners an area to record whether the facility has any *build-out capability*—that is, whether there are standing-room areas for which tickets may be sold, or other normally unutilized spaces that can be converted to safe, temporary seating, increasing the available inventory—and profit potential—beyond the standard seating manifest. Knowing this in advance can help organizers plan for the eventuality of selling out, and then expanding the seating to accommodate more potential ticket buyers.

In addition to paying a rental rate to the facility, there may be additional charges against ticket sales, as discussed in Play 2. This information should also be recorded on the survey form, along with information on the merchandising and catering contacts, each of which may be managed by a facility's own staff or by an exclusive concessionaire hired to manage these businesses on behalf of the building. The terms quoted by these entities may be noted here. Any capability offered by the facility to assist in the promotion of ticket sales may be recorded as well.

From city to city, and even from venue to venue within a single community, the cost of labor can vary widely. If not analyzed and adequately planned, facility labor can add considerable burden to an event budget. Organizers of large, complex events should consider hiring or identifying an event operations specialist who can estimate the number of man-hours that will be required from each type of worker, as listed in the Facility Selection Survey Form. Organizers without this capability can have the facility provide an estimate of what will be required if the management is provided with sufficient detail. Regardless, it will be easy to compare hourly rates, fees, and mark-ups between various venues by completing this section. Even small differences in hourly labor rates can prove significant when the total number of man-hours to load-in, stage, and load-out an event are tabulated.

Before budgeting estimates for labor, it is important to confirm whether the facility has entered into exclusive relationships with a labor provider. As is true of any vendor whose exclusivity is guaranteed by the facility, the organizer's ability to negotiate what are likely to be inflated rates and fees is severely limited. (As unpleasant as inflated rates can be, we have to understand this stakeholder's objective, as well. The exclusive vendor often must pay a percentage of its sales to the facility and must, in turn, charge these higher rates to make a profit.)

Higher labor costs and restrictive work rules do not necessarily indicate that these resources are unionized. Union labor is frequently more skilled and experienced in trade professions, and may actually be preferable with respect to a worker's familiarity with the facility and appropriate safety procedures. Riggers and electricians, presuming the minimum crews and work rules required by the union local are not unreasonable (e.g., when time-and-a-half and double overtime rates kick in, break times, meal allowances, minimum number of workers per crew, minimum number of hours per call, etc.), can fall into this category. But, union or nonunion, event organizers need to know all of the charges associated with labor, including the hourly rate, benefit payments (e.g., accruals for health benefits, insurance, vacation, retirement, etc.) charged to the promoter, and any administrative mark-ups imposed by the venue for managing the labor pool. Organizers of large events staged in a right-to-work state (i.e., states in which the event can hire anyone the organizer wants to perform work in certain capacities) and that have the potential to employ many union members to work significant hours preparing for and executing an event, may be able to negotiate a more favorable rate with the business manager of the union local.

Many facilities, particularly those with exclusive labor contracts, charge more per man-hour than is received by the worker, wages and benefits combined. The venue may be charging an "administrative fee," a percentage of the labor costs booked through its management, which also represents some degree of profit margin. This practice provides a common revenue stream for the facility, and is sometimes negotiable (depending on the overall profit potential of the event in other areas).

There are many sound reasons for a facility to enter into exclusive agreements with merchandisers and concessionaires and, to a lesser extent, labor. The venue usually receives a percentage of merchandise, food, and beverages sold by these external entities, occasionally against an annual guarantee. In addition, the venue takes no risk on the costs of inventory, equipment, or human resources. This is one reason why the costs to ticket buyers for food and merchandise is significantly higher inside the facility than outside. (This is only a contributing factor, of course. Having a monopoly on sales also creates captive consumers of people inside the venue.)

The next two sections of the Facility Site Selection Survey Form provide organizers with an area to record observations about some of the physical characteristics of the venue, as well as the equipment that might be available either as part of the lease rate or at some additional cost. Are there sufficient locker and dressing rooms and related facilities (such as showers and trainers' rooms) of the size required, and are they in good repair? Are the marshaling areas (back-of-house staging areas that are hidden from the public view used to hold sets, props, equipment, and people before they are needed) sufficient in size and security, safely lit, and easily accessible to the playing surface? Are these spaces filled with storage items belonging to the facility and, if so, will they be cleared by building management without the event incurring additional labor, shipping, or storage costs? Are there lockable and unlocked storage areas in the facility that may be used by the organizer, and how far ahead of the event may they be used? Are there score clocks, timing devices, and other equipment required for competition (e.g., nets, boards, baskets, goals, benches, etc.) in the facility's possession that may be used or modified for the event without additional charge, or will the organizer have to purchase or rent and install these items? Are there existing facilities for the expected media such as a press box, media seating areas, press conference facilities, workrooms, sufficient wireless communication and power access, a press lounge, and a location for broadcast trucks to park and plug in? How much parking for the public and special guests is located within reasonably close proximity to the facility, and how many complimentary spaces for staff can be included in the rental deal?

Does the facility possess a quantity of tables, chairs, and staging risers that may be used by the organizer, and will they add cost to the budget? Is there office space available for the event management staff? Does the venue have reliable WiFi and mobile device service for staff and fan use, and can those be made available at no charge to the event? If needed, how many phone or Internet lines (for VOIP phone systems) can the organizer rent from the building, and what is the cost to install the phones? (These costs can have a wide variance and can be considerable.) Does the building have a forklift or other equipment for material handling that may be used by the organizer's paid hourly labor during load-in and load-out, or will the use of such equipment incur additional costs? If marshaling or storage areas must be temporarily divided to create additional operational or hospitality facilities, does the building have pipe and drape units to lend or rent, and in what condition are they? Are there crowd control barriers, such as metal barricades, available for the organizer's use, or must they be rented? Many other venue-related questions should be answered in these sections, including those that are specific to a particular sport or event that will be utilizing the facility.

The presence or absence of sponsor exclusivities may figure prominently in evaluating the best venue for a sports event. Most every sports facility now has rules on what kinds of event sponsor signage will be permitted and precisely where partners' signs, banners and branding presence may or may not be exhibited. In most venues, the brand of beverages served (or "poured") is governed by an existing building sponsorship deal, and in the case of products containing alcohol, by the local liquor authority. The issues relating to sponsorship are many and varied, and will be discussed in detail later. In the interim, Figure 4.6 provides you with a checklist of some of the sponsor-related questions that should be asked during the site selection process.

Finally, examine the facility for areas in which hospitality functions may be staged to entertain VIP guests, athletes, sponsors, and others. Are there restaurants, cafeterias, cafes, or lounges that can be sectioned off for private use while the venue is open to the public? Are there on-site kitchens,

- ☐ What sponsors have "exclusive rights" to the facility? What do those exclusive rights include?
- ☐ Can event sponsors that do not conflict with facility sponsors be recognized on signage on or around the playing surface? What about event sponsors that do conflict?
- ☐ Can event sponsors that do not conflict with facility sponsors be recognized on temporary signage in the public concourses, or on the scoreboard and electronic displays? What about event sponsors that conflict?
- ☐ May nonconflicting or conflicting sponsors hand out sponsored premiums or product samples as people enter or leave the facility?
- ☐ May nonconflicting or conflicting sponsors set up tables or display kiosks in the public concourse areas?
- ☐ May nonconflicting or conflicting sponsors be recognized with announcements on the venue's public address system, on video screens and/or message boards, or on banners either inside or outside the structure? Is there any charge for this?
- ☐ Can event sponsor products that conflict with facility sponsors be served or distributed in back-of-house areas such as event offices, marshaling areas, and media facilities? (*Note:* It is common for a facility concessionaire to levy a "corkage fee," that is, a per-serving charge for accepting and serving free products from an event's sponsor in lieu of an organizer having to purchase inventory directly from them. This can sometimes be a negotiated item.)

Figure 4.6 Sponsor Exclusivity Checklist

or must food preparation facilities be temporarily installed? Are there meeting, conference, or board rooms easily accessible to audience areas that can hold smaller functions? Can part of the exterior grounds be reserved for tented functions? (*Caution:* Installing tents can be a very expensive option.) Is the provision of catering in these areas exclusive to the building concessionaire?

Obviously, the needs of every event and organizer will differ greatly. The Facility Selection Survey Form can be modified to include additional sections for any information that is pertinent to the specific project being planned to ensure that the same questions are asked of every venue under consideration. In this way, the answers may be compared and analyzed fairly and with relative ease.

Selecting a Facility

Usually, awarding a sports event to a city is coincident with the confirmation of a facility in which to hold it. Event organizers will weigh multiple factors in reaching their decision, including the costs of operating the event in each venue surveyed, whether the capacity of the facility is appropriate to the event, the reputation and geographic desirability of the venue (e.g., is the facility one that local ticket buyers would associate with a sports event?), and each party's flexibility with respect to protecting each other's sponsor relationships. Once a tentative decision has been reached, the event organizer will be forwarded a lease, or license agreement, that will list all of the agreed-to terms of the relationship. Because facility license agreements are considerably detailed, it is not unusual for a host of new issues to emerge that had not been discussed during initial negotiations. This is usually only a minor inconvenience, and these issues are better to surface and be settled during the negotiating process rather than closer to the event. It is almost certain that significant "boilerplate" language—that is, legal requirements for insurance, indemnifications, force majeure conditions (cancellations due to various unforeseen disasters or other conditions that would make moving forward with an event impossible), and other protections for the venue—will not have been previously discussed in detail. It is essential for event promoters to have qualified legal counsel review and propose redrafts of these points to ensure that they are as competently and fully protected as the facility. Although the nature of the facility license agreement will differ from venue to venue, as well as from event to event, a generalized sample facility license agreement may be found in Appendix 5.

Once the facility agreement has been signed and agreements are substantially in progress with other stakeholders without whom the event could not be staged (e.g., the local convention and visitors bureau and hoteliers), it is usually safe to announce the dates and host location of the event. Depending on the economic, political, and cultural significance of the event to the local community, the parties involved may stage a news conference or simply distribute an announcement via the event and venue's respective websites and by press release to inform the media and, through their various outlets, the public. Now, it is time to begin the production planning process, and building the team required to stage the newly awarded event.

Post-Play Analysis

A spirit of partnership between host cities, facilities, and event organizers is essential to success for all involved. It is incumbent upon all parties to develop an understanding of each other's wants and needs to achieve this level of cooperation. Host cities for events that travel or tour are most interested in the economic impact sports events offer, including how much in tax revenues and how many hotel room nights they will generate. They also pursue events for political, cultural, and emotional reasons peculiar to each respective market. Event promoters communicate their wants and needs through the development and dissemination of requests for proposal, documents that identify the minimum requirements for a community's or facility's bid to host an event to achieve success. Event facilities are generally interested in generating revenue, while event organizers are searching for the best and most cost-effective site to stage their event. A Facility Selection Survey Form is an effective tool for organizing, comparing, and analyzing information derived from surveys of each interested venue.

Coach's Clipboard

1. You are the organizer of an established and successful running marathon in a mid-size American city. Your organization receives an RFP from a similarly sized community in a neighboring state desirous of reenergizing its existing marathon race, which has lately experienced decreasing participation and mounting financial losses. The RFP is very basic—the city will provide no cash and take no risk. All revenues, expenses, and risk must be borne by the organizer. How can you establish a partnership with the community that lowers your risk while providing the city with what it needs—the execution of a successful marathon event with no outlay of cash?
2. You are the organizer of a regional high school track and field event for which there are limited facilities in your home city. Assuming the costs of staging the event in your local arena are too expensive, and the winter season during which it is held makes holding an outdoor event inadvisable, what venues in your city that are not traditionally associated with track and field meets might be investigated and approached to host the event?
3. Create an RFP for a statewide college ice hockey tournament that will attract teams from 16 universities, ideally using two venues in a single city yet to be selected. Include requirements for housing staff, participants, families, and fans within a 20-mile radius, as well as a sports memorabilia collector's show and fan festival envisioned to run concurrently during the tournament. Develop an economic impact estimate for the tournament and show.
4. Respond as the host city to the RFP you created in exercise 3. Your community can only offer one arena in which to hold the tournament and does not have a sufficient number of hotel rooms within the required radius. In what ways can you mitigate these shortcomings and provide additional relevant benefits to the event that will competitively position your hypothetical community to the organizer?
5. The best facility available for your minor league all-star game is sponsored by a soft-drink company that directly competes with one of your most important sponsors. Both your organization and the management of the facility want to stage the event there, but also want to protect their respective sponsor's rights. How can the two parties work to resolve the conflict? (Consider this exercise again after reading Plays 6 and 7.)

PLAY 5

Starting the Clock on the Sports Event Planning Process

"Excellence is not a singular act but a habit. You are what you do repeatedly."

—Shaquille O'Neal, NBA All-Star center

This play will help you to:

- Identify and plan for each of the critical tasks needed to manage your event.
- Create planning documents that will ensure your event stays on target to meet its deadlines.
- Create the organization you will need to execute your event.

Introduction

Professional and college sports teams prepare themselves for the pursuit of a championship by opening training camps and conducting preseason games to both identify and fortify areas of competitive weakness and take best advantage of their on-field strengths. Of course, the process of drafting the blueprint for the construction of a winning team does not begin the moment the first player reports to the training facility. The coaching staff spends the off-season evaluating the players on the team roster and reviewing scouting reports to identify positions that should be filled or reinforced as well as, and prospective rookies, free agents, and other prospects to invite to camp. Scouts must travel to a variety of games during the previous season to assess the abilities and potential of players on other teams and in lower-level leagues. Scouts will also attend the games of a team's upcoming opponents throughout the season to identify their rivals' strengths and weaknesses, and help the coaching staff prepare the system of plays that will best position the team for victory. Careful planning and adequate time are required to prepare a team for an important game, carried out against a strategic framework of interlocking deadlines and milestone dates. For coaches and players, far more time is spent preparing for a game than actually playing it.

As a sports event manager, you also will spend vastly more time planning than actually executing your event. By this point, you have defined what you want your event to accomplish and what it will cost to achieve your objectives. You have set a strategy on how you intend to finance the event and determined the optimal place to stage it. Now, it's time to begin the planning in earnest, and putting together the right organization together that will make it all happen. Sports event organizers must proceed down both paths at once because detailing the event management process will inevitably reveal how much and what kind of help you will require and when you will need it. While this chapter will explore these efforts independently, the notion of planning and building a team to execute the strategies and tactics are inextricably linked.

There are many outstanding resources worth consulting on the planning process, but we have found that two books that best apply the techniques of industrial project management to the world of corporate events are *Professional Event Coordination* by Julia Rutherford Silvers (John Wiley & Sons, 2003) and *Corporate Event Project Management* by William O'Toole and Phyllis Mikolaitis (John Wiley & Sons, 2003). O'Toole and Mikolaitis propose that many systems and decisions made in the planning process are interwoven and must be broken down into tasks and subtasks. Their technique separates the planning process into three key phases: (1) definition of the project, (2) the scope of work, and (3) a work breakdown structure, further subdivided into budgeting, scheduling, and risk analysis.

Identify and Analyze Management Tasks

The first half of this play explores the methodology of identifying management tasks, analyzing those tasks to discover all of the decisions and activities that must precede them, and setting a system of deadlines that will keep the project on schedule.

List Elementary Tasks

The best way to begin the event planning process is to develop a list of the primary or fundamental tasks that will need to be accomplished. Figure 5.1 offers a sample list of key tasks. The process of identifying the elementary tasks required to manage an event should start with a thorough examination of the tactics to be applied to meeting the program's objectives, as described in Play 1. Examine all of the event's strategies and tactics to ensure that a structure of elementary tasks to achieve them is in place. Then, apply the process of critical task analysis to explode them apart to expose all of the details required to make them work and succeed.

Every elementary task should have its own set of "key activities" identified and should have milestone dates assigned for these activities to be completed. The successful execution of these

- Develop an event budget
- Confirm event location details
- Develop attractions and activities
- Create a schedule of events
- Define staffing needs
- Sell sponsorships
- Create a floor plan
- Create a merchandise area
- Create a ticket sales area for next season
- Identify food and beverage offerings
- Book entertainment
- Invite dignitaries, VIP guests, sponsors, business owners, and other stakeholders
- Invite media to cover the event
- Advertise and promote the event to fans and nonfans
- Recruit, train, and orient staff
- Set up and install the event
- Operate the event
- Disassemble and move out the event
- Document the event for future sponsorship sales efforts
- Evaluate the event

Figure 5.1 Elementary Tasks

key activities is then dependent on the "supportive tasks" and "decision points" that must precede each of them, and that may be further subdivided to reveal additional required supportive tasks and decision points.

Let's go back to the fictional playoff pregame fan festival to which we applied the P-A-P-E-R Test in Figure 1.4 and develop some elementary tasks. The primary objective of the event was to reward loyal fans with a street festival preceding the team's first playoff game in three years, with the desired secondary objectives of exploiting the program for promotional and revenue-generating purposes (see page 18 in Play 1). Figure 5.1 lists the elementary tasks, in rough sequential order, that will form the nucleus of a critical dates calendar for this event.

Assign Deadlines to Elementary Tasks

It is usually helpful to assign preliminary deadlines, or end dates, before you begin to break the list apart to identify the many supportive tasks and decision points that will ultimately form the bulk of the planning calendar. Put the elementary tasks in the most logical sequence, starting with the first that will need to be completed, and ending with those whose completion will come last. The tasks listed in Figure 5.1 are presented in a rough chronological order. Now add deadline dates—that is, the date by which each task must be completed, as illustrated in Figure 5.2. The most helpful method for assigning deadline, dates, is to start from the end, those tasks that are completed closest to event day, and work your way backward.

Tasks that are to be completed after the event has ended, such as "document" and "evaluate the event," have been excluded from the balance of this process. It should be noted, however, that

FAN FESTIVAL EVENT DATE: April 15

Elementary Task	End Date
Develop an event budget	February 15
Create a schedule of events	March 15
Develop attractions and activities	March 27
Sell sponsorships	March 29
Create a merchandise area	March 31
Create ticket sales area for next season	March 31
Identify food and beverage offerings	March 31
Book entertainment	March 31
Create a floor plan	April 5
Invite dignitaries/guests/sponsors/business owners/stakeholders	April 8
Invite media to cover the event	April 8
Advertise and promote the event to fans and non-fans	April 14
Recruit, train, and orient staff	April 14
Set up and install the event	April 14
Obtain/confirm all permits, approvals, inspections, venue details	April 14
Operate the event	April 15
Disassemble and move out the event	April 16

Figure 5.2 Elementary Tasks with Deadline Dates

some subtasks for elements that will occur after the event is over might require scheduling before event day for their completion. To properly document the event, for example, a photographer or videographer would have to be hired in advance.

Although the list of elementary tasks in Figure 5.2 is in a logical, chronological order, the deadlines were assigned by starting with "operate the event." The organizer then worked backward through the list of tasks to "develop an event budget," estimating the time that must be allowed to complete each before the next on the list may be conquered.

Add Start Dates

Most teams in competitive leagues, both amateur and professional, do not clinch a playoff position until near the end of the regular season and the start of the playoffs. In our example, let's suppose the team is doing well enough to reasonably expect to reach the playoffs, but is not yet assured of postseason play. The team will want to set deadlines that are as late as possible so the event may be canceled with the least embarrassment possible, and with minimal or no financial exposure. In Figure 5.2, deadlines are set very close to event day to avoid having to pay for most requirements until the playoff picture is closer to resolution. It is suggested for most events, when and where possible, that deadlines should be set earlier than in this example, with extra time built in for the inevitable fulfillment of tasks that take longer than expected.

Just because end dates are set late does not mean that planning should also start late. Work on all of these tasks should begin as early as possible, even before the probability of the team's playoff appearance increases to even odds. For this reason, it is strongly suggested that critical

FAN FESTIVAL EVENT DATE: April 15

Elementary Task	Start Date	End Date
Develop an event budget	December 1	February 15
Create a schedule of events	December 1	March 15
Develop attractions and activities	December 1	March 27
Sell sponsorships	January 15	March 31
Create merchandise area	February 1	March 31
Create ticket sales area for next season	February 1	March 31
Identify food and beverage offerings	March 1	March 31
Book entertainment	March 1	March 31
Create floor plan	March 15	April 5
Invite dignitaries/guests/sponsors/business owners/others	March 15	April 8
Invite media to cover the event	March 15	April 8
Advertise and promote the event to fans and non-fans	March 22	April 14
Recruit, train, and orient staff	March 15	April 14
Set up and install the event	April 13	April 14
Obtain/confirm all permits, approvals, inspections, details	March 15	April 14
Operate the event	April 15	
Disassemble and move out event	April 16	

Figure 5.3 Elementary Tasks with Start and End Dates

dates calendars include start dates as well. Figure 5.3 expands the calendar for our fictional fan festival to include start dates for each elementary task.

Note that in our expanded list of elementary tasks, some action areas that have the same deadline date will take longer to plan and execute than others. The value of including a start date to the critical dates calendar allows event organizers to prioritize the order in which tasks with a similar end date should be initiated. In this way, planners will not run out of time to manage an elementary task because it was not initiated with sufficient lead time. By maintaining the critical dates calendar on a spreadsheet program, organizers can sort their tasks by either start date or end date—or maintain two calendars with identical information, each organized in chronological order by start and end dates, if desired.

Compile a Critical Dates Calendar

Many sports event managers begin the sports event management process by compiling all of the major component parts required to stage their event and assigning deadline dates to each task's completion. A critical dates calendar, or production schedule, is an efficient way of organizing all of these functions into a chronological order that begins to define the many paths of work required and checks the validity of each deadline against a structure of internal logic and

SIDELINE STORY

Planning for the Playoffs and Payoffs

The most critical and potentially lucrative part of the season for most professional North American sports leagues are the playoffs, or postseason, leading to the final series of games to determine the championship. In addition to their competitive importance to the leagues and teams, the financial significance of the postseason is without question. This is the period for a sport's greatest television viewership and media coverage, best attendance at the highest ticket prices, and greatest potential for increased merchandise sales. The postseason is as much a celebration for the fans as for the team, and they are generally more willing to devote the time and money to their passion at this time than at any other during the season.

Now, imagine planning logistics for the playoffs. Eight of 32 NFL teams discover they are in the first round of postseason (i.e., Wild Card Weekend) with a week to prepare, and only four will host the games. In the case of the NBA and NHL, half of the 16 teams that qualify for the postseason will find out that they will need to travel, and where, to meet their playoff rival with only a few days notice after completing their final regular season game. The remaining eight may not have to travel, but they will need to prepare for hosting the first two games of the postseason with little time to spare. The leagues, teams, and host facilities must prepare for an influx of inbound media, broadcasters, and operational staff requiring accommodations and work spaces and leverage, where possible, the increased interest in the games to realize additional revenue and business opportunities. Clearly, this planning cannot begin once the team clinches its spot in the playoffs.

The uncertainty of where games will be played is sometimes compounded by flexibility in the postseason game schedule. In the NHL, where every one of the four Stanley Cup playoff rounds is a best of-seven series, there is the possibility of starting subsequent rounds early if all of the games in preceding series end in four or five games so as not to have too great a gap in time in which no games are being played. As a result, the league's events department must begin planning for the postseason in the earliest stages of the regular season, identifying hotels in all 32 markets that can accommodate media, hospitality, and operational needs over a long range of dates (over as much as six weeks), paring back the number of cities in which these requirements are needed as teams drop from playoff contention. Very often, some host hotels will work for only certain dates due to other previously booked commitments, requiring different scenarios for hosting the first two games in a series or the next two, the full schedule of games, or an accelerated schedule due to previous rounds ending early. As a result, event planners for the Stanley Cup playoffs actually create many more plans for far more events well in advance than will ever be staged.

Clubs and their home arenas, for their part, have to plan well ahead of knowing whether they are hosting postseason games, and which ones, far beyond preparation for the players and teams to advance through the playoffs. In this environment of uncertainty, they must ensure they have left themselves sufficient time to plan for game operations, staffing, ticketing, hospitality, event presentation, and fan and promotional activities. Consider all the work that must be invested in before the playoffs begin and one begins to understand that the incredible disappointment of being eliminated from the postseason reaches through every level of the organization.

practicality. In other words, by listing all of the primary tasks that must be completed, the event director can assign deadline dates that logically and reasonably fit together, consistent with all the deadline dates of other activities that must precede or follow them.

This process, called *critical task analysis,* will ultimately help you determine the optimal dates by which to accomplish specific aspects of the event planning process. When complete, the calendar will be comprised of myriad details and deadlines that may appear so comprehensive as to seem daunting. However, the more detail devoted to assigning the completion of tasks and subtasks against realistic deadlines, the more effective the organizer will be in keeping the event planning process on schedule. Constructing the calendar starts with breaking apart each operational goal into its component subtasks that must first be completed through the application of the critical task analysis. Start with the end point of each process and when that work must be concluded. Then, work your way back through all of the many steps and decisions (subtasks) that must be taken or made to complete the task.

Let's take the seemingly simple task of inviting VIP guests to attend a sports event. Intuitively, we know that we will have to send invitations and receive responses. However, as Figure 5.4 illustrates, there are more than 20 other decisions that must be made, actions that must be taken, and procedures that must be determined before the first invitation can be sent. Every indented passage in the figure denotes a subtask or activity that must be considered and completed before plans for the task above it can be finalized.

Explode Calendar with Supportive Tasks and Decision Points

Now it is time to expand the critical dates calendar by exploding each elementary task into its component parts through critical task analysis, as seen in the example provided in Figure 5.4. Once you do this, you are likely to discover that many of your original dates are not early enough in the overall process to accommodate all of the activity and decisions that will be required between the start and end dates. You may also discover that certain supplemental tasks or decision points for one elementary task will need to be completed before the supplemental tasks of one or more other elementary tasks. It is perfectly natural for even the most experienced sports event managers to have to make these adjustments as the calendar is developed and refined.

Let's take a look at three elementary tasks from the current series of examples: "develop an event budget," "develop attractions and activities," and "sell sponsorships." Work on planning all three of these key elementary tasks must start early, and be developed concurrently. Figure 5.5 partially explodes each task into its component parts to illustrate.

These three elementary tasks were chosen for illustration because they are closely interrelated. To sell sponsorships, you have to create a package of benefits for the sponsor to buy. To create the benefits package, you will need to know what inventory, or the slate of attractions and activities, you will have to sell. To know what attractions you will have to sell, you will have to know what they are expected to cost. To know what they will cost, you will need to conceptualize what you want, contact potential suppliers, and solicit estimates. To sell attractions to a sponsor at the right price, you will have to know what they cost, what overhead costs will also need to be covered, how much your organization is willing to invest, and how much income you are trying to achieve overall. Later, you will have to order signage to acknowledge and expose your sponsors. To have the signage ready in time, you will have to have a deadline by which all of your sponsors will be finalized. (In real life, few sports event organizers will turn down late-arriving sponsors, and most will do everything in their power to accommodate them, even if it means incurring higher expenses and last-minute effort to get the deal done.)

Elementary Task: Invite VIP Guests to the Event Process: Invitations sent to VIPs, and RSVPs received

- Design invitations (Key Activity):
  - Allocate budget including design, printing, postage
  - Identify and engage designer/printer
  - Finalize logo to include in design
  - Identify to which events and activities the VIPs are being invited
  - Determine RSVP deadline date:
    - Determine when seating assignments must be made
    - Determine when unclaimed VIP tickets must be released to the public
  - Identify the RSVP mechanism (e.g., phone, web, e-mail, text, mail):
    - Determine how and where responding guests will pick up their tickets
  - Determine what information must be included with the invitations (e.g., hotel, transportation, parking)
  - Finalize hotel/vendor contracts and booking procedures
  - Determine how many VIPs can be accommodated:
    - Allocate complimentary seating for VIPs and remove tickets from public sale
    - Ensure the lost revenue from comp seating can be accommodated in the budget
  - Determine by what date invitations must be printed
- Print invitations:
  - Identify number of invitations required:
    - Generate and finalize the mailing list
    - Define the VIPs who should be invited (e.g., city officials, local businesses, celebrities, athlete families, media)
  - Determine time required for design, layout, proofs, production, and delivery
  - Determine by what date invitations must be sent
- Determine date by which invitees must receive invitations and send invitations:
  - Provide sufficient time for invited guests to clear personal calendars and respond
  - Identify the time that will be required to assign seating
  - Provide sufficient time for follow-up event information to be returned to the responding guest (e.g., confirmation, schedule of events, arrival location, ticket pickup, parking)
  - Create event information package for responding guests
  - Create VIP guest itinerary

Figure 5.4 Critical Task Analysis

After exploding each elementary task, begin filling in start and end dates for each of the supporting tasks and decision points of which they are composed, as illustrated in Figure 5.6. This is the step during which the event organizer must be particularly vigilant to ensure the calendar is internally consistent. In other words, all of the tasks that require other tasks to occur either as prerequisites or corequisites have start and end dates that are consistent and not contradictory. As a result, it is not unusual for some dates to slide earlier or later during this stage of the process to accommodate the need for consistency. In this example, the task of ordering signage must

FAN FESTIVAL EVENT DATE: April 15

Elementary Task	Start Date	End Date
Develop an event budget	December 1	February 15
Identify net income/loss goal		
Estimate total expenses		
Estimate total revenues		
Determine sponsor revenue needs		
First draft budget		
Finalize budget		
Develop attractions and activities	December 1	March 27
Identify attraction areas		
Request and receive cost estimates		
Confirm roster of attractions		
Order signage		
Sell sponsorships	January 15	March 31
Create sponsorship tiers and packages		
Create sponsorship presentations		
Solicit potential sponsor companies		
Finalize sponsors		
Order sponsor signage		
Order other sponsor fulfillment elements		

Figure 5.5 Exploding Elementary Tasks

slide to a slightly later date than originally anticipated by the list of elementary tasks because of the event organizer's need to delay activities that will incur costs just in case the team falls out of playoff contention. Moreover, the later date will also allow the organizer to accept new sponsors later in the planning process. The experienced sports event planner in this example has not simply assumed, of course, that his vendor can meet these later, just-in-time ordering and delivery dates. The vendor was made aware, and was accepting, of the delayed time frame.

Several additional examples of internal consistency may be noticed in Figure 5.6. The organizer must have a pretty good idea of the sponsor revenue needs before taking the event to market to potential sponsors, and would not be able to confirm the pricing of sponsorship packages until the budget is in some substantially complete, if not final, form. Because of the short time frame to bring the event to the attention of sponsors, the organizer is prepared to begin creating the packages to be offered to the sponsors as soon as the first draft budget is completed. The creation of a physical presentation to sponsors is underway as soon as the first draft expense budget is nearing completion. While the organizer waits for the development of the business end of the presentation (e.g., creating and pricing the package of benefits to be offered to sponsors), work may begin on the portions of the proposal that will build excitement and anticipation (e.g., introduction, graphics, background information). The presentations, therefore, are ready to go to market as soon as the budget and the business terms of the sponsorship package are finalized.

FAN FESTIVAL EVENT DATE: April 15

Task	Start Date	End Date
~~Develop an event budget~~	~~December 1~~	~~February 15~~
Identify net income/loss goal	December 1	December 8
Budget total expenses	December 1	January 2
Budget total revenues	December 10	January 17
Determine sponsor revenue needs	December 10	January 17
First draft budget	December 15	January 8
Finalize budget	January 8	February 15
~~Develop attractions and activities~~	~~December 1~~	~~March 27~~
Identify attraction areas	December 1	January 2
Request and receive cost estimates	December 15	January 8
Confirm roster of attractions	January 8	February 1
Order and receive signage	April 2	April 10
~~Sell sponsorships~~	~~January 15~~	~~March 31~~
Create sponsorship tiers and packages	January 15	February 1
Create sponsorship presentations	January 15	February 15
Solicit potential sponsor companies	February 15	March 22
Finalize sponsors	March 1	March 31

Figure 5.6 Exploded Critical Dates Calendar (Partial)

To get to this point, the roster of attractions must be confirmed. This, too, depends on completing at least the first draft of the budget. To ensure the budget contains all of the pertinent information relating to each of the attraction areas, vendors must be contacted to begin developing cost estimates. The roster of attractions and the budget are finalized simultaneously, and, not coincidentally, at the same time that sponsors first begin to be approached by the organizer.

Note that the original elementary tasks that were listed may now be removed from the calendar of critical dates. With all of the new detail added to the calendar, the elementary entries are now too broad to be very useful to the planning process, and are struck through in the figure for the purpose of illustration. Due to the fine level of detail in a truly functional critical dates calendar, the number of entries is generally very large. The three sample elementary tasks selected from the 17 listed in Figure 5.3 generated 14 entries on their own, and those are themselves abridged for the purpose of simplifying the illustration. Critical date calendars can contain lists of 100 or more tasks for even the simplest sports event. It is wise to add one more column to the spreadsheet to assist the event director in managing the planning process, as well as the various paid and/or volunteer staff members who will be recruited to execute it—the assignments of staff to each area of responsibility.

Add Responsibilities

Most sports event organizers must delegate responsibilities to a group of area managers, supervisors, helpers, and workers, whether paid professionals, volunteers, vendor companies, or employees of other partners. A column has been added to complete the critical dates calendar noting the individual

FAN FESTIVAL EVENT DATE: April 15

Task	Start Date	End Date	Responsibility
Identify net income/loss goal	December 1	December 8	GT
Budget total expenses	December 1	January 2	EN
Identify attraction areas	December 1	January 2	HR
Budget total revenues	December 10	January 17	GT
Determine sponsor revenue needs	December 10	January 17	GT
First draft budget	December 15	January 8	EN
Request and receive cost estimates	December 15	January 8	HR
Finalize budget	January 8	February 1	GT
Confirm roster of attractions	January 8	February 15	GT
Create sponsorship tiers and packages	January 15	February 1	TD
Create sponsorship presentations	January 15	February 15	FL
Solicit potential sponsor companies	February 15	March 22	TD
Finalize sponsors	March 1	March 31	TD
Order and receive signage	April 2	April 10	KD

Figure 5.7 Calendar of Critical Dates (Partial)

responsible to complete each task within the timeframe noted. Although in this case initials have been used, any desired identifier (e.g., full name, last name, job title) may appear in this column.

Note that the entries in Figure 5.6 have been re-sorted into chronological order, first by start date, next by end date. This is another strong reason for deleting the list of elementary tasks, as now the entire flow of work is integrated into a single organized chart in chronological order for use by all involved in the production, regardless of to what process each task belongs. The power of spreadsheet software for event organizers has probably been particularly apparent throughout this chapter as we sort the calendar by start and end dates. Additionally, software programs may be used to generate separate charts of responsibility for each individual listed in the calendar. This provides the sports event organizer and the managers responsible for each functional area with a ready and useful tool to ensure that workload is properly and equitably distributed, and access is available to information on exactly who is supposed to be doing what and when. Project management software can track the status of individual tasks and milestones with even more detail and generate flow charts and other graphic tools for presentation purposes.

Remember not to neglect those activities that occur *after* an event has been completed. Functions such as dismantling an event, vacating and restoring the event site, finalizing the budget settlement, scheduling postmortem event evaluations, documenting the event for sponsors, and releasing temporary seasonal employees are just a sample of the types of activities that happen postevent, and should also be included in the calendar.

Distribute Critical Dates Calendars

Critical dates calendars are most useful when they are distributed to as wide an audience as is practical, feasible, or desirable. Confidential or organizationally sensitive information, if any, should be deleted from these more widely distributed copies. At minimum, everyone listed in the responsibility column should receive a copy of the calendar. Staff in other areas of the organization with a need to know may be sent copies to assist them in demystifying what could well appear to be chaotic to those outside the event team. In this way, they may easily direct their questions, comments, and feedback directly to the individual overseeing a particular function, rather than solely to the event director. The question now is: "Who are the people doing all this work, and where are they coming from?"

Build a Support Organization

Whether you plan to use some combination of volunteers, part-time or full-time paid staff, or an event planning or production firm to staff your sports event, a structure needs to be put in place that will define areas of responsibility and accountability for each contributing individual. Many sports organizations exist explicitly to stage special events and are geared up 365 days a year to function as their own special events companies. Others are highly seasonal, in which a small core staff is retained on a permanent, full-time basis, periodically augmented by a more considerable temporary, in-season workforce. Still others (perhaps most) retain help from outside organizations, applying some combination of internal staff with resources such as vendors, consultants, temporaries, interns, freelancers, and volunteers. Because the structure of the event team should be defined by the workload ahead, event organizers frequently build their critical dates calendars early in the planning process to determine what human resources, skill sets, and talents will be required and when they must be applied. They can then create an organization plan that applies both internal and external resources, retaining those resources only for the period required to execute their responsibilities. Before they begin looking at areas of responsibility, however, it is important for the event organization to define levels of authority and determine how decisions, both short-term and long-term, will be made.

Define the Decision-Making Process

Frank Supovitz, one of our authors, recalls that many years ago as a freshman reporter for WQMC-AM radio at Queens College, City University of New York, he was assigned to cover a planned demonstration protesting the financially troubled city's decision to begin charging tuition at what was until then an institution totally supported by taxpayers:

> On the way to City Hall, I interviewed a student from campus I had come to know who seemed to represent—or at least belong to—a group called the Revolutionary Student Brigade (RSB). I cannot honestly remember whether the RSB considered themselves Trotskyites, Marxists, Leninists, or some other kind of *-ists,* but I do remember being stunned by the answer to the first question I asked—"Who is in charge of the RSB, and what do they hope to accomplish at today's protest?" "No one is in charge," he replied. "We are all in charge. Each and every one of our opinions is equal and valid." I don't recall what exactly he said he himself hoped to achieve.
>
> Although we embrace the notion of equality among all men and women, I knew then as I know now, that *someone* has to be in charge in order to keep things focused, progressing, and responsive to any number of lurking crises.

The decision maker may be an individual, a task force, or a committee, but there must be a structure in place that places the right amount of responsibility at each level of the organization and knowledge, recognition, and acceptance of that structure by all who operate within it. The genesis of every sports event organization starts with the ultimate decision makers—the individual or body of individuals, who have the authority to set objectives, determine strategies, and approve the spending of money to pursue and achieve them.

Frequently, a committee, task force, board of directors, or senior officer of a client organization occupies the top rung of the event team. It is particularly helpful to define the role of this individual or group, particularly with respect to what decisions must be presented for discussion and resolution. Defining these jurisdictions and limitations in the earliest stages will help the senior individual who reports to the group, in this case, the event director, to fully understand the responsibilities and authority he or she may exercise autonomously. Although *autonomy* suggests areas of total control over clearly defined areas, it does not obviate the complete accountability the event director has to the overarching group. It is essential, however, to move the majority of the day-to-day decision-making down below the committee, board, or client organization to enable the event team the freedom to quickly respond to the myriad challenges, changes, and opportunities that will inevitably present themselves often and suddenly during the event planning process. Figure 5.8 is a chart of typical authorities and responsibilities for an event's board of directors (which may take the form of an organization's chief executive officer, event committee, task force, or client organization), and the top individual charged with managing the event (in this case, the event director). This chart is for illustrative purposes, as authorities and responsibilities may slide from one category to another, depending on the needs of a specific event or the reporting structures of existing sports event organizations.

In Figure 5.8, a system of checks and balances is in place to empower the event director to make the day-to-day decisions required to manage the event without having to run every question, challenge, or issue past the board of directors. In this example, the event director has the broad authority to make operational decisions that will keep the event, or the business, running efficiently. The event director is totally responsible to the board, the governing authority. As the

Management Entity	Authorities and Responsibilities
Board of Directors	Definition of event objectives Approval of strategies and tactics Approval of event budget Approval of host city and venue selection Approval of sponsor, supplier, or broadcast and media deals with terms of more than one year Hiring and firing of event director
Event Director	Budget development and management Strategy and tactic development Approval of expenses Supplier selection, negotiations, and contract approval Sponsor solicitation, negotiations, and contract approval Broadcast and media solicitation, negotiation, and contract approval Hiring, training, and firing of event staff

Figure 5.8 Decision-Making Authorities and Responsibilities

individual held accountable for both triumphs and failures, the board may remove the director at any time for not meeting the demands and expectations of the position.

The board is in place to define the objectives for the event. The director is, in turn, responsible to develop the strategies, tactics, and budget required by the event to meet these objectives, although all three of these areas require presentation to, and approval by, the board. The event director in this example can approve expenses autonomously, but is responsible to inform the board if the budget is expected to experience any significant overall variance.

This illustration also limits the event director's authority to approving sponsor, supplier, or broadcast and media deals of only a single year's duration or less. This frees the director to manage the business of the most immediate event, enabling him or her to make a short-term deal without the approval of the higher authority. Having a free hand allows deals to be made that may help an organization respond quickly and authoritatively to emerging challenges such as unexpected budget overruns, supplier or sponsor defaults, unfruitful sponsor contract negotiations, or other previously unanticipated revenue shortfalls. Sometimes, a "fire sale" sponsorship at a below-market rate or a last-minute value-in-kind deal must be struck in order to reduce losses or cover shortfalls. Frequently, these deals are consummated late in the planning process and require the kind of rapid decision-making that board intercession would make unfeasible.

Although such deals may be justifiable and appropriate in the short term, they may not be in the best interest of the event promoter, client, or organization, over the long term. In the example offered in Figure 5.8, the deals with terms exceeding one year must be approved by the higher authority to ensure that they fit with the overall business objectives and strategies of the organization. As the event director serves at the pleasure of the board of directors, agreements made by this senior manager should not be able to long outlive him or her, in case that person's career proves to require abbreviation.

Create an Organization Chart

The substance of an organization chart will differ dramatically from event to event; the chart in Figure 5.9 illustrates a generalized presentation of a fictional sports event provided for the purpose of discussion. The boxes that are on the most common form of organization charts most often represent the names and titles of individuals, but may just as easily describe specific functional areas rather than individual staff positions. This latter format is useful for large events, where the simplicity of listing functional areas rather than names of individual staff members can make the portrayal of the organization easier to understand to those outside the organization. The position of each job on the chart and how the jobs are joined to those above and below symbolize the structure of their reporting relationships. There are many different ways to graphically portray an organization's structure, and several software tools are available in the market to assist in the preparation of professional-appearing charts.

There are three key reasons for taking the time to construct an organization chart for your sports event. The first is to define areas of responsibility and accountability. This will let everyone know what their job is and how they relate to other areas of responsibility in the organization. The second is to streamline decision making. Construct an organization chart with several management tiers so that not each and every issue need be presented to the event director for evaluation and definitive resolution. By limiting the number of staff members reporting only to the event director ("direct reports"), as well as those who report to each of the top managers in charge of each functional area (e.g., operations, guest services, marketing, presentation, etc.), top-level managers can delegate responsibility along clearly defined paths to those one level below. The third reason for institutionalizing an organization chart is to clearly communicate, both within the organization and outside, how each functional area fits into the event's overall management

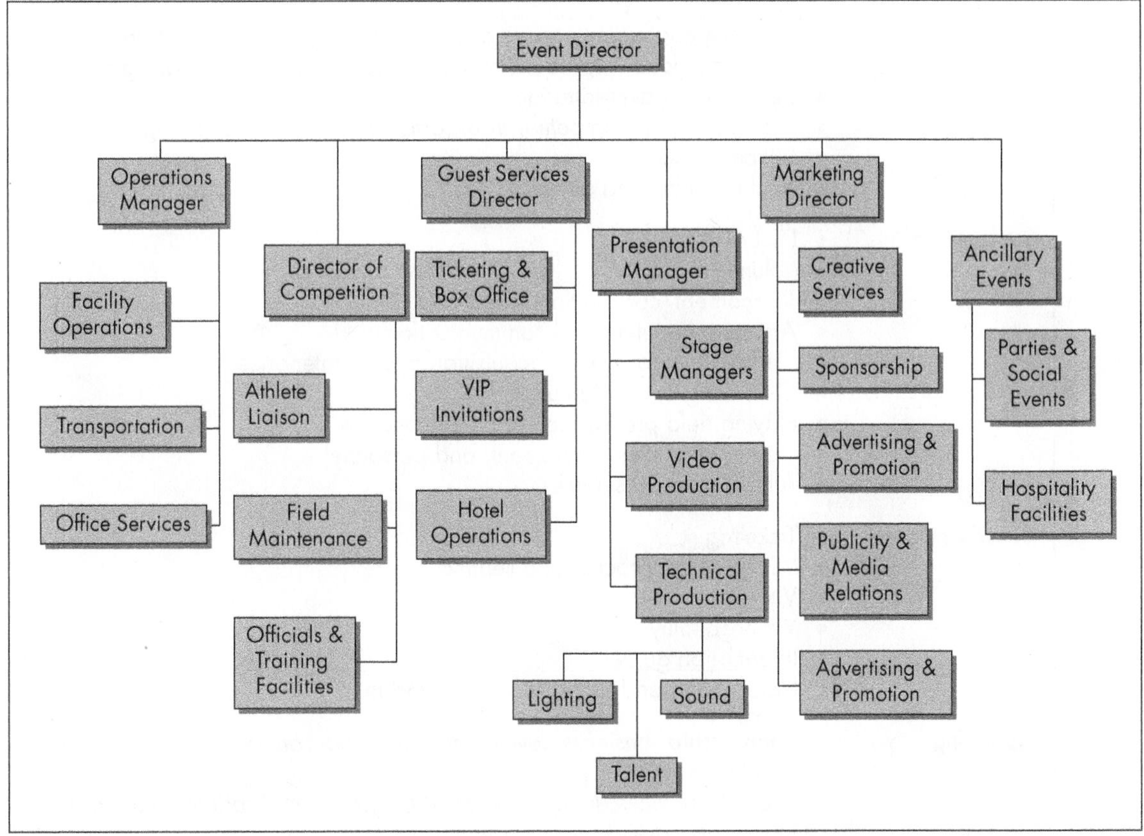

Figure 5.9 Sample Sports Event Organization Chart

structure. Distributing the chart to all those who work within it, as well as to key outside contacts ensures that the questions about, and any issues arising from, the event will be directed to the individuals who can best handle them.

The fictional sports event organization in Figure 5.9 divides the management team into six key functional groups: operations, competition, guest services, presentation, marketing, and ancillary events. While the structure of every event team will vary with the nature and needs of the program being managed, it is preferable to limit to as few as possible the number of functional areas reporting directly to a particular position. Although all members of the event team are ultimately responsible to the event director, this top manager has only six "direct reports," managers who are responsible solely to the director. Functions are grouped beneath each of these managers so that each of them, in turn, has fewer than six key areas for which they are responsible.

Regardless of the vast differences between sports organizations, events apply staff to the management of many common functions. Figure 5.10 lists some of the most common with key activities frequently undertaken by each. To meet an event's specific needs, some might be combined into a single area of responsibility, others more finely subdivided depending on the size, organization, and objectives of the event.

Operations	• Facility management: *space allocation management, load-in, installation, dismantle, load-out, labor (front of house staff), locker/dressing rooms* • Staff/vendor accreditation • Transportation: *competitor transportation, shipping/receiving* • Office services • Staff uniforms and attire
Competition	• First Aid/EMTs • Volunter Staff • Tournament/competition scheduling • Athlete scheduling and communication • Competitive equipment acquisition and maintenance • Officiating and judging • Playing field preparation and maintenance • Training facilities, equipment, and personnel • Athlete medical services
Guest Services	• Ticketing • VIP invitation process and seating • VIP gifts • VIP hospitality • Information guides • Hotel rooms and function space management
Marketing	• Sponsorship: *business development and sponsor sales, account service and fulfillment* • Creative services: *logo development, style manual, printed materials, marketing artwork, sponsor signage* • Advertising: *website, digital, newspaper, radio, television* • Outdoor: *billboards, banners, posters, marquees* • Promotions: *sponsor cross-promotions, retail promotions* • Publicity: *pre-event, media relations/accreditation, media center operations* • Merchandise and programs
Presentation	• Creative: *rundowns, scripting, music, costumes/wardrobe* • Production management • Talent booking: *announcers, entertainers, rehearsal scheduling* • Stage management • Scoreboard operations • Video production • Technical production: *staging, set construction, lighting, sound, special effects (i.e., lasers, pyrotechnics)*
Other Common Functional Areas	• Hospitality and social events: *receptions, parties, spouse programs* • Fan festivals and activities • Broadcasting: *television, web, radio* • Business affairs: *accounts payable, accounts receivable, purchasing, legal (i.e., contract negotiations, risk management, insurance)*

Figure 5.10 Functional Areas for Sports Events

Once you have identified the functional areas that are required for your sports event and they have coalesced into an organization chart, it is time to begin assigning staff to these various functions, or to search for, identify, and retain resources from the outside world to handle the workload.

Find the Right People

One of the wonderful things about sports events is there is usually no shortage of people who want to help staff them. Grassroots organizations tap parents, siblings, and friends of the participants to create the workforce they need to stage their events. Professional sports teams and their respective leagues are besieged by resumes—not just of those already working in the field, but also of sports and event management program students and graduates, career shifters, and job seekers willing to start off as interns, for little or no compensation, just for the work experience and credits on their resumes. The thousands of lesser-connected event organizers in between look to these same pools of experience, talent, and energy, and throw their nets even wider to meet their human resources needs.

Sports events staged by established organizations frequently draft full-time employees from other areas of their company to temporarily assist in the management and execution of key annual or one-time programs. This is the most common practice for the staging of a first-time event in an established organization. Borrowing internal staff helps the company test the event, allowing it to evaluate the desirability of holding the program again in the future without having to staff it with permanent employees the first time around. To keep costs down, they often supplement their on-loan event staff from other departments with temporary "seasonal" employees, individuals hired with predetermined start and end dates for their employment. Seasonal staff may be retained part time (under 35 hours per week) or full time (35+ hours), and may be paid either hourly or weekly.

Enlist Volunteers

In sheer numbers, there are easily more than enough men, women, boys, and girls volunteering to help staff and support sports events from the community ball field and the town rink to the campus gymnasium and the downtown arena. Volunteerism is what makes most sports events go, often providing the staffing glue that keeps the event together. Given the passion many feel for their favorite sport, school, community, or team, it is not hard to understand why. The practice of strategically employing well-briefed, enthusiastic volunteers is not restricted to small community grassroots events. Events staged by large amateur sports organizations and professional sports businesses also require the participation of motivated volunteers to provide short-term and event-day staff for their programs. At the most recent Olympic Games hosted in the United States, Salt Lake City's organizing committee for the 2002 Winter Olympics had approximately 8,000 volunteers for pre-Winter Games activities, 18,000 core volunteers for the Winter Games, and some 6,000 volunteers for the Paralympic Winter Games that followed, while more than 60,000 assisted during the 1996 Summer Games in Atlanta. From the major leagues' all-star game festivities and championship events to high school track meets and citywide marathons to professional tennis and local charity golf tournaments, volunteers are vital contributors to the success of virtually all sports events.

Staff for community-oriented grassroots events is often 100 percent composed of volunteers. The people recruited to fill positions ranging from those of great authority to those of more limited contribution are usually made up of friends, neighbors, and family members. Some participatory organizations, like running and skating clubs, have hundreds or even thousands of members, some number of which often assist with the coordination of their association's schedules of events as volunteers. Although volunteers are by definition unpaid, it is nevertheless recommended that their responsibilities be well defined as if they were paid staff to eliminate confusion and ensure that important tasks do not fail to be accomplished.

When a combination of paid and volunteer staff members works together, volunteers are best suited for positions that require intelligence and people skills, but little training beyond an orientation session or two. Professional event organizers must recognize that to the attendee, volunteers can be indistinguishable from paid staff. As ambassadors for the event organizer and often the first point of contact for participants, guests, and/or the audience, volunteers must be selected judiciously and provided with all the information and materials they need to do their jobs. But first, they must understand what their job is. Create a brief bullet-point job description for each volunteer position, as illustrated in Figure 5.11. Consider the personality traits and knowledge they must possess to fulfill these positions, and then identify the right resources in your market that can provide the body of volunteers most motivated to do a great job on your behalf.

As may be seen in these examples, volunteer jobs are not usually the most glamorous, and as such they may seem like they would be difficult to fill. But, don't underestimate the excitement that sports events generate. Most potential volunteers understand that they will not be running the show. They know they are providing the muscle and connective tissue that keeps everything together, and not necessarily the brain.

So, beyond the event staff's circle of friends, where do sports events find these masses of excited and devoted enthusiasts? That depends on the kind of functions you need to have filled by volunteers. Many local convention and visitors bureaus and sports commissions maintain databases of local residents who enjoy volunteering for special events and are experienced in dealing with the public, such as airport hosts (see Figure 5.11) and any position that will greet and provide information to incoming visitors. In some cities, the office of the mayor or the department of parks and recreation may maintain similar databases of potential volunteers.

If your city is blessed with sports teams, whether recreational, amateur, or professional, a highly motivated resource may already exist. Contact the recreational enthusiasts of your sport for the most enthusiastic pool of potential volunteers. In addition, many amateur and professional teams have booster or fan clubs that enjoy supporting sports events. Consider approaching their membership even if they are not specifically fans of the same sport as your event. Many members just enjoy being around a variety of sporting events. Do not overlook the power of *swag,* the exclusive event merchandise most organizers use as uniform wardrobe for paid and volunteer staff. An event golf shirt or T-shirt and cap can go a long way as an additional motivator to encourage volunteers.

Is there a university with a sports or event management program in the host community on either the undergraduate or graduate level? There are no more motivated prospects for volunteers than those who are looking to make contacts in the sports business and students training for future careers in this exciting, but hard-to-break-into industry. Contact the dean of the school under which these programs are offered to investigate whether an entire class or individual students can volunteer as part of a field experience. Many schools see great value in offering their students the ability to participate in a sports event as staff members.

These sources are the best and most proven for finding volunteers. Being targeted toward those most driven to serve, they usually bear the most fruit, but sometimes more effort is required to fill the ranks. Consider the use of a related organization's or event's website and social media to distribute a press release and basic details announcing the need for volunteers. Be sure to include information on how to apply. Advertise for volunteers through your own event's website as well as your print, radio, television, and/or Internet partners. You might even be able to get

Position: Airport Greeter
Description:

- Meet incoming athletes and VIP guests at the airport and direct them to the ground transportation provided for their convenience
- Assist with the recovery of luggage and equipment from baggage claim and with its transfer to the guests' transportation
- Offer to answer guests' questions about the event schedule, and dining and entertainment options in the city

Reports To: Event Transportation Dispatcher

Dates/Hours Required: At least two days between Thursday, April 13, and Sunday, April 16, for at least four hours per day as assigned

Position: Media Host

Description:

- Duplicate and distribute press releases, statistics, and other information to the working press
- Escort athletes to and from the press conference area
- Assist the public relations team in the Media Center during the event, as assigned

Reports To: Media Relations Manager

Dates/Hours Required: All days between Thursday, April 13, and Sunday, April 16, one hour prior to the start of event to one hour after the end of event

Position: Operations Center Representative

Description:

- Answer phones, direct calls, and take messages for event staff, athletes, and VIP guests
- Assist staff with copying, faxing, overnight packages, messenger services, and other office support functions
- Other office functions, as assigned

Reports To: Office Manager

Dates/Hours Required: At least two days between Thursday, April 13, and Sunday, April 16, for at least four hours per day as assigned

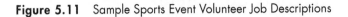

Figure 5.11 Sample Sports Event Volunteer Job Descriptions

media partners to provide these spots as public service announcements (PSAs), for which there is usually no charge.

There are many instances in which volunteer staff alone will not meet the human resources requirements of an event. Professional expertise not otherwise available within the existing organization may be required to plan, manage, and execute a successful program, and some number of talented temporary staff may need to be retained to achieve the desired result. A brief discussion of the temporary paid staff options available to event organizers follows.

SIDELINE STORY

The Power of Volunteerism

Super Bowl XLVI was Indianapolis's first-ever hosting of the National Football League's championship game. More than 8,000 volunteers were recruited, trained, and managed by the Indianapolis Super Bowl Host Committee to help staff *NFL Experience*, the league's massive interactive indoor fan festival, and *Super Bowl Village*, the committee's free outdoor street fair featuring nightly music acts, fireworks, food, and activities. Volunteers also blanketed the streets of downtown Indianapolis, the airport, and area hotels to provide greetings and guidance to fans unfamiliar with the city for the 10 days of festivities leading up to the game, as well as to direct fans from their parking lots and hotel rooms to the entrance to Lucas Oil Stadium on Super Bowl Sunday. Distinctively dressed and well-trained, these ambassadors for their community and the Super Bowl provided visitors with the "Hoosier Hospitality" experience for which Indianapolis is justifiably famous. Lead volunteers were identified by six-foot flags strapped to their backs and equipped with electronic tablets loaded with maps, schedules, restaurant recommendations, and other information to help showcase their community to the roughly 1.1 million visitors who visited the downtown area during Super Bowl week.

Spirited volunteerism did not end with the 8,000 frontline representatives of the community serving the visiting fans. Indianans from across the state contributed by knitting blue and white scarves, each individually different, to protect the volunteers from the cold. Over the course of a year, they generated 13,000 of them—enough to also outfit NFL staff, as well as the staff and players of the participating New England Patriots and New York Giants. Recognizing the great interest and power of its volunteer pool, the Indianapolis Host Committee also used the excitement of the upcoming Super Bowl to help revitalize the city's Near East Side, promote breast tissue donation at a nationally recognized tissue bank, and develop a three-block stretch of downtown street into a permanent pedestrian event venue.

Hire Freelancers: Employees and Independent Contractors

Freelance event staff may be retained either as temporary employees or independent contractors. If hired and compensated as employees, the event director may dictate work hours, set the policies and procedures to be followed, and supervise the freelancers as though they were regular full-time employees. Freelancers hired as temporary employees may also be entitled to all of the rights and protections offered to other employees, such as health insurance benefits and overtime pay—except, of course, that their last date of employment is known by both parties at the outset. Executing an employment contract with a freelance employee is not necessary, although having both parties sign a letter agreement defining compensation, basic work rules, and the date of termination is strongly recommended.

Independent contractors, by contrast, function as one-person vendors. A contract is typically negotiated, containing many of the same terms as the letter agreement used for temporary employees, but because the contractors are generally paid a rate for their completion of the project and upon presentation of an invoice, a payment schedule is usually included. The event manager does not directly supervise the work of an independent contractor, and, unless stipulated by the contract, has no control over what hours the contractor must invest at the event site. Contractors are free to work for more than one client over the course of their term, and have the right to hire and fire additional employees at their own expense to assist them in completing their assignment.

Independent contractors are particularly useful for very specialized functions in which the level and type of expertise exceed that of the event's senior staff. Such specialized contractors might include transportation system consultants, presentation directors, tournament competition organizers, construction or production managers, technical directors, and party planners, to name a few. It is preferable to put event team members on the payroll as temporary employees when the position calls for the execution of plans set by supervising managers or the event director. This by no means suggests that temporary event employees are any less skilled or professional than independent contractors. If supervisors hire wisely, they will always search for freelancers that add more firepower to the event team. If the culture of the event requires direct and constant interaction with management, retaining the freelancer as a temporary employee will usually be preferable. There are a number of additional procedural and legal differences between the retention of freelancers as temporary employees or contactors.

If it is determined that a temporary event employee is required, it is strongly suggested that a staff job description be created for each position. The job description should provide greater detail than the version used for volunteers (see Figure 5.11), providing both management and the employee with a clear understanding of the position's responsibilities, work rules, and limits of authority.

Use of Agencies

Some organizations consider staging sports events even though their main line of business may only be marginally or tangentially related to such activities as a sponsor or promotional partner. It may simply make good business sense for the company to own, develop, manage, and execute a sports event itself to further its corporate objectives, or to market a particular product. Event marketing agencies exist for the purpose of assisting such companies. They are advantageous to use as support organizations because they can apply an entire outside organization's resources toward the client's event marketing objectives without the company having to staff internally for what could be a costly and labor-intensive endeavor. The client company is strongly advised to exercise the greatest degree of discretion and thorough due diligence as to what event marketing agency to retain, checking references and pursuing independent research into the company's experience, achievements, and financial health before agreeing to any relationship. Most agencies will work on a fee-plus-expenses basis, and it is the client company's right to request an explanation of how the schedule of payments will be derived.

It is also not unusual for sports event organizations to retain specialized agencies to assume the management responsibilities of defined and specialized functional areas, such as sponsor sales, advertising, public relations, and group ticket sales, among others. Agencies that assume cost center functions (i.e., those areas that are represented by expenses in the budget) generally work on a fee-plus-expenses basis. Those that are charged with developing profit centers (i.e., those areas represented by revenues in the budget) usually work on some form of commission basis, and are compensated based on the amount of revenue they generate for the event.

Manage Your Support Organization

The acts of planning an event and building an event staff are very similar to launching an entirely new company, brand, or product. The event requires defined objectives, strategies, and tactics, a source of capital, and a staff to manage and execute it. The key difference between creating a sports event organization (with permanent, temporary, and volunteer workers) and staffing a startup company is that event teams are designed to be built up until they can meet an event's objectives and then are deconstructed, at least until the next event, when the building process begins anew.

The analogy of an event organization as a startup company is further reinforced by the working environment of long hours and work weeks, entrepreneurial multitasking employees who fill more than one function, guarded finances, and—to those of us who love this business—tremendous excitement. But startups can be confusing places without clearly communicated goals and procedures, and without constant communication between staff members. Event teams can be similarly confusing environments, and with a firm, climactic end date to their existence on the day of the event or soon thereafter, places of great anxiety if not properly managed.

Create an Event Staff Manual

Developing and distributing to the staff a manual with essential information about your event is a vital communications tool. Articulate and circulate a statement of your primary and secondary event objectives to your key event staff and, if you are not revealing confidential information unnecessarily, the results of your P-A-P-E-R Test (see Play 1). Your event's managers will not know how to hit the target if they don't know what or where the target is and how you expect them to reach it. This information will make up the first section of your event staff manual. Keep event manuals in electronic form or in a loose-leaf binder so sections can be periodically updated and corrected. The manual will serve as the definitive information source to which the event director and staff will constantly refer throughout the planning process, as well as during the event itself.

Add sections to the event staff manual that include the information you feel will be most useful to the team's planning and execution of the event. Most manuals will include a list of contacts, including each person's phone numbers, mail and e-mail addresses, and fax numbers. For ease of use, divide the contact list into four subsections: internal (members of the event team organization), facility, vendors, and external (non-vendors, such as city services contacts). Figure 5.12 provides a list of essential sections in sequence that will be common to most event staff manuals. The figure also lists several optional sections that may be included if applicable to your event, or appropriate to the level of employee receiving the binder.

Note that the list of essential sections for the manual includes an area for "policies and procedures." This section is particularly important for event teams that come together on a temporary basis, although it will be of value to virtually every organization. In this area, it is wise to include definitive information on how purchases are to be authorized and made, and how expenses incurred by event staff should be approved and filed for reimbursement. Include blank forms used for these procedures such as purchase orders and expense report blanks that may be downloaded or photocopied for submission, along with instructions on how they should be completed. If travel is required of the employee, include policies governing reimbursable travel expenses (e.g., preapproval procedures, class of service for air travel, hotel limits, food and beverage per diems). Minimum workdays and hours, codes of conduct,

Essential Sections

1. Event Mission and Objectives
2. Contact List
3. Calendar of Critical Dates
4. Emergency Procedures
5. Event Timeline or Schedule
6. Organization Chart
7. Maps and Floor Plans
8. Policies and Procedures

Optional Sections:

1. Financial Information
2. Contracts
3. Event Rundowns and Scripts
4. Facility Information
5. Sponsorship (List of sponsors and summary of benefits)
6. Transportation Plan
7. Travel and Hotel Information

Figure 5.12 Event Staff Manual Sections

attire guidelines, equal opportunity employment statements, and other administrative information should also be included. In the long run, taking the time to include these explanations in the event staff manual will avoid costly and potentially demoralizing misunderstandings for staff members and your organization.

A more concise variant of the event staff manual should also be created for volunteers. If volunteer workers are fulfilling functions of assistance rather than management functions, the nature of the policies and procedure sections should be changed to only those areas applicable to their position. More background information may be included, as well as a compendium of frequently asked questions (FAQs) and answers.

Schedule Regular Event Staff Meetings

It may seem obvious that the scheduling of staff meetings is the best way to keep event personnel current and updated to the constant changes of event life. Schedule meetings at regular intervals and include them in the critical dates calendar. If possible, set and circulate an agenda a few days in advance with a request for staff members to review and provide recommendations for topic additions at least 24 hours in advance. You will likely discover that these meetings tend to become less efficient as the number of attendees increases. Therefore, it is best to keep staff meetings compartmentalized for mid- to large-size events. One meeting unit should include the event director and the directors, managers, or heads of functional areas to share pertinent updates, announce tactical and schedule changes, set policies, discuss challenges faced by the event, and propose solutions. Each functional head should, in turn, conduct meetings with his or her own direct reports.

Another important meeting should be included on the critical dates calendar—the "tie-down" meeting (also called a final production, all-agency, or all-department meeting). Usually held just once, one to three weeks ahead of the event, the tie-down meeting includes all event staff, as well as representatives of important stakeholders such as key vendors and freelancers, agencies, operating departments, facility representatives, and broadcasters, among others. The tie-down is best organized as a communications tool to impart information and procedures, and to identify the remaining tasks ahead. With a potentially large assemblage of many dozens of event personnel, it is best not envisioned as a problem-solving session. Nevertheless, it is inevitable that some issues will be identified during the tie-down meeting as all pertinent functional areas report on how they will operate during the event. That is why holding this important session at least a week ahead of the event is so important. The time remaining until event day will give participants the opportunity to solve these late-emerging problems. It is recommended that the larger the event, the earlier the tie-down should be held to provide adequate time to solve the greater number of issues that are bound to surface. Scheduling and conducting a follow-up meeting is often necessary and useful.

Now, the event director has a road map and timetable for all of the many tasks and activities that must be executed in order to successfully manage and execute the event. Based on this more clearly defined workload, he or she can build an organization to undertake the challenge of producing a well-managed, flawlessly executed sports event. Before another moment expires, it is time to take the event to market and to start developing a roster of active, engaged sponsors to meet your event's revenue goals and to activate the program's promotional plans.

Post-Play Analysis

The framework of the event planning process is assembled by compiling a production schedule, or calendar of critical dates. This schedule lists the myriad essential tasks required to manage and execute the event and includes start dates, end dates, and the individual responsible for each entry. The best way to begin creating the schedule is to break up the tactics and strategies defined by the P-A-P-E-R Test into their component "elementary tasks." These elementary tasks are exploded into all of the supportive tasks and decision points required to meet them and then sorted into chronological order.

The process of building an event organization begins once the scope of the work is clarified by the critical dates calendar. Define the decision-making process and create an organization chart to begin adding muscle to the framework. Regardless of whether the organization will be composed of volunteers, existing staff, temporary staff, freelancers, or some combination thereof, create job descriptions for each position. Be sure to communicate essential information to all staff members through the creation of an event staff manual and by holding regularly scheduled staff meetings.

Coach's Clipboard

1. Compile a calendar of critical dates for the community all-star game discussed in Play 1. Create an organization chart and job descriptions for the all-volunteer team you will assemble to manage and execute this event.
2. Create an organization chart to organize, manage, and execute the 10K event discussed in Play 1. How many event-day volunteers do you think you will require? Assuming the

event is being held in your community, what specific resources will you employ to fill your requirements?
3. Create a job description for your volunteer director, the individual who will solicit, schedule, and manage all of the event staff referenced in exercise 2. What kinds of job backgrounds and professional skill sets would provide the most qualified candidates for this position?
4. What kinds of information would you include in the volunteer staff manual for the positions discussed in Figure 5.11?

PLAY 6

Understanding the Sports Event–Sponsor Relationship

"Champions keep playing until they get it right."

—*Billie Jean King, multiple American tennis champion & founder, Women's Tennis Association*

This play will help you to:

- Understand how revenue, cost avoidance, and activation generate the value sponsors can provide to sports events.
- Understand how sports events can provide a diverse menu of business solutions to a wide range of sponsors.
- Develop opportunities to strengthen the sports event–sponsor relationship with mutually advantageous activation platforms for consumer and business-to-business companies.

Introduction

In a free market economy, businesses, brands, and products devote significant resources to keeping their customers satisfied and wresting new ones from the grasp of their competitors. The stakes are as high as the life and death of the company, and the battle is joined on a multitude of fronts—in retail locations and with wholesale distributors, in digital, broadcast, and print media

SIDELINE STORY

Myron Cope's Terrible Towel

In 1975, broadcaster Myron Cope introduced to American football what many believe to be the first "rally towel" for a Pittsburgh Steelers playoff game. Before the game, local media and team players scoffed at the idea that fans twirling washcloth-sized swatches of gold and black fabric could intensify the excitement of the stadium experience and spur on their team. But, by the time the players were introduced and the stadium undulated with the color and motion of tens of thousands of spinning towels, it was clear that Myron Cope had ushered in a new Pittsburgh tradition. The Steelers progressed through the playoffs to win their second straight Super Bowl and the tradition was further cemented.

Rally towels are now a favorite fan souvenir and frequent sponsor giveaway at sports events across North America. Home team fans feel like contributors to successful play on the field, and sponsors that provide the towels to the fans entering the stadium help them feel that way.

advertising, and at trade events. Perhaps the most visible and intriguing battlefield of all is at sports events, where brand marketers spend millions on the attempt to transfer even a fraction of the avidity, excitement, and emotional engagement of a sport's loyal audience to the consumption of their product, service, or experience.

There is probably no more zealously sought-after, hard-fought, essential—and delicate—partnership in the business of event marketing than that which is forged between a corporate sponsor and a sports event. For participating companies, event marketing is a discipline all its own, an exciting, high-impact addition to the more traditional implements in the marketing mix tool shed—advertising, publicity, promotion, and direct sales. All of these common and conventional marketing elements have been part of the sports scene for more than a century. It is nearly impossible to remember a time when teams did not offer advertising signage in the outfield or ads in the team yearbook, promote "bat day" giveaways for weaker, tough-to-sell match-ups or stage wacky fan-friendly promotions to drive more fans into seats.

Today's marketers seek to deepen engagement with their customers by staging experiences in their own retail environments and at events outside of their own locations. In *The Experience Economy*[1], authors B. Joseph Pine II and James H. Gilmore write that a company "no longer offers goods or services alone but the resulting experience, rich with sensations, created within each customer." Companies seeking to differentiate themselves from their competitors understand the value of staging experiences that create lasting impressions in the minds of their customers. "The value of the experience lingers in the memory of any individual who was engaged by the event," they continue. Although Pine and Gilmore's landmark work primarily addresses why and how a company must engage at every point of contact with its customers, the notion may also be applied to how a marketer's association with sports events can provide the platforms that build memorable experiences and deeper relationships with a target market. A company sufficiently integrated as a sports event sponsor can benefit greatly from the strong emotional pull on fans during an event's progress and outcome, times at which customers are at their most engaged and excited.

---

[1]Pine, B. Joseph II and Gilmore, James H., *The Experience Economy Updated Edition*, Boston, MA: Harvard Business Review Press), 2011 Kindle Edition, location 569.

The Roots of Sports Event Sponsorship

Corporations have long recognized the powerful allure and marketing potential of sports events to highly engaged audiences on the field and at home (see Figure 6.1). For this reason, signage and advertising at stadiums and arenas and on broadcasts of sports events have been part of the sponsorship portfolio in one form or another for nearly a century. As sports event sponsorships evolved into progressively more sophisticated business opportunities, companies increasingly supplemented their in-stadium relationships by promoting their associations outside of the stadium and broadcast with additional exposure in retail locations, product displays, and their own advertising and promotional plans. To some degree, being able to access event tickets for a company's important clients had been part of the reason to sponsor an event, but the value of a sponsorship was primarily evaluated on the basis of tonnage—how many signs, advertisements, and promotions appeared in front of how many people and in how many places? Appropriately, companies next asked themselves about a sponsorship's return on investment—"How effective are these associations in developing customers and selling our products, whether the advertising appears inside or outside of the sports event?" This essential question led to sponsors seeking and demanding more activation opportunities that truly engaged the fan—their customer—and successful event organizers responded. The most impactful of today's sports event sponsorships invest organizers and partner companies in each other's success by immersing fans and sponsor clients in co-branded content at the event site (which still includes signage and advertising),

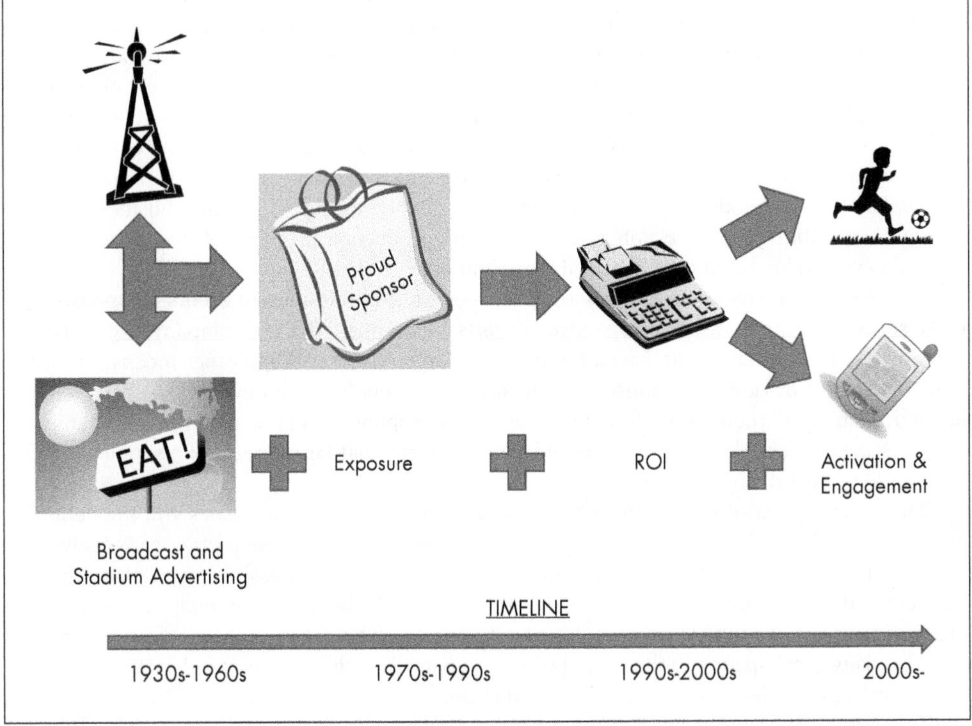

Figure 6.1 Evolution of Sports Sponsorship

offsite (which still includes retail and product promotion), and online to deliver sponsors with return on investment and fans with added ways to engage with an event.

The benefits of advertising a company's product at sports events have long been recognized because of the simplicity of their measurement and verification. The sports marketer can guarantee exposure to a number of fans in a facility based on the number of games played, or events staged over the life of an advertisement. The relative attractiveness and cost of an ad may vary based on its position. That is, how visible is the ad to how many fans, and how often is it in their field of view?

Television exposure, whether as dedicated event coverage or a result of news reporting, is also measurable based on ratings, the position of a particular sign, and the frequency of its appearance on the screen. These measures are still in common use today as key yardsticks for determining the value of signage at a sports event. Online advertising associated with the event, whether on the organizer's website, on mobile applications, or on other virtual platforms, may be similarly evaluated by measuring page-views, length of stay, and click-throughs to the sponsor's website. More traditionally, it is also simple to value an ad in an event program based on the number of copies printed and purchased and the position of the advertisement within the book (e.g., back cover, inside front cover, inside back cover, opposite or embedded in key featured stories). Marketers, both the advertiser and the event promoter, commonly use a "cost per thousand" (CPM) calculation to determine the value of an ad. Simply, the CPM represents the amount of money that is spent to purchase the ad for every thousand consumers who view it. In general, advertisers look for the lowest, most cost-efficient CPM when evaluating the attractiveness of purchasing a particular exposure opportunity.

Although the extent of an advertisement's exposure can be objectively measured by its CPM, it is more difficult to quantify its "stickiness," or how well a fan will remember the ad and how effective it will be in motivating someone to buy the product, visit the store, engage with the advertiser online, or employ the service being promoted. Because the excitement and emotional involvement generated by a sports event can add considerable glue to the stickiness of an advertising sign, banner, online ad, or commercial, some event organizers limit the ability to advertise at their events solely and exclusively to sponsors, those companies that are willing to support the event beyond simply buying an on-site or web advertisement to further their marketing objectives. In simplest terms, the ideal sponsor relationship is defined as one in which a business partner, through association with an event, realizes marketing benefits in excess of its investment and offers an event value beyond its financial participation.

Sports events are also competing with other sports and entertainment events for sponsors. To make sense from the sponsor's perspective, a sports event must offer the company more business opportunity than could be purchased for the same expenditure through other means. From the organizer's point of view, the sponsorship must provide benefits well beyond the costs that will be incurred to fulfill them. Therefore, both parties—the sponsor and the sports event organizer—are investing in each other, and both should expect returns that far outperform a simple cash-for-product (e.g., advertising) transaction.

Thus, although advertising continues to be an important—and sometimes still the central—component in the package of benefits enjoyed by a sponsor, the corporate partner can receive outstanding additional value and more ways to achieve improved "stickiness" for its message through an increased association and investment in an event. These benefits may include the ability to engage in pre-event promotions that increase the sales of both the sponsor's product and the event's tickets, participation in the event presentation itself, exclusive access to VIP tickets, receptions, parties, and other associated events, and more.

To justify this increased investment, event organizers must design and construct packages of highly attractive and tangible benefits that are available exclusively to sponsors. It is also a quid pro quo for a sponsor's increased investment that it should enjoy some measure of exclusivity that bars competitors from participating and promoting their products or message in any way associated with the event. The sponsor's ability to promote its product's superior and unique attributes without any interference from its competition is a valuable and essential ingredient in most sponsorship packages.

As companies have different marketing needs, event organizers must demonstrate some degree of flexibility in designing benefit packages that are individually tailored to their understanding of a particular sponsor's business objectives. A sponsor that markets a snack food to consumers may place more value on advertising, sampling, and direct sales opportunities. In contrast, a partner that sells high-priced technology solutions to other businesses may place greater value on exclusive access to the best tickets in the house, meet-and-greet opportunities with the athletes for its dealers and best clients, product demonstration kiosks near premium seating areas, and VIP hospitality opportunities such as insider parties and receptions, and place less emphasis on advertising.

What Sports Event Organizers Really Want from Sponsors

Before approaching a potential business partner with a program designed to meet what they believe are the company's objectives, sports event organizers should have a clear understanding of what they themselves want out of the relationship. Although it may seem obvious that sports events are in the sponsorship business to meet revenue goals, the organizer must recognize that in today's discerning, ultracompetitive sports event marketplace, more sponsors are demanding greater demonstrable results for their money. Consequently, sports event organizers have to work harder to provide more value for the sponsor. Savvy organizers know that there is more to what a sponsor can bring to the event than just cash. So what do sports event organizers really want—and need—from their sponsors? Three key things that organizers look for a sponsor to provide are *revenue, cost avoidance,* and *activation*. The first two attributes of the sponsor–event relationship have a direct impact on the financial success of an organizer's event. The last feature, activation, can have a no less profound, though sometimes indirect, effect on the organizer's success by framing how a sponsor will leverage the relationship for its own benefit, as well as for that of the event. Forging a sponsor relationship that offers a measure of all three can offer an organizer solutions to event marketing challenges with greater effect than can any alone (Figure 6.2).

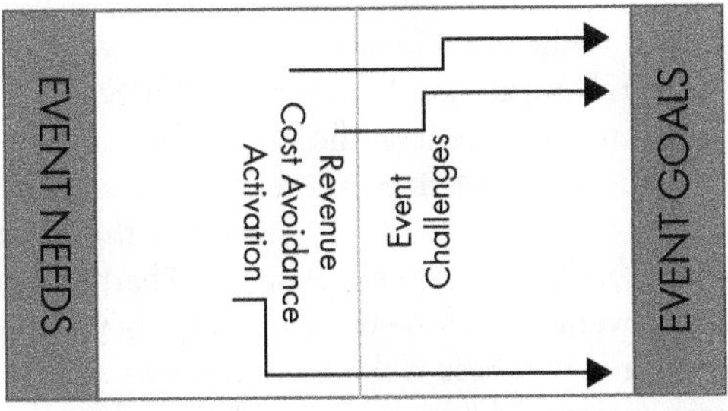

Figure 6.2 What Sports Event Organizers Need from Sponsors

Revenue

The vast majority of sports events that include corporate sponsorship as part of their business model do so to generate revenue. Generally, the fewer or more modest the other revenue streams (particularly ticket revenue and participation fees), the more an event will rely on some form of support from sponsors. An event that is free to participants and attendees, for example, will require a sizable portion of its revenue budget to be generated from corporate sponsorships.

It is very tempting for sports event organizers to view corporate sponsorship as "spackle for budgets," the great gap closer that will cover any shortfall on the balance sheet. A common approach of event promoters in determining how high to set a sponsorship revenue goal is to first estimate expenses, then set a reasonable and salable ticket price or participation fee, and finally, decide to cover almost all of the difference and profit, if any, with sponsor dollars. Although this is not a bad approach to start developing a sponsorship revenue goal, it can be a dangerous place to finish.

The amount of sponsorship revenue a sports event can generate is not a function of how much of the budget an organizer needs to cover, but rather, the event's intrinsic attractiveness to a sponsor and its potential effectiveness in achieving the sponsor's business objectives. The sponsor will compare the demographics of an event's audience with its own customers to determine whether various characteristics such as age, gender, income, education, and other consumer attributes complement each other. If they match well, the sponsor will then evaluate how effectively the rights and benefits offered by the event will deliver its message or sell its products to this common target audience. Organizers will need to make a candid and realistic assessment of how much interest an event will generate among the field of potential sponsors. Specifically, they will have to estimate how much money these companies are likely to spend to communicate with an event's ticket buyers, viewers, or participants, and what the event will have to deliver to its sponsors before finalizing their sponsorship revenue goals.

Cost Avoidance

Sponsors are increasingly attracted to the option of providing products and services in lieu of, or in addition to, cash in payment of some portion of their event sponsorship fees, particularly in a challenging economic environment. This practice is known variously as *barter, contra,* or *value-in-kind* (VIK). VIK sponsors provide products or services to an event and value them at the retail price an organizer would expect to pay if he or she had to expend cash to procure them. For the sponsor, this practice has multiple benefits. Obviously, it reduces the cash the company will need to spend in exchange for sponsorship rights. To sponsors, cash represents money that that has already been earned on past sales. Providing VIK, however, moves product inventory out of their warehouses, so sponsors are actually paying for their sponsorship with what amounts to new, *incremental* sales. VIK sponsors realize added efficiencies when using their products instead of cash. The real cost a sponsor incurred in manufacturing the product may only be 50 percent or less of the retail value provided to the event organizer.

Event organizers should, by all means, avail themselves of VIK opportunities that truly provide a level of cost avoidance equal to, or exceeding, the value of a cash sponsorship. In other words, make sure that the bartered products or services will really reduce your event expenses by at least an amount that equals your income goal had you been paid by the company in cash. Avoid deals that do not genuinely decrease budgeted expenses. Also avoid bartered products and services that add a level of operational inconvenience to the event. Ideally, they should be the actual products or services you would require and purchase if the VIK offer was not available. If the products or services are inferior to those that would have otherwise been selected, or are provided in excess of what is required or usable, a VIK deal can be more harmful than helpful.

To illustrate, imagine that a VIK arrangement is desired by an office equipment supplier, offering digital printer-copiers in place of cash, in exchange for its designation as an event sponsor. The top-of-the-line printer offered by the sponsor can generate 30 sheets per minute and collate 10 sets at a time. The event's media center, however, routinely copies large numbers of press releases, media clippings, and statistics, requiring a high-speed digital printer that can handle at least 50 sets at a time and at speeds of at least twice the speed at which the sponsor's printers can process them. If the proposed sponsorship deal is dependent on a VIK deal, the organizer must determine whether the lost productivity and greatly reduced speed so negatively affects the media center's ability to service the press that it would reflect poorly on the event. If it does, the event organizer would be wise to insist that the VIK deal exclude the provision of printer-copiers for the media center. Perhaps these reduced-speed printers can instead be used in lower quantity and in other functional areas. Because they would now provide less real value to the event, the pure VIK arrangement may have to be reconfigured into a combination of cash and products, or simply a sponsorship at a lower level.

If quality, quantity, and utility match up with operational and budget requirements, then accepting barter avoids costs, and that can be as good as cash. During economically challenging times, demonstrating the flexibility to consider incorporating VIK partners into the portfolio of sponsorships can mean the difference between closing a deal and watching one slip away. VIK is not just becoming a popular alternative to pure cash transactions in small and moderate-size deals. Its prominence is increasing in larger sponsor relationships, as well. Figure 6.3 lists potential barter opportunities commonly sought by corporate sponsors and sports event organizers. As previously discussed, planners are advised to budget for all expenses as though cash is required to acquire these products and services, but remain open to the opportunities that VIK arrangements can provide.

Activation

Activation is an industry buzzword that embodies a concept not easily described by a simple synonym. Best put, organizers need sponsors that will invest dollars beyond their sponsorship fee to promote their relationship with a sports event to build awareness of the event, drive ticket sales, and promote the purchase of merchandise, among other benefits (thus, their "activation"). The sponsor can similarly use the event to drive more customers to its brands or business through the placement of event-themed advertising in digital media, newspapers, on radio, television and its own website, through "outdoor" (billboard) advertising, in-store displays, and in sales promotions. The organizer, as a result, can enjoy the benefits of significant additional exposure through this associated advertising.

Increasingly, sports event organizers have been enjoying benefits from sponsors that, through their own activation strategies, are creating content-driven programming elements that add value to the events they support while engaging directly with the fan for their own marketing purposes. The traditional "sponsor village," an area set aside at events for sponsors to design, staff, and showcase products in a series of tents, kiosks, or table displays, is being replaced or supplemented by customized mobile marketing attractions sprinkled throughout the event site that can be easily set up, operated, and packed away for the next sponsored event in another city. Sponsors have discovered that they can best engage with fans attending a sports event by acknowledging and marketing to their passion—the sport itself. As a result, many sponsors now provide experiential attractions, content that can make the event better.

In today's sports marketplace, sponsor activation is an essential component of what makes the event–sponsor partnership work because of how effective it is in achieving the objectives of both parties. According to Jim Andrews of IEG, a Chicago-based authority on event sponsorship and

Operational Expenses

- Air travel
- Hotel accommodations
- Automobile rentals
- Fuel
- Office space
- Computer and printing equipment
- Office supplies
- Electronics (e.g., televisions, digital cameras, video equipment)
- Mobile telephones and service
- Staff and volunteer wardrobe
- Catering and refreshments (e.g., bottled water, soft drinks, beer)
- Legal, medical, financial, and other professional services
- Construction materials

Direct Event Expenses

- Sport-specific equipment (balls, bats, gloves, sticks, motor oil)
- Uniforms, footwear and performance gear
- Protective gear and equipment
- Timing equipment
- Locker room products
- Athlete participation gifts
- Event presentation services (e.g., audio, video, event planning services, etc.)

Marketing Expenses

- Television and radio advertising time
- Digital and newspaper advertising space
- Outdoor advertising space (e.g., billboards, mass transit advertising)
- Printing (e.g., tickets, invitations, brochures, fan guides, etc.)
- Fan giveaways and premiums

Figure 6.3 Typical Sports Event VIK Opportunities

the publisher of IEG Sponsorship Report, sponsors generally allocate between $1.40 and $1.90 in activation spending for every dollar spent on sponsorship fees. Some sponsors offer organizers "activation-only" associations, guaranteeing an event valuable advertising and promotion not otherwise available or affordable to the organizer. For the sponsor, this strategy can be an effective way of financing its partnership with an event by incorporating activation plans into existing advertising budgets at no incremental cost. Before an event organizer agrees to an activation-only deal, even if it provides outstanding media value, that organizer should evaluate whether the event's cash revenue goals can be met in other ways.

It should be noted that the ultimate objective of a sponsor's event activation strategies is to realize its own marketing objectives—winning new customers and selling more products. From the partner's perspective, "sponsorships are effective or ineffective based primarily on one thing—how they are activated," agrees David Grant, principal and co-founder of Team Epic. "Sponsors who are not getting full value either have selected the wrong sponsorship, or have developed the wrong marketing plans," he observes. Although a sponsor's activation strategies are geared primarily to fulfilling their own marketing objectives, working cooperatively to provide effective platforms for promotional activity can benefit both the event and its corporate partners.

Commitment to, or Prospect for, Continued Association

It may seem self-serving, and perhaps patently obvious, to suggest that some form of continuing commitment to future events is important to organizers in a sponsor relationship, but any list of event organizer's desires would be incomplete without mentioning it. Although not as essential as cash or activation campaigns in the short term, it is almost always in the best interest of a sports event organizer to sell the rights to more than a single year's edition as part of a sponsor's package of benefits. A multiyear deal reduces the expense and effort involved in selling each and every sponsorship annually and provides the organizer with a degree of certainty as to achieving at least a portion of the event's revenue goals for one or more succeeding years. (It is actually most beneficial if sponsorship terms are of varying lengths so that expiration dates are staggered over a range of years. In this way, although there will be a need to renew or resell some portion of an event's full sponsorship portfolio annually, the future of the event will not be endangered by the risk of having a single year in which every sponsorship must be renewed.) From the sponsor's perspective, a multiyear deal can provide the attractive benefit of price protection. The organizer of a successful event would be unable to increase the price of a sponsorship package beyond the terms of the contract for the years covered by the agreement. Nor would an event organizer have the opportunity to open the event for bidding to a sponsor's competitors, possibly replacing an incumbent that invested heavily in making an event a success with a newcomer promising additional activation, cash, products, or other benefits.

The continuity of a sponsor's involvement in an event from year to year builds a strong and valuable association between the partners in the minds of the consumers. Nevertheless, sponsors are frequently reticent to commit financial resources to events or event organizations that are not so singular or prestigious that protecting their investment over a period of years is an essential part of their corporate business plan. To encourage multiyear support, sponsors can be offered various escape clauses in their agreements. Such provisions may include "the right of first refusal," whereby a sponsor must formally turn down renewal before a deal may be finalized with any other company. Alternatives include a "right of first negotiation," whereby a potential renewal must be negotiated with the sponsor before any other company is approached, and a "right to terminate," permitting the sponsor or organizer to end the deal after the first event based on predetermined circumstances or measures (e.g., failure of the organizer to reach a defined attendance plateau, or the sponsor to achieve certain sales levels). These inclusions provide both parties with an explicit statement of intent indicating that a sponsor will consider extending its association if it does not wish to firmly commit itself for a number of years. (See Figure 6.4 for a summary of benefits that organizers seek from sponsors.)

The sports event business often seems as though it is rapidly approaching the point of saturation, a time when the clutter of too many sponsors in too many places at a single event interferes with making an efficient and effective impact on the audience. For this reason, sponsors have become justifiably more discerning and more demanding about the value of benefits offered by sports event organizers. Although they continue to accept the traditional and valuable features of advertising, signage, and tickets, many express the desire to receive an increased sense of "ownership" at a sports event. When sponsors refer to *ownership,* they are expressing a need to develop public perception of the company as the most dominant sponsor of the entire program, or of

- Revenue
- Cost avoidance (value in kind, or VIK)
- Activation
  - Advertising
  - Promotions
  - Publicity
  - Experiential attractions
- Commitment to, or prospect for a continued association

Figure 6.4 What Sports Event Organizers Really Want from Sponsors

specific event elements that can make a uniquely strong and memorable impact on the consumer. Not only can sports events offer sponsors a diverse menu of marketing opportunities to own, but also they now attract an increasingly broad and diverse group of companies, each of which may become business partners for a wide variety of reasons.

What Sponsors Really Want from Sports Events

Although sponsors have differing motivations for their participation in a sports event and vary as to the value they place on the specific benefits of involvement, what they do share is confidence in the strength of sponsorship as a powerful marketing tool. According to IEG's annual sponsorship review, North American companies spent $17.2 billion on event sponsorships in 2010, 3.9 percent more than the year prior, and global sponsorships totaled $46.3 billion, an increase of 5.2 percent. Spending on sports sponsorships, specifically, grew 3.4 percent overall in 2010.

George P. Johnson's 2010 EventView study[2], published in *Event Marketer* magazine and which surveyed corporate marketing executives on the importance of events as a component of their company's promotional spending plan, further validated the findings that sponsorship continues to grow as an effective marketing tool. When asked to list the top three marketing elements for establishing and enhancing relationships with their customers, event marketing was mentioned by 64 percent of those surveyed, followed by social media marketing at 55 percent and Web marketing at 54 percent. These results are particularly striking, as the survey was conducted at a time of deep and painful economic uncertainty during which corporate expenditures were under great scrutiny by company leadership, boards of directors, and stockholders. Although the same study ranked the perceived future importance of events to corporations' marketing efforts as increasing from 29 to 36 percent year-over-year, only 22 percent of respondents considered event marketing as the vehicle that provides the best return on investment (ROI), second to Web marketing, at 40 percent. The results indicate that there is great recognition in the marketing community that events provide outstanding opportunities to reach new and existing customers in deep and immersive ways. They also infer that event-marketing efforts are expensive, evidenced by the perception of a decreased ROI. It is essential, therefore, that organizers work tirelessly and collaboratively to maximize the effectiveness and efficiency of a sponsor's relationship with their event. Notwithstanding the modest overall growth of sponsorships in turbulent years, sports events are not immune to economic,

[2]http://www.mpiweb.org/Libraries/NTA-Reports/EventView_2010.pdf

social, and political pressures. They have, however, been proven to be powerful, effective, and compelling marketing tools because they are complex, multidisciplinary, multisensory, involving, and, when properly activated, motivational. To attendees and guests, a sports event may be enjoyed as a competitive contest, a live entertainment event, a television, radio, or Web-streaming broadcast, a social activity, or a meeting place to strengthen business ties. To a sponsor, they can be all of these, plus targeted, opportunistic, and high-impact advertising vehicles, promotional platforms, product demonstration and sampling opportunities, sales generators, forums for customer interactivity, and even fundraisers for a company's charitable endeavors.

Figure 6.5 lists some of the most often mentioned sponsor benefits that partner companies seek from sports events. They are presented in no particular order of significance, because the relative importance of these features will vary widely even among the sponsors of the same event. The first four—exposure, customer hospitality, sales opportunities, and fundraising for corporate causes—are sponsor benefits derived directly from an event. The organizer should carefully consider, during the negotiating process, how a prospective partner will value each type of benefit in order to design a sponsorship package that will achieve optimal success and return on investment (see Play 7). This is particularly important because prospective sponsors will already have determined their own strategies regarding how sports events fit into their marketing portfolio and how they will evaluate opportunities that work best for them.

Direct Sponsor Benefits

- Exposure
    - In-event advertising
    - Off-facility advertising
    - Social media, online, and app advertising
    - Product placement
    - Promotions
    - Publicity (media coverage, social network buzz)
- Customer hospitality
    - Event tickets
    - Reception/party invitations
- Sales opportunities
    - Direct sales
    - Product demonstrations
    - Sampling opportunities
    - Web links to and from event website
    - Database access (e.g., lists of attendees, survey respondents, mailing lists)
- Fundraising for corporate causes

Associative Benefits

- Exclusivity
- Ownership (de facto or perceived)
- Prestige and reputation
- Pass-through rights

Figure 6.5 What Sponsors Really Want from Sports Events

SIDELINE STORY

Xerox as an "Event Investor"

"Xerox has adopted the investment model approach to partnerships. Prior to 2009, the company bought sponsorships to use as hospitality and entertainment vehicles for customers and prospects," according to IEG's white paper *Invest, Don't Buy: A Smarter Way to Sponsor*. Rather than simply buying a package of sponsor benefits, IEG's paper describes how Xerox's adopted strategy supports its brand and meets these objectives:

- Apply unexpected and innovative ways of activating the brand and incorporating event partnerships into the company's own brand advertising.
- Reinforce closer business relationships with the event properties that Xerox sponsors.
- Provide VIP hospitality at events that surprises its clients

Three of the associative benefits listed in the figure—exclusivity, ownership, and prestige/reputation—are properties that may be associated with a sponsorship, but that will provide little in the way of easily measured results without formal studies being conducted, such as through the use of focus groups, intercept surveys, or the distribution, collection, and tabulation of audience questionnaires. These associative benefits reinforce the effectiveness of the more direct benefits, and can add considerable intangible value to the relationship between sponsor and event. As will be further described in this chapter, the associative benefit of pass-through rights can offer sponsors tangible cost savings, as well as the perception of a strong relationship with an event, in the minds of their customers.

IEG, which helps clients develop better relationships and results through sports and other entertainment properties, advises that sponsors should not view their association with events as "buying sponsorships," but rather, embrace more of an investment strategy in their event partnerships. "A buyer acquires something for limited use or to serve a single purpose—an arms-length transaction," states *Invest, Don't Buy: A Smarter Way to Sponsor*, an IEG white paper.[3] "An investor seeks to maximize its return, exploring and developing multiple ways in which it can earn dividends, and working in concert with the investment company."

This strategic shift from buyer to investor profoundly affects how companies define their sponsorship objectives in the sports event marketplace. IEG likens the increased emphasis on activation to the growth of information technology (IT) in the corporate culture. "Just as forward-thinking companies are re-engineering their technology infrastructure from top to bottom to become more interconnected, efficient, and effective, so must they redesign their sponsorship programs to optimize and better integrate partnerships, and align them behind growth and enterprise-wide impact."

Exposure—Advertising and Promotion

For new and emerging products and companies, exposure is frequently one of the most valuable components of the event sponsorship experience, although most established companies

[3] "Invest, Don't Buy: A Smarter Way to Sponsor" (c) 2011 IEG, LLC. 640 N. LaSalle, Suite 450, Chicago, IL 60654-3186. www.sponsorship.com. p. 3.

also recognize the value that can be realized by exposing their brands at sports events. Exposure opportunities at sports events abound and are most often manifest in advertising, promotion, and publicity programs, all basic and familiar pillars of the traditional marketing mix.

As previously mentioned, advertising opportunities are among the oldest forms of purchased exposure at sports events. It is widely accepted that repetition of advertising aids in viewer, listener, or reader recall, suggesting the repeated placement of ads in order for them to have their intended effect. However, some singular advertising opportunities at sports events can make more lasting impressions because, in effect, they are repetitive. Advertising signage within the audience's field of view may be seen repeatedly and over prolonged periods of time, requiring some modification in how value is normally measured for more traditional television, radio, or print advertising. In these more conventional forms, once an ad has aired or the page has been turned, the majority of its impact dissipates. Advertising opportunities during an event, however, can deliver impressions continuously and with varying impact throughout the two or three hours spectators are in the venue. On television, a single advertising location in the event venue comes into and out of view repeatedly throughout the program. Sponsors and their agencies have been measuring this effect in regard to television broadcasts for many years. Simply, the number of signage impressions can be multiplied by the number of seconds the ad is visible on television. This philosophy can be extended, to some degree, to a live audience as well. The most valuable advertising location will be in the place that the spectators will be looking the most often.

Another dynamic that greatly enhances the value of advertising signage at sports events is the degree to which its exposure is reinforced by other forms of a sponsor's advertising, promotions, and messages during the program. Public address announcements that recognize a partner's company or product, accompanied by logos displayed on the video scoreboard provide additional repetition and may aid in spectators' recall of the advertising. With even mid-size college and professional venues almost universally providing video playback capabilities on the scoreboard, the judicious airing of commercial spots for the live audience can provide bonus impressions and further reinforce the impact of static display signage. With the audience already familiar, prepared, and receptive to a sponsor's message, on-field or in-stand promotions can be all the more effective.

The different forms of advertising messages during the course of a sports event may actually aid in consumer recall beyond the effects of simple repetition. The Nordhielm/Dual Process Model of Advertising Repetition Effects, developed by Christie L. Nordhielm of the J.L. Kellogg Graduate School of Management at Northwestern University, proposes that the positive effect of repetition for some advertisements may actually begin to decline after three to 10 appearances, an effect known as *wearout*. At first, Nordhielm explains, repetition generates "familiarity and positive effect, but subsequent exposures eventually lead to wearout." Nordhielm's study ascertained that the practice of developing different forms and executions of an advertising message, with some number of common features such as the logo and brand name, but varying other components of the advertising vehicle, can greatly delay the onset of consumer wearout. It can be argued, then, that an advertising execution such as signage at an event can be reinforced and its effect on the audience enhanced with various complementary activities such as promotions, public address announcements, and direct sales activities such as sampling and product demonstrations, taking advantage of the benefits of repetition, and reducing or avoiding the effects of wearout.

Valuable advertising exposure may also be incorporated on the competitive field of play, on score clocks and timing devices, static or electronic signage bordering the playing surface, at start and finish lines, and behind goals, player benches, dugouts, and penalty boxes. The relative value of each of these positions is, again, determined by the frequency with which signage is in the spectators' or television viewers' active field of vision. During competitive downtime, such as intermissions, and between heats, innings, or matches, special video features and promotions and on-field fan activities may be "presented by" a sponsor that is both visually and verbally recognized during the promotion.

SIDELINE STORY

Gatorade's Event Exposure Strategy

Gatorade may be one of the most visible and effective companies to put the technique of multiple and strategically placed advertising messages into action at hundreds of sports events across North America and beyond. Gatorade's overall objective is to be the world leader in fueling athletic performance and working with professional athletes and leagues is one of the many ways for us to connect with athletes," says John Shumate, manager of brand strategy and marketing for the Gatorade division of PepsiCo. "The brand looks to partner with the most visible, influential, and highest-profile athletes and sports properties that will communicate to our core consumers that fueling your performance starts from the inside." Gatorade's partnerships include the National Football League (NFL), the Bowl Championship Series (BCS), and more than two dozen universities in the NCAA's Southeastern Conference (SEC) and Atlantic Coast Conference (ACC).

"At Gatorade, we look at every sports property and athlete spokesperson as a partner, not simply a sponsorship opportunity. Our relationships go deeper than an ad buy or a logo on the wall and we choose partners we can work with over the long term. We believe this approach gets us a much stronger return on our investment," adds Shumate. Gatorade's relationship with the NFL is a case study in exposure strategy. Every Gatorade bottle on the sidelines of all 32 teams and every cooler is a highly noticeable Gatorade orange. Players drink from Gatorade cups and wipe excess perspiration with towels sporting the brand's logo. Additional signage such as advertising and videoboard logo appearances are supported by players in full view of the live and television audience using these branded items of equipment through the entire length of the event. It further supports these efforts through partnerships with individual athletes that carry its message through to digital marketing, social media, and branded content, ensuring that Gatorade is top of mind as a performance brand not only at the event itself, but on the way to and from the venue, as well as at home and on mobile devices.

A sponsor's exposure benefits can also extend well before and beyond event day, both in advertising purchased by the organizer and in space arranged by the sponsors themselves in fulfillment of their activation strategies. Event advertising placed by the organizer may acknowledge just a primary, title, or presenting sponsor (see "Exposure—Publicity" on page 136), or may include a rotating list of other participating companies. Event promotions that at once help to sell tickets and offer dollars-off incentives with the purchase of sponsor products can provide both exposure and sales opportunities as direct benefits of sponsorship. Many event organizers also express appreciation for their sponsors' participation by scheduling a postevent "thank you" ad in area newspapers, sports periodicals, and in trade publications. This is a particularly effective practice when the ad is placed alongside the postevent editorial coverage of the event.

Properly designed online advertising acknowledging event partners has become a must in today's sponsorship environment. Potentially more effective than print advertising and static signage, online advertising provides sponsors with the opportunity to engage fans by strategically linking to the event's most-visited Web pages. Sponsors don't just want to be noticed on the event's website. They want those ad placements to provide interactive hyperlinks to their own websites, promotions, virtual product demonstrations, and direct sales platforms. The placement of these interactive ads can also be strategic. Restaurants might be most noticed on the webpage that provides directions to the event site, with a click-through to peruse their menu or print a special coupon for savings on the way to or from the event. Banks and financial services companies might enjoy the most targeted exposure by advertising on the page where fans order event tickets or merchandise, providing a click-through to apply for a new credit card.

Interactive advertising is no longer limited to web pages. The profusion of tablets and smart phones has encouraged the development of thousands of specialized applications ("apps") that organizers can use to enhance the fan experience before, during, and after events. Downloaded before or during an event, apps provide content such as maps and guides, schedule information, game rules, athlete and team information, background features, and other data suitable for reading on small portable devices. Advertising on these platforms might connect directly to a sponsor's website, a special offer, or provide information on where to find the sponsor's attraction, sampling, or demonstration area at the event site.

Exposure—Product Placement

One of the most valuable, sought-after, and closely protected advantages of sponsorship is the benefit of product placement. Sponsors attach great importance to the notion that their products, to the exclusion of any competitors, are those that will be used by the sports event organizer or are available to the public at, or through, the event. Food, beverage, and beer sponsors will require their brands be available at every possible venue location. Apparel manufacturers will likewise demand that their lines of merchandise be those affixed with the event's logo and sold at the event site. A cap manufacturer will want to see its logo on the side of the event caps worn by athletes during press conferences. Any product category that can be imagined to be useful in preparing for and executing an event is likely to have product placement provisions tied into the sponsorship deal—from airlines, car rentals, and hotels to telecommunications services, computers, and office equipment. In a returned spirit of partnership, of course, the event organizer can negotiate for preferred pricing on these products and services or accept some portion of an event's requirements as part of a VIK arrangement. Product placement requirements may also involve other manifestations unique to the product category. Examples include soft drink sponsor names on beverage cups and squeeze bottles, the use of sponsor vehicles in and around the event venue, and staff wardrobe sporting logos integrating the event and the manufacturer.

Sponsors often provide their products or services for consumer sweepstakes, promotions, and even awards for the athletes, to create excitement and exposure at the event and in publicity generated immediately following. A lucky fan may win an all-expenses-paid trip to a future event provided by an airline and hotel sponsor, or the free use of a smart phone with service for a year. When Century 21 Realty sponsored Major League Baseball's Home Run Derby, the top scoring hitter won a house worth $250,000 from Century 21 Realty for a sweepstakes contestant drawn at random. The "Most Valuable Player" at the Super Bowl wins a car presented postgame by General Motors. *(Caution: There are strict guidelines governing gifts, prizes, and awards to athletes, particularly amateurs and students, which could affect their future competitive status. Event organizers must be fully informed of any restrictions on a participant's acceptance of a sponsor gift or award.)* These benefits provide sponsors with exposure opportunities that are even more powerful than advertising, in the form of an endorsement demonstrating the event's strong preference for using a particular sponsor's product. The most innovative and compelling of these promotions can also add exceptional entertainment value and public and media interest in the event.

SIDELINE STORY

KIA's Product Placement Coup

The NBA All-Star Weekend's Slam Dunk Championship has been a fan- and viewer-favorite for many years. NBA players vie for top honors with stylish, gravity-defying acrobatic stunts evaluated by judges and the fans. The 2011 edition of the Sprite Slam Dunk Championship was particularly memorable for the winning basket and for the marketing bonanza that followed. In the final round of the event, Los Angeles Clippers forward Blake Griffin eclipsed runner-up JaVale McGee of the Washington Wizards by successfully jumping over the hood of a silver Kia Optima automobile on his way to a spectacular slam dunk.

It is not known how much more Sprite was sold as a result of this spectacular feat, but according to CNBC.com, online car sales marketplace Edmunds.com reported that potential car buyers "were 20 percent more likely to consider a Kia car, and twice as likely to consider the Optima model the day after the broadcast." Not wasting any time, the Korean automobile manufacturer created a television commercial incorporating the stunt immediately after the event. The positive publicity generated by this clever product placement effort continued for several months, culminating with an online auction of the car actually used in the Slam Dunk Championship to benefit "Stand Up to Cancer."

Exposure—Publicity

Sponsors spend millions of dollars each year to generate publicity for their products because they know that media coverage is generally perceived by the public as more objective and credible, and holds the public's attention for a longer period of time than a typical advertisement. The most effective way for a company to consistently capitalize on the publicity generated by a sports event is to literally appear within its name, as a *title* or *presenting* sponsor. Title sponsors are companies or brands whose names appear before or within the name of a sports event, such as tennis's *Sony Open, McDonald's All American Basketball Games,* the NASCAR's *Sprint Cup*, golf's *FedEx Cup, and hockey's Bridgestone NHL Winter Classic*. Presenting sponsors, companies with identities linked to the end of an event name, such as the Big Ten Fan Fest presented by Dr. Pepper, the NHL SuperSkills competition presented by Honda, and the WNBA Finals presented by Boost Mobile, also hope to increase their public exposure through a close association with the name of the event. Companies that invest heavily in title and presenting sponsorships recognize the publicity value offered by their elevated association, appreciating the likelihood that their brand will be routinely mentioned in news reports and sports articles during the normal coverage of an event. Title and presenting sponsorships command premium sponsorship fees for the organizer because of all of the extra public recognition the partner receives. These top-tier sponsors benefit from the inclusion of their identities within event logos and/or word marks, in advertising, on tickets, in information sent to participants and guests, and on virtually all printed and digital material generated by the organizer.

Title and presenting sponsorships supported by supplemental activation budgets tend to reach deepest into the public consciousness. However, this is not the only way that companies develop opportunities for enhanced publicity through their event partnerships. Sponsors often participate in intriguing and involving team, player, and fan promotions that can capture the imagination and active interest of both the media and the public. Insurance company Liberty Mutual announced the launch of the "Million Dollar Game" promotion for which the company offered a hefty financial donation to the charity of choice for qualifying college football teams that successfully competed in a regular season game without a single penalty call.

Watching an average spectator attempt a difficult athletic feat for an impressive cash prize, for example, has been a popular feature of major televised sports events. Dr Pepper and Pizza Hut staged a "Throw for Dough" promotion during the national broadcast of the ACC football championship game offering a scholarship to the student contestant who could throw the most footballs through a small hole at the top of an oversized Dr Pepper can. Toyota offered a free truck if a fan could score a basket from mid-court during halftime at a Portland Trailblazers game (both the fan and the team won that night). Some of sponsored promotions in which a finalist qualifies for a chance to win an astronomical cash prize are frequently designed as "insurance prizes" to keep the sponsor's costs within reason. That is, since the odds of someone winning the prize is low, but not zero, the sponsor can purchase an insurance policy to protect against the possibility of having to pay the enormous sum. Several agencies specialize in offering sponsors and organizers insurance prize policies, with premiums ranging from 10 to 50 percent of the prize value, depending on the difficulty of the contest. Obviously, the insurance agency will require involvement in the setting of contest rules to ensure there is a very good probability that the contestant will fail. As might be expected, the less difficult the test of skill and the greater value of the payoff, the higher the insurance premium will be. Alternatively, the sponsor can self-insure the prize by setting aside the full amount in advance if it desires to better the odds that a contestant will succeed.

Significant donations made to a worthy cause as a result of a sports event sponsorship can also generate significant media interest if properly promoted. Funds may be raised as a donated percentage of ticket sales, through silent auctions, via contributions made by fans or viewers and matched by the sponsor, or as a percentage of sponsor product sales during a specified period of time. Charitable promotions can firmly and favorably position both the sponsor and the event in the public's perception, are explored further on page 140.

SIDELINE STORY

2K Sports Takes Event Promotions Home

Baseball fan Wade McGilberry won $1 million by pitching a perfect game without setting foot in the stadium, thanks to Major League Baseball (MLB) licensee 2K Sports. Perfect games—a no-hit shutout in which the absolute minimum of 27 batters is faced—are among the rarest of baseball achievements, having only been accomplished by 23 pitchers as chronicled in more than 135 years of baseball record-keeping. No pitcher has achieved this feat more than once. The makers of the popular MLB 2K10 video game offered a million-dollar prize to the first perfect game played starting on the first day of its release, and to its surprise, McGilberry earned his reward on Day One of the promotion. Although 2K Sports enjoyed a significant burst of publicity for the stunt, having the promotion begin and end the same day was likely not what it had in mind. The licensee repeated the promotion for the release of MLB 2K11 the following year, but made several changes to ensure a longer life to the publicity it would generate and a better return on the investment. The most significant alteration provided for a warm-up period, allowing players to practice for several weeks between the first day of the game's release and the beginning of the promotion.

Customer Hospitality

Companies have long regarded sports events as excellent opportunities to extend hospitality and demonstrate appreciation to customers and important clients, dealers, distributors, franchisees, agents, and top salespeople. The George P. Johnson (GPJ) EventView study[4] concluded that events offer experiential platforms that "accelerate and deepen brand relationships" between customers and those staging or providing access to the events. An earlier GPJ study noted that events help sponsors close business deals faster, with sports marketing citied as a major "lead maturation" opportunity (i.e., effective venues to help convert business prospects into customers). For this reason, sponsors that most value sports events as customer hospitality vehicles expect access to what are perceived as "the best seats in the house" for the purpose of entertaining important guests and prospects. Customer hospitality is of particular importance to companies that transact most of their business with other businesses (commonly known as "B2B" companies). The average monetary value of a B2B sale by a company to its customer can be significantly greater than that of a sale from a business to a consumer. Therefore, the marketing efforts and dollars B2B companies apply to developing each new customer, and servicing existing ones, are often much greater than those of consumer companies. The experiential aspects of event sponsorship—that is, the ability to host "hot" prospects and reward current customers—is of increased importance and often represents a greater percentage of total sponsorship spending for B2B companies. Treating special guests with tickets for preferred seating locations, passes to private receptions or invitation-only hospitality suites, the ability to meet the athletes, and other exclusive and unique considerations can put B2B sponsors at a great advantage over their competition.

Sales Opportunities

Sponsors that have invested significantly in the success of a sports event expect organizers will, in the spirit of good partnership, afford them with opportunities to offset some of their costs with direct sales or the development of potential future sales. Most often, these objectives are achieved by engaging in on-site activities such as product demonstrations, sampling, couponing, or premium giveaways. Organizers who actively help a sponsor sell more of its products at an event are actually helping themselves. The more business a sponsor can develop at an event, whether manifest by direct sales or as leads for subsequent sales, the more likely the company will deem the investment a success and want to return as a partner for future programs.

For some companies, sports event venues offer an attractive marketplace for direct sales of their products, the most common being marketers of food, beverages, apparel, and collectibles. Other products and services also offer special event-day sales promotions and subscription drives. Bank of America, for example, a financial services company offering "affinity" credit cards, payment instruments that display the applicant's choice of sports team or other association on the face of the card, frequently offers free and exclusive event merchandise to attendees who apply for a card at the event. Recognizing the highly motivated viewing habits of sports fans, cable and satellite television services often offer special sports packages on a trial basis to those who apply at an event for their services. A mobile communications company that offers web-enabled devices can similarly promote the fan's ability to use its product to access scores of games in progress.

For many other marketers, both the organizer and the sponsor must apply some creativity to make the direct contact opportunity relevant for the consumer and potentially profitable for the

---

[4]http://www.mpiweb.org/Libraries/NTA-Reports/EventView_2010.pdf

sponsor. Although it is unlikely, for example, that an automobile dealer will actually sell a car at a sports event, it can offer a meaningful product demonstration by conducting test drives in the parking lot as fans arrive for the event. Fans who take the test drive may be given a voucher good for a free gift redeemable at the dealership, thus encouraging a visit by the consumer.

Many organizers offer sponsors areas for product demonstrations and sampling on the event facility's public concourses, in kiosks sprinkled through the event site, or in special tents or booths. The BolderBoulder 10K road race held each May in Boulder, Colorado, for example, opens a RaceDay Expo covering an entire athletic field with tents offering free samples of healthy lifestyle products and purchasable items for the 50,000 runners and the 100,000 spectators that cheer them on. The entrance concourse at the south gate of Indianapolis's Lucas Oil Stadium is a 26,000 square foot showroom for electronics retailer h.h.gregg, featuring sizable, interactive large-screen television displays where fans can check their fantasy football statistics, facilitated by a sales staff who can instruct visitors on the latest features of the newest devices and technologies. Many sports fan festivals include memorabilia areas for collectors sponsored by trading card companies such as Topps and Upper Deck, with such offers as a special card or set available only at the event. Or, a local restaurant may provide coupons and samples of appetizers to event attendees designed to drive traffic to their business location.

Marketers discover that sports events are effective places to reach their customers because attendee demographics are generally predictable and fans are in a highly excited, and therefore receptive, state of mind. The more the sponsor can associate its product or offer with the event itself, such as Bank of America's affinity cards, the better it can leverage that excitement and receptivity to influence sales.

SIDELINE STORY

Visa's Sponsorship Worldview

Visa, one the world's leading payment technology companies, has utilized the power of some of the world's greatest sports events to create stronger partnerships with their consumer and business clients. The company's association with the Olympic Games as a Worldwide Sponsor since 1986 has reinforced both global brand recognition for Visa, and significant sales opportunities as the only credit card accepted for event-related transactions such as tickets and merchandise sales. Its rights are not restricted just to the Olympic Games themselves, but also extend exclusively to all 205 National Olympic committees and each of their teams across the world. Recognizing the global appeal of football (or, soccer as it is known in the United States), Visa also partnered with the FIFA World Cup. In the words of the company's fact sheet on Visa's Global Sponsorship Portfolio, FIFA and Visa share "market leadership, global ubiquity, acceptance, and public awareness," making them ideal partners for both organizations' international ambitions for growth.

In addition to promoting card usage through payment arrangements with the Olympics and FIFA World Cup, Visa also offers "unique experiences" that fulfill some of sports fans' greatest desires. A "Go Football Experience" that was offered at the 2010 FIFA World Cup in South Africa enabled a limited number of Visa customers to tour the stadium before the match, or visit the playing field during halftime. Similar "unique experiences" are offered at the NFL's Super Bowl, enabling fans to visit the field and other behind-the-scenes areas otherwise inaccessible to the public.

Sponsors increasingly seek access to an event organizer's digital assets to generate sales and promotional opportunities. In addition to placing links on the event's website that can drive traffic to the sponsor's own digital platforms, partners often perceive great value in being granted use of the organizer's databases of event ticket buyers, guests, survey respondents, and invitation or mailing lists. Sponsors can use these databases to proactively contact fans who have demonstrated loyalty to a sport or event with offers customized to their interests. Accessing mailing addresses may be attractive to some sponsors, email addresses and mobile phone numbers for text messaging for others. It is also not improper for an event organizer to request a return courtesy—access to a sponsor's database for the purpose of sending ticket offers to a defined segment of its customers.

Fundraising for Corporate Causes

Some socially conscious companies combine their commercial involvement in a sports event with an effort to raise awareness and revenue for important causes and quality-of-life social programs. Whether the sponsor views the fundraising component of its participation as simply a public relations gesture or as part of its corporate philanthropic philosophy, sports events offer outstanding opportunities for doing good beyond the stadium gates.

Many sports event organizations are themselves not-for-profit associations that exist to promote a particular sport, lifestyle, or quality-of-life benefit. The International Special Olympics, the New York Road Runners Club (organizers of the New York City Marathon, among a number of events), the many national Olympic committees and national governing bodies, Little League, and hundreds of other not-for-profit sports associations are also organizers that stage sports events to promote their movements and messages. Although sponsor dollars are required to put on their events, most of their business models include raising needed revenues to fund operations, awareness programs, research and development, and other cause-related activities. Some events, like the *AIDS Run for a Cure*, are activities staged exclusively to achieve philanthropic and social missions, the sports event providing a compelling backdrop for the worthy cause.

Sponsors understand the enormous public relations benefits of funding cause-related activities and many reinforce their marketing investments with additional grants from their philanthropic budgets to ensure a sizable return for a charity. In addition to maintaining their good intentions, many corporate supporters may still want to take advantage of the rightfully attendant sponsor benefits that are due them through their association with an event regardless of from which budget the money originates.

The benefits of being associated with a not-for-profit cause or movement are well understood by event organizers as well. It is often the charitable aspect of an event that spurs ticket buyers into action and can attenuate one of the key components of a ticket-buyer's hesitation—price sensitivity. As long as the cost of admission remains within a range that is not completely unreasonable, members of the ticket-buying public will respond more favorably to an event whose proceeds benefit a charity with which they feel some affinity, than to a similar program without a not-for-profit beneficiary. Charitable objectives are especially helpful in generating ticket buyers—as well as athletes—for events that, without this association, might otherwise be of marginal interest to the public-at-large.

Associative Benefits—Exclusivity

With some few exceptions, business partners expect that their financial participation in an event will buy them some level of exclusivity—the ability to promote their company or brand without the interfering presence of their competition. This is not a universal truth, as demonstrated by

SIDELINE STORY

College Basketball on Deck

When the North Carolina Tar Heels and Michigan State Spartans took to the basketball court before a live national television audience on ESPN on Veterans Day 2011, they set sail on a new concept in college sports and cause-related event marketing. A multimillion-dollar temporary outdoor basketball arena, including court, video screens, grandstands, lighting, and public safety enhancements, was installed on the flight deck of the *USS Carl Vinson* aircraft carrier docked in San Diego Harbor to host the first Quicken Loans Carrier Classic.

The event "started as the spark of an idea in 2002 from Mark Hollis, the athletic director at Michigan State," recalls Morale Entertainment producer Mike Whalen. "Mark mentioned the idea to his coach Tom Izzo." Whalen and Morale, a not-for-profit whose "mission is to entertain and celebrate the men and women of the Armed Forces and to inspire appreciation and support across the United States," were brought on board to bring together all the elements—and to brave the financial risk—for the game. "The event was financed by the selling of sponsorships to many like-minded businesses and organizations who believed in the mission of Morale Entertainment, of celebrating our troops on Veterans Day," Whalen recalls. To achieve the mission of the event, however, television coverage would be essential. Sponsorship revenues helped Morale fund the purchase of broadcast time on ESPN (see Play 13), which, in turn, provided exceptional value to the sponsors and fulfilled the mission of creating a national spectacle to salute the military.

The results for sponsor-supporters Quicken Loans, State Farm, the US Navy, and ESPN were nothing short of stunning. The live audience of 8,000 seated on grandstands built on the ship's flight deck included President and Mrs. Obama, Secretary of the Navy Ray Mabus, and representatives of every branch of the US Armed Forces. The novelty of the setting and power of the message generated the highest-rated and most-viewed regular season college basketball match on the network in years, drawing almost 3.9 million viewers.

events such as auto racing, in which the participants themselves are individually sponsored, supported by companies that often conflict with the sponsors of the overall event. It is, however, true that although exclusivity is not a characteristic that can be ascribed a measurable financial value, its presence can constitute a significant portion of the sponsorship price tag. Sponsors understand that this premium is a necessary component of their fee. They know that once they enter into an agreement with a sports event, the organizer is no longer able to accept revenues from any other company or brand within their defined and protected category.

When a business partner enters into an agreement with an event organizer, the contract should define the exact corporate identity being granted sponsorship rights. For example, is it the company being recognized as an official sponsor (e.g., Anheuser-Busch), or is it a specific brand (e.g., Bud Light)? Because many companies market multiple brands and product lines, the agreement should also note the categories of exclusivity being protected by the sponsorship. For example, the corporate parent of an event's soft drink sponsor may also distribute snack foods and own chains of fast food, or quick-service, restaurants (QSRs). Sponsors often wish to prohibit the event organizer from entering into relationships with companies that compete with their other brands or lines of business, even though they are not represented at the event. Organizers, in turn, often respond by seeking to negotiate a higher sponsorship fee as recompense for the lost revenue opportunity forced by excluding these other business categories from a possible event partnership.

The exclusivity sponsors demand goes far beyond the walls of the event venue. A sponsor's exclusive rights must be protected in sales promotions, advertising, and other activities that take place before the event or outside of the facility. Organizers must pursue the perpetrators of "ambush marketing" activities, efforts undertaken by nonsponsor companies to give the public an impression of their being associated with an event. Common ambush marketing activities are characterized by the unauthorized use of the event name, logos and images, or terminology and artwork simply suggestive of an association with the event. Illicit techniques include the use of event tickets for promotional purposes, the creation and sale of unauthorized merchandise, and advertising that implies a relationship with an event without using any of the organizers' trademarks. Organizers with the resources to protect themselves and their intellectual property (i.e., logos, trademarks, artwork, etc.), frequently retain legal representation to stop ambush marketing activities that infringe on the rights of an event and its sponsors. The most common response after discovering such activities is to quickly identify the infringer and to have legal representatives send a "cease and desist" notice. This is most often in the form a letter from an attorney that outlines the believed infraction and instructs the ambusher to cease these activities within a certain period of time or risk legal action. It is often sufficient to stop blatant trademark infractions outright, or at least forces the ambusher to distance the themes of their promotional activities from the event. It is important that an attorney handle these communications to ensure the organizer is prepared to take the complaint to the courts if necessary, and to demonstrate to sponsors that their promotional rights are being actively protected.

Not all ambush activities are blatant infringements of an organizer's intellectual property rights. Over the years, many nonsponsor companies have identified perfectly legal ways to benefit from sports events without directly participating as a sponsor. Although the authors of this book do not condone such activities, as they do not accrue to the benefit of the event, it is important to understand how nonsponsors take advantage of these opportunities. With this understanding, organizers will not waste time pursuing legal options on baseless grounds, and will protect their rights, and those of their sponsors, by offering fans better value, entertainment, and promotional alternatives than the ambusher.

Strictly speaking, nonsponsor companies can stage private parties, receptions, meetings, or customer-oriented programs during the days leading up to and during an event as long as they do not infer a direct relationship and use no intellectual property of the organizer. It is easiest for a nonsponsor company to stage these activities in existing retail locations, hotels, restaurants, convention centers, and other places of public assembly and there is little an event organizer can do to stop them, even in close proximity to an event site. In these indoor locations, the visibility of nonsponsor events near the event site can be limited to some extent with a "clean zone" ordinance, as discussed next.

Nonsponsor companies will often seek permits to erect tents for parties, hospitality, or product sampling and demonstrations close to event sites, counting on the greatly increased number of fans and passersby in the area before, during, and after events. It is to the benefit of the organizer and its sponsors to work with the host city on establishing a "clean zone" ordinance that prohibits this more publicly visible, opportunistic activity in the immediate environs of the event site. Many large cities accustomed to hosting events already have some form of ordinance in existence that can be applied or modified for this purpose. These ordinances also limit the degree to which advertising or 'event signage can be added to temporary structures, or to permanent structures on surfaces not usually used for advertising. Establishing clean zones add great value to a sponsorship package, and the ability to obtain one for major events should be part of any host city negotiation before an event is awarded.

Billboards and other advertising locations near the event site are rentable by anyone, including nonevent sponsors. Organizers should be sure to identify billboards that are in clear view of an event site and encourage sponsors to lease them in order to block competitors from these attractive advertising locations. One of the most bedeviling developments facing event organizers today is the increasing frequency with which event sponsors and the marketing partners of a host venue are direct competitors. Conflicts between facility signage advertisers and competitive event sponsors are not new. The economically necessary practice of facilities renaming themselves, or sections of their building after one or more major sponsors, however, has created many more noticeable and high-stakes conflicts than those that existed between the signage advertisers of a facility and an event sponsor.

The economic realities of both the sports and facilities businesses have manifested themselves in the increasingly common practice of selling title sponsorship of new and existing sports venues to a corporate partner. This partnership is highly valuable to both the owner of the venue and the sponsor that buys the right to name it. The sponsor may contribute millions of dollars over the term of its contract to help finance construction or reduce some of the debt incurred during development of the facility. In return, the sponsor knows that thousands of newspaper articles, sports reports, and game broadcasts will make regular and frequent reference to the name of the facility without any additional purchase of advertising in those media. Millions of ticket buyers who enter the building will also be surrounded by the name and logo of the presenting sponsor on exterior signage, ticket faces, scoreboards, even highway signs directing drivers to its parking lots. There is probably no better or more positive way for a sponsor to become a household byword than by lending its name to one of a community's most exciting places of gathering.

How does this level of ubiquitous corporate identification affect a sports event organizer's ability to protect the organizer's own sponsor's rights? Like many relationships, it's complicated. A sports event's existing sponsor that competes with the naming rights partner of a facility will be concerned that the building sponsor will receive greater publicity exposure than it will. This is often the case. The enormous investment made by a facility's naming sponsor may well stretch the company's marketing budget to the point that additional sponsor opportunities may no longer be affordable. Since the namesake sponsor of a sports event facility will enjoy thousands of incidental references in the media, it correctly presumes that this recognition will provide additional exposure benefits before the fans of visiting events. A naming rights sponsor knows that its overarching presence can also effectively discourage competitor companies from entering into agreements with event organizers leasing the venue, further protecting its exclusivity. Naming sponsors, therefore, might not believe there is any need to participate as sponsors of teams or events inside their facility.

Event organizers should not be surprised if their sponsor values an organizer's event less overall at a competitively named venue, and the agreement between the sponsor and organizer may anticipate such circumstances and remedies. The sponsor may avoid using the event for customer hospitality. The sponsor may seek a reduced sponsorship fee or more opportunities away from the event site. For sponsors of televised events, they may push for more on-air visibility and commercial time. Whatever accommodation is made, there is little question that event sponsors will be uncomfortable in buildings with a competitive naming rights partner. It is up to the event organizer to provide additional value to overcome this understandable uneasiness. Organizers seeking new partners, however, are likely to find it difficult to impossible to attract a new sponsor in the same category as the host facility's naming rights sponsor.

Apart from building naming rights arrangements, sports facilities enjoy a large number of other partnerships of varying magnitude, ranging from gate, section, concourse, and club spon-

SIDELINE STORY

Let's Meet at the Game. Where Is That Again?

Sports events organizers can usually count on modern host facilities being maintained in good structural condition. What a stadium or arena might be called on event day, however, can be different from the name on the day the lease was signed. Sports events used to be held in places with romantic names like Boston Garden and Jack Murphy Stadium, the Montreal Forum and Mile High Stadium. Boston Garden is gone and replaced by a new arena that was called Shawmut Center until just weeks before its opening, but changed to Fleet Center named for a northeastern US bank that acquired the original namesake sponsor company. Fleet Center became TD Banknorth Center after those two banks merged, and a few years later, just TD Garden. Jack Murphy Stadium remains standing, and was renamed Qualcomm Stadium after the wireless chip maker in its home town of San Diego, California. The stadium was temporarily renamed Snapdragon Stadium to promote Qualcomm's mobile processor in an effort to reach an estimated 30 million television viewers during the 2011 college football bowl season.

The venerated Montreal Forum, built in 1924, could not withstand the growing economic pressures of the sports and entertainment business and was replaced in 1996 by an entirely new facility called the Molson Centre, later renamed the Bell Centre a few short years later. Mile High Stadium was razed and its replacement, Invesco Field at Mile High, created a furor that mobilized both the business and political communities in Denver, Colorado. The controversy was not caused because the old building was destroyed, but because the name of the new stadium bore the identity of a financial services company and not solely the moniker of its ancestor. Perhaps reflective of the community's sensitivity, for the first three years of the stadium's existence, the *Denver Post* referred to the facility only as Mile High Stadium. Less than a decade later, the stadium was again renamed Sports Authority Field at Mile High, after the locally based sporting goods retailer.

Miami's football and entertainment facility, opened under the name Joe Robbie Stadium, may have one of the longest histories of brand identities. In addition to bearing the name of the original owner of the NFL Miami Dolphins, the building has been known as Pro Player Stadium after a now-defunct sporting goods licensee, Dolphins Stadium, Dolphin Stadium, one year as Landshark Stadium, to be identified with musician Jimmy Buffet's beer brand, and Sun Life Stadium, named for a Canadian insurance company. After the last naming rights deal expires, the stadium will take on a new name as Sun Life exits the US market.

sors, to official soft drinks and beers, to lesser sponsorships that may include advertising signage and other exposure benefits. Some of these facility sponsor associations may also pose significant conflicts for event sponsors, especially in the case of soft drinks and other products or services that may have exclusive rights in the building. In most cases, however, event sponsors are accustomed to the notion that sports event facilities will contain a large amount of advertising and sponsor signage, some of which may conflict with their own.

Many stadium and arena operators have the flexibility to allow organizers to cover or replace signage belonging to some of their sponsors if the event is of sufficient magnitude and potential profitability and if the event will be awarded on the basis of a bid process that requires those rights. Even in such rare cases, the identity of the facility's naming rights sponsor is usually respected. (The Olympics is one of the few sports events that require even the name of the host facilities to be free of corporate identification.)

Presuming that the competitive issues between an event's sponsor and a host facility's namesake can be overcome, organizers are well advised to determine what restrictions a facility's manager will place on an event's corporate supporters before confirming the host venue. Beyond prohibiting the obscuration or obstruction of existing sponsor signage and displays, and insisting on pouring official beverages from their concessions (specifically soft drinks and beer), most facilities will put very few restrictions on event organizers. The sponsor that has purchased the naming rights to its building understands that it is in the venue's best interest to encourage organizers to book events there, even those with competing sponsors. Whether an existing sponsor will want to participate in an event facility named for a competing sponsor is a matter of corporate culture and strategy. Some relish the sweet irony and will expend even greater effort to generate publicity about being in "enemy territory," while others will opt to avoid being near a "competitor's building" completely.

Associative Benefits—Ownership

Sponsors are not vigilant solely about ensuring the absence of their competitors at a sports event. They also consider the degree to which other, noncompetitor business partners are present and recognized. As may be expected, the greater a sponsor's financial commitment, the more protective it will be about how its company or product will be perceived as compared with all others that are associated with the event. Sponsors will expect the organizers to protect them from excessive "clutter," a condition in which there are so many sponsors that the impact of their event identification is greatly diminished. To rise above the clutter of their fellow event partners, experienced sponsors strive to develop unique and innovative promotions or to pursue an association with specific event elements they can "own" exclusively. Such elements may include being identified as the presenting sponsor of a championship trophy, an MVP ("most valuable player") award, or some other form of participant recognition. Intermission or halftime entertainment, pregame shows, individual heats, races, or competitions, or in-venue promotions that benefit one or more fans are other components commonly offered to corporate partners that seek to rise above the sponsor clutter, even if only for a few minutes during the program.

Some companies in non–sports industries have taken event ownership to its purest form by developing, owning, and, in some cases, managing sports events themselves. Although the expense of assuming responsibility for all costs and risk is considerable, this strategy provides total control over every aspect of an event's development, management, and execution. The event may be fashioned to the exact specifications of the corporate owner, target fans of the precise demographics it seeks, and maintain a singular focus on its own goals and objectives. It may still provide opportunities for sponsorship and cross-promotions with other brands to help defray some of the costs, although some owner-sponsors prefer that 100 percent of the exposure opportunities belong to them alone. The company can customize sponsorship programs for its own business partners that can maximize sales opportunities for both. A soft drink company that owns its own sports event, for instance, might offer an opportunity for participation to a QSR to whom that company itself is a supplier. In this example, promoting the restaurants can have the secondary effect of increasing consumption of the company's own products at those locations. The corporate sports event owner can also define precisely how partners will enjoy exposure at the event and ensure that its own company or brand message dominates above its colleague organizations. As owner of the event, the company can limit consumer-directed activities to promotions that most effectively market its sports property, best enhance its sales, and control the clutter of too many advertising messages competing for the audience's attention.

SIDELINE STORY

Red Bull as a Sports Event Owner-Sponsor

Red Bull's imaginative lifestyle, music, and sports events bring to life its cutting-edge event ownership strategy to live audiences and viewers on digital and broadcast media worldwide. Lifestyle events are so integral to its marketing strategy that Red Bull's core product—an energy drink—is often nearly absent from a homepage visit to the redbullusa.com website. Many of its sports events are unique to its brand, such as The Red Bull Crashed Ice World Championship, a roller derby-style downhill ice skating competition introduced in 2001, and Red Bull Swamped, a wakeboarding race through the Louisiana bayou. Most of these events were distributed virally on digital platforms and rarely incorporate additional sponsors beyond Red Bull.

Strategic sponsor partnerships are now more commonly a part of the Red Bull–owned event portfolio. In 2006, the company purchased the MetroStars, Major League Soccer's (MLS) New York area franchise, and renamed the club the New York Red Bulls, which has attracted more than a half dozen other major sponsors. Beginning in 2012, Red Bull Media House, the company's media division, started presenting with the help of outside sponsors and advertisers the Red Bull Signature Series. This broadcast package presents some of the company's continuing portfolio, including the Crashed Ice World Championship and the X Fighters freestyle motocross event, to broader television audiences in 35 hours of programming per year on NBC and NBC Sports Network in addition to digital media platforms.

The advantages of corporate event ownership are clear. By controlling every aspect of the program, the corporate owner can ensure its dominance and avoid or manage the effects of multiple sponsor messages and clutter. Smaller-scale, precisely targeted niche events are prime candidates for corporate ownership because of their manageable cost and the relatively straightforward ability to measure the effectiveness of the program through increased sales. Grassroots and community programs involving local amateur athletes offer similarly attractive opportunities for corporate ownership by small local businesses for the same reasons—low costs easily compensated by incremental sales.

Corporate ownership of large-scale, high-budget events has not become as prevalent for a host of reasons. The financial risks are usually too great for a single company to assume. This is why sports event organizers must develop opportunities to attract multiple sponsors from a wide range of industries. In the professional and semi-professional sports world, an athlete's personal endorsement contracts can prove another obstacle to a sponsor corporation owning a sports event. Contracts signed with competitive companies can prevent a top-drawer athlete or team from appearing at a corporately owned event. In today's sports event marketplace, genuine, strategic, and effective partnerships between event organizers and corporate sponsors remain the business model standard because of the potential to realize at least a portion of the partner's corporate objectives without their assuming the financial risks of staging the entire program.

Associative Benefits—Prestige and Reputation

Another intangible benefit sought by sponsors is simply being associated with an event considered highly attractive by their most valued customers. The prestige and reputation of an event, its participating athletes, and, in some cases, its organizing entity can add significantly to its attractiveness to sponsors. The greater the public's interest in an event, the greater the hunger will be for tickets. The greater the demand for tickets, the more desirable the event will be for sponsors as an opportunity to entertain their important business guests. Prestige also adds to the effectiveness of consumer promotions and efforts that can increase the likelihood of media coverage that reinforces the association between a business partner and the event it sponsors.

This benefit becomes even more significant to companies that adopt the event investment strategy promoted by IEG in its previously referenced white paper. It states: "The criterion for a partnership investment is alignment of brand values on top of audience fit. As an investor, you must do your due diligence to understand your partner's brand: what it stands for; what its key attributes are; and its potential to impact the same elements of your brand."[5] Essentially, IEG is advising sponsors that the reputation and brand image of an event is crucial to the sponsorship evaluation and decision-making process. Further, sponsor-investors should do their due diligence to understand the passions, loyalties, and interests of the fans who most have an affinity with an event. IBM, one of IEG's many corporate clients, and a sponsor of the US Opens of golf and tennis, Wimbledon, and the National Football League, seeks partnerships with events that can engage with its current and prospective customers on an emotional level, and encourage a specific behavior—buying IBM products and services. Their investment principles appear in Figure 6.6.

Pass-Through Rights

Some sponsors whose businesses depend on the advertising or promotional efforts of other companies to bring their products to the consumer, such as retailers, media outlets, credit card brands, and software developers, among many others, favor securing pass-through rights to help make their event partnerships more efficient. Pass-through rights refer to the transference, by a sponsor, of some of its event benefits to its suppliers, distributors, retailers, advertisers, or other business partners. Such rights, however, can lead to serious misunderstandings if their limits and restrictions are not clearly defined before a sponsor enters into a final sponsorship agreement.

When a sponsor requests the inclusion of pass-through rights, what it really wants is to be able to offer a portion of its contracted entitlements to a third party. In so doing, the sponsor hopes to offset its financial obligations to the event or extend its reach to the consumer through co-promotions with its existing business partners. An electronics manufacturer, for example, may desire to offer pass-through rights to an electronics retail chain in return for that retailer providing advertising, in-store sales, and preferred aisle placement or point-of-purchase displays featuring the manufacturer's products and their joint association with the sports event. Similarly, a software developer may want to reduce its cash costs by sharing a portion of the sponsorship fee with a device manufacturer that offers its software with the purchase of every new device.

Media partners are particularly aggressive in pursuing pass-through rights. Being able to offer existing advertisers some limited benefit flowing from their association with an event often helps media sponsors offset their sponsorship fees, whether they are paid in cash or with the value of free advertising space or time. (See Play 8 for a closer look at media relationships.)

---

[5]"Invest, Don't Buy: A Smarter Way to Sponsor" (c) 2011 IEG, LLC. 640 N. LaSalle, Suite 450, Chicago, IL 60654-3186. www.sponsorship.com. p. 7.

Principles

- Showcase corporate "Smarter Planet" agenda within the partner's business environment (Accomplishes priority objective)
- Associate with leaders and innovators (Understands the partner's brand)
- Make the partner (event) more successful through IBM's technology (Shared responsibility for mutual success)

Characteristics

- Platform for demonstrating smarter enterprises
- Align with clients' personal passions
- Reach the target audience in significant numbers
- Balance cost and benefit

Evaluation

- Story relevance: Is the partnership truly telling a Smarter Planet story that will relate to clients' businesses?
- Marketing relevance: Are the marketing and communications teams using the story to further their objectives?
- Client engagement: Is the partnership drawing the right clients at the event or through other means? Is it impacting their impression of IBM?
- Revenue: Are clients further engaging with IBM postevent?

(Reprinted with permission from IEG)

Figure 6.6 IBM's Partnership Investment Principles, Characteristics, and Evaluation

Conferring pass-through rights to sponsors, if they are offered at all, is something that event organizers should consider both judiciously and selectively. When a third party agrees to an association with an event through a sponsor that passes rights to it, it is effectively removed from the universe of potential sponsors that can be solicited for revenues directly by the organizer. After all, why would a company make the large investment to be a sponsor if it can pick and choose only the benefits it absolutely needs, passed through by an existing sponsor at potentially a far lower cost? Perhaps more significant, this practice could remove an entire category of sponsors from the organizer's list of potential targets. If a quick-service restaurant enjoys an association with an event via pass-through rights from a sponsor (a soft drink company, for example), the event organizer would have a very difficult time selling a sponsorship to any other QSR. In addition, the event organizer must protect his or her current sponsors by guarding against the possibility of pass-through rights being offered to an existing partner's competitors. Much as is the case with maintaining an awareness of the activities of ambush marketers, an organizer's vigilance against competitors, regardless of how they may come to associate with an event, is an essential component of what a sponsor pays for.

Pass-through rights, on the other hand, can be very advantageous to an event organizer if they provide the potential for increased ticket sales, promotions, or exposure opportunities far beyond those otherwise available in the market. In the example just discussed, it may be that no QSR will make the commitment to support the event in cash. Working through the soft drink sponsor, however, the restaurant might agree to undertake promotions involving significant exposure for the event through tray liners, in-store posters, on-bag advertising, and online promotions. If the demographics of the event and the restaurant complement each other and there is a low probability of attracting a sponsor in the QSR category, there may be very good reason to accept a pass-through provision in the soft drink company's sponsorship agreement. The limits to which a sponsor will be permitted the right to pass through specific benefits should be clearly defined in its sponsorship agreement. It is recommended that every proposed third-party relationship be reviewed by the event organizer, and that none be permitted unless specifically approved in advance by the organizer in writing.

Know Your Sponsors

Armed with a familiarity of what sponsors generally seek from their sports event partnerships, it is now time to combine the organizer's sponsor revenue objectives with an analysis of what a specific prospective sponsor will want, need, and expect from its investment. Many event organizers begin by creating standardized packages of benefits for prospective sponsors at a number of different investment levels, assigning the quantity and quality of included features that correspond to the size of the proposed fee. Although presenting a package of consistent, predetermined benefits is often a good place to start the sales planning process, customizing a benefits package based on intelligence about a prospective sponsor's objectives is often a much more effective way to increase that sponsor's interest, and accelerate the closing of a deal.

Customizing a sponsorship package that includes the right features in the right quantities requires an understanding of a prospective partner's business objectives, its target market, and the marketing strategies it employs to communicate with and sell to its customers. Figure 6.7 provides a useful checklist of questions, the answers to which can help sports event organizers better understand the businesses of their prospective sponsor partners and the customers they serve.

Once in possession of the answers to as many of these questions as possible, the organizer can evaluate the prospect company as to whether it is a likely candidate for a sponsorship. Presuming the event presents a good opportunity for the prospect to reach its customers, the organizer is now better prepared to design a program that meets the sponsor's needs and provides the benefits of the greatest and most relevant value. What kinds of features can the event organizer offer, and in what quantity can they be made available to help the sponsor realize its business objectives? Would its sales efforts be better served by loading the deal with more premium-location tickets, trade or consumer advertising, sales promotions, or event promotions with publicity potential?

How can the event organizer meet the marketing objectives of the sponsor through activation opportunities at the event site? In what way can the event so effectively deliver results opportunities that the prospect might consider a position of greater ownership, such as a title or presenting sponsorship? The organizer can design both a presenting sponsor package as well as one or more less costly sponsor packages for its consideration, each combining the components that will be considered most attractive and best suited to the prospect at those levels of involvement.

The specific needs of prospective sponsors and the event elements that they will judge as best meeting their business objectives will vary widely from company to company. Although there are fundamental differences between the marketing practices most often employed by consumer-oriented businesses and those of B2B companies, some generalizations may be made regarding the types of sponsor benefits they seek from their event relationships. Contrast the overall characteristics of the consumer company sponsor package described in Figure 6.8 with the comparable features of a typical B2B sponsor package illustrated in Figure 6.9. Keep in mind that the relative importance of each type of benefit may differ between any two sponsors even within the same major business category, depending on those companies' individual marketing strategies.

- Who are the company's customers?
  - Do they transact most of their business with individual consumers (B2C) or with corporate clients (B2B)?
  - If they sell to both businesses and consumers, to whom do they want to direct their event marketing efforts?
  - What are the demographics (i.e., the objective statistical characteristics) of the customers they most want to speak to?
    - Are they young, middle-aged, or senior citizens?
    - Are they married, have children living in their household, or "empty nesters" (i.e., married with grown children living elsewhere)?
    - Is their disposable income modest, average, or appreciable?
    - What is their average level of education?
    - Do they rent an apartment or own a home?
    - In what parts of the country, state, or community do they live?
  - What are the psychographics, or behavioral characteristics, of the company's target customers?
    - In what kinds of sports do they enjoy participating?
    - How often do they attend sports events? What kinds of sports events do they most often attend?
    - What kinds of sports do they enjoy watching on television?
    - How avid are they as fans? How familiar are they with the sport and its athletes or teams? Are they the kinds of people who try or purchase new products and emerging technologies soon after they are introduced ("innovators"), or after most others have adopted and proven the worth of such innovations ("late majority")?
    - Do they enjoy an active lifestyle or do they pursue largely sedentary leisure endeavors?
    - What other kinds of entertainment do they attend or watch on television or stream to computers, tablets, or mobile devices?
    - What kind of music do they enjoy?
- What are the marketing and communications strategies the company applies to appeal to its target customers?
- Is the company's brand well established or new to the public? Is it declining or increasing in popularity?
- Does the prospective sponsor have a corporate culture or reputation for innovation and creativity?
- What other sports events does the prospect sponsor?
  - How does it use these events to achieve their objectives?
  - What promotional benefits associated with these events does the company find work successfully for them?
- What does the prospective sponsor want to gain from a sports event relationship in general, and from this relationship in particular, presuming the event provides opportunities that match its needs?

Figure 6.7 Getting to Know Your Prospective Sponsor and Its Customers

- With what events are their competitors associated? How successful have their competitors been in their event marketing efforts?
- With what other events has the prospective sponsor reduced or eliminated its relationship, and why?
- How will the company evaluate the success of its association?

Figure 6.7 *(Continued)*

- Event tickets
- Limited exclusive-access opportunities
- Consumer advertising in digital and print media
- Discount and premium sales promotions
- Direct sales opportunities
- Product sampling opportunities
- Commercial time (for events covered on television and/or radio)

Figure 6.8 Typical Sponsor Benefit Features for Consumer Product Companies

- Premium event tickets
- Broad exclusive access opportunities
- Business, trade, or specialty advertising and publicity
- High-value promotions
- Product demonstration opportunities
- Client hospitality opportunities:
  - Hosted by the event organizer
  - Staged directly by the sponsor

Figure 6.9 Typical Sponsor Benefit Features for B2B Companies

Consumer Products Company Sponsor Benefits

Consumer products companies are those whose end users are individual customers, marketing products they manufacture or sell at retail, with costs ranging from just a few cents to thousands of dollars—such as producers of candy bars, beer, mobile telephone carriers, makers of kitchen appliances and home electronics, real estate agencies, and automobile manufacturers. These types of companies commonly use event tickets to entertain their distributors, agents, wholesalers, retailers, and key executives, as well as for prizes in consumer sweepstakes and promotions. Their needs for exclusive access opportunities, such as "meet-and-greet" encounters with athletes and celebrities, visits backstage, and passes to receptions and media events, are usually limited in quantity as pleasing additional features for consumer sweepstakes promotions.

As a marketer of products or services to the public, advertising opportunities are usually the most beneficial to consumer-oriented companies. These advertising benefits may include public address and scoreboard announcements, commercials aired on the facility's video screen, print advertising in the event program, and display signage near the playing surface or elsewhere in the host venue. Acknowledgments and sponsor logo placement in advertising placed by the organizer in consumer publications to promote the event, as well as in digital and broadcast media, are also highly desirable elements for companies marketing primarily to a consumer audience. The use of time for airing sponsor commercials during television or radio coverage, or associated with online streaming of sports events, is usually a key component of major consumer company sponsorship deals.

The exclusive right to engage in promotional activities directed toward ticket buyers and other consumers, whether managed by the sponsor or presented by the event organizer under the sponsor's name, is highly attractive to these types of companies. Consumer-oriented promotions may include event merchandise or premium giveaways, ticket and/or travel sweepstakes, event admission or merchandise discounts with a sponsor's proofs-of-purchase, or store and print-at-home coupons. They may also feature opportunities to offer fans unique participatory activities, from trivia and skills contests to an honorary ceremonial role in the event (e.g., honorary batboy, honorary trainer, dropping of the first puck).

As outstanding opportunities for reaching fans directly, consumer products companies frequently take advantage of sports events as direct sales and sampling opportunities, passing out full- or trial-sized samples or coupons to enjoy discounts at an associated retail location. Consumer product sponsors also often distribute premium items such as event posters, visors, or other souvenir items prominently sporting their company or brand logo. These giveaway items are usually distributed to attendees on either entering or exiting the facility, although most venues prefer giving away products upon exiting to ensure that samples do not become projectiles or are left behind as trash. "Tabling," the ability to set up a table or kiosk for product sampling, direct sales, or demonstrations, is another form of direct interaction with the fan often considered appealing by consumer product companies.

Business-to-Business (B2B) Company Sponsor Benefits

Companies that market their products or services to other businesses (B2B companies) may find as attractive many of the same benefits as consumer products companies, but frequently with differing perspectives on their relative importance. The units of sale for B2B marketers are usually significantly higher in price and the purchasing decision maker often a more highly educated, highly compensated individual—someone who probably could have afforded to reach into his or her own wallet to purchase a ticket to the event. Therefore, the key attribute that contributes to providing a positive, exciting experience for the decision maker is exclusive access, something not available for purchase. This access begins with event tickets, and for many B2B companies, only the very best available will suffice. The B2B sponsor's target market must be entertained in seats they would have had difficulty procuring had they called the box office themselves. Therefore, an allotment of premium seats—field level, club level, luxury suites, or an analogous location in the event's host venue—is often an absolute requirement.

The kinds of exclusive access opportunities for a sponsor's VIP guests that are of greater importance to B2B companies go far beyond premium seat locations. "Meet-and-greet" receptions—exclusive opportunities for a sponsor's guests to interact with athletes or celebrities and other VIPs—backstage access, attendance at media events, and other behind-the-scenes inclusions provide great value to business marketers. These are the kinds of exciting experiences a company's prospective customers could not obtain without a prestigious invitation from the B2B sponsor, and, as such, are sometimes considered "must include" components of the deal.

B2B companies may consider the inclusion of consumer advertising benefits extremely attractive, especially those that also market directly to consumers. Few will turn down the opportunity for in-event signage, or public address and video scoreboard acknowledgments, if only to reinforce their integral association for the benefit of their own guests in the stands. Most B2B companies, however, will ascribe great benefit in any advertising placed by event organizers in business or trade publications and on websites directed toward the industries and decision makers they most often market to. In a multiple newspaper market, they will prefer placement of event advertising that contains recognition of their sponsorship in publications and on websites that most closely match the reading habits of the purchasers of their high-ticket products (e.g., the *New York Times, Wall Street Journal, Globe & Mail, Financial Times*). They will be less concerned about whether these same periodicals are also the best for communicating with the event's most typical ticket buyers.

Some B2B promotions may differ from those offered by consumer marketers in the average value of premiums, prizes, or awards. The sponsor may offer incentive awards, such as all-expense-paid trips to the event, to authorized dealers who reach a new, exemplary plateau of sales. Premier quality merchandise such as authentic jerseys or leather event jackets may be offered as premiums to top performing sales representatives who achieve significant percentages above their quota, or to retailers who have outperformed expectations. This is not to suggest that more modest promotions are not encountered in the B2B market. Event tickets and promotional premiums of lesser value may be offered to new clients and existing business relationships. Promotions of reduced value can also provide incentives to clients while respecting the ethical compliance regulations that guard against conflicts of interest in many corporations.

Product sampling opportunities often take the form of more sophisticated, personal, and comprehensive product demonstrations in a B2B sponsorship. Products targeted to other businesses may be too valuable to distribute for free or in bulk, and their market may comprise only a small fraction of the total audience. Therefore, rather than marketing to the entire event audience, these sponsors target their own guest list and other qualified attendees (such as purchasers of premium-priced tickets) for limited product or service demonstrations and even direct personal sales.

There is probably no more attractive opportunity to a B2B sponsor than the availability of exclusive client hospitality options. Receptions, parties, golf outings, luncheons, dinners, and walk-in hospitality suites provide sponsors with a direct and personal occasion to interact with clients and future business prospects. As casual entertainment experiences that surround sports events, these more insulated environments provide exclusive sales opportunities away from the clutter of other sponsors' messages more prevalent at the main event. Invitations to VIP events and activities hosted by the event organizer will be expected in quantity for client hospitality, although many sponsors will also often host their own exclusive events for their guests, either at the event site or at another nearby location.

Forearmed with an understanding of how corporate partnerships can work to the advantage of both the sports event and its sponsors, and recognizing the differing and highly individualized needs of consumer and B2B marketers, the organizer can begin to formulate a program of benefits that will convert prospects into sponsors. Effective marketing to prospective sponsors starts by identifying these wants and needs, and determining how the power of a sports event can deliver measurable results to satisfy their sales objectives and exceed their business expectations.

Post-Play Analysis

Like any good partnership, all parties benefit from a well-conceived and well-constructed event sponsorship. Organizers seek relationships with companies that can provide their events with a source of revenue and opportunities for cost avoidance. To stretch an event's promotional budget, organizers seek companies that will reinforce their association with a program of advertising in digital and traditional media, promotions, onsite engagement activities, and publicity at spending levels beyond their sponsorship fee, also known as activation. They also hope to create alliances with companies that demonstrate a commitment, or at least an intention, to continue their association with the event in future years.

Sponsors can derive a wide range of exposure opportunities from their event partnership, such as advertising at and beyond the event site, product placement, promotions, and media coverage. Sports events offer companies outstanding opportunities for customer hospitality through the provision of event tickets, VIP receptions, parties, and other exclusive access. They can also be a marketplace for direct sales efforts, product demonstrations, and sampling opportunities. Some companies also employ events as fundraising vehicles for corporate philanthropic efforts. Some of the attractive intangible properties of sports events sponsorships include category exclusivity, perceived ownership of event elements, an association with an event of prestigious reputation, and the ability to offer pass-through rights to other business partners.

Although the relative importance that each company places on the various elements in a sponsor package varies widely, prospective companies may be divided into two key groups, each with generally similar business strategies—consumer products companies and business-to-business marketers. Event organizers begin the process of designing a sponsor package by understanding how their prospective partners market their products or services to their customers, and what a company wants or needs from the relationship in order to achieve these marketing objectives.

Coach's Clipboard

1. You are organizing a tournament of regional police department baseball teams with the objective of raising funds for their Widows & Orphans Fund. What kinds of companies would be most likely to be attracted to the event? With projected admissions and donations revenue of $15,000 and operating expenses of $20,000, how can sponsor sales generate $20,000 net to the charity? Consider both cash and VIK sponsorship opportunities.
2. You are the marketing director for a consumer products company that supports esteem-building causes for physically disadvantaged children. Identify an existing sports event or create a new one, and explore how the company can help generate needed capital and exposure for the cause. Discuss how this effort can meet your company's marketing needs while supporting this worthy endeavor.
3. A marketer representing a major B2B corporation approaches an event organizer seeking a large block of premium seating, exclusive access, and hospitality opportunities for their upscale clients. The event already has a presenting sponsor under contract that paid more than the B2B company is willing to spend, and is receiving less in return than is sought by the marketer. How can the event organizer increase the value of the

relationship for the existing sponsor or increase the consideration offered by the B2B company to ensure that all partners are satisfied and treated fairly?

4. You are an event organizer who has enjoyed a long-term relationship with an electronics sponsor, which is set to expire the following year. Renewal negotiations for a new agreement are proceeding reasonably well. The host facility of your next event, however, has announced its new naming rights partner will be a competitive sponsor. How will you manage the relationship with your sponsor to maximize the chances of renewing your agreement successfully?

PLAY 7

Teaming with Sponsors

"Persistence can change failure into extraordinary achievement."
—*Matt Biondi, (American Olympic swimming champion, 1965–Present)*

This play will help you to:

- Design and customize sponsorship packages.
- Identify the costs and value of providing sponsor benefits.
- Engage in presenting and selling sponsorships.

Introduction

Once a sports event organizer has gathered all of the intelligence possible to gain an understanding of its prospective partner's business, the next step is to apply this knowledge to the development of a sponsor program that will meet the respective needs of all stakeholders—the event's organizers, participants, fans, and sponsors. The right program must not only provide demonstrable value and unique business opportunities to the sponsor, but must also help generate the net revenues required by the event organizer's budget.

Scaling and Pricing Sponsorship Packages

What benefits, and in what quantity, should an event organizer include in a prospective sponsor's package? How many tickets, and of what value? What kind of recognition should the company receive in pre-event advertising? How many scoreboard mentions, playing field signs, public address announcements, and in-event logo placements should it be given? What rights should be provided to the company, and what promotional opportunities should be included in its sponsorship package? What presence and prominence will the sponsor enjoy on the event's digital platforms such as websites and downloadable applications? How much of each of these elements will a sponsor enjoy relative to other event sponsors?

To sports event organizers, sponsor benefits may be divided into two basic varieties—those that will generate expenses against the event budget and those that, although offering value to the sponsor, can be provided without the organizer encountering any additional out-of-pocket expense. Before developing the sponsorship package, it is essential that organizers consider the actual costs of providing the benefits to sponsors that will impact the event's bottom line, also known as *fulfillment costs*.

Development and Fulfillment Costs

Among the most overlooked calculations by event organizers during the budgeting process are the costs of selling and fulfilling the package of benefits to which sponsors are entitled. The packaged goods and retail industries are quite familiar with the concept of ensuring that their prices reflect a "cost of goods sold" plus a margin of profit, as do most event organizers who sell merchandise as part of their business plans. Before fixing a price for a product, a manufacturer must identify the cost of materials, labor, tools, and equipment required for its fabrication, as well as for packaging, shipping, advertising, promotion, sales commissions, and other expenses encountered in bringing it to market. An allocation of overhead costs, such as for office staff and equipment, research and development, supplies, utilities, furnishings, and other expenses not directly associated with the manufacturing, marketing, or distribution processes must also be applied to truly reflect the cost of creating and selling a product for more than it cost the company to produce.

Retailers and sports event organizers demonstrate an understanding of this concept when they apply a price to the merchandise they sell. They consider the cost of acquiring the product, paying the sales staff and cashiers, acquiring the fixtures required for storage and display, allocating a sufficient percentage to cover overhead, and then add a profit margin before attaching the price tag. Sports events seeking corporate relationships to help fund their operations must plan in a similar manner. All of the various expenses expected to be incurred in marketing, creating, and delivering the product—an event sponsorship—must be identified and totaled, and a profit margin applied that is sufficient to meet an event's net revenue expectations.

Expenses incurred in selling a sponsorship, or development costs, include sales commissions, sales expenses, and the cost of market research. Obviously, these costs do not provide any value to the sponsor. They do, however, benefit the event organizer during the process of securing business partners and, therefore, should be factored into the "cost of goods sold" when setting sponsorship revenue goals and pricing benefit packages.

The many and varied expenses that are encountered by the organizer, but ultimately accrue to the benefit of the sponsor, are known as fulfillment costs. Fulfillment costs represent the actual out-of-pocket expenses that an event organizer will incur to provide the benefits to which the sponsor is entitled. Some of the most common development and fulfillment expenses encountered by sports event organizers are summarized in Figure 7.1.

Development Costs

- Sales commissions
- Sales expenses
  - Travel and accommodations
  - Business meals
  - Business entertainment (e.g., event tickets and hospitality during sales process)
  - Gifts, merchandise, and premiums
  - Presentation materials (e.g., printing, binders/folders, videos, web pages, file transfer protocol [ftp] sites)
- Market research

Fulfillment Costs

- Complimentary tickets
- Event signage and displays
- Printed and digital event guide and program advertising
- Pre-event advertising (e.g., Internet, print, radio, television, billboards)
- VIP hospitality
- Sponsor gifts
- Sampling and giveaways
- Discounting and couponing

Figure 7.1 Common Sports Event Sponsorship Development and Fulfillment Costs

Development Costs

Sales Commissions

Experienced event organizers may be consummate experts at planning, managing, and executing events, and perhaps even outstanding promoters in marketing their events to the public. They are often less adroit, or have only limited time available to invest, in cultivating the sponsors that will be needed to meet their budget's revenue expectations. Their relationships with the event marketing decision makers within the companies most likely to support their events may simply be too limited to successfully reach their sponsorship goals.

This is when sports event organizers seek professional help from the agencies and individuals who specialize in event marketing and maintain more intimate and regular relationships with contacts in a wide range of potential sponsor companies. There are a large number and variety of event marketing agencies to be found in *Sports Market Place Directory*, the massive and essential volume of contacts within sports and sports-related organizations available in print or digital form from Grey House Publishing Inc. (www.greyhouse.com). For detailed and the most timely intelligence on event marketing agencies and news about their current activities, outstanding resources include *Sports Business Journal, Sports Business Daily, IEG Sponsorship Report*, and *Event Marketer* magazine.

An event marketing agency can become the organizer's most important ambassador to the business community, and an extension of the event organization itself. As such, organizers are well advised to interview and check the references of several potential agencies to determine whether they have represented similar properties, the degree of their past successes, their assessment of the revenue potential for the event in question, and their cost schedules, before making a final selection. Once an agency or individual is selected, it will typically be the exclusive representative of the event to potential sponsors, so conducting thorough due diligence on their reputation, follow-through, experience, and contacts is essential.

Event marketing agencies are usually paid a percentage of the gross sponsorship fees they generate. In a well-functioning partnership, the organizer and the agency invest in each other's success. The organizer trusts that the agency is working diligently to recruit the sponsors that are needed, and the marketing agency invests considerable time and energy to turn over the revenue it generates to the event. It is, therefore, not uncommon for the agency to also require a monthly retainer as guaranteed income, often considered a "draw against commission."

If both the agency and the sponsors it develops continue to be associated with the event in future years, the agency generally continues to receive commissions on an agreed-to schedule defined by its contract with the organizer. The agency is usually still entitled to this percentage of future fees that result from its sales activities even if its own relationship with the organizer expires. In such cases, the agreement negotiated with the agency will often determine the period of time over which the commissions will remain payable to the marketer, and at what rate of compensation.

Most event marketing agencies prefer representing established, proven properties with high profit potential. The nature of community-based grassroots events sometimes suggests a more homegrown approach. No matter how lofty the aim, how warm the emotion, or how seemingly attractive the event is to the organizer, agencies are less drawn to events where the sponsorship revenue expectations are low, or set unrealistically high. Events with limited geographic appeal are also generally attractive only to the most entrepreneurial event marketing agencies, or those that specialize in a region's local events, because the revenues, and, therefore, the profits they can generate, are concomitantly limited. For events of modest budgets or geographically limited impact, retaining an event marketing agency may not be a preferred or realistic option. In such cases, event organizers needing help generating sponsorship revenues often reach out through the local chamber of commerce and/or create a business advisory group composed of influential individuals from the community who are motivated by local pride and a desire to see the event achieve success. Involving local business leaders in the management and marketing success of an event can help to leverage their relationships within the business community, provide introductions to other receptive business executives, and solicit advice on how to best approach them.

Sales Expenses

The agreement negotiated with the event marketing agency should also define the direct expenses beyond commissions or fees the organizer will consider reimbursable in connection with the agency's sales activities. Organizers may incur many of the same expenses whether they retain an agency to solicit and sell sponsorships, or market the event to corporate partners themselves. These may include travel and accommodations to meet with the organizer to plan sales strategy and with prospective sponsors to pitch the event, the preparation of sales solicitation materials such as presentation kits or binders, videos, website or ftp-site design, artwork and artist renderings, writers, printing and photocopies, gifts, office supplies, telephone charges, messengers, overnight couriers and postage, among others.

It is recommended that the agreement negotiated with the event marketing agency includes a budget or limit for total sales expenses. This may be accomplished by working with the agency to establish a detailed budget for sales expenses or requiring that individual out-of-pocket expenses beyond a certain limit (perhaps $500 or more) are approved by the event organizer in advance to avoid the potential of subsequent billing disagreements.

Market Research

Many event organizers conduct postevent market research to gauge ticket-buyer demographics, psychographics, buying behavior, price sensitivities, and perceptions of the quality of the event experience. These same research programs can also be applied to measuring the effectiveness of sponsorship, advertising, and promotional programs. Responses may be compiled by personal interviews during the event, and the distribution, collection and tabulation of questionnaires provided to exiting fans or delivered to them after the event by mail or email. Common questions include asking fans for their recollections of which sponsors supported the event, whether they visited various sponsored activities, and whether they participated in sponsor activation opportunities. The results can help organizers improve their event's business and marketing plans, validate the program's appeal to participating sponsors, and demonstrate its strength and value to future prospective business partners, as well as collect valuable data about attendees that can be used for future sales and communication outreach.

Fulfillment Costs

Complimentary Tickets

As discussed in Play 3, complimentary tickets are free to neither the organizer nor the sponsor. To the event organizer, they represent a lost revenue opportunity. Because complimentary tickets issued to a sponsor reduce the difference between cash received from ticket revenues and an event's gross potential, they actually "cost" the event budget their full face value. Likewise, when a sponsor analyzes the value of a package of benefits, it will regard the market price of complimentary tickets as value received in exchange for its cash or value-in-kind (VIK) payment to the event. For these reasons, it is common for sports event organizers to consider the face value of complimentary tickets as an expense paid in the fulfillment of a sponsorship agreement.

Complimentary tickets (*comps*) are often central components of sponsorship packages, but they should be used judiciously. Organizers want to fill the event venue with fans for the electric atmosphere that full houses provide, as well as for the generation of ancillary revenues such as merchandise, concessions, and parking. When provided to business partners in too large a supply, however, there is often a tendency for a portion of the complimentary tickets to go unused on event day. On top of the organizer realizing no sales of merchandise, concessions, or other financial benefit from an unused ticket, the event budget has paid for the ticket as a fulfillment cost. Provide the tickets that sponsors feel they need in order to embrace a sponsorship, but resist the urge to provide too many tickets for them to be able to effectively distribute or use for their own purposes. Have an understanding of how sponsors would intend to use their allotment of complimentary tickets. Would they employ them only to bring their own important guests to the event, use them in consumer promotions as sweepstakes prizes, or both? Providing comps that will be used for a sponsor's VIPs would often require better-quality tickets than those that will be used as consumer giveaways.

Signage and Displays

The exposure that companies receive in connection with their event sponsorship may include temporary signage on the playing surface or within otherwise conspicuous view of the audience. Corporate identification may be painted or applied directly on the walls, floors, boards, fencing, or structural fasciae of the host facility. Signage opportunities may also include banners located within and outside the event venue, on city street poles and over intersections, at headquarters hotels, and at area bars, restaurants, and attractions. The costs of designing, constructing, painting, printing, and installing signage with corporate identification, and any required space rental to display them, may not have existed had a sponsor not purchased those opportunities as part of its package. These benefits are, therefore, also considered fulfillment expenses. If street banners promoting the event would have been created and installed whether or not a sponsor purchased the right to be recognized on them, the expense should already be captured in the event budget and their cost would not be considered a cost of fulfillment.

Temporary signage mounted on specially designed trusses or frames or on structures installed specifically for the event may also be included as opportunities for exposure. As a general rule, if the truss, frame, or other temporary structure to which the signage is attached would be installed with or without the need to recognize a sponsor (e.g., signage displayed on speaker stacks, lighting trusses, or camera scaffolds), only the signage itself and not the cost of the structure on which it is supported should be considered a fulfillment expense. However, if the structure is installed strictly to meet the obligations of a sponsorship agreement, the costs of rent, fabrication, installation, and dismantling the structure would be added to the spreadsheet of fulfillment expenses.

Video screens and electronic message displays on scoreboards or other information displays around the venue can provide high-impact opportunities to expose and recognize a sponsor's association with the event. The costs of creating artwork for the video screens and programming for the electronic message displays should also be included as fulfillment expenses. The actual operation of these facilities, if they are also used for informational or entertainment purposes during the event such as play-by-play coverage, replays, the posting of statistics, and the airing of highlights, would not be included in the calculation of fulfillment costs.

Sponsor signage is one area where even highly experienced, well-intentioned organizers often overpromise and end up underdelivering to their partners. An overabundance of corporate logos and sponsor marketing messages at an event can create undesirable visual noise, clutter, and confusion. Some event marketers believe that "less can be more"—the fewer the sponsor logos that are present at any one location, the more impact each will have. There are a host of techniques that event organizers and venues use to reduce the clutter and maximize the impact of sponsor signage at sports events:

- *Gate sponsorships.* Name and theme the different entrance plazas and/or gates each for a single sponsor only. Use the dominant colors in the sponsor's logo in the décor and lighting design for those areas.
- *Quadrant, concourse, or walkway sponsorships.* Similarly, name and theme sections of seating, concourses, or walkways for one sponsor each.
- *Electronic signage dominance.* Display only one sponsor at a time on each of the video message boards and/or scoreboards inside the seating bowl, and rotate acknowledged sponsors at regular intervals. This provides particularly vivid visual impact in stadiums and arenas that possess electronic signs surrounding most, or all, of the seating bowl.

SIDELINE STORY

Cisco StadiumVision Changes Content Delivery

Cisco Systems, the San Jose–based information technology giant, introduced StadiumVision in 2009 as a content delivery system for stadiums, arenas, and other major event facilities. Simply put, StadiumVision enables facility and event organizers to manage every video screen throughout the building individually, often numbering in the hundreds and sometimes thousands in concourses, clubs, and suites, and at entrance gates and plazas, by assigning a unique Internet Protocol (IP) address to each display. This flexibility provides opportunities to display sponsor messaging to all locations at specified times (i.e., electronic signage dominance), or to specific screens based on location (i.e., gate, concourse, or quadrant sponsorship). The system is controlled in real-time, allowing for individual screens to shift to noncommercial programming such as welcome messages, wayfinding assistance, play-by-play coverage, statistics displays, exiting and parking information, concession stand menu boards, or virtually any purpose on a screen-by-screen basis. Cisco StadiumVision currently operates only in permanent installations and requires a trained staff to deliver this real-time content, but the unique and immersive opportunities it provides is well worth exploring by event organizers staging events in buildings featuring the system.

Of course, amateur and grassroots sports event organizers staging events in community facilities cannot avail themselves of Cisco's innovative and complex technology, but they can be inspired by its effectiveness, creativity, and flexibility. With recent rapid advances in computer and display technology, tablets or laptop computers, and high-definition television monitors can be used to provide some small-scale indoor events (or weather-protected locations at outdoor events) with the same flexible messaging opportunities using simple graphics software—a great cooperative project for your local university's information technology program!

Program Advertising

Organizers who publish and market commemorative printed programs or digital event applications (apps) often include advertising opportunities in their sponsor packages. To reduce financial risk, some organizers license the rights to publish an event program or app to a third party. The publisher, who may pay the organizer a percentage of sales, will absorb the costs of designing, writing, printing, and marketing the program. In addition to retaining a large percentage of sales revenues, the publisher is typically entitled to sell advertising space to help defray expenses. To control fulfillment costs, event organizers who license their publishing rights should negotiate for a number of complimentary advertising pages or positions, and a discounted rate for any additional space that may be required to fulfill sponsorship agreements.

Whether the program or app is created in-house or by a contracted publishing partner, it is recommended that event organizers assign both the creative and financial responsibilities of actually generating the advertisement to the sponsor. Sponsor companies frequently engage advertising agencies or maintain internal creative services departments that can easily and cost-effectively provide the artwork for the ad, removing the organizer from a potentially lengthy and expensive process of creative development and approval.

Organizers can also *up-sell* space in order to generate additional revenues. In other words, a sponsor entitled to a complimentary printed half-page ad may subsequently agree to increase the size of its space. Or, if a certain size ad in a digital edition is specified in the sponsor package, a larger or more prominently placed position can be offered. The difference between the rate for what the sponsor is already entitled to and the price for an ad incorporating its new advertising requirements may be invoiced back to the partner as an additional charge.

It is also recommended that one complimentary ad be reserved by the organizer to thank all of the event's sponsors, separate and apart from to any exposure guaranteed by their benefits packages. The inclusion of partner names and logos in a "thank-you ad" will add incremental value to each sponsor's existing exposure benefits while vividly demonstrating the organizer's appreciation.

Pre-event Advertising

Event organizers place advertising in a wide variety of media such as newspapers, magazines, online services, television, radio, handbills, and outdoor billboards to promote ticket sales, attendance, or increase the broadcasting audience, and often include one or more sponsor names and logos to provide increased value to their partner companies. Sponsorship agreements can include obligations for an organizer to place consumer or trade advertising with the more specific objective of overtly acknowledging a company's support of an event. These supplemental ads, which would not have otherwise been purchased, would be considered fulfillment expenses.

Many organizers enter into promotional relationships with media outlets that entitle the event to complimentary VIK advertising in return for an agreed-to package of sponsor benefits. In such cases, the organizer trades valuable consideration for the VIK advertising, such as complimentary tickets, signage, and other sponsor benefits for which the event absorbs the fulfillment costs. If the VIK advertising that flows from the media partner relationship is used by the organizer to pursue the event's own marketing objectives (e.g., increasing ticket sales, attendance, and broadcast ratings), only the direct expenses encountered in servicing the outlet need be captured as fulfillment costs (e.g., complimentary tickets, gifts, VIP hospitality). If, however, the VIK advertising is used to meet obligations to another corporate partner, these direct costs are considered fulfillment expenses against the gross revenues that accrue from that sponsor's agreement.

VIP Hospitality

Access to pre-game receptions, postevent parties, and in-venue hospitality suites has become a sponsorship entitlement of increasing appeal and significance, delivering to sponsors exclusive access and entertainment value for their own invited guests and conferring prestige upon the sponsors in the eyes of their invitees. Invitations to these highly desirable special-access opportunities have become a greatly sought-after status symbol. As a result, this is an area that event organizers must guardedly protect, otherwise an uncontrolled expansion of the guest list causes expenses to quickly skyrocket while the value of exclusivity declines.

A sponsor's package of benefits should guarantee a specific number of passes to these receptions and parties to ensure that the anticipated overall costs of entertaining sponsors and their clients do not exceed the budgeted limit. It should not be surprising when sponsors subsequently determine that they will need more invitations or passes to these limited-access events, especially as the event matures. One or two passes here and there probably won't amount to much added cost to the event budget, although one or two requests often develop into far more significant numbers. Assuming the reception is being hosted in an area where the available floor space will accommodate more guests, the organizer can establish a "buy-in" price to enable sponsors to purchase supplementary passes for their extra guests at a per-person rate. Sponsors can thereby be provided with the additional access they need, while the organizer protects the event budget from potentially costly overruns. A helpful and equitable formula used to set a buy-in price begins with the base per-person cost of food and beverage as charged by the caterer, plus gratuities, service charges, and applicable taxes. It is also fair to include an allowance for additional décor, rentals and overhead costs, inasmuch as more tables, chairs, centerpieces, floral decorations, dishes, silverware, and other decorative elements will be required as the number of attendees grows. For hospitality events that accommodate guests at dining tables of 10, a reasonable allowance per person is 10 percent of the estimated costs of adding a table unit (table rental, centerpiece, place-setting), plus a small additional charge for general room décor. This sample formula is summarized below:

Supplemental VIP event buy-in price per person =
Per person food and beverage cost
× Prevailing gratuities and/or service charge
× Applicable sales tax
+ 10% of additional per-table décor, rentals, and
other overhead costs

To illustrate, suppose a corporate partner requests an additional 20 party tickets to supplement the 30 to which it is already entitled. The cost of food and beverage, as estimated by the caterer, is $50 per person, plus 18 percent service charge ($9 per person) and 7 percent sales tax ($4.13 on $59), for a subtotal of $63.13 per person. As the event is a stand-up reception, only a small allowance must be added for additional décor, rentals, and printed invitations for which the event organizer in this example adds $6.50 per person, inclusive of taxes. Rounding off, the organizer can set a minimum charge of $70 per additional party pass. The value of establishing this policy becomes more obvious in considering the costs of entertaining even as few as 10 additional guests requested by each of five event sponsors, a total of 50 unanticipated, unbudgeted VIPs. Using the example in the preceding paragraph, the organizer would otherwise incur up to $3,500 in unbudgeted expenses to add this modest number of extra friends to the guest list. To each sponsor, however, the effective cost would total only $700. Access to an exclusive event is typically what the sponsors are after, and they are often willing to contribute to help defray the expenses of accommodating their additional guests. Although, in itself, the attribute of maintaining exclusivity to a top-quality sponsor hospitality event does not create additional costs, organizers often add a profit margin to the buy-in price to generate additional revenue and/or to discourage partners from purchasing an unreasonably large number of additional tickets. In this way, the organizer can maintain the exclusive nature and intimacy of the hospitality event, if desired.

Sponsor Gifts

Gifts of sports apparel and collectible merchandise displaying the event's logo are one of the requisite staples of sports events. Few sporting events fail to offer their special VIP guests a cap, t-shirt, golf shirt, tote bag, or a goody bag containing one or more of these items. Premium collectibles, such as tickets encased in Lucite, wristwatches, crystal paperweights, framed and autographed keepsakes, personalized jerseys, and other commemorative merchandise, are also frequently given to key sponsor contacts as gifts and expressions of gratitude. Organizers should be sure to include the costs of procuring these items in their estimate of fulfillment costs even though they most often fall outside of the benefits to which sponsors are contractually entitled.

Sampling and Giveaways

Companies are often granted *sampling rights,* the ability to distribute their product or a giveaway premium featuring their corporate or brand logos to the audience and/or athlete participants.

Conferring sampling rights does not necessarily mean that organizers are obligated to pay the material or shipping costs connected with this activity, or for the labor required for distribution. The organizer's agreement with the sponsor should clearly define where the financial responsibilities for sampling activities rest.

Before granting sampling rights to a sponsor, the organizer should consult his or her facility lease and the host venue's general manager. Some facilities restrict sampling activities to only those sponsors of an event that will provide products that do not compete with their own partners. A concessionaire's agreement with the building may also preclude events from sampling food or beverage items out of a concern that providing these free products would cut into their sales. It should be noted that these regulations might not be immediately apparent in a reading of the facility lease. Agreements protecting a venue's concessionaires' rights may be confidential instruments between the building and its food vendors. Additionally, some facility leases contain provisions that obligate the event organizer to adhere to the rules and regulations of the facility. To protect themselves against surprises, sports event organizers should not sign a lease agreement until they have been provided with a copy of those regulations. This is often where restrictions on sponsor activities such as sampling and the display of sponsor signage, as well as the stated rights of the event site's concessionaires and merchandisers, may be found. The lease may also reveal a charge for the right to sample or distribute sponsor products and limitations as to the product categories that may be prohibited as sample items.

It is not unusual for sponsors to agree to cover the direct costs of sampling their products at events. The staff required to distribute the samples may be provided by the sponsor, through the event organizer, by the facility, or contracted separately by either party so long as doing so does not violate building regulations or existing labor agreements. Volunteer organizations such as community sports teams, scout troops, and other youth organizations are excellent resources for providing labor for sampling at sports events. These groups usually come with their own adult supervision or leadership and will participate for the novelty and excitement of being involved in the event, plus a donation to their treasury. Another way to minimize the labor costs connected with sampling opportunities is to restrict distribution to the period when the audience is exiting. Ushers and other house staff are usually underutilized at this point and may be redeployed to execute sampling activities at the exits. In this way, the sponsor will incur only the small additional charge for perhaps an extra hour's time per staff member.

Facility and labor restrictions for premium giveaways, items of value that are not samples of the sponsor's product, are often similar to those for sampling. Try to avoid distributing commemorative balls, pucks, sticks, or other implements upon entry to the host venue as they could interfere with play or cause inadvertent injury to members of the audience. These items can be printed with event and sponsor logos and are great keepsakes, but they should be distributed to fans upon exiting. Some promotional items, such as rally towels, cheering cards, t-shirts, caps, and other materials that enhance the participatory nature of the viewing experience require distribution upon entry. Such objects should be sufficiently soft in substance so as not to create a safety hazard on the chance that fans cause them to become airborne during an event.

Secure the permission of the host venue before approving a sponsor's planned premium item to ensure that it does not violate house regulations or the facility's agreement with the merchandiser. In addition, try to avoid approving the sponsored distribution of premium items that are similar to merchandise being sold at the event. Free premiums can compete with souvenir sales and lower the "per cap" (see Play 3) for both the event organizer and the merchandiser.

The financial responsibility of purchasing the sponsored giveaway item should be defined by the sponsorship agreement. Some preparation ("prepping") costs may also be required, an area frequently overlooked by both sponsors and organizers. Posters, for example, must be rolled and bound with elastic bands or inserted into tubes for easy distribution to the fans and to prevent product damage. Plastic bags are often used to package a sample or giveaway item with product information, promotional offers, coupons, or future event information. Prepping the sample or giveaway item can be executed by an outside company or by a pool of volunteers. Also be sure to plan on deploying extra custodial staff to keep concourses, aisles, and other areas clean and service trash containers. Discarded giveaway items, wrappers, packaging, and couponing can create slip or trip hazards, debris blowing onto the playing surface, and a generally unpleasing aesthetic environment. Be sure to include these extra labor expenses and any additional refuse and recycling containers needed to support the giveaway in your fulfillment costs or the estimate of additional charges to your sponsor.

Discounting and Couponing

Corporate partners often activate their sponsorships by offering consumers added value with the purchase of their products—discounts on the price of event tickets or event merchandise. Ticket discounting is an extremely effective tool used by sponsors to drive customers into a retail outlet selling their products, or into a partner's own stores. A large portion of a sponsor's event activation strategy may focus on promoting the availability of ticket discounts. Ticket discount coupons may be incorporated into a product's packaging, printed onto shopping bags or on the tray liners of quick service restaurants, or attached to "point of purchase" displays promoting the product and the event. To further encourage product sales, the discount program may require customers to produce proofs-of-purchase of a sponsor's product to receive their savings at the box office, or provide a code that may be redeemed online.

To maximize the effectiveness of a discount promotion, sponsors may purchase advertising to promote the value they are providing to their customers, significantly extending the organizer's own advertising budget, and the discounts they promote can offer organizers excellent opportunities for incremental ticket sales. A sponsor can, in turn, benefit from being perceived by fans as the beneficent source of one of any number of discount options such as a fixed discount on the purchase of a ticket, a package price for a family of four, or the ability to buy one ticket and get one free, among many others. For multiday events, sponsor promotions can be employed to encourage improved attendance on nonpeak days and times by limiting the discount to less well-attended weeknights or for matinees. The difference between a full-price ticket and those sold at a discount through sponsor promotions is not usually figured into the costs of sponsor fulfillment, but must be considered during the budgeting process in the calculation of ticket revenues (see Play 3). To anticipate sponsor needs for discount offers, event organizers should set discount prices even before sponsors are confirmed and estimate the number of tickets that will likely be sold at these reduced prices. The usual expectation is for the sponsor to create, design, manage, and execute the advertising, point-of-purchase displays, coupons, and packaging in connection with its discount offer. It is highly recommended that the sponsor agreement articulate the requirement that all materials relating to the event must be reviewed and approved by the organizer before printing to ensure accuracy and creative consistency with other event communications.

Some B2B and high-end consumer companies activate their sponsorships by offering event merchandise and tickets *gratis* to their most important clients or as sales promotions designed to transform qualified prospects into loyal customers. An automobile manufacturer may want to promote its sponsorship with a free event ticket offer, providing consumers who take a test drive with a voucher redeemable for a pair of complimentary tickets. Or, a wireless services company may offer free event tickets to new customers who subscribe to its latest data plan. In cases like these, the quantity of redeemed tickets (the number of qualifying customers who actually exchange their vouchers for the free tickets and attend the event) is impossible for either the sponsor or the organizer to predict or budget for in advance. Promotions like these can be powerful advertising tools for an event as well as valuable incentives that sponsors can use to drive prospects into their sales locations and to convert potential customers into purchasers.

In most cases, however, the event budget cannot accommodate the issuance of what could become a significant number of these complimentary tickets. The sponsor's dealers, agents, or salespeople who control the distribution of the offer must also remain accountable for issuing complimentary vouchers only to justifiably qualified customers or prospects. For this reason, organizers can propose that sponsors desiring to distribute complimentary tickets or vouchers in connection with sales promotions reimburse the event for those actually redeemed by their customers. To make the promotion as cost-effective for the sponsor as possible, organizers may charge the sponsor the deepest discounted rate the budget will accommodate for redeemed tickets, coupons, or vouchers. This model places the financial responsibility for the redemption of vouchers with the salespersons or dealers, discouraging their distribution to anyone other than a qualified customer. The number of vouchers redeemed at the box office also provides the sponsor with measurable results by which to gauge the effectiveness of the promotion. It is strongly recommended that a disclaimer be included on the vouchers that clearly state that they are redeemable only while tickets remain available. Any restrictions on their validity (such as weekdays only, limits to certain price categories, etc.) should also be stated and positioned obviously on the coupon.

The Sales Process

A sports event director can be imagined as the coach of a football team, signaling plays to the quarterback from the sidelines, focusing the team's talents and resources on the pursuit of the goal—the sale of an event sponsorship to a prospective corporate partner. The quarterback, the individual or group empowered to make the snap on-field decisions, is responsible for executing the play. This person or squad must maneuver around a line of shifting obstacles and challenges, a defensive line filled with a prospect's objections, reticence, and apathy. The quarterback may be the staff member or internal department responsible for developing sponsors, a volunteer ringing the doorbells of neighborhood businesses, or an event marketing agency retained to take best advantage of its expertise and list of contacts. The very best are armed with an understanding of what specific sponsor prospects want from their sports event relationship.

The coach calls for plays that probe, test, and retrench, seeking the right way through these defenses. The opening play starts with the creation and presentation of a sponsorship program that lines up a series of benefits designed to provide business solutions to prospective partners. The first appeal to the sponsor prospect may move the ball close to the goal for a long gain, or perhaps at first only a few inches. Deficient intelligence or a poorly conceived presentation may result in a loss, the event's position moved even farther away from the goal. The ever-running time clock creates a sense of great urgency. There is only a limited amount of time available to bring the package into the end zone and to a victorious close. The quarterback reads the field and senses the potential areas of penetration. New plays are tried, strategies adjusted based on intelligence gained with each attempt and, eventually, the program presented is strong enough to score a touchdown. Or perhaps every play, no matter how strategic or creative, will fail and the game will have to be pursued with another, more receptive company. Alternatively, as the time ticks down to the event date and the final result appears in doubt, the coach may call for a field goal—a smaller sponsorship package to close at least some kind of deal before time runs out—a gain of only three points instead of a six-point touchdown. Three points—50 percent of the revenue the coach set out to realize—might be all that is possible to achieve at this point in this game. But, it may just be enough to help win the campaign.

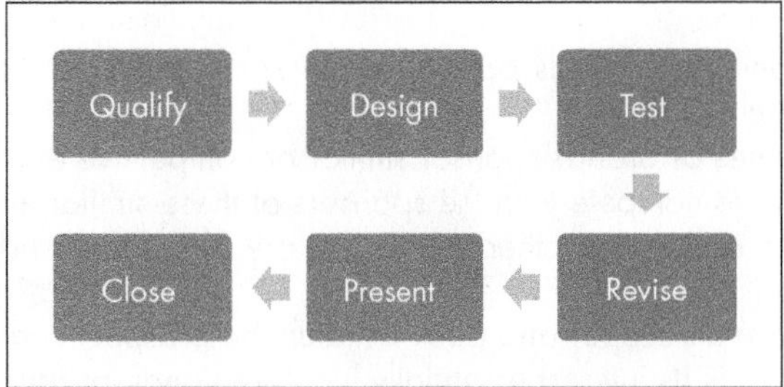

Figure 7.2 Six Steps in the Sponsorship Sales Process

In today's event management and marketing game, a USO philosophy, that is, understanding what this stakeholder—a potential sponsor—wants from a sports event, is the essential unpinning to the sales process. This philosophy is suffused throughout the six-step process of selling sports event sponsorships as described and in Figure 7.2: **(1) qualify, (2) design, (3) test, (4) revise, (5) present,** and **(6) close.**

QUALIFY and Target Sponsor Prospects

Too often, event organizers and marketing agencies create attractive but generic presentations featuring a standardized package of sponsor benefits. They blindly dispatch them to all corners of the business community with the expectation that some marketer, somewhere, will find the event and its promotional potential so compelling, so obvious, and such a perfect complement to their marketing strategy that it will instantly express interest in becoming a corporate partner. Easily separable levels of benefits define their sponsorship strata—sweeping, ubiquitous benefits for the highest-priced title sponsorship, significant exposure and hospitality opportunities for presenting sponsors, and diminishing levels of signage and ticket allotments for supporting partners. This practice is the classical "shotgun approach" to marketing, scattering shots over a wide area in hope of scoring a hit. The more labor- and capital-efficient "rifle shot approach," a precisely tuned campaign to reach specific target markets, is no less applicable to generating sports event sponsorship sales than it is to consumer marketing.

Most sports event organizers understand the fan base for their sports and events. The marketing agencies and outside consultants they retain to develop sponsorship revenue for these programs require no less familiarity with the product and its audience. This grounding helps marketing agencies and salespeople to recognize the unique opportunities and demographics that can be made available to the right event sponsors and better match prospects to the event.

The event marketer must narrow the vast universe of potential partners through a series of filters that qualify only those prospects most likely to perceive sponsorship of the organizer's event as an effective marketing opportunity and cost-efficient business solution. Figure 7.3 provides a list of questions that can be used to help refine the roster of qualified prospective sponsors. The sales process begins with the selection of target companies that may be approached to support the event. The ideal prospect should be one that shares a common or similar target market with the event, a company with existing or likely customers who are among those expected to either attend or participate. The demographics, lifestyles, interests, and habits of an event's guests or attendees should closely approximate those of the prospective sponsor's customers.

1. What companies or brands appeal to the same customer demographics and lifestyles as the event?
2. What companies or brands sponsor similar or competitive events?
3. What companies compete with the sponsors of these similar events?
4. What companies sponsor other events that are also supported by your existing sponsors?
5. What is the event's scope, and does it match the prospect company's marketing strategies (e.g., is its interest essentially local, regional, or national)?
6. What companies are launching new products or services that can be promoted by an event marketing partnership?
7. What companies are among those the event organizer doing business with that may consider cash or VIK sponsor relationships (e.g., vendors, companies represented by volunteer workers, or by members of the board)?
8. What companies embrace the same charitable or community-based causes that the event will serve or support?
9. Do the prospect sponsors possess the financial wherewithal to support the event?
10. What is the financial health of the prospective sponsors?

Figure 7.3 Top 10 Qualifiers for Sponsor Prospects

SIDELINE STORY

A Youth-Oriented Sports Marketer

Mountain Dew, acquired by Pepsi-Cola in 1964, is a carbonated citrus soft drink brand that has been marketed, in the words of the company's website, toward "young, active, outdoor types." The 55 mg of caffeine in each 12-ounce can is roughly 50 percent greater than the stimulant content in Pepsi's flagship cola brand and about half the content of a cup of brewed coffee. Pepsi reinforces its youthful perception in the marketplace through a major sponsorship of the Dew Tour and Winter Dew Tour festivals of action sports televised on NBC Sports, featuring BMX, skateboarding, and freeskiing, and other competitions targeting young active consumers. Mountain Dew's high level of sponsorship support provides the brand with title identification for the two national tours. It is joined by other marketers seeking youthful, active-lifestyle audiences that participate as location-specific title or presenting sponsors for individual stops on the tour such the Pantech Open, the Toyota Challenge, and the Dew Tour Championships presented by GoDaddy.com, to name a few. Mountain Dew's highly engaging event marketing efforts in online, print, and outdoor advertising campaigns, video highlights, games, and interactive content on its website, and product packaging work together to reinforce the image of a brand that appeals to the most creative, talented, and daring of today's young, homegrown athletes.

One of the quickest and easiest ways to get a sense of a company's target market, and frequently the types of events that are sponsored to promote its products, is to visit the websites and social network pages of the brand and its parent company. A visit to the website of the popular soft drink Mountain Dew, for example, demonstrates the brand's commitment to an active, cutting edge, youth-oriented culture, many of the sports events they sponsor that reflect this lifestyle, and other content directed to this audience, such as downloadable music and interactive games. The same brand's social network sites showcase up-to-the-second details about the athletes and events Mountain Dew sponsors, special promotions, and streams of interactive customer commentary on the product, and the lifestyles it serves. The Sideline Story on the opposite page describes this intriguing brand, its target market, and some of its featured events.

Revealing resources for identifying potential sponsors are the websites and social network pages of events that are similar to, or even competitive with, your own. Reach out to these sponsor companies, as well as those who compete with them for the same types of customers, to continue building your list of prospects. It is also worthwhile to visit the sites of unrelated sports, music, community, and cultural events that may appeal to audiences that share the same demographics and lifestyle characteristics as the fans of your own sport and event.

Consider the hidden members of your event's corporate family, any entity with a vested interest in the success of your event, such as your organization's suppliers and service providers. It is not realistic to expect that all, or even most, suppliers will be open to providing cash or VIK in return for a sponsorship position. After all, many are in business expressly to generate cash by selling their products and services to the event industry. Some, however, may see the value in reinforcing their partnerships with the event and its organizer for the development of additional business. For those sports event organizations that are under the supervision of a board of directors, advisory board, or other entity comprised of community and business leaders, a potential sponsor may already be sitting at your conference table, just a few seats away. Explore how the companies represented by these involved advisors can take best advantage of a more formalized business relationship with the event (especially if your event is a not-for-profit endeavor that accepts donations).

Have you read an article about an exciting new product or service that is being introduced at about the same time as your event? Product launches are usually funded with a temporary growth spurt of marketing dollars. Most companies, along with their advertising and public relations agencies, are always looking for new and unique ways to spread the good word about a fledgling product or service. Sports events can offer new product introduction campaigns the sampling, exposure, and engaging promotional opportunities that traditional advertising simply cannot match.

If your event is organized by a not-for-profit entity, is a program designed to improve the community's quality of life, or is a revenue generator for a charity, search for companies that support the same kinds of charitable endeavors. Check the charity's list of major corporate donors, as well as the supporters of similar charities to generate more leads for your list of prospective sponsors. Cause-related marketing—that is, the generation of funds for a worthy charity—can be a powerful motivator in developing corporate partners. Many companies have two discrete sources of support for events—a marketing budget for promotional opportunities and a community relations budget for supporting worthy causes. Is the event best positioned as a marketing opportunity, or might it have stronger appeal to a particular sponsor as deserving of charitable support?

The final considerations that should be infused into any process of qualifying potential event sponsors are the analysis of the financial wherewithal and health of targeted companies. Does the prospect company generate sufficient revenues to consider a sponsorship, and, if so, at what level of participation? If the company is healthy but possesses limited resources, a large

SIDELINE STORY

Founded to Promote Sports

Many not-for-profit organizations that generate revenues for distribution to worthy community or charitable causes embrace grassroots sports events, not just as recipients of their funding, but also as marketing tools for the promotion of their own agendas. The Florida Sports Foundation, for example, a division of Enterprise Florida, Inc., is a private not-for-profit corporation chartered to promote and develop professional, amateur, and recreational sports and fitness activities that support the state's burgeoning \$36 billion sports industry. Among its many endeavors, the foundation stages the Sunshine State Games, an amateur Olympic-style multisport event that not only provides an outstanding training and quality-of-life experience for 8,000 in-state participants, but also generates a sizable economic impact for the host region. Recognizing the state's attractiveness as a sports destination and the industry's potential for supporting the business community and generating tax revenues, the foundation offers event organizers the ability to apply for grants to attract sports events that are either up for bidding to interested communities, or are completely new. Essential requirements for a successful application include the potential for generating significant economic impact for the state of Florida and that any grant award be integrally necessary to the success of the event (i.e., the event might not be financially feasible to stage without it). As the foundation develops its own sponsors to fund the grants and continue promoting the state as a premier sports destination, organizers are obligated to acknowledge the Florida Sports Foundation as an event sponsor or supporter.

cash sponsorship is unlikely. Alternatively, a more modest cash sponsorship package, or some combination of cash and VIK might increase a company's receptivity. What is the state of the industry in which the company does business? If the industry is under economic stress, but the company is at the vanguard, VIK may, again, help to close a deal. What is the company's financial position—it is profitable or losing money? Is it hiring employees or downsizing staff? Do as much due diligence on the potential sponsor's corporate health as you possibly can. It is risky to partner with a company under financial stress because its presence may exclude other, more healthy companies from participating in the event. Slow payment or default by a distressed partner can cause an event to experience cash flow problems or fall short of its own budget expectations.

DESIGN a Sponsorship Program

It is now time for you to call for the right play that you, as coach, believe will run your team past the objections, reticence, and apathy of prospective sponsor companies. Sponsor revenue expectations projected during the budgeting process should anticipate the scaling of sponsorships into a number of price categories. Although there are many possible models for creating sponsorship tiers depending on the nature and structure of the event, Figure 7.4 illustrates a generalized pyramidal hierarchy of sports event sponsorships. The model divides available opportunities into four broad levels of participation: (1) title sponsorship, (2) presenting sponsorship, (3) category exclusive sponsors (also frequently called "official" sponsors), and (4) nonexclusive sponsors and

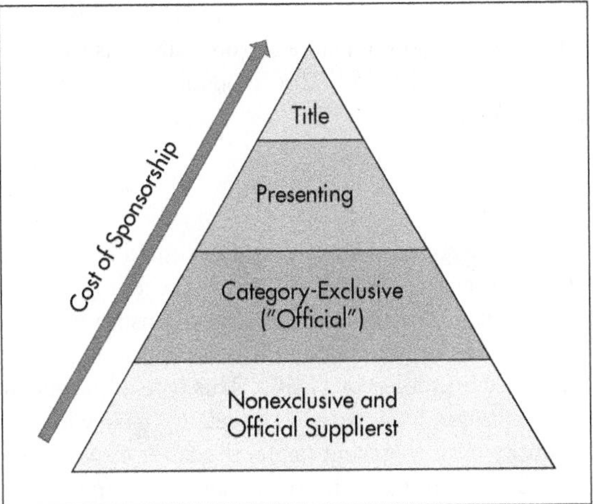

Figure 7.4 Sponsorship Pyramid

official suppliers. A subset of nonexclusive sponsors—donors—may also be available to not-for-profit events, and may provide an additional source of revenue to organizers who qualify.

Title Sponsorship

The level of greatest corporate support is *title sponsorship,* which, when available, is typically held by a single sponsor. Title sponsors can expect to reap the most valuable business solutions (i.e., customized package of benefits) as compared with an event's other corporate partners. What they are really paying a premium for, however, is to ensure that their corporate or brand name is uniquely and inseparably connected to the identity of the event. Whether motivated by the desire for maximizing exposure to its product's target market, bragging rights over its competitors, or demonstrating its pre-eminence in the community, title sponsorship can be a powerful, far-reaching tool for the corporate partner. A company that purchases a title sponsorship enjoys the singular benefits of appearing in all advertising, press releases (and, it is hoped, in the resulting media coverage), web pages, promotions, tickets, signage, and more. Examples of events with title sponsors include the Professional Golfers Association's (PGA) Cadillac Championship and Sony Open, college football's Maaco Bowl, Little Caesars Pizza Bowl and Beef 'O'Brady's Bowl; Major League Baseball's Taco Bell All-Star Sunday, Gatorade All-Star Workout Day, and SiriusXM All-Star Futures Game, the National Hockey League's Molson Canadian NHL SuperSkills competition, and the ING New York City Marathon, to name just a few.

Naturally, inclusion of the company identity in the event title and its graphic incorporation into the event logo clearly and definitively separate the title sponsor from all other partners to the widest possible audience. Some event organizers consider it important to maintain their own identity within the event title and logo to provide an historical context and continuity, as well as to make it easier to promote ticket sales and generate media coverage (e.g. college football's Tostitos BCS National Championship Game, AT&T Cotton Bowl, and Hyundai Sun Bowl, the Sprint NBA All-Star Celebrity Game, Bridgestone Super Bowl Halftime Show, Tim Horton's NHL All-Star Game, and Scotia Bank NHL Fan Fair), while other organizers place less importance on including their own identity (e.g., Atlanta's Chick-fil-A Bowl). This dominant position in the title provides the sponsor with added impact and importance. In cases in which the corporate sponsor's name provides the event's identity in its entirety (e.g., Sony Open), the event promoter can attach a significant premium. In such instances, journalists, as well as other sponsor partners in their own promotional programs, would find it impossible to refer to events without the title partner's corporate identification.

Presenting Sponsorship

Just beneath the pinnacle of the sponsorship pyramid occupied by a title partner is the presenting sponsorship. Instead of the corporate or brand name preceding the event identity, the sponsor's identity follows the title (e.g., the Senior PGA Championship presented by KitchenAid, the Military Bowl presented by Northrup Grumman, NBA All-Star Saturday Night presented by State Farm, and the NFL Experience presented by GMC). This type of participation is generally priced at a lower level than title sponsorship because of the relative ease with which media reports can separate the corporate identity from the event name, the latter of which retains a position of primacy. The premium value of a presenting sponsorship, however, is in the brand's relationship to the event and its logo, as well as the partner's ubiquitous presence in the promotions and marketing campaigns undertaken by the event organizer. But because the identities are so much easier to separate, it is considerably more difficult to insist that an event's other, lower-tier partners feature the presenting sponsor's name in advertising or promotion that activates their respective sponsorships.

In the eyes of other event sponsors, the presence of title and/or presenting sponsors can devalue the perception of their own participation. It is wise to disclose all levels of partnership available during the presentation phase, including title and presenting sponsorship opportunities, for two reasons. First, it may entice existing sponsors to consider a greater investment in the event. Lower-level sponsors will also evaluate their event relationship knowing in advance that a title relationship may subsequently be sold and will, therefore, have a clear and realistic picture of how other corporate or brand entities may enjoy greater exposure than their own.

Category Exclusive Sponsors

A title and presenting sponsorship can account for a sizable percentage, or even most, of an event's sponsorship revenue budget. The largest number of sponsor companies and brands, however, are most often found in the area of category-exclusive sponsors, also widely known as *official sponsors*. Because sponsorships of this type are more economically accessible to companies at more moderate price levels, events are usually blessed with more of them. Selling a title and/or presenting sponsorship are the ideal of most event promoters. If there are enough category-exclusive sponsors, though, the event can still meet reasonably set sponsorship revenue goals. For this reason, and as illustrated in Figure 7.5, the sponsorship pyramid depends on many more of these essential building blocks for a respectable amount of both revenue and promotional activation.

Note that the sponsorships in this area of the pyramid are much greater in number, and may even account for a cumulatively greater sum in revenue. The category-exclusive building blocks can include any variety of businesses, as illustrated by examples in the figure of those that commonly sponsor sports events. There is an almost limitless opportunity to expand sponsor categories to include companies in many other industries.

Sponsors buy into events to convert the benefits they provide into specific business solutions. What protects them from their competitors doing likewise is the exclusivity within their category guaranteed by the event organizer. It is essential to define exactly what category is being granted exclusivity. Will an automotive company's sponsorship offer exclusivity in regard to cars and trucks, or just cars? Will it preclude the event promoter from pursuing a sponsor relationship with a rental car company that does not feature the automotive sponsor's models? Would a

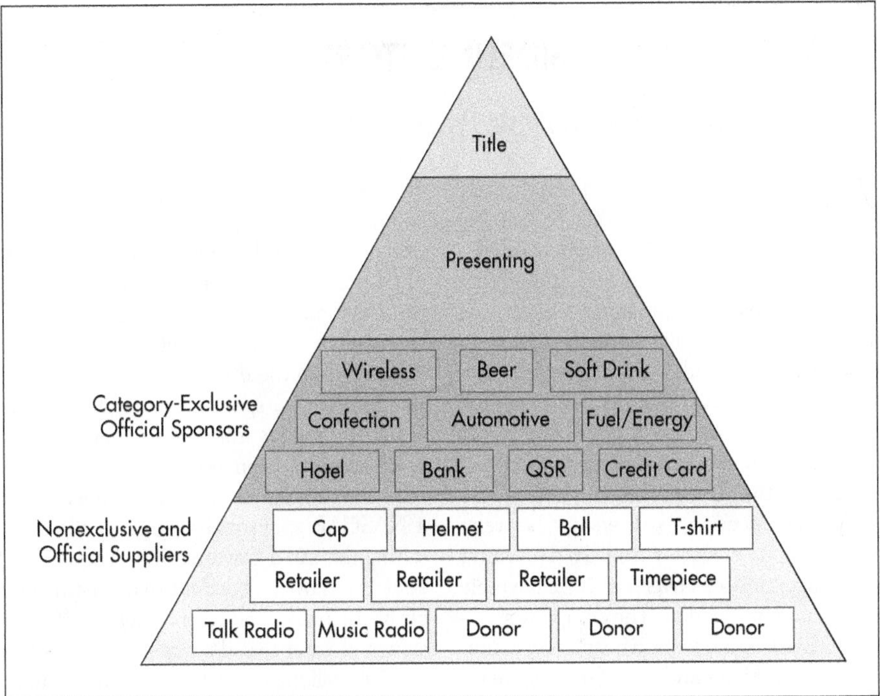

Figure 7.5 Building Blocks of the Sponsorship Pyramid

relationship with a motorcycle manufacturer still be permissible? Does the exclusivity extend to auto parts, prohibiting a deal with an after-market parts manufacturer or retailer? Will an airline partner's sponsorship prevent the organizer from pursuing a relationship with a railroad or bus line? If it is solely a domestic airline, can the organizer pursue a relationship with an international carrier? Does a deal with a soft drink company cover soda only, or will it include juices, water, coffee, tea, milk and dairy drinks, and isotonic sports beverages? If the company neither sells nor distributes these other beverage types, does the soft drink manufacturer's exclusivity still prevent you from selling sponsorships to other companies that do sell these products? Does the soft drink deal permit the promoter to pursue quick-service restaurant (QSR) sponsorships with any chain it desires, or only those that pour that brand? Will a mobile device manufacturer's package exclude deals with phone and data service companies that do not offer its products?

Obviously, from the promoter's point of view, it is most advantageous to limit a sponsor's exclusivity to the narrowest extent possible, enabling the event to attract sponsorships from a greater number of companies and industry types. From the sponsor's standpoint, the wider the definition of exclusivity, the more valuable the partnership will be. Event promoters will often place reasonable limits on areas of exclusivity in the first presentation they make to prospective sponsors, and may negotiate a higher purchase price if additional categories are later requested by a sponsor to make up for the loss in potential revenues.

Exclusivity granted by a sponsorship does not necessarily mean that the company can use the event to promote all the products it sells within protected categories. Thus, it is important to define the brands or product lines that are included in the sponsorship. Consider the fictional soft drink company again: Even if the sponsorship protects the company from the promotion of any other

SIDELINE STORY

Activating Multiple Procter & Gamble Brands

With a diverse portfolio of industry-leading consumer products, Procter & Gamble (P&G) focuses its sports marketing efforts on the promotion of individual brand identities rather than that of the parent company. Events with a series of venues, hospitality opportunities, or a schedule of events broader than the sports contest itself provide P&G with discrete, targeted opportunities to promote many of its brands with a minimum of clutter and competition.

In 2010, the US Olympic Committee (USOC) announced a partnership between Team USA and P&G for the 2010 Winter Olympic Games in Vancouver and 2012 Olympic Summer Games in London. The company sponsored the *P&G Family Home*, a hospitality center for Team USA athletes and their families, members of the media, and invited guests. The facility offered guests an opportunity to watch continuous Olympics coverage, refresh themselves with complimentary food and beverages, and enjoy an Internet café, among other features. Free laundry service was available to guests courtesy of P&G's Tide detergent, refreshments were provided in the Pringles Snack Lounge, and an onsite salon provided makeovers and relaxing spa services courtesy of Pantene shampoo, Cover Girl cosmetics, and the company's Olay (lotion), Venus (razor), and Secret (deodorant) brands. Toddlers could romp in a Pampers disposable diapers play area while parents sampled dental hygiene products at the Crest/Oral B (toothpaste) Smile Center.

The financial terms of the deal were not released, but it was disclosed that a combination of cash and VIK were components of the sponsorship agreement. P&G was granted promotional rights to Team USA over a wide range of its brands, which included the placement of the Olympic rings on the packaging of more than a dozen P&G products during the months leading up to the events.

Sometimes, sponsors derive broader, unanticipated benefits from a more narrowly defined association with an event. Perhaps one of the most famous such instances benefited P&G, a NASCAR sponsor through its Gillette brand, during the 2012 Daytona 500, when racer Juan Pablo Montoya collided into a dryer-truck parked off of the track. The crash touched off an explosion and extensive damage to the truck, spilling 200 gallons of jet fuel onto the course and resulting in a delay to the race that could not be resumed until the surface could be rendered safe. Racetrack maintenance crews quickly responded, dumping large boxes of Tide detergent onto the track and scrubbing the surface with brooms in the effort to clean the spill. Although not one of that particular race's sponsors, the deployment of the unmistakable bright orange boxes of Tide was captured and commented on by the national television broadcasters for up to 15 minutes during the wait to resume and was viewed by millions on various social networking sites. P&G quickly included this unexpected exposure bonanza into Tide's marketing plan, which included the creation of a television advertisement featuring footage of the cleanup effort that aired during coverage of NASCAR's subsequent Sprint Cup Subway Fresh Fit 500 race.

beverage at the event, can it promote only its cola brand or all of the flavors that the company bottles and distributes? Will it also be permitted to promote its citrus soda, mixers, fruit-flavored drinks or juices, and isotonic beverages? If not well-managed, a single sponsorship has potential to create a great deal of signage clutter, making it appear that there are many more sponsors than actually exist and devaluing the exposure of other, single-brand sponsors. However, as illustrated by the

Sideline Story on page 176, if properly priced and creatively designed, a multiple-brand sponsorship can provide a partner with significant impact and activation opportunities.

Category-exclusive sponsors desiring to stand out from their corporate peers frequently seek ways of exhibiting more "ownership" of an event, or an association that elevates them in some fashion above other sponsors. With a little creative thought, the title or presenting sponsorship of a specific event element may be devised. A trophy or award may be created that bears the sponsor's name, such as: the National Football League's "Pepsi Rookie of the Year," Major League Baseball's "Rolaids Relief Man, and the PGA's "FedEx Cup Trophy," Halftime or intermission entertainment, pregame festivities, and postgame parties often bear the identities of category-exclusive sponsors. Video or message board programming, event-specific apps and web pages, guest services areas and information kiosks, concessions areas, nearly any element of an event may be sponsored by one of the event's roster of corporate partners, providing the sponsor with the sense of ownership it desires.

Some category-exclusive sponsors are less concerned with the ownership of particular event elements than they are with preferential signage locations at the event site, inclusion in advertising, or access to hospitality opportunities. For this reason, event promoters should not feel compelled to include ownership entitlement to specific event elements in every sponsorship pitch. You may be giving away something of little value to a particular sponsor that can help close a deal with another company that places greater emphasis on this type of benefit.

Nonexclusive Sponsors and Official Suppliers

For financial, legal, or practical reasons, an organizer may desire to offer certain categories of sponsorship on a nonexclusive basis. For example, some local ordinances regulating the sales and marketing of alcoholic beverages bar beer companies from enjoying product-exclusive sponsorships that prohibit the sale of other brands of beer. For community-based grassroots organizations such as local Little Leagues, it may be not practical to have a single law firm, dentist, day camp, pizzeria, or chiropractor involved with an event to the exclusion of all other local concerns in their business categories. Being able to open the event to as many local businesses as possible, even those that are competitive with one another, keeps the cost of sponsorships to each community partner at a reasonable level and can help a volunteer organization close many more deals.

Retailers can also be prime candidates for nonexclusive deals. Providing opportunities to sell event merchandise at more than one retailer's locations is often in the best interest of an event organizer. Therefore, designating more than one "official merchandise headquarters" can be a good idea. Unique promotional packages can be developed to make each store's offerings unique and responsive to the specific needs and demographics of their customers. These activities may include a schedule of athlete appearances at certain stores or malls, an exclusive sales period granted to a partner store over a limited time (e.g., during the first week of product sales), or selected items being made available at only one location.

Media partners, more fully discussed in Play 8, are also good targets for nonexclusive relationships. Radio stations with sports talk formats and Top 40 music channels, for instance, may appeal to totally different listener demographics, and, as such, they would not be truly competitive with one another. It is, therefore, often possible to designate more than one "official radio station" for an event based on the broadcasters' formats.

Any sponsor relationship can be crafted as a nonexclusive partnership, presuming the participants are in agreement. This category is useful for generating last-minute revenues after it has been determined that no company will enter into a more pricey, exclusive relationship. It is also beneficial for smaller businesses and industries that cannot afford participating at an exclusive level. That is why official suppliers are often, though not always, nonexclusive. If it is relatively inexpensive for a supplier to provide its products as VIK to the event (sports equipment manufacturers, for example), the value to the event simply may not be great enough to warrant granting exclusive rights. Striking a nonexclusive deal, however, may be worthwhile to the supplier for the purposes of exposure, and to the organizer to reduce the expenditure of actual cash.

One note of caution: Once a nonexclusive deal is finalized within a specific sponsor category, it will no longer be possible to accept a competitor's offer to enter into a more lucrative exclusive deal later. Be judicious in determining what categories you ultimately decide to open on a nonexclusive basis to avoid potential lost revenues.

For not-for-profit events, a subset category of nonexclusive sponsorships—*donors*—may provide additional opportunities to generate revenue. The key distinguishing characteristic between sponsors and donors is generally the former's expectation of promotional benefits and/or the transference of rights to logos and other intellectual property between the parties. Donors, by contrast, simply support the event by *giving* money to the organization staging the event with no expectation of receiving tangible benefits in return. It is common to thank donors for their generosity in programs, on event websites, in advertising, and perhaps on signage at the event site. But, these acknowledgments come at the discretion of the event organizer, without a defined *quid pro quo* attached to the donation, promotional rights, or the rights to use event or corporate logos in promotional activities. Donations are simply that, monetary gifts that can come from any socially responsible or civic-minded person, family, or organization, with no expectation of exclusivity. They do, however, often come with the expectation of tax advantages, and, as such, are not available to for-profit events or organizers. For not-for-profit organizers and events, they can provide valuable fundraising opportunities to increase the charitable yield.

That's Not All, Folks—Create Innovations That Suit Your Event

Although the sponsorship categories described above are among those most commonly encountered, corporate relationships can take any creative form that a promoter can imagine. Devise new sponsorship concepts to suit your event and organization. For example, an event organizer can establish a partnership in which the sponsor becomes a *guarantor*. Guarantors promise to cover cash shortfalls, up to a certain level, at the conclusion of the event to ensure the organizer remains solvent or the program generates guaranteed revenues for charitable purposes. The company can fund this guarantee with a grant or agree to purchase a specified number of tickets, buying and using them outright or donating them to a deserving charity or worthy recipients such as active military families. Alternatively, guarantors can agree to cover the difference between actual sales and a predefined number of tickets to cover potential losses. A guarantor relationship is best established for events organized by not-for-profit groups or those designed to funnel a significant percentage of their proceeds to charity.

With the exception of donors, every sponsor relationship, regardless of whether it takes a traditional or an innovative, unorthodox form, will require some fulfillment inventory (e.g., signage, tickets, ad space, etc.) provided by the event in exchange for the sponsor's participation. Again, be sure that the inventory of benefits each deal consumes is commensurate with the benefits it provides to the event's bottom line.

How to Design the Sponsorship Program

Here is where understanding stakeholders' objectives—applying the USO Principle—pays the most handsome dividends. The sports event organizer now has a reasonably good idea of the business wants and needs of the prospective sponsor and knows what resources he or she can offer that sponsor through a relationship with the event. By matching the menu of event sponsorship resources to the business needs of the prospect, the event organizer is no longer selling just benefits, but *business solutions*!

On a spreadsheet, organize the menu of solutions your event can possibly provide to a sponsor. Then, create the number of levels of participation most appropriate to your event. In the example illustrated in Figure 7.6, sponsorships are divided into the four basic levels discussed in this chapter—title, presenting, official sponsor (category-exclusive), and official supplier. The latter two categories can be further subdivided into a series of price and benefit tiers, if desired, to provide more options to prospective sponsors. In this example, the levels are simply referred to as *title, presenting,* and *official* sponsors, but there is no particular importance to names of the various levels or subdivisions. They can just as easily be called gold, silver, and bronze, or diamond, ruby, and emerald, or identified as suggested by the sport itself (e.g., homer, triple, double, single).

The levels are then distinguished by the value of the benefits they include (which will be further illustrated shortly) and the degree to which they will be provided, always remembering that with most benefits come fulfillment costs. Contingent on these fulfillment costs, the organizer's desired return on investment and the overall revenue goals of the event, a base price can be assigned to each level. In this example, the title sponsorship commands a premium of three times that of the category-exclusive sponsorship, and just below twice the cost of a presenting sponsorship, because of the ubiquity of the company name in every reference to, and marketing program for, the event. The difference between the presenting sponsorship and the category exclusive package is slightly less than double the cost to entice official sponsors to consider upgrading to a presenting position at a reasonable increase in cost. Finally, a minimum value in cash and/or VIK has been set to qualify companies as official suppliers. (These multiples are for illustrative purposes only. Price differences between sponsorship levels are totally at the discretion of each event promoter.)

Remember that you are only organizing a basic framework for sponsorship packaging, as not all of the features of a particular partnership category will be of equal usefulness or value to any two companies. It is, therefore, suggested that the package price include a margin of contingency to cover unanticipated fulfillment costs. This will enable the promoter to demonstrate some flexibility in providing more value and different, more applicable business solutions for the sponsor during the negotiating process without necessitating an automatic increase in price.

A successful sponsorship presents marketing solutions customized for each prospective partner. Event promoters must remain flexible as they fashion the available benefits into packages that meet each company's fingerprint-different needs, ever mindful of the revenue and promotional requirements of the event itself. A package designed for a business-to-business sponsor may offer more opportunities for client hospitality, manifest by the inclusion of more tickets in premium locations and an increased number of invitations to VIP receptions. To offset the additional fulfillment costs encountered in accommodating these additional benefits, the organizer may offer fewer advertisements or on-site signage positions. If the fulfillment costs are still greater than were assumed at a particular sponsorship level, the promoter may increase the price of the package originally presented, or attempt to use these additional needs as an incentive for the prospect to consider a higher level of sponsorship.

Customizing a Sponsorship Package

An event organizer who is wisely prepared to customize sponsorship offerings to meet the business objectives of his or her target partners' brands has already determined how much profit needs to remain after a package is sold. He or she has calculated the cost of fulfilling each element of

ELEMENTS FOR SAMPLE SPORTS	**Title Sponsor**	**Presenting Sponsor**	**Official Sponsor**	**Official Supplier**
Event Identity	*Sponsor/Sample* Sports Event	*Sample* Sports Event presented by *Sponsor*	Official Sponsor	Official Supplier
Event Logo	*Sponsor* Integrated into Event Logo	"Presented by" tag	–	–
Use of Event Marks in Advertising (with event organizer's approval)	Yes, in all sponsor's advertising and promotions	Yes, in all sponsor's advertising and promotions	Yes, with Official Sponsor tag	Yes, with Official Supplier tag
Line of Sight Signage	10, plus integrated logo appearances	8	4	2
Public Address Announcements	10, plus integrated into every p.a. mention of the event	6, plus integrated into every p.a. mention of the event	4	2
Videoboard 30-second Spots	6	4	2	1
Event Website Exposure	Animated banner ad and link on top of home and ticket ordering pages	Column ad and link on right bottom of home page	Ad and link on site location to be determined	Acknowledgment with other official suppliers
Event Print Advertising	Integrated logo in all	"Presented by" tag in all	Name acknowledgment in three full-page ads	–
Event Radio Advertising	Mentioned with Event Name	"Presented by" tag in all	–	–
Event Television Advertising	Integrated logo in all	"Presented by" tag in all	–	–
Attendee Database	Access to ticket buyer database for one-time use	Access to ticket buyer database for one-time use	–	–
Other	Name on ticket front and ad on ticket back	Name on ticket front	–	–

Figure 7.6 Sponsorship Benefits Grid for Sample Sports Event

Program Advertisement	Back Cover	Inside Front Cover	Full Page, Color	Half Page, B&W
Event Tickets	100 VIP	50 VIP, 50 G.A.	20 VIP, 30 G.A.	4 VIP, 10 G.A.
Pregame Reception	100	50	20	4
Postgame Gala	100	50	20	4
Other Features	Sponsor name printed on all tickets; prominence on event app artwork; 10 all-access passes; integrated logo on all event merchandise and staff uniform apparel, street banners and site decor; sponsor representative to present trophies; 50 autographed balls; use of 20′ × 20′ tent for sponsor demonstration purposes; sampling rights; right to host private meet-and-greet reception with athletes; other benefits to be negotiated	6 all-access passes; "Presented by" tag on all staff uniform apparel; 25 autographed balls; use of 20′ × 20′ tent for sponsor demonstration purposes; sampling rights; right to host private meet-and-greet reception with athletes; other benefits to be negotiated	10 autographed balls; use of 10′ × 10′ tent for sponsor demonstration purposes; sampling rights; other benefits to be negotiated	2 autographed balls; sampling rights; other benefits to be negotiated
Base Price, as Listed	**$150,000**	**$85,000**	**$50,000**	**$20,000**

Figure 7.6 *(Continued)*

the offer, including a little extra for contingency and ensured that once costs and contingencies are deducted, the profit margin has met the event's goals. As discussed, what remains is to assess the *value* of each element *to the prospective sponsor*. Even if providing a certain benefit does not incur any out-of-pocket expense, a value may be assigned, representing its fair market worth. For example, screening a 30-second advertisement on the stadium videoboard may not incur a cash cost to the event organizer, but, like a complimentary ticket, it certainly has a monetary value. Value of a sponsorship package element may be calculated by factoring in how many people are engaged, for how long, and how deeply. Using the example of the 30-second videoboard commercial, an ad that is screened when the number of people expected to be in attendance is at its highest is most valuable. One that runs during a short break in the action when the audience is most engaged will be more valuable than one that is placed during an intermission or when the audience will still be arriving, typically times when fans are more focused on conversation or buying beverages than activity on the screen.

Figure 7.7 illustrates one way to organize your event's sponsor benefits by estimating the fulfillment cost of each inclusion, as well as its market value. In this example, we expand the table outlining the presenting sponsorship package described in Figure 7.6. The actual cost of providing each line item is estimated in the third column. For example, the cost of designing, fabricating and installing line-of-sight signage is $3,000 for each of the four signs, for a total of

Element	Entitlement	Cost to Event	Value
Line of Sight Signage	4	$12,000	$25,000
Public Address Announcements	4	$0	$5,000
Videoboard 30-second Spots	2 1 pre-event 1 in-event	$0	$5,000 $20,000
Event Website Exposure	Column ad and link on right bottom of home page	$0	$5,000
Event Print Advertising	Integrated logo in all	$0	$50,000
Event Radio Advertising	"Presented by" tag in all	$0	$50,000
Event Television Advertising	"Presented by" tag in all	$0	$100,000
Attendee Database	Access to ticket buyer database for one-time use	$0	$10,000
Program Advertisement	Full Page, Color	$2,000	$5,000
Event Tickets	20 VIP 30 G.A.	$2,000 $750	$2,000 $750
Pregame Reception	20	$1,500	$3,000
Postgame Gala	20	$4,000	$10,000
Other Features	Sponsor name printed on all tickets. Prominence on event app. 10 all-access passes. Integrated logo on all event merchandise and staff uniform apparel. Street banners and site décor. Company rep to present trophies. 50 autographed balls. Use of 20′ × 20′ tent for sponsor demonstration purposes. Sampling rights. Right to host private meet and greet reception with athletes.	$0 $0 $0 $0 $25,000 $0 $500 $4,000 $0 $10,000	$20,000 $10,000 $2,000 $50,000 $50,000 $10,000 $5,000 $25,000 $25,000 $20,000
Totals		**$62,250**	**$507,750**

Figure 7.7 Calculating Relative Value of a Sponsorship

$12,000. This is included as a fulfillment cost because the sponsor advertising signage would not be installed if a sponsorship was not sold. Public address (p.a.) announcements, however, have no real cost to the budget because the public address announcer and installing or operating the p.a. system would cost the same with or without a sponsor. The identical philosophy is continued throughout the "Cost to Event" column, identifying costs that would not be encountered if the sponsorship was not sold.

The estimates in the "Value" column represent the event organizer's best projection of how the prospect company will assess the attractiveness of the sponsorship. Sponsorship agencies and experienced sponsorship sales professionals are particularly adept at calculating the value of a package. If you do not have access to professional assistance, try some of these hints to estimate value:

- Use the prices you would charge to nonsponsors purchasing the same opportunities at your event to derive the value of tickets, advertising, memorabilia, and other easily priced items.
- Apply prevailing advertising rates in the local market can help you derive estimates for radio and television exposure, online advertising and signage (compare to rates for outdoor billboards with similar foot traffic).
- Compare the value of hospitality with prices charged for tickets to receptions, dinners, and other events that attract similar guests in your market. A premium may be added if the hospitality is particularly exclusive and available only to "insiders."

The presenting sponsorship package illustrated in Figures 7.6 and 7.7 is priced at $150,000 with fulfillment costs of $62,250, a 58 percent margin of profit for the event organizer. Assuming the components of the offer address the marketing needs of the sponsor's brand, however, the $150,000 price of the sponsorship provides a highly attractive $507,750 in real and promotional value, three times the prospect company's monetary and/or VIK investment. If further customization is needed to better meet the needs of the prospect, try to stay within a comfortable range of your desired profit margin with respect to fulfillment costs, while maintaining or even boosting the value to the sponsor. (*Note:* The profit margin and real/promotional value used in this example are for illustrative purposes only, and are not meant to represent target or ideal proportions.)

Apply your creativity to keeping the sponsorship price down—but net revenues high and the value even higher. If the event is regionally televised and the sponsor is a local company that would benefit less from this exposure, you can reduce the cost of that sponsor's package by positioning its signage in areas not as regularly visible to the television cameras. Those positions may be worth a higher premium to a sponsor that values the wider exposure offered by the broadcast. Identify other opportunities you can add to a sponsor's package that increase its value without increasing fulfillment costs or the price. Can you invent an opportunity that adds value to the event experience that also provides a sponsor with a business solution to a specific need or objective? Is there a special trophy or award that can be given to a participating athlete who embodies the attributes of the sponsor's company or product (e.g., speed, accuracy, courage, innovation, improvement, style, or leadership)? Can you devise an unusual exposure opportunity or cooperative promotion that combines the event's goals with the prospective sponsor's business objectives? Try promoting a fan poll and ticket sweepstakes on the sponsor's and event's websites with links to the company's online commerce page and the event's ticket service.

There are, of course, instances where the application of the USO approach will result in identifying companies whose business objectives will just never match the demographics, lifestyle characteristics, and opportunities of a particular event at that time. Every effort should be expended to search for synergies before ruling whether an approach to a financially qualified prospect is worthwhile.

TEST the Opportunity

Oftentimes diligent research, no matter how thorough, cannot uncover all you might need to know for a successful sponsorship pitch. You may not be able to glean from secondary sources many of the new product introductions, promotional campaign launches, and strategic shifts secretly being hatched in the offices and boardrooms of many potential sponsors. The only way to know for certain whether your own strategy is well-positioned to attract a potential partner is to test your approach before presenting the opportunity.

When practical, try to schedule a brief meeting or conference call with your target prospect to gain a better understanding of the company's most immediate needs and objectives. If you have already identified the decision maker, attempt to speak with that individual directly. If there is a team of decision makers, you may be able to interview just one. Let them know who you are and what property you represent and make it clear that, you are not scheduling a sales pitch. Rather, you respect their time and would like to ensure that if and when you return to provide details on how your event can provide effective promotional opportunities, it will be on target and worth the time for thorough consideration.

This step may be the most difficult to effectuate, especially for prospects with whom the event organizer has never had a relationship. Marketers are very busy executives and may not accommodate the request if they do not immediately see a benefit to their company. They may also be guarded as to what their objectives truly are to avoid having information leak to their competitors. Offer to sign a confidentiality agreement if you sense that this is the case. Unless the event or the organizer has had previous dealings with the marketer, do not expect to receive more than a very modest amount of time from the prospect. Prepare ahead of the first outreach and know what questions, as few and as focused as possible, you want to ask. Your only ability to test your assumptions may be that very first call. But, showing an interest in focusing your sponsorship proposal to the company's strategies and needs can increase the chances that it will be reviewed when it is received.

If you are only afforded a brief phone call, try to limit your questions to the fewest and most revealing possible. Figure 7.8 lists three such questions designed to provide you with the most information possible while generating the least resistance.

If your event is held annually, be sure to invite potential prospects to attend as your guests before pitching them a sponsorship. You can often discover much about what a company looks for in a sponsorship while you meet a decision maker in a casual setting and make that person feel like an insider walking around the site.

REVISE the Opportunity

The event promoter has now gathered the intelligence necessary to identify the objectives, needs, and attributes of the prospective sponsor company or brand. Demonstrating responsiveness and flexibility, the promoter must then line up the appropriate opportunities that the event can offer

- I notice that [insert prospect company's name] has sponsored [name or type of event(s)] in the past. What have you tried to achieve with these partnerships?
- How does [your company] measure the success of these event sponsorships?
- What is your vision of how a perfect sponsorship would help to achieve your company's objectives?

Figure 7.8 Three Sample Test Questions

to achieve a partner's goals. Now, it is time to create your own *flying wedge,* the customized proposal that will smash through apathy by clearly and inarguably illustrating the value the event can provide to the prospective sponsor, and sweeping possible questions and objections out of the play by anticipating and answering them before they can surface.

Taking all questions and feedback into consideration, and adding some creativity, flexibility and intuition, the promoter should tailor the package, incorporating the pertinent solutions in response to the additional information provided by the prospect. Now that the organizer knows as much as possible about the prospect, the offer may rely on additional background information and statistics that strengthen the appeal of the event in a way that will demonstrate your best understanding of the business objectives of the prospective partner. Reallocate the fulfillment costs of superfluous benefits to beef up those the company finds more appealing. Reinforce every facet of the presentation—not just "the opportunity"—to maximize its chance for success. Finally, reassess whether an upward revision in the sponsorship fee is required to adequately cover any new or expanded fulfillment expenses, or a downward revision is necessary to demonstrate responsiveness to the company's desire for involvement at a lower level.

PRESENT the Opportunity: The Sponsorship Deck

Your flying wedge is now ready to be designed and executed in a formal presentation to the sponsor prospect. The play will unfold through the development of a focused presentation that tells the story of your event and how it can best provide the prospect with effective business solutions designed just for that sponsor.

There are two components to your presentation—the personal, verbal demonstration that a sponsor's marketing wants and needs may be met by your sports event opportunity, and the physical, leave-behind materials that will keep selling well after the meeting has concluded. The written presentation is also widely known as a *sponsorship deck*, an easy-to-read restatement of the most important points of the presentation accompanied by relevant illustrations, graphs, and charts. An example of a sponsorship deck for a fictional regional multisport tournament may be found in Appendix 7.

An effective sponsorship deck demonstrates that the event promoter possesses at least a basic understanding of the company's event marketing objectives and builds a persuasive case for how sponsoring the event can provide solutions for the company's wants and needs. The deck should contain pertinent and comprehensive information that supports the promoter's arguments, organized in a logical, easy-to-digest format. How the information is presented is a matter of personal preference. We prefer to use short paragraphs and, where possible, use bullet points instead of, or preceding, the various sections of prose. This technique makes it easy for prospects to scan the deck after the presentation for the information they believe is most salient to their evaluation and ultimate decision.

It is essential that sponsorship opportunities be presented in person. There is simply no way to adequately communicate the excitement of your sports event through the mail, e-mail, or web links alone. Actually, there is no way to be certain that your delivered sponsorship proposal, regardless of how well composed, will even be opened or read. If it is read, there is no way to respond to questions or counter objections before opinions are formed. Whenever possible, the sponsorship presentation should be delivered during a live meeting with the company's event marketing decision makers. Without the organizer in the room, many prospective sponsors, if they open the deck at all, will look only at the last couple of pages—how much does it cost, and what do we get? Events are not commodities—they are experiences. Without experiencing your presentation, the sponsorship deck will, in fact, become a commodity. No one gets excited about a commodity. Remember that corporate marketing executives are besieged daily by sponsorship pitches by event promoters. E-mailed proposals can be deleted with a single keystroke. Links may never be accessed. And, mailed proposals do not remain long atop the stacks piled high on their desks; they quickly find their way to the bottom.

The written sponsorship deck is an organized, comprehensive summary of the event marketing opportunity, an outline that is presented in the same order as the verbal presentation. A picture is still worth a thousand words, so be sure to include images that illustrate the strengths and visual attractiveness of the event. A well-edited video is worth one hundred times that. Make sure that the video is as brief as possible. A video longer than two minutes becomes boring to everyone but the promoter. It should capture not only the excitement of the event, but also the various ways in which sponsors were recognized and how they activated their relationships. One or two brief case studies of sponsorship success with testimonials from past sponsors can be particularly effective.

Be sure to weave plenty of visual aids into your live presentation. If the event is completely new, consider hiring an illustrator to create a series of "artist's conceptions" and floor plans or maps. It is far easier for the prospect to imagine the event if he or she has materials through which to visualize them. Bring an event-logoed flash drive with the salient points of the presentation, plus electronic images of the supporting visual aids to leave with the prospect. Make sure the design of the presentation is as exciting and innovative as the content, and be prepared before you attend the meeting to send it again via email, with links to still photographs and video segments, as soon as you return to your office. If you are meeting at the prospect company's location, try to get permission to set up the meeting room at least 30 minutes beforehand. Bring and display enlargements of photos and artist conceptions. If you will be presenting graphics and videos, ensure that the projector for the presentation and the computer you will need are loaded, ready, and in perfect working order before the meeting begins. Don't count on accessing WiFi capabilities in the meeting room in order to make your presentation. Try to store and access everything you need—Microsoft PowerPoint files, video and photo files, and downloaded web pages—from your own computer.

Schedule an hour, but design your presentation for 20 to 30 minutes in length. The sponsor prospect may not arrive on time. Even if you are kept waiting for 15 minutes, you want to be able to deliver your entire presentation without having to make up for the lost time, and still have a period available for questions and further exploration.

Bring inexpensive gifts of event merchandise to the first meeting, such as t-shirts, caps, and balls or pucks in sufficient quantity to cover each meeting participant. (Be careful not to bring anything that has the name or logo of the company's competitor. If you use the company's logo on presentations or premiums, be 100 percent certain it is current and correct. Companies often change their corporate and brand logos in subtle ways without fanfare. A good place to check for logo accuracy is the company's own website.)

Remember that the deck has to keep selling after the live presentation is over. Make sure it is persuasive, organized, and comprehensive. Above all, make sure the assumptions and promises in the proposal are realistic and that hyperbole is minimized. Experienced corporate marketers have doubtless sponsored sports events that sounded better than they actually were, so assume that their hype detectors are turned to "high."

The points of emphasis to be included in sponsorship sales decks are as individually different as the events they represent. Some may have to include more in-depth background material to familiarize the prospective sponsor with the audience characteristics of the event or its featured sport. Presentations for reorganized or relaunched events may have to highlight changes in programming, staging, or entertainment value. Some may contain one or a handful of specific sponsorship opportunities, others a menu of opportunities from which the prospect may choose.

1. **Overview**—Capture the tone and significance of the event. Establish the legitimacy of the event and the credentials of the organizer.
2. **Introduction**—Summarize the opportunities presented by the event and objectives of the presentation.
3. **The Event**—Present a more complete (but concise) description of the property.
4. **The Opportunity**—Provide details on how the company can get involved.
5. **Next Steps**—Conclude with a call to action.

Figure 7.9 Basic Components of a Winning Sponsorship Sales Deck for Sports Events

Regardless of its ultimate format, there are several basic components of a winning sponsorship presentation (see list in Figure 7.9), organized in the same sequential, interest-building way in which a good novel unfolds. Capture the prospect's attention with the opening bullet points or brief overview paragraph, and then tell one of these simple stories:

> "Coming soon is a compelling and unique sports event. This is the story of what makes it compelling and unique, and how savvy sports marketers can realize their goals by being partners. Based on what we have learned about your company's strategies or plans, we believe you can be the next to profit by an association with the event. Here's what you can do to get in on it now!"
>
> or
>
> "An event that has provided outstanding results for sponsors that appeal to customers like yours can do the same for your company or brand. The reasons for these proven results are the compelling and unique ways we deeply engage our fans, and the cost-effective marketing opportunities we customize for our sponsors. Here are some of the ways you can use our event as an activation platform that will drive similar results for your company. We have some ideas to start with, and can work together to develop a host of other opportunities."

The **Overview** of a sponsorship sales deck is like the lead in a well-written newspaper story. It should grab the attention of the reader in its opening passage. Communicate genuine excitement and believable enthusiasm—not hype—in your verbal presentation. Establish the attractiveness of the event by portraying its past history and its growth in popularity, scale, and scope. Include brief quotes selected from media coverage of past events that reflect well upon the event. Demonstrate a basic understanding of the prospective sponsor's needs, if known, by describing what makes the event engaging, unique, appealing, and a great opportunity for the business partner. Provide a brief statement identifying the event organizer, the organizer's unique qualifications, and his or her successes in staging this and other events.

Now that you have the reader's attention, launch into a meatier **Introduction.** Demonstrate the attractiveness of the event's audience demographics and lifestyle characteristics. Include graphs, charts, and tables that portray the similarities between the typical ticket buyer or participant and the company's ideal customer. If the event has not yet debuted, describe these audience characteristics on the basis of similar events for the same sport(s) in analogous markets. Disclose the names of past and/or current sponsor companies and brands and, if appropriate, provide examples of how their association with the event proved successful to their marketing efforts. Showing a short, fast-paced introductory video of 60 or 90 seconds during this segment can vividly demonstrate the excitement the event will generate. This can transition very smoothly into the next component of the deck.

In **The Event** section, fully describe the program. Provide an organized portrayal of what the event is, where it will be held, and when everything happens. This is the point in the presentation when all the excitement and warmth of your product—the event—should come shining through. If appropriate, include a facilities map, a schedule of activities, illustrations, photographs, and graphics. Again, be sure to acknowledge and showcase images that feature visible recognition of existing sponsors. Describe the program so the prospect can sense the depth of your commitment to corporate partners. If your description sounds curiously like the copy you might use to promote the event to the potential public audience—it should! Although you are selling a corporate partnership and not tickets, you are still selling your event.

The event description must be as captivating and intriguing as possible, because it will lead directly into **The Opportunity**. This is where you will present the series of business solutions, entitlements, and benefits the event can provide to the prospective sponsor. If the promoter has a specific role in mind for a particular prospect, it should be fully described as an available option in this section. Otherwise, you may offer a series of possible customized packages from which to choose. If you know what the prospect wants from an event marketing partnership, demonstrate how the opportunity can help that company to achieve its marketing objectives. With this information, the company's decision-making process may be vastly simplified. Sponsorship packages that offer companies the right kinds of business solutions can then be evaluated on the basis of price and cost-effectiveness.

We prefer to call the last pages of the sponsorship deck **Next Steps** instead of "the conclusion." A conclusion implies an ending. If the promoter has done his or her job right, the sales process will be just beginning. In this brief summation, the deck should again emphasize the solutions the event can provide. Both orally and in writing, commit to working with the prospective sponsor to find the right solutions for the company if they have not already been presented. Be sure to provide a contact name and information for any questions that might arise after the presentation.

A fast-paced, uplifting wrap-up video of 60 to 90 seconds can punctuate your oral remarks and end the presentation on a high note. After the video, ask for questions and feedback. If questions are not forthcoming, ask a few open-ended questions to get the interchange going. If you were unable to gain input during the "test" phase, this is a great time to get it. Find out if the event, as presented, can meet the company's marketing needs and whether the opportunities outlined in the presentation are on target. If it is not, do not panic. It is rare indeed for a proposal to be so intuitively perfect that it is immediately accepted by the prospective sponsor "as is." Listen carefully to all questions, comments, and objections.

It is likely that a significant number of companies will simply pass on the opportunity outright. With prospects that seem even marginally engaged, try to determine what features they think are essential and which are superfluous to them. Ask where the sponsorship proposal falls short, and what could strengthen its appeal. Sense what level of involvement the company would be most likely to pursue if it did desire to become a partner and explore how the opportunities in the presentation may be better customized for that company's purposes. If you can elicit feedback during the presentation, propose a reasonable time frame for a second, more refined presentation that will better incorporate the prospect's thoughts. If you cannot gain feedback on the spot, propose a date by which you will contact the company for reactions and questions. Then, REVISE the proposal again and get ready for your next presentation.

CLOSE the Deal

When you return, use the overview and introduction sections to communicate what you learned from your last meeting and how you incorporated these insights into an opportunity more focused on the more specific needs of the sponsor. Present the newly fashioned opportunity and, again, ask for questions, comments, and areas of concern. Be prepared to negotiate on the spot if further revisions are requested or required, fortifying areas of importance and reducing components of less apparent significance. This is why it is so important to be familiar with the fulfillment costs and value of the various elements of all sponsorship deals. This may be your last chance to reach an agreement in principle, so be decisive and *make it count*! Respond immediately with solutions to the company's challenges.

More fine-tuning of the sponsorship solution may be required, and negotiations might eventually become complex and protracted. When it appears that a deal is possible, however, propose sending a letter of agreement to the prospect that will officially summarize the areas in accord. Negotiations will certainly continue once the agreement is sent, but this piece of paper may be essential to keeping the deal on track.

Don't Just Take Our Word for It

How do masters of the sports event sponsorship world put the processes and principles you have now learned into practice? Genesco Sports Enterprises' CEO John Tatum leads one of the nation's top sports marketing agencies, representing more than 30 corporate clients and hundreds of millions of dollars of spending in sponsorship, activation, and hospitality. "As a consultant representing, in my opinion, the best brands in the world, I am pitched numerous event marketing proposals every day," says Tatum. "The ones that get my attention and vetting prior to submission to our clients are the ones with the most innovative thinking, the ones that include a strategic solution that meets the needs of my respective client and delivers against their objectives. The key difference maker between a good pitch and a bad pitch is whether the property truly understands my clients' business challenges and can illustrate how this idea can deliver a solution that grows my clients' business. Too many sell "in-the-box" thinking and too many people sell what THEY want the client to buy—not what will truly help the client and serve the clients' needs." Tatum provides us with his "Top Five Dos and Don'ts" in Figure 7.10.

The Decision-Making Process

The decision-making process that a company undertakes to evaluate the attractiveness and suitability of an event marketing opportunity can be lengthy and arduous for both parties. After investing a significant amount of time and creativity, and crafting what would seem to be the ideal opportunity, the organizer may still find the result to be negative, often for reasons completely external to empirical analysis. It is, therefore, important to throw a wide net over the largest number of qualified prospects during the sales process, presuming there are no rights of first negotiation in force from previous sponsorship agreements. Don't limit yourself to a single company or brand within the same product category. Approach as many prospects as possible to enhance your

DO:

1. Your homework on the audience you are presenting to.
2. Include the sponsor's agency or other "influencer" to gain insights in advance.
3. Use research and analytics in your presentation (even if not 100 percent accurate—they will appreciate the effort you put into it).
4. Use as many "mock-ups" and/or creative renderings that may help the buyers visualize how this will come to life for them.
5. Include clear budgets and cost-transparency whenever possible.

DON'T:

1. Simply "sell" an off-the-rack solution—make them feel as if it was built exclusively for them.
2. Talk about or try to leverage the competition. If you refer to the buyer's competitor, simply reference it as if "this is what they are doing . . . I think we can beat them with this. . . ." Some of my clients shut down immediately when a salesperson mentions the competitor as a threat (veiled or otherwise).
3. Sell them something they haven't seen before. Cookie-cutter presentations are terrible. Every buyer of an event has its own DNA about why it wants to invest in the property.
4. Be a salesperson. Selling is an art that takes multiple engagement points. Rarely will someone buy on the first meeting. Be good at follow-up but don't badger/pester your potential customers or their agencies.
5. Leave out anything that isn't completely bullet proof (i.e., budgets, time tables, etc.). Make sure you don't overpromise and underdeliver.

Figure 7.10 John Tatum's Top Five Dos and Don'ts of Sports Event Sponsorship

chances for success. Waiting for one company at a time to evaluate the opportunity and evolve into a sponsor can be a costly mistake.

Present the opportunity to targeted prospects as far in advance as possible. There are thousands of great potential partnerships that wither and die because there was insufficient time available for the sponsor to fully evaluate the program, because the company's event marketing budget was already exhausted and committed to other events, or because there was not enough time for the sponsor to fully implement an effective activation strategy for its partnership. The event promoter is competing with dozens of sports and entertainment events for the prospect's consideration, and qualified companies are being approached regularly for every available sponsorship dollar. It is challenging enough to sell an event sponsorship—don't let insufficient lead time be the reason you are shut out.

How early is early enough? If the program is an annual event, it can be very effective to invite the decision makers from targeted companies to attend the most imminent edition as VIP guests. Greet them upon arrival and extend treatment befitting an actual sponsor. Make sure that they have access to on-site VIP hospitality, and provide them with some take-home souvenir or commemorative merchandise. Be sure to also invite the decision makers of companies that passed on the opportunity to sponsor the event if one of their competitors did not join the event partner family.

The quality of the event, the hospitality of the promoter, and the longer period of time before decisions must be made for the following year may persuade them to take another look. Try to set up a meeting to present the partnership opportunity as soon after their attendance as possible.

If it sounds as though you need a year or more to complete the process of securing sponsors, that can be absolutely true, particularly for midsize to large sports events and for deals of significant financial value. Simpler community and grassroots events, presuming their income expectations are reasonable, may be funded within a much shorter timeframe. Generally, the lower the cost of the sponsorship and the simpler the benefits, the less time is needed to generate sponsorships. For example, a local Little League all-star game charging a $500 sponsorship fee in return for a few banners needs only enough time to have the banner designed, printed, and delivered. Events that require advertising or promotional fulfillment activities such as consumer sweepstakes, discount programs, or commemorative merchandise, need more time to develop.

The Sponsor's Point of View

Sponsor prospects need time to fully analyze the potential advantages of supporting a sports event marketing opportunity. The evaluation period can take weeks or months, and the greater the degree of involvement and cost, the longer the process can be expected to take. A prospective sponsor will evaluate the offer on the basis of whether the event will provide the company with needed and desirable marketing opportunities and whether its marketing budget can accommodate the attendant financial commitment.

In addition to pure cost, an evaluation of the cost-effectiveness of the opportunity will also be of great importance to the sponsor. That is, will spending a given sum of money on this sports event produce a higher level of product sales than if the same sum of money were spent on another activity such as advertising, promotion, or even another sports event? The measure often used in this assessment, when product sales are the key determinants, is known as the return on investment, or ROI. Simply defined, ROI quantifies the number of additional dollars generated in sales for every dollar spent on the event's marketing fees and activation. If the ROI for an event marketing program can yield better results for the dollar than other components of a product's marketing mix, it will generally be regarded as a good buy by the prospective sponsor.

Of course, product sales cannot be accurately projected before a sports event sponsorship has commenced, only evaluated upon its conclusion. To improve the likelihood of a success, savvy sports event marketers measure potential partnerships against the strategies and standards that have yielded them best results in the past. Figure 7.11 provides a checklist of some of the criteria that sponsors may use to evaluate a new sports partnership opportunity. Be sure your research and proposal anticipate the answers to these questions.

Many of these event sponsorship characteristics can be applied equally well to sports events of global significance and to regional and community programs. It all depends on sponsors being able to generate an acceptable return on their investment. A corporate partner wants assurances that the respective target markets for the event and its business will be compatible and that a sufficient volume of the target audience or participants will attend to justify the expense.

Sponsors must also consider the timing of an event. Does the event schedule dovetail with other promotional opportunities (e.g., Fourth of July Sale, holiday shopping, clearances, new product introductions)? Do they already sponsor a sports event that adequately serves their target

- ☐ **Target Audience Alignment**—How well does the event's audience match with our customers?
- ☐ **Mass Reach and Appeal**—How large is the event's fan base? Does it reach into the communities, regions, or countries in which we do business?
- ☐ **Opportunity**—How can an affiliation with the event extend into other markets and business opportunities?
- ☐ **Compelling Broadcast Platform**—Do the event's broadcasting plans match with our existing media strategy?
- ☐ **Brand Fit**—Does the event's image, reputation, and character match those our customers associate with our brand(s)?
- ☐ **Leverageable Assets**—Does the menu of sponsor benefits provide opportunities for integration across our company's marketing mix?
- ☐ **Marketing Calendar Fit**—Does the event complement our company's existing activities?
- ☐ **Pass-through Rights**—Can our company involve our other business partners to help grow their businesses and strengthen our relationships?
- ☐ **Grassroots Opportunities**—Does the event provide a direct outreach to our consumers?
- ☐ **Cost-effectiveness**—Does this event offer our company good value for the money? Is it a more effective and efficient use of our marketing budget than spending the money elsewhere?

Figure 7.11 Sports Event Sponsorship Evaluation Checklist

market at that time of year, making the addition of another program an effort in duplication? Or does the opportunity fit a time of the year when an additional marketing program can help a company create a noticeable spike in sales?

Sports event promoters can provide prospective partners with answers only if they understand the questions. The overarching query will be: "How does this event marketing program offer my business unique and significant opportunity with sufficient and affordable value beyond its intrinsic prestige and attractiveness?"

How Companies Assess the Value of a Sponsorship

Except for making sure that the cost of selling and fulfilling the benefits promised to a sponsor do not exceed the revenues that are required from the relationship, there is no one right way of setting the price of a sponsorship package. Sports event organizers assign a price to a package of sponsor benefits based on how much it will cost them to fulfill their obligations, plus the net profit required to fund event operations, and calculate the value provided to the sponsor based on objective assumptions of the market value of the various components. Corporate partners, however, also perceive the value of sales and exposure opportunities in far more subjective terms. Although sponsors will place great importance on the prestige and reputation of an event, audience loyalty, the number of other event partners vying for attention, and the competitive protection offered by category exclusivity, they most of all want to be able to credit their event relationship with a measurable increase in product sales and/or an increase in market share.

Because most businesses have many more active marketing efforts in place than just a single relationship with an event, the direct effect of a sponsorship on sales is not always easy to quantify. It is easier to attribute an increase in sales for a small neighborhood business supporting a community sports program where anecdotal feedback from customers is personally received. At the opposite extreme, companies with global reach, spending great sums in support of sports event sponsorships of broad significance, also hope to experience a noticeable increase in sales and capture market share from their competitors. Sponsorship of sports events with national or international prestige, supplemented with wide-reaching, well-funded activation strategies, can perceptibly influence sales.

For the vast majority of companies that fall between the small neighborhood concern and the giant multinational corporation, it is often difficult to attribute an increase in market share to a single sports event sponsorship or to identify the portion of new sales it helped to develop. Therefore, it is to the benefit of organizers to devise opportunities that sponsors can use to measurably affect sales as a result of their partnership. These can include direct sales opportunities at the event and coded dollars-off coupons for products or retailers that may be distributed with tickets or upon entry, printed on the backs of event tickets, or included with the event program. Online visits and click-throughs from the event website to a sponsor's home pages and special offers can provide instant result metrics. Social network postings about the sponsorship can be easily tracked. Organizers can accept proofs of purchase from sponsor product packaging for discounted event tickets or merchandise and work with sponsors to execute cross promotions that demonstrate a direct cause and effect between the event and a product purchase. Any program that adds consumer value to the purchase of a sponsor's product or engagement opportunities before, during, or after the event can provide direct evidence that an event partnership helped to increase a sponsor's sales, adding great value to the relationship and strengthening the case for continuing the association in subsequent years.

Evaluation of Marketing Impact and Exposure

Sponsors will calculate the value of sports event partnerships in much the same way event organizers do (see Figure 7.7). Not surprisingly, a sponsor's assessment of value may differ, at least somewhat, from the organizer's calculations. Although many sports league sponsors conduct their own analysis of value with in-house personnel, companies that support programs with sponsorship fees in the six- and seven-figure range often retain an independent evaluation provider before and after the event such as IEG Valuation Service, or retain the expertise of a sports marketing agency. These companies use a vast database of sophisticated historical data to measure exposure time and value for a sponsor's logo, name, or product seen on broadcast, online and in print news coverage (see Play 13), on social networks, in advertising, point-of-purchase promotional displays, and presence at the event site. If exposure is among the company's strategic objectives for the brand it is marketing, each such exposure opportunity is assigned a value per impression, multiplied by viewership, circulation, and web page views. In some cases, it is multiplied again by a factor representing the length of time each corporate message is exposed.

The analysis of sponsorship value includes other key exposure points such as the brand's name and/or logo on event tickets, credentials, staff, crew and athlete uniforms, merchandise, letterhead, directional and welcome signage, street banners, event site entrance treatments, programs, invitations, posters, and many others. Print advertisements, online, television and radio commercials, ads on the videoboard, and public address announcements provide additional, easily measured value. The results generated by these agencies and valuation services will also demonstrate that not all signage is created equal. Organizers should ensure that sponsors investing the most in their event enjoy exposure opportunities that are in the most desirable, visible, and valuable locations to the media, particularly broadcasters, and audience.

Finalizing the Deal

The execution of a formal agreement between the sponsor and the event organizer or promoter, drafted and reviewed by competent legal counsel, is highly recommended immediately upon conclusion of negotiations. As a critical legal document, the agreement will include both the negotiated business points of the deal and various legal protections required by both parties. It is not unusual for attorneys representing the parties to identify dozens of further details and ramifications that must be defined (e.g., delivery date for tickets, approval processes, restrictions and limitations on promotions, fee and expense payment schedules, etc.). In addition, there are usually a significant number of necessary legal inclusions relating to insurance, liability, indemnification, cancellation terms, breach of contract penalties, and other safeguards that both parties hope never to have to use but are necessary to deal with unforeseen issues and emergencies. The agreement will also outline how intellectual property rights will be shared (e.g., the permitted usage of the logos and brand names of each party when used by the other).

Contracts and letter agreements used to finalize sponsorship deals generally remain confidential. Although proprietary and individual to particular event organizers, there are several areas that all sponsorship agreements should have in common, as described in Figure 7.12. This list highlights the most common and essential elements of sponsorship agreements. Many more sections may be added to meet the specific needs of the event and character of a sponsorship deal.

1. Definition of the Event, the Event Organizer, and the Sponsor
   - What corporate entities are entering into the agreement?
   - What event(s) or event element(s) does the agreement cover (this is particularly important for multivenue, multiday, and multiactivity events).
2. Identification of the Sponsor Identity
   - How is the sponsor being identified—by the corporate name or by one or more product or brand names?
3. Sponsor Designation
   - How have the parties agreed to recognize the sponsor in both event and corporate communications (e.g., as part of the event title, presenting sponsor, official sponsor, official supplier, or donor)?
4. Exclusivity
   - What product category or categories does the sponsorship extend to?
   - What kinds of relationships with other companies are made "off limits" to the organizer by the agreement?
5. Intellectual Property Rights
   - How and in what form may the sponsor use the event's name and logo?
   - How may the sponsor use the event organizer's name and logo?
   - How may the event use the sponsor's name and logo?
   - What approval process is required for each usage?

Figure 7.12 Essential Elements of the Sponsorship Agreement

6. Territory
   - Over what geographic territory does the sponsor's rights extend (e.g., community, state or province, national, continental, global)?
   - How is online promotional activity affected by these territorial limitations?
7. Term
   - When does the sponsor partnership begin and end?
8. Renewal Options
   - Under what conditions may the agreement be renewed?
   - Are there exclusive periods of first negotiation or first refusal?
   - Are there any price protections or other incentives offered to returning sponsors?
9. List of Entitlements
   - This list is frequently appended to the agreement as a separate schedule, outlining all of the agreed-to benefits (e.g., tickets, signage, advertising, hospitality opportunities, etc.) in exacting detail.
10. Marketing and Promotion Rights
    - What kinds of event-related consumer promotions are permitted by the agreement and over what period of time?
    - How may the sponsor use the event in product advertising, display materials, packaging, or promotions?
    - What online rights will the sponsor have with respect to the event?
    - Is the sponsor entitled to use photographs or video of the event or athletes in its marketing programs, and, if so, under what conditions?
    - How many event tickets and what merchandise are permitted to be used in consumer sweepstakes and giveaways?
    - Under what conditions, if any, may rights be passed through to the sponsor's other business partners?
11. Consideration
    - The sponsorship fee and schedule of payments, whether cash or VIK, must be included.
    - Fulfillment expenses payable by the event or sponsor, and any optional add-on benefits should also be defined.
12. Indemnification and Insurance
    - Under what procedure will lawsuits stemming from injuries or property damage in connection with the event, sponsor promotions, advertising claims, and other possible causes proceed, and under what state's laws?
    - To what degree will the event protect the sponsor against legal actions by third parties, and vice versa?
    - What minimum types and levels of insurance coverage do the parties require of each other?
13. Cancellation and Default
    - Under what conditions, if any, may the agreement be terminated?
    - What are the promoter's obligations, and the sponsor's rights, if the event is canceled or postponed because of conditions not under the control of either party (also known as *force majeure*)?
    - What happens if either the sponsor or the promoter defaults on its obligations to the agreement or declares bankruptcy?

Figure 7.12 *(Continued)*

Now, Service Your Sponsors!

Congratulate your sponsor and the responsible members of your organization on the successful conclusion of negotiations and the execution of your agreement. At this point, the work really begins. Too often, it is during the sales and negotiation processes when event organizers devote the most attention to their sponsors. Fulfilling the sponsorship agreement and investing in the sponsor's successful association with the event is a time-consuming but rewarding necessity. It is wise to appoint at least one staff member to serve as an account executive whose key function is to oversee the event's relationship with its sponsors. This individual should be empowered to ensure not only that the spirit and substance of the contract are met, but also that the sponsors feel they are appreciated and integral to the success of the event. Organizers should communicate with them often to share new developments and opportunities, to monitor their success, and to confirm they sense their obvious importance to making the event live up to its full potential. Investing the necessary time and effort in helping them achieve their objectives will pay future dividends as the event develops and grows in future years.

Post-Play Analysis

The best way to meet the objectives of prospective sponsors is to design a program of event benefits that provides solutions to their business wants and needs. Benefits of sponsorship may include tickets, exclusive-access activities, promotional rights, signage and advertising, online opportunities, and many others. An understanding of what the prospect hopes to achieve through its event association should help an organizer customize an individualized package that contains the most attractive benefits in the right quantities for each sponsor. Organizers should analyze and account for the fulfillment costs of delivering each benefit to ensure that their net sponsor revenue goals remain attainable. Likewise, estimate the value of these components to certify that what you present to a sponsor provides far more benefit than might be purchased separately.

Prospective sponsors should be qualified before being considered potential sales targets. Event promoters should create an organized and persuasive sponsorship deck for presentation to prospects that clearly outlines the opportunities available. Get the prospect's reaction to the presentation and make the revisions necessary to close a deal. Formalize the deal with a contract or letter agreement that clearly outlines the obligations of each party, sponsor benefits and promotional rights, and all financial and legal commitments. Understand how the sponsor will evaluate its success postevent, and ensure that the event meets or exceeds its expectations.

By teaming with sponsors and understanding their wants and needs, event organizers will be better positioned to manage events that will be teeming with sponsors.

Coach's Clipboard

1. A B2B technology company in a mid-size city has never sponsored a sports event in the past. It is not that the company has not been approached before; it has never seen the need. The company employs 1,500 local staff and a network of sales agents across

the country to sell its products and services. How can you position participation in your regional gymnastics event as an attractive business solution for the company?

2. You plan to present a B2C prospect with an opportunity to be the title sponsor of a state multi-sport recreational tournament. As a leader in its industry, the company has lesser interest in exposure opportunities than VIP hospitality for its dealers and retailers and fan engagement platforms at the event to enhance customer loyalty. The event site, however, does not offer significant space for sponsor activation or dedicated VIP reception spaces. How can you structure the sponsorship to deliver the appropriate business solutions to the prospect given these limitations of the event site?
3. An event promoter wants to approach a company with a history of spending generously on sponsorships for similar events. But the company's contact, however, refuses to provide any meaningful input on the firm's event marketing objectives and asks that all proposals be mailed before an appointment for any live presentation is considered. How should you proceed in preparing a pitch for this prospective sponsor?
4. A sponsor conducts a postevent evaluation, the results of which suggest that the demographics of the event did, in fact, match those of its target market and that the impact of the company's exposure met its expectations. The company's sales, however, showed no meaningful increase. What will you do to encourage the sponsor to return next year?

PLAY 8

Maximizing and Servicing the Media Partnership

"I always turn to the sports section first. The sports section records people's accomplishments; the front page nothing but man's failures."

—*U.S. Supreme Court Chief Justice Earl Warren, Sports Illustrated, July 22, 1968*

This play will help you to:

- Understand the opportunities to work with the news-gathering (editorial) and commercial divisions of media organizations to publicize and promote your sports event.
- Encourage media coverage before, during, and after your event.
- Service the needs of the media covering your event on site.

Introduction

The Roman god Janus is most often pictured in profile as a head with two faces. The deity of gates and doors, Janus also represented the concept of new beginnings. (Not coincidentally, this is why the month that bears his name is the first of each new year.) Ancient worshippers believed that one must pass through a gate or door before entering new places and, therefore, the guardian god of doors looks simultaneously in both directions—peering back into the past and ahead into the future.

To sports event organizers, the media often assume the countenance of Janus. Writers and correspondents look forward to event day, reporting on preparations and controversies, and speculating on how competition will unfold. They later look back on the results and provide analysis and perspective on the event's success and outcomes. The media can be an event's best friend or its worst enemy and, like Janus, they can sometimes assume both aspects at the same time. Much like the gods of ancient times, as perceived by their followers, the media can entertain well-directed appeals but cannot be controlled. To understand the delicate relationship between an event and the media, one must first grasp this key stakeholder's business objectives.

The Two Faces of the Media

A media outlet, whether a newspaper, magazine, website, radio station, or television network, exists for one primary purpose—to transmit information of interest to its specific target audience. Some of the information and how it is presented—in the form of advertising, promotions, and other joint marketing ventures—is under the direct control of the event organizer. Typically, the more valuable stream of information—in the form of news coverage and publicity—is under the total control of the media outlet.

The media provide event organizers with an essential platform to publicize and advertise their event, a vital component in the campaign to attract an audience and participants. When coverage of an event is positive, the media can generate the impact, influence, and credibility that advertising alone cannot achieve. Similarly, when its tone of coverage is negative, the impact, influence, and credibility can likewise be so persuasive that even the most creative advertising campaigns can have difficulty overcoming the challenge.

To preserve objectivity and journalistic integrity, while marketing themselves as an attractive platform for advertising and promotion, media outlets most often organize themselves into two separate, semi-autonomous halves: editorial and sales and marketing. The editorial half is charged with the responsibility of providing informational content by covering news and developing stories and features. This group is typically under the leadership of an editor or producer who, together with his or her writers, correspondents, and columnists, must compile and communicate information that is relevant and interesting to their readers, viewers, or listeners. Event organizers direct their publicity efforts toward this editorial side of the media, presenting and disseminating event information as news, press releases, story ideas, and opportunities for coverage during the event itself. Most editors and producers enjoy complete freedom in deciding which stories will be compelling enough to their audience to be written, published, or aired.

In business environments where the press is not financed, managed, or controlled by the government, operating a media outlet can be a very expensive proposition. In addition to selling individual copies and subscriptions, newspapers must sell advertising to cover their costs and generate a profit, or sell digital ad space or access to content on their respective websites. Electronic media such as radio and television also sell advertising to support their operations, or they charge viewers indirectly through carriage agreements with cable, satellite providers, or streaming services. Digital media producers sell subscriptions to users and/or advertising to commercial partners.

This second face of the media business is essential to enable the editorial staff the freedom and funding to pursue their journalistic responsibilities. This is the sales and marketing half of the media partnership, led in the printed media by the publisher and in the electronic media by a sales or marketing executive. Media outlets sell advertising, create and manage promotions, and pursue event-marketing opportunities as vehicles to promote sales, enroll new subscribers and sell additional advertising to event sponsors. Event organizers work with the sales and marketing side of media businesses to purchase advertising, create media partnerships and establish the consumer promotions that will drive ticket sales, revenue opportunities, attendance, and viewership.

To preserve the objectivity of reporting, an impenetrable Great Wall stands between the two halves of the media organization, particularly in the newspaper business in both their printed and online forms. In the model media outlet, the presence of a promotional relationship between a sports event and a news-gathering organization will not increase the interest of an editor in providing readers with news coverage. Conversely, its absence or partnership with a competitive media partner will not exclude an event from the editorial assignment calendar. An event–media partnership will neither provide organizers with a warranty against a lack of coverage or negative stories about the event nor encourage glowing reviews afterward. In the eyes of the editor, if the event is newsworthy, it will be covered; if it is well organized and executed, it may be covered positively.

Newspaper publishers, by contrast, see more than just the newsworthiness of sports events. They see unique business opportunities that can generate revenue and increase readership. They view events as attractive vehicles to sell incremental advertising and provide promotional platforms to benefit their business. Some create "special sections" that add value for readers and profits for the publication through increased circulation and incremental advertising revenue. The publisher and marketing staff are usually the key decision makers on whether to participate more broadly with an event. In addition to the goal of generating advertising revenues, their objectives may include increasing readership in their core market, expanding circulation, and attracting users to their website. Many magazines, particularly news and sports weeklies, are organized along similar lines as daily newspapers. National magazines are difficult to attract as marketing partners, but may be more accessible on the editorial front, assuming the event can generate stories or reportage that are nationally relevant. Generally, magazines with a local focus are much more open to working with event organizers as potential marketing partners.

Like magazines, local television stations and network affiliates are good targets for partnership opportunities with sports events. National networks normally get involved only in terms of providing news stories that are globally or nationally relevant. There is often a similar separation between the news and sports coverage side of their business, and the marketing and promotional side that generates the revenue that keeps them both operating. Where television outlets differ somewhat is in situations where a network holds the rights to broadcast the event. In such cases, the national broadcaster may engage in promotions that increase awareness for an event for the purpose of increasing viewership of its coverage.

Most business partnerships between sports event organizers and television broadcasters, unfold on the local level. On the one hand, the most obvious prospect is the local affiliate of the network that will broadcast coverage of the event. While other stations in the market may be approached if the affiliate passes on the opportunity, it can be more challenging to convince a television station to promote an event that will be seen on another channel. On the other hand, if the event is not a broadcast property, nearly any outlet will do. It is best, however, to align the event with a station that is the most watched in the market by the audience you most want to attract. Cable television affiliates can be outstanding resources, so it is wise not to overlook the local sports networks, regional affiliates of national sports networks, or local news channels.

Among potential media partners, radio is one of the most effective in generating local excitement, and is frequently the medium most agreeable to considering promotional partnerships. While entities like ESPN have established a network of stations with a mix of national and local personalities and content and many stations around the country provide nationally syndicated programming to their listeners, radio is primarily a local medium. Most advertising is sold locally and is usually far less expensive than television advertising. Radio advertising can also boast a far lower "cost-per-thousand" than newspapers when compared to full-page display advertising. (We compare radio spots to a full-page newspaper ad because they are similarly undistracted—there is only one radio ad on at a time and there is only one ad on a full page.)

The most efficient medium for spreading information—and arguably the most dominant—are web-based services, such as social media platforms, news aggregation forums, and media partners' websites. Web platforms have the distinct advantage over traditional media outlets by having the ability to be updated whenever and as often as the editor desires. The event organizer can offer information and have it disseminated to his or her target market virtually instantly. Conversely, the wide and instantaneous accessibility provided by online media enables them to report time-sensitive news to massive audiences, news that may be a tremendous advantage for promotion if the stories are positive and a burdensome challenge to the event's image if the stories take a negative turn. Web-based media have the power of nearly unlimited reach, so even if the event is locally focused, the event organizer has the potential of reaping benefits on a national, or even a global, scale. Social media sites give the concept of "word-of-mouth" new meaning by allowing individuals, journalists, and fanatics alike to share their thoughts and feelings to possibly millions of other people. Event organizers can leverage social media by curating specialized event pages or feeds, or, in some cases, partnering with popular bloggers—amateur and professional—to provide event content and coverage. Such content can deliver both journalistic information and a branded message to fans and customers.

Perhaps the greatest advantage of web-based media is that it enables direct interaction between the event's organizers and target audience, specifically in the form of social media platforms. This feature creates a more effective touch point than traditional advertising and provides a method of building a personal relationship between prospective customers and event organizers. Positive interactions with interested parties may serve to benefit the event as these individuals are influenced and, in turn, may relay their experience and interest to many of their friends and acquaintances via the same digital social medium. Social media essentially becomes free advertising, which is something every event organizer can benefit from, especially those with limited marketing budgets.

What an event organizer hopes media outlets will provide—both as partners and as communicators of news—will differ significantly as to the audiences these two partners seek to serve, as well as their respective corporate objectives. To understand what one can reasonably expect from the media, an organizer must comprehend what both halves of the media business want and need from a sports event.

What the Editorial Side Really Wants from Sports Events

It is important to recognize that because media outlets are typically bifurcated into independently managed editorial and marketing faces, their wants and needs can also diverge along very similar lines. Editors and writers, producers and correspondents, are charged with the responsibility of providing a conduit of information to their readers, viewers and listeners, and must cover events from perspectives they feel are newsworthy and interesting. To fulfill this mission, the editorial side needs compelling story ideas; accurate information to help support their reporting; good photo, video, or sound bite opportunities to add visual or audio support to their words; and facilities that will help them cover the event and submit their work to the editor or producer (see Figure 8.1).

I. Needs Prior to Event Day
- Compelling story ideas
  - Unusual or compelling stories about participating athletes
  - Interesting historical points on the event and past athletes
  - Significant business stories (e.g., economic benefits, intriguing or innovative partnerships)
- Accurate and comprehensive information
  - Press releases
  - Social media
    - Concise, regular updates
    - Timely and relevant information
  - Media guides
    - Background information
      - Participating athletes
      - Event history
    - Official rules and format of competition
    - Official statistics
    - Schedules of events
  - Access to senior event organizer management for interviews
  - A single point of contact for additional information

II. Needs on Event Day
- Appropriate, comfortable working conditions
  - Workstations with clear view of play
  - Timely access to official and accurate statistics, score sheets, athlete background information
  - Clear, unobstructed positions for photographers
  - Availability of required services and technology
  - Access to organizer management, coaches, and athletes at pre-event and postevent press conferences

Figure 8.1 What the Editorial Side of the Media Needs from Sports Event Organizers

Whether the sports event is a community tournament or a multinational invitational competition, event organizers must approach the media in a professional manner that demonstrates an understanding of their needs and expectations and represents the organization as competent and knowledgeable. Put another way, sports event organizers should provide no excuse to editors and producers to overlook covering the event. Fostering an amateurish impression to the media can seriously damage a sports event organizer's overall marketing plan. Diminishing the perception of an event's importance and credibility in the mind of the editor and producer can jeopardize the placement of essential pre-event reportage and even coverage of the event itself, or worse, generate negative impressions of the event or organizer through instantly accessible social media. As pre-event media coverage provides the public with a strong first impression of an event and, by extension, reinforces the perceived value of attending, organizers should ensure that every contact and communication with the editorial side is clear and confident, accurate and appropriate.

Like sports event organizers, editors and reporters, producers and correspondents must operate within the boundaries of limited financial resources. On the editorial side, budget constraints are manifest in the amount of space (newspapers, magazines, and web) or time (radio and television) that may be devoted to coverage of an event. The amount of space or time allocated to any story is determined by the editor or producer and is a clear indication of their perception of the item's importance to their readers, viewers, or listeners. Demonstrate the professionalism of the event and its organization and convey the importance of the event to the host community with every media contact. "Space in most newspapers is limited. Some organizers, understandably enthusiastic about their ventures, simply fail to realize that others might not share their enthusiasm," notes *Los Angeles Times* columnist Helene Elliott. "I think the drama and importance must be inherent. Don't send me demographic studies that men 18 to 34 love this event and so we must cover it. The event should be compelling enough on its own that it doesn't need false hype." Maintain frankness and credibility, as well as your reasonable expectations as to the intrinsic newsworthiness of your event.

Like sports event organizers, editors and reporters, producers and correspondents also work against immutable deadlines that must be recognized when planning campaigns to generate publicity. Daily print, television, radio, and digital media work on continuous deadlines, while deadlines for inclusion in weekly media may be only a couple of days prior to publication. Social media sites have especially demanding time constraints requiring updates on a minute-to-minute basis as news developments break. Monthly non-news periodicals are also sometimes called "long-lead" publications. You will need to provide information weeks or months before a particular issue is published, frequently long before press conferences are scheduled or releases are written. Demonstrate sensitivity to these deadlines by not wasting the media's time. Provide them with the information they want and need when and how they require it.

Information, Please

It is up to the sports event organizer to identify the newsworthy opportunities that exist for media coverage throughout the event-planning process and to effectively communicate these possibilities to any combination of editors, writers, columnists, producers, correspondents, and others. A campaign of strategically spaced press announcements should be planned over the days and weeks leading up to the event, during the event itself, and even afterwards to build interest among the media and, by extension, their readership, viewers, or listeners— your actual and potential audience. A sample campaign is presented in Figure 8.2 in a generalized, chronologically structured order that will be applicable to many sports events. Organizers may combine any number of these announcements into the same release and schedule additional announcements that are appropriate to their specific event property.

It is probably obvious that the first communication to the media should officially announce the event. Even existing events with a long tradition in the host city should plan to release a statement announcing the date(s) of the event, location(s), ticket sale details and background information such as historical highlights and economic impact estimates, if applicable. A press release distributed to a comprehensive list of media outlets or a news conference for invited media are standard methods to make the first announcement. In addition, before you can communicate this vital information, a digital platform and infrastructure should also be put in place from which you can simultaneously make an announcement. The best way to disseminate this information rapidly to mass audiences is via a robust web presence that includes a customized event site and connectivity with various social media outlets. This will provide a number of avenues for your potential ticket buyers and other targets to access crucial, up-to-the-second event information. If the event is introducing a new logo, it may be inaugurated at this time to begin the process of

I. Event Announcement
   a. Event Description, Host City, Location, Dates
   b. Logo Introduction
   c. Economic Impact
   d. Charitable Association
   e. What's New
   f. Web Presence (event website, social media, other digital assets)
II. Announcement of Participating Athletes or Tryouts
III. Major Sponsor Announcements
IV. Human Interest Stories (may be multiple releases)
V. Ticket Sales Date Announcement
VI. Credential Application Process
VII. "Hard Hat" Tour Invitation (an opportunity to tour the site during set up)
VIII. Participant Media Introduction
IX. Postevent Announcements
   a. Official Results
   b. Attendance Figures
   c. Amount Raised for Charity
   d. Continued Web Presence for Future Events and Follow Up

Figure 8.2 Sample Sports Event Press Announcement Schedule

building awareness for this refreshed identity, although a later logo launch is sometimes planned to provide the event with an additional media opportunity. Here, too, an organizer can announce any associated charity that will become the beneficiary of an event, along with information on the contributions the event has provided to charities in the past. As a reminder, don't forget to include when and how to purchase tickets if the information is known at that time.

The first announcement should introduce the media to the event, concisely describing the competition or program of activities. If the property is an established sports event, this description should also include information on what is new and exciting about the upcoming year's edition. Is the competition format different? Are there new activities or attractions planned for existing or new audiences (e.g., children, families, groups, or at-risk youth)? Will there be noted champion teams or players competing? Do not assume that all media are completely familiar with the event or sport, even those with a long tradition in the marketplace. "Event organizers need to provide members of the media with comprehensive background on the event, easy-to-understand chronologies of the event, and comments from participants, where and when applicable," says *Bloomberg News* reporter Allan Kreda.

The introductory announcement takes on particular importance for events that were open to bidding by prospective host cities. The first announcement is the organizer's best opportunity to excite the local media, and, through them, the community at large and area businesses. Winning the competition to host an event can be big news but, except for the most major of sports properties, that alone may not be enough information from which to fashion a compelling story. Include additional details on how many other cities competed for the honor, and why the city was selected. Include economic impact data (see Play 4) and the number of hotel room nights event staff, participants, guests, and fans will occupy. If there is a charitable partner or beneficiary of a portion of the event's proceeds, this could be a good opportunity to announce that, as well.

Delivering the Announcement—Press Releases

Sending press releases via e-mail or other means is an effective way of distributing key event information to the media before the event. Most direct communication with media members or partners is likely to be by press release—a concise, well-written missive that provides basic information in convincing, but factual, form. Because press releases are most effective when they are as brief as possible (either between one and three double-spaced pages), they cannot provide a full and comprehensive overview of a sports event. That said, a press release should include as many answers to the "who," "what," "where," "why," "when," and "how" details of the event, heralded by an attention-grabbing headline and subheading.

It is essential that the headline and subhead entice the reader to go further. Press releases are marketing and sales documents, though of a more subtle nature than sponsorship decks. To maximize the chances that a release will become a story, it must be compelling and credible—starting with the headline, subhead and opening sentences. As the *Los Angeles Times'* Elliott suggests, the credibility of a press release is dependent on its being convincing without any suggestion of hype. Above all, preserve your perception of professionalism by ensuring the release is 100 percent error-free, typographically, grammatically, and factually.

Because some media outlets will use the press release as their primary source of information about the event (and might even use the press release as is), it is important to include one or two quotes from reliable and respected authorities. It is appropriate that one or more points of information be provided in the form of a quote from the most senior official of the organization staging the event. A second quote may be included from another important stakeholder, such as a participating star athlete, a key city official, or a representative of the benefiting charity. Don't try to fit every piece of event information into the release, just those items that provide a complete framework outlining what the program is all about. Writers, reporters, and correspondents may want to incorporate more details, quotes, and information beyond those provided in the press release. Be sure to include a contact name, phone number, and e-mail address either at the top of the first page along with the desired release date or at the end of the document. The best stories are almost always generated by writers who look for perspectives that will be unique from those of their competitive colleagues. See Figure 8.3 for a sample press release that officially announces the fictional Big Street Sports Tournament described in the Host City Request for Proposal (RFP) in Appendix 2.

Some sports event organizers will have the budget available to retain the services of an outside public relations agency to help manage the publicity campaign, write press releases, and coordinate press conferences. Others, with limited financial resources and unable to afford public relations assistance, will be faced with the task of creating and distributing their own releases. Figure 8.4 provides organizers working with restrictive budgets with a brief checklist to consult before distributing the first press release.

Delivering the Announcement—Social Media

Press releases provide a means of formal communication with legitimate media outlets but, given the nature of web journalism and the realities of a 24-hour news cycle, you should also be prepared to offer information through more informal channels. To this extent, social media networks afford the means of mass communication to media members, as well as to thousands of amateur, semiprofessional, and professional bloggers, journalists, and your most avid and engaged fans—across the web. These groups may contribute higher speeds of information transmission and

(Insert Event or Organizer Logo Here)
LEDUC SELECTED TO HOST
THIRD ANNUAL BIG STREET SPORTS TOURNAMENT
More than 1,000 Top Amateur Athletes from Across the Nation
To Compete against Hometown's Best This Summer

Contact: Dan Sommer
dsommer@mnosports.com
888–000–000

The City of Leduc has been named as host of one of the nation's fastest-growing street sports festivals and national invitational tournament, the Big Street Sports Tournament, in the summer of 2014. The selection of Leduc as the host city for the Big Street Sports Tournament was announced in a joint statement by the Mayor of Leduc and MNO Sports of Washington, D.C., the promoter of the event.

The Big Street Sports Tournament will bring more than 1,000 top-ranked amateur athletes to compete at Leduc's Civic Sports Complex this July 23 to 27. The visiting athletes will also take on the city's own premier competitors in skateboarding, in-line skating, roller hockey, and BMX bicycle contests for all age, gender, and skill levels, ranging from "8 and Under" to "18 and Older" divisions.

"The Big Street Sports Tournament has found the perfect host in the City of Leduc," said Arthur Andrews, executive director of the event. "Action sports athletes from across the country will enjoy the outstanding hospitality for which the city has become famous."

"Leduc has again proven itself to be an active and exciting sports city," said Mayor Angie Arturo. "The Big Street Sports Tournament will attract thousands of families and sports enthusiasts from the local and surrounding communities to watch and enjoy the competitions, as well as to take advantage of a full weekend of great entertainment, interactive activities, and pure fun."

Sports fans and entertainment-seekers will be welcome to attend the event free of charge. In addition to the competitions, visitors will enjoy BMX half-pipe exhibitions, an extreme sports video arcade, "kids-only" clinics and activities, free in-line skating and braking lessons, nonstop musical entertainment, a bicycle tune-up area and obstacle course, a street sports product expo, special guest appearances, food provided by local restaurants, and more.

This will be the third edition of the Big Street Sports Tournament, which has been previously held in Providence, Rhode Island, and Orlando, Florida. An average of more than 30,000 visitors attended the festival and tournament in each city.

The full schedule of events and additional information for the Big Street Sports Tournament will be released at a later date.

Figure 8.3 Sample Sports Event Announcement Press Release

potentially great influence among your event's demographics. Although some of these individuals or outlets may not be accredited media, they nonetheless provide targeted outreach and drive the dissemination of information. It may be prudent to tailor your message specifically to social media platforms in order to deliver the most authentic and securely branded message. You may want to distribute links to the official press release via means of social media sites such as Twitter. Sending

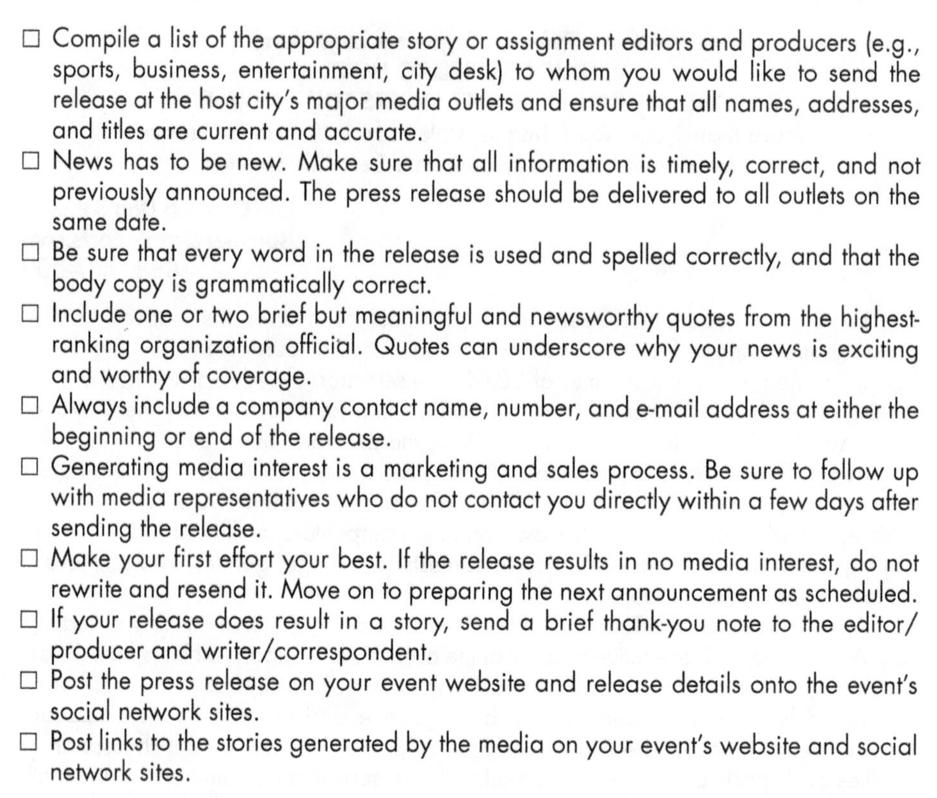

- ☐ Compile a list of the appropriate story or assignment editors and producers (e.g., sports, business, entertainment, city desk) to whom you would like to send the release at the host city's major media outlets and ensure that all names, addresses, and titles are current and accurate.
- ☐ News has to be new. Make sure that all information is timely, correct, and not previously announced. The press release should be delivered to all outlets on the same date.
- ☐ Be sure that every word in the release is used and spelled correctly, and that the body copy is grammatically correct.
- ☐ Include one or two brief but meaningful and newsworthy quotes from the highest-ranking organization official. Quotes can underscore why your news is exciting and worthy of coverage.
- ☐ Always include a company contact name, number, and e-mail address at either the beginning or end of the release.
- ☐ Generating media interest is a marketing and sales process. Be sure to follow up with media representatives who do not contact you directly within a few days after sending the release.
- ☐ Make your first effort your best. If the release results in no media interest, do not rewrite and resend it. Move on to preparing the next announcement as scheduled.
- ☐ If your release does result in a story, send a brief thank-you note to the editor/producer and writer/correspondent.
- ☐ Post the press release on your event website and release details onto the event's social network sites.
- ☐ Post links to the stories generated by the media on your event's website and social network sites.

Figure 8.4 Press Release Development Checklist

a complementary "re-tweet" from a member of the media creates the benefit of speaking to an audience with a diversified voice—information delivered informally to all, yet traditional in nature.

Utilizing social media to communicate your message can do more than cut out the clutter involved in sending information only to conventional media outlets for dispersal. Beyond adding efficiency to the process, social media platforms offer the unique opportunity to generate a buzz among consumers. Sites like Facebook allow events to create customized profiles with interactive message boards for fans to converse with each other and with the event organizer. As the organizer, you will be in position to encourage interaction and, possibly, action before the event even begins, providing a powerful touch point and access to your customers and guests. Microblogging sites like Twitter also provide the ability to drive engagement with and between event guests and help in the spreading of information. The organizer will also get an inside look at what discussion topics are trending and what "followers" are talking about. For examples of Facebook and Twitter pages for the FIFA 2014 World Cup, see Figure 8.5. Organic information transfer of this kind provides individualized word-of-mouth marketing that is second to none.

In essence, social media serve as a bridge between events, media outlets, and the end users. These sites can add efficiency and effectiveness to your relationships with the event's media partners, while also decreasing your dependence on the traditional outlets to properly deliver your

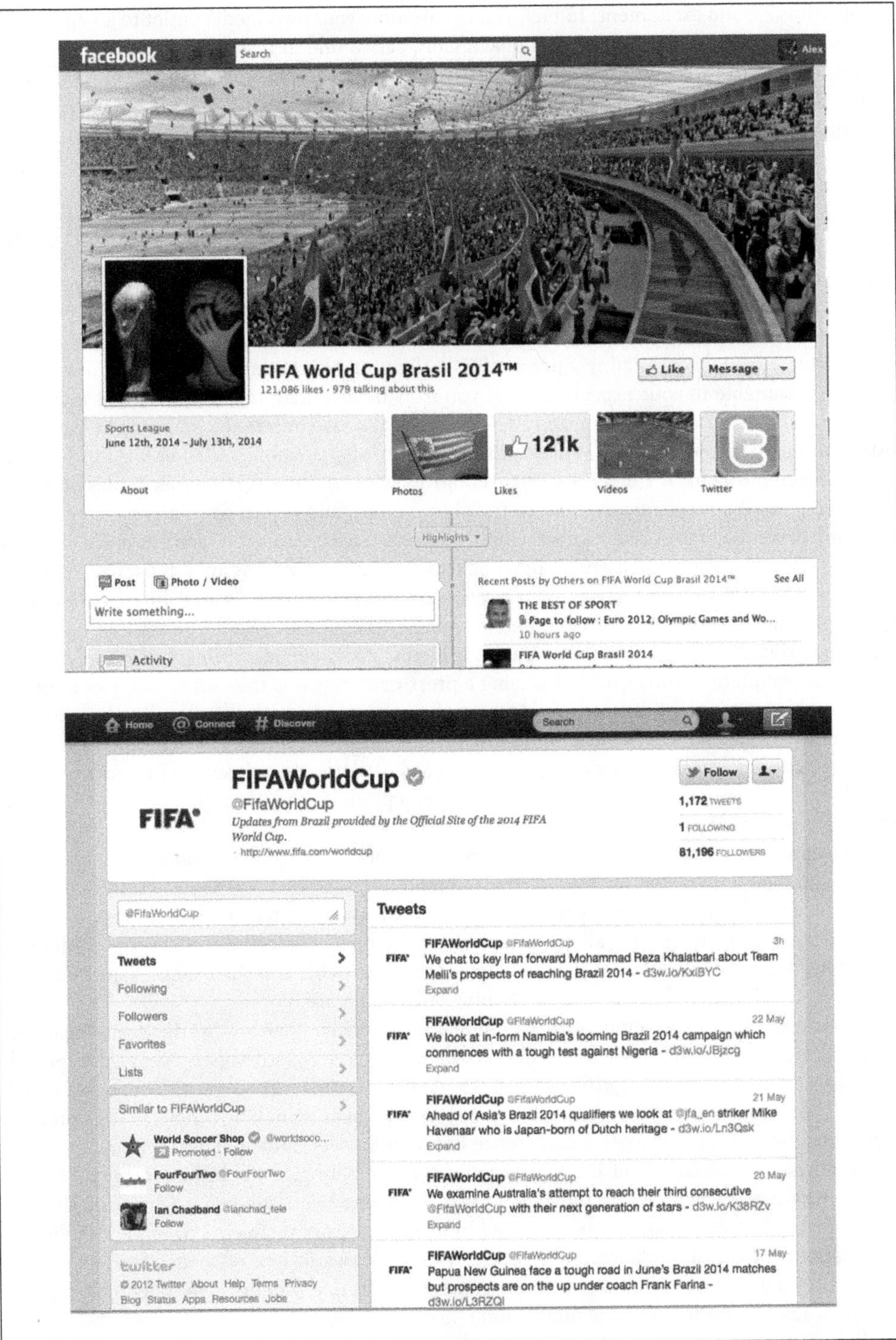

Figure 8.5 Examples of Event Social Media Pages (Facebook Fan Page for FIFA 2014 World Cup in Brazil; Twitter Feed for FIFA 2014 World Cup in Brazil)

event's message and excitement. In fact, you can become your own media outlet to a degree. The 24-hour news cycle demands that you play a more active role in disseminating event news and details along with your traditional media partners, though it is still important to cultivate strong relationships with trusted media members in order to accelerate the consumption of the event's announcements and other critical event information by the public.

Delivering the Announcement—Press Conferences

The first announcement of a sports event and the subsequent issuing of the most meaningful and important event information in succeeding weeks are often communicated at press, or news, conferences. Although press conferences can be far more effective in generating media attention than simply circulating a press release, they can also be far more involved and expensive. Be reasonable in your expectations. If you truly believe that an announcement is news of genuine significance to the community, it may merit a press conference and may be worth the extra coordination and expense. Will details be revealed that are compelling enough to be worth the time commitment of the media representatives who will attend? It takes far less time for someone to read a press release than to travel to, attend, and return from a press conference. (Of course, you will never really know whether a press release has been read.) Are the individuals delivering the announcement(s) newsmakers themselves, worthy of a personal interview, capturing for later video coverage for television or digital use or in "sound bites" (brief audio clips) for radio reports? Will there be other stakeholders at the press conference that the media will want to interview such as participating athletes, coaches, celebrities, or politicians? You should be completely confident that staging a press conference is the correct approach for any particular announcement, as poor media attendance suggests to those who did show up that the message delivered was of little importance. There is only one opportunity to do this right. If the announcing press conference is poorly staged, if there are no new or interesting details revealed, or if few media actually attend, the perception of the event in the market can be seriously and irrevocably damaged.

Recognize, too, that attendance at a press conference is a significant time commitment for editors and their writers and photographers, and producers and their correspondents and camera crews. News is happening everywhere, and there are only a limited number of personnel and equipment available to cover it all. Make sure the time being dedicated to the press conference will be well spent. Start as close to the announced time as possible and make it quick, no more than 20 minutes, as illustrated in the sample running order in Figure 8.6.

Press conferences are announced by circulating a "media advisory" to the same local contacts that were compiled for the distribution of press releases. An advisory is designed to provide enough information to encourage the attendance of media outlets without providing the key details that will be announced at the press conference as news. It should include a generalized statement describing the subject of the press conference (without inadvertently making the announcement in the advisory), the names of those who will be participating in the announcement, and, of course, where and when the announcement will be made. Again, a contact name and the best way to reach the contact should be provided to enable advisory recipients to request additional information, confirm attendance, or to receive press releases in lieu of their attendance. Send the advisory a day or two prior to enable assignment editors and producers to schedule a reporter and/or a camera crew to cover the press conference.

Select a venue for the press conference that is convenient to those attending and, if possible, meaningful to the event. Remember that reporters attending the press conference want

Time	Item	Duration (mins:secs)
10:00 A.M.	Host Welcome and Press Conference Rundown	1:00
10:01 A.M.	Introduction of VIPs, Special Guests and Tournament Representative	1:00
10:02 A.M.	Announcement of Event by Tournament Representative	3:00
10:05 A.M.	Mayoral Address *(introduced by Host)*	3:00
10:08 A.M.	Event Description and Details (with video presentation) by Tournament Representative *(introduced by Host)*	4:00
10:12 A.M.	Questions and Answers (with Tournament Representative)	5:00
10:17 A.M.	Host Wrap-up with Acknowledgments	1:00
10:18 A.M.	Breakout for One-on-One Interviews	

Figure 8.6 Running Order for a Sports Event Announcement Press Conference

little more than to hear the announcement, receive the details they need to develop a story, and write their article or broadcast their report. They generally will not want to have to endure lengthy commutes, nor will they desire a sightseeing tour of the event facility. If the host venue is conveniently located, by all means schedule the press conference there. If it is difficult to reach, efforts to generate media attendance may be more successful by staging the press conference at a more centralized location such as a downtown convention center, hotel, city hall, restaurant, or an appropriate local landmark. If the conference is being held in a facility other than the event venue, try to select a room that will not dwarf the audience. Oversized rooms can give the impression of sparse attendance. If space permits, invite a reasonable number event staff and local stakeholders to attend. Their presence will improve the appearance of the conference and may even provide additional interview subjects for the media. Press conferences are also usually "limited access" events, so inviting a small number of senior-level sponsor executives, business partners, and community leaders can also provide an exciting bonus that demonstrates gratitude for their involvement. But, try not to exceed the number of media members with the number of guests. Request that nonmedia guests and staff understand that questions to the participants and interview opportunities are restricted only to members of the media. Also, it is appropriate to make seating assignments to reserve specific locations for expected media only.

Some press conferences include a morning breakfast or midday luncheon, or at least snacks, coffee, and soft drinks, to enable the organizer to interact with the media over a longer period of time. Reporters have to eat, too, so this is the one instance when an event of greater duration is acceptable. Once the meal is consumed, though, the clock begins ticking again. Again, make sure the actual presentation is brief and to the point. Try to schedule the announcement on a day and time that does not compete for media attention with other sports or special events being held in the community. Check your local sports and other event calendars to reduce the chance of staging the conference concurrent with some other activity that can steal attention and media away from the delivery of your message. Avoid scheduling press conferences on a Friday because Saturday newspaper readership and television viewership are generally weaker than during weekdays or Sundays. Scheduling the start of press conferences for weekday late mornings or early afternoons are usually best for meeting late-afternoon and evening television news and newspaper deadlines.

Ensure that all media members who attend the press conference sign in as they arrive. Prepare and distribute a media kit that includes the press release, background information, photos, illustrations of the event site, and other appropriate materials that will help reporters prepare their stories. Be sure to remember to e-mail or otherwise deliver these items immediately after the press conference ends to media outlets that were unable to attend. Providing media members with a small takeaway token such as an event cap, pin, T-shirt, or tote bag is not inappropriate so long as its actual value is minimal.

Select an articulate host or master of ceremonies, preferably from the community such as a sports radio personality or disk jockey from a station that appeals to the same target market as the event. The host should introduce a senior organizer executive to deliver the majority of the information that is contained in the announcing press release. This segment should be as brief as possible to enable a guest speaker to be included, such as a city official, community host committee leader, or featured coach or athlete. After the guest speaker's brief remarks, the event executive can continue, providing additional event details. The description of the event can be supported by audio and visual aids. If graphics are used to support the presentation, the visual should provide a bright enough picture to be seen clearly without having to turn off the lights in the room. Provide hard copies of the supporting graphics to the media and be prepared with copies of the video on flash drives, or e-mail a digital link to enable attendees to access the graphics and video on demand.

When one or more people are scheduled to have speaking roles, be sure to review each participant's talking points, the broad topics they will address, and the statistics they will use in their remarks. It is best to provide each speaker with a brief written explanation of their role and the subjects they will discuss. Include factual information pertinent to their role to ensure that multiple speakers will not cover the same subjects or, worse, provide the media with contradictory information (e.g., expected attendance, economic impact figures, hotel room occupancies, etc.).

These guidelines are most applicable to the scheduling of pre-event press conferences. During the event itself, press conferences are frequently staged to service attending media with pertinent information, official results, and interviews. Technical requirements and a floor plan for staging press conferences are provided later in this chapter.

The Campaign for Attention

Experienced sports event organizers recognize that the announcing press conference or release is only the opening salvo in a campaign to maximize media attention. Publicity, by itself, is not a marketing panacea. It is an essential, but not the sole, component of an event's marketing plan and is reinforced by advertising, promotion, and event marketing campaigns. Audiences presume that news organizations are candid, objective communicators of important news and, therefore, the information they present is often perceived as more credible than the hype of advertising. Organizers need the media to generate the stories that will create a sense of believable importance and relevance to their events. In between the first announcement and event day, there may be myriad possibilities to present the media with additional story ideas from a number of different angles or perspectives, as presented in Figure 8.2. Create a schedule of opportunities to "pitch" reporters who had expressed specific interests after the announcing press release or conference. For maximum effect, try to time these efforts to lead up to or coincide with important pre-event milestone dates, such as the first day of ticket sales, the debut of paid advertising campaigns and promotions, or as player or team registration begins. Other announcements might be timed to generate publicity after the pace of ticket or sponsor sales has ebbed or when the event date is approaching and a little extra boost of public awareness is required.

SIDELINE STORY

Creating Coverage Creatively

In the mid-1980s, monster truck shows became popular events in arenas throughout the United States. The success of these attractions, whose "stars" were colorful vehicles with giant wheels and grandiose monikers that elevated into the air before landing forcefully and spectacularly on doomed cars and other defenseless objects, caught the attention of booking executives at Madison Square Garden. Originally considered to be an event appealing more to suburban and rural audiences and unlikely to be able to draw large crowds into New York City, the Garden decided to take a chance by booking a show on a February weekend in 1985. Early ticket sales were less than robust. Determined to improve sales in the final days leading up to the event dates, the Garden's public relations department met to brainstorm a "stunt," the kind of high-visibility publicity spectacle the staff often staged for one of its events to attract the attention of the demanding, hard-to-impress New York media.

On an Eighth Avenue sidewalk outside the Garden and the busy Pennsylvania Station train terminal, the media and the public were treated to a fantasy-come-true, the midweek demolition of the city's most ubiquitous vehicle: a "Cab-tastrophe" was staged with a monster truck crushing a New York City taxicab. The television and newspaper coverage of the stunt was enormous and the attention helped attract unexpected and welcome capacity audiences.

Encouraged by the successful weekend, the Garden booked the monster truck show again for a weekend in January 1986. Following its flamboyant publicity stunt for the first event, the Garden's public relations staff had to come up with another tour-de-force exploit, especially since the target audience for the show, young men, would undoubtedly be distracted by the coming weekend's NFL playoff game between the New York Giants and the Chicago Bears.

Rather than ignore a game that sports fans and the media were highly anticipating, the PR team decided to use the Giants-Bears matchup as the theme for another stunt. One of Chicago's most popular players was William Perry, an immense defensive lineman with a mammoth nickname to match his frame, "The Refrigerator." The media found the enthralling image of a monster truck driven by a Giants fan crushing six refrigerators in a quiet Greenwich Village location, Perry Street, in front of number 72, The Refrigerator's uniform, irresistible. The extensive coverage included national as well as the local outlets and was a highlight of an effective campaign to bring to the Garden great New York crowds who wound up enjoying the weekend monster truck shows more than the football game, which the Bears won on their way to a Super Bowl title.

Quite often, the trick to pulling off an effective publicity stunt and attracting attention for an event is being creative in finding fresh ways to connect with your audiences.

Human Interest Stories

One of the key focal points for pre-event publicity should be the development of stories about the participating athletes. Putting a human face on a sports competition can make an event more interesting to the potential audience and, as a result, appealing to reporters such as *Bloomberg News'* Kreda. "To me, the human interest angle always makes a sports event compelling," he observes. "Every event has the ability to produce the unexpected. I go into every sports event realizing that it can provide a drama or situation I've never before encountered." The human perspective on how an athlete prepares for and participates in an event provides the drama Kreda often uses in his reports. "The subtle human stories behind any event are of most interest to me," he adds.

Kreda understands the value of building relationships between his readers, the fans, and the athletes competing in the sports events he covers. The public wants to know who the athletes are, how they came to compete at the event, and why their performance is worthy of the spectators' interest. Roone Arledge, president of ABC Sports from 1968 to 1986, recognized the awesome power of connecting fans to athletes through the use of personal storytelling and revolutionized the way sports events were presented on television. Widely credited as the progenitor of many of the now familiar features of today's sports television landscape, Arledge was responsible for the creation of such landmark programming as *ABC's Wide World of Sports* and *Monday Night Football*, and such techniques as slow-motion replay. While supervising production for 10 Olympic Games, he pioneered the practice of interspersing in-depth personal features on world-class athletes into coverage of their competitive performances. To this day, networks continue to embrace and build on this programming philosophy as a way of riveting viewers to competitions, establishing powerful emotional bonds that involve the audience beyond simple appreciation of athletic excellence.

Sports event organizers should harness this power by familiarizing the media with their event's participants and identifying the human-interest stories that may abound. They must identify these opportunities through press releases, advisories, and personal phone calls to editors, producers and reporters, either directly or through the efforts of their public relations agency. Athletes need not be Olympians or famous to have engaging or emotional stories to tell, tales of triumphs over tragedy, and courage in the face of personal adversity.

Is there a registration or try-out process for participating teams or athletes? If so, prepare a release or advisory inviting the media to attend, and circulate a press release announcing the final roster of competitors. Are there never-before-told stories about a local participant who has overcome personal challenges to excel on the playing field?

"Event organizers who have local connections or star performers who have local connections are interesting," observes the *Los Angeles Times'* Elliott. Are there visiting athletes who have unique stories or perspectives on the local community to share? Traveling participants seem to get more fascinating the farther they have to journey to the event. Will they spend any time sightseeing or learning about the local culture? Is there a contestant who is poised to break a performance record or personal best? Perhaps there are teams seeking to end a particularly long championship drought or athletes focused on extending a winning streak. Don't overlook developing stories from the perspectives of event alumni or beloved greats of the sport. The history of a sports event is frequently best communicated in the words of former athletes.

Although sports event organizers and their agencies can encourage the development of human interest stories by circulating press releases, arranging for personal interviews are far more effective and usually far more appreciated by the media. Include an offer to set up an interview—in person, by phone, or another available mode—with the individual(s) featured in the release. Reporters will often want interviews to be held privately in an attempt to draw out answers or information that will provide exclusive content or stories that other media members may overlook. If you expect an unusually large number of media to desire interviews with the subject, however, a small informal gathering, breakfast, luncheon, or reception may be scheduled with the interview subject and interested reporters. Be prepared to stage brief one-on-one interviews immediately after the larger session. Television news and sports reporters will want to capture the athlete on video to support their stories. Likewise, radio media will want to record sound bites to make their reports more compelling to listeners.

Another convenient interviewing option for the media is to schedule a dial-in conference call. There are any number of companies that offer call-in services that provide a special phone number and access code through which a large number of reporters can listen to and ask questions of a subject. Alternatively, the Internet can be used for media-only sessions including the audio and video capabilities available on such sites as Skype, discussion "chats" with an exchange of media questions and interviewee responses in writing on your website or on one belonging to a sponsor, or interaction via social media. Access to the session can be restricted to the media with password controls, and later opened to the public for additional publicity value. Media conference calls and the Internet capabilities can be the most useful and cost-effective when the interview subject is traveling, or lives far from the host city.

Business Stories

The benefits and value that an event can provide to the business community should be promoted to both sports and business media early in the campaign. The articles they generate can be particularly useful for attracting local sponsors and promotional partners. "Economic impact stories are always good," notes Elliott. Even if impact figures were released during the announcing press conference, additional statistics can make for good reading. Typical minutiae and fun facts may include the number of hotel room nights expected to be sold as a result of the event, the number of staff and volunteers who will work on the program, projected attendance, and even the number of media expected to cover the event. Include historical information about the success of the event in previous years and past host cities.

Sponsor announcements are best directed to business reporters and trade publications and must be relevant to local commerce or the partner's industry. Is the sponsor celebrating a major anniversary of its association with an event? If so, talk about what has made the relationship so valuable to both parties. Perhaps a major sponsor decided to become involved with a sports event because of the cross-promotional potential with other sponsors. Is there is a new or intriguing special promotion that the organizer or sponsor will execute in fulfillment of their partnership?

Is there something new or unique about the sport or event organization? Stories can be pitched that discuss the vigor and longevity of the organization, the growth of the sport or the event's popularity, shifts in fan demographics, the advances in equipment, training, and technology associated with the sport, even the success of the organization's leadership.

Creating an Engaging Web Presence

Making fans aware of an event is only half of the battle. Public announcements and stories driven by mass media are great for generating publicity, but driving genuine fan engagement can be the difference between a casually interested individual reading about the event and an event ticket buyer or attendee. The web, and social media in particular, provide event organizers an excellent opportunity to develop a relationship with their potential customers and fans well before the event begins. The reach goes beyond any story or advertisement because the event organizer can directly and personally interact with prospective spectators. The power of web-driven influence can have a tremendously positive effect on your event, if used tactfully. But when this power is misused or abused, it can have quite the opposite effect. As such, it is important that a strategy is devised to make the event's web presence a tool and not a threat to the event's marketing.

The goal of creating a web presence is twofold: to drive excitement among potential event attendees and to start building a relationship with your customers. Driving excitement starts by developing features for the event's website that will encourage fans to visit and spend time perusing the site. This content can take many forms, including videos, pictures, and fan-generated multimedia. Media coverage and press releases should also be archived on the site for fan access. Offering rich content serves as a preview to the event, so it is important to deliver material that is representative of the event's product and philosophy and also provides sensory engagement for viewers. Updating the site on a regular basis with information about the event and fresh content will help drive continued, repeat traffic. The timing of these updates should coincide with important dates, such as the beginning of ticket sales, in order to draw high levels of traffic that may be more easily converted into sales. Content updates should be broadcast across social media platforms and the exchange of the information should be openly encouraged through the use of "share" buttons and easy access links.

Building a relationship with fans requires more than simply offering content and informational updates. Sharing news and features is a positive start, but it's only a start. Social media's ubiquitous presence in our society allows even the biggest corporate brands to become "friends" with their consumers. A sports event is no different. It is up to the event organizer to come up with ways to engage fans on a personal level. Posting thoughtful, intimate updates on social networks like Facebook and microblogging sites like Twitter will give the event a personality. Create interactive engagement by asking your fans and followers questions. Who is your favorite player? What was the best event you've ever attended, and why? Direct the questions to lead into event-relevant discussion. Include polls and encourage answers. What activity on Friday are you most looking forward to? Another useful tactic is to generate contests that encourage fans to participate in some way for the chance to win a prize. Such contests can be trivia related, or may require fans to send in a picture. Request that fans register by signing up or logging in and collect a judicious amount of non-sensitive personal information. This presents an ideal opportunity to capture valuable data, such as e-mail addresses, for later marketing and sales uses. In sum, the goal for creating a web presence is to get potential customers involved and to show them that there are people and personalities behind the title of the event. This will create goodwill and make people feel as though they are part of the event and the brand before they really begin interacting. It is this connection that will compel people to appreciate what the real event is all about.

A word of caution: Social media are extremely influential, and this may not always be a good thing. As a society, we are overwhelmed by the amount of information, content, and requests presented to us on an everyday basis. Be careful not to become part of the clutter by sending too many messages, generating irrelevant updates, or abusing the privilege of your customers' privacy and contact information. Web and social media can develop lasting relationships, or insensitive overuse can destroy them twice as fast. Listen to and learn from your digital and real-life interactions with your consumers to figure out where the proper balance of digital engagement lies. In the end, a well-developed and thoughtfully executed web and social media strategy can be the most effective tool in an event organizer's campaign for attention.

Countdown to Event Day

As event day approaches, an organizer's need for media attention typically grows exponentially. Publicity over the final few days can help to significantly boost attendance, increase last-minute ticket sales, and, for broadcast events, drive viewer and listener ratings higher. To maximize excitement, pictures best tell the story. Offer the media opportunities to cover preparations as the event moves into its host venue. If the installation of the playing surface or decoration of the event facility can provide good photographs or video footage, be sure to invite the media to capture them. Schedule a media preview or "hard-hat tour" to take interested reporters, photographers, and camera crews through the event site (providing there is something to see), or invite them to dry runs, technical run throughs, or tests of important operational systems. If entertainment is a prominent element of the event (e.g., opening and/or closing ceremonies, halftime or intermission acts, special presentations), invite the media to rehearsals and schedule interviews with the cast or featured performers. For participatory activities, such as at sports festivals, allow the media to preview these attractions the day before the public. If a sufficient number of media are expected to cover the event, invite reporters to participate in a media challenge edition of the competition right on the playing surface. Games or skills competitions can be staged between the media and athlete alumni, print and digital media against television and radio counterparts, or one media outlet against another. Noncompetitive sports events like 10K runs and other amateur events can even incorporate the participation of media contestants into the competition. The outlet will not only cover the event as it unfolds from a unique insider's perspective, but it may even generate advance publicity about how its representative in the event is training or otherwise preparing for his or her participation.

The arrival of teams or athletes previously featured in human-interest stories may generate additional photo opportunities. Be sure to include some media availability time in the event schedule to provide access to the most intriguing participating athletes. Opportunities may be scheduled as press conferences with a representative handful of participants just before or after a practice, at a welcome reception, during public appearances or even sightseeing tours of local points of interest. Alternatively, media availability time can be scheduled in which the participants are scattered throughout a hotel ballroom, on the playing surface, or along a host venue concourse beneath signs displaying their name, allowing reporters to guide themselves to the people they want to interview most. Try to arrange these opportunities at times that will still permit pre-event reporting for last-minute promotion, even if it will appear in the media just an hour or two prior to the competition. Every bit of coverage can be beneficial.

Servicing the Media at the Event Site

As noted in Figure 8.1, media members who cover a sports event expect appropriate, comfortable working conditions and the ability to view the competition from locations conducive to observing, writing, note taking, or uploading. Of equal importance are access to official statistics and score sheets, athlete and event background information, and the ability to avail themselves of facilities and technological services to file stories and broadcast reports in a timely and professional manner. Members of the media also anticipate being granted access to locker rooms, press conference locations, and other areas where athletes and officials may be interviewed, photographed, and observed.

Media Guides

A media guide, whether printed or digital, can provide all reporters with a consistent, uniform presentation of history, facts, participant information, and statistics. Start with the most basic of information—do not assume that the reporters assigned to cover your sports event or pre-event press conferences are completely familiar with the sport, its organization, rules, participants, or the format of the program.

Rosters, line-ups, and/or the order of competition should be provided to all media as they arrive or, at the latest, before the event begins. Include such information as a detailed event schedule, packages of statistics, past event results, milestones or records, biographical information on the athletes and coaches, and historical background on teams. Competition rules, copies of all press releases distributed since the first announcement, and information on upcoming events should also be available. Many sports event organizers compile all of this information in the form of a media guide, which may be as simple as a loose-leaf binder with section dividers, as professional as a spiral, saddle-stitched or perfect-bound publication, on a flash drive, or immediately accessible and updatable as an online version. Media guides are usually published as late as possible to allow for last-minute revisions, which is why loose-leaf binders and online editions can be particularly useful for events where changes are frequent and inevitable. The appearance and organization of the media guide must maintain a level of professionalism. For printed versions, create eye-catching graphics such as a specially designed cover using the event name and logo, number all pages, and include a table of contents for easy access to the information within. For digital editions, compose attractive home pages with tables of contents that link the user directly to the information desired.

Accreditation

For the purposes of maintaining a safe, exclusive, and professional work environment for the media and to maintain a reasonable level of security for the athletes and others working in nonpublic areas, an accreditation system is strongly recommended. Establishing an accreditation system involves the design and distribution of credentials to authorized personnel that visually identifies the bearer and his or her affiliation, and permits access to restricted areas. The media accreditation plan must be integrated into an overall system that event security and operations personnel will use to control access to all nonpublic areas of the site for staff, volunteers, vendors, reporters, broadcasters, and other stakeholders.

It is useful for staff to be able to visually identify members of the media to direct them to the facilities set aside for their convenience, as well as for the distribution of press information. The mechanics of setting up a comprehensive event credential system are more fully explored in Play 14, "Managing for the Unexpected." The process of qualifying media who wish to cover an event and using an accreditation system to manage their activities on the event site, however, is more appropriately discussed here.

Distribute an advisory to the target media listed in your press release database that invites media representatives to apply for credentials at least one month prior to the event. Larger and more newsworthy events that anticipate a significant media response should circulate this advisory with even more lead time. Include event schedule information and an application requesting the name of the media member(s), the affiliation, and full contact information. If the event is of the magnitude that media will be traveling to the host city, you may also include information regarding hotel accommodations.

In democratic societies, it is the right of the media to cover and report on any event that is open and available to the public. It is similarly the right of any event organizer to limit access to the event site to anyone who does not possess a ticket or credential. Organizers should assess the extent to which they can physically accommodate the media before accepting applications for accreditation. Although it is usually advantageous to maximize an event's opportunities for coverage, the number and nature of media members who should be provided with workspace and professional access and courtesies is completely up to the event organizer and may be limited by available support space and budget resources. It is perfectly acceptable to limit the number of credentials to those who can be accommodated safely and effectively. However, it should be kept in mind that competing media outlets within a particular territory (e.g., each of the daily newspapers or radio stations in a given market) will demand access that is fair and equal to that provided to their competitors. As a general rule, it is recommended that all bona fide media be accommodated if at all possible. Where the organizer has perhaps a little more leeway in evaluating whether to provide access is with regard to media with small niche readership or viewership or a questionable relationship to the event audience. If an organizer has never heard of an organization or individual requesting access, it is strongly suggested that the background of the entity or person is checked. Remember that once you provide someone with a credential for access to restricted areas, you also undertake certain liabilities in exposing participants and staff to unfamiliar or potentially questionable individuals. Media that cannot be accommodated in limited-access work and press conference facilities or who are unfamiliar to the organizer may be alternatively provided with complimentary tickets without additional access. While it is highly unusual for them to pay for tickets, media members who are not accommodated as above are still free to attend the event as ticket holders or members of the public and may subsequently write stories without having to apply for and receive credentials.

Be sure to set and clearly state a deadline for returning completed media credential applications. It is up to the organizer how strictly one will adhere to the deadline, balancing the desire for coverage with the necessity to control access to non-public areas. As a general rule, the organizer is not obligated to admit media to controlled areas if they appear on event day without having applied for credentials. It is, therefore, essential that all media outlets that may cover the event have an opportunity to receive and review the advisory and application with sufficient time to respond.

For major sports events, barcode technology is often used to store information about an individual media representative that was provided in the application for credentials. The barcode is part of the credential and can be scanned to verify authenticity or to provide access to restricted areas.

The organizer should carefully review applications and respond to approved applicants with information on where and when credentials may be picked up (nonapproved applicants, if any, should also be notified). It is recommended that the physical distribution of credentials be delayed until the day before they are actually needed to enter the venue, or on the event day, to reduce the chance of their being counterfeited and duplicated. Credentials should be worn and visible at all times, particularly in restricted areas. They may take the form of a pressure-sensitive printed sticker (acceptable for limited budget, one-day events), simple laminated cards with a safety-pin back or lanyard to enable it to be worn about the neck (essential for events that are longer than a single day), or a digital identification badge loaded onto a mobile device. An example of an event credential is pictured in Figure 8.7.

As previously mentioned, when a sports event organizer provides someone not under the event's direct supervision with access to restricted areas, the organizer assumes a greater level of liability. Therefore, it is recommended that some deterrents to the possible counterfeiting of credentials be considered. For low-budget events, unusual typefaces and multicolor, event-specific artwork can be inexpensive measures, although the widespread availability of software and inexpensive scanners and color printers means only that a counterfeiter has only to spend a little time

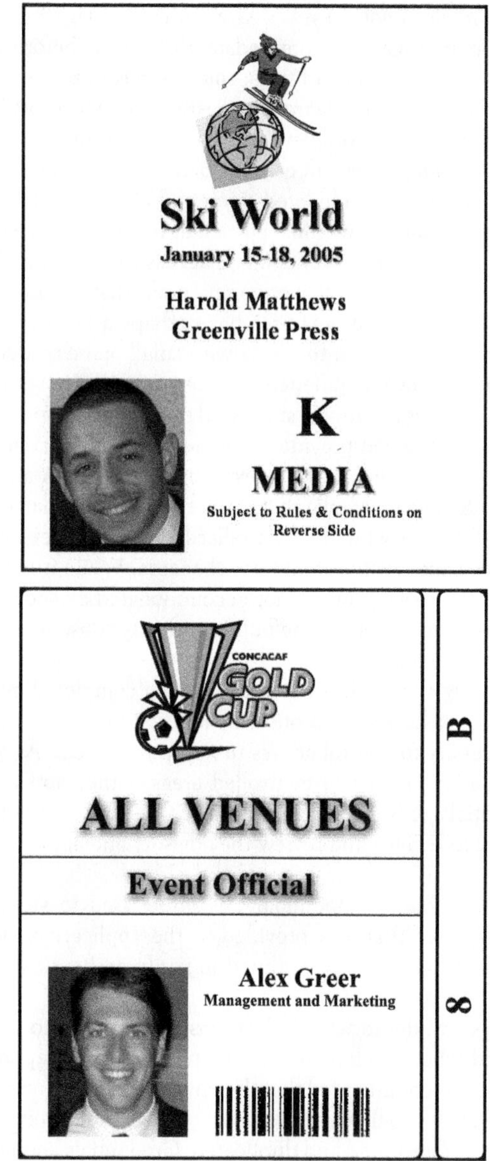

Figure 8.7 Sample Sports Event Media Credential

to craft a reasonably close facsimile. The application of small holographic stickers or holographic printing on the credential is another, better measure for organizers of events with greater security concerns. Printing the credential on special paper with unique weaving is yet another common deterrent to counterfeiting.

The inclusion of a small headshot photo of the approved media member on the credential is standard practice and strongly suggested for major, high-exposure events. Most media outlets are prepared to respond to this requirement and have the ability to digitally supply a jpeg headshot to include with the application for a credential. If unavailable, digital photos can be taken by event staff and applied to the credential on site. The best and most secure method of using photo identification is to digitally print the image directly onto the credential. For organizers with more modest budgets, the photo can be affixed to the credential and the entire card laminated to discourage counterfeiters removing the photo and replacing it with another. Be sure to confirm the identity of the individual receiving the credential by requesting that every person presents a government issued photo ID before receiving credentials. There are companies that specialize in providing accreditation services and can be engaged to handle the multi-faceted requirements of sports events.

If the event security plan is more complex than simply allowing credential-bearers unfettered access to all areas, a color and/or letter code may be included on the face of the credential. This code will provide security personnel with information on the specific areas of access to which the bearer is entitled (see Appendix 15). It is not generally necessary, in fact it is preferable not, to explain the meanings of the codes to non-security personnel.

On printed event credentials, such as those being worn with a lanyard, the reverse side of the credential often includes legal disclaimers that transfer the risks of injury during attendance at the event, and as a result of being granted access to restricted areas, to the wearer. The right of the organizer to remove the credential from the bearer for inappropriate behavior should also be included in this language. It is essential that a qualified attorney develop and approve this protective language.

In addition to providing an exclusive, professional work environment for the media and an essential level of security for the event, the accreditation process will also prepare organizers with an advance understanding of how many media will want to cover the event. Armed with this information, the organizer can install sufficient media center facilities and seating for the number of writers, broadcasters and other working media representatives.

Media Center Facilities

As has been discussed, representatives of the media expect comfortable and appropriate working conditions during the event. Most arenas, stadiums, and other regularly utilized sports venues have ready-made facilities designed expressly for this purpose. Others offer a selection of multipurpose rooms or empty spaces that can be allocated and outfitted to fulfill various functions based upon a specific organizer's needs. As you assign spaces to meet your sports event's many requirements, try to keep the facilities that are being set aside for the media in as close proximity to each other as possible. Be sure to post printed, not handwritten, directional signs along the route between the entrance the media will use and all areas to which they require access, including the media workroom, the event office, press conference location, the media lounge or hospitality area, the press box or other event seating designated for the media, and (if the media will have access) athlete locker rooms.

Media Workroom

Media seating at the event should be provided with a clear, unobstructed view of the playing surface whenever possible. Reporters for newspapers, magazines, websites, and others who must "file," or submit their stories to their editor under often tight deadlines, should be provided with "tabletop" seating, that is, seats that are located at tables or countertop working surfaces.

Draped, half-width folding tables can be installed in areas where reporters will be working to provide them with a flat surface for their laptops or writing tablets. Multiple outlet power bars with surge protection should be run atop or beneath the tabletops to provide writers with access to power for their laptops and other equipment. Task lighting should be added if the lighting conditions in the area are not conducive to reading statistics and score sheets. Event-day media also require reliable service for mobile devices and WiFi capability for making calls and uploading written stories and digital photography to editors. Other media, such as radio stations for game broadcasts or on-site updates, can be invited to arrange for dedicated phone or data lines to be installed at their expense during the accreditation process. To control costs and the possibility of abuse, it is recommended that any lines offered by the event organizer restrict access to local and toll-free numbers only. If a code is required to access an outside phone line or WiFi network, post this information on or near the phone. If the event is televised or if an in-house video feed of the action is available, place video monitors within convenient view of the media seating sections, as well as in the media workroom and any spaces set aside as press conference areas. A table stocked with media guides and multiple copies and past and current event press releases should be within visible reach of the workroom to provide reporters with memory-refreshing background information. Provide photocopies of pre-event print coverage, as well as transcripts of recent press conferences, if available. It is also recommended that a bulletin board or easel be located near the entrance to the workroom to post the event schedule and transportation information, if provided.

When the media contingent is so large (or the venue is so small) that it is not possible to accommodate all of the media with working space in direct view of the event's proceedings, a secondary media workroom may be constructed elsewhere, such as in a large, open space defined by a curtain wall along the event level of an arena or stadium or outdoors in a tent. All of the requirements set forth for media seating sections—tables, power, WiFi, phones, etc.—are equally important in these areas but, for such events, television monitors providing coverage of the event, appropriate heating/air conditioning, and security are absolutely essential.

Members of media expect and demand instant access to information as the event progresses. If the media are seated in a single area during the event, a separate, localized public address system can be installed to communicate pertinent information exclusively to them. Use the system to announce official results, advise the media on changes in schedule, explain the decisions of judges and referees, update statistics, provide available information on athlete injuries, and communicate post-event press opportunities. Having a media-only public address system is particularly important if an auxiliary media workroom is installed for an overflow of journalists, ensuring that all receive the same information at the same time. In areas where the media tabletops are in public seating areas, the speakers should be sized, placed, and balanced so only the media can hear the announcements that are directed to them. Most importantly, be sure to test all systems—electrical power, technology services, and broadcast feeds—several times before the media arrive to be certain that all are functioning properly.

Media Lounge or Hospitality Area

Keeping the media comfortable is of the utmost importance. Reporters and crews often arrive at the event venue early to grab interviews with arriving athletes and depart late after the event has concluded, postevent press conferences have been held, and their stories have been written and filed, their reports have been broadcast and their photographs have been uploaded. Provide water, coffee, soft drinks, and snacks throughout the day. Meals appropriate to the time of day can be provided either as an expense to the event or, at a modest charge to cover costs, to the media. Most venues with their own in-house caterer or concessionaire require organizers to purchase food, even in backstage areas, only from their service provider, typically an expensive proposition. If the event is able to bring its own food into the facility, an organizer's options become wider. "For a limited budget, grocery stores make sandwich trays," says Toronto-based media consultant David Job of Media Concepts. "Whole fruit and beverages can also be purchased and picked up."

Try to set up the refreshments in an area separate from the workroom if space permits. "Too often, workrooms become social gathering places and noise levels reach points that are distracting to writers who are working on deadline after others may have finished," observes Elliott. "Workrooms are workrooms, period. Set up a separate area, if available, where you have coffee or water and make sure there's a distinction between these areas," she suggests.

To determine what refreshments should be provided, consider what time most of the media will report to the event site and when most will depart. Estimate arrival at least 30 minutes before pre-game player availabilities and departure at least one hour after postevent press conferences to permit them time to complete their work. Do not assume the media will be able to visit concession stands—their job is to cover the competitive event, difficult to do if standing in line for a hot dog and soft drink. With this in mind, sandwiches and salads might be provided during lunch hours and a hot entrée can be served if work will take place through normal dinner hours. Soft drinks (the sponsor's brand!), coffee, and light snacks such as pretzels, popcorn, chips, and cookies should always be available. Figure 8.8 provides a handy checklist of media workroom requirements, followed by a real-life example of press box setup protocols from Soccer United Marketing's Media Operations Guide in Figure 8.9.

Media Relations Office

Be sure the media are looked after by knowledgeable staff members or representatives of the event organizer's public relations agency. A media relations office should be located within close proximity of the media workroom to enable reporters access to staff for additional information or special requests. It is recommended that the media relations office be divided into two spaces, one that is separated by closed doors in order to conduct internal, confidential conversations with the event director or other senior managers in the event of a crisis or controversy. It is also helpful to have this quieter separate workspace available to the staff for writing and proofreading press releases without distraction or interruption. A secure storage closet or small room is another necessity.

- ☐ Seating with tabletops (preferably with unobstructed view of event)
- ☐ Multiple power outlets and surge protectors
- ☐ Phone lines
- ☐ WiFi access
- ☐ Workspace (task) lighting
- ☐ Video monitors
- ☐ Small, localized public address system
- ☐ Refreshments (preferably in a separate hospitality area)
- ☐ Schedules, rosters, and line-ups
- ☐ Press releases
- ☐ Media guides

Figure 8.8 Checklist of Media Workroom Requirements

Game Day—Press Box Setup

Three (3) hours prior to first kickoff at each venue, the following must be in place:

I. Seating chart—hung in elevator, media seating area, and placed on stats table
II. Placards—one placard placed at each seat signaling name and affiliation of media member
III. Wireless Internet, DSL lines, or phone lines—check all lines for activation
IV. Game programs—one game program placed at each media member seat
V. Game notes—one game program should be placed at each media member seat
VI. Stats crew—dedicated computer for stats crew connected to printer; headphones to TV trucks; index cards available; flash stats. CONCACAF statistics rules will be adhered to.
VII. TV compound / TV and radio booths—game notes, rosters, and game programs delivered to broadcasters, to be overseen by broadcast liaison. VPO (Venue Press Officer) should nevertheless check in with liaison to make sure TV and radio crews are covered appropriately.
VIII. In-house feed—broadcast of the game should appear on press box TV monitors as well as be taped in press box VCR. Should it be requested from a media member, the press box supervisor should allow for in-game reviews at halftime and following the end of regulation.
IX. Catering (press box and photo workroom)—see "Game Day Stadium Needs."

Figure 8.9 Press Box Setup Guidelines (From Soccer United Marketing's 2011 CONCACAF Gold Cup Media Operations Guide)

The office should be staffed at all times the media are at the event site. Additional copies of press releases and other printed materials provided in the workroom should always be available from the office. The phone numbers and e-mail addresses for the media relations office and staff should be posted in the media workroom, as well as at the security office and the media entrance. No reporters, camera crews, or any other member of the media should be admitted to the event site without the knowledge of the staff in this media control center. Camera crews should always be escorted by a member of the media relations staff anywhere in the event site if at all possible.

The media relations office is an essential workspace from which to manage media center operations. Desks or draped and skirted tables with chairs should be installed to provide the staff with a functional workspace. Provide computers and networked printers if staff will not be using their own laptops and portable printers. Reliable service for mobile devices and WiFi capability should be available. At least one television monitor should be installed to follow the progress of the event and other developments. For large-scale events, ensure there are at least two telephone sets with multiple lines if possible.

It is also essential to have convenient and exclusive access to at least one mid- or high-speed copier with collator, stapler, and a more than adequate supply of copy paper. Along with the printer, a scanner, and a facsimile machine are other needed equipment. Depending on the anticipated use of each, a three-in-one unit might be most efficient.

- ☐ Easy access from media workroom
- ☐ Desks or skirted folding tables
- ☐ Chairs
- ☐ Multiple power outlets and surge protectors
- ☐ Laptop computers or tablets
- ☐ Phones (minimum of two, preferably with multiple lines)
- ☐ WiFi access
- ☐ Workspace lighting
- ☐ Television monitor
- ☐ Mid- to high-speed copier with collator and stapler
- ☐ Copy paper
- ☐ Scanner and fax equipment
- ☐ Office supplies
- ☐ Copies of all printed materials
- ☐ Secure storage closet
- ☐ Refreshments

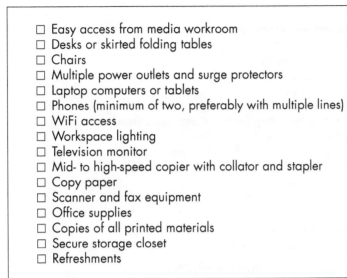

Figure 8.10 Checklist of Media Relations Office Requirements

Plans for refreshments or providing meals for the media also should include the media relations staff, who will be working the same long hours as the people they are serving on behalf of the event. Don't forget one of the most mundane of details—a carton or two of essential office supplies, including writing implements, folders, paper clips, staplers and staples, writing pads, message pads or Post-its, and any other consumable item that makes any functional office go (see Figure 8.10 for a typical checklist of media office requirements).

Press Conference and Interview Facilities

The press conference location provides a focal point for pre- and postevent interviews, the spot for dissemination of any information that is best delivered by a spokesperson throughout the program, and for any interactive exchange between the media and senior organization management. The press conference facility may occupy its own separate room, preferably close to athlete locker rooms and easily accessible from the media workroom. If such space is unavailable, an area can be created in a draped-off, column-free backstage space as conveniently located as practical. Regardless of its location, it should be situated in an area that is inaccessible to the public and as noise- and distraction-free as possible.

A checklist of requirements for a sports event press conference facility may be found in Figure 8.11, and a typical layout in Figure 8.12. Set up enough chairs in view of the stage to accommodate the media expected to cover the event. It is acceptable, but not necessary, to provide tabletop surfaces for laptops or writing tablets in the press conference area. The focus of attention in the room is a stage or dais constructed of riser platforms, commonly available through the event venue, at many hotels and convention centers, or through audiovisual rental agencies. Plan to design a stage that is only as large as required to accommodate the number of participants envisioned. Most stage riser platforms are available in 4-foot by 8-foot sections, and at heights

- ☐ Quiet, column-free, limited access space
- ☐ Media seating
- ☐ Stage riser(s) (preferably skirted)
- ☐ Camera/photographer riser
- ☐ Skirted tables for stage
- ☐ Podium (with optional logo)
- ☐ Pipe and drape backdrop (with optional customized drape)
- ☐ Public address system with technician
- ☐ Table microphones with mic flags for interviewees
- ☐ Wireless mics for moderator and interviewer questions
- ☐ Lighting for stage wash
- ☐ Video camera and monitors
- ☐ "Mult" box
- ☐ Video presentation equipment (optional)

Figure 8.11 Press Conference Requirements Checklist

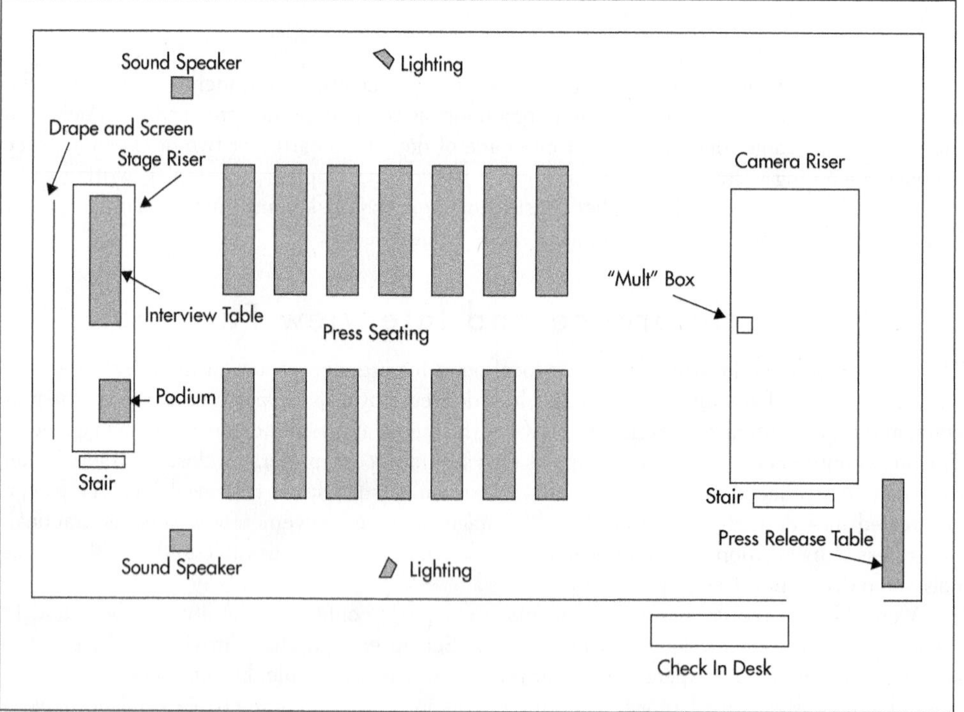

Figure 8.12 Sports Event Press Conference Room Layout

generally ranging from 18 inches to up to 36 inches. If the interview subjects will most often be standing at a podium, risers that are 18 inches or 24 inches high are probably sufficient, raising the participants sufficiently to be easily seen by all media in attendance without seeming to overpower the room. If, instead, the subject(s) will be seated at draped tables, the risers should be set at a minimum of 24 inches in height. For the most professional appearance, the legs of the stage riser should be skirted. It is not uncommon to set the press conference stage with both a podium and draped tables to enable the organizer the flexibility to quickly schedule multiple participant interview opportunities and statements without additional, last-minute setup. The podium should be in good, clean condition, and include a top shelf for speaker notes and water. If one is available, an event logo should be centered facing the audience on the top portion of the podium, professionally printed on a lightweight board (and affixed in a way to not damage the podium) to maximize exposure on any video footage used from the press conference. *Mic flags,* small plastic tiles imprinted with the event or event organizer's logo, can also be attached to the microphones on the podium and interview tables to increase visibility.

The microphones should be connected to a high-quality public address system with sufficient speaker cabinets to provide clear, uniformly distributed sound throughout the media seating section. It is strongly recommended that the press conference audio system be installed and operated by a qualified audiovisual equipment supplier that will have a technician remain on-site at all times the area may be in use. Be sure that all systems are periodically tested before the media arrive, as well as immediately before any press conference begins.

Drape the wall behind the stage with a dark, nonshiny background. "Pipe and drape" units, fabric panels suspended on a frame of sturdy metal frames, are commonly available from many event facilities and rental companies in royal blue, navy blue, and black. Blue drapes look best in photographs and video. A banner with the event logo can be suspended from the pipe centered in front of the drape on a thin monofilament line. Up to two additional banners might also be displayed; they might feature the logo of the event organization, a title or presenting sponsor, or another essential stakeholder, as desired. Any more than three banners will appear cluttered. Since the primary reason for affixing a banner to the drape is to increase its visibility in photographs and video footage, it is best for it to be positioned behind and just above the spot where the most important participants will be addressing the media. Make sure the banner is hung at a suitable height so that any logo is clearly visible, depending on whether someone will be standing at the podium or sitting at a table, A banner or entire panels of drape can be custom printed with *step and repeat logos* to increase the likelihood that at least one logo will make it into each recorded image of the press conference. Step and repeat drapes are like wallpaper – they feature small versions of one or two logos, usually for the event and a sponsor, at frequent intervals across the entire surface. Although the logos might not be particularly readable from a distance, they can be very effective in photographs and video.

A "camera riser" may be positioned behind the media seating area, centered at the opposite side of the room from podium and sufficiently large to accommodate the number of video and still photographers expected. It should be set at an equal height to the stage risers to enable camerapeople to shoot over the heads of the seated reporters. While most media who cover sports events will be equipped with lenses that will capture the close-ups they need from the back of the room, it is also acceptable to place the media riser closer to the stage so long as those making use of it will not obstruct the view of those seated.

An audio *mult box* should be available and located on or adjacent to the camera riser. A mult box is a small, briefcase-sized unit that distributes the sound directly from the press conference's public address system to any plugged-in television camera, radio line, and audio recording device. This unit is essential to providing the media with top-quality, interference-free sound from the press conference microphones. If your event venue does not own one, a unit can be rented.

Press conference areas should be lit for television coverage. The organizer's audiovisual supplier should be asked to light the stage with a "wash" (an even distribution) of television-friendly light. Lighting should be focused on the speaker standing at the podium and/or at the speakers sitting at the tables and never face directly into the eyes of the participants. Rather, they should be hung from a position 8- to 10-feet high, or on lighting "trees" (free-standing poles topped with lighting instruments) and placed at 45-degree angles to the stage's center on either side of the room. Whether hung or placed atop trees, lighting must come from two different positions to eliminate the harsh shadows that can distort or under-expose resulting photographs and footage.

If a large contingent of media is expected, the organizer may be well advised to install television monitors at regular intervals in locations distant from the stage and fed by a camera on the riser. The same feed can be sent to the video monitors in the media workroom to enable those in the process of writing their stories to cover the press conference, as well. If the press conference requires the presentation of event highlights or another video segment, large television monitors are essential. A large screen or monitor may also be installed to the side of the stage riser, if needed. The organizer's audiovisual supplier can provide the necessary equipment to professionally present video elements as needed. An event representative should work with the technician to ensure cues to run the video are smoothly handled.

Questions from the media can be captured by wireless mics passed into the audience by event staff members. At least two mics are recommended, assigned to staff on either side of the room for quick deployment. As these mics are also tied into the public address system, the questions will be easier to hear within the room and through the recording devices plugged into the mult box.

Depending on the situation, many postevent press conferences are broadcast live on television and/or streamed on websites, making the quality of all production elements associated with the press conference even more important for all concerned.

A Note about Talking to the Media

It is essential to appoint a key contact to serve as a spokesperson for the sports event organizer throughout the event planning process, right up through event day and beyond. All media inquiries and requests for interviews should be funneled through this single individual who can then schedule other event staff, athletes, and other stakeholders to speak with reporters. Be sure that all event staff and volunteers know the identity and responsibilities of this main contact, and refer all media inquiries to this person. No staff should provide interviews or insights to reporters before this essential step is taken to ensure that the event organizer speaks with a consistent tone and viewpoint, and always provides accurate information. This will also alert the organizer's management of any controversies that may be brewing in relation to the event, its sponsors, and other key stakeholders, as well as to any circulating rumors or potential crises on the horizon. The contact will screen and set up interview requests, determining the ideal and most appropriate individual to provide the media with the information they require.

The media having a single point of contact is a necessary first step to the management of disseminating event information, but controlling the message delivered to the media requires full understanding and cooperation from every member of the event staff. Given the speed at which information is transmitted, it is important that everyone on the event team is educated on the use of social media, specifically any policies that are in place governing how or if information is permitted to be shared. While taking an active role in social media is important in engaging and informing your guests and customers, delivering the wrong message, bad information, or the wrong tone can be devastating to your event. The event organizer should inform his or her staff of the issues that mismanaged social media can create.

Media Coverage and Media Partners

Although journalists' livelihoods ultimately depend on the financial health and business performance of the media entity for which they work, this face of Janus sees not the business and marketing needs of the employer. Conversely, the editorial staff will neither expect nor demand that any benefits be accorded them as a result of a media partnership between their employer and an event. Journalistic ethics would preclude any such expectation. Although great sensitivity needs to be exercised, it is possible for organizers to demonstrate such appreciation for the partnership. For instance, it is possible to provide a media partner with exclusive story ideas and supporting information for advance publicity purposes (although it is unethical to withhold this information from other outlets if they request it). An organizer can also provide media partners with accreditation for a quantity of reporters and photojournalists in excess of what is offered to other outlets, and can provide preferential locations from which they can cover the event.

It is essential to ensure that other media outlets covering the event feel no less accommodated in preparing their coverage. Although some feature story ideas and information may be shared with a media partner's editorial staff, it should come as no surprise that after a story appears in one media outlet, it may no longer be considered news, or newsworthy, by others. Every media outlet wants to be the first to release a story, and it may seem accommodating on the part of the event organizer to provide information to its media partner(s) first (something to which the media partner will rarely say no). However, it is important that all media in the market feel accommodated, appreciated, and integral to the day's activities in the event's pressroom. Therefore, if an organizer feels compelled to break a story first to the event's media partner, the selection and timing of the story should provide the greatest benefit to the organizer's promotional plans, with the least effect on the attitude of the rest of the media. Consequently, writers, reporters, and broadcasters will not feel that the organizer is withholding information from them and serving the media partner preferentially. In most cases, it is best to treat everyone on the editorial side of the media partnership as close to the same as possible.

Post-Play Analysis

Sports event organizers need the media to help publicize an event from the moment it is introduced, throughout the planning process, and after event day. A campaign of key, newsworthy event announcements and milestones should be scheduled to promote the event at strategic times, such as prior to the first day of ticket sales or participant registration, and with increasing frequency as event day approaches.

The editorial side of the media needs access to reliable and comprehensive information, statistics, and background to enable them to generate accurate stories. Event organizers must identify opportunities for human interest and business stories to further enhance pre-event coverage.

During the event, the media require access to even more information, as well as comfortable working facilities in nonpublic areas that will help them file and broadcast their stories on a timely basis. Refreshments and meals should be offered at appropriate times of the day for events that require the continuing presence of the media. Visual access to the field of play and free access to the event site are essential elements for providing a positive environment for the media. The media also require access to services and technology to enable them to do their work and to press conference facilities for important announcements and interview opportunities.

Coach's Clipboard

1. Create a publicity campaign for the fictional 10K run in Play 1, including a schedule of key announcement dates. Where should you hold the announcing press conference? What kinds of human interest and business stories will you propose to the media, and how? Where will you place the media office, workroom, hospitality area, and press conference area for this outdoor event?
2. Consider the hypothetical playoff fan festival in Play 1. How will the publicity campaign for this event differ from the 10K run above? What kind of pre-event stories might be generated for this event? How should this be managed, given the possibility that the team might not make the playoffs?
3. Write an announcing press release for the playoff fan festival above. When should this announcement be made, and what should it include? How can you keep interest high on your event website and on social media networks?
4. In what unique ways would you use social media networks as pre-event engagement opportunities for the 10K run? How can you utilize these networks during the event to provide enhanced coverage to the families and friends of the participants, and opportunities for your business partners?

PLAY 9

Activating the Sports Event Marketing Plan

"Study the rules so that you won't beat yourself by not knowing something."

—*Babe Didrickson Zaharias, six-time Associated Press Woman Athlete of the Year between 1931 and 1954*

This play will help you to:

- Develop a marketing plan for your event to best suit your resources and needs, using a combination of advertising, publicity, promotion, event marketing, direct sales, and social media.
- Discover how media partnerships can help advance a sports event's marketing objectives.
- Understand why and how media partners use sports events to meet their business objectives.

Introduction

To get their products into the hands of consumers, corporations develop and activate marketing strategies, applying tactics that include a combination of publicity, advertising, promotion, direct sales, event marketing, and social media campaigns. To the sports event organizer, the event is the product and the consumers may be ticket buyers, attendees, corporate partners, the media, and even participating athletes. Like companies that sell goods to consumers, sports event organizers must be more than just managers and manufacturers. They must also be marketers and

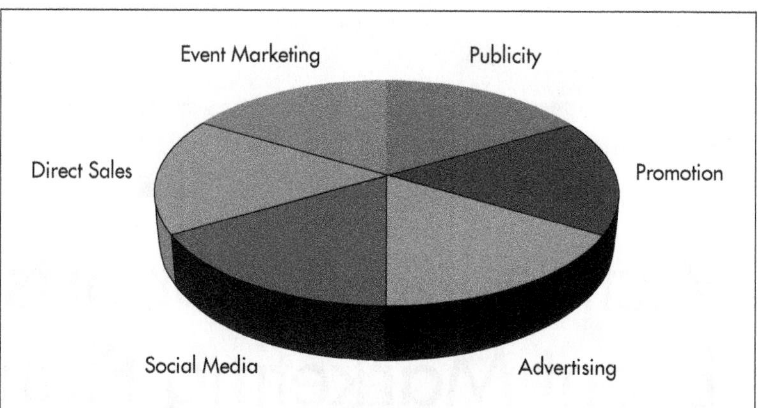

Figure 9.1 The Sports Event Marketing Plan Wheel

promoters, employing various forms of media and other mass communications devices to "sell" their event to the public.

The marketing plan fashioned to promote a sports event comprises the same tools as are used by consumer companies in varying degrees, as illustrated in Figure 9.1. The proportion of each event's resources that will be dedicated to various components of the marketing plan will vary widely by market and the type of event, and are totally at the discretion of the organizer.

Play 8 described in detail the infrastructure that is required to service the editorial side of the media and energize an effective publicity campaign. The core attributes of the news media industry, journalistic integrity, and a responsibility to report on reality in objective terms, have little impact on the essential truth that a media outlet is also a business, an entity that has to generate revenue in excess of expenses to remain in business. Although some revenues flow from subscriptions and single-copy sales, most of the revenue that maintains print media businesses is through the sale of advertising space. Much the same holds true for television, radio, and the Internet. Most of the income for commercial stations and websites flows from advertising time or space, although many sports television channels also charge cable systems a per-subscriber fee in addition to receiving advertising revenue.

What Media Partners Want from a Sports Event Relationship

Viewed in its most simplified form, advertising rates are predicated on both the number and the demographic quality of a media outlet's readers, viewers, or users. Therefore, any opportunity that can increase readership or viewer or listener ratings, increase usage, or generate measurable incremental advertising, is highly desirable to the owner, publisher, or general manager of a media concern. A marketing partnership with the right sports event can present many such powerful possibilities to print, broadcast and digital media businesses.

"Sports marketing offers newspapers the ability to become a part of a local event that typically appeals to families, youth, and ethnic markets," observed Sheri Wish, while serving as the former director of advertising, new business development, multimedia, and sports for the *Los Angeles*

Times. "These can be somewhat different than the typical core newspaper reader, offering branding and circulation opportunities to passionate fans and crossing income, race and geographical issues in the marketplace." Executives at broadcast and digital media entities share similar views. They agree that opportunities provided through effective sports marketing can expand their audience, positively contribute to their community, and increase revenue. As previously discussed, event participants, attendees, and viewers can be defined along demographic and lifestyle characteristics and, by taking advantage of an association with a sports event, a media outlet can reach into new markets comprised of loyal, passionate, and motivated fans. In order to effectively reach them, however, the media outlet must promote its association with the event, and provide fans with value not found elsewhere, including expanded coverage, special features, timely, exclusive, and, in some cases, live content and relevant advertising and promotions.

In well-served markets, newspapers, radio stations, local television outlets, and websites also view themselves as ambassadors of the community, businesses in a unique position to help promote the vigor and vitality of their readership, viewers, listeners, or user area. There is no hint of conflict of interest or imperiled journalistic integrity because they will still cover news as news, whether it is good or reflects poorly on the condition of the local market. Marketing activity that promotes their community, however, is good for area businesses and increases the relevance of the media outlet as an effective place to spend advertising dollars. The outlet is free to participate as a booster of local commerce while the editorial side reports on the news in a community. After all, working behind the scenes to promote economic growth and an improved quality of life directly helps the media's business. An invigorated market can encourage advertisers to move into the community or seek to do more business there. More business can mean more jobs, more jobs can mean more growth, and more growth means a larger universe of readers, viewers, and users. In the long term, attracting more positive attention to their community through sports event marketing efforts is simply a good strategy for media entities, and, since such efforts are undertaken without the direct involvement of the editorial staff, there is no risk of jeopardizing the company's objective journalistic standards.

Publishers, programming, and digital media executives also know that the excitement that sports events bring to a community can rub off on the companies that take an active role. The media are where potential event attendees and viewers naturally go for information, so establishing a strong, recognizable association with a sports event in the minds of the consumer can generate powerful results for both the media outlet and its advertisers. Readership, listeners, viewers, and users are the gold standard upon which the media's currency—advertising rates—is based, and sports events can provide outlets with outstanding promotional opportunities that can make a partnership both worthwhile and profitable. Sports events are particularly valuable properties with which to be associated for digital media services, as fans will return frequently to the featured event pages, often several times in a single day or even during a single website visit, for the latest exclusive content, event schedule updates, and other detailed event information. Beyond the sheer quantity of visits, or page views, the repetition of promotional messages on these pages when fans return adds incremental value to the advertiser.

Media outlets that become media sponsors can be afforded every benefit befitting their level of participation without endangering the objectivity of their editorial coverage. The greater the media company's financial involvement, whether provided in cash or as VIK, the more promotional exclusivities the organizer can offer. For example, a sufficiently robust partnership can enable a media outlet to be the sole source for reader, listener, viewer, or user benefits such as ticket giveaways, sweepstakes, contests, and discounts. At the same time, the division of news media into mutually exclusive editorial and marketing functions helps to protect a sports event from being ignored by nonpartner media due to promotional relationships with competitors. In a perfect world, media partnerships should not jeopardize basic editorial event coverage that will be provided by other newspapers or broadcasters.

- Revenue generation
  - Advertising
    - Directly from the sports event organizer
    - From sports event sponsors
    - Incremental advertising opportunities from nonsponsors
- Promotion
  - To increase circulation, listeners, viewers, or users
  - To increase the subscriber base
  - To expand into new markets
  - To promote new writers, talent, shows, or online services
- Event activation
  - Event site signage
  - Event promotional presence
  - Event presentation/fan activity element(s)
  - Inclusion in event advertising
  - Engagement with fans/readers via social media outlets
- Category exclusivity
- Sampling opportunities
- Exclusive hospitality opportunities for advertisers
- Pass-through rights

Figure 9.2 What the Media Want from Sports Events as a Marketing and Promotional Partner

A formal marketing partnership with a sports event can offer a media outlet many of the same featured benefits that other sponsors enjoy, including: signage at the event, the ability on site for an online service to promote enrollment for free or paid subscription accounts, a newspaper to distribute copies or special sections created for the event (sampling) or for a radio or television station to stage a live broadcast with popular on-air personalities (promotional presence), visibility associated with an in-event element (event presentation/fan activity), and the capability of providing special hospitality opportunities for customers or advertisers. As discussed in Play 6, media partners also seek the ability to offer pass-through rights to advertisers, using event benefits to add exceptional value to their existing marketing efforts to sell more space or time. Running a media outlet is an expensive proposition, so it is reasonable to presume that the decision of whether to pursue a marketing partnership with a sports event will be based on the economics of the deal—can the company enjoy direct financial benefits from an association with an event or develop new revenue opportunities as a direct or indirect result of the partnership?

What Sports Event Organizers Want from a Media Partner

Experienced promoters know that an event will never reach its full potential through publicity efforts alone. The role of the media-event partnership is to enable both parties to exert more control over the message they want to communicate, control that even the best publicity campaign, and resulting press coverage, cannot fully provide. Typically, the message the organizer wishes to convey is a call to action: "Please attend, purchase tickets, and/or tune in to this exciting event." The message the media partner wishes to communicate will vary based on its corporate objectives, but, at its core, it is a reminder of reliance: "Keep reading or watching this space. We will provide you with news and information on events and other happenings that are of interest to you, as well as with outstanding value (e.g., ticket discounts and other offers) that will more than compensate you for your attention."

Media outlets are no less mercenary about event partnerships than are event organizers, who also evaluate media partnerships from an economic point of view. Simply put, event organizers must also be event promoters to attract an audience and recognize that media outlets are the key suppliers of the advertising space and commercial time they will need to market their properties. Establishing a partnership with one or more media outlets can offer significant event sponsor benefits in exchange for advertising on a VIK, combined VIK and cash, or a preferred-rate basis. This can help drive marketing costs down for the promoter or expand the budgeted advertising and promotion plan to achieve greater results than just spending cash can do.

In addition to the ability to realize savings on advertising the event, organizers may direct the incremental advertising they must place to satisfy sponsor fulfillment obligations to their media partners. In addition, sponsors also perceive value in placing the advertising that activates their associated promotional campaigns with the websites, newspapers, or stations that support the event, adding increased presence, credibility, and relevance to the media outlet's users, readers, listeners, or viewers (presuming this audience also complements the sponsor's own target market).

Many media outlets, particularly online and print media, maintain a database of account holders or subscribers. This information may be comprised of e-mail and I.P. addresses only, or contain more robust data including zip codes or mailing addresses, and demographics such as age, household income, and special interests. Event organizers want access to account holder databases to promote ticket sales via e-mail or mail messages to the most likely buyers. These databases may have an extremely large and diverse membership, and may need to be filtered so they reach the most qualified account holders. They will be closely guarded by the media outlet, and your offer may have to be sent directly by partner to protect the privacy of its account holders. Nevertheless, using media partners' subscriber databases to help boost ticket sales can be a very important element of your marketing plan and you should make every reasonable attempt to come to an agreement to use them. Although the event's ticket holder database will not typically be nearly as large as theirs, media outlet partners may request this courtesy in return to help their own marketing efforts.

Media outlets represent the most consistent and continuous source of information about the past successes and failures of other sports events held in the marketplace. Event sponsors come and go, but the media in a given community are often a constant—they are always on hand to cover events and report on them. The members of media organizations almost always have observations as well. Archival information, that is, articles and blogs written and accounts broadcast about past events as they unfolded, only tell part of the story. Editors and writers, producers and correspondents can share their unvarnished perspectives on what made past events work in their city, or not achieve their full potential. Although these points of view usually do not often find their way into the published record, as they do not represent objective reporting but opinions, they are no less valid. While they might represent pure opinion, their perspectives and points of comparison are based on experience, and, therefore, worthy of serious consideration. Members of the editorial staff are usually not shy about sharing their event encounters. Usually being limited to reporting only substantiated facts, many media executives and journalists actually appreciate being able share their personal views. Expect and welcome a wide-ranging conversation—from how the competition was perceived by the press, to treatment of the media on site,

- Advertising space or commercial time devoted to promotion of the event
- Access to subscriber database
- Intelligence regarding local market sensitivities and perspectives
- Preferred rates for advertising purchased for sponsor fulfillment purposes
- Promotions designed to promote ticket sales, increase attendance, encourage broadcast viewership, and/or drive traffic to digital platforms
- Expanded pre- and event-day coverage to encourage a perception of increased importance
- Provision of added value to attendees (i.e., sampling)
- Co-promotion and fan engagement through partners' social media platforms

Figure 9.3 What Sports Event Organizers Want from Media Partners

to consumer reaction to the organizer, to the value of the event to the community. Be a sponge! These are the guardians through which information and perspective on sports events are filtered and communicated to the public. Few resources will be able to provide better, unbiased feedback. (For the same reason, be sure to speak with these same stakeholders after your event is over—the quantity of intelligence you can gain about your own event can be incredibly revealing!)

Members of the media outlet's marketing staff are equally excellent sources of intelligence regarding past events in their community. Their expertise in advertising and promotion can provide added perspective from a marketing point of view on where events succeeded and fell short in capturing attention and establishing relevance. This is particularly useful for organizers who are staging an existing event that is new to a particular community. Listen and learn from the mistakes or miscalculations that others have made. Potential ticket buyers and event attendees in different markets do not necessarily follow the same patterns or behaviors and may respond positively to certain advertising or promotional activities in one town and negatively to the same marketing endeavors in another.

Experienced marketing professionals from media outlets, like their editorial counterparts, can help organizers decode what has worked best in their community, although their agenda may be totally different. They are in the business of selling advertising space or time and an event organizer with marketing needs—and a budget—can be an attractive prospective client. They also recognize that broader promotional campaigns to enhance revenue potential for their newspaper, station, or website can be designed around an event, its sponsors, and its business partners because of the potential to generate even more advertising income from these event stakeholders. This part of the media business is focused on sales, so organizers should not be surprised when a meeting scheduled to explore the marketplace takes on a very positive and enthusiastic tone and then morphs into an equally enthusiastic sales pitch for advertising space or time. Figure 9.3 provides a list of what sports event organizers expect from media partners.

Selecting Media Partners

Organizers should concentrate their quest for information and insights, and ultimately their event marketing campaigns, on media outlets whose demographics and lifestyles most closely match the target market of the event. Radio stations are so easily segmented based on their programming formats (e.g., news, talk, sports, top 40/pop, urban, rock, soft rock, country, ethnic, easy listening) that the fit between event audience and listener can be almost intuitive. Magazines and Internet websites are similarly segmented among obvious populations and interest niches. Daily newspapers, on the other hand, are more limited in easily identifying demographic fits and their readers are often defined more along geographic lines. Their demographic segmentation may instead be delineated by what sections and stories their readers access (e.g., news, sports, entertainment/arts, editorial, and opinion), and whether they read them in print or online.

Communities served by multiple newspapers can sometimes exhibit additional demographic segmentation based on the publications' content and style. For example, *The New York Times* offers as comprehensive a sports section as the *New York Daily News,* but appeals to a higher income, more highly educated reader. Every outlet under consideration will have a marketing information kit available in print and/or online upon request that presents the demographics and lifestyles of its readers, listeners, viewers, or users, the size of the market, and, in many cases, consumer spending behavior. Based on this information and the demographics of an event's target audience, the organizer can select the most suitable media outlets to approach as prospective event partners.

What does a partnership between an event and the media really mean, and what various forms can it take? As discussed, a media outlet can legitimately assume the role of an event sponsor, although the decision to do so will usually have no bearing on the quality and tone of event coverage. However, if properly developed and managed, the partnership will probably affect the quantity, depth, and diversity of coverage. In exchange for enjoying all of the benefits normally accorded to a sponsor, plus others that uniquely meet its specific wants and needs, the media partner may provide the event with advertising space or time, a vehicle for promotional activities, cash, or some combination of all three.

Exclusivity Versus Nonexclusivity

The notion of forging a traditional sponsor relationship with a media partner should be, by now, familiar territory. It is important to recognize, though, that the provision of advertising by a media outlet without the exchange of cash is no more cost-free to the outlet than complimentary tickets are to the event organizer. Like "free" tickets, "free" advertising represents lost revenue potential to the outlet. Media outlets, therefore, expect significant value in exchange for their most attractive and marketable asset—access to potential ticket buyers or attendees through their respective platforms. If sufficient advertising opportunity is provided, the organizer can designate an outlet the "official online partner," "official newspaper," "official radio station," or provide some other similar partner identification that implies category exclusivity. It is important, though, that sponsorship agreements with "official" media partners do not prohibit the organizer from purchasing advertising from competitor outlets. The pace of ticket sales or other market conditions may require the organizer to place advertising on more than one website, newspaper, radio station, or television channel, and restricting marketing efforts solely to a single media partner can later prove debilitating. It is very likely that official print and broadcast media partners will want to also be designated as official online media partners, as most of these traditional outlets also publish digital editions. A media partner will often seek to protect its investment in an event by insisting on a provision in the sponsorship agreement guaranteeing that advertising placed with competitor media be met with an equal or greater amount of paid advertising with "the official" outlet.

There are instances when providing category exclusivity to a media outlet makes less sense because the value of advertising, cash, and other assets offered to the organizer is just not sufficient to warrant a sponsorship. In addition, sometimes realizing an event's sales and marketing objectives require having the ability to communicate with equal force among a broader variety of readers, listeners, viewers, or users than a single outlet can provide. In such cases, organizers can seek to patch together a number of smaller, nonexclusive promotional relationships with a series of media entities. This scenario is most often manifest in the form of a promotional partnership in which limited benefits are provided to a media organization in return for similarly limited VIK advertising, deeply discounted advertising rates, or outlet-specific promotions. The promotional partner may receive a quantity of tickets and event merchandise for use in sweepstakes or advertiser incentives, limited rights to use the event or organizer's logo, and perhaps some reduced level of on-site presence at the event.

The most effective method of signing a series of complementary nonexclusive media partners is to grant each some exclusivity with respect to one or more event elements. A media partner targeting families or children might be the only outlet permitted to promote a special family ticket package, or authorized to create an event-related educational or skills development program. These rights might include a sweepstakes geared to the specific interests of the outlet's audience, such as an opportunity to attend a special kids-only clinic coached by a star player, alumnus, or celebrity, or exposure at an on-site attraction geared for families with young children. This approach of segmenting media partners by offering them limited exclusivities provides the event organizer with the option to award others promotional rights to elements more suited to their specific target market. For example, a Top 40 music radio station could be granted rights to a sweepstakes for a ticket giveaway that includes passes to an exclusive winners-only post-game party. A sports talk station partnered with the same event might conduct a promotion that rewards winners with a behind-the-scenes tour, plus an athlete meet-and-greet session, and a visit to the play-by-play booth during the event, all elements of greater intrigue to the hardcore fan.

The strategy of pursuing nonexclusive media partners is most common in the highly segmented radio industry. In a given market, nearly everyone listens to the radio at some time in the day, although only one or two stations in a given day. Meanwhile, there are dozens from which to choose in a variety of programming formats. While there is little audience crossover between formats, there is enormous competition between stations that appeal to the same tastes. Therefore, best success will be enjoyed when pursuing nonexclusive radio partnerships that are exclusive at least within the same programming format (e.g., only one sports talk AM station, one Top 40 FM, one Spanish-language station).

Ownership of stations in the radio industry has also consolidated to a great degree. A sports event organizer might be able to forge a deal with a single company that owns a variety of radio stations within the same community, providing a wide range of partners in various formats and great value to both parties. Such a partnership was created between the National Hockey League and Clear Channel Radio, the owner of large family of stations in South Florida, during NHL All-Star Weekend. A group of four Clear Channel stations participated, each popular among different audiences, offering distinct demographics. Figure 9.4 lists the partner stations with the key listener characteristics that, when combined, saturated the market with a series of advertising

Station	Format	Demographics
WBGG-FM (BIG 106)	Classic Rock	Men 25–54
WHYI-FM (Y100)	Contemporary Hit Radio (CHR)	Young Men and Women
WRFX-AM (FOX Sports Radio)	Sports Talk	Hardcore Sports Fans
WZTA-FM (Zeta 94.9)	Alternative Rock	Men 18–34

Figure 9.4 Example of a Nonexclusive Radio Partnership

campaigns and promotions specifically appealing to the tastes and interests of targeted listeners. An All-Star Game ticket giveaway was staged in association with Clear Channel's sports talk station as the prize of most intense interest among loyal sports fans. Promotion of the NHL All-Star Block Party, a family-oriented outdoor fan festival, received more emphasis on the two stations with formats most appealing to men and women likely to have young families, while a fan concert starring rock icon Sheryl Crow was more heavily promoted by the station with a contemporary hit rock (CHR) format.

Nonexclusive media partnerships are much more difficult to achieve in the print sector than in radio. When there is more than one daily newspaper in a given community, they are almost certain to be highly competitive with one another for readership, advertising dollars, and, yes, even attractive promotional relationships with sports events. In cities where only one newspaper monopolizes the available readership, receptivity to participating as a sponsor or promotional partner will vary with the nature of the outlet's marketing objectives, community relations strategies, and its assessment of the event's attractiveness as a platform to achieve its aims. Some will immediately grasp the promotional opportunities and business solutions an official association with a sports event will offer. Others will desire involvement simply as active supporters of quality-of-life-enhancing events in their community. Still others, knowing they face no competition in their marketplace for an event's advertising dollars, will perceive no value in investing or participating as a media partner.

Television can offer opportunities for nonexclusive media partnerships, though on a more limited basis than radio. Unlike radio, there is a great deal of crossover in television audiences. That is, members of the same target market will change channels frequently to view or stream the shows, movies, or events that most interest them at the time that they air, or, much to the chagrin of both broadcasters and advertisers, record their favorite programming for later viewing irrespective of what channel they can be seen. However, sports events remain appointment viewing at the time they are broadcast and, therefore, continue to be powerful programming for broadcasters. Even nontelevised sports events can be compelling local opportunities for coverage and sponsor support because of their ability to generate interesting and topical content of relevance to the local community. Sports events can usually segment their television partnerships into two generally noncompetitive halves—an exclusive "over the air" broadcast partner and an exclusive cable sports channel partner. Of course, if the event is televised, it is most likely that the only promotional partnership possible will likely be with the channel serving as host broadcaster and the distribution services that provide it (e.g., cable, satellite, online streaming service).

US cable sports giant ESPN has established itself as a brand on multiple platforms—television, radio, and online—cementing a presence in key markets around the country through dozens of local sports talk radio stations that feature a combination of national and local personalities and programming. Although they are local radio affiliates, the well-known and highly regarded ESPN brand can add substantial value to an event and offers the potential of stretching local news into stories with national reach. Local affiliate programming can also be accessed nationwide on smartphones with an ESPN Radio "app," extending the reach through WiFi and mobile phone technology. Also for mobile devices, there is a Watch ESPN app to view events live and an ESPN ScoreCenter app to follow sports results as they happen. ESPN provides one prime example of how the lines between television, radio, and online content have blurred, making it difficult to unbundle exclusivities across these electronic media platforms.

Recognizing that broadcast and print media partners often have their own online platforms, the Internet can offer many mutually advantageous media opportunities for the same event, both on an exclusive and nonexclusive basis. To the benefit of the media partner, the event website can feature a range of highly visible options such as a banner advertisement across the top or bottom of a home page and interactive content including information, contests, trivia, video, and features, all of which can be sponsored. Event and sponsor messages can also be extended to friends and followers on social networks such as Facebook and Twitter.

The exclusivity an online media partner may seek can be better defined by the nature of the content the organizer can provide, features that can only be found on a particular online sponsor's website and nowhere else. In other words, it is advantageous to have a presence for the event on as many online sites as possible, and, since it is nearly impossible to withhold online rights from an existing print, television, or radio partner, the key to developing additional online partnerships beyond the sites of these more traditional media partners is to find a way to provide each with content that is exclusive to them.

Sports Event Promotions

Sponsors often activate their event relationships with consumer promotions that can support both the corporate objectives of their brand and enhance the success of the event. Most consumer promotions are supported with advertising in various media placed and purchased by the sponsor. Promotions offered by the media in support of their own partnership with a sports event takes the outlet out of the role of the middleman and puts it in control of event marketing programs that can benefit its objectives directly. Media marketers put great value on event promotions that can generate a database of readers, listeners, viewers, or users. For this reason, media promotions are commonly manifest in sweepstakes that require entrants to register by e-mail, text, code-scanning, or via an Internet website. The possibility of winning sports event tickets, experiences, merchandise, and memorabilia are strong incentives for the public to take the time and trouble to submit an entry that will later be compiled into a database for the partner's subsequent direct marketing campaigns. While the number of entries received is a good indicator of the effectiveness of the promotion, the outlet's ultimate, underlying objective will be to use this database to increase subscription sales, webpage views, or ratings.

A promotion that drives visitors to an outlet's website can be a strong selling point for a media partnership. As discussed, most traditional media outlets also maintain an Internet site that provides visitors with important news and programming information (editorial side), and sells incremental online opportunities to their existing advertisers (marketing side). To set the highest possible rates and create the best value for their online advertisers, media outlets must generate the greatest possible number of "unique visitors" (individuals visiting the site) and "page views" (how many different web pages on the site an individual downloads during their visit). Event organizers and their media partners will realize the best success when they design their Internet event promotions with these objectives in mind. Don't forget to include links on the media website to attract visitors to the event's website and vice versa. If tickets are required for attendance, be sure to also include a link directly to the site where visitors can purchase their tickets to the event online, and, ideally, print them at home.

From the sports event organizer's perspective, the most effective promotions, whether placed in the media by other sponsors or as the direct product of a partnership between the event and a media outlet, should be designed as tools to sell tickets or build an audience. Sponsor promotions, while clearly helpful to the organizer's sales and marketing efforts even if simply as additional exposure opportunities, are primarily designed to promote and sell the sponsor's brand through its association with the event. If the media partner is granted pass-through rights to leverage its event promotion, the marketing message will be subdivided among the various objectives of a potentially great number of partners. Promotions that result from the simple partnership between the media outlet and the event, with no other participating third party, can, therefore, be the most effective in building an audience.

Sales

- Discount offers
- Specially priced family packages
- Multiple-day admission packages
- Premium giveaways
- Bounce-back coupons

Key Messages: Value and Urgency

Awareness Building

- Ticket giveaways
- Merchandise giveaways
- Sports trivia contests
- Essay contests
- Social media engagement promotions or contests
- Press box or press conference access prizes
- Guest columnist or color commentator contest
- Athlete "meet-and-greet" opportunities
- School field trips
- Newspapers in Education (NIE) outreach programs

Key Messages: Inform and Excite

Tune-In

- "Watch and win" sweepstakes (i.e., tune in to see if you're a winner!)
- Insurance prize contests (e.g., million-dollar shots)

Key Message: Appointment Viewing

Figure 9.5 Fulfilling the Sales, Awareness, and Tune-In (S.A.T.) Objectives of Sports Event Promotions

One other important benefit a promotion can provide is data collection, a highly coveted prize for event organizers and sponsors alike. Any promotion that can include large numbers of participants providing their names and contact information can translate into a treasure trove of potential new customers. "One of the essentials we have for measuring ROI in a sponsorship relationship is how well we are able to collect consumer information," says Shana Gritsavage, Under Armour's director of global events. "We don't consider a promotion with an event a complete success without data mining. Even one new email address is an opportunity. When we look at sponsorship activation, we look to generate hundreds and even thousands of them."

Organizers, sponsors, and media partners can be as creative as they wish in constructing promotions. It is important, however, for the organizer not to lose sight of the key message he or she wishes to communicate or the desired call to action the organizer wishes to precipitate. Identify what you want the reader, listener, or viewer to do, and what value you are prepared to provide to reward them for doing it. Promotions, whether offered by corporate sponsors or media partners, can be divided into the three general categories as illustrated in Figure 9.5, categorized by the key objectives the program seeks to achieve. Tactics employed to fulfill the easy-to-remember "SAT" objectives of sports event promotions are those designed to increase sales (S), build awareness (A), and for events covered on radio, television, or digital streaming service, encourage tune-in (T).

Sales Promotions

The most common promotions designed to generate sales feature cost-saving ticket discount offers. (*Note:* In order to maintain sound financial control over the event's revenue budget, an allotment of promotionally priced tickets should have already been included in the calculation of the gross potential—see Play 3). Coupons entitling the bearer to dollars off ticket purchases may appear in print advertisements, on stand-alone retail displays (also known as "POP" or point-of-purchase promotions), on sponsor product packaging, or on a partner's website for disseminating special codes for online ticket purchases or downloading and printing coupons for physical redemption. To increase the rate of coupon redemption, that is, the number of sales ultimately generated from the promotion, include a web address or telephone number and code that will enable purchasers to conveniently access the discount through online and telephone ticket services. The importance of being able to offer consumers a mechanism to take advantage of an offer immediately cannot be underestimated. Try to ensure that as few steps and as little time as possible are needed between receipt of the discount offer and the actual purchasing transaction to enhance the effectiveness of the promotion.

Ticket discount promotions can be designed to achieve any of a number of specialized objectives. Place the fewest possible restrictions on redeeming coupons, except for prohibiting the use of multiple discounts on the same transaction, to increase overall attendance objectives. Alternatively, sales promotions can build attendance for less well-attended periods during multiday events by restricting discounts to weaker midweek dates or preliminary rounds only, or deepening the cost savings for these harder-to-fill dates. A coupon expiration date set before opening day can be applied to the offer if the objective is to increase the urgency to purchase tickets in advance. Another variation is a "family package" promotion, a multiticket deal that offers a specific number of admissions (typically four or more) at a lower combined price than if purchased separately without a coupon. Package promotions can be particularly powerful tools, as they can also increase the average number of tickets sold per transaction.

Whether a cost-savings coupon or a package deal, it is recommended that all discounts be identified as a courtesy made available through a sponsor or media outlet, and not as an offer provided directly by the sports event organizer. Discounting through a sponsor offer is a practice generally accepted even by ticket buyers who failed to participate in the promotion. Discounting offered directly by the organizer can cause customers who purchased tickets at full price to feel unfairly treated and to seek partial refunds. Also, try to time the introduction of the discount offer for a date *at least* a few weeks after the sale of event tickets begins. Promotions that result in a discount ticket being purchased by the same guest who would have otherwise purchased a full-priced ticket make little financial sense. Let the first weeks of ticket sales maximize the yield of full-priced tickets to the fans who want the best seats and add the discount promotions to the marketing mix later, when the rate of ticket sales can be expected to slow and fewer potential incremental ticket buyers need an incentive to purchase.

Promotions designed to increase sales can also include the offer of a premium item with every ticket, or with some minimum number of tickets purchased. These offers can create added value for the ticket buyer and may, again, be designed to achieve any number of specific objectives. Advertising in advance that all ticket buyers will receive a valuable premium upon entry to the event (e.g., a bobblehead figure, commemorative patch, pin, ball, etc.) can generate greater overall sales. Events on a more modest budget sometimes offer premiums to a limited number of attendees, such as only to fans who download a special offer from a sponsor's website, or to the first 1,000 to arrive. In addition to saving money on premiums, the latter technique encourages early arrivals to the venue, which has the secondary operational benefit of spreading the flow of incoming guests, as well as increasing pre-event food and beverage sales. To encourage advance ticket sales, the premium item, or a coupon redeemable for the premium at the event site can be e-mailed to those who purchase tickets before event day. The cost of the premium can be paid for by a sponsor or promotional partner, directly by the organizer as a marketing or sponsor fulfillment expense, or split between a partner and the organizer. The key to the success of any premium promotion is to ensure that this opportunity is communicated in advance to potential ticket buyers through advertising and other effective marketing platforms so it has the intended effect of increasing ticket sales.

A variation on this type of promotion that is of particular appeal to sponsors is the opportunity for ticket buyers to receive a "bounce-back" coupon with each admission. A bounce-back coupon is distributed to attendees at the event site, via mail, or through the Internet with advance ticket purchases, and offers a valuable discount or premium item courtesy of a sponsor if redeemed at a specific location. A consumer electronics store can distribute a coupon at the box office or upon entering the event site that is redeemable at its retail locations for a deep discount or gift item. Bounce-back offers can also be made during the event, offering discounts or premiums at sponsor-designated locations upon presentation of a ticket stub after the event. While such offers may provide exceptional value to an event sponsor and may be worthwhile creating as a cost-free benefit of the relationship, ticket stub bounce-back offers are rarely advertised in advance and, therefore, do not usually help organizers to sell tickets.

The messages communicated by effective sales promotions are "value" and "urgency." These programs stress value first. By taking advantage of the promotional offer, the ticket buyer or attendee will save money or receive some other valuable incentive such as merchandise, collectible memorabilia, or cost savings on sponsor products or services. To maximize a sales promotion's effectiveness, however, it should also communicate a sense of urgency. The offer should be taken advantage of as soon as possible to ensure that the ticket buyer will be able to fully enjoy it. Expiration dates and a limited number of premium items available only "while supplies last" can help to convey such urgency.

Awareness-Building Promotions

Sales promotions work best when building attendance for events that have some history or familiarity among potential ticket buyers and may be less effective for events that have a lower level of awareness. The key messages for awareness-building promotions are to inform or familiarize the community with the event, and to present salient information in a way that will excite or intrigue them into considering attendance. Although the call to action is *"Look over here at this exciting event!"* rather than *"Get your tickets now!"*, awareness-enhancing promotions can support attendance-building efforts profoundly, if indirectly. The timing of awareness promotions should be coordinated with the publicity and advertising sections of the marketing wheel. Publicity efforts can be very effective in generating awareness, and advertising is most efficient in driving attendance. Awareness promotions, therefore, are best timed for introduction coincident with the kickoff of the event's publicity campaign, or early in the advertising campaign.

Ticket and merchandise giveaways through a random drawing sweepstakes, a contest of knowledge or skill, a radio "call in to win," or a contest requiring fan response on social media sites are among the most popular forms of awareness building programs. To have the intended effect —ultimately promoting the sale of tickets—the mechanism for giving away tickets or other valuable prizes must be associated with communicating the message of ticket availability. To achieve optimal results, the process of registering to win should be surrounded by a campaign that involves the potential entrant in the event and at the same time educates the public about what the event is, and where and when it will happen. Awareness-building promotions help create what event promoters like to call a "buzz" surrounding an event, that is, a palpable level of excitement building in the marketplace.

Giveaways are highly prized by media sponsors and promotional partners, as they reward their viewers, listeners, or readers with value, and, if the "buzz" about the event continues to build, can help build their own readership, ratings, or page views. Radio stations are particularly effective partners for giveaways, and many are involved with multiple giveaway promotions simultaneously. For event promoters, radio campaigns are also highly valued because of the large numbers of listeners to whom the offer is communicated, plus the number of times the promotion—and the event—is mentioned on the air. Radio hosts can not only educate their audience about the upcoming event, but their often-enthusiastic delivery can also excite their listeners into entering the contest and ultimately attending the event. Developing a good relationship with the on-air personalities and providing them with the information they need to promote the event is essential to maximizing the effectiveness of a radio promotion and "building the buzz." Consider involving these individuals in the event itself as guest emcees or hosts. Their personal participation in the event is outstanding promotion for both themselves and their station, and almost guarantees frequent, enthusiastic endorsements on the air.

Sports trivia and essay contests are just two of the many varieties of knowledge- and skill-based competitions that can be used as promotional devices. Trivia contests work equally well as print, radio, and Internet promotions and frequently take the form of entry blank activities for print media, "call in to win" activities for radio, and fan voting platforms online. Essay contests, by contrast, are great vehicles for involving students and better-educated fans, and are best executed as newspaper, magazine, and website promotions. Entrants can be given a choice of topics or perspectives from which to write an essay of defined length to be judged by a celebrity panel. (To best manage the judging process, it is recommended that essays be limited in length; approximately 500 words is a reasonable standard.) As campaigns co-promoted with print or Internet media partners, contests such as these serve to supplement the event's schedule of paid or VIK advertising. As a radio or broadcast promotion, they can fulfill this same purpose, but are additionally effective as awareness- and excitement-generating vehicles. The excitement of the contestants who participate live as well as the enthusiasm of the broadcast hosts can vividly help to convey the event's relevance to the listening audience.

As stand-alone promotions, or as prizes for winning essay entrants, behind-the-scenes access opportunities are rewards with a high level of perceived value. These limited-access possibilities can include a backstage tour, a visit to the press box, attendance at a post-event press conference, or the ability to serve as a guest columnist, among others. (It is recommended that if the winner is designated a "guest columnist," the qualifying essay or column be posted on a website or elsewhere on the Internet rather than in the newspaper to preserve the latter's journalistic integrity.) Meet-and-greet opportunities with athletes before the event, at practices, or during warm-ups can also be particularly attractive prizes.

Effective promotions geared to younger audiences can include school field trips to the event site during nonpublic hours for tours, practices, or a formal educational presentation. These opportunities must be arranged with school districts well in advance to be considered for the academic calendar. Most districts are budgeted for a limited number of trips per year, sometimes only one or two, so the event promoter should contact local educators perhaps as much as a year in advance. Working with a newspaper or online news partner, event organizers can also gain entry into the classroom by developing and circulating academically relevant materials featuring the event as a theme. This, too, is a lengthy, as well as potentially expensive, process, and should be created in partnership with the local board of education. Be certain the schools will accept this material on behalf of their students before spending the time and money to create it. If the program must be sponsored in order to exist, be sure to understand the restrictions the school district or board will place on how sponsors may be recognized, if at all, and what kinds of sponsors might be prohibited. A less expensive and more widely accepted option is to investigate whether a

SIDELINE STORY

Newspapers in Education

In the 1930s, New York City public school teachers, wanting to expand social studies curricula to include daily lessons on current events, approached the *New York Times* to regularly bundle and deliver newspapers for classroom instruction. From these humble roots grew Newspapers in Education (NIE), a program coordinated by the World Association of Newspapers with approximately 700 newspapers in more than 40 different countries. Thousands of schools in the United States offer the NIE program to students from kindergarten to 12th grade through their local newspaper. Publishers have the flexibility to design the NIE program content for their own purposes, but all are designed to expose children to newspapers as a powerful and reliable source of information on current events. This flexibility enables newspapers to feature stories, background information, games, and photographs of events they sponsor or promote in the special NIE supplements they periodically publish. With sports so prominently featured in newspapers every day, providing information on upcoming sports events is directly on-strategy for a print partner's NIE program. Sports event organizers who want to expose their program to children and their families, have sufficient lead time, and can demonstrate the relevance and appeal of their event to this important audience, should investigate whether their town newspaper offers an NIE program in local schools, and do everything possible to be included. Interested event organizers can explore more details on the NIE program at the NIE Online website.

local daily newspaper participates in the Newspapers in Education (NIE) program. An association with this well-established and highly respected program can further reinforce the legitimacy and relevance of the event to the local community.

Social media platforms provide excellent outlets for fan engagement. These sites offer a number of benefits over the aforementioned media sources in terms of reach and financial consideration. Social media platforms are often free to use and offer features that allow direct interaction with fans. Promotions such as those outlined in this section can be conducted easily and cheaply with the potential to reach large numbers of fans quickly. For example, an event organizer or sponsor can run a contest requiring users to respond to a question or post with a clever comment or picture in return for a prize. The event organizer will then review the responses and choose a winner. Promotions of this kind can garner a great degree of exposure and sometimes thousands of responses, building hype for the event by incentivizing fans to participate even before the event begins.

Utilizing social media can serve to benefit both the event promoter and the event's media partners (see Figure 9.6). Conducting contests and promotions through social media outlets offers the benefit of contact information collection, instantly, with one simple interaction. This information is valuable for short- and long-term use for the event and its partners. It can be stored in a database for future use when developing and promoting similar events. As will be further explored later in this chapter, the event organizer and his or her partners will better understand their fans and what they are thinking by utilizing this information and, therefore, will be better able to serve their fans' needs and desires at future events.

Social Networks (i.e., Facebook, Google+)

- Build an event or brand profile with general information and space for fan interaction.
- Collect consumer data such as contact information and preferences to use for future events and marketing.
- Engage fans by asking open-ended questions, serving polls, or requesting action.
- Deliver media-rich content including videos, images, and links back to the official event/brand website.
- Offer updates about the event/brand on a regular basis.
- Create contests or promotions to drive traffic and "likes" to the profile page.
- Share links to news and media promoting your event and brand.
- Encourage sharing between fans and other consumers by incorporating share buttons on the official website and other sponsors pages.
- Sell goods or tickets to the event on the profile page or via links—especially effective for exclusive pre-sales.

Professional Networks (i.e., LinkedIn, Meetup)

- Create a buzz amongst industry professionals by creating a profile and/or event specific page.
- Create job postings and recruit potential event volunteers and/or employees.
- Keep industry professionals up to date and informed on the latest news about the event and brand.
- Encourage sharing between industry professionals by incorporating share buttons on the official website and other sponsors pages.
- Collect consumer data such as contact information and preferences to use for future events and marketing.
- Deliver media-rich content including videos, images, and links back to the official event/brand website.
- Share links to news and media promoting your event and brand.

Microblogging Sites (i.e., Twitter, Tumblr)

- Provide up-to-the-second information about the event to keep followers informed.
- Though abbreviations are commonly used due to character/space restrictions, be sure to deliver messages with proper grammar and spelling when possible.
- Write messages in a way that conveys the personality of your event or brand.
- Write updates on a daily (or more) basis.
- Encourage followers to share content with others and across social networks.
- Create interactive contests and promotions to engage fans and influence actions such as posting event/brand relevant pictures, videos, or blog posts.
- Deliver media-rich content including videos, images, and links back to the official event/brand website.
- Share links to news and media promoting your event and brand.

Mobile-Based Networks (i.e., Foursquare, LevelUp)

- Encourage "check-ins" and offer rewards for participation.
- Collect data on consumer behavior such as number of check-ins to specific locations.
- Capture customer contact data upon once they check in to the event.
- Create customized, branded content such as a badge or video that can be unlocked only upon checking in.
- Communicate and interact with customers while they are checked in to the event.

Figure 9.6 Social Media Platforms and Their Effective Marketing Uses

Tune-in Promotions

For televised sports events and the sponsors that support them by purchasing advertising time on the broadcasts, building viewer ratings can be as important as drawing a live audience. Ratings are based on the number of viewers who tune into the broadcast live. (Audiences who record the program for later viewing or download it from the Internet are not factored into television ratings.) Marketing campaigns designed to increase television ratings seek to create "appointment viewing," a desire on the part of the audience to attend the event via television at the time of its original broadcast.

For the most popular of sports programs, events can be relevant and compelling enough by their very nature to generate appointment viewing. The most obvious examples include the National Football League's astronomically rated Super Bowl and the biennial Summer and Winter Olympic Games. But, even these premier mega-events strive to maximize ratings, ever vigilant against even the most modest slide in viewing popularity. In this way, broadcasters can keep their advertising rates high enough to justify the rights fees they pay to the sports event organizer. (For a detailed discussion on the event organizer-broadcasting relationship, see Play 13). Most events, however, do not approach the perceived relevancy of a mega-event like the Olympics, the Super Bowl, or many league championship games, and need a variety of compelling reasons for the audience to tune in, essential to any continued viability of the program as a broadcasting property.

Among the most popular tune-in devices are sponsored "watch and win" promotions that require viewers to respond to some form of prompt during the live broadcast to win prizes. To be effective, the activity must be promoted, advertised, and publicized well in advance of the event. Typically, the more valuable the prize is the more compelling the reason to tune in and wait for the cue to participate. A sponsor might distribute game cards or advertisements with a serial number, phrase, or other code, along with the instruction to watch for an announcement of the winning variable during the event broadcast. A promotion requiring fans to use their tablets or mobile devices to text a code, quiz answer, or vote for their favorite player, team, or other option to a certain number can be effective on the broadcast, as well as at the venue itself. A similar tune-in scheme requires viewers to register in advance through a mailed, e-mailed, or Internet entry form, or advertisement, and then to tune-in for instructions on how the winner must claim his or her prize during the broadcast.

Another promotional device that enjoys periodic popularity is the "insurance prize" contest. This type of promotion qualifies a sweepstakes winner to compete in a contest of skill for a prize so impressive and valuable that the very fact that an average member of the public—someone just like the viewer—can win is a sufficiently compelling reason for appointment viewing. Although the value of the prize can range from $100,000 to $10,000,000, the event budget need not set aside such a prohibitive sum to cover the possibility of having to pay an extremely lucky contestant. The organizer can contact an insurance broker to purchase a special policy that will pay the contestant should he/she win. The premium for the prize can range from 10 percent to 50 percent of the payout, depending on the insurance company's assessment of the odds of winning. Insurance companies, being in the business of keeping more money in premiums than they pay in claims, will absolutely require input into the contest rules and procedures. Once these requirements are incorporated into the rules, the odds will, of course, dramatically favor the insurance company. That said, the possibility of a fellow fan winning a fantastic prize, however unlikely, can create another exciting reason to watch an event.

Many events also encourage fan interaction via social media during television or online broadcasts. During the broadcast, Twitter hashtags (identifying subject-matter markers) and handles (individualized name markers) may flash on the screen indicating to fans a means for sending their thoughts and questions to the event organizers or partners. Other integrations may encourage fans to share on other social media outlets the content that they are enjoying. Social media integration can be a powerful tool to mobilize fans, both physically and cognitively. The 2010 FIFA World Cup in South Africa is one compelling example of how social media can be leveraged to drive viewership and fan activation. The 2010 World Cup was the first major sports event to record over 3,800 tweets (Twitter messages) each second during the broadcast of a match between Japan and Denmark. Other major sporting events have since expanded on these participatory rates using many of the same social media integration strategies. Super Bowl XLVI, played in 2012 between the New York Giants and New England Patriots, for example, peaked at over 12,200 tweets per second.

The high degree of Internet traffic and conversation about the event also benefits official event sponsors. World Cup sponsor Coca-Cola received over 86 million impressions for its sponsored World Cup Twitter hashtag, *#WC2010*. Additionally, nearly one-quarter of the entire online buzz generated by the event's social media integration was focused on the official equipment sponsor, Adidas, during the first two weeks of the event. During other high-profile broadcast events, sponsors have profited by using similar social media integration strategies on their signage and in their commercial spots. The benefits of employing social media as a tune-in technique include greater viewership, stronger fan connections, and more valuable sponsorship packages from media partners.

This phenomenon of social media integration goes beyond the conventional means of "tuning in" to a broadcast. More commonly, events are integrating social media presence into the event itself. During the course of the event, fans may be asked to engage in real-time interaction through means of social media services like Twitter using their mobile devices. Select fans' responses will then be broadcast at the event, perhaps on the video boards, for other fans to see. Sometimes these interactions are part of a contest or promotions, while other times the event may request fan engagement simply to drive activity. People tend to respond to such requests from event organizers during the event for the prospect of momentary recognition amongst their peers. Even without formal calls-to-action, fans may react and respond to Twitter hashtags and handles that are placed around the event space like sponsor signage. Utilizing in-event social networking tools can be an effective way to add an interactive layer to your events and extend the tune-in effect to the live event.

Effective Sports Event Advertising

Regardless of how talented a sports event's public relations staff might be, no matter how well connected an agency, the ultimate control over what and how much pre-event publicity an event will receive is under the complete control of story editors and producers who have no other agenda than presenting presumably objective, newsworthy content to their audiences. While sponsor and media partner promotions provide opportunities to better control the marketing message, the objectives of those campaigns are formed from a composite of event organizer and sponsor partner needs. The event organizer will often have a singularly important objective that a promotion, because of its compromised agenda, is less well equipped to achieve. If an organizer, for instance, wants to inform the public that event tickets are about to go on sale, simply circulating a press release is relying upon the hope that editors will deem such information newsworthy. (Most will not.) Creating a promotion at this early date diverts attention away from the most important fact—tickets are going on sale—and may detract from full-priced ticket sales during the time they are most likely. The only way to be absolutely certain that the message gets through to the greatest possible audience is to place advertising in targeted print, broadcast, online, and other media, either on a paid or VIK basis.

By all means, imbue your advertising with creativity and style, but do not sacrifice the effective communication of essential information in favor of originality for its own sake. The purpose of effective sports event advertising is to incite a reaction, most often the sale of tickets. Provide all the information and motivation that is necessary for the readers or viewers to want to buy their tickets, and direct them to the most convenient way to make their purchase—immediately. The checklist in Figure 9.7 provides guidelines on what information is absolutely essential to include in effective event advertising, as well as additional elements that can be added to enhance the event's position as a "must see" entertainment opportunity. Identifying the name of the event and displaying the logo and essential data like the date, time, and location may seem obvious, but this information is nonetheless critical to include. Be sure to use the day of the week in addition to the date when advertising one-day events to provide absolute clarity to the reader or viewer.

Do not neglect including an obvious call to action. That is, what do you want to tell the reader, listener, viewer, or user to do? If the advertisement is designed to inform the public that tickets are now on sale, say so explicitly and make it easy for them to purchase or order them. Include an easy-to-remember website address and phone number so they are able to order tickets immediately or to gather the information they need to make a purchasing decision. Regardless of the call to action, provide all of the information required to enable the public to react as desired.

Advertisements for sports festivals and demonstration events in which the competitive elements represent more than one sport, involve sports or athletes that are unfamiliar to the public, or are only part of a broader series of attractions should include a brief list or description of compelling features to promote attendance. Descriptions should be short, imperative sentence fragments beginning with verbs that emphasize some form of interactivity with the event. Include only the best sales points, and those that are perceived as necessary to position the event as an exciting way to spend the fan's day or dollar. Use words like those in Figure 9.8 to influence your target audience into taking your desired course of action.

Essential:

- ☐ Identify the event by name and logo (if available).
- ☐ Include the day, date, time, and location.
- ☐ Make an obvious call to action (e.g., buy tickets now, make plans to attend, watch the event on television).
- ☐ Include a website and phone number to assist the public in reacting in the desired way (e.g., purchasing tickets or gaining more information).
- ☐ Include copy points that describe compelling event features to encourage reaction to the call.
- ☐ Post event and action photo(s) or footage.
- ☐ Integrate social media outlets and encourage fan participation.

Additional Elements for Consideration:

- ☐ Highlight the names and/or likenesses of featured athletes (be sure to secure the athlete's permission to use).
- ☐ Include player and fan testimonials.
- ☐ Recognize sponsors with appropriate prominence.
- ☐ Include quotes from coverage of past events.

Figure 9.7 Checklist for Designing Sports Event Advertisements

Add these influential words to your starting line-up of descriptive copy points:

- See. . .!
- Experience. . .!
- Enjoy. . .!
- Watch. . .!
- Meet. . .!
- Join. . .!
- Win. . .!
- Save. . .!
- Get. . .! (or Receive. . .!)
- Hear. . .!
- Play. . .!
- Try. . .!
- Cheer. . .!

Figure 9.8 Starting Line-up of Sports Event Advertising Copy Point Influencers

As influential as these commands might be, nothing is more persuasive than exhilarating photographs and action-laden film or video footage. Communicate the excitement of your event with one or more still images that bring life to your print advertisements. A single dynamic photograph is best for most applications, but multifaceted festivals might be better served with three or four smaller images to more fully represent the broad variety of activities to experience. Try to ensure that your images and copy points complement one another. Use images that communicate a specific story, message, or feeling to the reader. Post a gallery of still photos and video highlights in online advertising and on websites. The more times a user clicks to explore new images and footage, the more likely you have a hot prospect for tickets sales and attendance.

Be certain you have the rights to use whatever image(s) you select. Unless you own the images outright from a previous edition of your event, the photographer or the photographer's agency must provide permission and will commonly require payment for such use. In addition, any participant or audience member who may appear in the photograph or footage must also provide consent to appear. The permission of athletes and other participants is often secured in advance with a waiver that provides such written consent, or, in the case of more notable personalities, should be included in their appearance agreement. The consent of members of the audience whose images might be incidentally included in future advertising is obviously much more difficult. It is strongly suggested that legal language be included on the back of all event tickets and credentials that includes a statement that using the ticket and attending the event infers permission for their image to be used in advertising, promotion, and other marketing applications. Free events that do not use tickets should post similar permission language in conspicuous positions at all event entrances to protect against future claims for illegal use of a fan's image. (It is not a bad idea to post this disclaimer even when it is also included on the ticket back.) Finally, individual audience members interviewed on camera or photographed during an event may be asked to sign permission forms at the time they are recorded for future possible use. Regardless of how audience image permissions are sought, be sure to utilize the services of an experienced attorney to provide the protection required.

What if the sports event is brand new or no images from prior editions are readily available? If it is impractical or too expensive to stage photography simulating the event, consider using an action image of a participating athlete from another. The same permissions, and perhaps additional ones, will be required and some features of the photograph may require some alteration to disassociate it from the other event (specifically, avoid images displaying the logos, uniform designs, or other intellectual property of other event organizers or sponsors). Failing the availability of this option, the databases of stock photography agencies can be searched to identify and acquire the rights to use a suitable image. Some of the best databases are available online, including thumbnail-sized images, to help speed and simplify the selection process.

Television commercials and video clips used online should be well edited, exciting, and fast paced. Avoid subtleties and creative elements that overwhelm the ad's essential information. Employ the same action words to describe the event's compelling features and attractions, enthusiastically delivered by a professional announcer (or featured athlete). Use up-tempo music to add excitement to the delivery. The rights to use popular music in commercials (known as "sync" or "synchronization rights") can be very expensive. Less expensive stock music is available through most video editing houses. Promoters will need the same permissions for video and film as are required for still photography and may be able to secure stock footage in the same way stock photography is made available. Remember that the information presented in television advertisements is less "sticky" than print ads—you cannot tear a television or radio ad out for future reference. While it must be memorable, it cannot be expected to impart as much information as a print ad. Promoting an easy-to-remember website address for more information can help. Refer to Figure 9.9 for more tips on creating your event's television commercial and online highlight clips, as well as special information specific to advertising in print, radio, and outdoor, or billboard, advertising.

Organizers may be obligated to recognize their sponsors in event advertising. For title or presenting sponsors, integrated recognition within the event name and logo is always expected. Promoters may also have included similar rights for other, or perhaps all, official sponsors to help in their sales efforts. If the family of sponsors is broad and lengthy, some definition to their rights of recognition in event advertising is required to avoid having to fulfill sponsor obligations at the cost of excessively cluttering advertising creative. For example, the sponsor agreement can define the size of the ads in which the sponsor will be recognized (e.g., title and presenting sponsor logos in all ads, official sponsor logos in full- and three-quarter page ads only and listed by name in type in all others). The promoter can also schedule ads so a rotation of logos or sponsor names can be established in which each official sponsor is equally recognized over the course of the entire campaign, but not all sponsors in every ad. This practice is very useful in minimizing clutter and actually increases the recognition of a sponsor's brand when it appears in the company of, a lesser number of other partners. All or a designated level of, sponsors can have visibility on an event's website.

The right advertising campaign will be as unique as the event it is designed to promote. Evaluate whether the headlines or copy points should use terminology most familiar to passionate fans of the sport, and whether using these colloquialisms is the most effective way to reach the particular audience an advertisement is targeting. Sport-specific terminology could intimidate or turn off the more casual fans and ticket buyers and may be best used in niche publications or on web pages that appeal more directly to the sport's most avid audiences. Existing sports events, such as festivals and demonstrations that target a general, entertainment-seeking audience, may include quotes from news coverage of previous editions, a common practice in the motion picture and live entertainment businesses. It is important that the quotes are from sources that will be perceived as credible by the audience. (One creative variation is using quotes from past attendees.) Quotes can also be used to reinforce the legitimacy of a relatively lesser-known competitive event. Consider soliciting quotes and permission to use them from media, athletes, and other participants that enhance the perception of the event's importance.

Print Advertising

- Advertise in the newspapers and magazines that your target audience is most likely to read.
- Place advertising in the part of the newspaper your target audience is most likely to read (e.g., sports section, entertainment/calendar section, community section). Try to avoid less expensive "run-of-paper" (ROP) ads that will appear in whatever location the newspaper has available space.
- Don't count on one placement of an ad being all you will need to achieve your marketing aims.
- Integrate the timing of promotional advertising placed on behalf of sponsors into the overall advertising campaign.
- Keep the design simple and eye catching.
- Use still action photographs reflective of the event's excitement. (Be sure to clear the rights to an athlete's image from both the photographer and the athlete.)
- Remember that print advertisements are excellent reference tools for the readers. They may clip it out of the paper to retain the information they need, so include as much as possible without cluttering the ad.
- Be sure to include a website or code that can be scanned (e.g., QR code) to provide the reader with easy access to further information, content, and ticket ordering capabilities.
- Don't overlook weekly special interest newspapers and magazines such as community papers, local entertainment weeklies, parent publications, and sports-oriented weeklies.

Radio

- Run ads on stations and programs and at the times of day ("day parts") your target audience is most likely to be listening. As with print advertising, try to avoid a "run-of-station" schedule.
- Include an easy-to-remember website address and phone number for ticket purchases and further information.
- Engage a station's disc jockey to record reading the script with enthusiasm! (You may not be able to use this recording on other radio stations, however.)
- Use upbeat music under the voiceover that captures the excitement of the event.

Television

- Select television programming and special-interest channels and networks that your target audience is most likely to be watching at the time they are originally broadcast. (Programs likely to be recorded may be viewed after the usefulness of the call to action has expired, or may not be viewed at all during playback.)
- Include a screen graphic during the last five seconds of the ad with the event name and logo, day, date, location, and an easy-to-remember website and/or phone number for ticket purchases and further information.
- Use footage from previous events that show action, excitement, and fan reactions.
- Include images for which you have obtained rights from both the athletes and the owner of the footage.

Event Website

- Present all key information about the event, including how to purchase tickets and the schedule of activities, in a clear, visible, simple manner.
- Include an easy-to-find link that directs the user to an opportunity to transact a ticket purchase on every page. If the text is lengthy and greater than a full-screen image, include the link on at least the top and bottom of the page.

Figure 9.9 Sports Event Advertising Tips

- Use photos and/or video to their full eye-catching, attention-grabbing effectiveness. Include galleries of multiple images and video clips.
- Provide venue information including seating and parking diagrams, maps, and directions for transportation options.
- Refresh the information and feature content regularly to keep users up to date and to encourage repeat traffic to the website.

Event Social Media

- Present time-sensitive information about the event, including changes to the schedule of activities or updates for fan safety, in an easy-to-read, real-time format.
- Post photos and/or video of fans and their live engagement with past events or pre-event engagements to encourage interest.
- Provide general event and venue information from the event website with easy access to redirect for more in-depth information.
- Create contests, promotions, and polls that encourage fan involvement and response.
- Feature content that keeps fans aware of event-related news and to encourage their reciprocal interaction on the site before, during, and after the event.
- Highlight positive fan interactions on the site to express appreciation and inspire further fan communication and loyalty.

Outdoor (Billboards)

- Keep the artwork simple and readable, and avoid subtleties. Design the billboards with the understanding that people might drive by them at high speeds, so the copy points should be few, but large.
- Ensure an easy-to-remember event information and/or ticket purchase website address is one of the dominant elements of the billboard. Phone or text numbers may be added if they are also easy to recall.
- Don't try to cram so much information on a billboard that it becomes cluttered.
- Remember that billboards are excellent tools for generating awareness for an event, and less effective as ticket sales generators.

Figure 9.9 (*Continued*)

Special Sections

The two faces of Janus in newspapers and other print media—the editorial and advertising sides of the publishing business—delicately converge in the creation of special sections and advertorials. Special sections come from the editorial side. An editor or publisher might believe that an event can provide an opportunity to sell significant incremental advertising in a stand-alone or pull-out section of expanded coverage. As an editorial product, the special section will include items the editors find newsworthy, and the coverage might include stories calling attention to the event's history and highlights, and providing helpful information such as venue points of interests and parking maps.

In the United States, freedom of the press constitutionally guarantees that newspapers can generate as much and any editorial coverage they desire and, therefore, they need not be media partners to enjoy the right to publish a special section of expanded coverage. They may also sell advertising to anyone they choose, including those that are competitors to an event's sponsor partners. Sponsors understand that no outside party can have control over a free press, but organizers can still make the effort to enhance, if not protect, their sponsors' association with their event. An approach to newspaper marketing executives should be made to offer introductions to a sports event's sponsors, potentially the best target for selling advertising space in special sections publicizing an event, whether or not the newspaper is a media partner.

For high-profile events in competitive multi-newspaper markets, it is entirely possible that more than one will undertake the creation of a special section. Care should be taken to provide additional value that supports the special section under development by the event's media partner, including official site maps, detailed schedules of activities, and other exclusive opportunities. While the event organizer has no obligation to make as much information as readily available to a nonpartner, the enormous publicity value of a special section in a nonpartner newspaper cannot be overlooked. Be sure to provide whatever information will still help to make the nonpartner's special section intriguing reading and a good publicity vehicle for the event. Remember: The quality of any special section reflects on the event. Readers cannot be expected to reason that expanded coverage is poorer in one newspaper because it is competitive with the event's media partner.

Advertorials

A hybrid concept, the *advertorial,* has been finding its way into newspapers and magazines with increasing frequency. An advertorial can be a single page, series of pages, or an entire section of a publication that is at once an advertisement and a collection of feature articles. In contrast to a special section, it is the event organizer or sponsor that purchases 100 percent of the space for the advertorial. The organizer, in turn, can resell advertising opportunities in the advertorial to sponsors or deliver space as part of a sponsor's benefit package. Since all of the space has been paid for by the event, the organizer can write or exert significant control over the preparation of editorial copy, inserting articles that best suit the event's marketing objectives. Many organizers commission their own writers, or apply their public relations agency or staff, to write the articles for the advertorial. For those publications that require that their own staff write the copy and are concerned about distinguishing its content from true, journalistically objective editorial (e.g., the *Los Angeles Times*), the writers applied to advertorials are frequently distinct from the core editorial staff.

To ensure that the advertorial's articles get read by the public, organizers should provide or encourage stories that are no less compelling than if they appeared in editorial sections of the publication. Features should not be copies of press releases. However, because the event has total control over the content, every advantage should be taken to make sure the organizer's message is clear. Decide what you want the readers to do and what you want them to know. Provide every detail that will help them to make the decision you want them to make—to purchase tickets, come to the event, watch it on television, listen to it on the radio, or stream it live on the Internet.

Event Marketing

Sponsors employ sports event marketing campaigns to promote their products, so why can't event organizers do the same to sell theirs? Strategically scheduled mini-events that provide a taste of the big event to come can excite the public, encourage the purchase of tickets, and generate added publicity coverage. Schedule a fan participatory competition coincident with the campaign to sell tickets or encourage viewership, one that will foster an appreciation for the talents of the athletes featured in the main event. Create an exhibit on the history of the sport being featured, placed in a popular downtown destination. Consider creating a public opportunity out of, or beside, an already scheduled media event. Or, create events that will excite crowds already present in high-traffic areas at high-traffic times of day, as illustrated by the Pro Bowl marketing campaign Sideline Story.

Rights to these ancillary event marketing activities may be included in sponsor packages to provide additional value to prospective partners, or can provide promoters with additional "inventory" they can up-sell to existing sponsors. Be sure that these sponsorships provide incremental revenues beyond those required for funding the main event. Event marketing programs should be anticipated in the expense budget, funded by new sponsors or supported with incremental dollars from existing ones.

Are there other events, sports and nonsports alike, being staged in the host city that attract a similar target audience? Consider staging a mini-event or a promotional attraction on their event site to capitalize on the audience they already spend money to draw. Interactive activities— appearances,

SIDELINE STORY

The Pro Bowl Event Marketing Campaign

For 30 continuous years, the Pro Bowl, the NFL's all-star game, was played at Hawaii's Aloha Stadium, drawing approximately half of the 50,000 fans at the game from the US mainland. The game was dependent on the engagement of the local community to sell the remaining tickets and the support of the local government and businesses to energize the market to welcome fans, players, and business partners arriving for the event. Of particular importance was the sale of remaining tickets during the week leading up to the main event. To generate excitement in the market, encourage pre-event media coverage, and promote walk-up ticket sales, the *Pro Bowl Block Party* was staged on Waikiki's Kalakaua Avenue, the main thoroughfare through the resort area, the night before the game. This section of Honolulu is typically busy with tourists and young locals visiting the area's most active nightspots each evening. A half dozen temporary stages presented contemporary, jazz, and Hawaiian music, sports talk, cheerleader performances, and more, and official merchandise tents and food vendors dotted the six-block length of the event. More than 70,000 tourists, fans, and residents filled the streets for this one-night extravaganza, becoming one of the state's best-attended festivals.

Earlier the same day, *'Ohana* (Family) *Day*, a free, public NFL player practice annually drawing more than 10,000 fans, was held at Aloha Stadium, enabling fans to see the players close up and hear interviews from the on-field host. (Fans could very conveniently buy Pro Bowl tickets at the stadium box office when they arrived or departed *'Ohana Day*). These events, among others, not only generated incremental merchandise and ticket sales, but also created an air of celebration and excitement throughout the Honolulu market. Reflective of the mix of in-state and visiting fans, a combination of national and local business partners ranging from Hawaiian Airlines to Anheuser-Busch sponsored stages at the *Block Party* and promotions at *'Ohana Day* as components of their overall Pro Bowl event activation strategies.

autograph sessions and photo opportunities with athletes, batting cages, football tosses, slapshot booths, fan skills or trivia contests, to name just a few—are most effective in creating excitement. A promotional takeaway item with the event date, location, information, and ticket ordering website address and phone number, is highly recommended. Be creative and pick an item that itself represents the sport or event, but, if cost is an issue, the items need not be a permanent keepsake, such as a refrigerator magnet or key chain. After all, from a marketing perspective, the usefulness of the item expires when the main event is over. The premiums and the activity can be fully or partially funded by a sponsor, especially if the partner is common to the host event. Additional elements, such as sampling, can also be included, pending the permission of the host organizer. Try having a supply of tickets available and a mechanism to accept payment, if possible and permitted.

Are there parades, street festivals, civic gatherings, special holiday revelries, ethnic celebrations, or other activities in the host city that bring large numbers of people together? Consider contacting the organizers of these events to create a presence at these festive occasions, presuming the demographics of the audience complements your target market. Fitting into the cultural fabric of the host city, even if it is the home city of the event organizer, is essential and explored in detail in Play 10.

Social Media

As is abundantly apparent in the foregoing discussions on the more traditional components of the marketing wheel, it can be argued that social network media is as much a subset of publicity, advertising, promotion, and even direct sales, as it is a discrete spoke. In many ways, social media marketing does share attributes of these other marketing tools, but the dynamics and characteristics of these digital forums suggest applying a further and separate focus to use them to their full marketing potential. A social media campaign is similar to publicity because event organizers can disseminate information about themselves and their events to their most engaged fans, but different because the fans can respond or react – not just to the organizer, but also through conversation with every other fan with whom the organizer engages as well as their own circle of family and friends. It is similar to advertising because the promoter can provide information directly to users without the middleman of editors or journalists selecting whether, or how much, to provide to their readers or viewers. But, it is also different because organizers have to actively develop the "friends" who will read their social media entries. As has been illustrated, the social networks can be used to support promotions and promote sales with links to transactional ticket purchase sites.

To restrict our consideration of how to leverage the social media networks as simply an extension of traditional marketing would be overlooking the full potential of how they may be used to support the organizer's efforts. We view social media networks not as an outward-facing marketing tool, but as a two-way conversation directly between the organizer and any number of "friends." Because the fan is free to react publicly to the promoter's message, it is essential that the promoter monitor and respond to the fan's excitement, questions, or concerns. Assign a staff member to monitor the social networks, and watch the nature of fan conversation. Is it supportive or derisive? Are fans asking questions and getting accurate answers? Are they sharing bad information? Are rumors emerging, or are fans complaining about inconveniences? Once posted by users on the social networks, comments become facts if not corrected by the organizer.

There is no marketing tool that can create the depth and intimacy of engagement with your fans that social media can (See Figure 9.10). Create accounts on the most popular social networks and provide fans with the latest official information. Slowly drip insider tips onto the sites to keep them relevant and visited often. Read all user posts and if they ask questions, answer them and encourage your fans to engage further by attending the event and posting their observations while the event is underway. Post behind-the-scenes photos as preparations for the event advance and ask fans to post their own images while on site and after the event has concluded. Keep the site active all year for annual events and give fans a reason to check back regularly.

SIDELINE STORY

Social Networks and the NFL's Pro Bowl

To combat years of declining attendance, the NFL's Pro Bowl was moved in 1980 to Hawaii where it enjoyed three decades of success. The mid-Pacific tropical destination in the middle of the North American winter drew tens of thousands of fans from the US mainland for a week-long football vacation, filling 48,000-seat Aloha Stadium each year and generating significant tourism dollars for the State of Hawaii. In 2010, the Pro Bowl was moved from the week after the Super Bowl to the week before in an attempt to boost sagging television ratings. The event was also moved back to the US mainland for the first time in 30 years to further invigorate the game. The 2010 Pro Bowl was played in South Florida's Sun Life Stadium—the host of Super Bowl XLIV to be played the following Sunday—and positioned as the first major event of Super Bowl Week.

A comprehensive marketing plan was developed to build national and local awareness of the schedule and location change, sell tickets, and promote television viewership, utilizing most of the traditional marketing tools. The plan included television advertising during late NFL regular season and playoff games, local newspaper ads, in-store ticket promotions at presenting sponsor McDonald's locations, and pre-event features on NFL.com. For the first time, facilitating fan conversation over social networks was also an important component in the campaign to build awareness and build relevance for the Pro Bowl as the "kickoff" event to Super Bowl Week. The NFL retained Extreme Marketing, an Internet marketing company, to develop non-NFL-branded Pro Bowl fan micro-sites designed to seed and facilitate fan conversation about the event. Once established, the sites built their own following and authentic fan conversation about the Pro Bowl and participating players on the social networks. From time to time, game-day tips and behind-the-scenes photos were posted by "Pro Bowl insiders" showing players arriving in Honolulu, practicing, and visiting military basis. The sites developed thousands of followers and helped build the relevance of Pro Bowl among the most avid football fans.

Television viewership for the 2010 Pro Bowl increased more than 45 percent over the previous year, and more than 70,000 fans attended the game, the best-attended Pro Bowl since 1959. The social networks surely didn't account for most of these increases, but this then-burgeoning marketing tool certainly helped build incremental awareness, providing a platform for real fans to engage with one another in authentic debate and conversation. When the 2011 Pro Bowl returned to Hawaii, this social network platform was applied again to spur fan conversation and awareness about the all-star game's return to the Islands. National television ratings increased an additional 9 percent over the previous season's high levels.

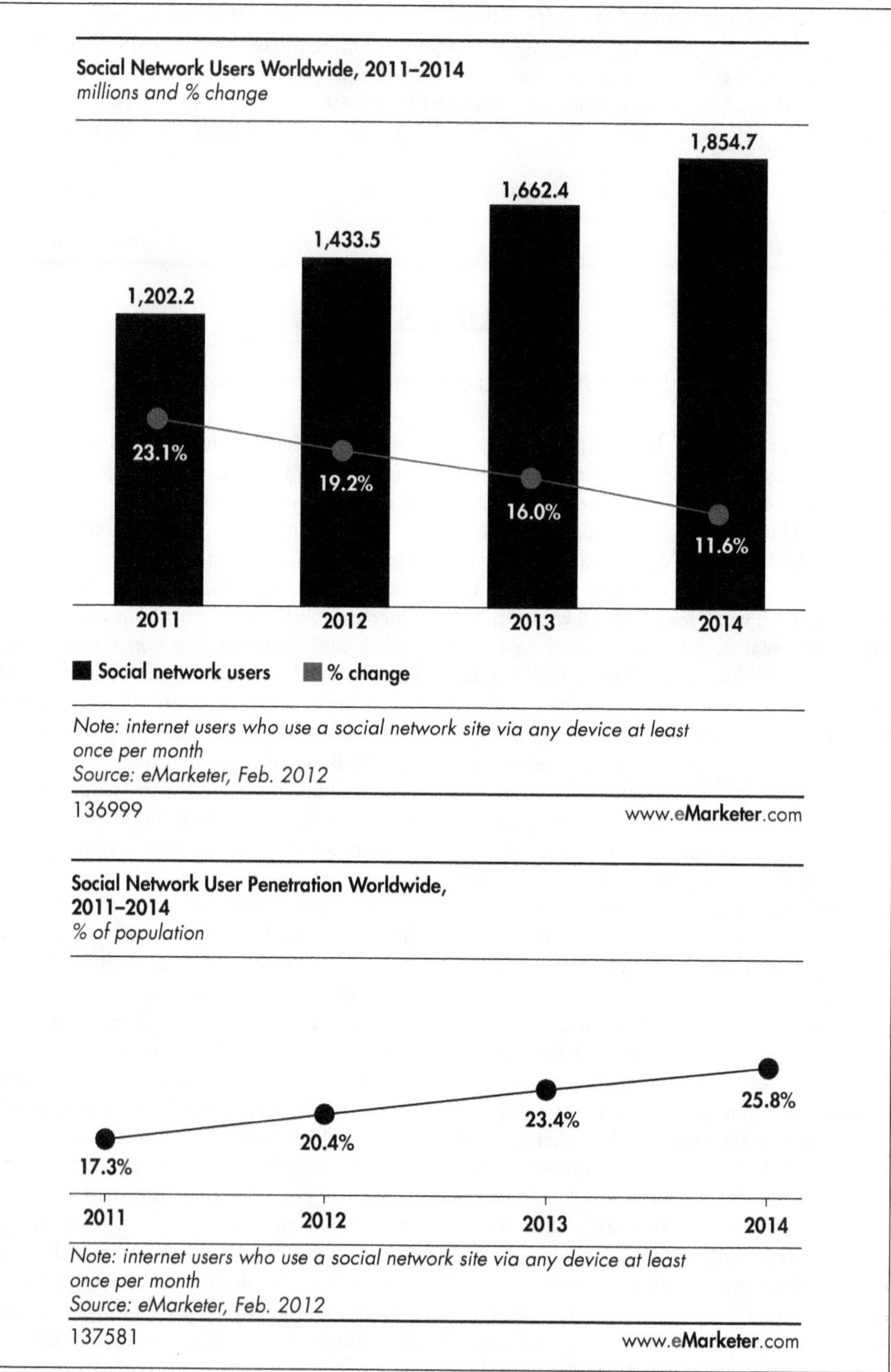

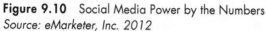

Figure 9.10 Social Media Power by the Numbers
Source: eMarketer, Inc. 2012

Social Network Users Worldwide, by Region and Country, 2011–2014
millions

	2011	2012	2013	2014
Asia-Pacific	**493.5**	**615.9**	**745.6**	**853.7**
China*	256.5	307.5	366.2	414.5
India	50.2	76.1	105.0	129.3
Indonesia	34.4	52.1	67.1	79.2
Japan	39.5	44.7	47.8	50.7
South Korea	20.7	22.7	24.6	25.9
Australia	8.8	9.8	10.7	11.6
Other	83.4	102.9	124.1	142.4
Latin America	**164.9**	**191.8**	**215.9**	**236.9**
Brazil	66.2	75.7	84.0	90.7
Mexico	23.7	27.9	32.6	37.2
Argentina	14.1	15.9	17.0	17.9
Other	60.9	72.3	82.4	91.1
North America	**163.9**	**174.7**	**181.9**	**189.2**
US	147.8	157.8	164.2	170.7
Canada	16.1	16.9	17.7	18.5
Eastern Europe	**139.0**	**157.4**	**176.5**	**192.7**
Russia	52.1	57.9	64.2	69.3
Other	87.0	99.5	112.3	123.4
Middle East & Africa	**111.1**	**148.5**	**183.0**	**211.6**
Western Europe	**129.8**	**145.3**	**159.4**	**170.8**
Germany	25.7	29.2	32.4	34.7
UK	23.9	25.9	27.7	29.4
France	19.9	21.9	23.6	25.0
Italy	15.8	17.8	19.7	21.3
Spain	15.5	17.5	19.5	21.2
Other	29.0	32.9	36.5	39.3
Worldwide	**1,202.2**	**1,433.5**	**1,662.4**	**1,854.7**

Note: Internet users who use a social network site via any device at least once per month; numbers may not add up to total due to rounding;
**excludes Hong Kong*
Source: eMarketer, Feb. 2012

137001 www.**eMarketer**.com

Figure 9.10 (*Continued*)

Post-Play Analysis

An effective marketing plan cannot rely on pre-event publicity alone. Additional tools, including advertising, promotions, and event marketing, must be employed to achieve your event's marketing objectives. Establishing business partnerships with media outlets can help to maximize exposure for an event at a greatly reduced cost. Newspapers and other print media open to participating as partners generally insist on exclusive relationships. Multiple radio, television, and online partnerships can be designed, with exclusivity protected by programming format or content elements. Promotions can be created with both media partners and sponsors that encourage ticket sales or build attendance, generate awareness of the event, or increase ratings for broadcast events. Ensure that event advertising has a clear message, with an obvious and compelling call to action. Consider working with newspapers and other print media to create special sections and advertorials to increase exposure for, and reinforce the importance of, your sports event. Apply best practices to social media network marketing. This tool incorporates many of the benefits of advertising, publicity, and promotion, but also provides a platform for direct and instantaneous two-way communication with your fans that can generate awareness, excitement, sales, and engagement like no traditional marketing medium.

Coach's Clipboard

1. Create an advertising campaign for the 10K run described in Play 1. Include an introductory ad to solicit participants, and another designed to appear the day before the event to encourage the attendance of spectators. How many times and when should each ad run? Write a 30-second radio spot to complement the print campaign.
2. At what other kinds of sports and nonsports events could the organizers of the 10K run stage event marketing activities to maximize spectator attendance? What kinds of activities should they stage, and what kinds of premiums could they distribute to help build attendance on event day?
3. How could the 10K run organizer reach into avid and casual running fans using the social media networks to generate participants? In what other ways can social media assist the organizer in creating excitement in the marketplace before, during, and after the event?

PLAY 10

Engaging the Community

"Individual commitment to a group effort—that is what makes a team work, a company work, a society work, a civilization work."

—*Vince Lombardi, Hall of Fame NFL coach, 1913–1970*

This play will help you to:

- Understand the motivations and apprehensions that influence a community's engagement in sports events.
- Develop programs that benefit and strengthen ties with the host community, including environmental and business development opportunities.
- Invest and involve the host community in the success of your event.

Introduction

Too often, sports event organizers overlook the many resources available in communities that are justifiably proud of the events they stage, as well as those they host. A talented organizer with sufficient resources can stage and promote an event without the active engagement of local government, businesses, and civic organizations. However, ignoring the role the community can play is to ignore the greater impact that can be achieved with the mobilization of these local resources and the greater benefits an event can provide to the region that plays host. Some of the same sports event organizers who are aggressive about pursuing sponsorship revenue in the community fail to notice the vast human resources and valuable services often available simply for the asking.

Programs that showcase the talents and athletic prowess of family, friends, and neighbors can be incredibly appealing to elected officials and local governmental agencies. After all, both the "stars" of the event and the people who come to see them compete are members of their voting constituencies. Local politicians strive to represent happy, vibrant communities, and any event that can improve the quality of life in their jurisdiction—within reasonable cost—is almost always welcomed enthusiastically. By extension, the governmental agencies required to support a sports event—police, fire, sanitation, streets, parks and recreation, and others—apply themselves with equal vigor as long as their use is kept within acceptable limits. Although they, too, may cooperate in a selfless, community-minded spirit, the agencies' supervisors also know that their annual budgets are often voted on by the politicians who support the event and those that vote for them.

By the same token, the larger the event and the greater its impact on local infrastructure and municipal services, the more likely that some sectors of the community will come to view it as less desirable, bothersome, or even intrusive. It would be overstating the case to suggest that amateur and professional sports events that draw participants and spectators from an area wider than the local market can develop a love-hate relationship with their host communities. It is true, however, that some constituencies have more to gain from their presence and others perhaps arguably have a bit more to lose. Sports event organizers should, by all means, accentuate the positive and beneficial aspects of their programs through various marketing and publicity efforts, as well as participate in efforts that can improve the local quality of life and enhance the health of the local business community. At the same time, they must recognize the areas of potentially negative impact, realizing that communities are composed of a wide variety of individuals and businesses, each legitimately affected by a sports event in their own unique ways (see Figure 10.1).

Local governments seek and support sports events for a host of emotional and practical, economic reasons that include instilling community pride and elevating both the self-image and the reputation of their municipality. The availability of entertainment and recreational options improves the perception of the community's quality of life and keeps its citizens within their hometown borders more often, spending money with local businesses and generating incremental tax revenues. Municipalities are not only competing for spending within their city limits but also for state, provincial, and federal grants designated for building, refurbishing, and maintaining recreational and entertainment facilities. An established history as an active focal point for sports and other entertainment events can portray a community as a vibrant, vital hub of economic and tourism activity that is worthy of further funding and development. Finally, do not underestimate the value of bragging rights. Beyond the purely economic competitiveness, politicians, city officials, and even area residents simply like to portray themselves as being from a place that is superior to that of their neighbors.

As explored in Play 4, sports events can generate economic impact across a wide spectrum of businesses, including restaurants, hotels, retailers, ground transportation operators, and other services. The more people an event can attract to a host city, even if only for a day, the greater its impact on the business community and, by extension, the greater the latter's support for the program. Keeping the host community's citizens in town raises the excitement level of the event, but also encourages their money to be spent with local merchants rather than outside the city limits. This helps spike tax revenues for the city, and may help fund future capital improvements not just for event facilities, but also for infrastructure the community citizenry uses in their everyday lives, such as roads, parks, and public spaces. In addition, successful sports events help attract more sports and entertainment events, keeping facilities well utilized and developing an increased flow of consumer spending and tax revenues for the future.

Reasons They Like Them	Reasons They Dislike Them
Community pride	Congestion
Quality of life	Crowds
Self-image	Traffic
Promotion of city to the outside world	Noise
Competitiveness with rival communities	Interference with normal business
Showcase of local talent	Security (fear/incidents of unruly behavior)
Business opportunities	Setting of precedents (apprehension of future events)
Retail	Pollution and litter
Hospitality and accommodations	Political opposition from disenfranchised neighborhoods
New business	Expenditure of taxpayer funds in support of events
Future events	Degradation of existing facilities
Tax revenues	
Grants for capital improvements	
Existing facility utilization	

Figure 10.1 How Communities React to Sports Events

The presence and proportionate importance of each of these motivators varies from city to city, and even from one elected administration to the next. What is almost as sure is that at least some constituents will be less enthused about the presence of a sports event, though the magnitude of their dissatisfaction and the degree of their ability to obstruct or otherwise affect its planning will differ. Residents living near event venues may be concerned about how both human and vehicular traffic, noise, and potentially boisterous fan behavior may affect their homes and neighborhoods. Businesses may be concerned about the added difficulties their employees may encounter in reaching their offices, and some retailers about the obstacles their customers could face due to heavy traffic, road closures, or detours.

In almost every community, there is likely to be some number of disenfranchised neighborhoods composed of economically distressed families, underemployed workers, and at-risk youth. Cities and developers often place sports facilities in or on the fringe of these areas, taking advantage of initially lower land values and, in some cases, fostering hopes of revitalizing an area to invite more businesses, more jobs, and improved housing. The residents of these neighborhoods may be profoundly affected by sports events staged in immediate proximity to their homes and businesses, suffering from the realities of game-day noise and congestion, and, if the event is economically exclusionary, on an emotional level, as well.

Many of these issues will be lurking beneath the surface and may become apparent suddenly and without warning in local newspaper reports or from various members of local government as a result of discussions held behind closed doors, in town and city council meetings. Events staged by organizers from outside the community and those that attract participants and spectators from beyond the city limits are particularly susceptible to political criticism and local suspicion. An experienced sports event organizer will identify, acknowledge, and address these challenges early in the planning process to minimize any real or perceived negative impact on the community, demonstrating an understanding and sensitivity to the issues facing potentially affected businesses and residents.

Identifying the Gatekeepers

The most effective way of identifying these concerns before they surface is to engage local government officials, business organizations, and community leaders early in the planning process. Forge a genuine and functional partnership based on open communication and acknowledgement of each party's respective agenda. Step 1 is to identify the *gatekeepers,* the influencers whose opinion and leadership help build consensus in the community. The value of finding and building relationships with a community's gatekeepers is illustrated in the next Sideline Story; although it comes not from sports but from the world of civic celebrations, and is a tale several decades old, it is no less relevant and reflective of the influence of gatekeepers and the importance of their role.

Various sectors of the community can throw obstacles in the path of staging a well-conceived sports event, interfering with any number of its logistical component parts, such as venue selection, transportation, parking, or even event marketing and promotion. Gatekeepers are community business or political leaders who can help decode local sensitivities to a sports event before they surface publicly and can help to ease or even eliminate possible areas of frustration for everyone involved. It is important to note that the onus is not on simply finding ways to develop the community's acceptance of the sports event organizer's plans. It is also up to the organizer to incorporate the intimate intelligence provided by the gatekeepers into plans that will well serve the local area and its residents with significant benefits to host the event with a minimum of inconvenience and with no diminution of any measures required for public safety.

As important as gatekeepers are for advance intelligence, organizers should recognize that they are also advocates for the citizens and businesses in their jurisdiction. They will know what kinds of marketing and community relations programs will work in their city and what will be received tepidly or negatively. They can advise the organizer whether to ignore an obstacle, work around it, or involve the source of potential criticism more closely in the early stages of planning. They can help identify the true needs of both local residents and industry and show how best to integrate them into the event for the gain of all involved. Figure 10.2 lists some of the most common gatekeepers of the community and where they can be found.

The larger a sports event and the greater the impact it will have on a community's normal operations, the more essential it is to identify one or more highly placed gatekeepers as early in the planning process as possible, perhaps even during the event bidding phase. The local sports commission or the convention and visitors bureau, whose constituencies may have already demonstrated their commitment to the success of the event, can help organizers identify and contact the gatekeepers most important to the tasks and challenges at hand. Certainly, a contact in the office of the mayor, perhaps the city's own chief executive, may be able to provide the highest of level of active leadership and personal oversight. Members of city council, or representatives of the analogous body in the community that represents the geographical areas most affected by the event, are also essential partners in order to gain the support of the municipality and the citizens living in its environs.

SIDELINE STORY

The Influence of the Gatekeeper

Playbook author Frank Supovitz recollects that the Radio City Music Hall Productions event team commonly referred to him as "Dr. No." The insidious Dr. No was a Philadelphia Police Department senior officer assigned to serve as the liaison to the "We The People" Parade, the nationally televised celebration of the United States Constitution's bicentennial, of which Supovitz was associate producer. One of the largest parades ever staged, the event featured 25,000 marchers and dozens of parade floats, including hand-built, horse-drawn recreations of those constructed for the original Grand Federal Procession of 1787. Perhaps to a greater degree than any other special event, parades depend heavily on the cooperative and integrated efforts of dozens of city agencies and hundreds of city employees. Without the active participation of the police and the departments with oversight of streets and sanitation, it is hard to imagine how a parade might ever hope to occur.

"Whether Dr. No understood the significance of this national celebration to the tourism and economic development efforts of the City of Philadelphia to this day remains unknown," recalls Supovitz. "What was evident is that he was a skillful master of yielding the powerful word that became his alias and employed it liberally as the answer to nearly every inquiry or request." For the record, it should be stated that the authority and expertise of the local police and fire departments, among other government agencies charged with the responsibility of security and public safety, should generally go unchallenged. These professionals know their city, understand their mission, and are charged with the uniquely weighty burden of protecting the public. This is a partnership where the rationally exercised authority of the law should be unquestioned.

"There did come a time, however, that it became apparent that Dr. No's use of his chief weapon had less to do with public safety and more to do with an abhorrence of personal inconvenience and ambivalence toward the event. His refusal to suggest alternatives, make recommendations, or provide feedback that defined the limits to which he was prepared to agree further supported this perception. This is a very unusual occurrence when dealing with our heroes in blue," Supovitz notes. It also became apparent that no operations plan submitted to him would ever be approved, thus seriously endangering the viability of the event and the city's ability to exploit it for its own purposes.

"Dr. No unwittingly taught me the value of identifying a gatekeeper." In this case, the keys to the gate were in the possession of an influential deputy mayor who served as City Hall's direct liaison to the We The People 200 Committee, the event's organizer. "Our encounters with Dr. No were related to this committee member during a hastily called meeting scheduled to review the operational plans for the parade. Within a day, Dr. No was reassigned, probably as much to his relief as ours, and a new event liaison, whose mantra was more akin to 'Let's figure this out together,' appeared." Working more closely as partners, with an understanding and respect for each other's needs and responsibilities, the parade drew an estimated four million people to Center City Philadelphia to celebrate this landmark date in the nation's history.

City Officials

- Mayor and/or city manager
- Deputy mayor
- Communications director
- Marketing director
- City council president and representatives (for impacted districts)
- Executive director, convention and visitors bureau
- Police commissioner or chief of police
- Fire commissioner
- Parks and recreation/other event oversight departments and agencies (i.e., sanitation, emergency medical, traffic/transportation, transit, permits)

Business Development Organizations

- Convention and visitors bureau
- Chamber(s) of commerce
- Business improvement districts or business partnerships
- Downtown or merchants associations
- Restaurant associations

Civic Groups

- Rotary International
- Kiwanis
- Masonic Lodge
- American Legion and Veterans of Foreign Wars
- Labor union(s)
- Religious group(s)

Sports Organizations

- Amateur sports federations
- Academic sports organizations
- Grassroots and recreational sports leagues
- Sports and entertainment commission

Figure 10.2 The Gatekeepers of the Community

The interest and support of city hall is particularly important to sports events that are not held in the same location each year. Finding out that the community is not behind an event on the highest levels after it has been awarded can be a major disappointment and perhaps even a mortal blow to its eventual success. With this in mind, it is recommended that a letter of support from the appropriate senior local official, such as the mayor, city manager, county supervisor, or board chairperson, be required for inclusion as part of the request for proposal (RFP) response. It is important to recognize and respect that city officials are responsible first and foremost to their voting constituents, both residents and business owners. The event's benefits to the community must be genuine and measurable to expect the involvement of top elected officials. This is especially true during an election year, when officials assume a more political mien, pushing through programs that provide great and obvious benefits to their communities or pulling away from almost any program at the hint of controversy.

If possible, arrange a meeting with the highest city official possible before the event is awarded or announced. Prepare an oral presentation of no more than 10 to15 minutes—that will likely be all the time he or she has—outlining the event and its benefits to the community. (Don't be surprised if that official is already aware of the program as a result of the bidding process.) Because such busy administrators will want to ask questions of specific pertinence to them within this brief timeframe, expect to be interrupted frequently. Emphasize your most important points—how the sports event will serve their city, its residents, and businesses—within the first few minutes. Additional information, descriptions, and illustrations may be left behind in a written summary document. The idea is to communicate sufficiently and succinctly with these officials so they are prepared with answers for their constituents' questions and can represent to their community that they have ongoing, constructive, and direct dialogue with the organizer. At the end of the presentation, offer to answer any remaining questions and, in return, request the official to provide a main liaison through whom all questions and requests to and from his or her office should be channeled. This may also be a good time to further engage city hall with an offer for the mayor and/or an appropriate councilperson to participate as a featured speaker in the announcing press conference or other upcoming media opportunity.

Failing the ability to successfully arrange a meeting with key local government officials, sometimes simply inviting these senior civic gatekeepers to participate in the sports event in a significant and meaningful way can help to open doors. The next Sideline Story illustrates this point.

SIDELINE STORY

Hockey Hall of Fame Grand Opening

Three days of festivities were scheduled when the Hockey Hall of Fame was due to open in the historic Bank of Montreal building at the busy northwest corner of Front and Yonge Streets in downtown Toronto, Ontario. Among the many and varied celebrations planned included a televised unveiling of the "Honoured Members Wall," the etched glass monument upon which the names of inductees to the Hall were enshrined, a procession of the then-90 living members to the new facility in open-air convertibles, and the "world's largest face-off," a photo opportunity in which the honorees would pose holding hockey sticks in the broad crossroads, forming an arc around a giant commemorative puck. Two street closures were required to execute the event. First, Front Street would have to be closed to accommodate the parade of convertibles. A few minutes later, Yonge Street, one of the city's busiest north-south thoroughfares, would need to be closed to set up and execute the face-off.

At that time, jurisdiction for each of these intersecting streets was under the control of two different government entities—the City of Toronto and Metro Toronto (the latter was a multicity regional government which has since merged with the City). Because of this circumstance, permits were required from each of the two administrations to stage an event in the intersection, but one refused to rule on the application for many weeks and reasons unknown, greatly delaying planning for the event. When Canada's then-Governor-General Ray Hnatyshyn accepted an invitation to ride in the lead car for the procession and pose with the hockey greats in the face-off, however, the permits were hurried through to approval.

Chambers of Commerce and Merchants Associations

Other important gatekeepers are the senior executives representing various sectors of the business community, some of whom may perceive an event as an opportunity and others as an obstacle to their enterprises. The local chamber of commerce represents the interests of area businesses and is responsible for attracting new companies and jobs to the community. Chambers often organize member breakfasts, luncheons, and other regular meetings to impart news, share ideas, and present information on emerging promotional opportunities. Make it a point to meet with the chamber's executive director and marketing director to introduce them to the event and its potential impact on local business. Explore with them the many opportunities—as sponsors, promotional partners, or simply as supporters—for area businesses. Request whether the chamber would consider entertaining a presentation about the event to its membership at an upcoming gathering. Bring promotional materials and giveaways to the meeting, as well as videos and printed summaries, which will communicate the program's excitement and promotional potential to business owners. Leave plenty of time for questions and answers and be prepared to liberally exchange business cards with attendees. Invite feedback and be open to new ideas—you never know where a dynamic and new promotional concept will come from (see Figure 10.3). If being able to speak at a membership event is not available, request the ability to be introduced to the membership through the chamber's newsletter, website, social media, or mailings.

Some groups of neighborhood businesses have more intensive, specific, and localized needs than a chamber of commerce with a citywide constituency. Local not-for-profit organizations with names that contain phrases like "business improvement district (BID)," "downtown association,"

- Provide opportunities for official sponsorship. Consider adding a less-expensive tier designed expressly for local businesses at national or regional events.
- Provide opportunities for local businesses to serve as contractors or subcontractors for the event. Consider launching or supporting an existing local business development program for small businesses and certified minority- and woman-owned business enterprises (MWBEs). (See Sideline Story.)
- Place posters or window cards in retailer windows.
- Conduct a window-decorating contest—participating retailers can win tickets and prizes for decorating their windows (or having children do so) with a theme relating the sports event.
- Request that businesses post welcome greetings to fans and athletes on company-owned electronic message signs and marquees.
- Offer advance event ticket purchase opportunities to member businesses and their employees.
- Encourage sports-event-themed menus at area restaurants and pubs.
- Consider developing cross-promotions with local attractions.
- Supply lapel pins or buttons with the event's name or slogan to be worn by employees of local businesses prior to and during event days.
- Arrange for event promotion or welcome banners to be hung on streetlight poles along major thoroughfares in the city.

Figure 10.3 Involving Local Businesses

"merchants association," and "business partnership," among others, concentrate their development efforts on just a handful of streets or blocks. If an event is scheduled within their area of influence, these local merchants could be among the most interested in exploiting the event to further their own business objectives. They will also be the most concerned about whether the event will create unwanted inconvenience, confusion, congestion, noise, and litter during their operating hours. Marketing and promotional programs undertaken with businesses located near sports event venues can be particularly effective, as both their employees and their customers are accustomed to traveling to, and spending time on, those few blocks. Creating a promotional incentive to buy tickets specifically for customers and employees of businesses with close proximity to the host facility, either on a website or at the venue's nearby box office, can help establish goodwill and support for the event.

Making opportunities for local businesses to provide goods and services in support of a sports event provides direct economic benefit to the community and can often realize cost efficiencies for the organizer, as well. After all, the cost of shipping supplies and equipment and transporting service providers can be wasteful if equally good materials and people are available right there in the local community. Regional business associations, as well as the host facility, are excellent resources for identifying qualified vendors and contractors from the community. The local government may also maintain a list of certified MWBEs—minority and woman-owned business enterprises—that can likely benefit greatly from an association (i.e., contracts) with the event.

SIDELINE STORY

The Super Bowl Emerging Business Program

The Super Bowl drives significant economic impact when the National Football League's championship game and its associated events unfold in a host city. To ensure that every segment of the community has a meaningful chance to participate from a business perspective, the local host organization and NFL offer enrollment to certified MWBEs (minority- and woman-owned business enterprises) in the NFL Emerging Business Program. The cornerstone of the program is a searchable vendor database that is made available to contractors, league sponsors, broadcasters, hotels, and other event organizers, as well as all league departments. This database helps procurers find qualified local suppliers and its use is required by the league's agreements with Super Bowl key contractors, which must provide periodic reports on their utilization of local MWBEs.

On any given year, anywhere from 400 to 1,000 MWBEs qualify for the Emerging Business Program. With such a large number of participants, it is made clear that not everyone, not even a majority, will actually receive a contract for the Super Bowl. The program, however, offers significant additional value to enrolling businesses. Several workshops are held throughout the year to help companies better prepare for competing on a larger scale through professional development forums, and learn how to read and respond to requests for proposal (RFPs). On several occasions, the NFL's Emerging Business Program database has been made available to other sports events to further enhance results for local MWBEs. The database for Super Bowl XL in Detroit, for instance, was provided to contractors for Major League Baseball's All-Star Game held the previous summer.

Restaurants

Not everyone views the crowds generated by sports events as a negative. A particular group of businesses that welcomes congestion, at least in the form of foot traffic, is restaurants and taverns. Ask the host city's convention and visitors bureau (CVB) to identify a key contact at the local restaurant association. Try to meet with the owners or managers of area eateries and bars to create mutually beneficial cross-promotions that will drive ticket holders into restaurants and their patrons to the box office. Does your event offer an app, post a downloadable information guide, or publish a similar resource for guests, participants, volunteers, or staff? List participating restaurants that agree to offer dining discounts (e.g., 15 percent off the bill, a free appetizer, or complimentary beverage) to fans and athletes upon presentation of a ticket stub, credential, or coupon. The organizer can further enhance the promotion in the venue with some combination of signage, public address announcements, souvenir program mentions or ads, or messages on video boards or electronic displays during the event, adding even more value to the relationship for participating restaurants.

In exchange for the organizer's promotion, these establishments may also decorate their own spaces in an event-oriented motif, hang event posters, offer event-themed menu items, or help promote the program by offering their regular diners coupons redeemable for ticket or merchandise discounts during the month leading up to the event. To maximize exposure for the event at area restaurants, the organizer may agree to provide digital artwork for the establishments to include on daily menus and welcome banners. A simple one-page permission agreement, drafted by an attorney, that defines how the restaurant may use the event logo (or other graphic material) is strongly recommended for this purpose. The agreement can provide the eatery with the right to use the logo for its own promotional purposes or for decorative uses, presuming an existing sponsorship agreement with another restaurant or chain does not preclude cross-promotions, as described earlier. To protect existing or future event sponsors, it is also suggested that the agreement prohibit the restaurant from including any third-party name or logo on banners or printed materials that feature the event name or logo. For example, a banner displaying the phrase, "Bob's Restaurant Welcomes the Big Street Sports Tournament," would be completely acceptable under such an agreement, while the same greeting from "Bob's Restaurant and Barley's Beer" would be expressly forbidden. In addition, the restaurant should not be permitted to pass through sponsorship rights for any event promotion to a third party, whether paid or unpaid, without the written permission of the organizer. Agree on a reasonable expiration date for the promotion, and make sure it is recognized in this simple agreement, as well as on downloadable or printed coupons and any other promotional materials or signage.

Area Attractions and Events

Events that draw tourists and one-day visitors to a community can be highly desirable to an area's sightseeing and cultural attractions, including local landmarks, amusement parks, museums, theaters, and natural wonders. Cross-promotions similar to those described for restaurants and bars may be pursued with these area attractions. The simplest way of reaching out to attractions will be through the local CVB, whose membership roster will include the operating entities of the city's most significant points of interest. Develop programs with high-volume attractions that appeal to similar audience demographics as your sports event. Concentrate on those that can promote the event or a promotional offer to the most residents and one-day visitors during the weeks leading up to event day. In exchange, the attractions should offer admission discounts to the sports event's fans, guests, participants, volunteers, and staff during the period immediately surrounding the program, most often a few days immediately before and after the event. Attraction offers may be communicated at the event site, but are at their most effective when promoted in advance of the planned arrival of inbound guests on apps, websites, and printed materials. As a result of these available opportunities, travelers may determine to extend their stay in the host city to take best advantage of the entertainment, cultural enrichment, and additional cost savings they can enjoy.

Consider designing promotions with professional and amateur sports teams in the host city, particularly those with crossover appeal to the sports event's target audience. Offer discounts on advance event ticket purchases to the loyal fans of major and minor league organizations, and participants in youth and adult recreational leagues. Send event posters to local recreation centers, park information centers, fitness centers, rinks, and other sports-oriented facilities. Promote group ticket packages to teams and associations that use these venues regularly and include an information telephone number, e-mail address and website. Some organizers offer not-for-profit groups such as junior leagues, scouts, hospitals, and other charitable institutions the ability to purchase a block of tickets at a discounted rate for resale to their membership at full price for fundraising purposes. (*Hint*: These discounted tickets will show a full price on their face. They should be coded so that, in the unlikely necessity of having to provide a refund, box office personnel will know the tickets were sold at a discount. It is further recommended that if refunds of fundraising tickets are determined to be necessary, they be transacted between the charity and the box office rather than with individual ticket holders.)

Be sure to identify the other events and celebrations being held in the host city during the time when most of your pre-event marketing activities are being planned. Sports and cultural events, festivals, civic and holiday celebrations, parades, fairs, and expositions can provide excellent platforms for additional cross-promotions and publicity. Staffing exhibits and information booths or tents or providing a printed flyer that can be distributed at these events can help to raise awareness for your program. In addition, attendees of conventions, trade shows, and special interest shows that attract out-of-town delegates are always looking for extracurricular activities during their visit. Concentrate promotional efforts on those that are scheduled during or around the same week as your sports event as a great source for additional attendees.

Welcoming Often-Overlooked Neighbors

Often-overlooked opportunities to build an event's relevance and popularity may be available in neighborhoods that are, simply, habitually forgotten by other organizers. Disadvantaged families and at-risk youth may be found in every city, and frequently in the shade of sports facilities. Extending a welcoming hand to these sometimes-unnoticed segments of the marketplace at sports events can provide an array of benefits, foremost among them, just doing good works in the community. Activities designed specifically for the disadvantaged can further a host city's own objectives for promoting inclusiveness, can develop positive public relations and new fans for an event, and can diversify the sport's fan base, to name just a few.

Providing special access or programming for the residents of lower-income neighborhoods and those most impacted by the event (i.e., residents living or working closest to the venue) can also help to gain the support of the community and its elected representatives. Organizers can offer exclusive athlete meet-and-greet opportunities, a special luncheon or barbeque with sports personalities, sports clinics, pre- or postevent access to the playing field, or even a number of unsold tickets on a complimentary basis to help improve the lives of those not fortunate enough to have economic access to event tickets or those who might be inconvenienced the most by event activities. Hosting or sponsoring programs such as these, beyond their purely philanthropic effect, adds immeasurable value to the main event in the eyes of city government and the community at large.

Consider, too, the impact that can be enjoyed by all parties by involving the participation of groups serving physically and mentally challenged individuals. Area recreational organizations, charities, hospitals, and schools can assist sports event organizers in identifying these groups and their specific special needs. Organizers may discover active local associations providing recreational programs to Special Olympians and Para-athletes who can be included either as participants or as guest spectators. Incorporating these inspirational athletes into the program can significantly add to the quality of a sports event. If this option is not within the scope of the event, consider offering special clinics or workshops conducted by featured competitors, or showcasing their inspiring skills during a pregame or intermission demonstration. Finally, many sports organizations and organizers invite military veterans to attend their events as guests and schedule opportunities to acknowledge them for their service during the event.

Impacting the Local Environment

"You go home after your event is over. We have to live here."

This is a comment we often hear when managing events away from our home cities. Sometimes, it is offered as an admonition to be aware of the region's political sensitivities while planning an event, sometimes about the inconveniences that local residents face during the program. It is equally applicable to the notion that events can impact the local physical environment in either positive or negative ways. There is no question that applying sustainable environmental practices is the right thing to do for the host region and our planet. It is also true that recycling, reuse, and recovery programs are vivid and public demonstrations of a sports event's sensitivity to the community. When you go home after your event is over, leave the environment at least no worse off than when you arrived, just as though you actually were going to continue living there.

Are you using wood, plastic, cardboard, fabric, or metal products in temporary construction, décor, or signage? Work with the local sanitation agency or an environmental services firm to recover those materials for recycling after the event if they would have otherwise entered the general waste stream. Allow fans, staff, and athletes to participate by providing recycling containers in offices, locker rooms, and event spaces. Replace disposable plastic water bottles for staff, crew, and participants with reusable water bottles with a sponsor or event logo on them. They can be filled from water coolers that reuse their large glass or plastic water jugs and make great keepsakes while significantly reducing waste. Collect and donate unused office supplies to a school or hospital rather than throwing them away when the event is over. If permitted, recover prepared, unserved food and beverages for a local food pantry. There are dozens of opportunities large and small to leave a positive impact on the host community (see the next Sideline Story). For a comprehensive and revealing review of the industry's best sustainable event practices, consult *The Complete Guide to Greener Meetings and Events* by Samuel deBlanc Goldblatt (Hoboken, NJ: John Wiley & Sons, 2012).

Focusing and Managing Community Enthusiasm

Almost immediately after a city or neighborhood has been named the host for a prominent sports event, a swell of community pride can cause leaders and influential citizens to seek outlets for their enthusiasm. Each believes that he or she has a role to play, a contribution to make, and insightful ideas that need to be realized. Word can quickly spread of plans for fundraising dinners,

SIDELINE STORY

The Super Bowl Environmental Program

On-site construction for the National Football League's annual Super Bowl begins about a month before the game, broadening the capabilities of a state-of-the-art American football stadium to include facilities for 30 international broadcasts and work spaces for more than 5,000 visiting media. The stadium also becomes a theatrical venue for the year's most technically and operationally complex 12-minute entertainment extravaganzas, the Super Bowl Halftime Show, and its immediate surroundings a center for world-class hospitality at the 10,000-guest NFL Tailgate Party and 5,000 guests attending through the NFL On Location sports travel program. The stadium and all of the functional areas required to accommodate these activities are enveloped by a high-security perimeter featuring two-and-a-half miles of fencing covered with decorative fabric, punctuated by tents containing more than 130 airport terminal-quality magnetometers to process more than 90,000 fans, workers, and participants. The amount of recyclable and reusable material generated by four weeks of construction is quite significant, so much so that the NFL hired Jack Groh, an environmental consultant, to oversee the reclamation project. Groh works with NFL departments, broadcasters, contractors, and others to recycle plywood, cardboard shipping boxes, miles of fence fabric, hundreds of street banners and way-finding signage, metals, plastics—anything that can be removed from the waste stream and reused. Wallets, shopping bags, and other items have been made of Super Bowl fence wrap material. More than 90,000 pounds of prepared, but unserved, food is recovered from parties held throughout the host city and sent to local food pantries to help feed the hungry.

Groh's environmental program goes still further. A sports equipment reclamation project collects truckloads of outgrown sports gear representing all sports and provides these used items to children in needy neighborhoods. He also oversees an annual carbon mitigation project that, recognizing the greater emissions of hydrocarbons from charter buses and increased traffic, plants more than 2,000 trees in the local community that will both absorb carbon dioxide over the lifetime of these plants, and beautify a needing area or help to control erosion in an environmentally damaged ecosystem.

What can your event do to leave a positive environmental legacy in your community?

public rallies and parades, concerts and clinics, pickup games, and corporate challenges. As unbelievable as it may sound, the actual sports event organizer is frequently among the last to know about these preparations.

Dynamic, involved, and enthusiastic boosters of the community begin to formulate ambitious plans to exploit the event for largely positive and selfless purposes. Those allowed to expand and develop unchecked and without the active involvement of the organizer can drain human and financial resources away from the main event, creating a muddle of mixed marketing messages to fans and potential sponsors. If poorly realized, these additional community activities can even taint the core sports event in the eyes of some segments of the marketplace. Simply put, the more active, interested, and involved a community, the more likely there will be a tendency to want to do too much.

It is in the best interest of the event organizer to channel this enthusiasm, not curb or obstruct it. Consider yourself lucky when the community gets so behind an event that it begins to mobilize spontaneously to support and take best advantage of it. A community's ambivalence, in contrast, can make the road to event success much tougher. Reach out and communicate with these fervent and excited souls. Validate the community's desire to become involved and provide focus for their efforts. Demonstrate your USO (understanding stakeholders' objectives) sensitivities—show that you appreciate and support the community's desires and help them understand yours. Channel its members' energy so they are working in support of the actual objectives of both the community and the sports event, rather than what they think those objectives should be. Help organize key local supporters into an advisory board to provide you with counsel and insights into the needs of the community. Or, engage the most driven and energetic individuals into task forces known as organizing or host committees.

Advisory Boards

If it is early in the planning process, organizers can form an advisory board comprising influential businesspeople, community leaders, and other individuals whose expertise, contacts, and familiarity with the host city can prove invaluable to event operations. Forming an advisory board creates a legitimate, official group of counselors to the event organization who can be relied on for valuable advice and insightful recommendations, perspectives on the community, and past event history. Embracing and engaging these leaders can serve to preempt any unauthorized ad hoc group, no matter how well intentioned, from pursuing a separate agenda in the name of the event. Advisory boards are also useful when the event and its organizing entity have little recognition in the community or among potential sponsors. When it is vital to establish the legitimacy of the event and its organizer, the composition of the advisory board is of more significance than merely managing and monitoring community activities. Members selected for the board should be well regarded as individuals whose presence will immediately reinforce the importance and benefits of the sports event to the community—leaders who are trusted and respected by local government, residents, businesses, and sport. In short, the event advisory board is an organized collection of gatekeepers.

When approaching the people targeted for membership on the event's advisory board, be sure their respective reputations in the community are beyond reproach. The host city's sports commission can provide the insights into potential candidates who are necessary to protect the event's own reputation by association. Be sure the role of the advisory board is well understood by those who are requested to serve. It is a body of experts to give *advice*, not direction, and to provide *recommendations,* not requirements. When an organizer believes the formation of an advisory board would be beneficial to the smooth management and operation of an event, letters soliciting participation should be sent as soon as possible after confirmation of the host city. Explain the significance of the event to the local community and the reason for soliciting the recipient's participation. Allow approximately two weeks to pass before making calls to follow up on each invitee's level of interest. A sample letter outlining the roles and responsibilities of an advisory board member appears in Figure 10.4.

It is important to note that the advisory board invitation makes no reference to empowering members to make policy decisions or provide any form of service to the event other than attendance at a monthly update meeting. On the surface, the advisory board will serve as a source of wisdom, but its members' time investment and active engagement can provide influence when needed. As the event approaches, members may also represent a network of gatekeepers who can help overcome challenges on a case-by-case basis.

Dear (Insert Addressee Name Here):

As you may know, Township Village has been named the host city of the upcoming Major Stick Sports Tournament, an event that will attract 500 visiting athletes and up to 2,000 spectators to Civic Gymnasium. The Major Stick Sports Tournament is in its 12th year, and Township Village has committed to making next February's event the very best ever.

The tournament will provide area hotels with a beneficial mid-winter boost, and local businesses with a unique opportunity to meaningfully enhance their first quarter marketing campaigns. The event will also generate needed funds for the Civic Gymnasium renovation project scheduled for next summer.

The Major Stick Sports Tournament requested recommendations from the Township Village Sports Commission for potential candidates to the Major Stick Sports Tournament Advisory Board. I am pleased to cordially invite you to be a member of the advisory board.

Members will assist us in ensuring the success of the community's participation in the event. The board will convene for a brief breakfast meeting once monthly through next February to review our plans and progress, and to provide the members' insights, recommendations, and expert opinions on various topics of interest and impact to the people and businesses of Township Village. An agenda and minutes will be circulated to all members approximately three days prior to each meeting which will take place on the first Tuesday of each month.

As an expression of our gratitude, actively participating advisory board members will enjoy attendance and VIP privileges at the Major Stick Sports Tournament with our compliments.

Please indicate your acceptance of this invitation to participate as a valued member of the Major Stick Sports Tournament Advisory Board by signing and returning a copy of this letter in the stamped envelope provided. We look forward to the prospect of your involvement in this important event for Township Village.

Yours very truly,
Sports Event Organizer

Please check one:

☐ I accept appointment to the Major Stick Sports Tournament Advisory Board.
☐ I am unable to participate at this time.

Figure 10.4 Sample Advisory Board Invitation Letter

Organizing and Host Committees

Organizing and host committees differ from advisory boards in that, at their most effective, they are groups of individuals dedicated to providing time, work, and expertise on specific functions supporting an event (organizing committee) or fulfilling the city's responsibilities as host (host committee). An organizing committee should be directly responsible to the event organizer, while a host committee may report to a host agency such as the local sports commission or CVB. To use each to the best advantage of all concerned, organizing and host committees should function as fully integrated extensions of the event team.

Properly managed, organizing and host committees can contribute significantly to the overall event organization. At least one senior member of the sports event management team should attend every meeting of each committee to ensure the objectives of these primarily volunteer bodies and those of the overall event remain well coordinated. Unmanaged, organizing and host committees can run amok. A presence at committee meetings demonstrates the organizer's collaborative commitment to and oversight for the progress and quality of work being performed by these community participants. It should not be assumed that the responsibilities assigned and undertaken by a local, often ad hoc, event support organization will be successfully or sufficiently fulfilled without vigilant monitoring. The more an event relies on the work product of a committee, the more conscientious the organizer must be in maintaining an awareness of the committee's activities. It must be recognized that all-volunteer committees will require an investment of management time and energy and, later, expressions of appreciation such as event tickets, party invitations, and acknowledgment gifts. Organizing and host committees for major events may even require full-time professional staff and a budget to finance their operations. In such cases, the financial obligation is usually the responsibility of the host city. In addition, as sports event committees must often supplement their budgets by soliciting sponsorships and donations, the organizer must communicate strict guidelines outlining how they may raise funds and from whom, in order to avoid instances in which the organizer and the committee compete for the same needed corporate infusion of funds. Therefore, before forming or requesting the formation of a host or organizing committee, sports event organizers should be completely certain that the need for such support truly warrants its creation.

Identify the roles and responsibilities expected of the group, and create an organization plan that defines all reporting relationships. Be sure the sports event organizer is always indicated as the overall authority for the effort, with at least a dotted-line relationship with host committees that report directly to the local government. Although the specific mission of an organizing or host committee will differ from one event to the next, Figure 10.5 lists a number of the most common sports event support areas of responsibility for such committees. This should by no means imply that every committee formed must undertake every role listed, or that other appropriate functions cannot be added to the list.

Notice that each of the functions presented in Figure 10.5 can be undertaken directly by event staff that may already be under the organizer's immediate control. Even so, the formation of a committee is an attractive option when the event budget is insufficient to allow the organizer to contract and pay full-time professionals to manage such functions. Also, these support organizations are frequently formed when the scale of the program is so large or so dependent on local resources that some division of labor between an out-of-town organizer and a local body provides significant cost and management efficiencies. In such cases, committees are often staffed with a combination of experienced, paid event professionals and motivated volunteers. Regardless, organizers are well advised to maintain close control over the activities of their supportive committees to ensure they actually provide what they are charged to contribute and with the attention to detail, quality, and timeliness the organizer would expect of his or her own staff.

Host cities should resist the temptation to appoint representatives to the host or organizing committee for the sake of politics or expedience. The best committee is the smallest committee, and any participant who cannot provide wisdom, work, or experienced perspective to the process will drain precious time and resources, and sap morale from those who will invest their time and talents more fully. A committee chairperson should be appointed, one who enjoys the respect of the community, who can provide leadership and direction, and who can maintain constant communication with both the members and the event organizer. The structure of the membership into functional groups should generally mirror the event organization. The committee chairperson should communicate most regularly with the event director. Subcommittee heads (examples noted

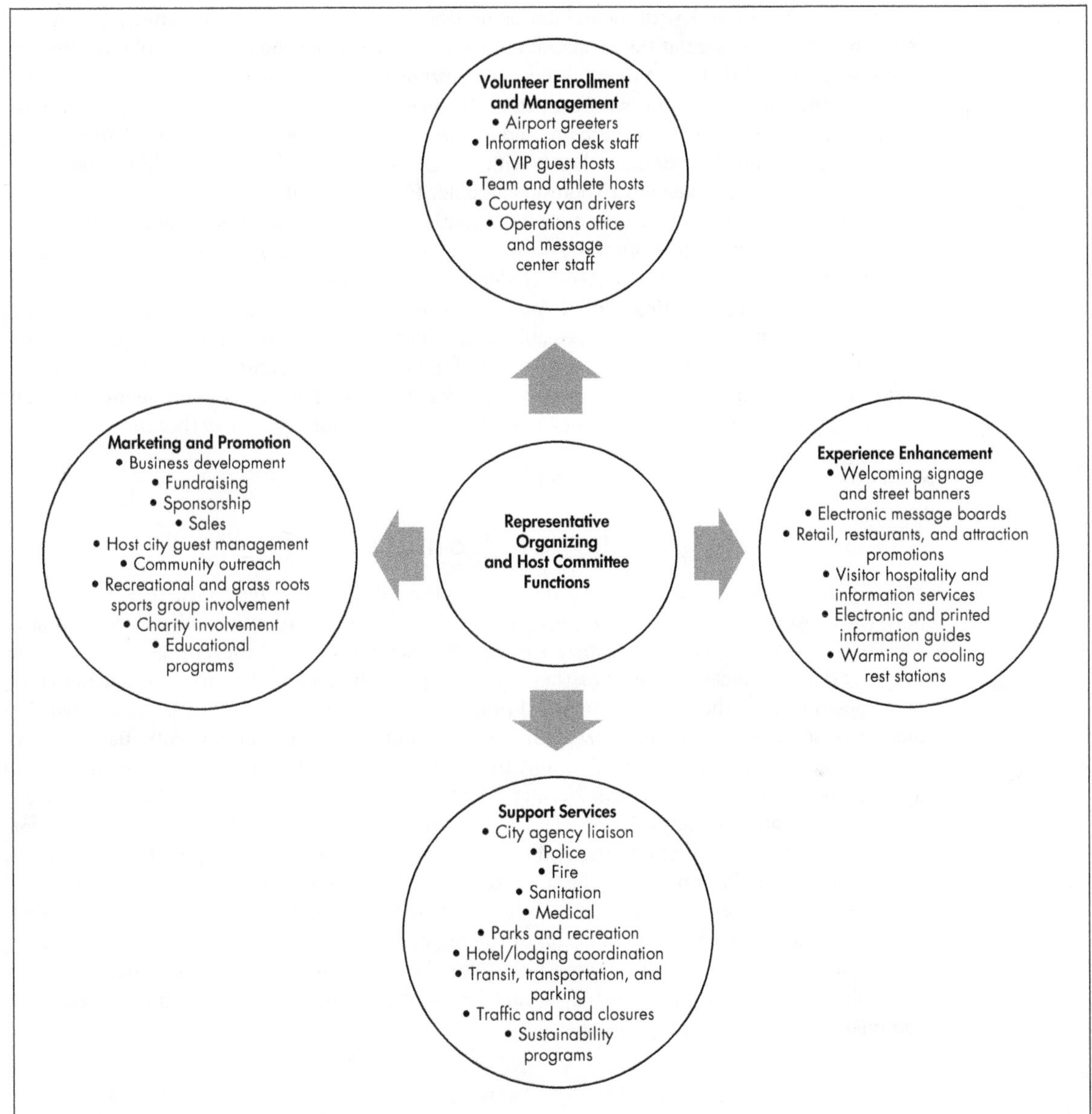

Figure 10.5 Representative Organizing and Host Committee Functions

in bold type in Figure 10.5) should report their progress to the committee chairperson at monthly meetings, but can also work closely with the event organizer's department heads whose operational responsibilities are most similar to their own. Although additional committee members may report to the subcommittee heads, it is recommended that the monthly or semimonthly update meetings be limited to the chairperson and subcommittee heads in the interest of streamlining the meeting agenda and maintaining efficiency. Subcommittee heads should hold subsequent regular sessions with those tasked to work with them, filtering updates down from the last committee meeting and receiving input to present at the next. Committee membership may be composed of city officials, business leaders, and other talented, influential citizens of the community whose common interest lies in the improvement or maintenance of the region's quality of life, and with a proven track record of contributing their time, energy, and talents to similar endeavors. The top positions (e.g., the chairperson and subcommittee heads with the greatest responsibilities) should be composed of the highest-level gatekeepers, wherever possible. Figure 10.6 illustrates some of the sources where organizers and host cities can turn for potential organizing committee members.

As discussed earlier, it is often the host city, sports commission, or CVB that will undertake the task of forming a host committee in order to help execute the specific responsibilities to a sports event without diverting a disproportionate share of city resources from their year-long missions. Thus, it is sometimes impossible or less desirable to prevent political appointments to the host committee. However, it is important for sports event organizers to make clear to the host city that, in order to truly support the objectives of both parties, the committee must be well integrated into the event team and must remain in close communication together throughout the planning process.

Local Promoters

When a sports event organizer's offices are located far from the host city, it is sometimes practical to work with a local event promoter to execute specific functions of the event operations and/or marketing plan. Organizers pursuing this option should exercise as much care in the selection of a local promoter as they would in pursuing a candidate for a senior management position with their own company. From the public's perspective, the promoter will be indistinguishable from the organizer. His or her reputation in the community, past history, and management style must complement that of the organizer to ensure that both they and, by inference, the event team will be viewed positively by all stakeholders. Well-connected promoters can be most helpful in marketing and selling event tickets, procuring local labor for event setup, operation, dismantling and other logistics, and providing insights into local politics and resources. Promoters may be hired on a fee basis and, if responsible for managing any cost areas, should be provided with a budget that by formal agreement may not be exceeded without the advance written permission of the organizer. If the promoter is solely responsible for the promotion and sale of tickets, then he or she may also be retained on a flat fee or on a fee-plus-bonus basis for achieving certain levels of paid attendance, or remunerated on a commission-per-ticket-sold premise.

Moving Forward

The sports event organization is now in place, and the enthusiasm of the community is focused constructively, via promotional partnerships, and on building mutually beneficial business opportunities. Advisory boards and committees of gatekeepers and hard-working volunteers are committed to the success of the community and the sports event to which they are about to play host. Costs are under control, marketing plans are in place, and sponsors are being signed. The production schedule shows the time remaining is growing short. Event day is approaching, and there is still much left to do.

Position	Resource
Committee Chairperson	Deputy mayor
	City council representative
	Major local real estate owner or developer
	President of local business concern
	General manager of local television or radio station
	Senior partner of local law firm
	Local business personality
Volunteer Enrollment and Management	Sports commission representative
	Convention and visitors bureau representative
	Sports team fan or booster club president
	Community sports program representative
	Community services manager for a local company (preferably a sponsor)
	Representative of an association with a community services mission (e.g., Rotary, Kiwanis, Lions)
Experience Enhancement	Creative director of local advertising agency
	Senior manager of local architectural firm
	Senior manager of an advertising firm
	General manager of local restaurant or attraction
	Senior manager of local chamber of commerce
Support Services	City director of special events
	City director of communications or marketing
	Police department community affairs officer
	Parks and recreation department manager
	Transit authority public affairs manager
	Local hotel general manager
Marketing and Promotion	Sports commission representative
	Convention and visitors bureau representative
	City director of communications or marketing
	Director of development for local charity (when the event benefits the charity)
	Senior manager of local chamber of commerce, business improvement district, or similar group
	Senior account executive of local public relations firm

Figure 10.6 Organizing and Host Committee Resources

Post-Play Analysis

Sports events are often staged in a vacuum, with little or no active participation on the part of local government, businesses, or groups that routinely operate in the interest of community service. Many of these sectors of the community recognize that sports events can provide powerful quality-of-life and economic benefits to their region, so organizers who have not engaged the local community on some level may be overlooking a valuable, motivated resource. Organizers should identify the *gatekeepers,* the influential civic, business, and neighborhood leaders who can provide intelligence on the perceptions of the local market and expedite requests to and approvals by city agencies and community partners.

Business development groups, such as chambers of commerce, neighborhood business partnerships, restaurant associations, and others, can provide excellent sources of exposure and supportive cross-promotions. Consider how to involve often-overlooked neighbors, such as lower-income communities, disadvantaged youth, and those with special needs, in the event. Be sensitive to the local environment and embrace sustainable event practices to recover, recycle, and redistribute materials that would otherwise enter the waste stream.

Respected members of the community who share an interest in the success of both the sports event and the host city may be fashioned into an advisory board to provide advice and counsel to the organizer. Task forces composed of local resources, known as organizing and host committees, can provide counsel, work, and accountability to a sports event organizer. The activities and responsibilities of these committees are overseen by a chairperson or executive director and must be continually monitored by the event organizer to ensure completion to desired standards.

Coach's Clipboard

1. Identify the gatekeepers in your local community who can prove helpful in planning and organizing a meet of visiting amateur swimmers. What obstacles to staging the tournament could be presented during planning and how would one or more gatekeepers help to advise and overcome them?
2. What organizations would you engage to develop cross-promotions and mutually advantageous exposure opportunities for the event above? How would they help promote the event and what would those business partners expect in return? What costs might be incurred by the event budget in activating these programs?
3. How would you apply best sustainability practices at the swim meet? What materials can be recovered and either recycled or reused? How else can you positively affect the quality of life and the environment before, during, and after the event?
4. How would you reach out to involve lower-income families, at-risk youth, and the mentally and physically challenged in the event? Presuming entrance to the meet is free, what value can you provide to these sectors of the community that will enhance their experience and further the objectives of the city and the event?

PLAY 11

Accommodating and Managing Guests

"It is not the critic who counts; not the man who points out how the strong man stumbled, or where the doer of deeds could have done them better. The credit belongs to the man who is actually in the arena."

—*Theodore Roosevelt, 26th President of the United States (1858–1919)*

This play will help you to:

- Develop your event's ticket sales strategy.
- Manage your event's guests and ticket buyers.
- Provide the best and most welcoming experience for your fans.
- Work most efficiently and effectively with host hotels.

Introduction

All the plans are in place; now it's time to manage and execute the event. During this period, event organizers put their production and marketing plans into action. "The devil is in the details," it has been said, and this is never more true than in the planning and execution of sports events. It is here that the needs of the events vary most. Every event requires clear objectives, a budget, a host venue and production schedule, a marketing plan, and the support of sponsors and other promotional partners. Some require the organizer to possess an understanding of the dynamics of ticket sales, the basics of broadcasting, and the tenets of technical production. Others require an understanding of the logistical elements of managing participating athletes and incoming guests and fans, still others the fundamentals of working with the hotels that will be employed to provide event offices, accommodations, and hospitality.

Although the remaining "plays" present specialized subject matter that may be more pertinent to some organizers than to others, a working familiarity with all areas of sports event planning is strongly recommended for all.

SIDELINE STORY

The Box Office's Virtual Revolution

Managing audiences at any sports, leisure, or entertainment facility has involved the use of tickets for centuries. For most of that time, virtually all transactions took place at the theater, arena, or stadium box office, which takes its name from the wall of cubby boxes that ticket managers used to keep tickets from different shows, games, or events organized and separated. Imagine the number of cubbies that Major League Baseball stadium box offices used to need to organize 50,000 tickets for 81 regular season home games!

In the late 1960s, computerized ticketing was introduced, but came into common use slowly and selectively at sports venues. Large off-premises computers began maintaining ticket inventories and slow, bulky printers rendered tickets on demand at box offices, as well as by telephone and, for the first time, at remote ticket-purchasing locations. Often, a combination of *hard tickets,* those printed tickets kept in inventory by box offices and computerized tickets released only for limited and predetermined seating locations, were in use simultaneously, and ushers (like a young Supovitz) encountered duplicated tickets—one hard ticket and one computer-generated ticket—and disgruntled ticket holders on a fairly regular basis.

Eventually, computer-generated tickets delivered by high-speed printers and using a single common inventory as those purchased off-site to eliminate duplications replaced the cubbies at stadium and arena box offices. Today, non-computer-printed tickets are used for low-budget events and as commemorative pieces for season tickets and high-priced sports events as much for anti-counterfeiting security measures. Remember that tickets can be very special to the people who buy them—even low-budget sports events can make a ticket a commemorative item using special fonts, simple artwork, or any design device that makes it a special keepsake, especially for the friends and families of the participants.

Computerized ticketing continues to evolve to the benefit of buyers and organizers. Tickets can be purchased from home computers, tablets, and mobile devices and either printed at home, or sent as a graphics file to a mobile phone suitable for scanning at the stadium gate. They can even be sold or traded through team sites and secondary ticket agencies such as Ticketmaster's Ticket Exchange, Stub Hub, and eBay, and transferred from one mobile device to another.

Although many experienced box office directors can amazingly and accurately count tickets by listening to the sound of a stack of tickets riffling between their fingers, we expect that the number of transactions using an actual paper ticket will continue to diminish steadily.

Selling Tickets

Sports event organizers should view tickets as monetary instruments. The ticket, whether printed on paper or displayed in electronic form on a digital device, represents value received by the purchaser in exchange for cash, so steps should be taken to protect the organizer and buyer against the possibility of loss, theft, or counterfeiting by unscrupulous opportunists. For major events, tickets should be generated only as needed by a computerized ticketing service or printed by an experienced, bonded ticket supplier such as Consolidated Printing, Mercury Ticketing, or Weldon Williams and Lick. Once tickets are received, every ticket should be counted to ensure the number ordered matches the exact number received. Tickets with specific seat locations or sections should also be checked for accuracy against the seating manifest, a list of every individual seat as defined by section, row, and seat number. (It is also recommended that the host facility be inspected on a seat-by-seat basis prior to selling tickets to ensure the manifest reflects the current physical reality of the venue.) Until sold, printed tickets should be stored in a secure location such as a bank vault or safe.

Computer-generated tickets do not exist in physical form until printed and, as such, require the same anti-theft measures prior to sale. They may, however, be more prone to the possibility of counterfeiting. The pervasiveness and quality of design and drawing software and inexpensive color printing can create an illegal market for phony tickets that can endanger the financial viability of an event and may put unsuspecting purchasers at risk of being barred admission when the counterfeits are detected. Anti-counterfeiting devices for printed (or hard) tickets that make it easy for organizers to detect a bogus ticket include such techniques as the application of holographic stickers, and the use of special security paper during the printing process (e.g., the inclusion of metallic threads, watermarks, and images viewable only under ultra-violet light). The most prevalent deterrents to counterfeit tickets, whether hard or electronic, have been the use of barcodes on tickets, commonly employed by year-round sports facilities and other venues that use laser scanners to read printed bar codes on tickets at their entrances. Once a unique bar code has been scanned by a reader device, no other ticket with the same or an invalid code will be permitted admission. Although no anti-counterfeiting measure can be completely effective against sufficiently motivated persons with criminal intent and any ticketing system will always have its flaws to overcome, "bar codes have streamlined the whole process," says Turnstyles Ticketing co-CEO Chris Hutson. "Anyone responsible for managing tickets can turn a bar code on or off. If a ticket is lost, stolen, or somehow duplicated, the bar code can simply be canceled, making the ticket useless. For a series of events, such as a tournament or playoff round, ticket bar codes can be activated on a round-by-round basis, which is very efficient and easy for an event and venue."

Ticket Types and Admission Policies

There are two basic types of ticket policies—reserved seating and general admission. Reserved seats guarantee the purchasers specific seat locations. Some sports events, most notably those held in professional sports arenas and stadiums, sell virtually their entire inventory as reserved seat tickets, regardless of price level. General admission (GA) tickets, in contrast, enable the purchasers to occupy any available seat on a first-come, first-served basis. GA tickets may be scaled like reserved seat tickets (see Play 3), with different prices for access to specific sections or levels. They are also sold for events during which the audience moves around the site or views the event from standing locations rather than occupying a seat. Because GA tickets only guarantee admittance, and not necessarily a specific spot from which to enjoy the program, managers of facilities hosting sports events that utilize this policy should be prepared for the formation of queues before the doors open, as audiences holding these tickets arrive early to claim the best possible seats or viewing locations. Some events offer both reserved and GA sections, providing for those who prefer the convenience of having a specific seat waiting for them when they arrive, usually at a premium price, and enabling others who do not mind planning for an earlier arrival to realize some economies at the sports event. Pursuing a GA seating policy can increase the risk of injuries, particularly if the organizer expects a potential crush of fans racing for the best seats when the venue's doors first open. For this reason, general admission ticketing is not recommended for professional or large-scale sports events. Work with your risk management specialist to determine whether this policy will potentially raise your insurance premiums or increase the likelihood of injuries (see Play 14).

When to Begin Selling Tickets

Regardless of the nature of sports event, whether it is an exhibition game, themed game night, skills competition, track meet, opening ceremonies, fundraising dinner, or a player draft, selling or distributing tickets in advance is an absolute must. Relying primarily on tickets sold as fans arrive on event day, also known as "walk-up" business, can put the organizer at serious financial risk. First, advance sales provide cash flow to cover pre-event expenses and deposits. The funds represented by walk-up ticket sales are not available before the day of the event. Second, advance sales reduce the potentially devastating effects of event-day weather conditions. Attendance is guaranteed by tickets sold in advance if atmospheric conditions threaten, but do not ultimately affect, event-day operations. Fans without tickets, however, have the total freedom to decide whether to attend on event day, based on either a whim and/or concern about impending weather conditions. Advance ticket holders have invested their money and will receive no refund unless the event is completely canceled, so, even if there is a small chance the sports event will go on, they will be far more likely to make the effort to be there.

Creating a sense of urgency is the key to generating advance ticket sales. You want fans to think: "If I do not get my tickets right away. . .

- "I will miss out on attending at all because tickets may be sold out later."
- "I will not get the best seats, which could diminish my enjoyment of the event." (A reserved seat policy must be in place to provide ticket buyers with the availability and choice of best seats.)
- "I won't receive an offered premium item or some opportunity available solely to advance purchasers, or only for a limited time."

The "when" of putting tickets on sale is inextricably linked to the "how" to put tickets on sale. You must have enough time to inform the public about the event and communicate the availability of tickets to potential buyers. Then you have to make it easy and convenient for them to make their purchase. You must leave yourself sufficient time to put the word out, let it permeate around the market, and have enough time remaining for them to order or purchase and receive their tickets. You also must give yourself enough time to react to the marketplace with new sales strategies should your initial marketing campaign produce fewer sales than expected.

A sample ticket sales timeline for a hypothetical event scheduled for mid-June is illustrated in Figure 11.1. Before a single sale can be made, a ticket manifest must be finalized. The manifest lists every possible seat location or ticket number that can be sold, including standing room, accessible seats, and seats identified as having obstructed views. It should also include every location that normally exists, but may ultimately be removed from sale because of total obstruction, removal for the installation of television cameras, scoreboards, other operational elements, or any other possible reason that a seat is not expected to be salable. These are known as "seat kills," and it is, of course, preferable to identify them so they may be removed from the manifest of tickets available for public sale well before the first ticket is sold. (Remember that if the tickets for killed seats are included in the event's gross potential, their removal from sale will represent an expense against the budget.) Be ready to have the tickets for killed seat locations available anyway, just in case plans later change (e.g., camera positions are shifted) and those seats, as a consequence, end up unaffected by obstructions. A best guest-service practice to follow is to have a small number of ticket locations not available for sale put aside to address any complaints or to solve thorny issues raised by purchaser. This will enable staff to relocate them to a more desirable area.

Note that in the hypothetical example given in Figure 11.1, the primary public campaign begins on April 1, approximately 10 weeks prior to the event. Four weeks before this date, an offer will be made to those listed in a database of past ticket buyers, a sponsor's customers, staff, and volunteers, presumably the most loyal and likely purchasers. This offer can reward your best customers and enhance a valued promotional partnership with an opportunity to purchase preferred seat locations ahead of the public sale date. Communicate urgency by establishing a reasonable deadline for response and leave your ticketing staff sufficient time to process orders between the deadline and the first day of public sales. It is important to keep in mind when this kind of advance accommodation is offered, it is wise not to sell all of the best seats to the presale database. It will be perceived as deceptive and unfair if the only seats available to the very first public ticket buyers are in less than prime locations. A common and fair practice as applied to this sample event would be to divide the tickets available so that at least some portion of the best available seats will still be available to the public on April 15.

Just as important as not setting the "on sale" date too late (i.e., too close to the date of the event) is to not promote tickets sales too early. Events with unusually strong demand for tickets, such as the Olympic Games, college and professional championship series (e.g., bowls, tournaments, etc.), and major league all-star contests, may not require adherence to this rule. Organizers

February 1	Inspect facility and finalize ticket manifest
March 1	Past-year ticket buyers, sponsor's customers, staff and volunteers receive offer (via e-mail, website, text, tweet, fax, and/or mail) for advance tickets purchase before general public
March 22	Response deadline for past-year ticket buyers
April 1	Marketing and communication campaign begins to promote public ticket sales
April 15	Public ticket sales begin
May 23	Sponsor ticket promotions and second wave marketing campaign (if necessary) begin
June 15	Event day

Figure 11.1 Sample Ticket Sales Timeline

for these uniquely successful events often make tickets available six, eight, in some cases even 10 months or more in advance. For most sports events, however, it is important to time the initial public sale just right. Identifying exactly when that should be will vary depending on the nature and date of the event. Note that first day of public sales for this hypothetical event is in the early spring (April 15). In this case, the organizer feels that the best time to begin selling a warm-weather event is when potential ticket buyers first start thinking about the imminent approach of warmer weather. Attempting to sell the public a far-off, outdoor, warm weather event in the coldest days of winter, when sports fans are in the midst of enjoying indoor and more rugged outdoor events, may prove to be a wasted effort. The database of past purchasers, though, can be approached by direct mail, e-mail, and social media campaigns at an earlier time. Their loyalty to the sport and strong, positive memories of past events make them more likely to be future purchasers and perhaps more motivated to procure their tickets ahead of the public rush. Customers and employees of participating sponsors represent another targeted audience who can be reached and are likely to be responsive to such a promotional benefit in advance. In our hypothetical example, these groups are granted a three week window to order their tickets in advance. Although past purchasers and sponsor customers may be given more time to respond, if desired, a relatively short advance sale opportunity is recommended, again to increase the sense of urgency. The longer a potential buyer is given to make his or her decision, the more likely the decision will be delayed or, possibly, forgotten completely.

How to Sell Tickets

As previously mentioned, it is essential to make it easy and convenient for potential buyers to purchase their tickets, and to encourage them to act immediately. Today's sports event audiences have become accustomed to purchasing event tickets using any one of several methods, from using the convenience of the Internet to traveling to a venue's box office. If a fan happens to be attending other events held in the same venue, or lives or works nearby, the box office can be an opportune option. However, event attendees have become quite comfortable with the Internet through desktop, tablets, and mobile devices and such conveniences as the ability to consult seating diagrams to find best available locations at different price levels, to securely use a credit card for ticket purchases, to confirm the purchase by printing or digitally saving tickets to their mobile device, and to obtain up-to-date event information, making the Internet a preferred and convenient ticket-purchasing destination.

A similar procedure is suggested for ticket sales to grassroots and community sports events that will be held in temporary facilities or those that maintain no permanent box office. A single, reliably available location with regular business hours should be designated for ticket sales. For example, a local merchant's retail store can be selected and promoted for this purpose. Even if the business owner makes no direct profit from ticket sales, the store traffic created by the sports event purchasers, and resulting incremental sales of the storeowner's retail products, can provide a strong incentive to participate as the event "box office." Additionally, ticket sales may be promoted on banners and posters displayed at the retailer's store, increasing exposure and sales for the sports event to their existing shoppers. This option is highly preferable to selling tickets for community sports events out of someone's home, as inconsistent hours of availability will reduce convenience for the potential buyer.

For events taking place at permanent sports facilities, sports fans routinely expect and demand instant access to tickets at the time they see the first advertisement or read the first announcement, lest their response to the call to action be delayed or forgotten. These venues offer or require use of their computerized ticket services, such as Ticketmaster, Tickets.com, or a similar system. The fees for transactions using these services are typically shared between the seller-organizer and purchaser, and are usually defined in the facility lease agreement (see Play 4).

These powerful services also provide event promoters the ability to offer ticket sales over the telephone, at remote locations throughout the host city, as well as via the Internet from anywhere in the world. It is wise to include the telephone number and website address for the ticket service in every event advertisement, promotional coupon, and poster, and to provide links from the event organizer's website directly to the ticket service's sales page.

Events that will be held in facilities with no permanent box office can attempt to negotiate an agreement with the dominant ticket services mentioned above to sell their tickets. Alternatively, you can take advantage of independent web ticketing services and software to manage your own electronic database of ticket inventory, provide fans with a convenient on-line mechanism to purchase their tickets, and maintain access to up-to-the-minute sales reports. Organizers may investigate the software and services offered by companies such as Tix.com, InHouse Ticketing, Vendini, Blackbaud, and Extremetix, among others.

Tickets ordered by phone or via the Internet, whether through an event facility's permanent system or a contracted independent operation, can be delivered using print-at-home services or standard mail at the purchaser's preference upon completion of the transaction. Print-at-home has become a popular option as it provides customers the convenience of instant access to their tickets. This method also greatly reduces the organizer's costs of handling and shipping tickets. If insufficient time remains between the date of purchase and the day of the event to be confident that tickets will be received in time (usually any less than two weeks), they may be printed by the service and left at the venue's "Will Call" window or at the organizer's "Guest Services" desk on event day. If tickets are picked up on site, or at the event's offices, it is strongly suggested they be transferred to the buyer only after presentation of a government-issued photo identification card such as a driver's license, and a matching signature to guard against possible fraud. Business cards should not be accepted as proof of identification.

Mobile technology is also being leveraged as a method of ticket transmission and access into events. Upon purchasing tickets, customers may choose to have their tickets sent to them digitally via email or link. In this instance, the customer has the ability to produce the ticket on his or her mobile device for presentation upon entry into the event. Each digital ticket is marked with a unique registration key or barcode for security and authenticity purposes. For this system to be utilized, an event venue must be properly equipped with compatible software and hardware to allow ticket takers to accurately confirm that the ticket is genuine and has not previously been used. This method has become popular because it provides a convenient transfer of the ticket with the added benefit of secure storage within one's mobile device.

Ticket Brokers

Ticket brokers essentially resell tickets they purchase from the organizer, the box office, or from other buyers. The laws governing acceptable business practices of ticket brokers and the maximum fees they may legally charge the public vary widely from one local government to the other. Some may be officially authorized to sell event tickets by the organizer, but by far most operate outside any chain of direct responsibility. Many brokers maintain websites that list all of the events for which they offer tickets, procured from a variety of sources. Organizers of successful sports events are constantly amazed at the extravagant prices brokers charge for tickets, particularly once the event is officially sold out. As long as the broker does not use the logo, proprietary artwork, or any other intellectual property of the event, there is usually nothing most organizers can do about what many perceive as overly inflated ticket prices. At the same time, the organizer, having had no direct role in the transaction between the broker and the purchaser, bears no responsibility beyond the face value of the ticket. Therefore, if refunds are necessary for any reason, typically only the face value of the ticket need be recompensed. Brokers are generally honest at least to the extent that the tickets they resell are genuine. There are, however, counterfeiters masquerading as ticket brokers that can perpetrate fraud against both the buyer and organizer. The organizer has no obligation to accept counterfeit tickets obtained from such sources and should encourage those who purchased them to seek the assistance of local law enforcement.

Digital services like StubHub have created a secure forum for resellers and second-hand buyers to do business. These "secondary ticketing services" have become popular by providing an expedient transaction environment, limiting and, in some cases, guaranteeing against illegal selling practices, and creating a structured marketplace to help set market prices. The entities selling tickets on these digital marketplaces range from single sellers to large-scale brokers. Businesses of this kind provide an open commercial space in return for commissions on sales and small fees charged to the purchaser and/or seller. These services typically do all of the work required in transferring the tickets between parties, as well. In addition, an event can sponsor secondary market sales through its own digital platform in order to take advantage of the revenue it may lose on the second-hand market. This practice has caught on with major professional leagues and teams, as the digital marketplace has become a more common and trusted consumer ecosystem.

Distribution of Tickets to Free Sports Events

Many sports events that embrace a free admission policy may still desire to distribute tickets in advance. Tickets serve as convenient reminders of the event's date and time, and can easily be slipped into wallets and displayed under kitchen magnets. The ticket policy for a free sports event is usually best offered on a general admission basis; reserved seats are not recommended. Free tickets are not usually redeemed at the same rate as priced tickets, as the bearer has exchanged no money or other value for its use. Therefore, organizers will often distribute as many as two or three times the number of free tickets as can normally be accommodated at the host facility in hopes of filling it with spectators. This is not possible with reserved seats. It is a near certainty that a reserved seat ticket policy for a free event would result in a significant and noticeable number of empty seats. The exact multiple of free general admission tickets that is advisable to distribute for a given event should be based on past history, the attractiveness of the event to the public, and the experienced opinions of the facility manager, organizer, and other trusted stakeholders.

Regardless of the number distributed, it is strongly suggested that all tickets include a disclaimer to avoid overfilling of the venue, such as: "This ticket is valid for admission on a first-come, first-served basis. The organizer and facility reserve the exclusive right to delay or deny admission based on crowding and concerns for public safety." In order to guard against overcapacity and to offer admission to fans not holding advance tickets if space permits, it is further suggested that tickets include an advisory that requires arrival at the event at least 30 minutes before it begins. Thus, late-arriving ticket holders may be denied entry if absolutely necessary to maintain safe conditions, while permitting the organizer the option of admitting non-ticket-holding fans in the final minutes leading up the event in order to fill empty seats. Depending on the anticipated popularity of the event, be prepared for an early-arriving crowd for any event admitting fans on a first-come, first-served basis, whether paid or free. Set up organized queue lines in advance, and have security and guest services personnel (i.e., people who can provide information and direction, and communicate with the organizer if necessary) arrive sufficiently early to manage any building crowd. If possible, have your facility and staff ready for a slightly earlier gate-opening time than published for the safety and convenience of your fans.

Free tickets may be distributed in all of the same ways that promotional material and discount coupons are provided to the community to encourage ticket sales. Point-of-purchase displays in area stores, website offers, and print-your-own tickets over the Internet are particularly effective ways of dispensing free tickets into the marketplace.

Packaging Tickets

Organizers marketing sports events that are held over a series of days should consider creating packages containing tickets for multiple matches. Packages can include admission for the most attractive event day (e.g., the final round of a tournament) and for one or more dates that are expected to be less popular. This practice can increase ticket revenues and encourage improved attendance during times that might otherwise be expected to draw smaller crowds. Consider selling multiday tickets ahead of the public offer for individual ticket sales to create urgency and provide the incentive of better seats for those purchasing packages.

For both one-day and multiple-day events that draw fans from outside the host area, packages may be created that provide value or one-stop shopping for their convenience. Consider

SIDELINE STORY

NFL On Location

Sports travel packagers have offered fans one-stop-shop opportunities to visit host cities and attend sports events for many years. Most packages are offered by companies that have expanded their core businesses by combining two industries—the proven travel package business familiar to most tourists and the burgeoning broker/secondary ticket business.

In 2005, the National Football League introduced NFL On Location, its own branded and internally managed sports travel business. The program, initially established as a business-to-business service, offered packages to companies hosting guests at Super Bowl XL in Detroit's Ford Field, including a hard-to-get game ticket, a four-night hotel stay, a pregame party across the street from the stadium at Comerica Park, merchandise, and other benefits. Package prices were scaled on the basis of seat location, the quality of the hotel room, and other factors, as well as the pricing established by the many other sports travel businesses already in operation and offering packages to the same event. Companies from across the United States purchased in excess of 900 packages, generally in increments of 20 or more per purchase, in NFL On Location's first year of operation.

In the ensuing seasons, fans hearing about NFL On Location wanted access to the same opportunities as corporations, though perhaps only two or four packages at a time. The NFL responded by making a version of the program available for individual sale. Additionally, many companies and fans wanted to be able to shop for their own accommodations, and locally based purchasers did not need hotel rooms. Game-day packages were created to respond to this need, retaining many of the other benefits and inclusions and lowering the overall cost. Within five years, the number of NFL On Location packages sold for the Super Bowl more than quadrupled, and, today, the program provides sports travel packages for several other league events, including the NFL Draft and the NFL International Series games.

Chances are, your events are smaller or less well-known than the Super Bowl. If you have fans or guests coming from out of town to attend or participate, you have a chance to generate revenues by packaging conveniences with your event tickets. After all, fans have to stay somewhere, eat, park their cars, or take home a remembrance. What can you add to the event ticket that can provide value and convenience to the purchaser, and profit for your organization?

a package price that includes a hotel stay in a property participating as a sponsor or marketing partner, a pre-event party, or postevent experience. (It is to the benefit of the hotel to offer event packages through its own database and marketing campaigns, as well, helping to extend the organizer's marketing campaign and filling the property's inventory of guest rooms. Be sure the hotel takes advantage of this opportunity.) Other features such as preferred parking at the host facility, athlete or alumni meet-and-greets, event merchandise, and concession food vouchers can be included, as well.

Creating and scaling ticket packages are similar to building sponsorship deals. Be sure that the fulfillment costs (e.g., the cost of tickets, hotel rooms, parties, food, merchandise, etc.) are fully covered by the package price, and add a reasonable profit margin for added revenues. For events that do not bring many fans from out of town, packages need not include hotel rooms, of course. Develop an "event-day package" that combines some of other elements mentioned, and others, to create a menu that provides value to the purchaser, and an attractive, exciting and convenient way to enjoy your event.

Losing Sleep 101—What to Do if Tickets Are Not Selling

Your revenue budget is dependent on ticket sales. A well-placed advertisement has already appeared in the local newspaper, press releases have been distributed to the media to announce the on-sale date, e-mail offers have been sent to your best customers, and the website highlights all relevant information. Yet, you are frustrated that advance sales are slower than expected. Is it time to start panicking? Use the decision tree in Figure 11.2 to plan your most appropriate response.

Two courses of action—the reduction of seating inventory and the wide distribution of complimentary tickets, also known as "papering the house"—are scenarios that should be employed after all marketing efforts have failed and the time remaining to sell tickets grows short. Complimentary tickets can still have a small positive effect on the net income of the event (or, perhaps due to disappointing sales, slightly reduce the net loss) through sales of merchandise and concessions, but will have the greatest effect on perception and public opinion. Simply put, they serve to make the audience appear larger and the popularity of the event greater. The practice of adjusting the reserved seat sales policy to skip every alternate row in the final days before the event [5c in Figure 11.2] can also make the audience appear larger.

Reduction of Inventory

If large numbers of tickets are expected to remain unsold, organizers may decide to reduce the quantity of empty seats by closing off less desirable seating sections. This enables the organizer to save a small amount of money on the house staff (e.g., ushers, security, guest services staff, cleaning) that would have to service the area on event day. Guests who have purchased tickets in those locations may be moved to unsold seats in higher priced sections, generally without any complaint from the public.

Events that are broadcast on television are usually seen from one primary direction. Try to fill the areas the television cameras will be facing first. If the event budget permits, cover empty seating sections with fabric or banners containing event artwork or perhaps a sponsor logo to turn a potential eyesore into pleasing décor and/or additional revenue. Better still, if seats are portable, consider physically removing selected rows and/or sections entirely.

Use this decision tree to plan your response to slow ticket sales. This model presumes that ticket prices are set at reasonable levels and are available to the public by convenient means. It also assumes that advertising and publicity campaigns, as well as the ticket sales date, were not set unreasonably early.

1. Is there still enough time left to sell the remaining tickets? *(YES—go to [**1a**] and [**2**]; NO—go to [**5**])*
   - **[1a.]** Did another sports or entertainment event compete for the fan's disposable income the week your ads were placed? *(YES—go to [**1d**]; NO—go to [**1b**]*
   - **[1b.]** Was the public preoccupied by a big news story the week tickets went on sale that diverted attention away from the offer? *(YES—go to [**1d**]; NO—go to [**1c**]*
   - **[1c.]** Does the current ad have a clear "call to action," communicate urgency to buy, have all pertinent information, and a convenient response mechanism for purchase? *(YES—go to [**1d**]; NO—go to [**1g**])*
   - **[1d.]** Is there more than one additional placement of the ad scheduled? *(YES—go to [**1e**]; NO—go to [**1f**])*
   - **[1e.]** **Action:** Consider running the ad again, or extending the campaign, and go to [**4**].
   - **[1f.]** Is the ad placed in print, radio, television, and/or the Internet in places, at times and on programming the event's target audience will be expected to see it? *(YES—go to [**2**]; NO—go to [**1h**])*
   - **[1g.]** **Action:** Make adjustments in the ad and buy additional space and/or time, and go to [**2**].
   - **[1h.]** **Action:** Consider purchasing additional advertising space and/or time in the media most likely to be read, heard, or seen by the event's target market, and go to [**2**].
2. Have past ticket buyers had time to receive and respond to their advance ticket offer? *(YES—go to [**2a**]; NO—go to [**2b**])*
   - **[2a.]** **Action:** Consider making follow up phone calls or a second mailing to past ticket buyers. Go to [**3**].
   - **[2b.]** Don't panic yet! Go to [**3**].
3. Are sponsor promotions offering discounts on tickets already in the marketplace? *(YES—go to [**3a**]; NO—go to [**3b**])*
   - **[3a.]** **Action:** Request increased promotion by media partners, if available. Investigate adding other discount admission partners. Go to [**4**].
   - **[3b.]** **Action:** Don't panic yet! Consider moving up the introduction of sponsor promotions to an earlier start date. Go to [**4**].
   - **[3c.]** Have you been actively communicating with fans in the social network media? *(YES—go to [**4a**]; NO—go to [**4b**])*
4. Work with International and external partners to develop more promotional opportunities on multiple platforms GO to [**4a**].
   - **[4a.]** **Action:** Increase fan engagement activities and publicize new promotional opportunities. Post trivia contests for prizes, and encourage fan conversations with polls and solicit opinions (e.g., who will win and why). Work with sponsors to activate new short-term promotions that build instant excitement (e.g., schedule and announce new athlete appearances at retailers and special last-minute ticket offers). Generate new storylines. Post pictures of arriving athletes, preparations at the host facility. Go to [**5**].
   - **[4b.]** **Action:** What are you waiting for? Go to [4a], fire up your computer, and get started!

Figure 11.2 Decision Tree: Response to Slow Ticket Sales

5. Are far more tickets still available than can reasonably be expected to be sold at this point in time? *(YES—go to [**5a**]; NO—go to [**5b**])*
   - **[5a.] Action:** Consider reducing seating inventory. Close unsold seating or viewing areas in the facility to save on operational costs. Go to [**5b**].
   - **[5b.] Action:** Consider distributing a large quantity of complimentary tickets to deserving groups to make the event day audience appear more robust (called "papering the house"—see discussion to follow). Go to [**5c**].
   - **[5c.] Action:** Consider selling tickets, or distributing complimentary tickets, in every alternate row to make the audience appear larger, and then fill in the empty rows if sales subsequently increase. Go to [**5d**].
   - **[5d.] Action:** Review all other expense areas to compensate for the expected shortfall in revenues.

Figure 11.2 *(Continued)*

"Papering the House"

Papering the house, that is, issuing and distributing complimentary tickets to fill unsold seats, is a last-minute, few-options-remaining strategy to make the event venue appear more full. If widely publicized, it can send a message to the public, and to sponsors, that the event was either not popular enough to support paid ticket sales or that the event could not justify using as big a venue. It can create dissatisfaction among an event's most loyal guests—those who actually spent money to attend. In addition, once the process of papering the house begins and the availability of free tickets becomes publicly known, the event organizer can usually bid farewell to any possibility of significant incremental ticket revenues. So why do it?

If the event organizer is reasonably certain that all possible avenues to generate additional ticket sales have been exhausted, papering the house effectively can provide a number of advantages. Whether having purchased a ticket or attending for free, audience members also purchase merchandise, concession items, and parking. If the organizer benefits from the sales in these areas, some additional income can be generated from the incremental audience. This is particularly important if budget assumptions require a larger audience to achieve merchandise revenue expectations now that the pace of added ticket revenues appears to be slowing.

A large crowd also creates more fan excitement, motivates the athletes, makes sponsors happier, and helps guests feel that they are attending an event of sufficient importance to have warranted their time and interest. Sparse attendance is almost always mentioned in media reporting. If the program is a multiday sports event, papering earlier rounds can generate more widespread and positive word of mouth and additional ticket sales for later dates. Finally, for televised and video-streamed events, nothing says, "This event is unimportant" more effectively than an empty grandstand.

Deciding to paper the house does not automatically solve these problems unless the strategy to distribute tickets is well reasoned and relatively discreet. The event promoter has also to guard against the biggest negative possibility of all: Complimentary tickets are widely distributed and the people who received them still don't show up. Such circumstances say, "Even the people who could have attended for free didn't think it was worth the bother." Unless you are reasonably convinced that papering will generate the audience you need to enhance the overall experience, minimize embarrassment, and increase merchandise and other nonticket revenues, consider other less-risky ways of making empty seats disappear, such as closing off and covering seating sections, before committing yourself to this last-ditch effort.

Distribute tickets to groups or through organizations that can be depended on to actually use them. Many communities have programs run through local government agencies that distribute event tickets to low-income and at-risk youth. If you use a ticket service such as Ticketmaster or Ticketfly, the local sales office frequently maintains relationships with special charitable programs that can channel tickets to qualified, dependable, not-for-profit groups. Blocks of tickets can also be distributed to area businesses through the local chamber of commerce and to hospitality industry employees such as hotel and restaurant workers, through the convention and visitors bureau. Distribution of tickets to groups is much more efficient than trying to dispose of tickets one pair at a time. Consider inviting hospital workers, scout groups, and youth organizations. Think of youth leagues and recreational programs focused on the same sport celebrated by the event.

Event vendors may also be able to use tickets for the promotion of their own business objectives. You can host military personnel and their families by working through the public affairs officer at nearby installations, or members of the police, fire, sanitation, and other service workers through the city government or their unions. Try to salvage some positive benefit from the papering effort by selecting one or more of these groups to receive tickets you may not otherwise be able to sell, and issue a press release that turns the donation into a positive publicity story. Again, be sure that the groups to which you make complimentary tickets available will have the time and ability to distribute them to people who will actually use them to avoid creating sections that, although not empty, are only sparsely populated.

Many of the techniques used to reduce inventory can also be applied to papering. If the event is televised, make sure that you concentrate distribution efforts on the side facing the cameras to give the appearance of better attendance. Invite the families of technical crews and talent working on the television production to attend as guests of the organizer. If tickets are printed with reserved seating locations, you can also distribute complimentary tickets in every alternate row.

Marketing Spaces on Tickets

The backs of tickets, ancillary page space on print-at-home tickets, and the body of e-mails containing digital tickets are often used as marketing opportunities, such as displaying presenting sponsor logos and websites, bounce-back coupons, or promotions for merchandise and future events. Perhaps more importantly, these spaces are frequently used for the inclusion of legal language that can cover a multitude of liability issues, including the right to eject the guest for inappropriate behavior, the right to use the purchaser's image in television coverage and future marketing materials, and, increasingly, the acknowledgment that the use of the ticket implies the guest's understanding that attendance at a sports event can possibly result in physical harm in the normal course of competition and presentation. The organizer's legal counsel must assess the need for any messages that should be included in these areas and draft all appropriate language. Computerized ticket services use standard legal language and may not offer as many options to customize these spaces.

Guest Management

The audience of nearly every sports event will include guests who attend at the invitation of the event organizer, host city, and other stakeholders. These invited guests may include sponsors, broadcasters, and other business partners whose agreements define a number of tickets to which they are contractually entitled. They may also include individuals whose invitations serve as expressions of gratitude for noncontractual contributions to the success of an event. Tickets in appropriate seating locations should be removed from the event's inventory to satisfy contractual obligations before the first tickets are sold to the public. Other discretionary requirements for special guests should also be estimated before ticket sales begin. Use Figure 11.3 to avoid overlooking some of your most important guest "audiences."

Note that the figure includes entries for holding both complimentary and tickets "for purchase." High-demand, high-profile, and charity-oriented events frequently invite the majority, or even all, of their guests to purchase their tickets before the public sale. Others invite guests on a complimentary basis to fulfill sponsorship obligations, express gratitude, and extend hospitality to both current and potential future business partners. Often, sponsors and other guests who are invited on a complimentary basis have additional needs, and the organizer will fulfill these extra requests on a "for purchase" basis, if available.

Sponsors and broadcasters often make up the largest percentage of guests. Be sure that every agreement defines an exact number of complimentary tickets each partner is entitled to receive, as well as how many may also be purchased. Review every agreement before tickets go on sale and remove the required number of tickets from inventory. Figure 11.3 also suggests entries for sponsor and broadcaster "guests," that is, key partner contacts to whom the organizer would like to

	Complimentary	For Purchase
Sponsors, contractual	________	________
Sponsors, guests	________	________
Broadcasters, contractual	________	________
Broadcasters, guests	________	________
Host venue	________	________
Promotional partners	________	________
Players/athletes	________	________
Coaches, officials, trainers	________	________
Alumni	________	________
Celebrities	________	________
Host/organizing committee	________	________
Local government officials	________	________
Influential community contacts	________	________
Prospective future partners	________	________
Key vendors	________	________
Organizer executives and staff	________	________
Miscellaneous (house seats)	________	________

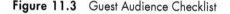

Figure 11.3 Guest Audience Checklist

extend additional, personal courtesies without their attendance counting toward the contractually obligated allotment.

Key host city officials who played a direct or indirect role in the success of an event may also be invited to attend, but do not be surprised if they refuse an offer of complimentary tickets. Many local laws prohibit municipal and state employees from accepting gifts in excess of a certain value. As a consequence, you should take no offense when some government employees offer to purchase their tickets, and others simply respond that they are unable to attend. Gifts of event tickets are also excellent expressions of gratitude for host or organizing committee members and influential community contacts who have provided helpful assistance in the planning, marketing, and execution of the event. Don't overlook potential future business partners in the host city. Consider inviting the key marketing executives of both local and national companies headquartered in the area from which future event partnership proposals might be solicited. Finally, has next year's sports event already been awarded to a new host city? Be sure to invite key contacts and gatekeepers from that community to witness event operations first hand and begin to spark their interest and excitement.

Value-in-kind (VIK) deals with vendors and media partners frequently involve the transfer of event tickets, which should also be held back from the manifest prior to public sale. The organizer may additionally wish to invite key vendors that have provided outstanding service or unusual value to the event. Keep a reasonable supply of "house seats" on hand, tickets in good viewing locations for last-minute requests and invitations. It is wise to reduce this quantity as the event grows closer, periodically returning unused house seat tickets to the inventory available to the public. Be sure to have an acceptance deadline for all guests, whether invited to receive free or purchased tickets, so you have a way to sell or otherwise dispose of tickets held for those who opt not to attend. Feel free to expand the form in Figure 11.3 to include columns that note the number of tickets needed for ancillary events, such as parties, receptions, workshops, clinics, and player practices. The organizer would be best served by maintaining the form on a spreadsheet or, preferably, in a guest management database using appropriate software or in a proprietary database program, as described later in this chapter.

Conflict Seats

Keep some quantity of tickets available on event day as "conflict seats." These tickets are actually used to resolve conflicts, such as reseating guests from areas that may have become unexpectedly obstructed by such elements as lighting towers, trusses, cameras, scoreboards, staging, or decorative props. Tickets for the seats the organizer is able to identify in advance as seats with obstructed views of the field and standing-room tickets, should be sold with their limitations clearly visible on the ticket front at the time of purchase, so conflict seats are not generally used for relocating these guests. Other uses for conflict seats include reseating guests upset by antagonistic neighboring fans, in the rare event guests bearing duplicate tickets for particular seats present themselves, or for any number of discretionary purposes deemed appropriate by the front-of-house staff. Conflict seats are typically not returned to the box office for public sale, as they could be required at any point during the event. The host facility can recommend an adequate number of conflict seats to hold, based on the venue's size and experience.

ADA Seats

Be sure to retain seats for your guests with mobility, visual, auditory, and other impairments. It is not only the right thing to do. It is the law, as defined by the Americans with Disabilities Act of 1990, and similar legislation in effect in many other countries. All large sports and recreation facilities already have a plan for accommodating "ADA guests" in various locations around their seating areas, and organizers should consult with the host venue's ticketing supervisor to ensure this inventory is properly managed. For small or nontraditional facilities that do not have a plan, it is up to the organizer to ensure that adequate and equal access to seating areas is provided including ramps for mobility impaired guests, where needed, and a selection of locations with unimpaired visibility to the event is provided. If possible, retain a legal consultant specializing in ADA law to help guide you.

Guest Management Systems

A guest management system encompasses more than the simple compiling of an invitation list, sending invitations, and assigning tickets to those who accept the offer. Whether the needs of guests are maintained on index cards, in a loose-leaf notebook, or in an electronic database, organizers must constantly monitor and manage guest needs, right up to event day. Administering the guest management process efficiently is of paramount importance. Money, goodwill, and reputation are at stake when inviting and hosting these influential individuals. Sponsors and business partners expect a flawless sports event experience in recognition of their participation, and the generation of future business may in part depend upon the organizer exhibiting proven guest management skills and capabilities.

The larger the guest list, the more imperative it is to organize the guest management process electronically. This will give the organizer the ability to access information easily, eliminate duplicate invitations and ticket assignments, generate management summaries, and include a more comprehensive record of information for each invited guest, such as portrayed in Figure 11.4.

The guest management database is comprised of records for each person invited. These individuals are frequently divided into "audiences," a categorical description of the type of organization they represent. Typical audience categories include many of those listed in Figure 11.3, but may be expanded or subdivided as the event and its guest list require. If the database is particularly large, the management of individual audiences may be split among event staff members who most often interact with those groups invited to attend (but cross reference all lists of invited guests to avoid duplications).

The guest database is a powerful, permanent record that can also increase future efficiency, serving as the basis for compiling invitation lists for subsequent sports events as well. For these reasons, it is important to include as much information in each record as possible. Request that invited guests provide the data for the items (or "fields") 2 through 10 to ensure you have the most up-to-date contact information. Track the invitation process in fields 11 through 13. If a follow-up e-mail, phone call, text, letter, or fax is sent because no response was received by the requested deadline, indicate the most recent attempt at communication in item 12. Fields 14 through 18 initially indicate how many tickets are being held, and ultimately provided for the guest, the seat locations assigned, whether they are to be *gratis* or on a paid basis, and whether payment has been received. If tickets to additional events, such as parties or hospitality programs, are to be provided, they should be inserted in item 19. It is recommended that separate fields be assigned for each ancillary event, giving the organizer with the flexibility of inviting each guest to only the activities desired.

In cases where sports event tickets represent significant monetary value, the organizer might be advised to not mail tickets to the invited guests, but rather, request that they pick up their tickets on site, either at the box office will call window or at an organizer's guest services desk, or, suggest printing the tickets themselves if the design or paper stock of the ticket is not a priority. Tickets may be lost in transit, and the use of overnight delivery or bonded messenger services can

1. Audience
2. Name
3. Title
4. Company
5. Address
6. E-mail
7. Phone (office or residence)
8. Mobile phone
9. Fax
10. Assistant name
11. Date invitation sent
12. Date of most recent follow-up
13. Date response (RSVP) received
14. Number of tickets offered
15. Number of tickets provided
16. Comp or purchase
17. Payment information
18. Seat location
19. Ancillary event tickets
20. Date tickets mailed/delivered
21. Pick-up authorization (i.e., who is allowed to pick up the guest's tickets)
22. Transportation
    a. Arrival information (airport, flight, time)
    b. Departure information
    c. Ground transportation requirements
23. Hotel
24. Hotel room type
25. Other guests in room
26. Credit card
27. Gift
28. Invited by
29. Notes

Figure 11.4 Guest Management Database Record Composition

add considerable operational expenses. Guests who have received their tickets in advance also often arrive at the venue with their tickets still atop their dresser, or left in their hotel rooms. Be sure to have access to the database and vouchers ready at the guest services desk on which to copy the seat locations for guests who arrive without their tickets.

It is also wise to establish a policy regarding who will be permitted to pick up a guest's tickets. It is recommended that guests pick up their tickets personally, upon presentation of valid photo identification such as a driver's license or passport, especially those seated in the very best locations. (Some may give their tickets away to someone unimportant to the organizer, or even sell their tickets, and this becomes much more difficult if the tickets must be picked up on site.) Many important guests, particularly celebrities, government officials, and senior executives, may find it inconvenient or undesirable to pick up tickets themselves. A representative may be identified to the organizer, and authorized in advance and in writing by the guest to receive tickets in his or her place (field 21). This representative should also produce acceptable identification and sign a log on receipt upon delivery.

The guest management database can also assist in the administration of transportation systems (22) and hotel accommodations (23–26), as well as any other special programs or privilege, such as the distribution of gifts to selected guests (27). Any additional information that suits the organizer's purposes may be included in the database such as the name of the staff member who invited the guest (28), and miscellaneous notes of interest (29).

The great power of an electronic guest management database is manifest in the organizer's ability to sort information by any individual field. Management reports can be generated identifying only "Players and Athletes," or just those guests requiring hotel rooms, individuals invited on a complimentary basis, or those invited by a particular staff member. In addition to the use of off-the-shelf software options such as electronic spreadsheet and database programs, there are a host of more specialized solutions. These include online event registration services and web-based software, some incorporating modules for the management of guest accommodations, such as those available from EventBrite, Evite, Cvent, and other well-regarded programs. These companies primarily service corporate and association events, but some of their services are easily adaptable to small and mid-size sports and recreational events, particularly for the registration of athletes and teams.

Management of Athletes and Players

For most sports experiences, there simply is no event without the athletes. Athletes should be managed like the most important of VIP guests. Make them feel appreciated, and their enthusiasm and excitement, their professionalism in meeting the media and other important guests, and their physical performance will shine through. The players, whether they are a group of 10-year-old track competitors, a team of college footballers, or members of a professional hockey club, are the ultimate ambassadors for their sport and the events in which they compete. They are the attraction the public comes to see and, in most instances, represent everything that is positive and good in sports. Therefore, no discussion on guest management would be complete without including this most important segment of guests—the athletes and their own guests and families. Manage them with the respect and treatment they deserve and they will come prepared to compete with clear and focused minds.

What athletes want most of all is to perform to their highest potential. Try to make the event a memory of a lifetime, if not only for their performance, then also for the experience. Make sure their families feel the admiration as well. Consider staging special events just for them. Allow families to attend practices and provide them with the best viewing areas that can be made available. If appearances at additional sponsor or fan events are part of a player's participation, transport the athlete to the event location in style. Ensure the player arrives early enough to stay on schedule, but not so early that he/she sits around waiting to participate. Make sure there are healthy refreshments available in an attractively decorated waiting area ("green room") before the appearance. Try not to schedule too many appearances, or for such lengthy durations, that the athlete tires before the athletic performance itself. Respect any physical routines an athlete must adhere to leading up to the event (e.g., practices, aerobic workouts, weight training) before scheduling other activities.

Sports event organizers who require athletes to make special appearances should also consider hosting a private reception, postgame meal or party, or open a hospitality lounge that is exclusive to players and their families, an oasis from the frantic atmosphere surrounding most events. Use the same guest management system to track the arrivals, departures, hotel, ticketing, and gift needs used for your most important guests. You may even add their uniform and equipment needs, ground transportation requirements, and ancillary event appearances as additional fields in the database.

Communicating with Guests

Communicate with your guests to ensure they have all pertinent event information before they leave home, and once they arrive at the event. Send a confirmation e-mail with preliminary event information after receiving indication of their attendance. Include instructions on how to book rooms at the event's headquarters hotels, information on ground transportation options in the host city, and a hotline number for last-minute changes to arrival plans. Be sure to maintain a web page and/or a mobile "app" that guests can access for up-to-the-minute information on event developments and reprints of pre-event newspaper coverage. Social media platforms can be especially effective in delivering time-sensitive messages, as these sites are checked regularly by users and are expected to provide the timeliest information. An event staff member should be dedicated to updating these sites to ensure the most efficient and accurate dissemination of information to guests. Publish a welcome package to be given to the guest upon hotel check-in or when the guest picks up tickets including a convenient pocket-sized event information guide containing final activity schedules, event office locations, e-mail addresses and telephone numbers, transportation schedules, dining and entertainment options, and discounts offered by local businesses. Open an information desk in each headquarters hotel lobby. In short, never leave the guest in a position where he/she neither knows the answer to a question nor knows how to be able to get one.

Hotel Management

Sports events that draw participants and guests from outside of the host community are the most likely to have to enter into a relationship with at least one host hotel. Hotels start to make their money on "heads in beds," but those heads also have mouths that eat in their restaurants, drink in their bars, talk over their telephone systems, and work in their business centers. Guests use their computers and tablets utilizing wireless or broadband Internet connections in the hotel's sleeping rooms and public areas, attend dinners and parties in their ballrooms, and use audiovisual services in conference facilities. Moreover, the hotel's catering department provides meal and refreshment services to all of these functional spaces.

What Hotels Really Want from Events

Most hotels want to attract groups that they know will fill sleeping rooms and generate restaurant and catering revenue. Sports events, like corporate conferences and conventions that can fill up to 70 to 80 percent of their total capacity, are the most welcome if they bring major food and beverage events such as parties and dinners along with them. Hotels rarely offer more than 80 percent of their rooms to a single group to reduce their risk in case of a poor turnout and to ensure they have a supply of guest rooms for what hotels call their "transient" guests—their loyal and frequent business travelers. In addition, many hotels have contractual agreements in place that guarantee a certain number of rooms to airline crews, visiting guests or transferring employees of local corporations, and other organizations year round. The more long-term contracts that a hotel has in place, the lower the percentage of rooms it will be able to make available for the guests and staff of one-time events.

Hotels are, in a sense, in the wagering business. They bet on the success of an event by agreeing to hold a certain number of rooms for the group's use. However, they do not want to commit to holding rooms for an event if the organizer is not equally, and contractually, obligated to use them. To improve their odds of success, hotels routinely investigate an event's *pick-up history*, the number of rooms the organizer has actually used in the past compared to the number that were originally held, by calling previous host cities and properties. A high percentage of actual usage makes an event very desirable and will encourage the hotel to offer an organizer a greater number of rooms. A poor pick-up percentage may cause a hotel to either offer fewer rooms or pass on participating at all. Hotels want event organizers to constantly monitor their expected needs and to advise the hotel as early as possible if they will not require as many rooms as were requested. If a hotel holds rooms for a sports event that do not materialize into occupancy by guests and it cannot subsequently resell them, it will want to be compensated for lost business.

What Events Really Want from Hotels

Organizers are also in the wagering business. They want to ensure their selected hotels will hold the number of rooms they will require to accommodate their athletes, guests, and staff with the least amount of financial risk. They want the best available accommodations at the lowest possible rate, and polite, attentive service for their guests. The quality of a sports event's selected host hotels reflects directly upon the overall event experience. Athletes and guests who encounter accommodations of poor quality or inferior service will have equally poor memories of their attendance at the event.

Sports event organizers also need places to work. They require hospitality suites to meet and greet their guests, rooms for participant registration, ticket distribution, accreditation, transportation dispatching, and information dissemination. If the event is being held in a city distant from their home offices, they will want to convert some hotel meeting rooms into full-service offices, with workspaces that feature WiFi connectivity, and access to printers, copiers, and fax machines.

Some sports events require too many rooms to be accommodated in a single hotel. Although guests may be dispersed into multiple host properties, organizers will most often concentrate their functional offices and staff in one "headquarters hotel." When organizers need to use more than one hotel, they prefer them to be adjacent to one another, or within a reasonable walk, to avoid having to allocate funds to shuttle guests and staff between more distant properties. If large numbers of hotels are required, organizers prefer they be located in clusters to similarly minimize shuttle transportation costs.

Unless the event is committed to using a specific property because of a sponsorship agreement, organizers should inspect as many hotels as possible to compare overall quality, rates, service features, and business policies. The local CVB or sports commission can save the organizer's staff significant time by coordinating inspection visits, or "site surveys," of hotel properties that the local representatives believe meet the stated needs of the event, from overall quality to guest room and space availability and the interest of the property in being considered as a host hotel. During the site survey, each of which might average up to two hours, the organizer will have the opportunity to evaluate the hotel on a wide range of criteria, such as those listed in Figure 11.5 and described in the following section.

Evaluating and Negotiating with Hotels

Among the first characteristics to evaluate is the geographic desirability of the hotel's location. Is it adjacent to, or reasonably close enough to, the event site to enable participants and guests easy

- ☐ Geographic location and proximity to event site(s)
- ☐ Overall hotel quality (via independent ratings and visual inspection)
- ☐ Suitability of rooms
- ☐ Sufficient rooms and suites available on first hold
- ☐ Room rates
- ☐ Suite rates
- ☐ Complimentary room ratio
- ☐ Function space availability
- ☐ Function space rates
- ☐ Technology availability and installation charges
- ☐ Business center services
- ☐ Shipping and receiving charges
- ☐ Room service hours
- ☐ Health club facilities and charges
- ☐ Room drop charges
- ☐ VIP amenities
- ☐ Sponsor sensitivities
- ☐ Newspaper delivery
- ☐ Valet parking availability
- ☐ Parking rates
- ☐ Hotel channel
- ☐ Signage policies
- ☐ Supplier exclusivities (e.g., technology, security, rentals, decorators)
- ☐ Space and systems for merchandise sales
- ☐ Deposit and payment schedule
- ☐ Cancellation policy
- ☐ Attrition policy

Figure 11.5 Host Hotel Evaluation Checklist

access? The farther the hotel is from the host venue, the more likely it is that the organizer will need to establish a shuttle transportation system. Transportation systems are most cost efficient when a single bus or van within a fleet may be used for multiple trips. The farther the hotel(s), the fewer round trips each vehicle will be able to make per hour and the greater the number of vehicles that will be needed. Is the hotel in an attractive location within the host city or on the edge of an economically depressed area? When choosing hotels, sometimes it is preferable to sacrifice proximity to the event site for a more pleasant or attractive location.

For many events, another geographic consideration will be proximity between the athletes' hotel and the location of practice facilities. Avoiding lengthy bus or shuttle trips for participants, coaches, and staff to get to and from training locations can be as a high priority for many event organizers as securing the quality practice sites themselves. "There is a balance of many factors in identifying the best possible accommodations for sports events, especially those such as international soccer with so many people who travel great distances," says Jill Fracisco, deputy general secretary of soccer's Confederation of North, Central American and Caribbean Association Football (CONCACAF) governing body. "In addition to considering the hotel's amenities, the time to transport between a hotel and a stadium and between a hotel and a practice location are among the most important."

Based on both personal visual inspection and ratings of independent hotel evaluation services that can be found in a variety of printed and online publications, is the property of a quality and reputation that will reflect well upon the sports event? What is the age of the hotel, and what is its experience in serving as a host location? How well is the property maintained, and when were the guest rooms, meeting rooms, and public spaces last renovated? Does the hotel offer all of the amenities demanded by the event's guests? Will some audiences of invited guests require a more elegant hotel and others a more value-oriented property? If so, should the group be split in two or more subgroups based on their price and quality sensitivities?

Is the hotel prepared to hold an adequate number of guest rooms, suites, and meeting and reception rooms for the event's guests? Until a hotel has a signed contract for the rooms, it will place them "on hold," a nonbinding agreement to provide the rooms until a specified deadline date for a final contract—unless someone else signs a contract first. The total inventory of all rooms reserved over all pre-event, event, and postevent days is called a *room block*. It is standard practice for a hotel to contact event organizers holding rooms that are not yet contracted if another group expresses interest in contracting over the same period. The hotel usually offers the organizer the opportunity to formally commit to using the rooms in the block before entering into a contract with another party, but will release the hold if the organizer does not agree in a timely manner. It is also standard practice for hotels to put a "second hold" on rooms, which will entitle the second group to automatically claim the rooms should the first decide to release its hold, fail to enter into a contract, or default on a required deposit.

What percentage of the rooms will be paid for directly by the event and what percentage by the guests? Are the rates within an acceptable price range for the purchaser? Few groups pay the standard "rack rate" for sleeping rooms. The more rooms an organizer will commit to using, and the more catered events they will hold at the hotel, the more negotiable the room rate may become. Will suites be required by the event for important sponsor guests, celebrities, athletes, performers, or senior executives, and are a sufficient number or adequately sized and appointed suites available? Hotels routinely offer a number of complimentary rooms for the organizer's use based on the number of rooms actually used. This ratio is somewhat negotiable and usually in the area of one complimentary room for every 45 to 50 paid rooms (suites are often counted as two or more rooms). Try to negotiate an additional room or suite on a complimentary basis for one or more of the organizer's top executives, and a number of free upgrades into higher-priced rooms, subject to availability.

Does the hotel offer an adequate amount of space for the various hospitality events (e.g., dinners, luncheons, parties, award ceremonies, and meetings) the organizer wants to host? Are there sufficient rooms for event office needs over the dates required for setup, pre-event preparation, and the postevent dismantle period? Every hotel has a standard rental rate for its meeting and ballroom spaces, but many will waive these rates if the event commits to a large enough number of guest rooms or a guaranteed amount of catering over the course of its stay. The cost of meeting room rentals can be a considerable, but often an avoidable, expense and can be a strong enough reason to select one hotel over another as a suitable host.

As part of evaluating the suitability of a hotel, it is certainly fair to ask the management if any inconveniences, such as renovation work in any part of the property, a noisy construction project next door, or road repairs outside the front door, are scheduled or can be anticipated around the dates of your event. Having this information may be an important factor in deciding among different hotels.

A key area to confirm in evaluating a potential host hotel is technology, specifically the availability of and any associated costs relating to these essential services. Is there WiFi connectivity throughout the hotel? Are guests assessed a daily charge for wireless or high-speed broadband access in their rooms or meeting facilities? Are there costs incurred by adding extra telephone and data lines into offices and meeting rooms? Can mobile devices work in all areas or is there limited reception in portions of the hotel? All guests attending an event will have the expectation to be technologically connected on demand so reliable service is required where guests will be staying.

In addition, guests, particularly sponsors and other business partners, will often require access to the hotel business center for many services including computers, scanners, printers, copiers, and fax machines as well as for local or overnight shipping. If your needs do not warrant the costs of renting and installing equipment in your meeting room office, try to negotiate preferred rates and extended hours of operation for the business center.

Are there charges for receiving event materials shipped to the hotel and delivered to the meeting rooms? If these charges cannot be negotiated away, will the hotel agree to a flat or maximum daily fee for received packages and faxes? Are there service charges for shipping materials from the hotel as well? Will the hotel permit courier and freight companies to pick up prepaid shipments without a service charge?

Room service hours, where available, should be compared to the times that guests and staff will most likely make use of in-room dining, particularly late hours after nonmeal events have concluded. Hotels will often extend hours at the organizer's request if the property can reasonably expect to profit from this accommodation. Are there high-quality, health-conscious menu items available? Some hotels may offer to provide special late-night, event-themed items and healthy food selections promoted on special in-room menus during the event. Sports events generally attract athletes, fans, and other guests committed to keeping in shape, so access to fitness facilities is also usually expected. Is there a facility located on the property with a sufficient quantity of aerobic and weight-training equipment in good working order, or is there a health club nearby with which the hotel has an access agreement? Is there a charge for using the facilities and, if so, can it be negotiated to enable event guests to enjoy privileges on a complimentary basis? If the facility is not available 24 hours a day, is it open at times that reasonably complement the event schedule? Can extended hours be negotiated?

Organizers may be planning to communicate with their guests by delivering information packets, letters of welcome or newsletters to their rooms. Surprise gifts such as T-shirts, caps, a basket of sponsor products can await guests upon their arrival or when they return to their rooms after the event. Most hotels charge a fee for these "room drops" that can range from $1.00 to $5.00 per delivery depending on the size or weight of the items delivered.

A less-expensive alternative is to staff a guest information desk in the lobby of the hotel. In addition, most hotels will not charge for the distribution of information packets to guests upon check in. The organizer can request that the hotel recognize a certain number of their most important guests with special welcoming amenities, such as a delivery of a themed basket of goodies, a plate of dry snacks, chocolates, fruit, beverages, or a souvenir cap, pennant, or T-shirt. Most hotels will agree to offer these hospitable extras to a limited number of the event's guests, as identified by the organizer, at the property's expense. Make sure that the hotel is aware of sponsor sensitivities, so they do not greet sponsor guests with a basket of their competitor's products. Be aware of the hotel's own sponsorship agreements, although most will agree to serve a sports event sponsor's products even if they have existing agreements with a competitor company.

Will the hotel deliver newspapers to the event's guests each morning? Can the organizer specify a particular newspaper, such as the event's print partner? Are valet parking and self-parking options available and, if so, at what cost? Try to secure a number of complimentary parking accommodations for staff vehicles or courtesy vans and in convenient locations if possible. Are there convenient places on the property for bus shuttles to load, off-load, and park?

Is there an available channel on the hotel's in-room television system for the organizer's own programming? Some hotels permit organizers to run footage of past sports event highlights, an infomercial presentation, and/or other entertainment or information to all guest rooms on an open television channel. There is usually a charge for this service.

What are the policies regarding the use of decorative event and directional signage or other branding elements in the hotel lobby, on the building exterior, and in other public spaces? Some hotels will permit freestanding signage that posts event and transportation schedules, and directs guests to various event offices. Will the property permit the organizer to hang festive welcome banners, display trophies, and outfit front desk staff, bellpersons, doorpersons, and waitstaff in event caps, golf shirts, or jackets? Some hotels endorse this level of staff participation, while others will restrict staff at most to wearing lapel pins or buttons.

Many organizers look for opportunities to sell official merchandise, such as selected attire and souvenirs, at designed locations away from the event venue. Is such an operation permitted in the hotel? If so, is there suitable and easily accessible space for a merchandise sales location? Can the organizer bring display units or tables or can the hotel provide them? What is the most convenient way for the organizer to accept credit card payments in the hotel and are there any associated costs?

Finally, are there exclusive suppliers that the organizer must use inside the hotel property? At minimum, hotels generally insist on providing all food and beverage and telecommunication/technology services on their campuses. Does the hotel require union electricians to distribute power or to install lighting for parties and hospitality events? Is the organizer obligated to use the in-house audiovisual company, or can an organizer's needs be bid out to others? In-house vendors with the exclusive right to provide these services will almost always be more expensive than those who must compete with companies that can be brought in from the outside. Can the organizer hire an outside security company to protect its guests and assets, or must all security be arranged through the hotel?

Attrition and Cancellation Clauses

Perhaps the most sensitive and financially risky points of negotiation are the hotel's policies on room attrition and cancellation. An attrition penalty is incurred when the number of guest rooms used by an event falls below an agreed-to percentage of the contracted number. Cancellation penalties, of course, are encountered if the organizer cancels the entire agreement after the contract is signed.

As previously discussed, the hotel wants to assume the least risk of being left with unused, nonrevenue-producing sleeping rooms, while the organizer wants to take on the least risk in having to pay for them. Hotels will generally refuse to be bound to hold rooms without defining financial penalties for organizers who cancel their agreement or fail to fill all or the vast majority of rooms they contract. Although the penalties may seem unusually onerous, it's a necessary business practice for the hotel. Consider this, sports event organizers: Would you allow another business to hold event tickets indefinitely without paying for them, understanding that even though there is demand for those tickets, there is a chance they would be returned unused and unpaid? Hotels need these safeguards to maintain their business; at the same time, event organizers need to minimize the financial risk of encountering cancellation or attrition penalties.

As a result, hotels will generally pressure organizers to get contracts signed, while organizers will try to delay executing a formal agreement as long as possible. This dynamic is sometimes reversed when an event is of such great regional, national, or international importance that a city expects a large influx of travelers who are not part of the organizer's room block, or when a particular hotel is strongly desired by an organizer due to quality, convenience, or value. In these cases, the organizer will want to protect a room block at a preferred rate, while some hotel managers resist, preferring to fill their rooms with other corporate or individual travelers, presumably at a more lucrative room rate. As surprising as it may sound, some hotels will simply prefer not to participate in sports event group bookings at all, or will hold only small-sized room blocks, because they expect to operate during that time at high percentages of occupancy, and at rates they need not negotiate.

Once a hotel contract is signed, it indicates that both parties are betting on the success of the other. It also means that the organizer is fully aware of the potential financial impact of the prevailing attrition and cancellation clauses. Thus, when it is time to execute the agreement, be sure the event is unlikely to be canceled or postponed, and that you hold only those rooms that you truly believe will be needed. Penalty provisions aside, hotel contracts actually work in the sports event organizer's favor—it typically does not permit the hotel to cancel or reduce the size of the room block. It may, however, allow the organizer to periodically reduce the size of the room block by a specified percentage without penalty on defined deadline dates well in advance of the event.

Be particularly vigilant regarding how cancellation and attrition penalties are calculated. Some will be calculated on the total number of room nights held during the contract period, or on the quantity of rooms contracted for what is called the peak night, the night when the number of a sports event's guests is at its maximum. Some agreements will demand payment not only for the unoccupied rooms, but also for an estimated amount of lost income from food and beverage operations. Organizers should attempt to assume only the risk for the rooms themselves, as lost income from food and beverage operations are simply assumptions that cannot be substantiated. Most attrition penalties are activated when the total room pick-up falls below 80 to 90 percent of the contracted room nights, a percentage which the organizer should attempt to reduce as much as possible during negotiations. Smaller and more up-scale hotels, however, frequently insist on an even greater percentage of pick-up, some as high as 100 percent. These penalties will be assessed during the settlement of the bill after the event.

On the other hand, cancellation penalties are payable immediately upon termination of the contract. The percentage of room revenue for which the organizer is responsible will increase at contractually defined deadline dates, beginning as low as 10 percent of room revenue upon execution the contract, and increasing to 25 percent perhaps a year in advance, then periodically to 50 percent, 75 percent, and up to 100 percent if canceled close to event day. Again, the contract proposed by the hotel may suggest that penalties include estimated food and beverage income, which the organizer should attempt to negotiate out of the agreement. If dinner functions, parties, and other hospitality events are included in the contract, some hoteliers will attempt to include some portion of the projected revenue for these functions in the cancellation penalty. Event organizers should resist this inclusion as no expenses are incurred against these events by the hotel until very close to the event (i.e., the hotel does not purchase food or contract labor for the hospitality function until just days before it occurs).

An essential element for the event organizer to include in the contract relating to cancellation and attrition is the notion that, if rooms are released by the organizer and subsequently resold by the hotel to other groups or to the public, the value received for those rooms will be deducted from the organizer's penalty. Requesting this inclusion is reasonable and puts no one at an economic disadvantage, as the hotel suffers no financial hardship if the rooms that were contracted, but unused by the organizer's group, were eventually sold to others. Without this provision, the organizer would remain totally unprotected against attrition, while the hotel would enjoy the benefits of essentially being paid twice for the same room.

Deposits

Like many business agreements, hotel contracts will often include a request for a nonrefundable deposit, perhaps 10 to 20 percent of the total value of the rooms on hold, upon execution of the contract. If paying this deposit is unavoidable, it can be applied to satisfying the event's "master account," a tally of all charges that will be paid by the organizer during settlement of the bill after the event. The size of the deposit is frequently negotiable if the organizer can produce evidence of an excellent credit history, or if the majority of the room block will be paid for directly by the event's guests.

It is advisable to set up a master account regardless of who is paying for the guest rooms. The organizer can specify which staff or guest rooms should be billed to the master account. It is recommended that organizers authorize only room and tax charges for these rooms so incidentals, such as room service and restaurant charges, shop purchases, WiFi access, minibar, pay-per-view movies, laundry, telephone, and other fees, are paid by the occupants, and selectively reimbursed after a thorough review of their expense reports. Master account charges may also include fees for catered meetings and receptions, technology and event office costs, delivery and room drop charges, business center usage, and other operational expenses.

Managing Hotel Operations for Sports Events

Once the hotel contract is signed, the property's sales department will take a less active role in the event, replaced by convention services and reservations department representatives who will remain in contact with the organizer on a daily basis. The convention services contact will work with the organizer on the assignment and installation of office, hospitality, and reception facilities, and will often coordinate the event organizer's catering needs.

The reservations department will work with the organizer to manage the room block and guest registration. Many organizers prefer to manage the room block by requiring guests to arrange for hotel accommodations through its own staff rather than directly with hotels. This is particularly useful when a number of host hotels are involved. The organizer can assign guests and participants to the hotels that are most appropriate for them, or to distribute the audience among properties that require the greater number of occupied rooms to avoid attrition penalties. It is also the best way to identify which guests have indicated their intention to attend, but who have failed to make reservations. Event staff can contact these individuals to determine their housing needs as the deadline dates to release the sleeping rooms approach.

The organizer will then generate a "rooming list" for the hotels through a guest management database, updating the hotels with changes throughout the pre-event period. Be sure to work with the reservations department to ensure that the rooming list has all of the information the hotel requires, and to determine how best and often to inform the reservation department of the inevitable changes to the list.

If guests are given the responsibility of making reservations directly with the hotel(s), provide them with a code that will identify them as being associated with the event. The hotel can then provide a rooming list to the organizer indicating who has made reservations within the block. It is essential to regularly and vigilantly compare this list against the guest management system to ensure that all event guests staying in the hotel have identified themselves as being part of the block. Those who make reservations in their assigned hotel, but are not identified as event guests, may not be credited to the room block, which could result in the assessment of an otherwise avoidable attrition penalty. Organizers should provide guests with a reservation deadline well ahead of the key date to release rooms as defined in the hotel contract. Fix a response deadline that is at least two weeks ahead of the release date to give event staff the opportunity to contact those who have not yet appeared on a rooming list.

Finally, recognize that it is standard procedure to provide gratuities to hotel employees dedicated to the success of your event. The hotel sales manager can recommend the customary range of cash gratuities that may be offered to the convention services manager, catering managers, bell staff, and others.

Hotels and organizers share the common objective of ensuring that their guests enjoy the best possible sports event experience. The hotel's convention services department will create a resume of important information for the entire hotel staff regarding the event's operations at the property, which the organizer should review for accuracy. The convention services contact will also schedule a "pre-con" (preconvention) meeting a few days before the majority of the event's guests arrive. Among those invited will be key organizer personnel and each of the property's department heads (e.g., housekeeping, security, bell staff, room service, front desk, etc.) to ensure a direct and consistent flow of information between the two partners. The pre-con meeting is an excellent forum to express appreciation for the staff's hard work to come, and to surface any questions or concerns about hotel service encountered to date. The hotel will provide organizers with an "event resume," reflecting all of the details about their group, including who is authorized to approve charges to the master account, function space room usages, room service hours, VIPs entitled to amenities, special charges, and much more. Be sure to review it in detail! If the event has any policies regarding athletes or other guests (e.g., no autographs), this is the appropriate forum in which to communicate them. Leave the staff feeling excited, appreciated, and committed to success, and the organizer's guests will enjoy their stay as much as the event itself.

Post-Play Analysis

Marketing campaigns should focus on selling tickets in advance to enhance attendance and revenues. Utilizing the best combination of affordable and practical media elements for your event, design these campaigns to establish a sense of urgency, but allow enough time for the public to respond. Set a ticket policy—reserved seats or general admission—that best serves the needs of your sports event. If tickets do not sell well, a number of options may be considered to make the event venue appear more full, including the reduction of seating inventory and the distribution of complimentary tickets, also known as papering the house. Before sales begin, be sure to remove tickets required for business partners, athletes, and invited guests from those to be sold.

Keep track of all guest needs by establishing a guest management system that works best for your event. This database will indicate whether invitees have accepted their invitation and what tickets they will receive to which activities; it will include arrival information, accommodations assignments, and more. Athletes and event participants can often be managed using the same system, adding special activities, perquisites, and equipment needs as additional fields that are customized just for them.

Communicate with your guests and ensure they have all pertinent event details, such as activity and transportation schedules, dining and entertainment options, maps, and contact information for key individuals. Consider publishing a guide, as well as a web page and mobile device "app," that will provide easy access to the essential information required both during their visit as well as ahead of time.

Carefully evaluate hotels under consideration as host and headquarters properties. Negotiate the best contract possible, and hold only the number of rooms you are reasonably comfortable you will use. Financial penalties for using far fewer rooms than contracted, or for canceling a hotel deal, can be significant.

Coach's Clipboard

1. Ticket sales for a national skateboard competition, which were brisk when first put on sale, have slowed dramatically. Approximately 50 percent of the available tickets have been sold, but the budget had estimated 70 percent. With two weeks remaining until the event, what plans should be considered to balance the budget and fill the venue? Assume that one half-page advertisement is scheduled to appear in the local newspaper on the opening day of the weekend event.
2. A regional track and field event is best viewed from a section of existing bleachers that is open to the public. What viewing options can be considered to accommodate the attendance of sponsor guests? How would you begin to design a similar area on a public beach for a surfing competition?
3. Develop a social media plan to support your marketing efforts for one of the events above. How will you keep fans visiting and interacting from the time the event is announced through and including event day? In what ways can you use social media to continue to engage with fans after the event has concluded?
4. Design an event app that will provide fans with the information essential to their game day experience. What should be added for events that bring a majority of attendees from other regions?
5. A beachfront resort hotel would provide excellent accommodations for important guests traveling into the host city for your event, but the director of sales resists negotiating for preferred rates or anything less than 95 percent pick-up before an attrition penalty begins to apply. While guests will be responsible for their own charges, the organizer will remain liable for the unoccupied rooms. The event venue is located 20 minutes away by shuttle bus. What options should you explore to minimize the event's financial exposure?

PLAY 12

Presenting Your Event

"Sports is the only entertainment where, no matter how many times you go back, you never know the ending."

—*Neil Simon, American Playwright*

This play will help you to:

- Produce an entertaining environment for fans attending your sports event.
- Create the necessary documents required for good presentation planning, including event rundowns, scripts, blocking diagrams, and production schedules.
- Become familiar with the basic tools of sports event presentation.

Introduction

Today's sports event organizers recognize that audiences have certain minimum expectations when they attend a sports event. When people come to watch their favorite athletes, they expect to be able to see every moment and nuance of the performances and to share in the emotional excitement. They come to participate vicariously in the players' victories, to demonstrate their admiration with displays of appreciation, approval, encouragement, and support through hearty applause and throaty cheers. To enhance their sense of participation and enable them to react with knowledgeable enthusiasm, fans want to be able to visually comprehend, evaluate, and judge the progress of the contest. They want as much information as possible—rosters, official results, statistics, and the other interpretive data that can enhance and enrich their viewing enjoyment. Finally, they also want to be entertained. They want to feel they are personally involved and witnessing something unique and important, perhaps even historic. Regardless of the eventual outcome, a sports event must present an experience worthy of the fan's time and entertainment dollar.

It is not coincidental that the basic requirements of the live sports experience summarized in Figure 12.1 embrace philosophies that are similar to those underlying the way an event is presented on television. Sports event broadcasts inject the viewer into the competition, establishing an intimacy between the audience and athlete. Cameras remove distance, capturing the facial expressions that register accomplishment and disappointment, achievement and frustration. Announcers describe the progress of play, provide insightful analysis, and project opinion as to how athletes and their coaches can respond to competitive challenges. Replays reverse time to allow both announcers and audiences to dissect and evaluate a team's or athlete's performance. Hosts familiarize the viewer with the athletes, provide pertinent background information, present statistics, and summarize the event upon conclusion. Pulsating music, colorful graphics, and the skillful direction of camerawork keep viewers sufficiently engaged and entertained to ensure that they remain glued to their television screens even during commercial breaks. On-screen graphics note the quarter, period, or inning, which side possesses the ball, who is at bat, and how much time and how many timeouts remain. An information ticker crawling across the bottom of the screen shows scores of other games, individual player statistics, and news from other sports.

Whether or not they are televised, the most entertaining sports events are those that embrace the same production values, logical flow, and minute-to-minute attention to detail as a well-planned broadcast. Craft the event as though you were planning a live show on the world's largest 360-degree television screen, and then add the extra elements unique to the live entertainment experience that can enliven the athletes, as well as the audience. Give the event a sense of worth and importance by creating an environment of excitement from the moment the audience enters the event facility, through the pre-event entertainment and ceremonies, and during the competition itself. Remember that audiences experience sports events in a multisensory way. The sounds of a sports event can be as important as the sights in elevating the level of enthusiasm and enhancing the entertainment experience.

To fully capture the active involvement of the fans, the competitive activities at a sports event may require the support of technical systems including lighting, sound amplification, electronic message boards, and video image magnification (I-Mag), among others. The same technical support may also be used to captivate the audience with ceremonies and entertainment elements before, between, and after the competitions.

The in-stadium and in-arena entertainment experience is also becoming increasingly personal and customizable. Fans need access to fast and reliable mobile phone and WiFi service at the event venue to download statistics, check on scores from other teams and sports, and watch key replays from games being played in other cities. As much as personal technologies drive us apart,

To meet the minimum expectations of the audience, sports events must be presented so that fans are . . .

- Able to see the competitors they came to watch
- Able to visually comprehend the progress of the event or competition
- Kept informed of official results and critical information
- Excited and entertained

Figure 12.1 Basic Requirements of Sports Event Presentation

they also bring us together. Fans want to communicate with their friends and families about the events they are watching via social networks, check their statistics-driven sports fantasy teams, upload photos taken from their seat, and meet up with other friends attending the game. Having sufficient access to Internet and phone service has become essential to the entertainment experience at today's sports event facilities.

Ceremonies and Entertainment Elements

Every event has its own personality, every sport—even new and emerging ones—its own traditions. For some sports events (e.g., football, hockey, basketball), organizers want to get the crowd loud, energized, and excited. For others (e.g., golf, figure skating, tennis), a more conservative atmosphere is more acceptable and appropriate. In almost every instance, however, opportunities abound for celebrating the featured sport, setting a singular tone for an event, and making unique, lasting impressions with emotional opening ceremonies and pre-event festivities, intermission entertainment, and postevent finales (see Figure 12.2).

Many sports events, particularly those involving teams of athletes, are presented on large playing surfaces and, in some cases, before large audiences. The playing surface, the natural focal point for an event, can also serve as the stage for ceremonial and entertainment segments, as long as they do not affect the quality of the surface for the competition. Regardless of how impressive the entertainment, the actual competition is what the audience has come to see, and the safety of the athletes and quality of the surface are paramount when compared with any other consideration.

Whether it is made of grass, artificial turf, ice, wood, dirt, clay, or padded mats, there is nothing more important to a sports event than the quality of the surface on which it is played. The preparation and maintenance of these substrates before, during, and after an event is specialized and scientific, and the practitioners variously trained in the biology, chemistry, and physics of their craft. When in doubt, consult the specialists upon whose shoulders the feet, legs, and heads of amateur and professional athletes depend.

- Pre-event live musical entertainment
- Opening ceremonies
- Introduction or entrance of teams or athletes
- Presentation of colors and national anthems
- Sport-specific ceremony (first pitch, tip off, face-off, coin flip)
- Recognition of past champions, hall of famers, and event alumni
- Appearances and participation by celebrities and dignitaries
- Video features
- Programming during breaks in play
- Halftime or intermission entertainment
- Live musical performances
- Postevent presentation of awards and trophies

Figure 12.2 Presentation and Ceremonial Elements of Sports Events

Physical stresses on the playing surface can be considerable during the progress of a game, match, or meet. Grounds crews are prepared for the wear and tear on the playing field, and, in the case of outdoor events, to best care for the surface, when adverse weather occurs. They are less able to mitigate damage from heavy vehicles or equipment used during installation of the event or during pregame or halftime presentations, burns from pyrotechnics, or dangerous debris from special effects. Be sure that any entertainment element you plan to incorporate that can affect the field, ice, or court is reviewed and approved by whomever is chiefly responsible for the playing surface.

Pageantry

Most sports events are presented on a 360-degree stage, surrounded by an audience that may be dozens to hundreds of feet distant from the action. Because it is difficult to establish an intimacy with the athletes from such prodigious distances, most of today's large arenas and stadiums have installed large video displays to simulcast the action, deliver information and provide replays. These screens, known by such brand names as Sony Jumbotron, Mitsubishi Diamond Vision, and others, bring the action and the personalities of the athletes into sharper focus for the live audience. The large sizes of the playing surface and extraordinary distance from the audience create a similarly challenging environment in which to entertain and excite audiences before play and during intermissions. Pageantry—colorful, large-format entertainment with an emphasis on music and mass movement, sometimes supported by special effects such as lighting, lasers, digital projection, and pyrotechnics—is a popular solution in professional and top-tier amateur sports for these reasons.

Pageantry also needs big sound to go with the big visuals. Depending on the size of the facility, it may be difficult to see details clearly from all points, but it should never be difficult to hear. In a large sports venue, sound can provide ceremonies and entertainment with the ability to touch and energize an audience to perhaps an even greater extent than visuals, as will be discussed later in this chapter.

Amateur Entertainers

An enormous budget is not required to inject the vibrant and rousing pageantry that can give even the most homegrown sports programs the feel of a big event. The area's best high school and college marching bands can provide musical entertainment that can energize and inspire the crowd. Drill teams and kick lines can perform acrobatic and dance sequences that add a visual dimension to the thunderous presence of the band. For even greater impact, organizers can combine local bands or drill teams into a massed band, or a larger dance line, for an even grander presentation. Add colorful, waving flags of symbolic significance to the event (flags of countries, states or provinces, sports teams, or schools, and customized designs made especially for the program) for great, inexpensive props that can measurably increase the visual excitement on the field. With the exception of custom banners, you don't even have to buy the flags, poles, or holsters. Most items can be rented from a regional flag retailer. Drill teams and youth sports teams, groups that are used to working together as an organized unit, can be mobilized as flag and prop holders and marchers.

Using existing groups to provide large numbers of amateur performers is a manageable and efficient approach. Groups often come with their own infrastructure; members are used to following the instructions of their coaches, teachers, or the other adult supervisors who routinely coordinate and manage their activities. They usually have an established procedure for relaying information to their members, and are familiar with traveling, or at least arriving and marshaling, as groups. It is obviously easier to manage four coaches each responsible for 25 team members than 100 individual performers. Each participating performer should receive, review, and sign a simple one-page waiver prepared by the event's attorney, protecting the organizer against liability claims in case of injury or accident, and granting permission to use the performer's images in event photography, video coverage, and broadcast (for a more detailed discussion on participant waivers, see Play 14 and Appendix 9).

Treat amateur entertainers with the same respect and consideration as you would extend to those who are being paid to perform. Ensure that plenty of water is readily available at all rehearsals, as well as in staging areas, and that restroom facilities are easily accessible. If rehearsals or call times require participants to be on the event site throughout the day, be sure to provide meals or snacks, or provide reasonably long enough meal breaks for them to be able to find food elsewhere. The feeding of cast and crew members is a perfect opportunity to involve a food or restaurant sponsor. Where possible, it is a best practice to try to provide food for cast, crew, and staff members on site when events or rehearsals are located in areas that offer few dining options. Rehearsals cannot usually restart until all cast members have returned, so it only takes a handful of late-returning participants to hold up an entire show.

Celebrity Entertainers

Organizers of major sports events are incorporating entertainment provided by well-known bands and celebrity performers with increasing regularity. Musical performers who appeal to the same target audience as the featured sport can add significant excitement to pre-event, intermission, and even postevent festivities. Their celebrity stature and amplified sound can help bridge the physical distance between the event and the audience. Some will readily agree to appear during sports events with large live and television audiences to enjoy wide exposure for a new album or soon-to-be-released song. Keep in mind that a performer's fee is not related to the length of an appearance. To professional performers, the time investment is nearly the same whether they play a single song, or a full 90-minute concert. They still have to travel to the event, set up their gear, participate in a sound check and rehearsal, perform, and then travel on to the next stop. Their fees may be negotiable to some extent, but do not expect costs to be significantly reduced because of the brevity of their appearances.

Well-known musical acts are best procured through their national booking agency. You can usually identify the agency from the act's website. For the right price, performers will appear virtually anywhere as long as they are not on hiatus or working on an album. When bands take a break from touring, its members disperse and it is very difficult for their management to reassemble them.

Artists' fees can be very expensive, but that is only the beginning of the costs that can be incurred when booking recognizable talent. After receiving notice of the initial asking price, request a copy of the act's contract and rider. The rider is a list of all of the extra requirements that must be covered by the organizer, including the number of people for whom travel must be provided and at what class of service. The list typically includes members of the act, as well as backup singers and musicians, the manager, the road or tour manager, sound director, lighting director, and often others. Some acts additionally require such personnel as bodyguards, hairdressers, make-up artists, and wardrobe supervisors, and their rider will define whether the specific individuals to fulfill these roles must travel with the artist, or may be provided on site by the sports event organizer. The rider will also contain specific information about the act's requirements for hotel accommodations (which will likely include some number of suites at a top-quality property), meal and special dietary requirements, postevent hospitality, and complimentary event tickets.

Minimum production requirements are also provided in an accompanying technical rider, usually specifying the size of the stage, audio equipment, lighting, musical instruments (often referred to as *backline*), and other performance-specific needs.

Negotiate the fee and the rider at the same time, as it is the totality of their costs that is important. You may still be able to meet an artist's minimum fee requirements while reducing the expenses of fulfilling the rider, or partially cover the rider costs with a reduction in the fee.

There are areas of negotiation illustrated in Figure 12.3 that may be applied to the contracts for professional artists. Remember that most talent contracts and riders are generic documents. Other than including the date, location, the name of the buyer, and the length of the performance desired, they are not generally customized by the agency to the needs of a particular show or sports event. As a result, the contracts that organizers receive are generally designed to be applicable to events in which the act is performing as a solo or featured concert attraction. Sports events usually use professional artists in a much more limited way, integrated as an element of a much broader event. As such, the act's tour management may relax a significant portion of the technical requirements, such as the size of the stage, and supporting lighting, sound, and special effects. With fewer technical requirements, the organizer may be able to successfully reduce the number of technical personnel that must travel with the artist to the event.

The meal requirements that are outlined in the artist's rider are often exhaustive. They not only specify which meals must be covered and for how many individuals, but often identify the exact menu. To simplify event-day logistics, especially in temporary event facilities that are not equipped for fine catering, organizers can propose a flat fee (also known as a *buy-out*) payable to the artist that will enable the tour management to provide the meals desired on its own.

Finally, most artists will require a number of complimentary tickets to the event for their management, important business clients, and perhaps even local members of their fan club. As the event is not a typical concert, the organizer can usually negotiate a reduction in the number of tickets normally required by the artist.

Put the counteroffer to the agency in writing, but do not be surprised if it does not respond immediately. The agency will have to confer with the artist's management before accepting any reduced fee, and with the act's tour manager to discuss any alterations to the rider. Acts in high demand may also deliberately delay in responding in hope that a concert promoter or an event

- Talent fees
- Air travel
  - Reduce the number of people traveling
  - Convert a number of airfares at first and business class to coach
  - Seek to include sponsor-provided (VIK) tickets
- Hotel
  - Reduce the number of people traveling
  - Reduce the number of suites required
- Meals and snacks
  - Reduce or buy out
- Technical rider
  - Reduce technical requirements (e.g., stage size, lighting, special effects, audio) to levels appropriate to event and its host facility
- Complimentary tickets

Figure 12.3 Commonly Negotiable Talent Contract and Rider Terms

in another location will offer them more money for an appearance. It is not unusual for popular performers to refrain from accepting the terms of a counterproposal until 90 days before an event, when it becomes apparent that no more lucrative offer from another party for the same date is likely. Therefore, be sure that your counterproposal includes an expiration date for accepting the offer. While it may not inspire a performer's management company to act with any greater speed, it does enable the organizer to approach other alternative acts after the expiration date has passed.

Hosts and Announcers

Sports events frequently require a public address announcer to welcome and communicate with the audience, relaying official scores, and fulfilling marketing obligations to sponsors. A pleasant-sounding, authoritative announcer with a smooth, professional delivery will capture the attention of the audience and lend an air of importance to both the festivities and the competition. Quite often, the best sources for announcers are local radio and television stations, which can provide another exposure opportunity for a sports event's media partners. To save money on talent fees, an organizer can seek to incorporate the station's provision of an announcer as part of their media sponsorship deal. Make sure the announcer becomes familiar with the pronunciation of each of the participant's names to ensure they are presented with authority, sincerity, and confidence.

Some events also lend themselves to involving a host or emcee in addition to the public address announcer. Unlike the unseen announcer, a host has a visible presence and provides at least some of the focus of attention when speaking with the audience. A host can provide a more personal touch to welcoming the audience, interviewing players, coaches, and dignitaries, and delivering scripted monologue for pre-event and intermission festivities. Like a television color commentator, the host can add dimension and drama, information and insights, enthusiasm, and entertainment value to both the pre-event ceremonies and the contest itself.

If you want to add ceremonies and entertainment to your sports event, knowing what resources you can reach out for will help inspire your planning. But before contacting potential performers and other event participants, you have to know how you will use them and what you will want them to do. It is now time to begin the production planning process.

Production Planning

Planning the presentation and production of sports events is a complex process that often requires the appointment of an event producer or presentation director. This individual is charged with the responsibility of developing the program's creative approach, working with technical specialists to arrange for sound, lighting, staging, and other presentation tools, and, ultimately, overseeing the day-to-day details of event production. Once the producer has a reasonable understanding of the missions of the sports event's presentation and how they will be achieved, the planning starts with the preparation of lists—lots of them, including contact lists, rehearsal schedules, production schedules, cast lists, wardrobe lists, prop lists, audio and music play lists, video lists, and event rundowns. These documents help the producer to organize his or her thinking, identify required purchases, and communicate expectations to the cast, production staff, and crew. Developing and maintaining these many lists ensures that no detail goes unconsidered by the presentation director, and that every facet of the production is communicated to the entire presentation team. Figure 12.4 provides a summary of the most essential production documents, which are explored in detail in the following sections.

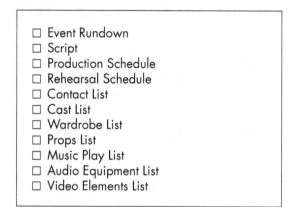

- ☐ Event Rundown
- ☐ Script
- ☐ Production Schedule
- ☐ Rehearsal Schedule
- ☐ Contact List
- ☐ Cast List
- ☐ Wardrobe List
- ☐ Props List
- ☐ Music Play List
- ☐ Audio Equipment List
- ☐ Video Elements List

Figure 12.4 Essential Event Production Documents

Event Rundowns

The key event presentation tool is called the *rundown* (also sometimes known as the running order or *run-of-show*), a document that outlines the precise details of how an event will unfold. The document is divided into rows that represent *segments* or *scenes,* descriptions of a major event activity, and columns that provide fine detail as to what occurs within each segment. A complete sample event rundown appears in Appendix 10, a small portion of which is represented in Figure 12.5 for the purposes of the discussion that follows.

During planning meetings, and in the midst of the event itself, it is simplest and most expedient to refer to production segments by its sequentially assigned item number. It also removes the possibility of error in case some segments are similarly titled. Following the item number is the time column, indicating the precise time of day that each segment will begin. It is advisable to synchronize all of the presentation staff's clocks and watches to "official event time" at least one hour prior to the entrance of the audience. Digital stopwatches that display the time of day to fractions of a second are highly preferred over analog timepieces with sweep second hands. If the event is televised, the official time is set by the broadcaster, as networks must time their programming and breaks with the highest level of precision. Official network time may be confirmed by a quick visit to the broadcaster's production truck.

The running time (R/T) indicates the amount of time required to complete each segment. In the preceding example, the running time is expressed in the most common form for televised sports events—"hours:minutes:seconds." Rundowns are easiest to customize and maintain on a spreadsheet program such as Microsoft Excel, enabling the event organizer to apply formulas that automatically calculate the next entry in the time column based on the running time in the previous row. As is true of all planning documents, revisions will be made constantly, and any change in a segment's running time will affect all the timings that follow. The ability to see the effects of these changes instantaneously is what makes a properly formatted spreadsheet essential. In the previous example, the running time of segment 1, which begins at 7:00 P.M., is 30 minutes. Segment 2, then, will begin precisely at 7:30 P.M. If the running time of segment 1 is changed to 35 minutes, the formula will automatically recalculate the start time for the player warm-up to 7:35 P.M., and carry the adjustment through the entire rundown document.

The next column gives a description of the activities occurring within the segment. The description should be detailed enough to provide a general sense of how the event site will appear

#	Time	Segment	R/T	Description	Audio	Video/Scorbrd
1	7:00:00	House open	0:30:00	Audience enters. Lights at preset levels. Gobos in corners. Stage managers to get players out of locker rooms at 7:25:00.	P.A. mic: Welcome and sponsor recognition (Pea Pond Mills, Pete's Pies, Faroff Airlines, Metro Daily News) over music bed #1	Event and sponsor logos in rotation; welcome; sponsor logos during recognition (Pea Pond Mills, Pete's Pies, Faroff Airlines, Metro Daily News)
2	7:30:00	Player warm-ups	0:20:00	Players enter and warm up on field. Lights on full.	Music bed #2	Event and sponsor logos in rotation; welcome

Figure 12.5 Setting up an Event Rundown

to the audience, as well as any details regarding what should be set up during this time period in preparation for the next segment. In this example, the field will be lit at some predetermined level specifically designed to create a desired theatrical effect as the audience enters. During the same segment, stage managers, the individuals responsible for the movement of people and materials on the field, will ensure that players are moved from the locker rooms with ample time to begin their warm-ups as scheduled in segment 2.

Columns for rundowns can be customized for the specific needs of a particular sports event. Most will include an "audio" column that will describe what the audience will hear during the segment. As will be made more apparent by referring to the complete rundown in Appendix 10, the audio column will describe whether the sound the audience should hear will come from a disc player, an audio file on a hard drive, or a particular microphone. Many permanent event organizers or their audio contractors use a "file server" on which music and prerecorded announcements are stored in a digital format for instant retrieval and play. Servers are especially useful when flexible, immediate access to a large library of music is required, often used to react to specific game or event situations.

A column may also be added for "video" if a large screen exists in the event venue upon which to run moving images. Many companies also rent screens that may be installed especially for an event on a freestanding scaffold, hung from overhead trusses, or mounted on the back of a tractor-trailer. Presentation directors for events of more modest scale can rent video projectors and screens, LCD video walls, or large-screen HD television screens, as appropriate for the size of their event and whether it is held in daylight, at night, or indoors.

The video screen can be used to simulcast broadcast coverage of the event or images from cameras operated solely for the consumption of the venue audience. Providing live coverage to the screens is commonly called "I-Mag," or image magnification. Although including I-Mag coverage of the event can be expensive, there are few presentation tools that can establish better intimacy and participation between the athletes and their fans. Pre-produced video highlights of past events, features on participating athletes, and special music videos can also be presented to add great entertainment value for the fans. Animations and still graphics can be designed to display player close-ups, background, trivia, and the informative statistics that have become so important in recent years. Video screens are also often used for displays of game operations information, including score, play clocks, and other essential play information when separate scoreboards are not present or in use. In such cases, it is best to display game information at all times on some portion of the screen so they remain visible for players and coaches when replays and other video features are being shown.

Sponsors also consider the ability to run commercials or display their logos on the screen as highly desirable exposure opportunities. In basic productions, videos may be run directly from DVDs, but are most often stored in a file server for instant access. The same column on the rundown can be used to describe the images displayed on the scoreboards or electronic message boards (also known as matrix boards, or, for displays located on the fascia of venue seating areas, ribbon boards), if available and appropriate. The sample event in Appendix 10, for example, takes place in a facility that is equipped only with a matrix board.

To customize the rundown to the needs of the program, presentation directors can add more columns to the spreadsheet. Additional columns may describe the activities of the broadcaster (of particular importance if the presentation director must keep the audience entertained during commercial breaks), performers entertaining in areas off the field, or any other major activity. It is also a good practice to add an empty column for comments to the right side so various production staff can insert notes regarding their own responsibilities for each segment.

The running order must be kept current and distributed to all production personnel with the date and time of revisions noted on all pages. A general announcement noting the date and time of the final revision should be communicated to all production staff before the event begins to ensure that all possess the correct, definitive version. It is important that the final revision is distributed at a time when everyone can receive and review it well before the production begins.

Scripts

The rundown defines the specific information that is required for the script, the document that contains the exact words to which the hosts or announcers must give voice. Scripts are best prepared with a heading on the top right side of the page showing the item number from the running order, as well as the segment description (see sample script page in Figure 12.6). Center the name or role of the individual who will read this portion of the script. Print the script in large, double-spaced type, and underscore or bold the key points of emphasis. This will also help to immediately identify the contents of the script page without having to read all of the copy.

Like the running order, the script must remain current with the date and time of any revision, noted as a footnote on all pages. Be sure the public address announcer and/or host has an opportunity to review the script—even if not completely finalized—before event day to enable that person to make his or her own notes, investigate pronunciations of names, and be familiar enough with the copy to deliver it confidently, enthusiastically, and error-free.

It is best to provide the script to the announcer in a loose-leaf notebook to allow the insertion of revised pages when changes are made without having to replace the entire script. Use a different color paper for sheets replaced each time a series of script revisions are released, and match the prevailing running order with the same color paper, using the recommended order in Figure 12.7.

Scripts often include contractually obligated sponsor acknowledgments and commercial announcements, usually delivered during the pre-event period, intermissions, and breaks in the action. Throughout a sports event, however, the audience is often waiting expectantly to know what's going on. Identify for the announcer those moments and situations during the competition when it is appropriate to relay information to the public. Think of how you watch a sports event on television—the announcers tell you everything you need to know. Why should your paying customers receive any less information? Such information may include upcoming matches, official results, explanations of judges' or referees decisions, important statistics, and records that have been broken. Establish a protocol as to when those announcements may be delivered—during play or only during a break

(1) HOUSE OPEN

ANNOUNCER

WELCOME TO THE FIVE COUNTY FOOTBALL TOURNAMENT, PRESENTED BY **PEA POND MILLS.** TODAY'S EXCITING EVENTS ARE ALSO BROUGHT TO YOU BY:

PETE'S PIES. MADE FRESH EACH DAY RIGHT IN PETE'S OWN KITCHEN. VISIT **PETE'S PIES' WEBSITE** AND ENTER THE CODE ON YOUR TICKET FROM TODAY'S EVENT FOR FREE DELIVERY OF YOUR NEXT FRESH FRUIT PIE ORDER. FRESH PIES FROM FRESH PERSPECTIVES, THAT'S PETE'S . . .

AND BY **FAROFF AIRLINES.** FAROFF IS GOING YOUR WAY WITH 15 FLIGHTS DAILY FROM FIVE COUNTY METRO AIRPORT. CONNECTING YOU WITH AMERICA. FOR YOUR NEXT TRIP, THINK FAROFF . . .

AND THE **METRO DAILY NEWS.** BE SURE TO STOP BY THE DAILY NEWS KIOSK BEHIND SECTION 101 FOR YOUR FREE COPY OF TODAY'S PAPER AND A 90-DAY TRIAL OF **METRO DAILY SPORTS ONLINE.** SEE FOR YOURSELF WHY WE'RE RATED #1 FOR FIVE COUNTY AREA SPORTS!

Figure 12.6 Sample Script Page

1. White
2. Pink
3. Blue
4. Green
5. Yellow

Release script changes in bunches, rather than one page at a time, when possible. After reaching the yellow revisions, return to the original order starting with pink, noted at the top of the page as "double pink," and so on.

Figure 12.7 Script and Running Order Release Color Order

in the action. Video screens are also often used to communicate important information when it is deemed inappropriate or too intrusive to the game to deliver it over the audio system.

Production Schedule

If the event rundown is the key tool for the actual presentation, the production schedule is its analog for the staff responsible for preparing the participants and physical site ahead of the event. The production schedule outlines all of the preparatory activities at the event facility. A sample production schedule is provided for illustrative purposes in Figure 12.8.

Cast List

Management of the event's noncompetitive participants and performers can be facilitated by a cast list, as illustrated in Figure 12.9. The cast list is a roster of the various individuals or groups, organized by their role or function as defined in the running order. The names in each unit appear in the next column, followed by the key contact for each. Note that the marching band in this example is made up of a total of 150 members from four different high school bands. The key contacts in this case are the band directors of the schools.

FIVE COUNTY FOOTBALL TOURNAMENT
PRODUCTION SCHEDULE
(as of Wednesday, February 7—12:30 P.M.)

Day/Date/Time	Activity	Location
Friday, September 9		
9:00 A.M.–12:00 P.M.	Phone and data lines installed	Room 156
1:00 P.M.–6:00 P.M.	Production office equipment (laptops, copier/printers) delivered	Room 156
Saturday, September 10		
2:00 P.M.–5:00 P.M.	*Calhoun vs. Kennedy H.S.*	Stadium Field
6:00 P.M.–11:00 P.M.	Production office setup	Room 156
Sunday, September 11		
9:00 A.M.	Security begins—Credentials required	All Areas
9:00 A.M.–6:00 P.M.	Banner and signage installation	All Areas
Monday, September 12		
9:00 A.M.	Production office opens	Room 156
9:00 A.M.	Distribute walkie-talkies	Room 156
10:00 A.M.–5:00 P.M.	Clean and set up locker rooms	Rooms 142/4

Figure 12.8 Sample Production Schedule

Tuesday, September 13		
9:00 A.M.–5:00 P.M.	Load in and install lighting	Stadium Field
	Load in and install sound	Stadium Field
7:00 P.M.–11:59 P.M.	Focus lighting	Stadium Field
Wednesday, September 14		
9:00 A.M.	Balance sound system	Stadium Field
9:00 A.M.–12:00 P.M.	Paint field markings and 50-yd. line logo	Stadium Field
9:00 A.M.–2:00 P.M.	**NO STAFF OR CREW PERMITTED ON FIELD!**	
9:00 A.M.–3:00 P.M.	Media workroom and lounge setup	Rooms 136/8
6:00 P.M.–11:00 P.M.	Technical rehearsal	Stadium Field
Thursday, September 15		
4:00 P.M.–8:00 P.M.	Ceremony rehearsals	Stadium Field
7:00 P.M.–11:00 P.M.	Equipment trailers arrive	Gate 5
8:00 P.M.–11:00 P.M.	Technical rehearsals	Stadium Field
Friday, September 16		
8:00 A.M.–3:00 P.M.	Team practices and photos *(No stadium audio!)*	Stadium Field
3:00 P.M.–7:00 P.M.	Ceremony rehearsals	Stadium Field
7:00 P.M.–9:00 P.M.	Dress and camera rehearsal	Stadium Field
Saturday, September 17		
6:00 A.M.	Television news trucks arrive	Gate 5
8:00 A.M.–4:00 P.M.	Team practices and photos *(No stadium audio!)*	Stadium Field
4:30 P.M.—5:45 P.M.	Ceremony rehearsals	Stadium Field
6:00 P.M.	**DOORS OPEN**	
7:00 P.M.	Opening ceremonies begin	
Sunday, September 18		
8:00 A.M.–10:00 P.M.	Tournament play	
Monday, September 19		
8:00 A.M.–6:00 P.M.	Load out all equipment and offices	
6:00 P.M.	All walkie-talkies returned	Room 156

Figure 12.8 *(Continued)*

FIVE COUNTY FOOTBALL TOURNAMENT

Cast Unit (#)	Name(s)	Key Contact	Coordinator
Marching Band (150)	Maxwell High School Band	Ethan Jacobs	Ryan Holzer
	Nathaniel High School Band	Harold Matthews	Ryan Holzer
Flag Bearers (50 + 3)	Andreas High School Drill Team	Catherine Arthur	Tiffany Richards
	McJames High School Drill Team	Jean Shirley	Tiffany Richards
USMC Color Guard (4)	U.S. Marines—Quantico	Capt. Mitch Field	Marc Levine
Army Parachute Team (5)	U.S. Army—Fort Bragg	Lt. Erwin Edwards	Marc Levine
Lieutenant Governor (1)	Lt. Gov. Jill Samuels	Art Frank	Bill Haufreitz
Coin Toss Celebrity (1)	Senator Jackson Litvak	Katerina Daniels	Bill Haufreitz
Anthem Singer (1)	Jill Andrea	Jill Andrea	Bill Haufreitz
Announcer (1)	Rob Roberts	Rob Roberts	Bill Haufreitz
Trophy Presenter (1)	Phil DeBasquette (Sponsor)	Maria Marconi	Bill Haufreitz

Figure 12.9 Cast List

Also notice that although the flag bearer unit requires 50 participants, three additional drill team members are included in the cast list. These extra individuals are "alternates," cast members who will attend all rehearsals with their units, so that they could easily replace those who drop out of the event due to illness, schedule conflicts, inadequate rehearsal attendance, poor performance, or subsequent disinterest. Alternates are strongly recommended for amateur performing groups in which the number of participants is critical. In this example, there are 50 flag bearers, each holding a flag of one of the United States. To have 49 states represented would be unacceptable; therefore, it is important to include alternates in case a member of the unit fails to attend the event for any reason. The marching band, however, requires no alternates, as missing members would not be as noticeable. (*Note:* Marching bands that perform intricate field formations, as is often the case in football game halftimes, may require alternates to eliminate the possibility of visible gaps in their routines.) Alternates, when required, serve a very critical function. However, as they may not participate in the actual ceremonies if ultimately unneeded, the organizer may assign them to other roles during the event that require little or no rehearsal preparation.

The cast list identifies the key contacts for each unit, the person to whom information should be directed for each group in the cast. Data such as the contact's phone number, e-mail address, and mailing address should be included on the list. The final column on the cast list denotes the talent coordinator (TC), an event staff member directly responsible for all aspects of the participation of specific cast units. Depending on the complexity of the program, the talent coordinator can serve other roles on the event staff as well. For example, the TC responsible for the participation of sponsors in event ceremonies can also serve as the individual responsible for sponsor-driven functions such as fulfillment, and guest management. A TC should attend all rehearsals for his or her assigned units and serve as the primary conduit of information to the group's key contact. Although a TC can be assigned to more than one group of participants, care should be exercised to avoid tasking one TC with groups that may participate simultaneously in sectional rehearsals that are held in separate locations (see "Sectional Rehearsals").

Wardrobe List

A wardrobe list can provide both the presentation director and the cast members with a clear understanding of required items of apparel, and who is expected to provide them. The wardrobe list, as illustrated in Figure 12.10, begins with the same units as the cast list, and includes any other groups that may also be visible to the audience. In this example, additional wardrobe guidelines are specified for the stage managers, stage crew, and camera people with their utilities (utilities are people who accompany camera personnel, handling the cables so they are neither tangled nor tripped on, or who aim the antenna that transmits images from a wireless camera to its radio receiver). These staff members are often forgotten until they show up at the event site in torn jeans and dirty T-shirts.

It is not unreasonable to require cast, staff and crew to supply wardrobe items that are commonly worn by the general population such as white sneakers, or black or khaki pants, as long as enough time is provided for participants to procure these personal items should they not already possess them. The event should provide items that are not in common usage, those that include event logos or specific designs, or that must match exactly with other members of the same unit. Stage crew, stage management staff, and camera crew are often dressed in dark clothing to hide or visually deemphasize their appearance as compared to the cast.

Wardrobe items provided by the event are best distributed to the cast and alternates on the day before the event, or the day prior to the dress rehearsal. This way, apparel is less likely to be damaged, soiled, or misplaced prior to event day. Be sure to include alternates in the wardrobe order. Cast members who lose or arrive without the proper wardrobe for dress rehearsal or on event day is yet another reason to have alternates waiting to take their place.

Scheduling Rehearsals

Rehearsals are essential to the smooth operation of any event. Even the most simple and straightforward presentation should be meticulously rehearsed to ensure smooth and professional execution. Several different types of rehearsals may be required including sectional rehearsals, technical run-throughs and dress rehearsals, as illustrated in Figure 12.11.

Sectional Rehearsals

Units that perform at sports events ceremonies may have different rehearsal requirements based on the complexity of their participation or the precision of their performance. For example, a marching band that must execute several different formations while playing, for example, would require a larger number of rehearsals than, say, the announcer. A series of sectional rehearsals expressly for the marching band and the flag bearing drill team members that must be integrated into their field formations has been scheduled in hypothetical example illustrated in Figure 12.11. In the early stages, it is not important for the band to practice on the same exact field on which it will ultimately appear. To enable the technical staff to install the sound, lights, and other equipment needed at the hypothetical event venue, these first sectional rehearsals are scheduled at a nearby high school.

Sectional rehearsals may be conducted with or without sets, staging, or props. It is wise, however, to simulate the position of any staging or obstacles (e.g., location and orientation of field entrances, team benches, lighting towers, added bleachers, risers, or constructed sets) that will be present during the event with traffic cones and construction tape to familiarize the cast with their locations throughout rehearsals. Later sectional rehearsals should include the actual props,

FIVE COUNTY FOOTBALL TOURNAMENT

Wardrobe List

Cast (#)	Wardrobe	Provided By
Marching band (150)	Full band uniform	Band director
	Clean white sneakers	Cast member
Flag bearers (50 + 3)	Black slacks	Cast member
	White shirt	Cast member
	Event jersey	Event
USMC color guard (4)	USMC dress uniform	US Marine Corps
Army parachute team (5)	US Army uniform	US Army
Lieutenant governor (1)	Sport jacket	Own wardrobe
	Shirt and slacks	Own wardrobe
Coin toss celebrity (1)	Sport jacket	Cast member
	Shirt and slacks	Cast member
	Event cap	Event
Anthem singer (1)	Blue skirt	Cast member
	White blouse	Cast member
	Red kerchief	Cast member
Announcer (1)	Sport jacket with event patch	Event
	Shirt and slacks	Cast member
Trophy presenter (1)	Sport jacket with event patch	Event
	Shirt and slacks	Cast member
Stage managers (2)	Khaki slacks (no jeans)	Own wardrobe
	Event T-shirt	Event
	Event cap	Event
Stage crew (3)	Black slacks	Own wardrobe
	Black event T-shirt	Event
	Black event cap	Event
	Black sneakers (no stripes)	Event
Camera crew and utilities (6)	Khaki slacks (no jeans)	Own wardrobe
	Event T-shirt	Event
	Event cap	Event

Figure 12.10 Wardrobe List

Five County Football Tournament Rehearsal Schedule				
Day, Date	**Time**	**Location**	**Rehearsal**	**Units**
Saturday, September 10	9:00 A.M.–12:00 P.M.	Calhoun H.S.	Pre-show sectional	Marching band (150) Flag bearers (50+3)
Sunday, September 11	4:00 A.M.–6:00 P.M.	Calhoun H.S.	Pre-show sectional	Marching band (150) Flag bearers (50+3)
Monday, September 12	4:00 A.M.–6:00 P.M.	Calhoun H.S.	Pre-show sectional	Marching band (150) Flag bearers (50+3)
Wednesday, September 14	4:00 A.M.–6:00 P.M.	Calhoun H.S.	Pre-show sectional	Marching band (150) Flag bearers (50+3)
Thursday, September 15	6:00 A.M.–11:00 P.M. 4:00–5:30 P.M. 6:00–8:00 P.M.	Five County Stadium Five County Stadium Five County Stadium	Technical rehearsal Announcer rehearsal Pre-show rehearsal	Announcer Marching band (150) Flag bearer (50+3) Announcer Parachute spotter (1)
Friday, September 16	8:00–11:00 P.M. 3:00–4:00 P.M. 4:00–5:00 P.M. 7:00–9:00 P.M.	Five County Stadium Five County Stadium Five County Stadium Five County Stadium	Technical rehearsal Entrance of athletes rehearsal Color guard and celebrity blocking Dress and camera rehearsal	Athlete stand-ins (50) USMC color guard (4) Celebrity stand-ins (3) Marching band (150) Flag bearers (50+3) Announcer Parachute team (5) USMC color guard (4) Celebrity stand-ins (5)
Saturday, September 17	4:30–5:00 P.M. 5:00–5:15 P.M. 5:15–5:45 P.M. 6:00 P.M.	Five County Stadium Five County Stadium Five County Stadium Five County Stadium	Anthem singer rehearsal Celebrity blocking Trophy presentation rehearsal Doors open!	Anthem (1) Lt. governor (1) Coin toss celebrity (1) Trophy presenter (1)

Figure 12.11 Rehearsal Schedule

sets, and technical production elements, and, if feasible, are best held in the venue in which the ceremonies will take place.

Blocking

Blocking is the process of determining entrances, movement, and positions during sports event ceremonies, as well as the exiting of all participants, props, and staging in sequential order. Blocking is best planned on the actual performance space, but may be simulated elsewhere. The first blocking run-through need not be done with the actual participants present. Stand-ins may be positioned and repositioned until the presentation director (and television director, if appropriate) is satisfied with the ceremony's flow and appearance. If stand-ins have been used and, if at all practical, a final blocking run-through should be scheduled with the actual participants.

The importance of rehearsing the entrance and exit of each unit cannot be overstated. Blocking will help to identify potential areas of congestion and confusion at ingress and egress points, and can indicate the length of time required for participants to move from their point of entry to their performance area, and then back out again. Blocking diagrams, such as those in Figures 12.12(a) through (c), may be drawn and distributed to cast members and staff to graphically demonstrate the proper movement of the cast, sets, and props on the field; these are particularly helpful tools for complex ceremonies that involve large numbers of participants. (In this example, a marching band and flag bearers enter the field to perform, at the end of which a color guard and anthem singer enter, deliver their performance, and all exit to clear the field for the game.)

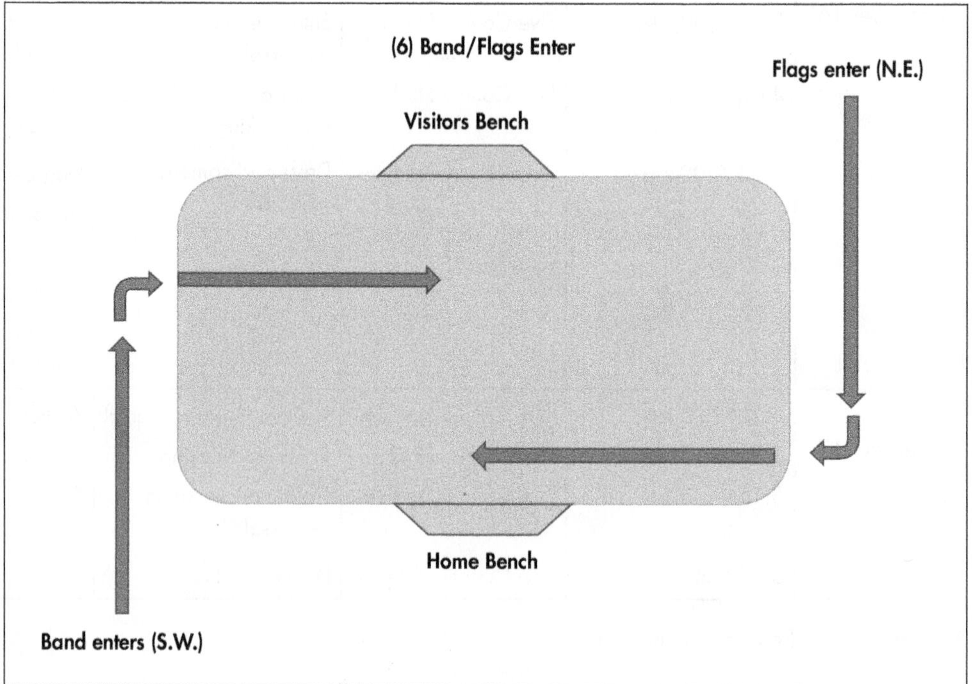

Figure 12.12a Blocking Diagram 1

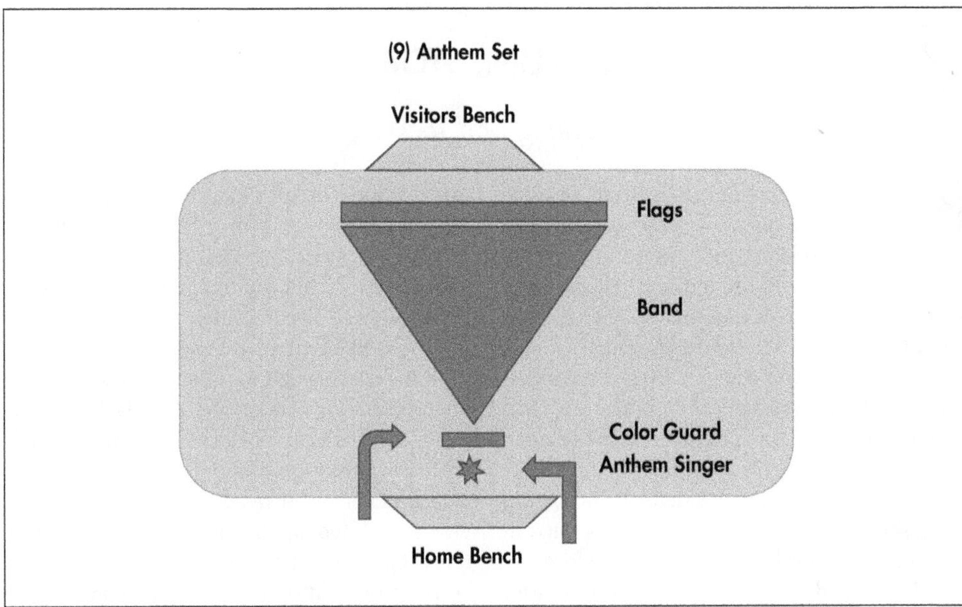

Figure 12.12b Blocking Diagram 2

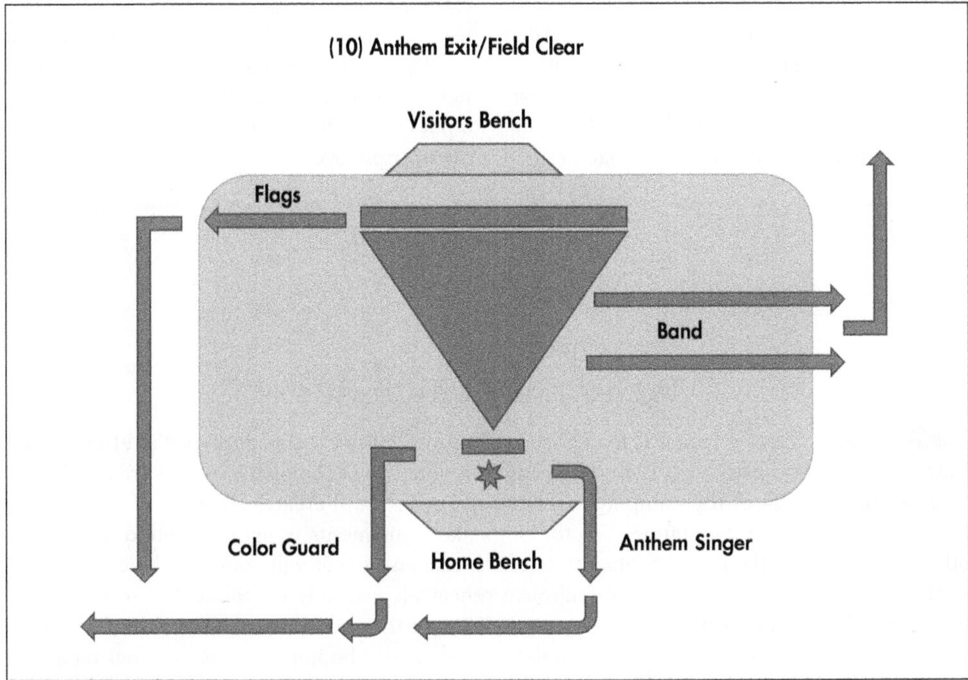

Figure 12.12c Blocking Diagram 3

SIDELINE STORY

Blocking and Tackling

Blocking sports ceremonies is often an exercise in scheduling and traffic control, and participating athletes and teams always get the right of way. Without them, there is no sports event and it is essential to manage the entrances on and off the field, court, or rink to ensure that pomp does not create a circumstance that interferes with their safe and unhindered access. Will a stage come down the same tunnel through which the players must exit? If there is room on the sidelines, bring the stage through the tunnel during a stoppage in play and temporarily place it in a safe location off of the field. Or, if time will permit, wait until the players clear the field before bringing out the stage.

Often, there are a limited number of access points to the playing surface and the competition for time and space can create significant complications. When the National Hockey League's Stanley Cup is awarded at center ice after the deciding game of the best-of-seven series, the crew that deploys carpet runners for dignitaries, the trophy table, and the trophy itself, is spring-loaded in a predescribed order, along with stage managers and participants in a tunnel that is frequently the same one that players will use to access their locker rooms. These elements are in place with five minutes remaining in the final period of play, and squirts quickly out onto the ice through what is typically a narrow one-person-wide door in the dasherboards when the game is declared officially over. If with one minute remaining, the game is tied and appears to be heading for overtime, the elements lined up inside the tunnel rapidly move back out of the way and into a service corridor or holding room so postgame preparations cannot be seen by players returning to the locker room. The process of reassembling the postgame ceremony in the tunnel, out of view of the fans and players, is repeated once the players return to the ice to begin the extra period, the stage managers and crew waiting expectantly to spring into action in sudden death overtime. Consider the frazzled nerves on both sides of that narrow door when a potentially deciding game extends into double or triple overtime.

Technical Rehearsals

The designers and technicians responsible for lighting, sound, video, and special effects need time to work toward perfecting their event-day presentation. Technical rehearsals are conducted to make sure that all of the equipment functions properly and creates the desired result. This is the time when the presentation director can make adjustments in lighting, sound, video, and other effects before the participants arrive for the rehearsals that will combine the cast with all of the technical elements. As such, technical rehearsals can only be conducted in the actual location where the event will take place. In addition, if the sports event is being held outdoors during any time when the sky is not completely dark, it will be important to conduct technical rehearsals at approximately the same time of day as the actual presentation to evaluate the effect of both the intensity and angle of sunlight on the visibility of added lighting, video, and other visual effects.

Dress Rehearsal

The final rehearsal is often called the dress rehearsal. This rehearsal should run through the event from start to finish in real time, that is, without stopping. This will help the presentation director verify the timings on the rundown and make adjustments as needed. The dress rehearsal should involve every participant in the ceremony, although it is not uncommon to again have dignitaries and celebrities represented by stand-ins. Dress rehearsal is the last, best time to see how the ceremonies will unfold exactly the way the audience will see it on event day. It is final confirmation that the production plan is as accurate as possible. For events that are broadcast on television, it is often also the best opportunity for the broadcast director to stage a simultaneous camera rehearsal to maximize the quality of the coverage of the show.

If an event's production is particularly complex, it is strongly recommended that one or more event run-throughs be scheduled in "stop-and-go" fashion. These are extra run-throughs of the entire program, held on the day or two prior to the dress rehearsal, involving all participants (or stand-ins) and technical departments, during which the presentation director may stop the rehearsal, request adjustments, provide direction, and restart the segment. Stop-and-go run-throughs should be scheduled to take no less than three times the expected running time of the event to accommodate the many pauses you can expect in the rehearsal.

Technical Tools of Sports Event Production

In addition to the ceremonies and entertainment of an event, the competition itself will require the installation and operation of technical systems such as sound and lights. Fulfilling their most basic objectives, a sound (or audio) system is responsible for communicating verbal information and musical entertainment to the audience, and lighting maintains optimal conditions for safe play and visibility for the audience, both live and on television. At minimum, the design of these technical systems must support and never impede competitive activities. This essential mission, often expanded by the theatrical needs of ceremonies and entertainment, is further explored in the following sections.

Staging

While the use of staging or risers for sports event ceremonies is not an absolute requirement, the elevation they provide above the playing surface for anthem and musical performances, speeches, or postgame trophy presentations, can imbue any element with a sense of greater visibility and importance. Staging postgame ceremonies on risers also provides the media with a more clear view for photographers and camera crews. For a small number of individuals, stages need not be very high. They can be custom built or fashioned from risers that can be rented in heights as low as six inches or as high as 36 inches and in rectangular panels or pie-shaped pieces that can create circular stages. If more than a few inches high, stages should have safety rails fastened on the back side and a stair unit with handrails for safe and easy access.

The method by which the risers will be deployed and where they will be set will play a central role in considering how to design a stage for sports ceremonies. Does it need to be deployed and removed quickly? Will it be placed directly on the playing surface, on the sidelines, or can it be installed in an unoccupied area within the seating bowl? Will the stage be wheeled into place or carried by a backstage crew or volunteers? Will it be stored out of sight when not in use, or will it be in plain sight throughout the event?

Obviously, using stages on the playing surface itself will involve the most sensitive considerations. If the stage risers are supported by legs, you must make sure they will not create pits or divots on the playing surface. This can be mitigated by placing bits of plywood or another hardboard material beneath the legs to better distribute the weight of the stage when fully loaded with participants. (Be sure to paint the plywood the same color as the playing surface so they do not stand out—green for grass, white for ice, tan for wood floors, etc.) You must also install it quickly when athletes are either warming up or playing, and in such a way as to not damage the surface. Staging will either be hand-carried or rolled out on wheels. It is recommended to hand-carry the stage(s) into place if it is not too heavy, large, or dangerous for the crew to do so. If must be rolled into place, be sure the tires are as large as practical and made of rubber—smaller, harder wheels create greater stresses on the playing surface. Additionally, be sure that wheels are not turned too sharply, which can tear grass and leave skids on wood floors and ice. The same goes for vehicles used in any on-field ceremonies—the combination of sharp turns and weight can cause significant damage, especially to a field made of natural grass.

SIDELINE STORY

Protecting the Players' Turf

Super Bowls are world famous for their halftime shows. Elaborate stages, technical effects, a cast of multitudes, and band gear for star entertainment are set in place during the roughly eight minutes television broadcasters use to recap the action of the game's first half and cut away for two sets of commercials. A crew of hundreds gets everything in place for the 12-minute show, and the removal of the staging in less than another eight minutes requires precise choreography and stage management.

Until Super Bowl XLIII in 2009, similarly elaborate pregame entertainment was offered to the audience from the field, sandwiched between player warm-ups and kickoff. To accomplish installation of the stage, the performance of the act(s), and removal of all elements within as short a period of time as possible, the time between the end of player warm-ups and kickoff bloated to in excess of 55 minutes at Super Bowl XLI. Players could hardly be warmed up for their most important game of the year nearly an hour after they left the field.

To reduce the amount of time between warm-ups and kickoff and still offer the television audience spectacular pregame entertainment, the star performance was relocated at Super Bowl XLIII to a stage in the NFL's Tailgate Party in the stadium parking lot, where it has been staged ever since. In this way, player introductions, the anthem performance and the ceremonial coin toss, among other smaller event elements requiring far less setup and running time could be incorporated into the pregame rundown in such a way as to reduce the time, between warm-ups and kickoff to a period similar to a regular season game. The concert performance moved outside of the stadium is shown live on the stadium videoscreens, or recorded and played back at a time that makes the most sense from a live event perspective.

Another way to reduce stresses on the players and playing surface is to stage entertainment elements on the sidelines or in an area off of the field entirely. For many years, cheerleaders at American football games have performed on the sidelines. At the 2009 NFL Pro Bowl, an all-star exhibition game, stages were build on scaffolds in the corners of Aloha Stadium, areas of the host facility not used for seating or obstructing the views of fans. These stages accommodated a lively band playing rock tunes entertaining live during television commercials instead of the game presentation director having to play recorded music. From time to time, other elements such as Hawaiian drummers and cheerleaders could entertain from these areas, bringing the show closer than ever to the fans in the stands.

Sound

Surprisingly, sound is one of the most often-overlooked production elements at sports events. Even many of today's largest professional sports facilities possess permanent installations that are substandard in terms of how well they amplify and distribute sound throughout the venue, or the range of sound they can reproduce. Many use loudspeakers that are well suited to project the range of the human voice, but are incapable of reproducing the wide range of bass and treble tones appropriate for playing live or recorded music. If music is integral to the entertainment of the audience, be sure to test any existing permanent systems for the quality of the sound they can provide, using various pieces of music with as wide a range of tones as possible. Orchestral soundtracks such as John Williams themes and digitally recorded pop tunes can clearly demonstrate the degree of a sound system's versatility.

Also test how well the sound is distributed throughout the audience. Sound reaches spectators in a "line of sight" fashion. That is, if you are in an area where you can see the front of the speakers, then sound should be able to reach your ears without the distortion of first being reflected off another surface. The system should be balanced so the volume and tone of the sound are essentially the same regardless of where a listener sits. A system has an insufficient number of speakers, or is unbalanced, when the volume in one area is very loud, but low, distorted, or inaudible in others. In addition, determine whether the sound should be projected onto the playing surface, the benches, or the athlete waiting areas. If so, additional speakers may be required, as many facility's systems are designed to amplify sound only into the audience and not onto the playing surface.

If the existing sound system is not up to required standards, work with a qualified audio designer or rental agency to supplement the number of speakers or add the right kinds of speakers to present clear, distinctive sound. Sometimes, however, it is best to start over and install an entirely new, temporary sound system that will operate independently from the permanent one. Audiophiles are familiar with the two major types of speakers (although there are more)—woofers for low, bass tones, and tweeters for higher pitched sounds. Woofers, are typically housed in larger speaker cabinets to achieve their characteristic deep and resonant tones. Without woofers, music can seem shrill and even irritating. Tweeters are needed to provide the clear, high tones that prevent the sound from seeming muffled. Do not be surprised if your audio company installs what looks like single speaker cabinets. Frequently, both types, along with speakers that provide the midrange frequencies, are housed in the same cabinet for easier deployment. Speaker cabinets are also often stacked or hung in a long series called *line arrays,* to better cover especially tall or wide areas with a uniform level and quality of sound.

Speakers project sound from amplifiers that receive audio information from a number of sources. The voices of announcers, hosts, and live performers are received from microphones that are either "hardwired" (have a cable that runs to the amplifier) or wireless. Wireless microphones, also known as RF mics, transmit the sound over a radio frequency (hence the *RF* abbreviation). RF microphones can simplify the staging of an event by allowing the performer to be located anywhere on the stage or playing surface without trailing a microphone cable. It is wise, however, to have back-up mics available (preferably hardwired) in case of a failure of the wireless system or unanticipated interference from another RF source. Note that there are usually many other pieces of electronic equipment at a sports event that will utilize radio frequencies, such as walkie-talkies used by the event and facility staff, and cameras and microphones being used by broadcasters, to name just a few. There may also be RF users outside, but near the venue, such as transportation dispatchers and others. It is, therefore, important that frequencies of all these users are coordinated to ensure the sound system broadcasts the signal from only those sources desired without interference from others on the same frequency. Many audio services vendors and companies specializing in RF frequency monitoring can provide coordination services before and during your event.

Recorded music at sports events is increasingly being played back from digital sources ranging from iPods to laptops to dedicated computer servers programmed to store musical tracks. Music loaded on a computer server system such as Click Effects and other professional playback and disk jockey programs, offers the great advantage of being able to access any desired piece of music instantaneously from a large library of songs. The software and technology required for music editing and storage of an enormous library of music has become inexpensive and widely available even to the home use market. At the time of this writing, a small Apple iPod device with 160 gigabytes of hard disk storage, sufficiently large to store up to 40,000 different songs, could be purchased for less than US$250. A large number of versatile programs for editing music and audio tracks is available for purchase from software developers and free from some shareware services, all offering capabilities that used to be available only from professional sound studios.

The sound from all audio sources is cabled to a mixing position, a console from which an operator can select which microphones, disc players, computer inputs, video sources, or computer servers (each dedicated to its own "channel") are to be turned on and those to be turned off. The mixing position can also blend the sound received from each channel to achieve the desired combination of sounds, such as an announcer's microphone and a selection of music in proper balance. The console should be located in the audience to allow the operator mixing the sound to experience the volume and balance between channels just as the audience does.

One of the unfortunate characteristics of the sound generated by large-scale pageantry is that may be difficult for participants to hear themselves and the other sounds of the event around them. Figure 12.13 provides a checklist of staging and production helpful hints relating to sound at sports events that will help to reduce the confusion.

Lighting

Lighting needs can be divided into three major categories—competitive necessities, television requirements, and theatrical or ceremonial needs. In this regard, the organizer's first and most important mission is to ensure that lighting is sufficient for the safe execution and viewing of the sports competition, with no areas of shadow that can affect the quality of play. Lighting must come from more than a single point in order to avoid the casting of shadows. Further, lighting sources must be elevated so they do not create blind spots by being projected from an area in the athletes' direct line of sight.

Televised sports events require a more powerful level of lighting for coverage of the competitive events. Most sports event stadiums and arenas that are home to organized professional, semiprofessional, or college sports teams are already equipped with lighting that will serve most television needs. Competitions held in venues that are infrequent sports event hosts and temporary outdoor facilities, however, may require added lighting for both general event and television lighting. Companies such as Iowa-based Musco Lighting can provide permanent and temporary installations. Their portable systems are often mounted on trucks, and are effective at distances of up to 1,000 feet. Temporary units may also be ordered with their own generators and equipped with booms to elevate lighting up to 150 feet high.

Events that are broadcast in high-definition format require an even greater flood of light than televised events of the past. The industry standard lighting level of 200 foot-candles (approximately 2,150 lux), long used in analog broadcasts, may now require a 50 percent increase or more

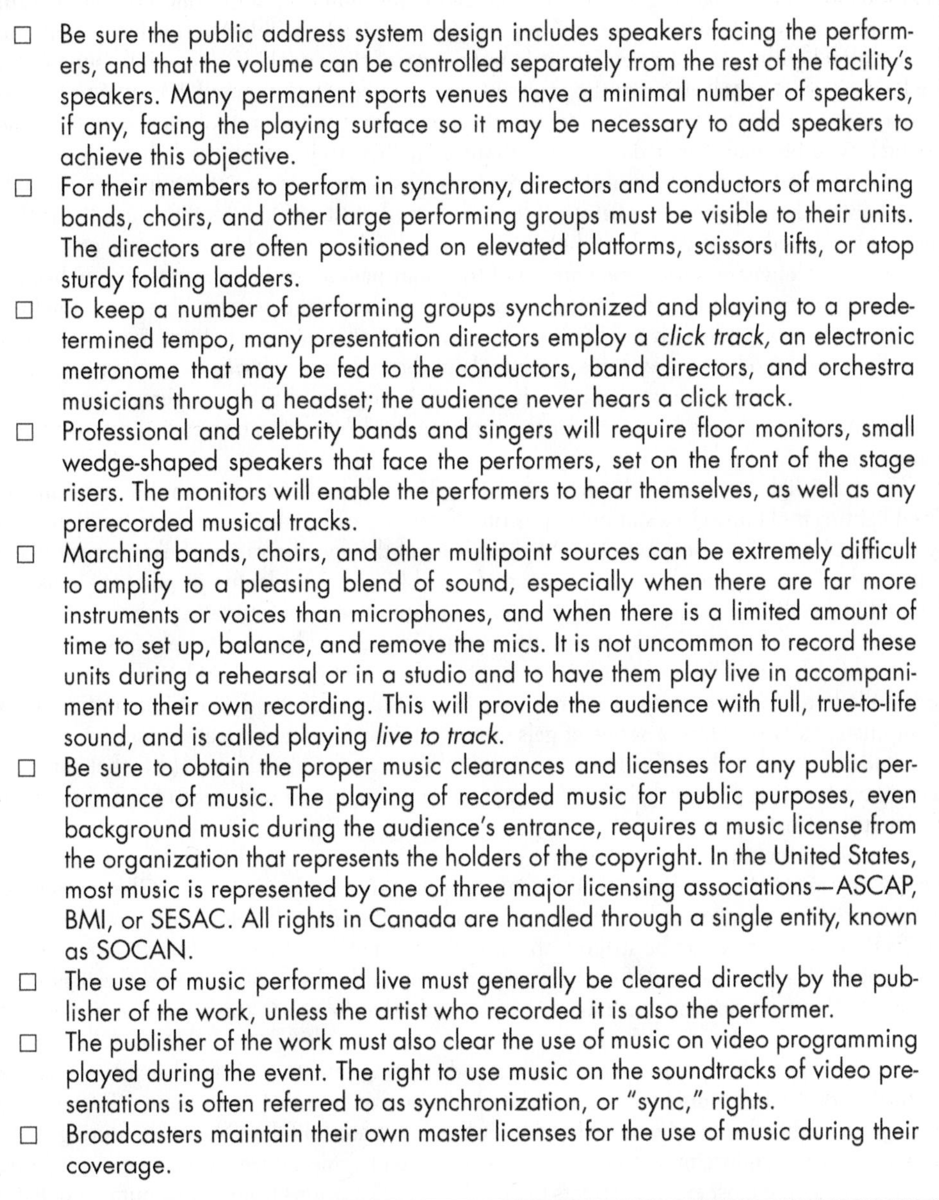

- ☐ Be sure the public address system design includes speakers facing the performers, and that the volume can be controlled separately from the rest of the facility's speakers. Many permanent sports venues have a minimal number of speakers, if any, facing the playing surface so it may be necessary to add speakers to achieve this objective.
- ☐ For their members to perform in synchrony, directors and conductors of marching bands, choirs, and other large performing groups must be visible to their units. The directors are often positioned on elevated platforms, scissors lifts, or atop sturdy folding ladders.
- ☐ To keep a number of performing groups synchronized and playing to a predetermined tempo, many presentation directors employ a *click track,* an electronic metronome that may be fed to the conductors, band directors, and orchestra musicians through a headset; the audience never hears a click track.
- ☐ Professional and celebrity bands and singers will require floor monitors, small wedge-shaped speakers that face the performers, set on the front of the stage risers. The monitors will enable the performers to hear themselves, as well as any prerecorded musical tracks.
- ☐ Marching bands, choirs, and other multipoint sources can be extremely difficult to amplify to a pleasing blend of sound, especially when there are far more instruments or voices than microphones, and when there is a limited amount of time to set up, balance, and remove the mics. It is not uncommon to record these units during a rehearsal or in a studio and to have them play live in accompaniment to their own recording. This will provide the audience with full, true-to-life sound, and is called playing *live to track.*
- ☐ Be sure to obtain the proper music clearances and licenses for any public performance of music. The playing of recorded music for public purposes, even background music during the audience's entrance, requires a music license from the organization that represents the holders of the copyright. In the United States, most music is represented by one of three major licensing associations—ASCAP, BMI, or SESAC. All rights in Canada are handled through a single entity, known as SOCAN.
- ☐ The use of music performed live must generally be cleared directly by the publisher of the work, unless the artist who recorded it is also the performer.
- ☐ The publisher of the work must also clear the use of music on video programming played during the event. The right to use music on the soundtracks of video presentations is often referred to as synchronization, or "sync," rights.
- ☐ Broadcasters maintain their own master licenses for the use of music during their coverage.

Figure 12.13 Sound Advice: Staging and Production Hints for Sports Events

in the level of illumination (at an increased price, of course) to at least 300 foot-candles (approximately 3,230 lux) for an HD broadcast.

Various types of lighting instruments and techniques can be applied to the presentation of a sports event, adding theatricality and excitement to opening ceremonies, athlete introductions, entertainment and anthem performances, intermission fan promotions, and more.

Before designing the lighting for ceremonies and entertainment, determine how the lighting to be used for competition and television purposes is controlled. Television lighting, and most competition lighting, is so bright that little in the way of theatrical lighting will be seen unless the lighting used for television or the competition is turned off or dimmed. Many of today's top indoor sports venues have installed electric shutters on their television lighting, which enables the facility to be temporarily darkened without actually extinguishing the lights. These shutters may be used for only a limited time, in some cases up to 15 or 20 minutes, to keep the lights behind them from overheating. Older venues and most outdoor facilities use lights that, once extinguished, must cool down before they can be relit, a period that can take as much as 15 minutes or longer. A noticeable amount of time may pass after the lights are turned back on for them to warm up to the temperature required for television coverage. The event's lighting designer should consult with the facility manager and test the house lighting for this *re-strike time*. There are also lighting systems that proclaim the ability to *re-strike* to the levels required for television coverage almost instantly. It is strongly suggested that any permanent lighting system not using shutters be tested for the time required for restoration to full intensity after being turned off.

Theatrical lighting can be divided into two major types—fixed and movable instruments. Fixed lighting is clamped in a stationary position, focused on a single nonmovable location. Leko lights, par cans, and fresnel (freh-NEL) lights are all of the specific variety. Lekos are spotlights that can be focused sharply on fixed areas of variable size. The lamps in par cans look like automobile headlamps, and basically function in a similar way—illuminating a larger area with a general "wash" of light. Fresnel lamps are adjustable and may be used for either spot lighting purposes or for achieving a wash of light. A sheet of colored gelatin (also known as a *gel*) can be installed on any of these fixed instruments to create light of the desired hue and intensity. Color changers or scrollers, a series of gels either manually or automatically operated, can also be installed in front of these fixed instruments. Strobes are specialized fixed lights that can blink once like a blinding flash of lightning, or at variable, sometimes rapid rates of speed to create stop-motion effects.

Dozens of stock patterns and custom-built logos can be projected by installing "gobos" on the lighting instrument, stencils that are cut from metal or etched on glass. Glass gobos can be fabricated in full color or less expensively in a single tone (with color added by a gel). The effects they can provide can be striking on either fixed or movable lighting systems. Sports event presentation directors can order custom gobos to project the logos of an event, the organizing entity, and their sponsors on the playing surface and other locations throughout and even outside the venue.

Movable lights can create more dynamic and exciting effects than fixed instruments, and are further divided into manually operated and computer-controlled instruments. Follow spots are large spotlights that can be moved manually by an operator to follow the action during player introductions and entertainment performances. The use of computerized, or intelligent, lighting, however, allows the most exciting effects to be achieved. The beams from a large number of lights may be moved in many directions at once, colors changed, the size and shape of the beams varied, gobos revealed and rotated. Different looks can be preset for the audience's entrance, athlete introductions, ceremonies, anthem performances, intermissions, and exits. The lighting designer "records" these settings into a computer, and can cause an entire segment's look to change dramatically with the press of a single button.

The production schedule may have to provide the designer with a significant amount of time to point and focus fixed lights in their desired positions and to program the complex looks that intelligent lighting can generate. As focusing must be done in darkness, the programming of lighting for events held outdoors must be done at night.

Lasers

A laser emits an intense beam of light that can be narrowly focused, bounced off mirrors, or filtered to create colors, prisms and cloudlike patterns. The output of a laser is best seen when the atmosphere contains moisture, as minute water droplets reflect the light that creates those brilliant beams. For this reason, the use of lasers often requires the use of fog or haze machines. A laser can be used to generate an arrow-straight beam focused on tiny mirrors located across the event facility, and the resulting reflections on additional mirrors to give the appearance of a great number of beams. Audiences often perceive they are seeing many laser beams when they are simply seeing a single beam split into dozens of reflections. Lasers can also be programmed to project logos or create animated effects when projected against a flat surface. These laser graphics are actually a single beam tracing the artwork at a very high rate of speed, which is why laser images seem to flicker as the design being drawn gets more complex. Lasers create a great amount of heat, and must be located where they can be cooled by a running water source. They must also be projected in areas away from the audience to avoid potential eye injuries to spectators. The operation of lasers requires experienced technicians and adherence to strict safety precautions.

Video and Projectors

As is true of audio, there are two ends to a video system. On one end is the source of the images, such as the television feed of a live broadcast, a sports event's dedicated cameras, and the playback of recorded materials and computer-generated animations. Recorded video can be played from the same kinds of computer servers and hard drives as recorded audio files, or for those with modest equipment budgets, from recordable DVDs prepared for the event. However, the great flexibility offered by instant access to a desired video clip offers has made storage of video images and animations on a computer's hard drive the most attractive alternative to sports presentation directors.

On the other end is the medium upon which the images are made visible to the audience. The various sources are cabled to a video switcher that enables an operator to select the images desired and change from one image to another by a desired effect, such as a cut (an instantaneous change from one camera or image to another), dissolve (a gradual fading out of one image as another fades in), or wipe (an animated effect that removes one image and replaces it with another). In a darkened indoor facility or an outdoor venue at night, video images may be projected on white screens. A projector is positioned either in front of or behind the screen. Rear projection (RP) screens are often preferred to eliminate the chance of shadows created by members of the audience or cast. The disadvantage of rear projection is the amount of space required behind the screen for the positioning of the projector so the image fills the screen. The distance between the screen and the projector is known as the *throw,* and, in most cases, the larger the screen, the greater the throw required. Rear screen projection is also best when the audience views the screen only from one side—the front. Fans who watch anything projected on an RP screen from behind will see a mirror image. It is also important to remember that to avoid casting shadows on the image, the area between the projector and the screen cannot be used for entering cast, participants, athletes, or the movement of any backstage crew.

Video projectors have become less expensive and more versatile in recent years. Projectors using LCD (liquid crystal display) technology can automatically switch from front screen to rear screen imaging without special lenses, and electronically correct the phenomenon known as *keystoning,* a common form of image distortion caused when the projector lens is not exactly centered on the screen. (A keystoned image may look wider at the top of the screen, for example, than at the bottom, or vice versa.) The same digital technology can also reduce somewhat the required throw distance through the use of digital algorithms that magnify the projected image. If projectors are to be used, it is recommended that two projectors be simultaneously focused and the images synchronized on each screen, if the budget permits. This will provide an important back-up system in case one projector fails. As viewed by the audience, a failure would cause the image to appear to dim slightly rather than go completely dark.

Most major sports and entertainment events have switched their loyalties to LED (light emitting diode) screens, large television screens that require no projector. Sports event audiences will recognize Jumbotron, Diamond Vision, Daktronics, and other brand names as representative of this type of display. As a group, they are sufficiently bright to present sharp and colorful images in sunlight or in full television lighting, as well as in the dark. If the facility does not possess an LED video screen, and the event budget permits, a temporary installation can be arranged. For outdoor events, and if the staging plan will accommodate it, consider using a mobile, truck-mounted screen to eliminate the labor costs of unloading, installing, and removing the rented screen. The companies that rent these trucks also provide an on-board control room complete with video switchers, tape decks, video servers, slow motion recorders, character generators (machines that can add graphics, such as player names, statistics, and other typed information to an image), and even cameras to feed images to the screens, providing additional cost efficiencies.

Although they can still constitute a significant expense, the cost of renting LED screens has generally been decreasing with technological advances, and the clarity, or resolution, of their images has improved. You can enjoy considerable savings if you can sacrifice a little resolution quality. Today's screens are much thinner than in the past, much like flat-screen televisions, and require comparatively little depth for the machinery itself. They do, however, generate significant heat and the area behind the screens must be well ventilated.

One new effect gaining in popularity is digital video mapping, in which a projector generates images that simulate objects in three dimensions on a flat surface. The surfaces can be traditional white projection sheets on the playing surface, the white of a rink's ice sheet, or even the interior or exterior structural elements of the host facility. Designing the images is the expensive and time-consuming part, but the effects are truly stunning.

Autocue

Participants who deliver speeches at an event, as well as hosts and emcees who are visible on camera, can be supported with device called an autocue or teleprompter. This equipment is composed of a large television monitor supported by a special word-processing program that scrolls through the script as the speaker reads. Because the autocue is positioned just below, to the side, or mounted directly on the lens that will capture his or her image, the speaker is able to read from the monitor's screen while appearing to be looking into the camera or straight ahead. Because users do not have to consult a written script or note cards, or memorize lines, they will appear more professional, confident, and believable when using an autocue.

Confetti and Balloons

The dropping of confetti, streamers, or balloons from the roof trusses of indoor facilities at the end of events can provide an inexpensive visual crescendo. For outdoor facilities without overhanging roofs, confetti cannons can be rented to launch colorful, lightweight tissue paper or Mylar high into the air that will flutter slowly back onto the audience or playing surface. Work

SIDELINE STORY

"Doing the Math" Takes on a New Prominence

Sports statistics used to be compiled for distribution to the media after a game, and read about in the newspaper by super-fans the following morning in tiny agate print. Today, fans enjoy sports on many levels, both inside and outside of the event, including fantasy games that require instant access to up-to-the-second statistics. Fans do not want this information the next morning, they want it now, either by downloading statistical data into their handheld devices and tablets or by watching scores and other statistics scroll across videoboards and electronic message displays in the venue. This often requires event organizers to retain a legion of statisticians in constant communication with officials, game presentation, information technology, and media relations personnel and with access to official, verifiable information. Frequently, statisticians are not only monitoring and disseminating data at the stadium in which they are located, but are also keeping current with their colleagues in other stadiums and arenas who are tracking other matches and events to ensure fans in the venue are receiving the broadest spectrum of sports statistics that they desire.

The National Football League took delivering current information about other games well beyond the out-of-town scoreboard when it introduced NFL Red Zone, a cable channel that switches between all NFL games in progress to show every potential scoring play as it happens. A feed of the channel was provided to all NFL stadiums beginning in the 2010 season so game presentation directors could show important plays from other games to the stadium audience during stoppages in the live game. This feed was also installed in London's Wembley Stadium for the 2010 NFL International Series game between the San Francisco 49ers and Denver Broncos, providing European fans of American Football with the same access to real-time highlights afforded to their counterparts in the United States.

with your groundskeeper to understand how these effects will affect the surface on which your sport is played. For instance, because confetti is unkind to ice (the small pieces of paper or metal can melt into the ice, discolor the surface, and create skating hazards), its use is not recommended unless the ice will be removed or scraped down after the event. Confetti can also clog drains used to pull water off of artificial and natural turf, and should be vacuumed off of playing surfaces as soon as is practical.

Pyrotechnics

Pyrotechnics, more commonly known as fireworks, can punctuate an event with spectacular color and heart-stopping sound. Fireworks displays can be designed to last just a few brilliant seconds as a visual and auditory climax for the closing moments of an event or to provide a visually rich and thunderous pageant of 20 minutes or more, synchronized to a musical soundtrack. In short, fireworks almost always imply a feeling of celebration and importance.

The catalog of aerial pyrotechnic effects, those launched into the air by electronically controlled mortars or rockets, is extremely varied, their names often reflective of their visual impact. It is easy to imagine the effects created by Yellow Chrysanthemums, Red Comets, Split Comets, Ring Shells, Stars, and Roman Candles, to name just a few. The size of the shell's burst is determined by the size of the shells—three-inch (diameter) shells are among the smallest and least expensive, larger shells in popular use reaching eight inches, 10 inches, and even 12 inches or more. Shells that create a loud noise upon exploding include a "report charge," although many can be designed to display without this loud bang.

Ground-based fireworks, such as gerbs or pyrotechnic fountains, do not launch shells into the air and, therefore, are the effect of choice indoors, because the precise position and the height can be more precisely designed and regulated. Small shells can also be suspended from roof beams on non-flammable cables to provide a controlled indoor "aerial" display. Graphics, such as logos and line art, can be executed in fireworks called set pieces, or pyrographics. These ground-based displays can create a brilliant finale moment, literally burning an event's or sponsor's brand image into the memories of thousands of spectators.

A gas flame projector uses a burner that releases and ignites a flammable natural gas, producing a bright orange flame and a ball of heated air that is perceptible for hundreds of feet. Obviously, it is important to keep all flames and pyrotechnics effects away from athletes, fans, staff, equipment, and décor that can ignite or be functionally affected by their heat or the byproducts of ignition. Gas effects usually burn clean, with no visible smoke or debris. Pyrotechnic devices, however, can leave behind ash, pieces of shell casings and ignition assemblies, and chemical salts and invisible gases that can irritate or injure if they come into contact with the audience, cast members, or athletes. They also create smoke, which can produce additional irritation and partially obscure the playing surface for both live and television spectators. The effects of smoke are particularly noticeable when using pyrotechnics indoors, as it often takes the host facility's ventilation system a significant and noticeable amount of time to remove it.

Pyrotechnics should be designed and fired only by experienced, licensed fireworks companies and technicians. These professionals will be familiar with the safety requirements governing the use of pyrotechnics and gas effects, as recommended by the manufacturer and the American Pyrotechnics Association or other national bodies. They will file for all needed permits (be sure to plan far enough in advance to accommodate for this application process), and arrange for the necessary test firings that are universally required by local fire marshals. Be prepared to produce certificates of fireproofing for all banners, sets, props, and other materials near the firing and spectator areas, as well as proof of liability insurance. Also make sure that the amount of smoke and debris generated will not interfere with the quality of the playing surface or the comfort and performance of the athletes.

Supovitz's Theory of Event Flow

Like nature, live events abhor a vacuum. When nothing is happening, audiences lose interest and begin thinking about being elsewhere. The television industry is very familiar with the tenuousness of its hold on the audience. There are rarely even a few seconds during which there is a total absence of movement and sound. If there is a gap of just a few moments, viewers know that someone has made a mistake. Take a cue from our broadcasting brethren, and *produce live events as though they were television shows.*

The running order and script reveal the visuals and words that will be used to support a sports event, but not necessarily how well they are stitched together. The cueing, or the second-by-second timing of how the event flows from one segment to the next, should be perfected during rehearsals. Be on the lookout for times when absolutely no visual or aural information is being exchanged during ceremonial elements, as well as during competition. Such a gap might last only a few seconds, but the excitement of the audience and momentum of the competition can quickly dissipate during that time and may require great effort to restore.

If an event is to be broadcast, embracing this philosophy will make the live event far easier to translate to television. Even if it is not, today's audiences are accustomed to fast-paced, multisensory experiences and constant access to compelling information. Many professional basketball, baseball, football, and hockey teams direct their everyday games in this manner, but this theory suggests that other sports events, including amateur and grassroots programs, can be easily and cost-effectively executed in this same way.

To continually engage the audience, have hosts conduct player interviews, play upbeat music, or stage promotions and contests that give away prizes. Start these elements as soon as a pause in the play begins, and cease just as the contest resumes. Fulfill sponsor obligations for public address announcements, but include a background of appropriate music. (Think of these as your commercials.) Play enlivening and inspirational music as athletes are introduced. Program fan participation activities between matches or during intermissions. Have a band perform, screen music videos, provide replays of highlights from the competition in progress, announce or show statistics. Cue these elements tightly together so as one finishes, the next begins. Don't just make the event as good as if you were watching it on television—make it better.

Sports purists often decry the loss of conversation between members of the audience, and the cultures of some sports require more sedate surroundings. Although producers should design the most appropriate presentation for entertaining their core fans, the notion of tying event elements closely together is no less valid. There should always be something for the audience to do or discover when competition is not in progress, even if the experience is in another location to which the audience has to direct its attention. Having activities and entertainment planned elsewhere on the event site, but not in the area of the athletic competition, is a good alternative for events whose culture frowns on noise where the sport is being played. In such cases, provide activity at corporate hospitality pavilions, public food areas, or at an on-site fan festival.

Some sports events, of course, are already television presentations. Producers who embrace the notion of designing their events as though they were television shows are well positioned to work side by side with their television counterparts and will be able to balance their needs with the unique requirements of this important medium. See Play 13 to better understand the needs of our broadcasting stakeholders.

Post-Play Analysis

Sports events are entertainment experiences. Audiences want to be able to support their favorite athletes or teams, comprehend the progress of play, be kept apprised of important information, and be entertained. Pageantry provided by marching bands, drill teams and kick lines, and other large-format performing units can add significant scale and excitement to pre-event ceremonies and intermission periods, their large-scale visuals and sound filling the often substantial void between the audience and the playing surface.

Sports event presentation directors or producers manage the production by generating important planning documents including an event rundown, production schedule, cast list, wardrobe list, and rehearsal schedule, among others. These essential tools help to organize the myriad details that must be managed while preparing the facility for event day. Consider all of the presentation tools that can help to excite, entertain, and inform the audience including lighting, sound, video, and special effects such as lasers and pyrotechnics. The use of each must be designed for maximum effect without affecting the quality of the playing surface.

Coach's Clipboard

1. An action sports competition featuring skateboarders, BMX bicyclists, and in-line skaters is scheduled for a local stadium of 5,000 seats. The competitors are composed of participants from the community and invited athletes who are coming from a significant distance. Create brief pre-event, intermission, and postevent ceremonies that will excite the audience and familiarize attendees with the fame of the visiting athletes. Include an event rundown and rehearsal schedule in your plan.
2. A statewide high school all-star football game marks 50 years of players advancing to college and professional football greatness. Design and draw blocking diagrams for a pregame and halftime commemoration that salutes the schools and 50 returning alumni.
3. What kinds of technical equipment, both for the competition itself and for presentation purposes, will be required to produce the event described in item 1? Create a production schedule to organize the facility for deliveries, installations, rehearsals, and dismantling of the event.
4. Your sponsors have requested recognition beyond signage at the host venue for the event described in item 1. What exposure opportunities can be offered to partners during opening ceremonies, intermissions, and during the competition itself? How can you use various technical presentation tools to provide unique impact for your top sponsors?

PLAY 13

Working with Broadcasters

"You're never as good as the praise or as bad as the criticism."

—*Gary Bettman, commissioner, National Hockey League*

This play will help you to:

- Understand what broadcasters want, need, and expect from a sports event.
- Explore the options for broadcasting your event.
- Learn how to work harmoniously with broadcast partners.

Introduction

Mass media such as television, radio, and the Internet can provide organizers with the incalculable benefit of broad geographic and demographic exposure for their sports event. The ability of a broadcast to make an event available to an exponentially larger audience than the live crowd alone can position a sport like no other promotional tool, achieving a degree of instant accessibility and notoriety and, in time, helping a sport to establish its cultural relevance. A sports event broadcast places the event in a superior competitive position, enabling the organizer to attract more and better athletes and teams, and package sponsorships at pricing levels far greater than nontelevised events. Even incidental television exposure can have a significant positive effect on a sponsor's sales, and guarantees of a viewing audience for a company's commercials, signage, and products are major selling points for potential sponsorships. As will be seen, this outstanding and enhanced exposure opportunity is difficult to achieve, and is becoming increasingly costly to execute on a number of levels.

SIDELINE STORY

Sports Television—Where It's Been, Where It's Going

Television's American debut gathered curious crowds to the RCA Pavilion at the 1939 New York World's Fair. A few weeks later, college baseball enjoyed the distinction of being the first sport ever featured on this then-nascent medium. A single camera on the third base line made broadcasting history when it transmitted images from a game that spring between Columbia and Princeton Universities on RCA's experimental television station W2XBS, the forerunner of New York's WNBC. It was a featherweight boxing championship that anchored the first network sports broadcast on NBC's *Gillette Cavalcade of Sports*. Neither pugilist Willie Pep nor opponent Chalky Wright could possibly conceive of themselves as pioneer athletes back in 1944, especially when there were only 7,000 functioning television sets in the United States. But, it was apparent even then, in the waning years of World War II, that corporate sponsorship of televised sports events would be necessary to cover the considerable costs of putting them on the air.

Decades later, rights fees would make up the majority of a broadcaster's expenses in covering the largest and most widely viewed sports events. In 1970, networks paid the National Football League $50 million for the right to broadcast NFL games, and, by 1985, those fees had risen to $450 million. In 1998, the NFL's broadcasting rights were sold in an eight-year package worth $17.6 billion. By 2011, the league's nine-year broadcasting rights extension was valued at nearly $4 billion annually.

Realistically speaking, the vast majority of the sports events currently being staged will never enjoy broadcast coverage. Only a select few will ever be attractive enough for broadcasters to invest the time and capital to cover an event, or for sponsors and advertisers to purchase the commercial time to make the venture financially viable. Even fewer will be so universally appealing that the broadcaster will invest beyond its costs of producing the program to add a rights fee payable to the event organizer simply for the opportunity to feature it on television, radio, and/or the Internet. Broadcast rights fees for the most popular leagues, teams, and events in an ever-evolving sports programming landscape continue to increase seemingly with no limitations.

What Broadcasters Want from Sports Events

For the most part, broadcasters are in the business of making money while serving their viewing and/or listening audience. Depending on the media entity, they earn the majority of their revenues by selling commercial time or advertising space by collecting subscriber fees from cable and satellite operators or through a variety of digital offerings. Additional revenue potential is realized by providing various forms of in-program recognition to broadcast partners, usually associated with programming elements such as replays, score clock and other graphics, special features, and other exclusive content or even virtual signage (superimposed artwork of a sponsor or brand logo that appears to be at the event site, but is visible only to the television audience). In short, the potential to make a profit by televising a particular sports event is generally the motivation for a broadcaster to desire covering it.

Viewership and Ratings

For most television broadcasters, profit potential is driven by how many viewers they can attract to a sports event. The more viewers they can draw, the more the broadcaster can charge their advertisers. In the United States, two standards are used to measure the quantity of television viewers—Nielsen ratings points and market share. Through a variety of data collection methods including instantaneous electronic monitoring and submission of written diaries by participating viewers, Nielsen Media Research assigns television ratings points that represent the number of households that watched a particular program within a specified area. (Nielsen also offers a similar service that calculates ratings for online usage and Arbitron, another media research company, provides similar ratings information for radio broadcasters). In the US, a nation of an estimated 116 million households, one national Nielsen ratings point is equivalent to one percent of the total, currently an approximate 1.16 million households. Ratings points are also compiled on a market-to-market basis, the value of which varies, depending on the local population. A single ratings point earned for a broadcast in a city of 2 million households would represent an estimated 20,000 households (again, 1 percent of the market). Ratings for nationally telecast events are compiled on both national and local levels, the data for which can help disclose to organizers and sponsors what regions are stronger and which are weaker for a particular sport or event. For example, a sports event with a national rating of 1.7 (1.972 million households) can present a much more impressive rating of 5.8 in a host city of 1 million households (58,000 viewing households), and yet only a 1.1 score in a more distant city of 4 million (44,000). Of course, sports events that are televised only in a single local market, such as a marathon or a high school game, do not generate national ratings.

After an event has aired nationally, two sets of ratings are released. The first, called "overnight ratings," represent a national estimate based on electronic viewing data gathered solely from the country's largest markets, released within hours of a broadcast. National ratings are released a few days later after more complete data have been collected and analyzed from all surveyed markets across the country. Depending on the nature of the event and the consistency of its appeal, national ratings may vary by as much as a full ratings point or more from overnight data.

Nielsen also subdivides ratings across several demographic categories to assist sponsors in better targeting their advertising purchases. Ratings can be tabulated strictly for male viewers of ages 18 to 34, for example, a highly prized market for many sports event advertisers. Low national ratings, however, are not always indicators of weak programming choices for a broadcaster. Depending on the sponsor, national ratings points may be less important than local ratings in their most important geographic markets or exceptionally good viewership among their products' target demographics (such as specific age groups or gender).

Another common reference point used in determining the effectiveness of a program in attracting television viewers is a number that represents the *share of market*. The number often quoted as a *share* is the percentage of televisions tuned to a particular program compared to all of the televisions being watched during the same time period. Programs that are scheduled to air late at night may generate only modest ratings (because many people are asleep), but a strong share of market (because a large percentage of those who are awake and watching television are viewing a particular event).

Event organizers can also increase viewership numbers by utilizing streaming video on the Internet. Streaming video sites like YouTube offer cheap, and often free, alternatives to television broadcasts and can provide wide-reaching exposure. These sites can be used as a primary source of broadcast or as a complement to the television broadcast of the event, streaming the video content of the broadcast and, increasingly, accompanying "second-screen" programming on a digital platform. Some large-scale events, such as the NCAA college basketball tournament, and leagues, such as MLB, have created successful and lucrative online offerings of live broadcast content.

Commercial Sales Potential

From the broadcaster's perspective, the profit potential of covering a sports event is almost always dependent on the ratings it can be expected to generate. The ability to identify past years' ratings performance among audiences with various demographic characteristics determines how much the broadcaster will be able to charge for commercial time. A more detailed demographic analysis of the ratings also can be used to target companies that want to position themselves before the types of viewers a sports event attracts.

The most likely companies to purchase commercial time on a sports event broadcast are the sponsors that already enjoy a business relationship with the organizer. Many corporate partners will have already planned to "activate" their event sponsorship with the purchase of commercial time. Other companies will have spent their budget assuming that their on-site signage will already be highly visible during the event broadcast, and that no additional purchase of commercial exposure is necessary. Overall, the attractiveness of broadcasting a sports event increases with the receipt of commitments to purchase commercial time from current event sponsors.

The broadcaster will also evaluate whether the program has enough appeal to convince new advertisers that are not sports event sponsors to consider purchasing commercial time. If event sponsors do not elect to participate as advertisers, the broadcaster will want the flexibility to sell the opportunity to any company willing to spend the money—even those that are competitors of event sponsors. In most cases, it is a good practice for organizers to ensure that their sponsor contracts provide exclusivity only at the event site. However, agreements should guarantee sponsors the right of first refusal on opportunities to purchase commercial time on any event broadcast that may subsequently be scheduled. That is, the organizer's agreement with the broadcaster would obligate them only to present event sponsors with an opportunity to buy commercial time before offering the same deal to a sponsor's competitors. If the sports event sponsor waives its right to purchase commercials on the broadcast, or fails to respond within a certain amount of time, the broadcaster would then be permitted the latitude to approach competitor companies. There are many major events that offer broadcast advertising as part of their sponsorship entitlements, in which case such exclusivity may be preserved. These packages are generally priced expensively, and include the purchase of broadcast advertising as a sponsorship fulfillment item.

Streaming broadcasts on digital platforms can increase overall exposure numbers, but often have trouble generating the sales dollars of a television broadcast. This may be due, in part, to the evolving nature of the digital broadcast industry and relative audience sizes. However, the digital broadcast creates opportunities to pursue additional sponsors or increase the package values of the sponsors of the television broadcast that see value in advertising during the online broadcast. The digital broadcast also opens up new opportunities for event organizers and producers to engage their fans through interactive and social media that coexist with the streaming video.

Exclusivity

Broadcasters that have invested the considerable capital required to produce televised coverage of a sports event want assurances that their right to exclusivity is protected. They will vigorously defend their rights against any other mechanism by which a fan can visually experience the event, in whole or in part, on other television stations and over the Internet. Any simultaneous transmission of the sports event within their viewing territory will detract from their ratings and make it more difficult to sell advertising at the highest possible rates. The presence of radio broadcasters and still photographers are usually not problematic for the broadcaster, but any video cameras, even those desiring to record only pieces of the event for news coverage, can create significant issues for the rights holder. Simply, the broadcaster will want to be the exclusive source of all video footage for news highlights, sports magazine shows, and any other programming. Even the presence of the organizer's own video cameras that are dedicated to recording the event for archival or promotional purposes may be addressed in the agreement between the organizer and the broadcaster to clarify the definition of broadcast rights holder exclusivity.

SIDELINE STORY

The Conundrum of Mass Public Viewing

There are few opportunities to demonstrate the popularity of a major sports contest more than public viewing events, rallies, and parties. Gatherings of thousands, even tens of thousands, have watched and celebrated national championship games and international competitions with fellow fans in open plazas, on streets, in arenas, and at stadiums across the globe.

Federation Internationale de Football Association, globally known as FIFA, the international governing body of football (soccer), recognized in 2002 that unofficial mass viewing areas showing games on giant television screens were popping up on public plazas in Japan and Korea, hosts of that year's World Cup. For the following edition, held in Germany in 2006, FIFA introduced "Fan Fests," officially designating focal points in each German host city where mass viewing of broadcasts could take place. The notion was expanded further at the 2010 World Cup in South Africa. FIFA added six locations in key international cities—Berlin, Mexico City, Paris, Rio de Janeiro, Rome, and Sydney—to nine South African cities hosting World Cup for Fan Fest viewing events. According to FIFA's official website, more than six million fans enjoyed a 2010 World Cup match from an official Fan Fest location.

There is no question that mass public viewing of a broadcast can demonstrate the powerful reach and appeal of a significant sports event. The NHL's 2011 Stanley Cup was similarly simulcast to an audience gathered for public events in the streets of Vancouver, British Columbia. These are events unto themselves, and require a sufficient budget, meticulous planning, a focus on crowd control, public health and safety, adequate facilities (including access to restrooms and drinking water), local government support, a marketing plan, and on-site direction and technical support. They also require the permission of the event organizer and the broadcaster that hold the rights to the match and broadcast.

Event organizers assume a great deal of risk when they create a mass public viewing environment, as excited—or disappointed—crowds can get out of hand. Additionally, for many broadcasters, mass public viewing can be an anathema. Although the fans who are watching the broadcast in a public location would also have likely watched the event at their own homes, viewership ratings can be misleadingly skewed downward by an out-of-home simulcast. Even a handful of fans leaving homes with metered televisions in favor of a public viewing event can generate a decrease in ratings. This can cause broadcasters to miss the ratings they promise advertisers—even if the on-air advertisements are shown at the public site. As a result, some sports event organizers and broadcasters withhold permission for mass public viewing of broadcasts.

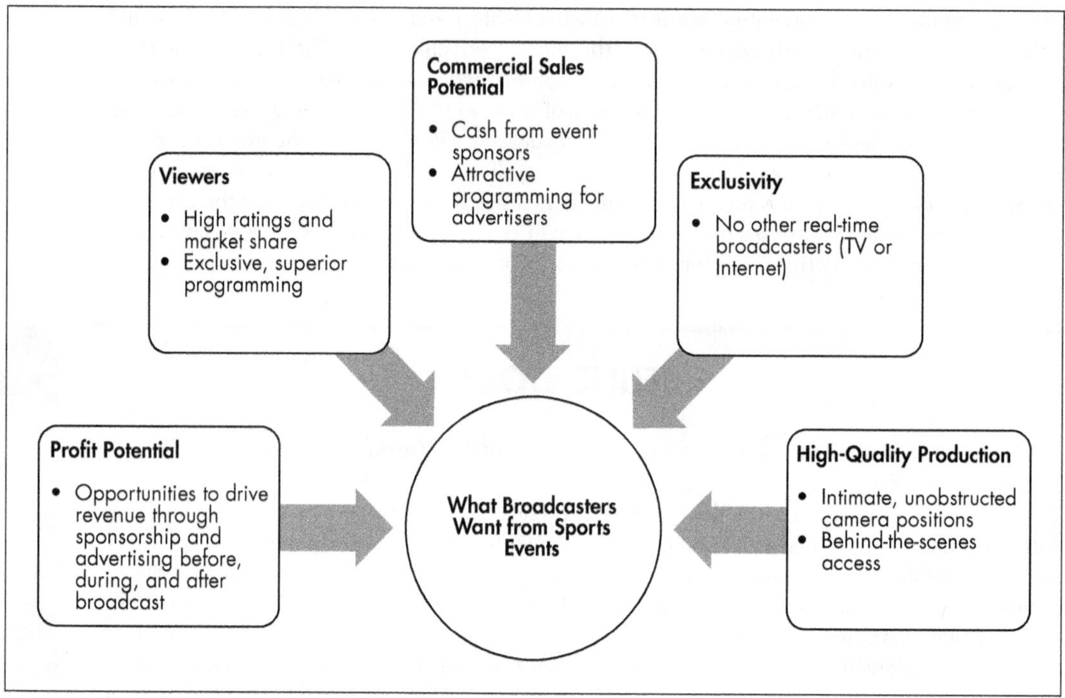

Figure 13.1 What Broadcasters Want from Sports Events

Even when observing broadcast exclusivity, organizers should be open to welcoming video crews from other media outlets, but must limit their access to defined areas with no view of the playing surface, such as news conference rooms and other back-of-house areas, to preserve the rights of the host broadcaster. (Enabling media to videotape segments of the competition if there is no host broadcaster is completely at the discretion of the organizer.) The broadcaster may also wish to be protected with respect to any video simulcasts of the sports event on the Internet. The broadcaster may wish to include in its agreement the right to simulcast video coverage of the sports event on its Internet site. If not, streaming video images and audio on the organizer's website is a great way to expand the event's reach globally if broadcast coverage is limited only to a modest geographical region. Because global access includes the region where the broadcast may also be seen, the rights holder may require that Internet coverage be delayed from a few minutes to hours to give the broadcaster the window of exclusivity it requires to generate ratings.

Opportunities to Provide High Production Values

If it has been ascertained that providing coverage of a sports event represents a viable business proposition, the broadcaster's next objective is to ensure the product it can deliver to viewers is of the best quality possible. Generally speaking, producing television coverage of a sports event is an expensive proposition. It requires an enormous expenditure in labor for on-air talent, camera operators, electricians, video editors, sound engineers, graphics designers, statisticians, drivers, and support staff, to name just a few. Cameras and production trucks with video and audio control rooms must be rented and/or moved to the event site, scaffolds or sets for anchor positions and studios built, lighting and audio systems installed, recorded features edited, and host scripts written. With all that effort and expense, broadcast producers want to make sure they can position cameras in locations to cover the event from the best and most intimate of perspectives.

Although there are producers who well understand that energized audiences make for compelling television, the agenda of many television executives sometimes neglects to take into account the quality of the experience for the live audience attending the event. These producers want their cameras in the best possible locations, regardless of the visual obstructions they might create for those who may have purchased tickets for seats immediately behind. For this reason, it is best to know where camera locations will be before tickets are put on sale. The seats immediately behind the cameras may be removed from public sale (or "killed"), or be made available to the broadcaster for entertaining its own complimentary guests. Broadcasters also want unlimited access to athletes before the event to conduct interviews and provide behind-the-scenes glimpses of the event. Both are perceived to add great value to the viewing experience. As a general rule, if providing access will not interfere with the operation of the event, the safety or performance of the athletes, or the quality of the viewing experience for the live audience, it is best to grant these rights to the broadcaster. Figure 13.1 summarizes what broadcasters are looking for in sports events.

While there are any number of elements that broadcasters need or want from event organizers, there also are significant philosophical and format differences between competing broadcast entities in styles and substance, even when covering the same sport. "One key thing to remember is that every broadcast company is different and will operate that way," says veteran NBC Sports producer Fred Gaudelli. "Hearing the line, 'That's how network X does it and it's good enough for them' would be akin to a sports event organizer hearing, 'That's how the major leagues do it,' from TV."

What Sports Events Organizers Want from Broadcasters

Sports events can provide broadcasters and their viewers with outstanding entertainment, but in today's business landscape, it is clearly a buyer's market. For their part, organizers desire the greatest and broadest exposure possible for their sports events (see Figure 13.2). From a brand positioning perspective, this exposure provides legitimacy and validation that the event and its featured sport are relevant enough to merit broadcast coverage, and provides them with outstanding opportunities for self-promotion. Television exposure does not come without a potential downside, however. Televised programs must be compelling enough to ensure that the local paying audience will still come to witness the event live. Simply, purchasing tickets and parking cost money, and attendance costs time in traveling to the event and returning home. Television, by contrast, provides virtually no-cost access to the event and the convenience of a quality viewing experience while never having to leave your home. Recognizing this reality, the National Football League since 1973 has routinely blocked television coverage within local markets in which tickets for games have not sold out. (Prior to 1973, no NFL game could be broadcast in the home team's television territory whether or not it was sold out.) The convenience and absence of cost in consuming a sports event on television is yet another reason to ensure that the live presentation of the event is even more exciting and provides greater value than the broadcast version, as discussed in Play 12.

The exposure provided by television coverage also makes an event more relevant and attractive to potential and existing sponsors. The positions granted by the organizer for sponsor signage

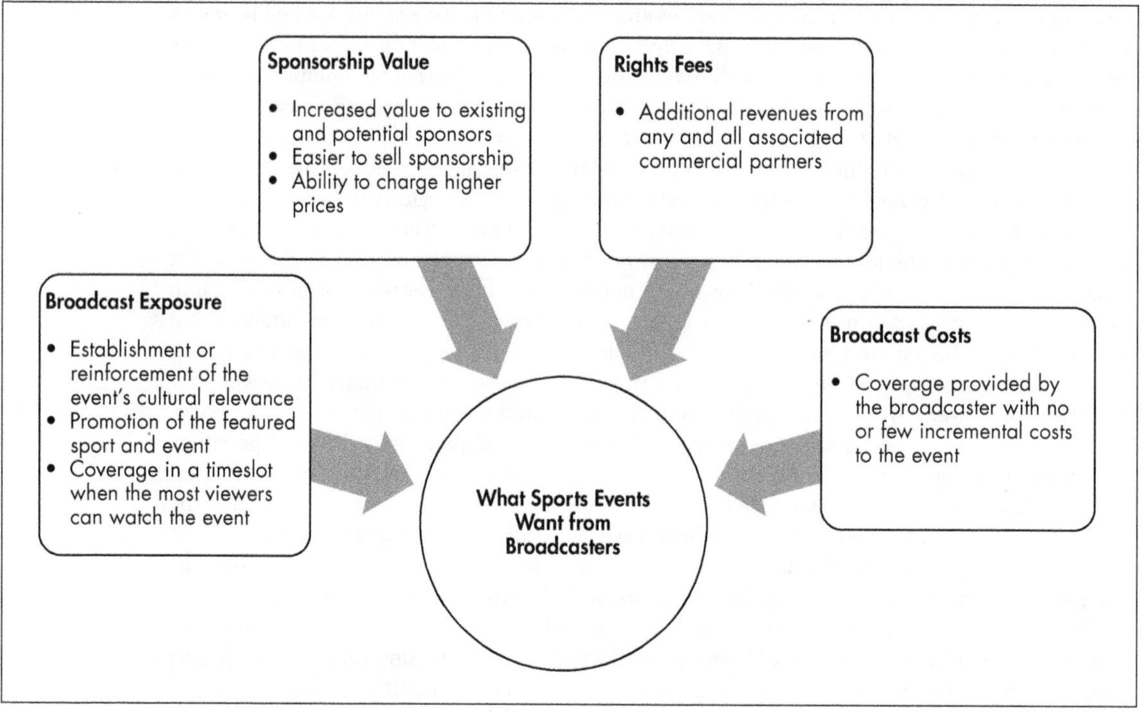

Figure 13.2 What Sports Events Organizers Want from Broadcasters

at the event site becomes even more significant: Those with the greatest probability of being seen on television command higher fees or are included only within premium-priced partner packages. Presuming that sponsorships are priced competitively for the expected number of viewers, television coverage generally makes events far easier and more desirable to sell to potential sponsors.

Broadcaster–Sports Event Business Relationships

In addition to increased sponsorship fees, sports event organizers hope to profit from rights fees paid by the broadcaster. At the very least, they want to enjoy the remarkable benefits of television exposure without experiencing any net increase in their costs. Agreements with broadcasters should define what fees, if any, would be paid to the organizer, and which expenses would be assumed by the broadcaster. These parameters define the four basic relationships between a broadcaster and the sports events they cover, as listed below.

- Fee-based rights holder
- Fee-free rights holder
- Time buy provider
- Owner or co-owner

Event organizers who represent properties with an extremely high perceived value, typically those of global or national importance, often offer broadcasting rights to interested bidders in exchange for a cash payment, or rights fee. A broadcaster that purchases the rights to televise an event (the *rights holder*) is confident that the program, by virtue of its expected ratings and viewer demographics, will appeal so strongly to advertisers that it will be able to charge the high rates for commercial time that will cover the production costs and the rights fee, and still leave a profit. Needless to say, there are precious few sports properties that can command such significant rights fees.

Other events are attractive enough for broadcasters to consider airing, but are not expected to generate sufficient profitability to enable them to offer the organizer a rights fee. Some event organizers will nevertheless award the rights to the broadcaster on a no-fee basis to take advantage of the broadened exposure for promotional purposes, as well as for the incremental value a broadcast will generate with respect to the sponsor fees they can charge. Organizers may also be able to negotiate receiving a commercial spot or two on a complimentary basis in no-fee deals, which, in turn, can be used for their own advertising, resold to a sponsor, or included in a high-end sponsorship package.

Organizers who can provide no-rights-fee programming for broadcasters are discovering more opportunities for television coverage of sports events than at any time in the past as broadcasters expand their sports channel offerings and professional and collegiate sports leagues and teams establish their own proprietary regional sports networks (known as RSNs). Through acquisition or expansion, broadcasting and cable networks have expanded their sports programming menu by introducing dedicated day-long sports channels (e.g., NBC and NBC Sports Network, CBS and CBS Sports Network, ESPN, ESPN2, and ESPN Deportes in the United States; Sky and Sky Sports in the United Kingdom; and TSN and TSN2 in Canada). On a more regional basis, RSNs such as Madison Square Garden's MSG Network and The New York Yankees' YES Network in the New York City metropolitan area, the Mid-Atlantic Sports Network (MASN) co-owned by the Baltimore Orioles and Washington Nationals, the Big Ten Network and the University of Texas's Longhorn Network, provide unique programming appealing to enthusiastic and demographically specific fan audiences and generate substantial local revenues. Additionally, professional leagues in North America have established special-interest sports and sports news channels for cable, satellite, and Internet distribution, including NFL Network, NBA TV, NHL Network, and MLB Network. Sports broadcast industry insiders predict a wave of digital technology giants such as Apple, Google, Yahoo!, and others entering into exclusive sports content deals in the not-too-distant future.

If broadcasters pass on the opportunity to televise a sports event, not all hope is lost for an event to receive television exposure. Many organizers negotiate with broadcasters to purchase a timeslot in return for a flat cash payment, and then produce and air their own coverage of a sports event. These productions can air live or may be re-edited in a compressed form for later broadcast. Entering into a "time buy" relationship releases the broadcaster from all risks of having to generate viewers and advertising revenue, placing those responsibilities squarely on the shoulders of the organizer. In return for the purchase of the airtime, the organizer will usually receive all of the available commercial time, perhaps minus one or two spots the broadcaster will hold back for promoting other programming. The organizer, in turn, can sell the commercial time to sponsors and other advertisers, either independently or through a third-party marketing agency. Alternatively, the value of the commercial time can be included in the fulfillment costs of event sponsorship packages, a benefit perceived to be of great value to business partners.

Obviously, time buys are dicey propositions. The organizer assumes the significant financial risk of purchasing the airtime, as well as the costs of producing the event for television—basically all of the expenses the broadcasters themselves were not confident enough to be able to offset through their own marketing efforts. Before committing to a time buy, event organizers are well advised to confirm the timeslot being purchased in writing. The advertising rates, or the value of commercials granted to sponsors, that an organizer will be able to charge to offset costs will be dependent on the customary advertising rates charged for other programs during the time and day an event will air, the overall interest in the event among the viewing public, and the channel upon which it will air. Production costs will remain the same whether a program airs at 1:00 A.M.

on an overnight Monday or 8:00 P.M. primetime on a Thursday. The value and attractiveness of the airtime—and the rates that can be set for advertising—will obviously be much greater for the latter timeslot than the former.

Time buys have become somewhat more affordable as the cable television industry continues to subdivide into increasingly smaller special interest and niche viewer markets. That does not necessarily mean, however, that the economics of producing a sports event for special interest cable channels are becoming more attractive. Dozens of regional and specialty sports networks and channels are now available as partners, many of which are hungry for new and inexpensive programming, and new broadcasters are entering the marketplace regularly. The limiting factor, of course, is the number of viewers that smaller, niche broadcasters can attract and the concomitantly reduced advertising rates that organizers can charge sponsors to offset the production, even with cheaper airtime costs. Although production costs will be the same no matter where the program airs, the smaller the potential viewing audience offered by the broadcaster, the less valuable the commercial time will be. Therefore, another important point to negotiate in a time buy agreement is the network's or channel's willingness and ability to promote the event telecast with free commercial spots in the days and weeks leading up to the program, as the most likely audience for a televised event may be the viewers already watching that channel.

With increasing regularity, broadcasters themselves are becoming event organizers and owners of original sports programming made expressly for television. ESPN's wildly successful X Games

SIDELINE STORY

ESPN'S X Games

In 1995, ESPN, the most popular all-sports cable network in the United States, staged the first Extreme Games across four cities in Rhode Island and Vermont before an estimated 198,000 spectators. This eight-day multidisciplinary tournament included nine competitive action sports such as windsurfing, bungee jumping, and mountain biking. The following year, ESPN announced that a new winter sports festival would be added to the now familiar X Games brand starting in 1997. By 1998, the X Games franchise went truly global, the organizers staging an Asian X Games exhibition in Phuket, Thailand, during which qualifiers advanced to the Summer X Games in San Diego. Although ESPN does not release attendance figures, reports suggest that, at its peak, as many as 275,000 spectators attended the summer games, and more than 80,000 attended the winter edition. More significantly, these various X Games events and qualifiers continue to provide ESPN with hours of television programming including direct event coverage, highlights featured on its flagship SportsCenter broadcasts, and incorporation into magazine show features. As both the organizer and rights holder, ESPN can assert total control over the event schedule, invited athletes, featured sports, sponsorships, and staging.

In 2012, more than 20 hours of X Games coverage was broadcast live on multiple channels owned by the rights holder, including ESPN, ESPN2, ESPN-3D, and ABC in the United States, plus additional live broadcasts in Africa, Asia, Australia, and South America. Additionally, the X Games and Winter X Games provide many opportunities for broad and extended coverage on ESPN's robust digital platforms, media with which the network's technically savvy young audiences are comfortable spending hours consuming sports content.

franchise, featuring both cold- and warm-weather competitions, provides this broadcaster/owner with a sports event over which it can exert total control. ESPN can feature the sports it feels its viewers want to see most, eliminate those that rate less popularly, and convert advertisers into event sponsors, rather than the other way around.

Working with Broadcast Producers

While ESPN and others in the industry own and present their own events, in most cases broadcasters are engaged in the sole business of broadcasting events, not staging them. A close working relationship between the organizer and rights holder, based on a mutual understanding of each other's objectives, is essential to ensure a positive and beneficial outcome for all involved. It has been stated that events should be presented just the way they would be seen on television to keep the live audience energized and engaged. Similarly, broadcasters want to capture the excitement and dynamism of the live event experience, first to attract viewers and ultimately to keep viewers from changing channels to other programming alternatives or tuning out altogether. "Through my experience, I have found that live event coordination and television producing is in many ways similar," observes Canadian Broadcasting Corporation sports producer Sherali Najak. "In television one of my jobs is to extract the passion and emotion an event can create." If a sports event is televised, the organizer should work cooperatively with the television producer to find ways to help the viewers feel like they are there, and perhaps even wish they were. "I always find that because events are so detail oriented and time consuming to organize that the execution and planning of the event often takes priority over the thrill and amazement that television tries to cover," Najak asserts. "This can't be manufactured but certain steps can be put in place to give the event a chance to tell its own story."

If the organizer has done his/her job well, the live audience will feel the pulse of excitement from the moment they arrive. The event environment is loaded with visual and auditory cues that something special is about to happen, and the audience will react vociferously at predictable points in the running order—when athletes first enter the arena, for example. For live broadcasts, it is essential to coordinate the timing and staging of these focal points with the broadcaster so the television production also can take best advantage of them, rather than having viewers watching a commercial when highly anticipated activities take place or the most climactic moment happens. Live audiences enjoy the sense of participation in an event—let them know when the television audience is also joining them at the event, and prompt them to demonstrate their enthusiasm at that very moment with hearty cheers of excitement.

The broadcaster and presentation director should also remain in communication during the competitions themselves to coordinate when commercial breaks will be taken, preferably during stoppages of play. Many sports that are regularly televised in real time have adopted protocols that determine when television breaks can be taken, and delay the resumption of play until the broadcast has returned from airing commercials. The competitive cultures of others totally preclude stopping play for commercial breaks, and, as a result, the broadcaster must decide whether commercials will air only during intermissions, or during unpredictable but potentially decisive moments in the competition.

Remember that when a sports event is televised, there is no real "backstage." Anything and everything can be captured on television or recorded unless specific instructions regarding access are communicated and understood. Clearly define whether a broadcaster's cameras will have access to the athletes' locker rooms and, if so, during what periods. Can they enter the locker room pre-event to tape interviews? Will they be able to broadcast live from the dressing rooms during intermissions, or will they be limited to a location outside the door? What kind of access will they be permitted postevent? Dress the nonpublic areas in which cameras will be permitted to shoot with event banners and posters, perhaps with sponsor identification, for additional logo exposure.

Ensure that either the organizer or the host facility has determined what kinds of production trucks and trailers the broadcaster will require for its coverage of the event and identified where they will be positioned. The truck contains all of the technical equipment required for producing the broadcast coverage, and the positioning of cameras or where the truck can conveniently connect to existing utilities and cabling will often determine its location. Understand how cables will be routed between the truck and the cameras. If they are run through public areas, determine whether they must be hung from the ceiling or placed beneath temporary cable chases to ensure they are not trip hazards for anyone, especially the athletes, fans, or staff.

Speaking from experience, CBS Sports Executive Vice President, Operations, Engineering, and Production Services Ken Aagaard is familiar with the commonly recurring challenges that need to be anticipated and addressed. "Probably the least understood of the broadcaster's basic needs are setup time, parking, and access to the venue," he says. Television producers need the time to install their cameras, cable them to the truck, establish communication with the network, and for the director and his or her crew to rehearse. At the same time, the most experienced producers understand the many competing demands for time and space in the host facility. "Broadcasters least understand the multiple of conflicts the organizer encounters from stadiums, team owners, players, and local organizers," says Aagaard. By appreciating and solving the other's concerns, a smooth and collaborative relationship resulting in the best possible event can be achieved.

Integrating Audience Needs

When dysfunctional relationships develop between sports event organizers and their broadcasting counterparts, they are often over the lack of the basic understanding that there is really only one audience being served simultaneously by both parties. When a difference of opinion emerges between the live presentation director and a television producer, it is far from unusual to hear this argument surface: "To whom would you rather promote your product—the few thousand people here or the millions watching on television?" The right answer is: "Both!"

The need to appeal to both sets of audiences is mutually beneficial and, in fact, finding the proper balance is crucial to creating a vibrant and exciting entertainment environment. Organizers are responsible for delivering value and an emotional payoff to the loyal fans of their sport to keep them engaged, entertained, and energized to return for future events. Without respecting and embracing the needs of an event's core audience, loyalty is bound to wane and disinterest is sure to take hold. These devoted fans are the same people who will later watch coverage of events they cannot attend on television or via Internet streaming, so ultimately, even home viewership will ebb from cavalier neglect. Keeping fans coming back is as much a ratings concern for broadcasters as a financial one for the organizer. Simply, a full event venue also makes for good television. Nothing says, "This event is not important enough for me to spend time watching it," than empty grandstands on television. Provide only good reasons for the live audience to keep coming back for future events.

"Nothing will enhance your event more than great television coverage," says NBC's Gaudelli. "Understand how you may use TV to benefit whatever event you're organizing. On the flip side, TV should understand that the integrity of the event can't be compromised to make 'better TV.' The common goal we share is for the event to be great. Together we can make that happen for both parties. Understand that if the event fails on either platform (on TV or at the venue), the event is a failure."

Broadcasters have concerns similar to those faced by sports event organizers, but with a significant added challenge. Like live sports event organizers, they must keep their viewing audience entertained and their interests served at all times to keep them coming back to watch future events. But, their concerns are more immediate and acute with respect to a sports event broadcast. A fan who has already invested the capital, time, and effort to pay for a ticket, given up a day or evening, and traveled to see a sports event live has far greater staying power than those fans watching from home. The fan in attendance will likely remain at the event a far longer period of time, even if the contest proves disappointing, than a television viewer with ready access to a remote control. Television producers must be concerned with attracting and holding their audience on a minute-to-minute basis, lest viewers switch to alternative sports programming on another channel or another leisure-time option. Understanding this important stakeholder's key objective is paramount to the future business of the sports event organizer—potential ticket buyers are watching the event on television! Organizers should do everything possible to help television producers keep their coverage interesting, informative, and entertaining. Give them the unique access they need to bring the viewer closer to the athletes and the sport. Make sure they do not miss a second of action. And, work closely with them on developing new camera positions to give viewers fresh perspectives on the coverage of your sport.

Similarly, sports broadcasters should also take note: "Prime television viewers are watching the event live!" The most likely viewers for coverage of future sports events are seated in the grandstands. Ensure that your game presentation director brings replays, player features, and interviews to the fans in the stands. Fans like to associate with others who are devoted to their favorite sport. Demonstrate your own knowledge, respect, and loyalties to the sports they love, and they will devote an allegiance to your coverage and on-air talent, as well.

Glenn Adamo, the NFL's Vice President of Broadcasting, Production, and Media Operations, and veteran of sports broadcasts ranging from national championships to Olympic competition, is a master at working closely and collaboratively with live sports event producers to achieve mutual objectives. He notes five areas of "Must Dos" for sports event organizers when working with broadcasters (see Figure 13.3).

1. Communicate during planning.
2. Integrate timings and other broadcasting needs.
3. Remain flexible.
4. Rehearse together.
5. Communicate during events.

Figure 13.3 Adamo's Top 5 Broadcasting "Must Dos" for Sports Event Organizers

"One Event—One Audience"

Sports event organizers must let the broadcaster know what activities are being planned before live coverage is scheduled to begin. Pre-event fan activities can provide outstanding footage (known as "B-roll") that can be integrated into recorded features that can air during event coverage, or incorporated into the opening of the broadcast. Make sure the broadcast producer is offered an opportunity to send a camera crew and reporter to all press conferences and other media events, excellent opportunities to capture interviews with the athletes. Engage the broadcast producer in discussions regarding the development of the event rundown so everything can be planned from camera positions and commercial breaks to segment timings and scripting. Familiarize the producer with every aspect of the event to ensure that the television show can portray the sport with the impact, if not all of the imagery, presented to the live audience. If organizers strive to stage the event with the precision of a television production, the only way to ensure that both parties remain in lockstep is to integrate their timings so that each understands what the other can expect as the event unfolds. "Timing is always underestimated," says the CBC's Najak. "Five seconds of a dead house can be a lifetime on television. It's magical to the viewer when events or introductions happen exactly on cue without a second of silence or hesitation." As Najak, Gaudelli, and Adamo can attest, there may be two productions being presented simultaneously (i.e., television and live), but there is still "One Event—One Audience."

In order to achieve this unity of purpose, both parties must remain flexible and understanding of each other's objectives throughout the planning process. A segment may need to be moved to provide a broadcaster with time to break for commercial, another may need to be shortened or lengthened to accommodate other requirements and realities. Broadcasters, similarly, should maintain some flexibility to ensure that the event neither loses its focus or momentum for the live audience. "Remember, the event producers have spent days and even weeks planning their execution so it is perfectly timed for their purposes. Asking them to 'scrap' their show for TV will not work," says Adamo. "They can be flexible but need you [broadcasters] to also understand their issues."

In this spirit, accommodating commercial breaks cannot result in a total cessation of activity for the live audience. While the broadcaster is fulfilling its advertiser and sponsor obligations, the organizer can likewise use the opportunity to do the same. But, sometimes the momentum, especially with regard to pre-event entertainment activities, must continue to keep the audience engaged. It is helpful for both the broadcaster and the live presentation director to agree in advance on what segments might be missed, and over what period of time. Providing broadcasters with an opportunity to review rundowns, scripts, and other presentation plans well in advance gives them the opportunity to create their own rundowns and surface challenges, requests, and requirements during the formative stages of planning. By crafting the rundowns together, the presentations are more likely to appear seamless, both on television and at the sports event venue.

Camera Rehearsals

There is only one way to test whether these integrated timings will, in fact, work to the benefit of both audiences: rehearse all critical segments together! For example, decisions should be made in advance as to whether the broadcaster will use the event's announcer or its own during athlete introductions, how they will be covered by the cameras, whether hand-held cameras will be temporarily permitted on the playing surface, and at what pace they will progress to accommodate the needs of television. For the live-event audience, athletes could be announced more rapidly, but if being planned for television, a pace must be determined to allow for smooth direction of the cameras, graphics, and the announcers. Staging a camera rehearsal for segments such as this is by far the best way to establish these parameters. The athletes themselves are rarely available for these essential rehearsals. Use stand-ins to simulate the timing and assist in the blocking of player introductions and other important ceremonial elements for the purposes of both the live event and broadcast producers. Schedule joint rehearsals far in advance—like the producer of the live sports event, the broadcast producer has many more rehearsals that must be staged during the time leading up to the program (e.g., host rehearsals, tape cues, animations, and graphics).

The camera rehearsal will also establish whether the lighting conditions planned for various segments will be conducive to television coverage. Live presentation directors love to stage events in the dark. Lighting and special effects shows are often at their most dramatic and emotional when they are executed in an otherwise completely dark facility. For television, however, dark environments are horrendously limiting. The impact of a light show on a television screen does not approach the excitement it generates in the facility. As wonderful as they might be live, light shows often appear indecipherable on television, so these theatrical openings are frequently the points in the rundown at which broadcasters will be doing something else.

Television directors also don't like concentrating on a single shot or subject for a long time. The response of the audience at a sports event and during pre-event introductions is a great visual opportunity for television directors. If the fans are in total darkness, the director will have difficulty portraying their enthusiasm at key moments in the broadcast. Consider partially lighting fans in selected seating sections during times and segments when the rest of the audience is otherwise in the dark to give broadcasters an option to show spirited audience reactions. Broadcasters should also demonstrate what lighting they plan to use during various theatrically illuminated portions of the event. Thousands of dollars in lighting and special effects can be ruined by floodlights used during an unanticipated interview at the edge of the playing surface, or in an anchor position overlooking the field.

Installing temporary television lighting into indoor facilities that are not specifically designed for television can provide its own challenges. Simply put, lights are hot. "Temperature is something I never thought about till I saw all lights it takes to put on a television event in a large venue," observes the CBC's Najak. "If the audience is too warm (or too cold), then it affects the perception of the product. Many of the shows we do are in excess of two hours. The audience starts fidgeting (in the heat) and becomes disinterested in the production of the show. I always make it a rule to cool down the house right up until show time." Not only can lighting affect the comfort of the audience, it can also dramatically impact the performance of an athlete. Ensure the air handling systems of the host facility can adequately cool or vent the heat from the indoor environment. If it cannot, temporary air conditioning units can be rented, albeit at a potentially prohibitive cost.

The Importance of Communication during the Event

Close and regular communication between the organizer and broadcaster must extend well beyond the planning process. It is also essential to maintain open lines of communication throughout the event and broadcast as they progress in real time. The game presentation director should appoint an individual on staff to maintain contact with the producer in the television truck during the event to receive the concerns of the broadcaster, as well as to communicate any required changes in timings by either party. Accidents or unforeseen issues happen during events, and aberrations in timing, order of competition, and athlete appearances, to name a few, are to be expected. "If your show, or theirs, goes awry you need to be able to communicate in order to execute the integration without embarrassment," observes Adamo. Install a "PL," a private line phone, headset, or other wired device between the truck and the presentation director's position, to keep a flow of communications going during all phases of the event. Know when the broadcaster has, in fact, departed the event site to accommodate a commercial, and definitively when the broadcast coverage has returned to ensure no part of the action is missed. Communicate the substance of judging and referees' decisions so the broadcaster is as well informed as the live audience. Provide game statistics and confirm historical milestones. Make sure the broadcaster has access to all essential information to make the coverage genuine, authoritative, and reliable.

Post-Play Analysis

Broadcast coverage of sports events can exponentially increase the audience that witnesses a competition and provide tremendous additional value to event sponsors. To present a viable business opportunity to a broadcaster, sports events must be able to generate revenues in excess of production costs and any rights fees that might be paid to the organizer. As a result, very few events become broadcast properties compared to the total number staged. Alternatively, sports event organizers can invest in a *time buy,* the outright purchase of time from a broadcaster. In exchange for a cash payment, the organizer typically receives the inventory of commercials available during the time period, which can be resold to sponsors or other advertisers. The organizer, however, must pay the costly expenses of production and, in the case of recorded events, the postproduction editing of the event.

Sports event organizers and broadcast producers can create a seamless production by embracing the "One Event—One Audience" concept. The future viability of both the sports event and its broadcast coverage depend on simultaneously serving the needs of both the live and television audiences. Both parties should communicate with each other regarding their plans before the event, and exhibit reasonable flexibility to ensure that the needs of both the live program and its televised alter ego are met. Rehearse important television moments with broadcast cameras operating, and be prepared to make adjustments to enhance their coverage. Keep the lines of communication open throughout the planning process and establish a real-time communications system during the event broadcast to minimize the effect of accidents, mistakes, and oversights, and to inform the broadcaster of all pertinent developments.

Coach's Clipboard

1. Both national and regional broadcasters have decided not to take advantage of the opportunity to televise a top-tier skateboarding competition. The event's presenting sponsor is keenly interested in having the program featured on television, but the organizer has no available funds to risk buying the time on the regional sports network that is willing to air it for a price. What can the organizer do to improve the chances of the event being broadcast? What other options exist if television broadcast coverage remains elusive?
2. A television producer has been assigned to cover your one-day track and field meet just two weeks before the competition will be held. A pre-event ceremony has been scheduled and publicized to begin at 3:00 P.M., with the first race stepping off at 3:20 P.M. During the first conference call to review the event rundown, the producer indicates that for the broadcast's purposes, the first race must begin at 3:08 P.M. What options are available to you as the sports event organizer?
3. A major news event has suddenly preempted live television coverage of an organizer's sports event while in progress. What kinds of risks may the organizer be subject to, and what protections should it have in place, to minimize the financial impact?

PLAY 14

Managing for the Unexpected

"If they expect us to expect the unexpected, doesn't the unexpected become the expected?"

—*Anonymous*

"The unexpected always happens."

—*Proverb*

This play will help you to:

- Analyze your event's risk exposure and manage those risks.
- Develop security and accreditation plans for your event to protect participants, fans, and property.
- Understand the types of insurance available to protect the organizer from unanticipated crises.
- Develop an emergency response and communications plan.

Introduction

As game day approaches, the countless hours of intense and detailed planning have laid a solid foundation for an entertaining, smooth-running, and rewarding experience for the athletes, audience, sponsors, and staff. Regardless of how simple a sports event may appear to be, rest assured that there will be dozens of unfulfilled details and inadvertent omissions that will come to light in the final days, hours, and minutes, from just about every direction. Some may even become evident as the event itself progresses, a natural byproduct of a detail-laden, multidisciplinary process. It remains the sports event organizer's job to predict, project, and plan for these issues and challenges before they present themselves, and to establish a plan to deal with those that nevertheless emerge unexpectedly.

Risk Assessment and Management

Every sports event carries elements of risk—and lots of them. Athletes may be injured in the course of competition or resulting from accidents caused by noncompetitive circumstances. A spectator can fall from the bleachers at a community activities field, or an errant ball can cause unintentional physical harm. Organizers add risk factors for almost every benefit they offer their audiences and any accommodations they make for the athletes. Despite meticulous planning and all good intentions, a caterer can unwittingly serve tainted food, trusses supporting lighting can tip and fall, loudspeakers can become detached and drop to the ground, a bus or van carrying participants can become involved in a traffic accident. Fireworks can drop smoldering debris on unsuspecting people or damage parked cars. Spectators can wander into nonpublic areas, trip on cables, or fall down stairs. In short, absolutely anything can happen.

The comforting news is that although organizers cannot totally eliminate the possibility of an injury or damage to property as either a direct or indirect result of a sports event, they can exercise the good judgment and sensitivity required to evaluate and manage risks and to greatly reduce the potential of their occurrence. Among the essential resources for incorporating this philosophy into all phases of sports event planning is *Event Risk Management and Safety*, by Dr. Peter E. Tarlow (Hoboken, NJ: John Wiley & Sons, 2002). In this book, Tarlow outlines a formalized risk management process, which is summarized and expanded in Figure 14.1.

Analyzing Risk Exposure and Possible Outcomes

Identify the many areas in which an event and its various participants, spectators, stakeholders, and organizations may be placed at risk. Issues can be separated into three broad categories: (1) areas that may affect the health, safety, and security of spectators, staff, and participants, (2) financial and legal issues that can threaten the ability of the organizer to complete the event, and (3) potentially catastrophic occurrences that can cause the event to be canceled completely. See Figure 14.2 for a summary of the discussion that follows. Although the areas of concern may seem as limitless as the imagination, the probability of such risks occurring may range from the infinitesimal to the

1. Identify areas of risk exposure and the likelihood of their occurrence.
2. Project possible outcomes flowing from areas of risk exposure.
3. Determine possible remedies.
4. Act on feasible remedies to prevent possible outcomes.
5. Identify possible reactions to potentially unavoidable crises.
6. Formalize crisis management and communications procedures.

Figure 14.1 Risk Management Process

A careful and comprehensive evaluation of the areas listed can help sports events manage potential risks that could impact the safety of the public and participants, as well as the financial health of the organizer.

Safety and Security

- Crowd control
- Organized queuing of early- or rapidly arriving spectators
- Sufficient points of ingress and egress
- Sufficient front-of-house staff for directing and providing information to guests
- Emergency evacuation plan
- Dissemination of instructions and information to staff and the public
- Clearly marked emergency exits
- Reassembly area for staff
- Security of athletes and playing surface from spectators
- Security of assets and property
- Lockable storage and office areas to prevent theft of equipment and materials
- Adequate security personnel to safeguard equipment and materials that cannot be protected in lockable areas
- Public safety
- Policies regarding banned materials and substances at the event site (weapons, alcohol, bottles, cans, drugs, etc.)
- Degree of audience screening upon entering the event facility (e.g., visible inspection, patdowns, magnetometers, wands, bag x-rays or searches)
- Inspection of vehicles entering restricted areas

Financial and Legal Issues

- Labor disputes
- Unavailability of required labor
- Jurisdictional disputes between the organizer, facility, and labor
- Picket lines and protests
- Legal challenges
- Court injunctions
- Failure to secure required permits
- Intellectual property right infringements
- Criminal investigations
- Civil suits
- Public protests and civil disturbances
- Preparation in event of civil disturbance
- Law enforcement assistance during public disturbance
- Designation of free speech zones
- Bankruptcy
  - Organizer
  - Host facility
  - Other stakeholders (e.g., vendor, sponsor, broadcaster)
- Refund policies
- Conditions under which refunds will be issued
- Procedures for obtaining refunds post-event or cash on hand for on-site refunds

Cancellation Scenarios

- "Acts of God"
  - Weather conditions (snow, ice, rain, lightning, wind) that make playing, attending, or traveling to the event inadvisable
  - Flooding
  - Earthquake
- Power failure
- Structural damage to, or collapse of host facility
- Irreparable damage to playing surface
- Toxic waste spills
- Catastrophic political or cultural events
- Global or national tragedy
- Acts of terror
- War
- National day(s) of mourning
- Inability of teams or participants to appear or play for any reason
- Emergency conditions apparent before the event vs. those occurring during the event
- Inaccessibility of event facility to participants or fans due to roadway or parking area closures

Figure 14.2 Managing Sports Event Risk Factors

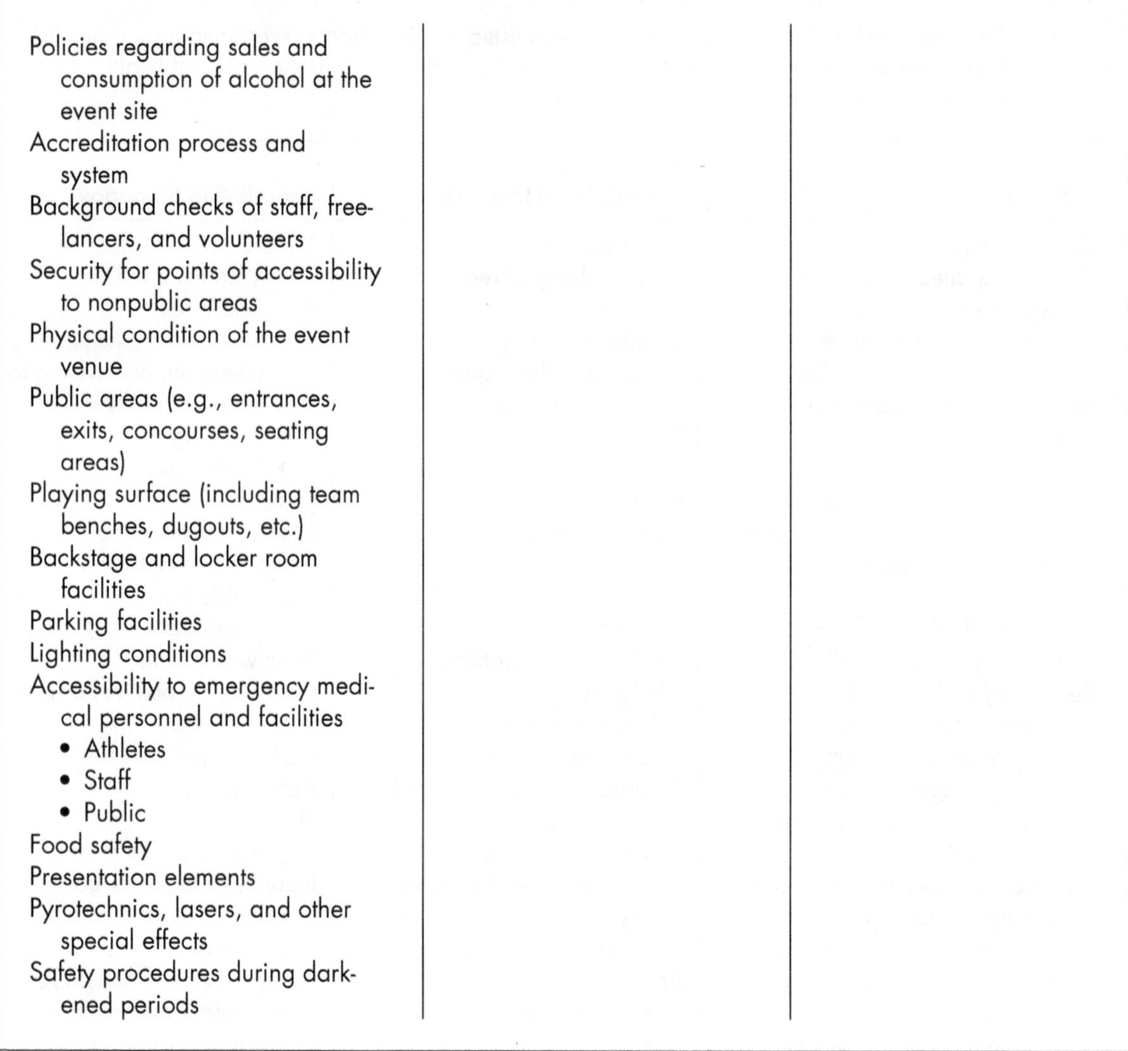

Policies regarding sales and consumption of alcohol at the event site		
Accreditation process and system		
Background checks of staff, free-lancers, and volunteers		
Security for points of accessibility to nonpublic areas		
Physical condition of the event venue		
Public areas (e.g., entrances, exits, concourses, seating areas)		
Playing surface (including team benches, dugouts, etc.)		
Backstage and locker room facilities		
Parking facilities		
Lighting conditions		
Accessibility to emergency medical personnel and facilities • Athletes • Staff • Public		
Food safety		
Presentation elements		
Pyrotechnics, lasers, and other special effects		
Safety procedures during darkened periods		

Figure 14.2 *(Continued)*

quite possible. It is the responsibility of the organizer to ensure that all plans minimize the risk potential to the greatest degree possible through a process of thorough self-examination.

Safety and Security

Next, project the possible outcomes that can develop from areas of potential risk. Some may simply create nuisances that could affect the enjoyment of those in attendance; others may pose the potential for more serious health and safety concerns. First and foremost, the safety and well being of all who attend a sports event, from participants to spectators to staff, is of paramount importance. With all other considerations treated as secondary, determine whether you, the organizer, and the venue are providing a sufficiently safe environment for the event from the time and point of arrival until departure. Have operational plans created an environment that will encourage fans to arrive extremely early and rush into the facility when the doors first open (such as first-come, first-served general admission seating)? How early will spectators arrive, and will they begin crowding around the entrances to position themselves to get the best possible viewing locations? How early should the facility plan to queue the spectators into orderly lines? Can temporary weather conditions cause crowds to appear at the gates late and all at once? (These types of crowd control issues can also exist on the day event tickets are first placed on sale at the box office.)

How early should the public be admitted to the venue on the day of the event? Will there be sufficient time and front-of-house labor to ensure that all arrivals can find their seats before the event begins, or within a reasonable period of time? Are trained, informed personnel available to keep crowds moving, to direct spectators, and to answer questions? Is there pre-event entertainment to encourage early-arriving guests to take their seats, rather than rushing in from the concourses as the competition begins? Are there obstacles, either physical objects or security presence, between the spectators and the athletes to protect each from the activities or enthusiasms of one another?

Are concessions open to enable fans to purchase refreshments and merchandise while they wait for the event to begin, or to occupy them during breaks in play? Are there sufficient staff and points of purchase to keep waiting times as short as possible and queues arranged to keep those in line from blocking areas of public concourse? Is alcohol being served only to adults who present required proof of age? How late into the event will alcohol be served, and are there trained personnel among the concessions staff who can determine whether a spectator's reasonable limit of alcohol consumption has been reached? Are there limits to the amount of alcohol that may be purchased per transaction?

Most permanent event venues maintain a written evacuation plan in case of fire and other extreme conditions, such as storms with lightning, or credible threats to public safety. Become familiar with the plan and understand under what circumstances they might be required. What procedures are necessary if an evacuation becomes necessary? How will the public know the best routes to vacate the building? What role does the event's staff play during and after the facility is being cleared? Who makes key decisions, and by what method will the venue and event decision makers meet to consider the options and required courses of action?

Does the celebrity status of the sports event's participants require the separation of the public from the competitors to ensure their safety? What can happen if the event's accreditation plan is compromised and a fan accesses a nonpublic area? Is there a plan to screen those arriving at the facility and to search bags and other carried items to ensure that no one enters with materials that can be used to intentionally—or even accidentally—injure participants and other spectators? Does the screening system create long waiting lines at the doors, or are there adequate personnel and entrances to handle the numbers of spectators expected? Do plans also call for athletes, media, and support staff to be screened and searched?

Does the event's system of designing and distributing credentials discourage the possibility of counterfeiting? Is there an approval process in place that requires review or oversight of the list of credential applicants before individuals are approved to control the number and nature of those receiving them? Are there different levels of credentials that allow access selectively to some of the most sensitive areas? Does the system of soliciting and hiring staff, freelancers, and volunteers include some form of background or reference check? Do event staff drivers or vendors providing transportation services have valid and appropriate licenses and acceptable safety records, or a history of traffic violations?

Is the event facility in good physical condition, or are there areas that require upgraded lighting or the removal of potential sources of injury? Have temporary event venues been designed to permit

SIDELINE STORY

Protecting Event Participants

If you think a violent incident involving spectators and athletes cannot happen at your sports event, consider this abbreviated, but sobering, chronology:

- On April 30, 1993, 19-year-old tennis star Monica Seles was stabbed in the back by a spectator who rushed through the grandstands and jumped into a courtside rest area while she waited for her next game to begin at the Hamburg Open in Germany. Rushed to a nearby hospital, Seles recovered, but would not play again for 27 months.
- During the last game of the 1995 NFL New York Giants' season, fans launched dozens of hard-packed, icy snowballs onto the field, striking and knocking a San Diego Chargers assistant unconscious. The team identified 75 season-ticket holders and their guests among the perpetrators and revoked their ability to renew their accounts for the following season.
- The playing field was abandoned for a half hour after fans at a 2001 Cleveland Browns football contest against the Jacksonville Jaguars began throwing beer bottles onto the field. The game was halted with only 48 seconds to play, following a disputed call by the officials. The game was completed after the stadium had been almost completely emptied.
- In 2002, fan violence erupted in the stands during a game between the Washington Redskins and Philadelphia Eagles. Police attempted to control the crowd by using pepper spray, which drifted onto the Philadelphia bench and into the players' faces, causing respiratory symptoms and vomiting.
- In April 2003, Chicago's US Cellular Field witnessed an attack on first base umpire Laz Diaz, when a fan leaped

the flow of people through safe, well-lit areas? Have cables and temporary wiring been distributed in such a way as to eliminate or minimize the possibility of ensnaring or tripping passersby? Are lighting towers and other upright structures sufficiently weighted down or secured with guy wires to keep from upending in wind or as the result of a collision? Are there wind load limits for temporary structures that would require closure or evacuation in the event of threatening fronts, and is there a system in place to monitor approaching weather? Is the weight of equipment elevated above a stage, playing surface, or audience within approved safety limits? Are the poles and pegs for tented areas secure and weighted? Are tower and tent guy wires strung in areas away from public access? Are there sufficient restroom facilities, and are they serviced regularly? Is there sufficient parking or nearby access to mass transportation systems to accommodate participants and spectators? Are there sidewalks present or is there a clear path off the street from parking areas to the event venue? Are shuttle buses a safer alternative to move spectators onto the event venue property?

Is the playing surface in good condition or are corrections, modifications, or renovations required to guard against injuries to athletes and game officials? Are there holes, metal covers, gratings, or depressions in the surface that must be filled, capped, or repaired? Is there a clear, unobstructed path between the locker room or athlete preparation areas and the playing surface? Will there be easy access for athletes, game officials, and spectators to medical personnel, equipment, and supplies,

onto the field and attempted to tackle the official during the eighth inning of a game against the Kansas City Royals. It was the fourth time the game was halted that night while stadium security rounded up fans running onto the field. Just the previous season, a fan and his 15-year-old son assaulted then-Royals first-base coach Tom Gamboa on the very same field.

- In September 2003, in an effort to reduce threats to athlete security and the incidence of injury, the New York City Council overwhelmingly approved legislation that imposed penalties of up to $1,000 in fines and one year in prison against fans who illegally enter playing surfaces at professional sports events.
- In November 2004 at The Palace at Auburn Hills, the Indiana Pacers and the Detroit Pistons were involved in one of the ugliest incidents in NBA history, an altercation that will be forever remembered as the Malice at the Palace. With less than a minute left in the game, a fight between players on the court was broken up, but a cup filled with a drink was thrown from the stands and hit visiting Pacers player Ron Artest while he was lying on the scorer's table. Artest charged into the stands and participated in a brawl between players and fans. As a result of the incident, nine players were suspended; five of the nine, who also were charged with assault, were sentenced to one year of probation and community service; five fans faced criminal charges and were banned for life from attending Pistons home games; and the NBA altered league security procedures and moved to limit the sale of alcohol at its venues.
- In 2012, fans of Germany's Dynamo Dresden played a game against Ingolstadt at an empty Gluckgas Stadion. The German soccer federation ordered the stadium closed after fan violence marred a contest the previous autumn. Although no one saw the contest live, 32,066 fans purchased tickets—an official "sell-out"— but watched the game on large video screens set up outside the empty stadium.

and a system in place to direct help to where it is needed? Is an ambulance on site for dispatch of the injured or ill to a nearby hospital or clinic? If not, how long will it take for emergency vehicles to reach the event venue in the traffic conditions that will exist at various times on event day?

Are there presentation elements that can pose a threat to safety, such as pyrotechnics, flame effects, lasers, or trusses or towers containing lighting and sound equipment? Has the design and installation of all technical elements been executed or supervised by professional, experienced personnel? Are all potentially dangerous special effects stored and displayed in areas that are of sufficient distance from the public as to minimize any possible mishap? Have experienced, licensed riggers installed all equipment that is suspended over the playing surface or spectator viewing areas?

Remedying and Responding to Risk Exposure

Considering the many potential areas of risk exposure and analyzing the impact of the dozens, or even hundreds, of hypothetical circumstances that could befall a sports event will help organizers to crystallize possible responses before the intense pressures of necessity and immediacy prevail. Some answers may seem patently obvious. For example, if an unsafe structural condition exists in the facility, it is the responsibility of the organizer to bring it to the attention of the venue management and request or demand its repair. Conditions that are insufficiently safe or secure should be reinforced, removed, or repaired or before they can present clear threats to safety. Access to nonpublic areas should be obstructed or staffed by security personnel. Challenges to maintaining positive cash flow in the event of default by a sponsor can be mitigated in advance by securing letters of credit from a bank or investors. Options for issuing refunds in case of a sudden, unavoidable cancellation are best considered before fans start lining up at the ticket window, when there is still time to determine how cash can be made available given the enormous financial impact such an eventuality will have on the organizer.

The answers to other hypothetical questions may be less obvious, requiring great forethought and the application of sound, ethical, and responsible judgment. It is impossible to predict, for example, how outside events beyond the control of the organizer might affect the safe conduct of the event, or even the advisability of opening the doors to the public at all. These are the concerns for which insurance was invented.

Financial and Legal Issues

Safety is of the utmost importance, but there are other areas of risk that can affect the conduct of a sports event. Are the contractual agreements governing workers at the event facility and hotels and with major vendors in full force and effect, or is there a possibility of a strike, lockout, or work slowdown due to labor unrest? How could the potential of labor actions affect the safe and smooth conduct of the event? Is there a possibility of a picket line or protest being staged outside of the event facility, and what effect will the presence of protestors have on spectators or other labor groups associated with the event? Have you worked with public safety officials to set aside an area that can be designated as a "free speech zone," a place where protestors can exercise their rights without interfering with the safe conduct of participants and fans?

Have legal challenges been filed against the event, organizer, host facility, or major sponsor? Is there a claim being levied against any stakeholder associated with the event that could cause the program to be postponed, delayed, or altered in any way? Are all required permits secured or in the process of review? Have all appropriate licenses for the public performance of music, video, or design elements been acquired, or do any outside parties claim intellectual ownership of the event or any element contained therein?

Are any stakeholders, including the organizer, venue, major sponsors, vendors, or media partners, in particular financial distress? Are any in imminent danger of filing for reorganization or bankruptcy? How much cash has been issued in the form of deposits or progress payments already paid to or received from financially shaky stakeholders, and may, therefore, be at risk of partial or total loss? Are there legal actions pending against any stakeholder that has failed to meet past contractual obligations?

Does the organizer have a written refund policy and procedure for fans to follow for compensation if an event is interrupted, postponed, or canceled? Will there be sufficient cash on hand if refunds are to be made on site?

Cancellation Scenarios

What kinds of occurrences can cause the event to be canceled or postponed? Is the event's successful completion subject to favorable weather conditions? At what minimum and maximum air temperatures may the event proceed? Does an outdoor contest require the existence of dry field conditions, or can it take place regardless of precipitation? What extreme precipitation conditions could cause the event to be subject to cancellation or postponement? What effect would extended electrical storms, accumulating ice, or high wind conditions have on competition? Would decisions be made differently before the event begins versus once fans were on site and the event was underway?

What is the likelihood at that time of year of a weather postponement? If the event must be postponed, is an alternate "rain date" included in the facility lease? Is it practical to move an outdoor contest to an indoor location? What additional costs would the organizer have to bear to hold the event on an alternate date or in an alternate space? Will the organizer be liable for issuing refunds for rescheduled or canceled games? What is the financial exposure associated with a total cancellation? In addition to refunding ticket revenues, what portion of sponsorship, broadcast, and other revenues will need to be returned? What extreme weather conditions might cause cancellation or postponement for indoor events—a blizzard, ice storm, hurricane, lightning, damage stemming from tornados, flooding due to torrential rains, or impassable roadways? Is the

SIDELINE STORY

Moving Minnesota

On early Sunday morning, December 12, 2010, a massive and rapid accumulation of snow resulting from a blizzard that struck Minneapolis, Minnesota, caused the air-pressure supported dome over the Hubert H. Humphrey Metrodome to tear and collapse, rendering the stadium useless for the balance of the NFL Minnesota Vikings' season and, most immediately, for the team's home game scheduled for the same afternoon. A weather emergency task force of league and team personnel quickly convened by conference call to explore the options—find another NFL stadium that could be mobilized to host the game or find a neutral site in which to play for a rescheduled game against the New York Giants on Monday evening. The Detroit Lions, just hours from opening the stadium doors for their own Sunday afternoon game, began preparations to schedule staff and develop an operations plan for their own Ford Field to host the game. While Minnesota fans shoveled away nearly 18 inches of snow from their homes and watched the contest on national television, more than 40,000 fans from the Detroit area were admitted free to enjoy the game.

Simultaneously, work began to relocate the one remaining Vikings home game on the schedule, set for the very next Monday night. The open-air University of Minnesota's TCF Bank Field had already been winterized for the deep cold of the north Midwest winter, its field under several feet of accumulated snow from several winter storms and all utilities shut down for the season. Through a heroic effort by the school, team, and league, hastily arranged contracted and volunteer staff removed hundreds of truckloads of snow from the stands and field, reactivated the stadium, contacted game-day staff, and readied the facility to host the Vikings' last home game of the season against the Chicago Bears amid another fresh snowfall in the Minnesota cold.

Although it is unlikely that such drastic measures will be required for your event, be sure to consider what your weather contingency plans will be— will your event be postponed, moved, or canceled in case of extreme weather? What measures must you take to protect your facilities, equipment, and playing surface should adverse weather be expected?

event facility in a seismically active zone prone to earthquake activity? Does the venue have its own power-generating capability, or would it be subject to even the remote possibility of power outages? Is there adequate illumination of the playing surface and spectator access areas in case a daytime event must be delayed until after sunset? Are there local curfew ordinances that require the event to be completed by a specified time?

How would the organizer react to the great unknowns of catastrophic political or cultural events, such as a global or national tragedy, acts of terror, or the sudden outbreak of war or epidemic? Would the event continue to be held on a national day of mourning following tragic circumstances?

Liability Insurance

In its most basic form, an insurance policy is issued by a company that agrees to assume the financial risks of unforeseen, unfortunate, and even cataclysmic occurrences on behalf of the organizer, in return for a fee (the premium). Depending on the amount and type of protections an event organizer chooses to procure, a significant portion of the budget can be spent on satisfying insurance premium expenses.

SIDELINE STORY

Simulating Emergency Reaction and Response

Many large event organizers and public safety agencies stage emergency simulation exercises to test their decision-making systems and preparedness for the unexpected. Since 2006, senior game-day managers for the NFL's Super Bowl, for example, participate in such an exercise approximately 10 days before the game. A hired facilitator interviews representatives from all major operational areas (e.g., facilities, security, guest management, game operations, law enforcement, fire marshal, medical services) over the course of several weeks to gain a thorough knowledge of every facet of the event, and tests weaknesses in the system by presenting the group with emergency scenarios to be solved in real time. The half-dozen cases that will be presented by the facilitator over the half-day exercise are kept confidential until they are revealed to the group to ensure that solutions are developed under the pressure of time, and as a team. Over the years, many solutions developed in response to simulated scenarios have resulted in permanent changes to the emergency preparedness plan for the Super Bowl.

The simulation also builds trust between the event management team and the public safety officials overseeing the event by defining how different decisions are made, and by whom. Oversight on matters of public safety and law enforcement, for instance, appropriately belong to the government agencies with ultimate authority, and the event organizer's staff will support their decisions as directed with human resources and physical assets. Decision making on most other operational contingencies, such as postponement or cancellation for reasons other than public safety, belongs to the event organizer. Organizers for events large and small should define an emergency operations plan, and work with the host venue's management and public safety agencies that have jurisdiction over the event to establish a process for clear decision-making and response. Can your events benefit from an emergency response simulation?

At minimum, event organizers should procure liability insurance to protect themselves from direct expenses and legal actions that may result from injuries to spectators, athletes, and volunteers. Proof of insurance against property damage is also essential and will be required by event facilities, sponsors, equipment rental companies, and/or other business partners to help protect their own assets against risks related to the event.

"Policy forms are non-standard in nature and are often specifically tailored based upon the type of event, location, duration, the ability to postpone and/or reschedule, and prevailing insurance market conditions," says Bill Bannon, Vice President of Advisory and Special Risk Services for BWD Group, LLC, an agency based in Plainview, New York, with expertise in sports event insurance. Organizers should investigate coverage options for sports events early in the planning process, not just to ensure an adequate budget is set aside for this purpose, but also to guarantee locating the protection needed at the lowest possible cost. "The insurance marketplace for coverage of sports events is small and specialized," Bannon notes.

The amount of liability insurance that should be procured for a sports event is both a budgetary and business decision based on its size and complexity. Most event liability policies should carry minimum protection ($2 million is a suggested amount) per occurrence, although larger events and those that are deemed to present more risks to spectators or participants should seriously consider policies offering coverage of $5 million to $10 million per occurrence, or even more. Most policies have an aggregate ceiling as well, limiting the total amount of coverage per event to a stated figure. Just like personal auto, medical, and homeowners insurance, a deductible will usually apply. That is, the organizer will be responsible to pay the deductible amount to satisfy claims against an event before the policy's protections begin providing the balance.

Check the policy carefully and speak with your insurance representative to determine whether additional insurance coverage is advised. Is the organizer providing its own independent transportation services, or are staff members required to drive vehicles for VIP transports, deliveries, and on official business? Perhaps, then, special automobile coverage should be obtained. Are alcoholic beverages being served? Liquor liability insurance is strongly advised in such cases. Are checkroom facilities being provided for spectators' coats and bags? Coat check insurance is available to protect against theft or loss of furs and other expensive personal property. Is the organizer serving food or selling merchandise? Consider product liability insurance to guard against the risk of tainted food or covering injuries and accidents related to souvenirs (even miniature bats, balls, sticks, and flags on sticks can hurt bystanders or become missiles). Working closely with an experienced attorney and insurance agency is essential to identifying the types and limits of coverage that are advisable for a particular sports event.

The need to procure insurance for participating athletes will depend on the nature of the event, participating governing organizations, and other factors. As a general rule, such an insurance policy must be in effect or be obtained whenever an athletic competition is staged. Organizations such as USA Cycling, for example, offer approved event organizers the option to purchase insurance through the governing body's own broker, or they may act independently as long as coverage meets the organization's minimum requirements. Coverage is especially recommended for exhibition activities, such as "alumni games," "amateur invitational tournaments," and "celebrity games," among others. Athletes who do not daily train for regular competition are especially susceptible to injury.

Make sure your own vendors are carrying adequate insurance, as well. Legal actions against an uninsured vendor working on the organizer's behalf can cause the supplier to go out of business, leaving the organizer exposed to pay 100 percent of a plaintiff's damages. Proof of coverage, in the form of "certificates of insurance" that include definitions of their policy limits, can easily be obtained from vendors. Check all of your leases and agreements for requirements to name the host facility, sponsors, vendors, and other stakeholders as "additional insured" parties. Your insurance company will issue a certificate that identifies the party requesting coverage as also covered by your insurance. In return, your attorney and insurance broker will help you identify which of your business partners should also name your organization as an additional insured. Commonly, these will include event facilities, as well as vendors in "high risk" businesses, such as rigging, lighting, and pyrotechnics companies, among others.

Cancellation Insurance

Cancellation insurance recompenses an organizer for event expenses if the program is unable to proceed or be held at all. The various, often necessary forms of cancellation insurance can be very expensive and may be subject to a number of significant restrictions and limitations imposed by the insurer. Because policies vary, it is wise to work with an experienced broker or agency to shop and compare the coverage available and premiums charged by a number of different insurance companies. Cancellation coverage can be used to repay sponsors and ticket buyers, satisfy vendor invoices, and fulfill other financial obligations that will protect the organizer from economic ruin due to unlikely and unforeseen circumstances. The premium charged is usually a percentage of the total amount covered, which can range from protecting gross receipts to simply recompensing the organizer for irrecoverable expenses. A provision should also be included to cover any reasonable expenses an organizer may encounter in an attempt to prevent a cancellation, whether or not that attempt was ultimately successful. An organizer cannot simply cancel a sports event and expect the insurer to honor a claim. The policy will define specific acceptable reasons an event may be canceled, many of which are described in Figure 14.2.

Cancellation insurance premiums have increased dramatically since 2001, and areas of coverage have narrowed or become better defined. Availability of insurance protection for "certified acts of terrorism," for example, is now guaranteed in the United States through 2014 as a result of the Federal Terrorism Risk Insurance Act of 2002 (see Figure 14.3 for the government's definition of certified acts. This act is set to expire unless renewed or modified by the US Congress in 2014). For an additional premium, many insurance policies can also offer coverage against

FEDERAL TERRORISM RISK INSURANCE ACT OF 2002

Note: This legislation is set to expire in 2014 unless renewed or modified by the US Congress.

Section 102(1)(A): Any act that is certified by the Secretary (of the Treasury), in concurrence with the Secretary of State, and the Attorney General of the United States (i) to be an act of terrorism; (ii) to be a violent act or an act that is dangerous to (I) human life; (II) property; or (III) infrastructure; (iii) to have resulted in damage within the United States, or outside the United States in the case of (I) an air carrier or vessel described in paragraph (5)(B); or (II) the premises of a United States mission; and (iv) to have been committed by an individual or individuals acting on behalf of any foreign person or foreign interest, as part of an effort to coerce the civilian population of the United States or to influence the policy or affect the conduct of the United States Government by coercion.

Figure 14.3 Definition of "Certified Act of Terrorism"

"noncertified acts of terrorism," basically defined by the same circumstances, but without the Treasury Department's official certification. Insurers can offer different levels of coverage for noncertified acts based on occurrences within certain distances from the event venue (e.g., 250 miles), or within a specified time before the start of an event (e.g., seven days). Both time and distance variables are frequently negotiable, but the wider the coverage, the more expensive the premium will be. The location of the host facility will also be considered when the insurer sets the premium. Generally, sports events held in major cities are considered as more likely targets by insurance companies than those staged in less-populated areas.

Additional protections can be added to cancellation insurance policies at the organizer's request and expense. Sponsor revenues dependent on television coverage, for instance, can be insured against preemption due to matters of national attention, such as breaking global news stories and tragedies. An outbreak of a virulent communicable disease can also cause spectators, sponsors, and athletes to reconsider their plans to travel to a host country or city for a sports event. In 2003, the FIFA Women's World Cup soccer tournament was forced to move from China, in the throes of a SARS outbreak, to the United States. The same medical predicament had stunning effects elsewhere. According to the Canadian Broadcasting Corporation, the loss to the local economy in Toronto, Ontario, during the SARS outbreak topped an estimated $1 billion. The effect on travel and tourism alone was expected to reach in excess of $570 million. Mexican facilities went empty during the global 2009 swine flu scare, causing the outright cancellation of the CONCACAF (Confederation of North, Central American and Caribbean Association Football) Under-17 championship round and the closing of all stadiums to the public nationwide for 176 professional league games. (The latter were broadcast, but played in empty stadiums.) Although the total economic damage to the event organizers, stadium operators, leagues, and teams from lost ticket and concessions revenues was not officially released, one report on NBC estimated that refunds of more than $500,000 were issued for a single professional league game (Chivas-Pumas) and that lost concessions revenues, particularly beer sales, for the anticipated crowd of 50,000 were expected to be significant. As a result of such catastrophic losses, communicable diseases are now often excluded from regular cancellation coverage, requiring the negotiation of additional premiums.

Weather Insurance

Weather insurance is another type of coverage to carefully consider for outdoor events that can be affected by such meteorological events as rain, snow, temperature, lightning, high wind speeds, and fog. This type of cancellation protection specifies under what conditions the insurer will honor claims to recover expenses. "This coverage is typically written on an all-or-nothing basis," says BWD Group's Bannon. "If specified unwanted conditions occur at the location as determined by the closest National Weather Station or on-site independent weather observer, the policy would pay the limit purchased." Typical measures include how much rain and snow must fall over a defined period, sustained wind speeds, and trigger levels for extreme temperatures. These specifications are negotiable based on how much the organizer is willing to spend. A policy that will honor claims for events canceled due to rainfall of four inches over two hours immediately before the event will cost less than one that protects against two inches during the same period. If it seems more like wagering than the usual process of making a sound business decision, you are not mistaken. Insurers want to improve the odds that they will be able to keep your money and reduce the probability you will collect on a claim. Nevertheless, cancellation coverage is often essential for ticketed and sponsored events to avoid the possibility of financial disaster due to weather. Some sponsors will actually require the organizer to carry cancellation insurance to ensure their marketing investment will be repaid if the event is not ultimately executed.

Waivers (Releases)

Simple, single-page documents designed to provide sports event organizers with limited, but specific, protections from legal actions are called waivers or releases. Signed waivers are usually requested from individuals who will engage in some participatory aspect of a sports event, such as amateur athletes, performers, volunteer staff, promotion contestants, and fan participants in certain physical demonstrations and activities. An experienced attorney should craft an organizer's waiver that is most appropriate to the type of event and the protections desired. A parent or legal guardian must sign waivers required from minors. Waivers should include language indemnifying the organizer against claims arising from injuries that result from participation in the event. A participant's receipt of the document infers acceptance that some level of risk is involved in the event experience and his or her signature essentially acknowledges that this has been taken into account when making the decision to participate.

Another common purpose of the participant waiver is to provide agreement that the image of the signatory at the event is the property of the organizer. This grants the organizer permission to use a person's image in video footage and photography for live or recorded broadcasts, website clips or images, advertising, promotions, and printed or online materials. The participants will not be paid, nor will further permission be required, if their images are used in any of these or other materials. This language is also frequently printed on sports event tickets to remove the risk of legal challenges to the future use of the audience's images in these same media. Many sports event organizers also post similar consent language on large posters prominently displayed at the host facility's entrances to further reinforce their ability to use audience images in broadcast(s) of the event.

Accident Response

The presence of first aid personnel, such as qualified first aid practitioners, emergency medical technicians (EMTs), and physicians, is essential to protect the safety and well being of all in attendance at any sports event. Sports events are inherently risky, especially for participants in athletic competition, but also in some respects for the spectators. It is strongly recommended that wherever possible an ambulance be present or accessible to the event site for the timely transfer of the injured or sick to full-service medical facilities. At minimum, an ambulance service or nearby hospital should be identified and aware of the event in case of the need for the rapid dispatch of an emergency vehicle. All staff and volunteers should be familiar with the procedure and mechanism to summon early-response assistance to the scene of an injury or other situation requiring medical attention.

If an accident occurs on the event site, whether involving athletes, spectators, staff, crew, volunteers, or vendors, ensure that affected parties are referred to first aid personnel whether injuries appear to exist or not. An incident form should be filled out to provide complete contact information for the affected party, as well as a description of the injury or situation, the location and circumstances surrounding the occurrence (see Figure 14.4). If possible, the facts recorded on the report should be reviewed and verified by the injured party. Most permanent event facilities have a standard incident report form and will provide the organizer with additional copies for the organizer's files and possible future reference. The accuracy and comprehensiveness of this document is essential, as it will certainly play a role of major importance if any legal action is taken in the future.

Accreditation

Event credentials and the access they provide to nonpublic areas are neither a right nor perquisite to be automatically granted to staff, stakeholders, or important guests. Although they are often

(Event, Organizer, or Host Facility Name)

INCIDENT REPORT FORM

Date of Incident:____

Name of Person Assisted:____________________________________

Home Address:____

Local Address (if different from above):_________________________

Phone (Day):____________________(Night):____________________

E-Mail:__________________________________Male/Female:______

This person is ______a guest ______staff member ______volunteer ______event participant _____other (describe:)________________________________

Emergency Notification Contact & Number:_________________________

____

Description of Injury or Complaint:______________________________

____

Location of Incident (as detailed as possible):_______________________

____

____

Details of Incident (use back of form if additional space is required):________

____

____

____

____

Assistance Provided & Actions Taken:_____________________________

____

____

____

Name of Responding Individual:_________________________________

Signature:__________________________Date:__________________

This form must be submitted to the Event Operations Office as soon as possible following the incident.

Figure 14.4 Sample Incident Report Form

perceived as the foregoing, credentials are first and most importantly a method of controlling access to areas of the event venue that require a measure of security or safety. They can help an organizer improve security at an event by prohibiting unauthorized access into sensitive locations such as the area around the playing surface, player benches and sidelines, locker rooms, media facilities, and others over which operational control is essential. The form of the credentials should not be designed until their end purpose, the method by which they will be distributed, and how they will be enforced are clearly defined (see Figure 14.5 and online Appendix 13).

The accreditation process begins by defining what areas of the event facility require restricted access, and how strictly controlled those areas must be. Make copies of the event venue floor plan and separate public areas from those to which access should be limited. Note where checkpoints—the points at which credentials must be presented to security personnel for access to restricted areas—will be required. Make sure that there are no other ways of gaining access to these restricted areas (i.e., back doors, elevators, staircases) without first encountering a checkpoint.

The simplest credential system is one in which only a single level of access is indicated—an "All Access" credential. For many events, however, different levels are required to provide extra security and crowd control measures. For example, it may be desirable to more strictly limit access to the locker room corridor from all but team staff and a handful of essential event personnel. The area immediately surrounding the playing surface might be off limits to all media except authorized photographers and television camera operators, requiring a different level of credential and method of display such as a bib or armband.

The general design of all accreditation, regardless of access level, should look essentially the same to enable security personnel to identify bona fide credentials at a quick glance (see sample credential in Figure 8.6). A best practice is to visually distinguish credentials that provide special access with a headshot photo of the bearer, a band of a specified color, and a large letter or number code that can immediately confirm its status to security personnel from a distance of several feet. Post a chart at each checkpoint that identifies for both security staff and credential bearers what color bands and codes are permitted to pass into the adjacent restricted area. This practice eliminates confusion and obviates the need to print exactly the significance of codes and color bands on the credential. As it is wise to consider the egos of credential holders, it is often best not to label credentials with access level codes that are obvious in hierarchy (e.g., A, B, C). Finally, remember that working representatives of the police and fire departments in uniform should not require credentials to gain access to event facilities.

Like event tickets, credentials should be designed and printed so they may not be easily counterfeited. The bearer of a credential has even more privileged access to an event site than a ticket holder, and a breach of security by someone with bogus credentials can have incredibly

- Define areas of access
- Identify levels of access
- Design credential (anti-counterfeit, photo, code)
- Confirm display method (i.e., lanyard, clip, lapel pin, bib, armband)
- Create and communicate application procedures
- Validate and distribute
- Manage and enforce

Figure 14.5 Designing an Event Accreditation System

serious results. For this reason, it is strongly recommended that credentials include the name and affiliation of the wearer and photo identification that is sealed onto the card under a plastic laminate. Without this measure, it is too easy for the recipient to pass a credential to someone else and for the photo to be replaced. It is also helpful to use design elements such as embossed metallic logos or holograms, or special papers with colored or metal threads that are common anti-counterfeiting devices.

To further reduce the possibility of counterfeiting, it is recommended that credentials be distributed at the latest possible moment, preferably at the actual event site and on the day before or the first day they are required. Whenever possible, though, credentials should be prepared in advance. To speed this process, an electronic file with a photograph of the recipient can be emailed to the organizer ahead of time. It should be required that credentials be picked up in person. A valid government-issued ID card, such as a driver's license or passport, should be presented as proof of identity before the credential is released. Prepare a log listing all who have been received their accreditation and require a signature beside each name to indicate the credential has been picked up. Credentials should be worn about the neck or clipped to clothing in a visible location at all times to identify the wearer as authorized to be in restricted areas. As an added security measure, it may be advisable for some staff, vendor, and volunteer personnel to undergo background checks. This is of particular importance for individuals who are not well known to the organizer, but may be placed in proximity to star athletes, celebrities, and dignitaries.

Audience Security

Is your event of sufficient public importance or visibility to consider screening all who enter the venue? Should audience and those entering through the loading docks, employee entrances, and the media gate be subject to scans with electronic wands, bag searches, and x-rays, or required to pass through magnetometers (metal detectors)? While these measures can increase the sense of security at an event, they can detract from the fan experience and significantly delay the entrance of the audience if there is insufficient security staff or equipment. Be sure you have enough of both because such security measures prevent the possibility of criminal activity, and the use of these procedures may even reduce the premium for liability insurance.

The sense of a safe and secure environment is essential for the enjoyment of the audience. Are security staff members within easy reach of all seating areas in case of an altercation between athletes or members of the audience? Are crowd management teams properly assigned to prevent or discourage fans from attempting to enter the playing area? Are trained security personnel on the lookout for pick-pocketing, thieves, and shoplifters? Are they in radio contact with a supervisor in case of a need for additional assistance?

Reacting to Emergencies

Risk assessment and management methodologies can be very effective in reducing the chances of accidents and emergencies, but they cannot completely eliminate their possibility. Despite thorough planning and the remedying of their most probable causes, incidents beyond the control of the organizer may still occur. Prepare to meet these challenges head on by establishing a chain of command and a crisis communications plan.

Establish a Chain of Command

Sports events are fast-moving environments, where unpredictable situations can develop from any quarter—among the athletes, the audience, or the staff. Things happen quickly, and appropriate, decisive response must be handled rapidly, responsibly, and authoritatively. Establish a chain of command that identifies the decision makers who are empowered to manage areas of responsibility, and define the scope and limits to their authority. Determine what kinds of issues should be communicated further and immediately to the most senior members of the organization and identify how they can be reached. The most important document in managing the operations of an event is a contact list—the list of event, venue, and organization staff with accompanying e-mail addresses, and mobile, office, and home phone numbers. Ensure that all personnel have the most important information on event day stored in their mobile devices or on tablets, and have a pocket-sized version printed on a small laminated card, two sided if necessary, that also is issued to all staff.

Develop a Crisis Communications Plan

A written communications plan should be developed to formalize how the organizer will manage major challenges internally, and the method by which the media and public will receive information in case of a crisis. The plan should outline the step-by-step process by which a potential crisis will be identified, managed, and communicated (see Figure 14.6).

The organizer will have already completed the first part of this exercise—the identification of potential crises—during the risk assessment process (see Figure 14.2). Beyond those conditions listed, the organizer must be prepared for the totally unexpected, as well. Identify in writing the ultimate decision maker who will ascertain whether an event should be canceled, postponed, resumed, or in any way altered. Some organizations will require those decisions that can affect their financial health or public image to be made by the board of directors. However, convening a quorum will often be impractical as crises often arise quickly and responses may be required just as rapidly. It is recommended that only a single decision maker be designated if possible. If the organization's bylaws require board approval, this may be assigned to the chairperson, who may have the authority to act in the interest of the full board and in consultation with the event director or president of the organization. Also select a second-in-command to take this individual's place if the decision maker is incapacitated, missing, or otherwise unavailable.

These top-level officials may comprise, at least in part, the Crisis Assessment Task Force, a small, select group of experts with whom the decision maker will consult in case of an emergency. At minimum, the individuals in charge of security and operations, the event facility, media relations, broadcasting should be included in this group of consultants. The function of the task force

- ☐ Identify areas of crisis potential
- ☐ Identify the decision maker(s) and crisis assessment task force
- ☐ Establish a command center
- ☐ Identify critical stakeholders and their representatives
- ☐ Assess appropriate responses
- ☐ Create a media communications plan

Figure 14.6 Crisis Communications Plan

is to receive information and analyze any developments related to the crisis and to make recommendations to the decision maker. It is suggested that this group be kept to as small a number as possible to streamline discussion, consultation, and decision making.

Remember that there is usually more than a single decision and response required in managing a crisis. There may be many second-to-second judgments that are necessary as an emergency develops and its aftereffects become known. Identify a command center to which appointed members of the Crisis Assessment Task Force and the decision maker will report when an emergency condition becomes apparent. This facility should be in a secure area out of public view, but within easy reach by those who will require access. The control center should be equipped with a number of hard-wired telephones in case of an interruption of service for mobile devices or a radio/walkie-talkie network. Having a laptop, printer, and scanner/fax machine is also recommended.

The courses of action formulated in the command center may also affect the businesses of important event stakeholders. It may be appropriate to alert some of these stakeholders to the crisis and the anticipated responses before the media or public are apprised. If an announcement is determined to be of sufficient importance to communicate to the media, consider whether a limited number of top sponsors and broadcasters should be informed simultaneously or immediately before the media so they have time to prepare their own responses to the crisis.

If a major emergency emerges, you probably will not have to worry about calling the media to inform them—the media likely will already be calling you. Select a spokesperson to provide them with a consistent source of information and communication. Who that spokesperson should be can depend upon the nature and severity of the crisis; that said, credibility and authority are key. The greater the potential impact of the crisis, the higher into the organization you may want to reach for the spokesperson. If the media are already on site, convene a news conference and prepare a press release with consistent information for immediate distribution upon completion of the session. If the media are not on site, circulate brief statements and updates via a press release with a contact name and number for further inquiries. The contact should not be the spokesperson, but someone who will screen and prioritize calls and schedule interviews for the spokesperson. A news conference may be subsequently scheduled at a time and place the media can attend. Identify the cause for concern (e.g., athlete injury, potential cancellation/rescheduling of the event, etc.), and how and when the organizer will respond (if known at that time). The spokesperson should only make truthful, to-the-point statements of fact and offer no speculation. If details regarding the crisis and its response continue to develop and additional information should be provided at a later time, provide an estimated time frame to the media as to when they might be updated.

Acknowledging the World Condition

Globally significant events, whether occurring in the host city or hundreds, even thousands, of miles away, can affect an organizer's plans and program. In the days following the tragic terror attacks on the World Trade Center and Pentagon in 2001, dozens of amateur, college, and professional sports events were canceled or postponed. As emphasized throughout this book, sports events are very public reflections of our cultures and, as such, must sometimes mirror society's moods and expectations as they exist outside the arena. After a respectful pause in the staging of many sports events, both to reflect on the September 11 tragedies and to make necessary adjustments in security procedures, play was resumed, many preceded by "moments of silence." Flags flew at half-staff, black bunting draped the walls of many arenas and stadiums—in later days replaced with patriotic red, white, and blue—and intermission sponsor promotions were replaced by the singing of "God Bless America." As a gathering of human beings with common interests (i.e., fans of a sport or team) and the values shared by all people, a sports event is also expected to provide opportunities for public reflection.

Thankfully, few world events match the horrors of September 2001. But, other tragedies of cultural significance can develop at any time. It is important for organizers to demonstrate their own sensitivities, as well as those of their nation and local community, when such occurrences present themselves. Carefully review all aspects of the event presentation plan—ceremonies, production elements, public address announcements, decorative components, and advertisements—to ensure that no inadvertent lapse of judgment is apparent to the participants or members of the audience when such unfortunate circumstances occur.

Applying sensitivity in the wake of a tragedy is simply common sense. It is, on one hand, incumbent upon sports event organizers to entertain their guests and ticket buyers. To do any less would be a disservice to their loyal, paying customers. On the other, difficult times call for a candid assessment of how appropriate a celebration of sport may be in light of the world condition. Here is hoping you never have to make such decisions. But, be prepared to act quickly, thoughtfully, and decisively in case you do.

Communications

From both operational and risk management perspectives, there is an essential need for information to be exchanged continuously between the event director and various areas of responsibility. Communications systems—two-way radios/walkie-talkies, ClearComs, mobile devices and phones, private line (PL) communicators, and others—provide much of the connective tissue that keeps an event together and running smoothly.

In 1949, United States Air Force Captain Edward A. Murphy, an engineer working at Edwards Air Force Base, inspired the now-infamous and oft-quoted "Murphy's Law"—"If anything can go wrong, it will." Murphy was working on an Air Force project charged with the responsibility of determining how much sudden deceleration a human being might be able to survive in a crash. Inspecting the device that would be used in the experiment, Murphy found it wired incorrectly. When he expressed his annoyance at the technician who installed it ("If there's a way to do it wrong, he'll find it," he fumed), his famous namesake principle was immortalized.

We believe there is a corollary to Murphy's Law relating to what has too often been experienced as the most common source of grief in the execution of special events—"The area with which you cannot communicate is the place where things will inevitably go wrong." Events are living, dynamic organisms where challenges are presented in real time and must be solved before the audience or athletes can notice them. So, as you plan your event, consider Supovitz's Corollary, perhaps as appropriately expressed in the vernacular of Sun Tzu, the author of *The Art of War*: "You have already lost control in the area where communication does not exist."

You are simply not in control of your event if you do not have a reliable system of communication in place that will provide instantaneous contact to and from every area where decisions must be made and directions transformed into action. It is sometimes tempting to skimp on walkie-talkies and phones to avoid cost when, in fact, not being able to communicate with event staff, and their not being able to communicate with the event director, can result in the entire budget being wasted on a completely failed event.

It may not be possible to provide communication devices for staff in every location. However, every staff member, volunteer, or participant should know how to reach someone in a position of

SIDELINE STORY

The Space Shuttle Columbia Disaster

The author Frank Supovitz recollects preparing for final rehearsals just hours before the pre-game ceremonies were to begin for NHL All-Star Saturday in February 2003, just as the space shuttle *Columbia* disintegrated over Texas at a height of 200,000 feet. The shuttle was due to land at Cape Canaveral, only 200 miles north of the host arena in Sunrise, Florida. In the early hours after the tragedy, there was scant detail and no confirmation from NASA as to whether anyone had miraculously survived, or whether the debris had caused catastrophic damage to towns in Texas and neighboring states along the shuttle's trajectory. "Time was growing short, and we could not wait for official news before evaluating plans for our event in every detail. We had to move, and fast. If the impact of disaster included devastation on the ground, we thought, the event might have to be canceled completely."

Assuming the tragedy was restricted to the unfortunate souls on board, the production staff was quickly assembled in the arena. Production director Steven Hubbard arranged to hang black drape from the arena's upper level fasciae in four corners. A moment of silence would be written into the script. A military color guard was already scheduled for the pre-event ceremonies. Scriptwriter John Kannengeiser contacted the public affairs officer in charge of their appearance to ensure adherence to protocol regarding the display of the American flag on a day of national tragedy.

The opening ceremony for the All-Star Game was planned to include a series of giant "postcards from Florida" projected onto the ice. The lighting director was to ensure that images of Cape Canaveral or the space shuttle were not included. Every second of video and screen graphics were reviewed. "One feature, an animated logo for the NHL SuperSkills competition, featured stars dashing across the night sky, leaving comet trails very similar to the images of incandescent wreckage millions of viewers had just seen falling on CNN. Our video director and his staff moved quickly to render an entirely new animation without this potentially evocative and disturbing imagery."

Game presentation director Sammy Choi pointed out that the opening ceremony preceding the player introductions drew heavily from space imagery. "The more we thought about it, the more we realized that 75 percent of the already heavily rehearsed show was no longer appropriate." The opening ceremonies featured enormous projections of rotating stars, while a video of NHL players skated against a night sky. The hockey all-stars on video were to transform into constellations of shooting stars falling to the ice surface in lasers and lights to a soundtrack of Moby's *We Are Made of Stars*. "Regardless of how hard everyone had worked to develop, design, and rehearse these spectacular effects, it was a unanimous opinion that hockey players appearing to fall from the sky would be too reminiscent of the morning's tragedy." Lighting designers David Agress and Paul Turner, who had been awake all the previous night focusing the original show, worked feverishly to reconstruct a light show that would be as spectacular as possible, just not as obviously themed.

Finally, it was the NHL's plan to treat fans to a colorful, celebratory fireworks show as they exited the arena. After a day filled with repetitive replays of explosions in the upper atmosphere on every television channel, the league decided to quietly cancel this surprise event element. "After all was said and done, however, our assumption remained that people bought their tickets to be entertained and, if they chose to attend, their expectations were that we would do so. If we had any doubt whether all this self-examination was even necessary, it vanished just minutes before the event when I received a phone call at the timekeeper's bench from a reporter from the Associated Press inquiring whether we had reconsidered any of our plans for the presentation."

authority and responsibility. There should likewise be a way to reach each and every individual empowered to execute a job at an event. For event participants, this pathway of communication may be through an area supervisor or stage manager who can relay messages and information between the event director and the coaches, athletes, officials, or cast.

The most common devices in use for event site communications are two-way radios, or walkie-talkies, and Clear-com systems. Two-way radios are advantageous because they are wireless, permitting the user mobility throughout the event site. Test the radios well in advance to determine if there are any areas in which transmissions cannot be heard. Such "dead spots" are common in indoor facilities, where radio signals may have difficulty penetrating concrete walls. Consider working with your radio supplier to install a repeater antenna, a device that essentially receives the transmission, and then rebroadcasts it into hard-to-reach or more distant locations.

Walkie-talkies are radio frequency (RF) devices, as are wireless microphones and remote television cameras. There may be many groups that have independent two-way radios in the same facility, such as the production staff, broadcasters, the front-of-house staff, transportation dispatchers, parking lot staff, and even entities outside in the immediate area, such as taxis and delivery services. Work with your radio vendor to "clear channels," ensuring that the communications system used by each group does not interfere with any other. The most illuminating "Sideline Story" illustrating the results of a failure to provide clear channels of communication can be found in the Old Testament tale of the "Tower of Babel" (found in chapter 11 of the book of Genesis). Similarly, interference between different communication groups using the same radio frequencies can prove confusing and disastrous. They can also render the pictures and sound from wireless television cameras and microphones useless.

Closed-circuit, wired systems, such as Clear-coms, are commonly used in areas where continuous and simultaneous two-way conversations are required. Users of walkie-talkies cannot hear anyone else when they are talking. Clear-coms, however, operate more like telephones. Both parties can hear each other continuously. Wireless Clear-com stations are also available for users who require more mobility.

Tie Down the Details

Another way to manage for the unexpected is to make sure that all staff and stakeholders have a clear understanding of all event details before the actual program takes place. Schedule a "Tie-Down Meeting"—also called a production meeting or an all-agency meeting, depending on the sport and event—two to five days prior to the event and invite both event staff and representatives of each functional area and agency (e.g., security, marketing, public relations, insurance, information technologies, parking). The meeting should systematically review the schedule of events, the production schedule, event rundown, athlete and competitive issues, transportation systems, communications, sponsorship fulfillment plans—literally any and every detail that should become common knowledge to the event staff. During this meeting, the staff should feel free to ask questions, request additional information, and surface issues and challenges. Therefore, the larger and more complex the event, the farther in advance of event day you will want to schedule the tie-down to permit sufficient time to make adjustments based on issues that will come to light during the meeting. Be sure to communicate any changes to the plan made after the tie-down meeting. Prepare and distribute an event manual that contains all of the pertinent information and schedules discussed.

Volunteers and event-day staff should have an orientation meeting that is a more condensed version of the tie-down. They, too, should receive a volunteer manual that provides appropriate information in an easy-to-access reference document.

Post-Play Analysis

Subject all aspects of the event to a thorough risk assessment and management process. Identify areas of risk to athletes, officials, spectators, and staff, as well as financial risks to the organization. Project possible remedies to potential crises flowing from these risks and take actions that will reduce the likelihood of their occurrence. If your event will be held outdoors, be sure to have a weather contingency plan to determine under what conditions the event will be postponed, canceled, or continue to move forward. Procure liability insurance and, if necessary, event cancellation insurance to reduce the financial burden on the organization in case of accidents, emergencies, and circumstances that could cause the program to be canceled or postponed. Prepare to respond to emergencies by establishing a chain of command and a crisis communications plan.

Be sure to have a system available for communication between the event director and major areas of responsibility. It is impossible to control an event or respond to the unexpected without the ability to communicate. Information is power and its accessibility the best defense against confusion. Schedule a staff tie-down meeting and an orientation for event-day staff and volunteers to review event details and surface conflicts and inaccuracies. Circulate an event manual with all pertinent schedules, contacts, and information that may be used as an easy reference tool.

Coach's Clipboard

1. A statewide high school football tournament has been moved to a nearby college campus, having outgrown the available facilities in the host community. As three games are scheduled each day, temporary locker rooms have been set up in the gymnasium with drapes separating each of six team dressing areas. An audience of 5,000 is expected, while the full population of college students is living on campus. What security and safety factors should be considered during the three-day tournament?
2. A regional track and field event is scheduled for Sunday morning at your local high school gymnasium. Three days before the event, the national weather service issues a forecast calling for a 50 percent chance of blizzard-like conditions beginning after sundown on Saturday. What courses of action should be considered by the event organizer?
3. You are organizing a marathon race through a major downtown area. Analyze and list the risks you could likely encounter. What kinds of insurance coverage should be secured?
4. Your marathon budget is dependent on having 75 percent of the revenues derived from sponsorships. The presenting sponsor, which was to provide 50 percent of total sponsor revenues, has filed for bankruptcy and will default on its final payment. How will the organizer continue to pay the bills? What steps might have been taken during the event planning process to avoid this crisis?
5. Create a crisis communications plan for the marathon. Who should the Crisis Assessment Task Force include? Where is the best place to locate the command center? How would you respond if threatening weather appeared likely to turn dangerous during the course of the event?

PLAY 15

Reviewing the Game Tapes

"I firmly believe that any man's finest hour—his greatest fulfillment to all he holds dear—is that moment when he has worked his heart out in a good cause and lies exhausted on the field of battle—victorious."

—Vince Lombardi, Hall of Fame NFL coach, 1913–1970

This play will help you to:

- Create a post-event publicity plan.
- Prepare for your event's financial settlement.
- Plan for conducting effective post-mortem meetings and interviews.

Introduction

The final moments of the score clock have expired, the final heats have been run, and the tournament champion has been crowned. The crowds have gone home, the athletes' buses have pulled away, and the equipment, décor, and added seating are in the process of being disassembled and removed. Reusable and recyclable materials and supplies are being captured and diverted from the waste stream, and unserved prepared food is en route to local food banks. Rented equipment is being recovered and returned to vendors, and the host facility is undergoing the transformation back to its pre-event condition. Congratulations are in order for the event's managers and staff, and sincere gratitude due to all those whose participation and hard work have contributed to an event that was rewarding for the athletes, fans, sponsors, host city and facility, broadcasters, and the organizer. But the work is far from over. There are people to thank, stories to tell, bills to pay, opinions to solicit, and analysis to complete of how every system, process, and detail performed before the time comes to consider staging the event all over again.

Post-Event Publicity

Stage a press conference after the event has concluded, with statements by key stakeholders and interviews with winning athletes and team members. Although the press coverage that can be generated after the event can no longer help an organizer sell tickets, it can help enhance awareness, recognition, reputation, and revenues in the long term. In many cases, a press conference is conducted within minutes after competition concludes to provide the media with an opportunity to interview the winning and losing coaches and players. Because these are the stories of most immediate interest to the media, it is often best to limit the content of this first post-event press conference to the match or contest itself. Additional press availabilities can be scheduled to share aspects of the event that are newsworthy, such as exemplary achievements or apparent failures, officiating controversies, or injuries to participants or spectators. It is essential that the spokesperson meeting the media on behalf of the organizer, ideally the most senior event organizer staff member, is prepared with as many factual details as are known, whether delivering good news or bad.

If the event is of sufficient importance to the host community or beyond, another press conference may be scheduled after the event to generate additional coverage. For events that attract press beyond the host market, try to schedule this second media availability on the morning after the competition, before the participants and media travel home. By that time, the media will have filed their stories about the competition and competitors and they will be looking for new angles now that the event is over. If the event is primarily local, it is acceptable to schedule the last press conference later on the day after the event, or even the second day following, if necessary or beneficial. Hosting a wrap-up press conference is not an exercise in event organizer ego or self-promotion. It is an opportunity to start promoting next year's event by demonstrating its worth to the community while stakeholders are reveling in this year's accomplishments. Invite the senior political leader who has been most helpful to the event, such as the mayor or county executive, and share pertinent details on how the event was received by live and television audiences, participants and fans, local citizens and the business community. A sample rundown of a post-event press conference may be found in Figure 15.1.

If you do not stage a postevent press conference, be sure to circulate press releases with the official results, attendance figures, milestones and records broken, and any amounts that may have been raised for charity, no later than the day after competition concludes. Include quotes solicited from local government and business leaders that reinforce the value of the event to the community.

Collect both pre- and post-event news clippings from websites, newspapers and magazines, and recordings of television coverage, reports, and interviews for both archival purposes, as well as for circulation to current and prospective sponsors and other stakeholders. Check all of the websites of local television and radio stations and print media. Use news, image, and video search engines such as google.com and bing.com to find coverage beyond the host community's borders, and check all of the social networks to capture fan reaction, photographs, and links to additional coverage.

FIVE COUNTY FOOTBALL TOURNAMENT
Post-Event Wrap-Up Press Conference

#	Time	Segment	R/T	Description
1	8:00	Press Conference Room Pre-set	0:57	Room opens for media. Coffee and light refreshments set in back of room. Camera risers, mult boxes, and lighting accessible for set up. Press clippings, newspapers, and releases set on side table.
2	8:57	Participants Seated on Dais	0:03	Winning team captain, team coach, mayor, and event organizer take seats on dais.
3	9:00	Welcome and Opening Statement	0:05	Event organizer provides greetings and opening statement from podium: congratulations to winner(s), success of the event, attendance, records broken. Congrats and thanks to host facility and city. Organizer introduces mayor, shake hands, and return to dais.
4	9:05	Mayor Statement	0:03	Mayor congratulates winner(s) and speaks on the event successfully meeting the goals of the host city and the importance of the event to the region. May include statistics provided by organizer such as number of visitors, hotel rooms booked, etc.
5	9:08	Introduction of Winner(s)	0:01	Organizer returns to podium as mayor takes seat. Remarks about quality of competition. Introduces athlete and/or coach for their remarks, then returns to dais.
6	9:09	Winner Remarks (Participant and/or Coach)	0:05	Participant and/or coach remarks about their experience in host city and at event, as well as competition.
7	9:14	Concluding Remarks	0:02	Participant and/or coach returns to seats; organizer returns to podium to wrap up remarks about this year's event. May provide brief comments about next year's program, if appropriate.
8	9:16	Question & Answer (Q&A)	0:10	Media ask questions from audience. Staff hands wireless mics to reporters asking questions; dais guests answer questions from their seats using tabletop mics. Organizer says one final "thank you" at conclusion of Q&A period.
9	9:26	Photos	0:04	Photographers take group shots after Q&A of dais participants in front of event banner.
10	9:30	One-on-one Interviews and Photos	As needed	Press conference concludes. Media interview and photograph winners, mayor, and organizer as desired.

Figure 15.1 Sample Post-Event Press Conference Rundown

- Gifts
  - Game ball, puck, or other symbol of the sport
  - Poster
  - Tickets encased in Lucite
  - Crystal paperweight with event logo
  - Staff photo
  - Photo album
  - Wall plaque
  - Highlights video or copy of the event broadcast
  - Goody bag
- Personal and signed note of thanks from senior management

Figure 15.2 Common Forms of Postevent Recognition

Recognition

Try to budget recognition for key staff members, volunteers, and vendors, especially those who invested effort far beyond expectations (see Figure 15.2). A small keepsake can go a long way toward making sure that those who have worked countless hours, or gave freely of their time, feel appreciated. An effectively managed event team develops into a family. The stresses and rigors of event planning, management, and execution can have the same effects that challenges have on a real family—the experiences its members have encountered together can either bind them inseparably close or drive them irreversibly apart. As the extended event family parts at the close of an event, a party—even if it's just pizza and soft drinks—can help to seal these relationships forever.

Although everyone involved should receive some expression of appreciation, the more essential the contribution, the more important the gift. Consider sending a piece of game-used equipment to the mayor and other government officials without whose support the event might not have been possible or as successful. Frame the piece or display in a ball case with a small, personalized, engraved name plate expressing your thanks. Chances are it will be displayed in the recipient's office, where it may become a conversation piece, further promoting your event and cementing your relationship with the stakeholder for possible future support. Similar expressions may be sent to the decision-making broadcasting, sponsor, and host facility stakeholders.

Settlement

Enjoy the accolades, but there are almost certainly bills left to pay, and perhaps even some revenues to collect. The process of receiving, reviewing and paying invoices, collecting money yet to be received, and fulfilling all remaining obligations is called the *event settlement*. The more complex the event, the longer the process can be expected to take. Like the organizer, the host facility, hotels, and major suppliers will receive invoices for materials procured and labor expended during the process of preparing for their own involvement in the event. It is not uncommon for facility and hotel settlements to require a few weeks, or even several months, to complete. Be sure to review every charge and compare the terms of leases, contracts, and letter agreements to make sure that all costs are within the understandings they outline. There may also be charges that should have been sent directly to other stakeholders, such as sponsors and broadcasters. If possible, have these charges deducted from the settlement and invoiced directly to these third parties unless they were arranged or requested by the organizer on their behalf. In the latter case, it is often more appropriate to pay the charges and then invoice the stakeholders. Finally, if you have amortized capital expenses, don't forget to carry the proper percentage forward to future events.

Postmortem

Soon after the end of the event, conduct a series of postmortem meetings among staff and key stakeholders. This extremely valuable process can help isolate areas and circumstances that were executed less well than planned, and recognize the success of those elements that achieved their goals and objectives. Annual events should begin planning their next edition no later than the end of the last, so use the postmortem less as a critique of what has passed and more as a springboard for that which will follow.

Conduct postevent meetings with sponsors, broadcasters, and other stakeholders as well. A candid discussion of the triumphs and tribulations of their respective experiences can help organizer improve his or her performance in the future. Recognize sponsors' and other partners' participation with special gifts and collectible items from the event that can adorn their lobbies and offices, vivid reminders of their partnership with the program. If sponsors have agreed to support the event only until the most recent edition has concluded, this is the perfect time to demonstrate your interest in their success and renew their relationship. Come prepared to learn how you can better meet their business objectives, and get them reconfirmed before their excitement can wane. Don't be surprised, however, if they prefer want to await the results of any marketing research or event promotions they may have conducted.

We have found that conducting a series of postmortems in small functional groups, rather than a room filled with staff and stakeholders with differing agendas and opinions, maximizes quantity, quality, and value of information these meetings can provide. When practical, try to schedule focused one-hour discussions with stakeholders with like interests, such as found in Figure 15.3. Schedule these meetings in advance so each stakeholder can conduct their own postmortems

- Key event staff
- Competition staff and officials
- Facilities operations
- Broadcast and media operations
- Logistics (housing, transportation, government services)
- Sponsorship and media partnerships
- Marketing and promotion
- Ticketing and guest management
- Event presentation

Figure 15.3 Sample Schedule of Sectional Postmortems

directly after the event to present you with the most comprehensive input possible. Meet with your department heads and key staff first for the broadest feedback, then the other stakeholders for more narrowly focused viewpoints.

Compile observations by taking copious notes and meet again with key event staff after all other postmortems have been completed to discuss all of the feedback received. There will likely be many areas for which improvements have been recommended. Prioritize those that can be effected for the next edition within the financial and staffing constraints of your event plan. Compare the final results with the objectives, strategies, and tactics as defined by your P-A-P-E-R Test (see Play 1) to determine if your event realized all you set out to achieve, and rewrite your objectives, strategies, and tactics with the experiences of the last event fresh in your mind.

If you have conducted marketing research among your fans and spectators, share the results with your partners, and ask that they do the same for you. The event family is not limited to your staff and volunteers. It extends to your best partners, as well. Stay in touch throughout the year, and discuss plans for future events and improvements you seek to make. Engage them in the planning and development process, and they will feel involved, invested, and embraced.

The Game Ends . . .

Sports events are massive consumers of time, labor, and capital. They can be hard on the physical, mental, and emotional state of those who compete, plan, promote, manage, sponsor, broadcast, publicize, present, and otherwise participate in these uniquely exciting and stimulating environments. Everybody wants the same thing—a successful event that is a positive experience for everyone it touches. Sports events can engender an infectious passion and intense conscientiousness from all who are involved. It is a competitive environment to be sure. Everyone wants to record their personal best—the best athletic performance, the best promotion, the best event presentation.

Supovitz recollected in the *First Edition* of the *Sports Event Management and Marketing Playbook*: "If my own experience is any guide, there will be countless mornings when you will arise before the sun after a seemingly endless string of 18-hour days. You may stumble toward the shower and, with what seems like every remaining ounce of your strength, turn on the hot water. You may let the water stream down your body while leaning motionless against the tile as time seems to stand still, the battle joined to fight the fatigue and clear the cobwebs from your mind. You may at this point ask: 'Why am I doing this to myself?'

"Under the circumstances, it may take a while for the answer to come. Then, the event is finally underway, the fans are cheering, and the athletes are giving it their all. Your own heart is pounding and the adrenaline is surging through your bloodstream. In a rush, it is suddenly done and the energized crowd leaves abuzz, still cheering, laughing, singing, and reminiscing over memories just moments old, but lasting a lifetime.

"Then, you'll think back to that morning shower, and smile inwardly.

"Yeah . . . that's why!"

Post-Play Analysis

The work on sports events does not end when the contest is done and the crowds go home. Prepare your plans for postevent publicity, postmortem evaluations, staff and participant recognition, and the schedule for financial settlement before the event has taken place.

Coach's Clipboard

1. Make a list of the positions in your organization and the types of stakeholders that will be deserving of recognition for their contributions to the success of the Five County Football Tournament. You may wish to identify different levels of recognition to express appropriate appreciation to separate groups.
2. Create a schedule for postmortem meetings that should be conducted following the Five County Football Tournament, including when they should take place and who the attendees should be. Include a plan for how often and when to reach out to key stakeholders between the end of this year's event and the date for next year's tournament.
3. Create a postevent publicity plan for the tournament. What positive messages will you try to reinforce? How will you deal with potential negative results (e.g., traffic and parking issues, poor officiating, serious injuries to athletes or spectators)?

PLAY 16

Planning Your Future in Sports Event Management and Marketing

"Ninety percent of life is just showing up."

—*Woody Allen, film writer, director, actor*

"If winning was easy, losers would do it."

—*Brad Keselowski, American auto racing driver*

This play will help you to:

- Learn and develop the skills and traits for a successful career in sports events management and marketing.
- Plan your path to position yourself for job opportunities in sports events.
- Identify resources that will help you to grow and advance in the sports event business.

Introduction

From the wide and varied perspectives of objective observers to experienced executives and occasional onlookers to intensely avid fans, it is clear that the growth of the sports industry has exploded to unimagined heights with no apparent sign of slowing. Sports have become an enormous, global, multidisciplinary business. There are more leagues, teams, athletes, media outlets, events, workers at events, venues, workers at venues, and people covering, talking about, attending, participating in, following, and otherwise consuming sports. It is also undeniable that it is more competitive than ever before to enter and/or advance in the industry because there are so many more people attracted to sports as a career path. Although there are no guaranteed courses or sure-fire techniques to assure success in pursuing a position or advancing in sports event management or marketing, there are some suggestions to offer that have proven to be helpful, based on many years of meeting, interviewing, hiring (and rejecting), and mentoring sports industry aspirants.

There are truisms in any industry and this certainly applies to sports, especially when it comes to managing and marketing events and operating the venues that host them. Perhaps the best concept to understand before training for or embarking on a career in this wonderful industry is, "We work when other people do and we work when other people don't." Most sports event and venue managers are on duty whenever events take place, and that most often occurs when other people can attend them, the times when fans are not working, on some combination of weeknights, weekends, and holidays. Events and venues are also businesses, so, in addition to operating during "leisure time" for everyone else, the professionals who run and staff them are also expected to be at an office during "regular business hours." In addition to the extraordinary time commitment, event and venue management and marketing requires passion, energy, creativity, attention to detail, communication and organizational skills, the ability to solve problems and think on one's feet, the flexibility to work with a wide range of people and personalities—embodied in a well-rounded maestro of many disciplines. Know what the specific job that most interests you entails, the sacrifices that may need to be made, and the attributes that are required for someone in the event business.

There are several traits that will only and always serve to enhance anyone's job prospects in the sports industry. If they sound like you, and you have the drive, passion, and determination to be the next sports event management star, we look forward to the possibility of you joining us in this incredibly exciting industry.

Communication Skills

Among the most important requirements for those who organize and manage events is having the ability to clearly inform, train, and lead the people who work for them. Strong communication skills are essential tools to be able to do so. Writing well—be it an e-mail, a news release, a memo, a business plan, a sponsorship proposal, an event recap—and speaking well—whether at a planning meeting, a news conference, a marketing presentation, a social function, or a room with a small group or a large audience—are proficiencies that can be found in outstanding leaders, like successful event organizers and managers, who are good at motivating, inspiring, convincing, informing, and focusing others.

In event management and marketing, the most effective writing is delivered in a clear and concise style. This can be achieved through patient practice, attention to writing basics such as the use of good grammar, sentence structure, punctuation, and spelling, and taking the time to read over your written work as a reader, not as the writer. Having someone else read, proofread, and even edit your writing can be extremely helpful.

Whether speaking before prospective sponsors, the media, your colleagues, or a potential employer, three of the best sales tools are to appear calm, confident, and comfortable. To be comfortable when speaking in any setting requires preparation, organization, and three essential steps: rehearse, rehearse, and finally, rehearse. First, know what you want to accomplish with every interaction—are you selling an idea, a philosophy, a call to action, or a sponsor package? What information do you need to help sell your message and encourage the result you are looking for? How can you present this information to build your case? Write everything down and practice! How long did it take to deliver your message? Can you be more effective by being more concise or by adding more information? A speaker who is prepared with the appropriate information and details, who can call upon thoroughly researched background information, and who has mastered key techniques such as making and maintaining eye contact and using visual aids and technology can have confidence in front of any size audience with sufficient rehearsal.

Gaining Experience

As Woody Allen's famous observation, "Ninety percent of life is just showing up," suggests, you can't get somewhere if you're nowhere. This is especially true in sports event management and marketing. Anyone looking to enter this highly competitive field should be looking for ways to gain valuable experience, to demonstrate personal initiative to a prospective employer, and to distinguish himself/herself from others seeking the same job. For any given opportunity, there will only be one winner. Here are several suggestions to help you win the game.

Use Some of Your Free Time to Volunteer on the Staff of a Sports Event

Whether it's a major tour golf tournament, a national marathon race, a local recreation league game, or staffing an information booth at a minor league game, you'll learn something by doing something. What the actual events are and which volunteer jobs you will be assigned are almost secondary elements to just having an opportunity to get into the game at an event. Find opportunities to learn about different events and different jobs associated with the management of an event. Through this exposure, you might find out any number of things: what you like or don't like, where you excel and have interest or not as much. In addition to absorbing every detail relating to the event, you also are able to add the experience to your resume. Employers seeking goal-oriented, results-driven, self-starting potential employees will likely identify an individual who has demonstrated the desirable quality of initiative to be a coveted candidate. Learn about the individuals who are advancing or continuing their careers at the event. What paths did they take on their roads to success? Meet and interact with the paid staff. As you will soon see, networking with those who can one day help your career can certainly begin at the arena, ballpark, or gymnasium where you also gain your first working event experiences.

Attend a Higher Education Institution with a Respected Sports Management Program

As Appendix 11 highlights, there are well over 300 colleges and universities in the United States alone that offer degrees in sports management or administration. There is a wide range of programs, including some that are academically and theoretically structured with scholarly instructors and others concentrating on a more applied curriculum with faculty consisting of industry practitioners who teach what they know and what they've done. These programs can be found in every corner of the country, at public and private universities, and at community colleges.

By earning a degree in sports management or administration at a higher education institution, you will have an impressive credential to add to your resume, a depth of knowledge based on academic achievement, and a set of peer and industry contacts that can be called on throughout your career. Many colleges and universities also offer continuing education courses and certificate programs to provide those who have already launched a career with greater accessibility to academic training in sports event management. Although they might not add measurably to your resume, they can provide more insight and knowledge that can make you a better performer in our industry.

Take Advantage of Internship Opportunities

Many sports organizations offer internships, or practical training supervised by an executive or mentor, to students and young job seekers. Most often, internships are another benefit available as part of the sports management program at many college and universities, although some internships are available directly from employers through an application process. Internships may be paid or unpaid, may provide students with academic credit upon successful completion, are usually for a defined period of time, and almost always have limitations on the number of hours per week one may work. As different business and college publications describe, internships may also be called externships and apprenticeships but, no matter the name, these programs offer opportunities for young people to work in a professional, career-related environment and acquire valuable experience. In addition, an intern has chances to interact with executives at different levels of an organization. These connections can lead to a full-time position, an expansion of one's professional network of contacts, or the establishment of an ongoing relationship with a mentor. The essential value of an internship is the experience gained, no matter the sport or organization. So, individuals looking for an internship should start with a series of questions, among them:

- In what department of the organization is the internship?
- What responsibilities are assigned to the intern?
- To whom does the internship report, and what opportunities will there be to meet other executives?
- Will this internship provide relevant experience, skill building, and learning for career development?

A positive, enriching, career-enhancing internship can result from satisfactory answers to these questions.

Another consideration to keep in mind is that valuable experience can be gained through internships with organizations outside of high-profile or major professional leagues, such as in minor and development leagues, intercollegiate athletics at any level, city or county recreation departments, tournament sports such as tennis and golf, and team sports looking to gain traction. Within these organizations, you will have the opportunity to work in a position that may assume multiple roles and responsibilities on any given night and/or event. This experience will expose you to all aspects of sports management, and provide you with a broad perspective of the overall operations. "A candidate with this type of past experience, and the fresh perspective of another league, could well be viewed as a valued candidate for an eventual position with one of the major league teams, leagues, or venues," says Mary Davis, former president of employee and administrative services of Washington Sports and Entertainment, once the owner of the NBA Wizards, NHL Capitals, WNBA Mystics, and the Capital Centre and Verizon Center arenas. She is also an instructor with Georgetown University's Sports Industry Management master's program.

SIDELINE STORY

The Power of an Internship

Internship opportunities for young industry hopefuls come in many forms, from administrative work in a league or organization's front office to event-day duties with a special event or team. These positions are often unpaid, and a great deal of passion and dedication is required to successfully manage demanding hours of work. On the surface, the proposition of working long hours for free might not seem very appealing, but internships offer resume-boosting experience, invaluable access to build relationships, and unbeatable auditions for jobs many young professionals dream to secure. Perhaps most importantly, internships provide hands-on exposure that may be instrumental in guiding the future career path of an industry rookie.

In 1982, an ambitious and excited youngster began an aggressive letter-writing campaign to the National Football League's then 28 teams begging for a job. After writing hundreds of letters, he was finally awarded an internship with the NFL's front office. After working hard for a year in the league's administration, the young man accepted another internship with the New York Jets before returning to the league office as a public relations assistant in 1984. He never looked back, taking on challenges and pursuing all opportunities to move up the company ladder. Twenty-five years after his first internship, in early 2007, Roger Goodell was voted in as the Commissioner of the NFL. His story is by no means typical, but it exemplifies the importance of securing a good internship and working with inspired dedication every day, no matter the task. In the business of sports, hard work, enthusiasm, learning, and diligence can pave the path from unpaid intern to the managerial ranks—even to chief executive.

Burnish Your Personal Brand

Every sports event management or marketing situation offers opportunities for any young aspirant to burnish a personal brand that can leave a positive and permanent impression on colleagues and prospective employers. Develop a sterling reputation of being reliable, dependable, punctual (or even early) in producing quality work, thorough, accurate, enthusiastic, always presentable, and available. Being considered a go-to person can lead to being considered a can't-do-without future employee.

"Employers look for leadership skills and for accomplishments," says Buffy Filippell, the founder of TeamWork Online, the respected online recruiting network serving the sports and live event industry. "They want people who have led, who have stepped up to accept responsibility. They also look for people who have had success at something, not just done something. These things differentiate an outstanding job candidate from everyone else."

Start Building Relationships

The sports industry is a relationship business. Deals are struck, people get hired, information is shared, recommendations are made, and trust is built—through relationships. Whether it's through volunteer service, taking graduate school classes, during an internship, or pursuing other opportunities, it is never too early to start building your network of contacts, peers, mentors, and executives. When there is a reception, seminar, or conference that will include industry representatives, make sure you attend, and make every effort to engage and exchange business cards with those individuals.

Filippell suggests that a college graduate should get to know alumni from his or her school who might be helpful. People with positions in sports represent a good starting point, but making and maintaining contact with individuals not necessarily from your own educational or desired professional discipline can be similarly effective. For example, someone who is interested in a job in sports public relations might reach out to alumni from the university's journalism school, or a sports administration graduate seeking an event management position could start connecting with alumni with business degrees. "You don't necessarily need to meet just the big guns, the highest level executives," adds Filippell. "Getting to know people closer to your own age and sharing experiences can be extremely helpful." To that end, you should use social networks such as Facebook and LinkedIn to expand your network. But don't just collect names and "friends"; make connections, form bonds, and communicate regularly with people in your network.

It will make a strong impression when you speak to anyone in a position to help your career if you're ready with a 30-second overview—the elevator speech—about yourself that highlights two or three important points. If you know something about the person you're engaging, such as a recent accomplishment, this can naturally lead to your offering a compliment or an expression of admiration. Ask questions . . . be ready with them . . . and listen to the answers so that you can respond thoughtfully and professionally. This kind of give-and-take becomes a conversation, a far more desirable and potentially productive exchange. Also, Filippell advises, "A positive, can-do personality can trump a lot of other things. Use your personal presentation skills to their best advantage and let that personality come through." After you've had an opportunity to speak with individuals you've met, be sure to follow up by sending a short note of appreciation via e-mail . . . the very next day.

Outreach, preparation, presentation, and follow-through are always appreciated and are excellent ways to get noticed and to be remembered. Take the initiative and be ready. You never know where your next encounter may lead.

Watch and Learn

If you want to organize and manage sports events, attend events whenever you can. As baseball great and philosopher Yogi Berra once said, "You can observe a lot just by watching." When you attend an event, any event—a game, concert, show, wedding, graduation—you can do more than root for your team or sit in the audience. Watch and learn how each event is organized and managed. Observe the people performing the functions that are contributing to a smooth operation. Consider the timing of the flow of the event. Appreciate and critique the event's creative elements and think about what you might do differently. Mentally go through your own event checklist to see how the organizer measures up in covering key details. Every event you attend can also serve as a workshop to test your event management knowledge and skills.

Choosing the Right Company

There are many sources that offer helpful instruction on how to construct an effective resume and cover letter. However, there are few sources better qualified to provide some guidance for your job search in the sports industry than Mary Davis.

SIDELINE STORY

More than Just an Affinity

The saturation of college sports marketing and management programs followed the emergence of sports marketing as a viable career field starting back in the early 1990s. Truth be told, most of the industry's senior executives never enrolled in an undergrad or graduate-level sports management program. So what is the real value of a sports marketing-focused degree today?

Several years ago, sports industry veteran Glenn Horine founded the Center for Sports and Entertainment Studies at Iona College, 30 minutes north of New York City. His vision was to introduce graduate students to the myriad job opportunities beyond just the professional sports teams and leagues, which grabs the attention of many students, especially in the New York area. Like other respected college undergraduate and graduate programs such as at Ohio University, New York University, University of South Carolina and Georgetown University, Iona has engaged senior industry leaders from the world of corporate marketing, digital media, public relations, research, and event management, among others, as adjunct professors and guest lecturers. This wide array of talent and experience has helped students learn first-hand how and why companies still value academic performance and work experience over one's affinity for a sports or an entertainment property.

Since the startup, Horine has found himself as both a career counselor and teacher. "Most students, who are interested in a sports career, profess their 'love' for a team as a primary asset in their job qualifications. They struggle to recognize that their attraction is not a value proposition, but just an affinity," says Horine. "Most entry-level hiring managers continue to look for well-rounded students with demonstrated record of academic performance, no matter what the school of study, along with related work experience. Ultimately, employers want an individual who either delivers value (e.g., revenue) or reduces risks and has personal advocates to support their story."

No surprise, breaking into the sports and entertainment industry is very competitive due to the number of students seeking "social currency" (e.g., tickets, brand association, etc.) that this field often yields. Horine believes that during a college career, students can put themselves in a favorable position for a job opportunity by:

- Earning academic accomplishments
- Building a network with the assistance of the college's alumni association
- Conducting exhaustive research on industries, companies, and executives of interest
- Landing at least two-to-three meaningful internship/trainee positions, and
- Letting people know what you're focused on.

"A couple years ago, I brought my class around to a few of the New York sports teams and historic venues with no expectations about our hosts offering any internship/trainee opportunities to the students," states Horine. "I always remind students to respect our hosts and to follow up with them. You'll never know about opportunities, unless you ask. Sure enough, one student did, and he landed a prime internship at a major event that summer where he performed well. So well, our hosts helped him land a permanent job in hospitality with one of the local professional teams. Sports and entertainment is a highly competitive field, but one can break in with a disciplined approach in and out of the classroom."

"When you are interviewing for opportunities in sports event management, you should also be interviewing the company that is interviewing you," she suggests. "Research the organizational structure, corporate culture, vision and mission statements, and determine if this organization is a right fit for you and your career path. Choose an organization where you believe you can work for at least three years, which shares your values and ethics, and offers career promotional opportunities.

"Three seasons pass by very quickly in a job you enjoy," she adds. "At the end of three years, you will be an attractive candidate for organizations looking to fill key management positions at the next levels."

As has been described in the previous chapters and elsewhere, sports is a very broad field. Very often, good opportunities to get started with a major league team may be found in sales. "If you can focus all of your attention on being a top salesperson and commit to one to two seasons, you can make a good living as well as learn a great deal about the team, product, and brand," Davis says. "Great companies tap into the sales force to promote individuals into public relations, marketing, and event management, appreciating that these individuals' experiences in sales have given them a depth and perspective that were learned on the job." When organizations need to streamline their operations and reduce their workforce, an unfortunate inevitability even in sports, decision makers are likely to keep people who have built a solid record of generating revenue and productivity over those who primarily add to expenses.

You will find in Appendix 12 a helpful list of resources to consult as a good starting point for your career search. As the list indicates, there are multiple ways to start and advance in sports management and marketing. "Consider, evaluate, research, choose wisely, work hard, demonstrate respect, and have ethics," says Davis, "and you will have a very rewarding career and achieve your goals."

A sports executive, flush with frustration, burst into a colleague's office seemingly at the end of her patience with a new crop of interns. "Why is it our interns get dumber every year?" she vented. "They don't," her colleague replied. "Interns will always come to the project with no knowledge of what we do. The gap between your own knowledge and experience and theirs keeps getting wider because you're growing as a professional. They will always come as new students of the industry."

A Final Story

Twenty years ago, there were only a handful of institutions of higher learning that offered degree programs in sports business, even fewer that trained students for careers in event management. Today, intern and entry-level job applicants are arriving with degrees in sports management offered by hundreds of institutions and/or credible work experience. They arrive with a firm grounding in the history, philosophy, and practice of the industry, armed with skills and understandings that their predecessors had to make up mostly with drive and determination.

The discipline of special events parallels the exciting growth in sports as a dynamic entertainment business. Today, interns and graduates are no longer arriving as blank slates. They come to the industry with fresh perspectives and refreshing questions, new ideas, and no less drive and determination. For those of us who may serve as their mentors, the wisest will be listening as much as they teach.

Post-Play Analysis

Embarking on and growing a career in sports event management and marketing will take dedication, persistence, and hard work. Be sure to develop excellent written and oral communication skills. They will serve you well from writing cover letters that accompany resumes sent to prospective employers to demonstrating your promotion potential as you expand your career. Gain experience by getting involved as a sports event volunteer, and/or as an intern. Observe, learn, and emulate what the best in the industry do to help establish your own brand reputation. The authors wish you the very best of luck—we look forward to seeing you on the sidelines!

Coach's Clipboard

1. You are planning to attend an event at which you can expect to meet a number of executives who are prospective employers and you need to prepare your 30-second elevator speech. Make a list of the five attributes that you feel are your most notable qualities. Be prepared to select two or three to highlight, depending on the individual to whom you're speaking. Practice what you want to say.
2. As you start seeking a job or an internship and begin researching various companies, consider the qualities that you're looking for in an organization. Write them down in priority order. Consider this a "living document," a list to which you can add, subtract, and/or re-order qualities that are important as your search proceeds. Most importantly, consult your list from time to time as you look to match your qualifications with those organizations that fit your goals.
3. To prepare for your job or internship search, consider your personal strengths and also traits about which you're less confident. Make a list of up to five areas where you'd like to improve and create a plan—focusing on proactive steps and a timeline—for achieving results.

APPENDIX 1

Event Expense Budget Worksheet

ACCT. NO.	EXPENSES	BUDGET	FORECAST	ACTUAL	VARIANCE	COMMENTS
1000	PLAYER COSTS					
1001	Player Appearance Fees					
1002	Player Prize Money					
1003	Player Gifts					
1004	Player Travel, Air					
1005	Player Travel, Ground Transfers					
1006	Player Travel, Hotel					
1007	Per Diem					
1008	Player Scheduled Meals					
1009	Player Guest Expenses					
1010	Uniforms & Equipment					
1011	Insurance					
1012	Officials					
1013	Officials, Travel Expenses					
1014	Trainers					
1015	Trainer Expenses					

ACCT. NO.	EXPENSES	BUDGET	FORECAST	ACTUAL	VARIANCE	COMMENTS
1016	Medical Staff					
1017	Ambulance					
1018	Player/Athlete Transportation/Parking					
1049	Miscellaneous Player Costs					
1050	TICKETING EXPENSES					
1051	Capital Replacement Costs					
1052	Sales & Amusement Taxes					
1053	Box Office/Ticket Processing Labor					
1054	Remote Ticket Fees					
1055	Credit Card Commissions					
1056	Ticket Printing					
1057	Group Sales Commissions					
1058	Mailings, Creative					
1059	Mailings, Printing					
1060	Mailings, Postage					
1099	Miscellaneous Ticketing Expenses					
1100	FACILITY EXPENSES					
1101	Facility Rental					
1102	Facility Labor					
1103	Carpenters					
1104	Electricians					
1105	Laborers					
1106	Riggers					
1107	Cleaners					
1108	Groundskeeper Crew					
1109	Ushers & Guest Services					
1110	Ticket Takers					

ACCT. NO.	EXPENSES	BUDGET	FORECAST	ACTUAL	VARIANCE	COMMENTS
1111	Security					
1112	House Supervisors					
1113	Medical/First Aid					
1114	Scoreboard Crew					
1115	Video & Matrix Crew					
1116	Stage Hands					
1117	Spotlights					
1118	Changeover Crew					
1119	Miscellaneous Facility Labor					
1120	Bleachers/Additional Seating					
1121	Playing Surface Prep Expenses					
1122	Game-Required Equipment					
1123	Rope & Stanchion					
1124	Barricades					
1125	Fencing					
1126	Security Equipment (wands, cameras)					
1130	Utility Costs					
1131	Generators					
1132	Power Distribution					
1133	Water					
1134	Waste Receptacles & Dumpsters					
1135	Portable Toilet Facilities					
1140	Host Facility Décor & Wayfinding Signage					
1141	Tenting					
1142	Flooring & Carpeting					
1143	Pipe & Drape					
1199	Miscellaneous Facility Expenses					

ACCT. NO.	EXPENSES	BUDGET	FORECAST	ACTUAL	VARIANCE	COMMENTS
1200	GUEST SERVICES					
1201	Invitation Design & Printing					
1202	Invitation Postage					
1203	Guest Management Expenses					
1204	Guest Transportation					
1205	Guest Gifts					
1206	Guest Hospitality					
1207	Complimentary Tickets					
1208	Information Guides					
1209	Event Guide App Development					
1210	Non-Stadium Directional Signage & Info Desks					
1250	Hotel Lobby Décor					
1251	Hotel Staff Gratuities					
1253	Hotel Attrition Contingency					
1299	Miscellaneous Guest Services Costs					
1300	EVENT OPERATIONS					
1301	Temporary Staff & Interns					
1302	Volunteer Staff Expenses					
1303	Staff Travel Expenses					
1304	Staff Meals or Per Diem					
1305	Staff Wardrobe/Uniforms					
1306	Site Surveys/Planning Trips					
1307	Pre-Event Planning & Tie-Down Meetings					
1308	Event Location Office Rent					
1309	Event Location Office Furnishings					
1310	Computer & Printer Rental					
1311	Copiers & Fax Machines					
1312	Televisions, DVD & DVR Players					

ACCT. NO.	EXPENSES	BUDGET	FORECAST	ACTUAL	VARIANCE	COMMENTS
1313	Phone Lines					
1314	Data/Broadband Lines					
1315	Phone Equipment					
1316	Phone Service & LD Charges					
1317	WiFi/Wireless Internet					
1320	Event Location Office Supplies					
1321	Radios					
1322	Mobile Phone Rental & Service					
1330	Accreditation					
1340	Postage & Overnight Services					
1342	Storage					
1343	Shipping & Trucking					
1350	Liability Insurance					
1351	Event Cancellation Insurance					
1352	Legal Services					
1360	Police					
1361	Sanitation					
1362	Fire					
1363	Other City Services					
1364	Permits					
1399	Miscellaneous Event Operations Costs					
1500	MARKETING/PROMOTION					
1501	Logo Development					
1502	Advertising Agency & Creative					
1503	Advertising Agency Expenses					
1504	Advertising, Print					
1505	Advertising, Radio					
1506	Advertising, Internet					
1506	Advertising, Outdoor					

ACCT. NO.	EXPENSES	BUDGET	FORECAST	ACTUAL	VARIANCE	COMMENTS
1507	Posters & Handbills					
1520	Website Development, Design & Management					
1521	Social Network Marketing Campaign					
1540	Public Relations Agency					
1541	Public Relations Agency Expenses					
1550	Telephone Information/800 Service					
1560	Street Banners, Design & Printing					
1561	Street Banners, Installation					
1562	Airport Greeting Signage					
1570	Promotional Items (caps, pins, t-shirts)					
1599	Miscellaneous Marketing Expenses					
1600	MEDIA EXPENSES					
1601	Press Conferences					
1602	Media Pre-/Post-Game Meals					
1603	Media Center F&B					
1604	Media Tabletops, Phones, Internet Access					
1605	Photocopier/Fax					
1606	Media Office Expenses					
1607	Media Office & Support Supplies					
1610	Media Guide					
1611	Photography					
1620	Media Gift					
1699	Miscellaneous Media Expenses					
1700	SPONSOR FULFILLMENT COSTS					
1701	Agency Commissions					
1702	Sales Expenses					
1703	Banners & Signage					
1704	Complimentary Tickets					

ACCT. NO.	EXPENSES	BUDGET	FORECAST	ACTUAL	VARIANCE	COMMENTS
1705	Sponsor Hospitality					
1710	Sponsor Activation Expenses					
1720	Sponsor Gifts and Post-Event recognition					
1799	Miscellaneous Fulfillment Expenses					
1800	BROADCASTING					
1801	Broadcast Expenses					
1802	Airtime Purchase					
2000	PRODUCTION COSTS					
2001	Stage Risers & Platforms					
2002	Set Design					
2003	Set Construction/Rentals					
2004	Set Refurbishment					
2005	Lighting					
2006	Audio					
2007	Special Effects & Pyrotechnics					
2007	Props & Flags					
2008	Draping					
2009	Floral					
2030	ClearCom					
2040	Video Production					
2041	Video Projection					
2050	Production Management Fees					
2051	Production Management Expenses					
2052	Production Labor, Installation					
2053	Production Labor, Rehearsal & Event					
2054	Production Labor, Dismantle					
2060	Equipment Rental					
2070	Talent Fees					
2071	Talent Expenses					

ACCT. NO.	EXPENSES	BUDGET	FORECAST	ACTUAL	VARIANCE	COMMENTS
2075	Costumes & Wardrobe					
2099	Miscellaneous Production Expenses					
3000	ASSOCIATED EVENTS & PROGRAMS					
3001	School/Educational Outreach					
3100	Welcome Party					
3200	Closing Party					
3300	VIP Hospitality					
3400	Spouse Program					
4000	OTHER EXPENSES & ADJUSTMENTS					
4100	Amortization of Prior Year Assets					
4200	Deferral of Capital Assets/5yr.					
4300	Deferral of Capital Assets/3yr.					
4400	Contingency					
TOTAL EXPENSES						

APPENDIX 2

Event Revenue Budget Worksheet

ACCT. NO.	REVENUES	BUDGET	FORECAST	ACTUAL	VARIANCE	COMMENTS
0010	ADMISSIONS					
0011	General Admission Tickets—Type A					
0012	General Admission Tickets—Type B					
0013	General Admission Tickets—Type C					
0014	General Admission Tickets—Promo Price A					
0015	General Admission Tickets—Promo Price B					
0016	General Admission Tickets—Family Deal					
0018	VIP Seating					
0020	Party Area Rental					
0021	Picnic Area Rental					
0029	Miscellaneous Admissions Revenue					
0030	CONCESSIONS					
0031	Food & Beverage Sales					
0032	Catering Sales					
0035	Merchandise Sales					

ACCT. NO.	REVENUES	BUDGET	FORECAST	ACTUAL	VARIANCE	COMMENTS
0036	Program Sales					
0041	Coat & Bag Checking					
0043	Parking					
0049	Miscellaneous Concessions Revenue					
0050	SPONSORSHIP					
0051	Title Sponsorship					
0052	Presenting Sponsorship					
0053	Exclusive Sponsorship					
0054	Non-Exclusive Sponsorship					
0055	Official Suppliers					
0056	Value-In-Kind					
0058	Donors/Donations					
0059	Grants					
0060	Sponsor Activation Revenue					
0061	Advertising—Program & Printed Materials					
0062	Advertising—Signage & Banners					
0063	Advertising—Website					
0064	Advertising—Event App					
0065	Supplemental (buy-in) Hospitality					
0069	Miscellaneous Sponsorship Revenue					
0070	TOURNAMENT & PARTICIPATION FEES					
0071	Tournament Fees					
0079	Miscellaneous Participation Fees					
0080	MEDIA REVENUES					
0081	Television Rights Fees					
0082	Radio Rights Fees					

ACCT. NO.	REVENUES	BUDGET	FORECAST	ACTUAL	VARIANCE	COMMENTS
0083	Online/Streaming Rights Fees					
0085	Footage Licensing					
0089	Miscellaneous Media Revenues					
0090	MISCELLANEOUS					
0099	Miscellaneous Revenues					
TOTAL REVENUES						

APPENDIX 3

Sample Host City Request for Proposal

MNO Sports Events, Inc.

Request For Proposal To Host The Big Street Sports Tournament Summer, 2015

MNO Sports
123 S.W. 2nd Avenue
Biggtown, MD 00000

Request for Proposal
Big Street Sports Tournament

Table of Contents

I. INTRODUCTION

MNO Sports is pleased to offer communities with an active interest in world-class amateur sports events and festivals the opportunity to host a proven, exciting, and crowd-pleasing concept in amateur street sports: **The Big Street Sports Tournament**.

The Big Street Sports Tournament will attract thousands of families and sports enthusiasts from local and surrounding communities free-of-charge, as well as participating amateur street and professional extreme athletes from throughout North America for a full weekend of entertainment, interactive activities, competition, and pure fun, including:

- Age-Bracketed Skateboard Competitions
- BMX Half-Pipe Exhibitions
- In-line Skating Demo Zone
- Extreme Roller Hockey Rink
- Street Sports New Product Expo
- "Kids Only" Clinics and Activities
- Bicycle Tune-Up Area and Obstacle Course
- Extreme Sports Video Arcade
- Special Guest Appearances
- Nonstop Musical Entertainment
- Food Concessions
- . . .and more!

The Big Street Sports Tournament is totally new for 2015 with more to see, more to do, and more to enjoy than ever before! Your city can capitalize on the expanding interest and phenomenal growth in street sports within your community and beyond by participating as the host of this outstanding street sports festival and national invitational tournament.

II. THE BIG STREET SPORTS TOURNAMENT: A New Tradition Continues

The Big Street Sports Tournament enters its 12th year in 2015, combining visually exciting, heart-stopping athletic demonstrations by top street athletes with an invitational tournament matching local amateur players with visiting teams from across the continent in all age, gender, and skill levels ranging from "8 and Under" to "18 and Older" divisions. The tournament draws approximately 1,000 top amateur athletes from all over North America, accompanied by their friends and families. Past host cities include Orlando, FL, Providence, RI, Syracuse, NY, Potomac, MA, and Appleton, WI.

This document has been prepared to provide prospective host cities with uniform and comprehensive guidelines and specifications to assist them in the preparation of a proposal to host The Big Street Sports Tournament. For your ease of preparation and to assist us in the evaluation process, a questionnaire is included that, when complete, will form the core of your proposal. The questionnaire must be completed and requested materials attached for successful consideration. You are, however, welcome to append any additional information to the questionnaire that you believe will present your community as the best possible host for The Big Street Sports Tournament.

Please submit your proposal by November 15, 2013, to the address noted on the last page of the questionnaire. Once all proposals have been received, MNO Sports will analyze submissions and evaluate whether site visits will be required prior to final selection of a host city.

If you have any questions regarding this document or the preparation of your proposal, or wish to receive a copy of this document via e-mail, please do not hesitate to contact Nathaniel Jacobs, Vice President, MNO Sports, at (202) 000-0000, or by e-mail at njacobs@mnosports.com.

III. EVENT SCHEDULE

The next available edition of **The Big Street Sports Tournament** will be held on a single weekend in Summer 2015. Potential host cities should select first- and second-choice weekends that are the optimal dates for staging the event in their community.

Most in-bound participants and their guests will arrive on Friday evening. The host city is welcome to provide a hospitality reception sponsored by a local restaurant for arriving players, if desired.

The public is welcome on the event site beginning with the first tournament games at 8:00 A.M. on Saturday. The site will close at 7:00 P.M. Saturday, reopen at 8:00 A.M. Sunday morning and remain open until closing ceremonies conclude at 6:00 P.M. Sunday evening.

Special events and entertainment will be scheduled throughout the weekend at times to be determined.

IV. ROLE OF MNO SPORTS

MNO Sports will work closely with the host city, its designated agencies, and local corporate partners to ensure that **The Big Street Sports Tournament** offers a positive and rewarding program for all visitors, athletes, sponsors, and business partners, while providing a major sports showcase for the host city.

MNO Sports will:

- Design, manage, and produce The Big Street Sports Tournament at its own expense.
- Install, operate, and dismantle all event attractions, equipment, and other elements.
- Work with the local sports commission, convention and visitors bureau, and/or other authority to promote and publicize the event on a national basis online, in print, and on ESPN radio affiliates.
- Manage the tournament invitation and registration process.
- Work with area hotels to provide attractive, reasonably priced accommodations for visiting athletes, fans, and event staff.
- Promote extended visits to the host city and local points of interest to visiting athletes and their families in their invitations and registration packets, as well as on a mobile phone app for visiting fans and in web links for e-mailed materials.
- Provide benefits to the host city as outlined in Section VII.

V. ROLE OF THE HOST CITY

The host city will play a prominent role in helping to shape the character of **The Big Street Sports Tournament**:

A. EVENT SITE RECOMMENDATIONS

It is an objective of MNO Sports to attract the largest audience possible for the event. The ideal event site will provide a minimum of 50,000 usable* square feet of space in a location demonstrably familiar to the local community as a major event site and/or one that regularly experiences high pedestrian traffic during a weekend or featured event.

Up to seven (7) performance and street sports competition areas will be installed on the event site, requiring level footprints of clear, flat, unobstructed blacktop free of pot holes, street lamps, utility poles, planters, and manhole access covers. This space is required to accommodate the playing and demonstration surfaces, team benches, and spectator viewing areas. Competition areas range from the smallest at 30′ × 50′ to the largest at 110′ × 160′.

Preference will be given to event sites that reflect the unique culture and qualities of the host city.

B. EVENT SITE SERVICES

The host city will ensure that the site is delivered in clean condition to the event before the scheduled onset of installation. The city will provide sufficient refuse and recycling containers, maintain sanitation services during and after event hours, and will supervise cleaning of the site immediately after the removal of event elements by MNO Sports at no cost to the event.

The host city will schedule sufficient police, fire, and emergency medical service coverage during the event, and during installation and dismantling operations, to protect the health and safety of the public, participants, and event staff. Adequate overnight security staffing by either bonded guards or on-/off-duty police is essential. These requirements will be provided by the host city at no cost to MNO Sports.

C. HOTEL RECOMMENDATIONS

Approximately 350 quality and competitively priced hotel rooms will be required on peak nights. A preliminary schedule of room requirements appears below:

	Mon–Thurs.	Fri.	Sat.	Sun.	Mon.–Tues.
Rooms	10	350	350	350	10

Host hotels will also make available the meeting rooms or function space required for the management of the event during the days listed above at no cost. To be considered as a prospective host hotel, function space should be put on a tentative hold per the following schedule:

*Required gross square footage may be higher to avoid the presence of street lamps, medians, planters, sewer grates, or other obstructions.

Office	Min. Sq. Ft.	Occupancy
Operations Office	1,500 sq. ft.	7 days prior through 2 days following event
Event Storage	1,500	7 days prior through 1 day following event
Gift Bag Distribution	1,500	7 days prior through 1 day following event
Sponsor Hospitality	1,500	1 day prior though final event day

The event headquarters hotel will permit event organizers to place welcome and directional signage in the hotel lobby area and on the exterior of the building in mutually agreed locations. The event will be permitted to staff an information desk in the lobby of the hotel within line-of-sight of the guest registration area.

The headquarters hotel(s) will provide a total of 30 complimentary room-nights for pre-event planning trips, the fulfillment of which will be administered by the local convention and visitors bureau (CVB).

During the event and for up to four (4) weeks prior, a discounted "staff rate" will be available to event staff, up to a maximum of 80 room nights.

Hotels will agree to provide the event with a rebate of $10.00 USD per room night occupied by visitors assigned to the event room block during the period listed above, excepting the discounted staff rate rooms as defined above.

The headquarters hotel will agree to make broadband and wireless Internet access and health facility services available to the management and staff of the event at no cost. The event will look favorably upon hotels offering this policy to all guests in the event's room block.

While the host city should identify hotels that are interested in being considered as a headquarters hotel after they have reviewed and agreed to these specifications, MNO Sports will negotiate and contract with any and all required local hotels directly.

D. PROMOTION AND PUBLICITY

The host city will undertake all efforts to publicize the event in advance to promote attendance. The promotion plan should combine advertising on local television and radio, in local magazines and newspapers, as well as additional promotion through the installation of street banners, outdoor advertising, websites of local interest, and other mechanisms. MNO Sports will consider—but must approve all—proposals for media partnerships (e.g., the naming of one or more media outlets as **"the official television station, radio station, newspaper, etc. of 'The Big Street Sports Tournament"**).

Please enclose letters of support and/or interest from media interested in participating as promotional partners for the event with your proposal, containing commitments to provide advertising time or space. Host city websites will actively promote and prominently feature the Tournament at least ninety (90) days prior to the event through the last day of the program.

E. WELCOME SIGNAGE

The event will look favorably upon proposals that include welcome signage installed to greet inbound players, sponsors and special guests at airport locations, on street poles in major business districts and near headquarters hotels, and approaching the event site over key intersections or on outdoor advertising billboards. Event sponsor identification may be included, following the guidelines discussed in Section F below. (*Note:* MNO Sports may, at its sole discretion, require inclusion of the event's national presenting or title sponsor(s) of the event in the design of all welcome signage wherever local sponsors are included.)

F. LOCAL SPONSOR PARTNERS

The Event maintains an impressive list of national and regional sponsors entitled to marketing and promotional rights at The Big Street Sports Tournament (see Section VIII for the roster as of the date indicated).

MNO Sports will consider—but must approve—any local sponsors and the package of entitlements proposed by the host city. The sponsors may provide either cash or value-in-kind to the host city to offset the latter's expenses. Notwithstanding the above, MNO Sports maintains its rights to procure local sponsorships or value-in-kind arrangements at its sole discretion.

The host city will retain all revenues from local cash sponsorships from the agreements it generates, providing they are approved in advance by MNO Sports. All costs in fulfilling said sponsorships will be borne by the host city. The event is appreciative of trade or value-in-kind deals provided by the host city that can supply additional value to the event. MNO Sports, however, cannot offer cash payments or commissions to the host city for such donated goods and/or services.

Notwithstanding the above, MNO Sports will not approve local sponsorship deals with companies that, in MNO's sole opinion, are competitive with the event's current or prospective business partners, as listed in Section VIII.

G. HOST CITY FEE

There is no fee required to submit a proposal for consideration as host city of The Big Street Sports Tournament. A $10,000 fee will be paid to MNO Sports by the selected host city, due upon execution of a letter agreement between the host city and MNO Sports. This fee is not refundable if the host city cancels its participation for any reason after the letter agreement is executed.

MNO Sports may waive the host city fee if, in its sole opinion, the host city is providing exceptional value in equipment, products, or services that will benefit the event beyond the minimum requirements of this Request for Proposal.

H. VOLUNTEER STAFFING

MNO Sports will provide all management and paid staff for the event. The host city will be required to provide approximately thirty (30) volunteer staff members per event day to work under the direction of MNO Sports for the proper, safe, and efficient operation of the event. The host city should identify how it will assist MNO Sports in the solicitation of volunteer staff. Volunteer staff members will receive an event cap and t-shirt, both for their use on-site and as a take-home memento. Meals and refreshments appropriate to the time of day will also be available to working volunteer staff.

I. FOOD VENDOR MANAGEMENT

The host city will be responsible for the identification of licensed, reliable, and experienced food vendors for the event site. MNO Sports will be entitled to a $75 fee per vendor per location. The host city may assess an additional fee to vendors to offset its own expenses.

J. KEY POINT OF CONTACT

The host city should identify a key staff person to serve as a high-level liaison between the local government and the Event Director. This key contact will interact directly with the municipal departments required to successfully stage the event, expedite any and all local permitting requirements, and ensure that the event complies with all applicable municipal ordinances, where appropriate.

K. AVAILABILITY OF EVENT EQUIPMENT AND SUPPLIES

The host city should identify any event equipment and services it will agree to make available to the event at no cost.

The following items are essential to the operation of the event, and their provision at no cost to the event would significantly improve the chances of a successful bid. Please enter the quantity of items available on the attached questionnaire:

- Folding tables
- Folding chairs
- Staging platforms and/or risers
- Power generators or access to power sources
- Bleachers
- Portalettes
- Golf and utility carts
- Water trucks
- Forklifts
- Dumpsters
- Waste receptacles
- Ice and ice storage
- Tents and canopies
- Shuttle buses between player hotel and event site (may be municipal transit vehicles)

VI. THE IDEAL EVENT SITE

The recommendation of an appropriate, attractive, and highly desirable event site is among the most important considerations in preparing a successful event proposal. As previously discussed, it is a mutual objective of the event organizers and the host community to attract the largest local and in-bound audience possible for the event. Therefore, the ideal event site will showcase the unique aspects and culture of the host city, and will possess a combination of many of the following attributes:

- An area in or adjacent to, a normally high pedestrian traffic flow during the operating hours of the event;
- An area in or overlooking a landmark or nationally recognized buildings, scenery, skylines, or natural wonders;
- A flat, smooth, and well-maintained paved surface with sufficient drainage and contiguous space to accommodate the various playing surfaces and entertainment areas, plus safe pedestrian flow through all areas of the event site (as determined by the local fire marshal);

- A player equipment drop-off location and visitor access to nearby free or reasonably priced parking and/or mass transportation;
- Visitor and participant access to on-site or nearby restroom facilities (or the ability to install portable restroom facilities provided by the host city at no cost to the event);
- Sufficient weight-load capacities to enable fully laden tractor-trailers to park and off-load at the event site (*Note:* Several decorated trailers will remain on the event site for the duration of the program.);
- Complete access for installation beginning Thursday afternoon at 5:00 P.M. and completion of dismantle by Monday morning at 8:00 A.M.;
- No rental charges, permit fees, or other financial obligation payable by the event to the city and/or private owner of the property;
- No broadcast origination fees or media restrictions for the event of live or taped telecasts or news coverage;
- Permission for the sale of event merchandise to the public with no additional charges levied against gross proceeds other than normally payable local and/or state or provincial sales taxes;
- No site-specific sponsor exclusivities that conflict with the business partners of the event as described in Section VIII.

VII. HOST CITY BENEFITS

- **Host City Designation**

  The host city will be able to use its designation as **"Host City of The Big Street Sports Tournament"** in all advertising, promotions, and publicity prior to, during, and one year following the event, each such use subject to the approval of MNO Sports.
- **Use of Marks**

  The host city will have the right to incorporate the logo of "The Big Street Sports Tournament" into all printed and Internet advertising and promotional material, as well as in the production and distribution of premium items, such use subject to MNO Sports approval.
- **Promotional Opportunities**

  The host city will have the opportunity to utilize the event to promote tourism, or in other marketing campaigns undertaken by the local government and its agencies among both participants and visitors. Opportunities may feature the inclusion of a premium item in visiting player gift bags, city attraction and restaurant maps, coupon books and/or product samples delivered at check-in for visiting players, and the inclusion of a special promotional brochure in the player solicitation package sent to potential participants during the team application process, all such materials and use subject to MNO Sports approval.

  The event organizer will promote the host city on the **Big Street Sports Tournament** web page at www.bigstreetsports.com in banner advertising, pre-event publicity, and coverage of the event. All printed and electronic materials designed to promote the event will prominently feature the host city, including press releases, participant applications, and advertising.
- **Event Site Benefits**

  The host city will receive significant and prominent recognition at the event site on signage boards located throughout the area and in scheduled public address announcements.

  The host city will receive a 10′ × 10′ tent on site for its own exhibition purposes for the duration of the event. Alternatively, the host city may utilize its own existing structure for such purposes, which may exceed the 10′ × 10′ footprint, subject to the approval of MNO Sports.

The host city may enter one athlete or team in each amateur tournament event at no cost. This opportunity may be used for internal or promotional purposes, at the discretion of the host city.

- **Database Access**

  MNO Sports will make the database of all tournament participants and MNO Sports-run sweepstakes entrants, if any, available to the host city for postevent marketing purposes, as permitted by law. The event organizer will make two one-hour appearances of five visiting street sports athletes available to the host city, for attendance at a city-run reception, hospital visits, or other opportunity to be mutually agreed upon.

VIII. BIG STREET SPORTS TOURNAMENT PARTNERS

Big Street Sports Tournament Partners

(Effective August 30, 2013, and subject to change)

The companies listed here are the national sponsors of the Big Street Sports Tournament and are entitled to exclusive promotional benefits in connection with the event. Additional national event sponsors may be confirmed by MNO Sports at any time without notice. The host city may seek to secure local sponsors in product categories other than those listed below, with the prior approval of MNO Sports:

SOFT DRINK COMPANY
ISOTONIC BEVERAGE COMPANY
BICYCLE COMPANY
IN-LINE SKATE COMPANY
SKATE WHEEL COMPANY
SKATEBOARD COMPANY
SAFETY EQUIPMENT COMPANY
FIRST AID SUPPLIES COMPANY
QUICK SERVICE RESTAURANT COMPANY
MOBILE PHONE COMPANY

Note: In an actual RFP, the real names of sponsor companies would appear above.

IX. THE BIG STREET SPORTS TOURNAMENT

Request for Proposal Response Form

Prospective host cities are invited to prepare their proposal in any format desired. However, a fully completed Request for Proposal Response Form should be included as the first section of the submitted document. An electronic version of this form is available upon request. To receive a copy via e-mail, please contact Nathaniel Jacobs at njacobs@mnosports.com.

Please submit all applicable forms and accompanying materials by November 15, 2013, to the name and address noted on the last page of the Response Form.

I. CONTACT INFORMATION:

HOST CITY: ____

APPLYING ENTITY (E.G., CVB, SPORTS COMMISSION):

____

PRIMARY CONTACT: ____

TITLE: ____

ADDRESS: ____

____

TELEPHONE: ____________________ FAX: ____________________

E-MAIL: ____

Weekend(s) applied for:

1st Choice: ____________________________

2nd Choice: ____________________________

The applying city agrees to all terms as outlined in the bid specifications for **The Big Street Sports Tournament** _______YES ______NO

(If "no," please attach a detailed description of exceptions)

Are there other city festivals or events scheduled on the same weekend(s), or on the weekends immediately prior to or following these dates? _______YES ______NO.

(If "yes," please note or attach further information)

II. PROPOSED EVENT SITE

SITE NAME: ____

SITE OWNER: ____

EVENT SITE CONTACT NAME: ________________________________

CONTACT PHONE:____________________ E-MAIL:______________________

Please attach a description of how the proposed event site fulfills the "Ideal Event Site" characteristics described in this RFP (include photos, floorplans, and elevations, as available):

SEATING CAPACITY: _______________________________________

TAXES AND FEES ON SALES OF TICKETS: ______________________

LABOR AND UNION EXCLUSIVITIES: ___________________________

HOURLY LABOR RATES (including benefits and management fees):

Ushers: _____________

Security: _____________

Electricians: _____________

Carpenters: _____________

Riggers: _____________

CATERING EXCLUSIVITIES: ______________________________

CONCESSIONS EXCLUSIVITIES: ______________________________

MERCHANDISE EXCLUSIVITIES: ______________________________

OTHER RESTRICTIONS: ______________________________

III. HOTEL

Hotels participating in the bidding process must hold space on a first-option basis until the determination of a host city is made. Please complete one hotel form for each property participating in the bid.

HOTEL NAME: ______________________________

TOTAL # ROOMS: ______________________________

TOTAL HELD FOR EVENT ON A FIRST-OPTION BASIS: ______________________________

PROPOSEDROOMRATES:SINGLE:______________ DBL/DBL:______________

TAX RATES ON SLEEPING ROOMS: ______________________________

YEAR OF LAST SLEEPING ROOM RENOVATION: ______________________________

YEAR OF LAST PUBLIC/FUNCTION SPACE RENOVATION:______________________________

If selected, the hotel agrees to provide function space in the quantity, and as described in this RFP _____YES _____NO

Please attach description of any exceptions or exclusions

HOTEL CONTACT NAME/TITLE: ______________________________

PHONE: ______________________________FAX: ______________________________

E-MAIL: ______________________________

CONTACT SIGNATURE: ______________________________

IV. HOST CITY

CITY SERVICES LIAISON: ______________________________

TITLE AND PHONE: ______________________________

CONVENTION & VISITORS BUREAU CONTACT: ______________________________

TITLE AND PHONE: ______________________________

AVAILABILITY OF EVENT RESOURCES (SEE SECTION V.(K)).

Item	# Available	Comments (e.g., size)
Folding tables	________	
Folding chairs	________	
Staging and/or risers	________	
Power generators/access to power	________	
Bleachers	________	

Portalettes ________

Golf and utility carts ________

Water trucks ________

Forklifts ________

Dumpsters ________

Waste Receptacles ________

Ice and ice storage ________

Tents and canopies ________

Shuttle buses ________

REGIONAL POPULATION: ____________________

AVERAGE HOUSEHOLD INCOME: ____________________

EFFECTIVE STATE AND LOCAL SALES TAXES: ____________________

ADDITIONAL NON–HOTEL-RELATED TAXES: ____________________

Proposed Media Partners:

Please enclose letters of interest or support

PRINT: ____________________

TELEVISION: ____________________

RADIO: ____________________

OTHER: ____________________

SOURCE OF VOLUNTEER POOL: ____________________

Please submit all applicable forms and accompanying materials no later than November 15, 2013 to:

Nathaniel Jacobs
MNO Sports
123 S.W. 2nd Avenue
Biggtown, MD 00000
njacobs@mnosports.com

APPENDIX 4

Request for Proposal Evaluation Form

Sports Organization
Event Name

RFP Evaluation Form

Selection Criteria	CITY A	CITY B	CITY C	CITY D
Contact Name and Title	_______	_______	_______	_______
Contact Phone	_______	_______	_______	_______
Contact Email	_______	_______	_______	_______
Agree to All Bid Specifications (Yes/No)	_______	_______	_______	_______
Exceptions:	_______	_______	_______	_______
	_______	_______	_______	_______
Other Events Scheduled within Time Period	_______	_______	_______	_______
Event Site Information:				
Name of Event Site	_______	_______	_______	_______
Location of Event Site	_______	_______	_______	_______
Size or Seating Capacity	_______	_______	_______	_______
Contact Name and Phone	_______	_______	_______	_______
Meets Ideal Event Site Requirements? (Yes/No)	_______	_______	_______	_______
Exceptions:	_______	_______	_______	_______
	_______	_______	_______	_______

Selection Criteria	CITY A	CITY B	CITY C	CITY D
Effective Taxes on Ticket Sales				
Other Fees on Ticket Sales				
Labor and Union Exclusivities				
Hourly Rates (incl. Benefits and Management Fees)				
Ushers				
Security				
Electricians				
Carpenters				
Riggers				
Catering Exclusivity?				
Merchandise Exclusivity?				
Concessions Exclusivity?				
Hotels:				
Hotel Name (# Rooms)				
Overflow Hotel (# Rooms)				
Room Rates				
Tax Rate on Sleeping Rooms				
Will Hotels Meet Minimum Requirements? (Yes/No)				
Exceptions				
Host City:				
Will Host City Provide Support Required (Yes/No)				
Exceptions:				
Size of Market (Population)				
Average Household Income				

Effective State and Local Sales Taxes	______	______	______	______
Letters of Support Included	______	______	______	______
Additional Pertinent Information	______	______	______	______
	______	______	______	______
	______	______	______	______
Evaluator Comments	______	______	______	______

APPENDIX 5

Sample Facility Event License Agreement

This Facility Event License Agreement is provided for illustrative purposes only, and is an abbreviated representative composite inspired by a variety of actual contracts. This document is not intended for use as a legal instrument. A number of additional legal details may appear in actual Facility Event License Agreements. Event organizers and facilities should retain the services of competent and experienced legal counsel for the process of creating, negotiating, and agreeing to any contract, including a Facility Event License Agreement. The words, passages, and figures in italics denote inclusions of details for a fictional event to better illustrate the appearance of a typical Facility Event License Agreement.

* * *

XYZ ENTERTAINMENT CENTER EVENT LICENSE AGREEMENT

This agreement (the "Agreement"), made and entered into on this ____ day of __________, 20__, by and between *XYZ Sports & Entertainment, Inc. ("XYZ"), a Florida* corporation, and hereinafter referred to as **Licensor**, and for the use of *XYZ Center (the "Center")*:

JKL Sports Events, Ltd.
123 S.W. Fifth Avenue
Cityview, FL 30000
954-000-0000 (Tel); 954-000-0001 (Fax)
Harold Matthews, President

Hereinafter referred to as **Licensee**.
The Licensor and Licensee hereby agree as follows:

1. EVENT (the "Event")

Event Name/Description: ________________________________

Move-In/Rehearsal Day(s): ________________________________

Event/Performance Days & Times: ______________________________

Move-Out Day(s): ______________________________

Ticket Prices: ______________________________

Estimated Gross Potential: ______________________________

Move-in, Rehearsal, Event and Move-Out days shall collectively be referred to as the "License Period." Use of *XYZ Center* in excess of the time described herein may result in additional charges to the Licensee.

2. LICENSE FEES

(a) The Licensee agrees to pay to the Licensor the following License Fees (the "License Fees"):
   1. Basic License Fee: *$30,000*
   2. All other fees referenced in this Agreement, including, but not limited to, the Television Origination Fee and Souvenir Merchandise Fee;
   3. All such additional fees, charges, and other amounts payable by the Licensee, including, but not limited to, event staff service charges, food and beverage service charges, ticket sales commissions, cleaning, maintenance, and conversion charges.

(b) The Licensee agrees to pay all taxes levied on the License Fees or as a result of the Licensee's use of the *Center* including, but not limited to, admission taxes, amusement taxes, and sales taxes on the ticket price. The Licensee agrees to pay *$15,000* as a nonrefundable license deposit. The deposit is due and payable upon the return of this executed Agreement.

(c) The Licensee will be responsible for paying in full the amount of the Licensor's actual costs on settlement in accordance with the provisions herein. The Licensor will, upon request, provide the Licensee with estimates of projected Event costs. Such estimates are reasonable attempts at identifying costs made in good faith by the Licensor based on information provided by the Licensee and are not binding on the Licensor.

(d) The License Fee has been determined based on the Ticket Prices and Estimated Gross Potential as defined above. In the event that the Actual Gross exceeds the Estimated Gross Potential, the License Fee shall increase by *0.5%* for each *1.0%* positive difference between the Estimated Gross Potential and the Actual Gross. Regardless of the Actual Gross, the License Fee will not be decreased.

3. LICENSE AREA

(a) The Licensor hereby agrees to grant to the Licensee the nonexclusive right to occupy and use the following areas (the "Licensed Areas") of the *Center* during the License Period: *the Center bowl, concourse, locker rooms, and all other non-office spaces in the Center.*

(b) No other areas shall be occupied by the Licensee unless authorized in advance in writing by the Licensor. The Licensor reserves the right to license or use all areas of the *Center* not expressly assigned to the Licensee during the License Period for any purpose whatsoever. The Licensee acknowledges that the *Center* or various parts thereof may or will be used for the installation, holding or presentation, and removal of other activities or events. It may be necessary for the use of the *Center*, including, without limitation, all common areas, to be shared by the Licensee and others as designated by the Licensor.

The Licensor shall have the authority to establish the schedule for the use and availability of such services and accommodations.

(c) The Licensee shall use the Licensed Areas solely for the purpose of preparing for and presenting the Event during the License Period. The Licensee will not permit the use of the Licensed Areas or any part thereof for any other Event, business, or purpose.

(d) The Licensor shall have the right to the free access of any and all areas of the *Center* including, but not limited to, the Licensed Areas at all times during the License Period.

4. SERVICES TO BE PROVIDED BY THE LICENSOR

(a) The Licensor shall provide lighting, heating, air conditioning, and water, as installed at the time of this agreement, and at such times and in such amounts as shall be necessary in the Licensor's sole opinion acting reasonably, for the comfortable use and occupancy of the *Center*.

(b) The Licensor will provide equipment, staffing, or services for this Event at its discretion, taking into consideration Event information provided by Licensee and at the Licensee's sole cost. Such staffing and services include, but are not limited to, ushers, ticket takers, guest service hosts, security, police, ticket sellers, conversion crew, cleaning staff, carpenter(s), laborers, electrician(s), riggers, and emergency medical personnel. The Licensor retains the right to determine the appropriate number of personnel necessary to properly staff the *Center* and protect the public. All personnel provided by the Licensor shall remain employees of the Licensor and will be under the Licensor's direct supervision.

(c) All utilities, including, but not limited to, electricity, water, gas, telecommunications, cable television, data and Internet service, and other equipment and services needed by the Licensee, must be ordered through the Licensor.

5. EVENT TICKETS

(a) The Licensee acknowledges that the Licensor has an exclusive agreement with *Ticket Service, Inc. ("TS")*, a computerized ticket service company, whereby the Licensor/*TS* will jointly act as exclusive agents and be responsible for maintaining control over the inventory, distribution, and sale of all tickets for the Event through the Licensor's Box Office and *TS* outlets, unless otherwise agreed to in writing by the Licensor.

(b) Regardless of whether tickets will be sold on a reserved-seat or general-admission basis, the number of tickets printed shall not exceed the maximum capacity of the *Center*, which the Licensor shall determine in its sole discretion.

(c) The Licensor shall at all times maintain control and direction of the ticket office, ticket personnel, and ticket sales.

(d) The Licensee acknowledges that tickets purchased over the Internet, by telephone, by mail order, at *TS* outlets and through the Licensor's Will Call Office are subject to service charges payable to *TS* and/or the Licensor in addition to the basic ticket price.

(e) The Licensee shall pay to the Licensor all applicable credit card service charges, based on gross credit card revenues, including applicable taxes, of *two and a half percent (2.5%)*.

(f) Following the Event, the Licensor shall provide to the Licensee a full report of ticket sales by the Licensor/*TS* for the Event, and prepare the Preliminary Settlement Summary. The Licensor shall then pay to the Licensee the proceeds of all tickets sold by the Licensor/*TS*, less the following amounts:

i. The total of all applicable taxes, service charges, and Facility Usage Fees (the latter fee will be deducted from gross ticket proceeds at a rate of *$0.50* per ticket);
ii. The total identified by the Licensor as owing pursuant to this Agreement, in accordance with the Preliminary Settlement Summary. To the extent that ticket sales proceeds can be applied in full against the payment obligations of the Licensee to the Licensor hereunder, those obligations shall be deemed to have been satisfied. The Licensee shall submit payment for obligations of the Licensee not so satisfied to the Licensor at the completion of the Event.

(g) The Licensor shall provide to the Licensee a Final Settlement Summary thirty (30) days after the final date of the Event indicating any adjustments due to either party to this Agreement.

6. COMPLIMENTARY TICKETS AND PASSES

The Licensee shall provide to the Licensor *sixty (60)* complimentary tickets for the event, at least fifty percent (50%) of which will be located in prime seating areas, the value of which shall not be included as part of the proceeds from ticket sales.

7. REFUNDS

(a) As a result of cancellation or postponement of the Event, *TS* and the Licensor shall refund the ticket price of any unused tickets, and may, in accordance with *TS* and/or the Licensor's policy, refund applicable service charges and/or handling fees at the point of purchase.
(b) In the event that part of the Event is cancelled or postponed, Licensor may in its sole discretion determine what, if any, portion of the ticket price shall be refunded.
(c) Any amounts forwarded to the Licensee by the Licensor with respect to ticket sales shall be returned immediately to the Licensor after the Event has been cancelled or postponed.
(d) The Licensor shall retain the right to make ticket refunds for cause or maintaining the public faith. This right shall include, but is not limited to, seats blocked by equipment of the Licensee, its broadcasting partners or sponsors, when exchange for comparable locations is not possible. Refunds will not be made if tickets for such seats were sold clearly marked for sale at a discounted price, and clearly marked as "Obstructed View" seats. If the Event is cancelled, the Licensee shall permit the Licensor to reimburse any amount that ticket holders paid for tickets. The Licensee shall pay the licensor a mutually agreed on ticket handling charge on tickets sold up to the time of cancellation as compensation for the task of refunding tickets to the cancelled Event, except if cancellation was caused by a force majeure, as described in this Agreement.

8. MERCHANDISE AND PROGRAM SALES

(a) The Licensee or the Licensee's designated agent(s) shall have the exclusive right to provide souvenir merchandise and programs to the Licensor for sale by the Licensor on a consignment basis during the Event on behalf of the Licensee.
(b) The Licensee shall not sell, authorize, or permit the sale of any souvenir merchandise and/or programs during the License Period within a one (1) mile radius of the outside of the *Center*.
(c) At the conclusion of the Event, the Licensor shall return all the unsold souvenir merchandise and programs provided by the Licensee or the Licensee's designated agent(s). The Licensor shall retain a commission of *20%* of Net Revenues on merchandise and program sales, less all applicable taxes and credit card commissions.

(d) The numbers and locations of the merchandise sales areas in the *Center* for use of the Licensee or the Licensee's designated agent(s) will be at the sole determination of Licensor.
(e) Notwithstanding Section 5(a) above, the Licensor retains the exclusive right to operate and maintain its concessions, store, and concourse merchandise kiosks during the Event to sell souvenir merchandise and programs not related to the Event, and without any payment due to the Licensee.

9. ADVERTISING AND SPONSORSHIP

(a) The Licensor retains the exclusive right to conduct, sell, and retain all revenues from all advertising and promotion whatsoever in and about the *Center* including, without limitation, on the public address system, video screens, main scoreboard, auxiliary scoreboards, matrix message signage, other electronic and display signage, posters, banners, and promotional displays during the Event and without approval by or payment to the Licensee. The Licensee shall not obstruct or cover any such advertising or promotion.
(b) The Licensee shall not display or grant to Event sponsor(s) or others any right to display advertising at the *Center* without the prior written consent of the Licensor, and which consent may be withheld for any reason.
(c) The Licensor consents to and grants the Licensee a limited license to use the logo and name *XYZ Center*, as applicable, in Licensor's approved typeface as the site designation for the Event in advertising and other material promoting the Event. All such usage shall be subject to the Licensor's prior written approval and shall be accompanied by applicable trademark notifications as designated by the Licensor.
(d) The Licensee shall not permit the distribution of any free samples or promotional merchandise, programs, food, beverages, or printed material of any kind at the *Center* during the Term without the prior written consent of the Licensor, which consent may be withheld in the Licensor's sole discretion.

10. VIDEO AND/OR AUDIO REPRODUCTION

Licensee and Licensor hereby agree that there shall be no electronic media exploitation of the Event whatsoever without the prior written permission of the Licensee. The term "electronic media exploitation" shall be defined as the exploitation of the Event, whether on a live, delayed, or other basis, through any means of signal distribution including, but not limited to: broadcast television, basic or premium tier cable television, direct-by-satellite television, pay-per-view television, radio, basic or premium tier Internet service, or home video.

11. LABOR AGREEMENTS

Licensee shall not perform any work or employ any personnel in connection with the Event except if such work or employment conforms to labor agreements to which the Licensor or its contractors are a party. The Licensor may deny access to the *Center* to any person whose admittance could result in a violation of any such labor agreement.

12. FOOD AND BEVERAGE CATERING SERVICE

The Licensor reserves the exclusive right to provide all food, beverage, and catering service outlets within the *Center* including alcoholic and other beverages, and to retain all revenue derived therefrom.

13. INSURANCE, INDEMNIFICATION, AND DAMAGES

(a) The Licensee agrees to assume, defend, indemnify, protect, and hold harmless the Licensor, and its affiliates, shareholders, officers, and employees against any and all claims, or causes of action arising or resulting: (i) from the use, occupancy, or licensing of the *Center* by the Licensee, its contractors, subcontractors, exhibitors, or other invitees or persons attending the Event; or (ii) out of any personal injury or property damage occurring in or upon the *Center* due to any contravention of the provisions of the License, the said rules and regulations, or any applicable laws, rules, regulations, or orders of any governmental agency having jurisdiction over the *Center*, or due to any negligence or willful act by the Licensee or those for whom the Licensee is in law responsible.

(b) The Licensee shall obtain and maintain, at its own cost and expense, for the duration of the License Period, a Comprehensive Public Liability and Property Damage Insurance policy along with the required Workers' Compensation, Automobile Liability and Umbrella Liability coverages. A certificate of insurance shall be provided to the Licensor a minimum of thirty (30) days prior to the starting date of the Event. The Licensee shall name the Licensor and its respective shareholders and officers as additional named insureds on the insurance policy. Such insurance shall be provided by a comprehensive general liability insurance policy including personal injury, contractual liability, cross liability, and occurrence property damage with a combined single limit of at least $5,000,000 for each occurrence.

(c) The Licensee shall not make any alterations of any kind to the *Center* without the prior written consent of the Licensor, which consent may be withheld in the Licensor's sole discretion. The Licensee agrees that if the *Center* is damaged by the act, default, or negligence of the Licensee, or those persons for whom the Licensee is responsible in law, or any person admitted to the *Center* by the Licensee or Licensee's agents, then the Licensee shall pay to the Licensor upon demand such reasonable sums as shall be necessary to restore the *Center* to its original condition.

14. FORCE MAJEURE

None of the parties shall be in breach of this Agreement if the performance by that party of any of its obligations hereunder is prevented or preempted because of an Act of God, accident, fire, labor dispute, riot or civil commotion, act of public enemy, governmental act, or any other reason beyond the control of that party. In any such event, this License shall terminate and the Licensee and the Licensor shall each only be responsible for their own expenses. The Licensee hereby waives any claim against the Licensor for damages or compensation by reason of such termination.

15. OBSERVANCE OF LAW AND PUBLIC SAFETY

(a) The Licensee, its employees, agents, and all other persons connected with its use of the *Center* shall comply with all laws, statutes, regulations (including, but not limited to, police and fire and regulations and occupational health and safety regulations), and all requirements of governmental and regulatory bodies.

(b) The Licensee will obtain all necessary permits, licenses, and approvals relating to the use of and the conduct of the Event in the Licensed Areas and provide the Licensor with satisfactory evidence of the licenses and approvals.

(c) The Licensee will obtain at its expense the right to use any patented, trademarked, or copyrighted materials, dramatic rights, or performance rights used in the conduct of the Event.

(d) The Licensee agrees that it shall not use any pyrotechnic devices without the prior written consent of the Licensor, which consent may be withheld in the Licensor's sole discretion. If such consent is granted, the Licensee shall comply with all laws, rules, regulations, criteria, and policies of all federal, state, and municipal authorities or agencies applicable thereto. The Licensee shall deliver all supporting documentation confirming the Licensee's compliance with the above requirements at least fifteen (15) days prior to the first performance of the Event.

(e) The Licensor reserves the right to make announcements in the interest of public safety, to provide safety information to attendees, and, in coordination with Licensee, to announce and otherwise promote upcoming events at the *Center* during the Event.

16. TERMINATION

(a) If the Licensee is adjudicated bankrupt, or adjudged to be insolvent, or a receiver or trustee of the Licensee's property and affairs is appointed, or the Licensee is in default of any of its obligations under this Agreement or pursuant hereto, then this license may at the option of the Licensor be cancelled by delivering to the Licensee notice to that effect.

(b) Upon any termination, the Licensee shall immediately pay to Licensor the License Fees as liquidated damages, together with all costs, losses, expenses, and damages, as determined by the Licensor. Deposits and payments received are nonrefundable in all instances including, but not limited to, a termination.

THE LICENSOR:

XYZ SPORTS & ENTERTAINMENT, INC.

By: ______________________________

Name:____________________________

Title:_____________________________

THE LICENSEE:

JKL SPORTS EVENTS, LTD.

By:_______________________________

Name:____________________________

Title:_____________________________

APPENDIX 6

Facility Selection Survey Form (simplified)

PROPOSED EVENT: ______________________________

Date(s)/Time(s): ______________________________

Load-in Date(s): ______________________________

Load-out Date(s): ______________________________

FACILITY: ______________________________

Facility Address: ______________________________

____

Key Contact: ______________________________

Title: ______________________________

Phone: ______________________________

Email: ______________________________

Fax: ______________________________

Date Availability for Load-in: ______________________________

Event Date(s): ______________________________

Date Availability for Load-out: ______________________________

Available Seating by Scale/ Level: ______________________________

Total Manifest: ______________________________

Manifest by Break: **Section:** ____________ **Tickets:** __________
____________ **Tickets:** __________
____________ **Tickets:** __________
____________ **Tickets:** __________
____________ **Tickets:** __________

Total ADA Seating Included Above: ______________________

Temporary Seat/Build-Out Options? ______________________

RENTAL COSTS/TERMS: ______________________

Tax Rate on Tickets: ______________________

Capital Replacement Fees on Tickets: ____________ **paid by** ____________

Other Service Fees on Tickets: ____________ **paid by** ____________

Credit Card Processing Rate: ____________

Other Box Office Fees: ______________________

Merchandise Contact: ______________________

Merchandise Sales Exclusivity? ____________**Terms:** ____________

Concessionaire/Caterer Contact: ______________________

Concessionaire/Caterer Exclusivity? ______________________

Food/Soft Drink/Beer Exclusivity? ______________________

Event Promotion Services: ______________________

HOURLY LABOR RATES:

Electricians: __________ **Union:** __________
Carpenters: __________ **Union:** __________
Riggers: __________ **Union:** __________
Stagehands: __________ **Union:** __________
Decorators: __________ **Union:** __________
Security: __________ **Union:** __________
FOH: __________ **Union:** __________
Medical: __________
Scoreboard/Video Crew: ______________________

Estimated Conversion/Cleaning Costs: ______________________

FACILITY NOTES:

Locker Rooms: ______________________________

Dressing Rooms: ______________________________

Marshaling and Storage Areas: ______________________________

Scoreboard/Videoboard/Other Displays: ______________________________

Media Facilities: ______________________________

Parking Facilities: ______________________________

Concourse Information Displays: ______________________________

Exterior Electronic Signage/Marquees: ______________________________

BROADCASTING NOTES:

Number of Loading Docks: ______________________________

Broadcast Truck Docks or Compound(s): ______________________________

Permanent Camera Positions and Baskets: ______________________________

____

Broadcast Booths for Television and Radio: ______________________________

Broadcast Origination Fees? ______________________________

CONNECTIVITY:

Number of Available Phone Lines: ______________________________

Available Internet Capability and Available Fiber Optic Capacity: ______________________________

Mobile Phone Cellular and WiFi Capacity: ______________________________

AVAILABLE EQUIPMENT (quantity/cost):

Tables: ________________ **Tablecloths:** ________________

Chairs: ________________ **Risers:** ________________

Forklifts: ________________ **Barriers:** ________________

Pipe and Drape (lgt/ht/color): ______________________________

Crowd Barriers (lgt/type): ______________________________

Other: ______________________________

____

____

____

SPONSOR EXCLUSIVITIES AND SIGNAGE RESTRICTIONS:

____

____

____

____

____

____

HOSPITALITY OPTIONS: ______________________________

____

____

OTHER NOTES: ______________________________

____

____

APPENDIX 7

Sample Sports Event Sponsorship Deck

D.E.F. Sports & Entertainment

An Introduction to
SPORTSFEST 2015
A Mid-States Regional Multi-Sport Festival
presented to
Mid-States Car Dealers Association

August 2014

An Introduction to Sportsfest 2015

Table of Contents

I. SportsFest—An Overview

Mid-summer weekends in the Mid-States Region changed forever with the area's first test drive of SportsFest in 1998.

SportsFest has annually provided the region's children and their families with an exciting, highly anticipated weekend of wholesome fun and friendly competition enveloped in a festival atmosphere featuring great entertainment, fantastic local food, and a midway filled with interactive exhibits, intriguing displays, thrilling rides, and involving activities.

More than just a sports festival, and much like the Mid-States Region Car Dealers Association, SportsFest is a celebration of our region's diverse cultural heritage, our active lifestyle, and our vibrant business community.

More than 50,000 active, attractions-seeking families are expected to ***GET INTO IT*** by participating in SportsFest 2015, returning to enjoy their favorite sports events, plus a host of new programs, activities, and entertainment.

SportsFest is a favorite location for local television and radio news, a magnet for dozens of live remote broadcasts throughout the weekend. The event also generates significant newspaper coverage throughout the Mid-States Region.

SportsFest provides participating businesses with outstanding opportunities to reach a large number of the area's active consumers, introduce new products, host important customers, and demonstrate their support of community recreation programs. The Mid-States Regional Car Dealers Association (**MSCDA**) can drive qualified buyers into its members' showrooms, conduct test drives right on the event site, and explore limitless options for a wide variety of promotional opportunities at the Mid-States Region's most anticipated sports and active lifestyle festival.

The net operating proceeds of SportsFest 2015 will be donated to the Mid-States Region Sports Council for the redevelopment of recreational facilities, the acquisition of new sports equipment, and funding of physical fitness programs for the area's disadvantaged youth.

SportsFest 2015. . .

. . . ***GET INTO IT!***

SportsFest was founded by D.E.F. Sports & Entertainment, a Mid-States Region corporation that specializes in the organization and management of sports tournaments and events for youth. D.E.F. Sports & Entertainment is also the producer of the Mid-States Region Invitational and the Grain City Wheat Festival.

II. INTRODUCTION

The appeal of SportsFest has grown steadily since its inaugural model rolled out in 1998. Now in its 18th edition, SportsFest will expand to over 10 acres of the Old Fairgrounds, featuring full tournament competition in nine team and individual sports.

Our goal is to attract more than 60,000 participants in 2015, more than triple the number of attendees of the inaugural year. Preliminary attendance for the recently completed SportsFest 2014 is projected to reach 55,000.

Most recent market research indicates:

94% of attendees intended to return to SportsFest the next year

87% rated their experience at SportsFest good to excellent

74% reported visiting the Hometown Market Midway

62% stated they expected to patronize sponsors of SportsFest

95% attended with other family members or friends

73% said they would return with more or the same number of family members or friends next year

78% of families have school-age children involved in one or more organized sports activities

45% of families have school-age children involved in two or more organized sports activities

Of attendees surveyed:

71% are 18+ years of age

58% are between 18 and 45 years of age

68% have a household income of more than $75,000 per year

84% have completed high school

63% have completed college

Source: Intercept surveys conducted during SportsFest 2013. Additional statistics and background are available upon request.

III. SportsFest 2015—Why Everyone Is "Getting Into It!"

SportsFest 2015 will combine proven fan favorites with attractions and programming that are totally new for its biggest year yet. There will be more to see, more to do, and more to enjoy than ever before! **Admission is free**. Tournament participation requires a registration fee to cover uniform t-shirts and other competition expenses.

This year's schedule includes nine sports tournaments for all age groups:

1. The Plainside Journal Baseball Classic
2. The Pyne Brothers Department Store Softball Tournament
3. The L&M Garden Center Field Hockey Championships*
4. Basketball*
5. Flag Football
6. P.B.F. Shoes Track & Field Meet
7. Shuffleboard*
8. Archery*
9. ***Freestyle Skateboarding (New for 2015)****

**Includes paralympic competition*

Plus . . .

- All-age clinics for all nine featured sports
- An expanded 350-seat multivendor food pavilion, presented by FF Supermarkets
- The Hometown Market Midway
- The KMMM-FM Radio Main Stage
- The Angel's Cola Entertainment Band Shell
- Three additional entertainment stages
- The Bob's Burgers Kid Zone
- The Mid-States Region Sports Hall of Fame Traveling Exhibit
- The SportsFest Country Store
- . . .and more!

IV. EVENT SCHEDULE

The 2015 edition of SportsFest will be held on the weekend of July 24–26. For our SportsFest partners and their guests, the fun will start right away!

Friday, July 24: 3 P.M. to 10 P.M.

3 P.M. Corporate Challenge SportsFest sponsor companies may participate in our Corporate Challenge Ironman Tournament at no charge. Each company may register a team of up to 20 participants to vie for Mid-States Region dominance, competing in skills competitions in each of our nine featured sports areas. The event site is open exclusively to all sponsor-company employees and their guests.

5 P.M. Grand Opening The public is officially welcomed to the event site when our 2015 SportsFest Grand Marshal arrives in a procession of **MSCDA**-provided convertibles to cut the "starting line" ribbon. Guests enjoy entertainment throughout SportsFest as they explore our 10 acres of sports and activity areas.

6 P.M. Mid-States Regional Media Challenge Newspapers, television stations, and radio stations compete for bragging rights in skills competitions within each of our nine featured sports areas, broadcasting live remotes and covering their stories from inside the dugouts and on the sidelines.

7 P.M. Grand Opening BBQ Celebration, presented by Angel's Cola The Mid-States Region's gastronomical event of the summer! Spread out the picnic blanket as you settle down to enjoy pit barbecue, ribs, chicken, roasted corn and local vegetables, fresh hearth-baked bread, ice cream, and apple pie with thousands of your potential customers, neighbors, friends, and family. While you eat, watch featured musical entertainment on the nearby KMMM-FM Radio Main Stage. Frisbees and beach balls optional!

Saturday, July 25: 8 A.M. – 10 P.M.

8 A.M. Let the Fun Begin! Mid-States Regional athletes of all ages begin competing in nine sports— baseball, softball, field hockey, basketball, flag football, track & field, shuffleboard, archery, and freestyle skateboarding.

Because competitors and their ardent supporters are always hungry, our Food Pavilion, presented by FF Supermarkets, opens with limited breakfast and coffee service at 7 A.M.

9 A.M. All Entertainment and Activity Areas Open There is truly something for everyone at SportsFest 2015!

Before and after checking out all the sports event action, guests will be able to explore the many products and services offered by our world-class sponsors at the **Hometown Market Midway**. The increasingly popular Midway is an outstanding opportunity for the **MSCDA** and each of our participating companies to meet thousands of SportsFest participants and attendees first hand, to demonstrate innovative models, products, and services, and to develop new customers!

Entertainment will abound at SportsFest 2015 with featured performers at the **KMMM-FM Radio Main Stage** and the **Angel's Cola Band Shell**, as well as **three additional entertainment stages** located throughout the event. Whether your interest is old-time rock and roll, country western, jazz, pop, blues or blue grass, SportsFest 2015 has become almost as much a showcase of local musical artists as it is of athletics and regional businesses. Don't be surprised to see your local high school band suddenly march across the Old Fairgrounds to the thundering cadence of drums and horns!

Kids from 5 to 12 are welcome to discover **Bob's Burgers Kid Zone**, a supervised activity center filled with safe play opportunities evocative of each of SportsFest 2015's nine featured sports. Parents can relax with a cup of Bob's famous coffee while their children enjoy either structured games or free play, inflatable bounces, and arts and crafts stations. Each young visitor receives a participant's gold medal, courtesy of Bob's Burgers.

Every area athlete will want to visit the **Mid-States Region Sports Hall of Fame Traveling Exhibit**, an inspirational exploration of the rich sports heritage of our communities. Four generations of trophies, memorabilia, and photographs of great moments in Mid-States sports are sources of great local pride—as are the achievements and memorabilia on display of Mid-States alumni in college and professional athletics throughout the world!

A wide range of delicious food will be available at our multivendor **Food Pavilion, presented by FF Supermarkets**. From burgers and wings to grilled sandwiches and healthful salads, the Pavilion will offer delights to suit the most discriminating palate. Although most SportsFest guests enjoy eating under the sun—or on the run—the dining area under the Pavilion tent has been expanded to accommodate those wishing to consume their meals in the shade and at a more leisurely pace.

Guests will shop for official SportsFest merchandise, local crafts, and take-home confections at the **SportsFest Country Store**. Concessionaires will also be on hand to offer sundries including, batteries, sunscreen, sunglasses, and other items to make the day at SportsFest that much more memorable and enjoyable.

11 A.M. All-Age Clinics Begin You're never too old and never too young to learn the rules of the game and get pointers from our region's accomplished athletes in all nine featured sports at the Sports Clinic attraction. Forty-minute sports clinics for a range of age groups are offered every hour on the hour until the evening's events at 6 P.M.

1 P.M. Picnic on the Green, presented by Angel's Cola Bring your blanket for a trip back to a simpler time. Enjoy a five-cent glass of Angel's Cola as the Mid-States All-Star Brass Band plays a tribute to the music of the early 20th century at the Angel's Cola Band Shell. Prizes will be awarded for the best circa-1920 costumes!

6 P.M. Mid-States Region Pasta Cook-off, benefiting Starlight Foundation Replenish yourself after a full weekend of watching or playing in athletic competition at SportsFest's now-famous pasta feast! Bring the whole family for heaping bowls of salad, spaghetti, meatballs and sauce, garlic bread, and other treats. Tickets are $10 for adults and $5 for kids, with proceeds benefiting the Mid-States Region chapter of the Starlight Foundation. Save room for dessert!

7 P.M. Mid-States Region Fruit Pie Bake-off, benefiting Youth Sports Who bakes the best fruit pies in the Mid-States Region? You be the judge, and then destroy the evidence! Proceeds benefit our community's youth recreation programs.

8 P.M. Headline Concert at KMMM-FM Radio Main Stage A top-name musical artist (to be announced in late Winter 2014) will round out a full day of fun. Past performers have included: *Cheryl Byrd, Second Ear, Cryptic Message*, and *Two for Holding*.

Sunday, July 26: 9 A.M. – 9 P.M.

9 A.M. Let the Fun Continue! Competition in all nine sports—baseball, softball, field hockey, basketball, flag football, track & field, shuffleboard, and archery, freestyle skateboarding continues.

9 A.M. All Entertainment and Activity Areas Open

11 A.M. All-Age Clinics Begin Forty-minute sports clinics for various age groups are offered every hour on the hour until 5 P.M., with "elite" clinics available for more seasoned athletes at 1 P.M. and 3 P.M.

7 P.M. SportsFest 2015 Parade of Athletes & Medal Ceremonies Cheer on all of your SportsFest 2015 neighbors, family and friends. All registered tournament participants are welcome to march to the KMMM-FM Main Stage for a salute to the athletes and the presentation of medals. Everyone who participated in the nine featured competitive tournaments will be recognized.

8 P.M. SportsFest 2015 Ice Cream Social, benefiting the Mid-States Shelter Relax after the pomp and pageantry of the medal ceremonies at the SportsFest Ice Cream Social, a place to greet your friends and meet new ones. The $3.00 sundae buffet, with do-it-yourself toppings, benefits the Mid-States Shelter. Take your sundae to your favorite location at SportsFest for the excitement at 9:00 P.M.!

9 P.M. SportsFest 2005 Grand Finale Fireworks Spectacular Tens of thousands of Mid-States Region citizens and guests will enjoy a spectacular fireworks extravaganza visible for miles around, set to a sports theme soundtrack broadcast on KMMM-FM radio. When the show is over and the smoke clears, you will wonder just how you will be able to wait another full year to see what SportsFest 2016 will have to offer!

Additional special events and entertainment will be scheduled throughout the weekend at times to be determined.

V. HOW THE MSCDA CAN *"GET INTO IT!"*

The **MSCDA** can GET INTO IT in a big way as a title or presenting sponsor of SportsFest 2015, as a tournament sponsor, activity area sponsor, or as a nonexclusive event participant.

SportsFest 2015 can provide the **MSCDA** with outstanding opportunities to feature your new models, offer test drives, raise awareness, promote special sales and financing incentives, and entertain important fleet customers.

In addition, the **MSCDA** can reinforce its position as a major corporate citizen in our community, joining a proud family of sponsors that includes: Angel's Cola, Bob's Burgers, FF Supermarkets, KMMM-FM Radio, L&M Garden Center, P.B.F. Shoes, Pyne Brothers Department Store, the Plainside Journal, Community Bank, Tomvel Ice Cream, Dell's Sports, and a host of official suppliers.

The pages that follow describe just some of the ways the **MSCDA** can **GET INTO IT!**

GOLD MEDAL—TITLE SPONSORSHIP

- SportsFest 2015 will be renamed **MSCDA SportsFest 2015**.
- The **MSCDA** will be integrated into the highly recognizable SportsFest logo and featured in all event site signage, banners, promotional point-of-purchase displays, newspaper advertising, television commercials, and event merchandise. All event press releases will include acknowledgment of the **MSCDA** as the title sponsor of SportsFest 2015.
- All third-party sponsor promotions authorized by the event organizer will be required to include the **MSCDA** identification in the event name.
- The **MSCDA** will be given the exclusive right to promote itself as the **"Official Car Dealership Association of SportsFest 2015."** All member dealers will be given the exclusive right to promote themselves as **"Members of the Official Car Dealership Association of SportsFest 2015."**
- The **MSCDA** and its member dealers will be granted exclusivity as sponsors of SportsFest 2015 in the automotive sales, service, and after-market parts categories.
- The **MSCDA** will be granted the opportunity to conduct test drives, subject to safety restrictions, in a mutually agreeable area adjacent to the event site. The **MSCDA** will have the right to provide shuttle transportation from the main entrance of StreetFest to the test drive site.
- An **MSCDA** representative will be given the opportunity to participate as a featured speaker in the grand opening ceremonies, as well as during the closing addresses prior to the Fireworks Spectacular.
- An **MSCDA** representative will participate on stage during the Medal Ceremonies on Sunday night.
- The **MSCDA** will be granted a 40' × 40' exhibit area in the Hometown Market Midway. Up to twelve (12) automobiles may be parked around the Midway as static displays, with signage promoting the test drives and dealer promotions.
- The **MSCDA** may additionally select one available tournament area to be recognized as the presenting sponsor. Currently available tournaments include basketball, flag football, shuffleboard, archery, and freestyle skateboarding.
- The **MSCDA** may additionally select one available entertainment activity to be recognized as the presenting sponsor. Currently available entertainment activities include the

fireworks spectacular, ice cream social, pasta cook-off, fruit pie bake-off, and the medal ceremonies.

- The **MSCDA** will be granted to right to conduct an exclusive SportsFest 2015 sweepstakes promotion in the Plainside Journal (see below).
- The **MSCDA** will have the exclusive right to provide the weekend's grand drawing prize of one-year's use of a brand new car for one lucky winner.
- The **MSCDA** will receive two hundred (200) complimentary tickets to each of the pasta cook-off, the fruit pie bake-off, and the ice cream social.
- The **MSCDA** will receive one (1) complimentary team registration for the **MSCDA** SportsFest Corporate Challenge.
- The **MSCDA** will receive ten (10) complimentary athlete registrations for each of the tournament's nine featured sports.
- The **MSCDA** will have the exclusive use of a 40' × 40' VIP tent for private receptions and entertaining. (Furnishings, food, beverage, entertainment, signage, and decoration are at **MSCDA**'s cost.)
- The **MSCDA** will receive two hundred (200) complimentary daily passes to the SportsFest 2015 VIP Hospitality Tent.
- The **MSCDA** will receive twenty (20) backstage passes for the Headline Concert, including a meet-and-greet opportunity with the artist (subject to the artist's contract restrictions). Fifty percent (50%) of these backstage passes must be given away as part of a consumer promotion by the **MSCDA** and its member dealers.
- The **MSCDA** will receive fifty (50) VIP seating passes for the Headline Concert. Guests will be seated on a first-come, first-served basis.
- The **MSCDA** will receive one hundred (100) VIP SportsFest merchandise packs, including a t-shirt, cap, pin, and commemorative poster. Fifty percent (50%) of these merchandise packs must be given away as part of a consumer promotion by the **MSCDA** and its member dealers.

MSCDA SPORTSFEST 2015 GOLD MEDAL TITLE SPONSORSHIP: $150,000

SILVER MEDAL—PRESENTING SPONSORSHIP

- SportsFest 2015 will be renamed **SportsFest 2005, presented by MSCDA**.
- The **MSCDA** name will be associated with the SportsFest 2015 logo (e.g., SportsFest 2015, presented by the **MSCDA**), and featured in all event site signage, banners, newspaper advertising, television commercials, and event merchandise. All event press releases will include acknowledgment of the **MSCDA** as the presenting sponsor of SportsFest 2015.
- The **MSCDA** will be given the exclusive right to promote itself as the **"Official Car Dealership Association of SportsFest 2015."** All member dealers will be given the exclusive right to promote themselves as **"Members of the Official Car Dealership Association of SportsFest 2015."**
- The **MSCDA** and its member dealers will be granted exclusivity as sponsors of SportsFest 2015 in the automotive sales, service, and after-market parts categories.
- The **MSCDA** will be granted the opportunity to conduct test drives, subject to safety restrictions, in a mutually agreeable area adjacent to the event site.
- An **MSCDA** representative will be given the opportunity to participate as a featured speaker in the grand opening ceremonies, as well as during the closing addresses prior to the Fireworks Spectacular.

- An **MSCDA** representative will participate on stage at the Medal Ceremonies on Sunday night.
- The **MSCDA** will be granted a 20' × 20' exhibit area in the Hometown Market Midway. Up to six (6) automobiles may be parked around the Midway as static displays, with signage promoting the test drives and dealer promotions.
- The **MSCDA** may additionally select one available tournament to be recognized as the presenting sponsor. Currently available tournaments include basketball, flag football, shuffleboard, archery, and freestyle skateboarding.
- The **MSCDA** will be granted to right to conduct an exclusive SportsFest 2015 sweepstakes promotion with SportsFest 2015 in the Plainside Journal.
- The **MSCDA** will have the exclusive right to provide the weekend's grand drawing prize of one-year's use of a brand new car for one lucky winner.
- The **MSCDA** will receive one hundred (100) complimentary tickets to each of the pasta cook-off, the fruit pie bake-off, and the ice cream social.
- The **MSCDA** will receive one (1) complimentary team registration for the **MSCDA** SportsFest Corporate Challenge.
- The **MSCDA** will receive five (5) complimentary athlete registrations for each of the tournament's nine featured sports.
- The **MSCDA** will have the exclusive use of a 20' × 20' VIP tent for private receptions and entertaining. (Furnishings, food, beverage, entertainment, signage, and decoration are at **MSCDA**'s cost.)
- The **MSCDA** will receive one hundred (100) complimentary daily passes to the SportsFest 2015 VIP Hospitality Tent.
- The **MSCDA** will receive ten (10) backstage passes for the Headline Concert, including a meet-and-greet opportunity with the artist (subject to the artist's contract restrictions). Fifty percent (50%) of these backstage passes must be given away as part of a consumer promotion by the **MSCDA** and its member dealers.
- The **MSCDA** will receive twenty (20) VIP seating area passes for the Headline Concert. Guests will be seated on a first-come, first-served basis.
- The **MSCDA** will receive fifty (50) VIP SportsFest merchandise packs, including a t-shirt, cap, pin, and commemorative poster. Fifty percent (50%) of these merchandise packs must be given away as part of a consumer promotion by the **MSCDA** and its member dealers.

SPORTSFEST 2015 presented by the MSCDA SILVER MEDAL PRESENTING SPONSORSHIP: $100,000

BRONZE MEDAL—OFFICIAL SPONSORSHIP

- The **MSCDA** name will be recognized on a rotational basis in banners, newspaper advertising, television commercials. All event press releases will include recognition of **MSCDA** as an official sponsor of SportsFest 2015.
- The **MSCDA** will be given the exclusive right to promote itself as the **"Official Car Dealership Association of SportsFest 2015."** All member dealers will be given the

exclusive right to promote themselves as **"Members of the Official Car Dealership Association of SportsFest 2015."**

- The **MSCDA** and its member dealers will be granted exclusivity as sponsors of SportsFest 2015 in the automotive sales, service, and after-market parts categories.
- The **MSCDA** will be granted a 10' × 10' exhibit area in the Hometown Market Midway.
- The **MSCDA** may select one available tournament to be recognized as the presenting sponsor. Currently available tournaments include basketball, flag football, shuffleboard, and archery.
- The **MSCDA** will be granted to right to conduct an exclusive SportsFest 2015 sweepstakes promotion in print media of its choice at its own expense.
- The **MSCDA** will receive thirty (30) complimentary tickets to each of the pasta cook-off, the fruit pie bake-off, and the ice cream social.
- The **MSCDA** will receive one (1) complimentary team registration for the **MSCDA** SportsFest Corporate Challenge.
- The **MSCDA** will receive two (2) complimentary athlete registrations for each of the tournament's nine featured sports.
- The **MSCDA** will receive twenty (20) complimentary daily passes to the SportsFest 2015 VIP Hospitality Tent.
- The **MSCDA** will receive four (4) backstage passes for the Headline Concert, including a meet-and-greet opportunity with the artist (subject to the artist's contract restrictions).
- The **MSCDA** will receive eight (8) VIP seating area passes for the Headline Concert. Guests will be seated on a first-come, first-served basis.
- The **MSCDA** will receive twenty (20) VIP SportsFest merchandise packs, including a t-shirt, cap, pin, and commemorative poster. Fifty percent (50%) of these merchandise packs must be given away as part of a consumer promotion by the **MSCDA** and its member dealers.

The MSCDA—The official automobile sales, service, and after-market parts sponsor of SPORTSFEST 2015: $60,000

ACHIEVER MEDAL—OFFICIAL SUPPLIER

- The **MSCDA** name will be recognized on a rotational basis in banners, newspaper advertising, and television commercials.
- The **MSCDA** will be given the right to promote itself as the **"Official Supplier to SportsFest 2015."**
- The **MSCDA** will receive ten (10) complimentary tickets to each of the pasta cook-off, the fruit pie bake-off, and the ice cream social.
- The **MSCDA** will receive one (1) complimentary team registration for the **MSCDA** SportsFest Corporate Challenge.
- The **MSCDA** will receive four (4) complimentary daily passes to the SportsFest 2015 VIP Hospitality Tent.
- The **MSCDA** will receive four (4) VIP seating area passes for the Headline Concert. Guests will be seated on a first-come, first-served basis.
- The **MSCDA** will receive eight (8) VIP SportsFest merchandise packs, including a t-shirt, cap, pin, and commemorative poster.

THE MSCDA: An official supplier to SPORTSFEST 2015 $25,000

VI. NEXT STEPS

SportsFest 2015 and D.E.F. Sports & Entertainment are excited about the possibility of welcoming the **MSCDA** to our prestigious family of sponsors.

Please note that only one title sponsorship, one presenting sponsorship, and a limited number of exclusive official sponsorships are available at this time. Additional official sponsors may be confirmed subsequent to the presentation of this proposal.

The sponsorship packages described in this proposal have been prepared to reflect the **MSCDA**'s stated desire to increase the exposure of its member dealerships to area residents and to encourage test drives by potential car purchasers. Additional sponsorship opportunities may be customized to best fit the needs of the **MSCDA**. We look forward to working with you to create a dynamic partnership that will help the **MSCDA** meet its marketing objectives, and exceed its expectations.

Please call:
Jack D'Andrea
Executive Director
SportsFest 2015
1836 Adams Street
Brownsville, MO 00000
Tel: 000-000-0000
Fax: 000-000-0000
Jdandrea@sportsfest.net

APPENDIX 8

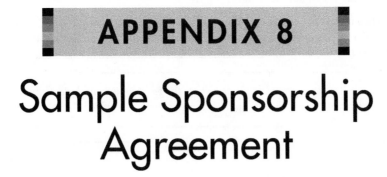

Sample Sponsorship Agreement

Note: This sample abbreviated sponsorship agreement is provided for illustrative purposes only. It should not be used as a legal document without the review and advice of competent legal counsel. Additional sections should be added to memorialize any additional elements agreed to during negotiations.

* * *

DATE__________

Corporate Name of Sponsor
Attn: Contact Name
Address
Re: *Name of Event*

Dear ____________________:

This letter, when executed by the parties, shall set forth the agreement (the "Agreement") between ____________________ (the "Company") and ________________ (the "Event Organizer"), relating to the Company's sponsorship of ________________________ (the "Event").

1. DEFINITIONS

As used herein, the following terms shall have the following meanings:
1.1. "Event" shall consist of *(Insert a full description of the event here, including dates, times, and location)* ____
____

1.2. The Company acknowledges and agrees that, subject to the Event Organizer's obligations to the Company as set forth herein, the Event Organizer shall have complete creative and operational control over every aspect of the Event.

1.3. "Marks" shall mean the following: (i) the name and logo of the Event, (ii) the name and logo of Event Organizer, (iii) any marks developed after the date of this Agreement that describe elements of the Event or contain the name of the Event.

1.4. "Term" shall mean the period beginning as of the date of this Agreement and ending on *(insert the expiration date of the sponsorship agreement, typically shortly after the last event the sponsor has agreed to support if multiple years)* ____

____.

1.5. "Territory" shall mean *(specifically describe here the geographic boundaries defined by the sponsorship, i.e., the name of the community, state, or broader territory in which the sponsor will have marketing rights to the event)*____

____.

2. MARKETING RIGHTS

The Event Organizer hereby grants to the Company the following sponsorship rights in connection with the Event in the Territory and during the Term, subject to and in accordance with the terms and conditions set forth in this Agreement:
2.1. The Event shall be referred to as *(insert the official title of the event here, including title or presenting sponsor references, if applicable)*________________________________. This title shall be used in all promotional, advertising, and other materials prepared by each of the Event Organizer and the Company, in connection with the Event.

2.2. The Company shall have the right to use the Marks in connection with Event-themed advertising and promotional programs in print, online, radio and television media, at retail locations, and points of purchase in the Territory during the Term at its sole cost and expense. Each such advertising or promotional program shall be subject to the approval of the Event Organizer in its sole discretion.

2.3. The Company shall have the right to distribute product samples or premiums at its own expense using the Marks in the Territory during the Term. Each such product sample or premium prepared for distribution using the Marks must be approved by the Event Organizer in its sole discretion.

2.4. The Company shall be included in all print, online, radio and television advertising promoting the Event, including but not limited to press releases concerning the Event; signage placed in various locations throughout the Event listing corporate sponsors of the Event, and acknowledgment in the Official Program and on any mobile device applications made available to the public.

2.5. The Company shall be entitled to five (5) public address announcements during the Event, each of no more than twenty (20) seconds duration. The timing and placement in the program of such public address announcements is at the sole discretion of the Event Organizer.

2.6. The Company shall be entitled to two (2) commercial spots each of no more than thirty (30) seconds duration to be displayed during the Event on the scoreboard video screen and approved for use by the Event Organizer in its sole discretion. The timing and placement in the program of such commercial spots is at the sole discretion of the Event Organizer.

3. OTHER BENEFITS

(Note: Benefits outlined below are for a hypothetical sports event. Include all benefits other than Marketing Rights in this section.)

The Company shall receive, at no additional cost:

3.1. Number (#) tickets to the Event in the Premium Seating section of the Facility.

3.2. Number (#) tickets to the Event in other sections of the Facility on a best-available basis.

3.3. Number (#) tickets to each of the pregame hospitality suite and the postevent party.

3.4 Number (#) invitations to the VIP athlete meet-and-greet opportunity on the evening prior to the Event.

4. COMPENSATION

In full consideration for the rights granted and agreements made hereunder, the Company shall pay to the Event Organizer a fee equal to $____________ in the aggregate, which shall be payable as follows: $______________ upon execution of this agreement, $______________ on or before ______________, and $______________ on or before ______________.

5. REPRESENTATIONS, WARRANTIES, AND COVENANTS

The Company shall indemnify and hold harmless the Event Organizer, its owners, directors, governors, officers, employees, agents, successors, and assigns, from and against any claims, demands, causes of action, suits, proceedings, judgments, losses, liabilities, damages, injuries, costs, and expenses arising out of, resulting from, or which, if true, would arise out of or result from, any act or omission of the Company relating to this Agreement; or misrepresentation, breach of warranty, or other breach of any obligation or covenant made by Company in this Agreement. Without limitation of the indemnification hereunder, the Company shall maintain both general liability and product liability insurance, in customary amounts and on reasonable terms, which policies shall include the Event Organizer and its owners, directors, governors, officers, partners, partnerships, principals, employees, agents, successors, and assigns as additional insureds.

6. TERMINATION

6.1. The Event Organizer may terminate this Agreement by written notice to Company should Company fail to make any payment required hereunder when due, or observe or perform any of its other material obligations under this Agreement, in each case if such failure, if curable, is not cured within five (5) business days after receipt by Company of written notice of thereof.

6.2. This Agreement shall terminate automatically if either party files any voluntary, or if there is filed against either party an involuntary, petition in bankruptcy under the Bankruptcy Act.

7. MISCELLANEOUS

The Company shall not assign this Agreement to any person, corporation, or other entity without the prior written consent of the Event Organizer. The Event Organizer shall not assign this Agreement to any person, corporation, or other entity, other than to a parent, subsidiary, or other affiliate, without the prior written consent of the Company. This Agreement and all of the terms and provisions hereof, will be binding upon, and will inure to the benefit of, the parties hereto and their respective successors and permitted assigns.

Please indicate your agreement with the foregoing terms by signing and dating both of the enclosed copies of this Agreement and returning them to me. A fully executed Agreement will be returned to you promptly thereafter.

Sincerely,

Event Organizer

By: ______________________________

Name: ____________________________

Title: _____________________________

ACCEPTED AND AGREED, this ______day of __________, ____.

The Company

By: ______________________________

Name: ____________________________

Title: _____________________________

APPENDIX 9

Sports Event Participant Release

This sample participant waiver and release is provided for illustrative purposes only. It should not be used as a legal document without the review and advice of competent legal counsel.

Name ("Participant"): ______________________________

Address: ______________________________

____

Email: ______________________________

Telephone (Home): ______________________________

Telephone (Mobile): ______________________________

RELEASE FROM LIABILITY. By freely agreeing to participate in (name of event) (the "Event") as a volunteer, athlete, sports activity participant, or attendee, the "Participant," and if the Participant is younger than 18 years old, his/her parent or guardian, hereby voluntarily agree to release (name of organizer) (the "Sports Event Organizer"), each owner, operator, and management agent of each event facility, each sponsor, agency, vendor, independent contractor, and person, partnership, or corporation engaged by the Sports Event Organizer, and each of their respective parent entities, subsidiaries, stockholders, affiliates, and other related entities, and each officer, director, employee, volunteer, licensor, sponsor, partner, principal, representative, and agent of the Sports Event Organizer and each of the foregoing, and all of the foregoing's respective successors and assigns (collectively, the "Releasees"), from, and waive in respect of each Releasee and covenant not to sue any Releasee for any and all liabilities, losses, damages, costs, expenses, causes of action, suits, and claims of any nature whatsoever (collectively, the "Liabilities") arising from, based on, or relating to personal injury or death to, or damage to or loss of property of, the Participant sustained in connection with the Participant's participation in any activity or event associated with the Event, or travel to or from any of the foregoing activities or events. Such release, discharge, waiver, and covenant not to sue shall include, but not be limited to, any and all such Liabilities caused in whole or in part by the negligence of any Releasee in connection with such Releasee's involvement with the Event.

PARTICIPANT ASSUMES RISK. The Participant is aware of and understands the inherent risks and dangers of the Event in which he or she will be participating and the potential for injury that exists when participating in the Event, and agrees to assume all risk of and responsibility for personal injury or death to, or damage to or loss of property of, the Participant arising from, or relating to the Participant's participation in the Event. Such assumption of risk includes, but is not limited to, any personal injury or death, or damage to or loss of property caused in whole or in part by the negligence of any Releasee. The Participant understands and agrees that, in the event of any injury to the Participant, none of the Releasees will be responsible for any decisions relating to medical treatment for the Participant or for such treatment itself.

RIGHT OF PUBLICITY. Participation in the Event shall constitute permission to use the name, likeness, or any other identification of the Participant for advertising, publicity, or any other purposes in connection with the Event or the business of any of the Releasees, in any medium and at any time, in perpetuity, and without compensation to or right of prior review or approval by the Participant or his or her parent or legal guardian (except where prohibited by law). The Participant agrees, for itself and its personal representatives, executors, administrators, heirs, next of kin, successors and assigns, to release and discharge each Releasee from, to waive in respect of each Releasee, and not to sue any Releasee for, any and all Liabilities arising from, based on, or relating to any claim for invasion of privacy, violation of right of publicity, defamation, or appropriation in connection with any such use.

NO OBLIGATION OF RELEASEES. None of the Releasees shall have, or be deemed to have, any obligation to the Participant hereunder or otherwise in connection with the Event unless set forth in writing signed by the Participant and the Releasee.

MISCELLANEOUS. This Release shall be governed by and construed in accordance with the laws of _(state or province in which the organizer is incorporated)_____. If any portion of this Release shall be held invalid or unenforceable, the remaining portion hereof shall not be affected thereby and shall remain in full force and effect.

REPRESENTATIONS. The Participant and his or her parent or legal guardian states that he/she has had full opportunity to ask any questions regarding the Event that he or she may have, that he or she has read and understands this Release (or that his or her parent or legal guardian has read and understands this Release, and has explained it to the Participant), and that he or she has been given an opportunity to review this Release with anyone he or she chooses, including a lawyer, and has done so to the extent he or she wishes to do so. The Participant further states that he or she is in good physical condition, is physically fit to participate in the Event, and is not subject to any medical condition that poses or may pose any risk of harm or disability to others.

_________________________________ Date: ______________________

(Signature of Participant)

I am over the age of 18 as of this date: _________Yes _________No

Name of Parent or Guardian (Please Print) if Participant is Under 18:

_________________________________ Date: ______________________

(Signature of Parent or Guardian)

Emergency Contact Name:___________________________________

Emergency Contact Telephone Number:_________________________

Emergency Contact Email:___________________________________

APPENDIX 10

Sample Sports Event Rundown (pre-event)

MNO Sports, Inc.

FIVE COUNTY FOOTBALL TOURNAMENT
FINAL GAME RUNDOWN
(as of November 28)

#	TIME	SEGMENT	R/T	DESCRIPTION	AUDIO	VIDEO/SCOREBOARD
1	7:00:00	**House Open**	0:30:00	Audience enters. Lights at opening preset levels. Gobos in corners. Stage managers to get players out of locker rooms at 7:25:00.	P.A. Mic: Welcome & sponsor recognition (Pea Pond Mills, Pete's Pies, Faroff Airlines, Metro Daily News Online) over music file 1.1–1.9 (open mix)	Event & sponsor logos in rotation; Welcome. Sponsor logos displayed during recognition (Pea Pond Mills, Pete's Pies, Faroff Airlines, Metro Daily News Online).
2	7:30:00	**Player Warm-ups**	0:20:00	Players enter and warm up on field. Lights on full competition level.	Music file 2.1–2.6 (warm-up mix)	Event & sponsor logos displayed in rotation; Welcome.
3	7:50:00	**Set Up Opening Ceremonies**	0:10:00	Players leave field. Dim lights to house open level. Crew sets up opening ceremonies riser at 50-yard line. Band, flag bearers, and kick line at position on sidelines at 7:57:00.	Music file 3.1–3.3 (set up mix)	Event & sponsor logos in rotation; Welcome. Sponsor logos displayed during recognition.
4	8:00:00	**Five County High Schools All-Star Marching Band**	0:03:30	Lights on full. Massed Five County High Schools All-Star Marching Band, flag bearers, and kick line enter field from sidelines to drum cadence, then perform: "Remember the Titans."	Fade music. Marching Band plays live	"Please Welcome the Five County High Schools All-Star Marching Band!"

5	8:03:30	**Host Welcome**	0:01:00	Public address announcer welcomes J.J. Jayson. Jayson walks from sideline to opening ceremonies riser and welcomes audience. Jayson intros Superintendent of Schools Andrew Anderson.	P.A. Mic for Host Introduction; riser mic	"WFMS Host J.J. Jayson"
6	8:04:30	**Superintendent of Schools**	0:02:00	Superintendent Anderson walks from sideline to opening ceremonies riser and speaks from riser mic. Exits to sidelines when finished with remarks.	Riser mic	"Superintendent of Schools Andrew Anderson"
7	8:06:30	**Introduction of the Players**	0:06:00	Jayson returns to mic. Band plays on cue as teams run from sidelines (without helmets!) to their respective 20-yard lines. Jayson introduces each player; players wave.	Riser mic; Marching Band (live)	"The Five County High Schools All-Stars!"
8	8:12:30	**National Anthem**	0:02:00	Jayson introduces Betty Fumbles to sing National Anthem. Fumbles walks from sideline halfway to riser holding wired microphone. Players and singer face band's color guard. Fumbles sings.	Riser mic; Singer mic	"Our National Anthem"
9	8:14:30	**Ready to Go!**	0:02:30	Fumbles exits. Jayson thanks all, departs. Players to proper sidelines. Band, flag bearers, and kick line march off to "*On Wisconsin!*" Crew removes ceremony riser.	Riser mic; Marching Band (live)	"Welcome to the Five County Football Tournafest!"
10	8:17:00	**KICKOFF!**		Band continues playing until kickoff.	Marching Band (live) until kickoff	"It's Game Time!"

APPENDIX 11

Sport Management Programs: United States

Following is a list of universities offering sport management programs in the United States at the time of publication.

Name	Bachelor's	Master's	Doctoral
Adams State College	✓	✓	
Alfred State College	✓		
Alvernia College	✓		
American Military University	✓	✓	
American Public University	✓	✓	
Aquinas College, MI	✓		
Arkansas State University	✓	✓	
Ashland University	✓	✓	
Auburn University		✓	
Averett University	✓		
Baldwin-Wallace College	✓		
Ball State University	✓	✓	
Barry University, FL	✓	✓	
Baylor University		✓	
Bellevue University	✓		
Belmont University		✓	
Bemidji State University	✓		
Bowling Green State University	✓	✓	
Cal State University–Bakersfield	✓		

Name	Bachelor's	Master's	Doctoral
California Baptist University		✓	
California Polytechnic State University	✓		
California State University–Long Beach		✓	
California State University–Fresno		✓	
California University at Pennsylvania	✓	✓	
Canisius College		✓	
Cardinal Stritch University	✓	✓	
Castleton State College	✓		
Cazeenovia College	✓		
Cedarville University	✓		
Centenary College	✓		
Central Michigan	✓	✓	
Chowan College, NC	✓		
Christian Brothers University	✓		
Claflin University	✓		
Clemson University	✓		
Cleveland State University	✓	✓	
Coastal Carolina University	✓		
Colby-Sawyer College	✓		
College Misericordia	✓		
College of Mount St. Joseph	✓		
College of Saint Rose, Albany, NY	✓		
Columbia College Chicago	✓		
Coppin State College	✓		
Corban University	✓		
Daemen College	✓		
Dakota Wesleyan University	✓		
Dana College	✓		
Daniel Webster College, NH	✓		
Davenport University	✓		
Defiance College	✓		
Delaware State University	✓	✓	
DeSales University	✓		
Dowling College	✓		

Drexel University	✓	✓	
Duquesne University	✓	✓	
East Carolina University		✓	
East Central University		✓	
East Stroudsburg University of Pennsylvania	✓	✓	
East Tennessee State University	✓	✓	
Eastern Illinois University	✓	✓	
Eastern Kentucky University	✓	✓	
Eastern Michigan University	✓	✓	
Eastern New Mexico University		✓	
Elms College	✓		
Elon University	✓		
Endicott College, MA	✓		
Fairleigh Dickinson University	✓	✓	
Flagler College	✓		
Florida A&M University		✓	
Florida Atlantic University		✓	
Florida International University	✓	✓	✓
Florida Southern College	✓		
Florida State University	✓	✓	✓
Fontbonne University	✓		
Fresno Pacific University		✓	
George Mason University	✓		
George Washington University		✓	
Georgetown University		✓	
Georgia Southern University	✓	✓	
Georgia State University		✓	
Glenville State College	✓		
Gonzaga University	✓	✓	
Graceland University	✓		
Grambling State University	✓	✓	
Grand Canyon University	✓		
Guilford College	✓		
Hampton University	✓		
High Point University	✓	✓	

Name	Bachelor's	Master's	Doctoral
Idaho State University		✓	
Illinois State University		✓	
Indiana State University	✓	✓	
Indiana University of Pennsylvania	✓	✓	
Indiana University Purdue University Indianapolis	✓		
Indiana University, Bloomington	✓	✓	✓
Ithaca College	✓	✓	
Jacksonville University	✓	✓	
James Madison University	✓	✓	
Johnson & Wales University	✓		
Judson University	✓		
Kennesaw State University	✓		
Kent State University	✓	✓	
Keystone College	✓		
Kutztown University	✓		
Lake Erie College	✓		
Lancaster Bible College	✓		
Lasell College	✓		
Lees-McRae College	✓		
Lewis University	✓		
Liberty University, VA	✓	✓	
Limestone College	✓		
Lincoln College–Normal	✓		
Lindenwood University	✓	✓	
Lipscomb University		✓	
Livingstone University	✓		
Lock Haven University of Pennsylvania	✓		
Loras College, IA	✓		
Louisiana State University	✓	✓	✓
Loyola University, Chicago	✓	✓	
Luther College	✓		
Lynchburg College	✓		
Lynn University	✓	✓	

MacMurray College	✓	
Madonna University	✓	
Manhattanville College		✓
Marian College	✓	
Marian College of Fond du Lac	✓	
Marquette University		✓
Marshall University	✓	✓
Martin Methodist College	✓	
Marymount University	✓	
Maryville University	✓	
Massachusetts College of Liberal Arts	✓	
McDaniel College	✓	✓
Medaille College	✓	
Menlo College	✓	
Mercy College	✓	
Merrimack College	✓	
Mesa State College	✓	
Messiah College	✓	
Metropolitan State College of Denver	✓	
Miami University	✓	
Michigan State University		✓
MidAmerica Nazarene University	✓	
Middle Tennessee State University		✓
Midway College	✓	
Millikin University	✓	
Minnesota State University, Mankato	✓	✓
Mississippi State University	✓	✓
Missouri Baptist University	✓	✓
Mitchell College	✓	
Montana State University–Billings		✓
Morehead State University	✓	✓
Mount Ida College	✓	
Mount St. Mary's University	✓	
Mount Union College	✓	
Nebraska Wesleyan University	✓	

Name	Bachelor's	Master's	Doctoral
Neumann College, PA	✓	✓	
New York University	✓	✓	
Newberry College	✓		
Niagara University	✓		
Nichols College	✓		
North Carolina State	✓	✓	✓
North Central College	✓		
North Dakota State University	✓	✓	
North Greenville University	✓		
Northcentral University	✓	✓	✓
Northeastern University's College of Professional Studies		✓	
Northern Illinois University		✓	
Northern Kentucky University	✓		
Northwestern University, School of Continuing Studies		✓	
Northwood University	✓		
Northwood University Florida Campus	✓		
Nova Southeastern University	✓		
Ohio Dominican University	✓		
Ohio Northern Universtiy	✓		
Ohio State University		✓	✓
Ohio University	✓	✓	
Oklahoma City University	✓		
Old Dominion University	✓	✓	
Olivet Nazarene University	✓		
Otterbein College	✓		
Palm Beach Atlantic University	✓		
Post University	✓		
Quincy University	✓		
Radford University	✓		
Regis College	✓		
Rice University	✓		
Robert Morris College	✓	✓	

Rogers State University	✓		
Rutgers University	✓		
Sacred Heart University	✓		
Saint Augustine's College	✓		
Saint John Fisher College	✓		
Saint Leo University, FL	✓	✓	
Saint Mary's College of California	✓	✓	
Salem International University	✓		
Salem State University	✓		
Sam Houston State University		✓	
San Diego State University		✓	
San Jose State University	✓	✓	
Schreiner University	✓		
Seattle Pacific University		✓	
Seattle University		✓	
Seton Hall University	✓	✓	
Shawnee State University	✓		
Shepherd College, West Virginia	✓		
Siena Heights University	✓		
Slippery Rock University	✓		
Southeast Missouri State University	✓	✓	
Southeastern University	✓		
Southern Illinois University	✓	✓	
Southern Methodist University	✓		
Southern Nazarene University	✓		
Southern New Hampshire University	✓	✓	
Southwest Missouri State University	✓		
Southwestern Christian University	✓		
Southwestern Oklahoma State University	✓	✓	
Sport Business University	✓		
Sports Management Worldwide	✓	✓	✓
Springfield College	✓	✓	
St. Ambrose University	✓		
St. Cloud State University		✓	
St. Edwards University		✓	

Name	Bachelor's	Master's	Doctoral
St. John's University	✓	✓	
St. Thomas University, FL	✓	✓	
Stetson University	✓		
SUNY at Brockport	✓	✓	
SUNY at Canton	✓		
SUNY at Cortland	✓	✓	
SUNY at Fredonia	✓	✓	
Syracuse University	✓		
Temple University	✓	✓	✓
Texas A&M	✓	✓	✓
Texas A&M University–Corpus Christi	✓		
Texas Tech University		✓	
Texas Woman's University		✓	✓
Thomas College	✓	✓	
Tiffin University	✓	✓	
Towson State University, MD	✓		
Troy University	✓	✓	
Tusculum College	✓		
U.S. Sports Academy, AL	✓	✓	✓
Union County College	✓		
University of Alabama		✓	
University of Arkansas at Little Rock		✓	
University of Arkansas, Fayetteville		✓	
University of Central Florida (College of Business Administration)		✓	
University of Central Florida (College of Education)	✓	✓	
University of Charleston	✓		
University of Cincinnati	✓		
University of Colorado at Colorado Springs	✓		
University of Connecticut	✓	✓	✓
University of Dallas Graduate School		✓	
University of Dayton	✓		

University of Delaware	✓	✓	
University of Denver		✓	
University of Findlay	✓		
University of Florida	✓	✓	✓
University of Georgia	✓	✓	✓
University of Houston	✓	✓	
University of Illinois	✓	✓	✓
University of Indianapolis	✓	✓	
University of Kansas	✓	✓	✓
University of Kentucky		✓	
University of Louisiana at Lafayette	✓		
University of Louisville	✓	✓	✓
University of Mary Hardin–Baylor	✓		
University of Maryland		✓	✓
University of Massachusetts	✓	✓	✓
University of Memphis	✓	✓	
University of Miami	✓	✓	
University of Michigan	✓	✓	✓
University of Minnesota	✓	✓	✓
University of Minnesota, Crookston	✓		
University of Missouri	✓		
University of Nebraska at Kearney	✓		
University of Nevada–Las Vegas (College of Education)		✓	✓
University of Nevada–Las Vegas (College of Hotel Administration)		✓	
University of New England	✓		
University of New Hampshire	✓	✓	
University of New Haven	✓	✓	
University of New Mexico		✓	✓
University of New Orleans	✓	✓	
University of North Carolina		✓	
University of North Florida	✓		
University of Northern Colorado		✓	✓
University of Oklahoma		✓	

Name	Bachelor's	Master's	Doctoral
University of Oregon	✓	✓	
University of Pittsburgh–Bradford	✓		
University of Saint Mary	✓		
University of San Francisco		✓	
University of South Carolina	✓	✓	
University of South Dakota	✓	✓	
University of Southern Indiana	✓		
University of Southern Maine	✓		
University of Southern Mississippi	✓	✓	
University of St. Francis	✓		
University of St. Thomas, MN		✓	
University of Tampa	✓		
University of Tennessee	✓	✓	✓
University of Tennessee at Chatanooga	✓		
University of Texas	✓	✓	✓
University of the Incarnate Word	✓	✓	
University of the Pacific	✓		
University of Washington		✓	
University of West Florida	✓		
University of West Georgia	✓		
University of Wisconsin–LaCrosse	✓	✓	
University of Wisconsin–Parkside	✓		
Virginia Commonwealth University		✓	
Viterbo University	✓		
Warner Southern College	✓		
Washington State University	✓	✓	
Wayne State College (NE)	✓	✓	
Wayne State University		✓	
Webber International University	✓	✓	
West Chester University of Pennsylvania		✓	
West Virginia University	✓	✓	
Western Carolina University	✓		
Western Illinois University		✓	
Western Kentucky University	✓	✓	

Western Michigan University		✓
Western New England College, MA	✓	
Wichita State University	✓	✓
Widener University	✓	
William Penn University	✓	
Wilmington College	✓	
Wilson College	✓	
Wingate University	✓	
Winston-Salem State University	✓	
Winthrop University	✓	
Xavier University, OH	✓	✓
York College of PA	✓	

Note: There are similar lists for Canada, Europe, Australia, New Zealand, India, Africa, and Asia

Source: North American Society for Sport Management, 2012, www.nassm.com

APPENDIX 12

Sports Industry Career Resources

Following is a list of important resources that can be helpful to anyone pursuing a career in the sports industry. There are other resources that career-seekers are encouraged to consult as well.

Associations and Organizations

International Association of Venue Managers (iavm.org)

International Facility Manager Association (ifma.org)

North American Society for Sports Management (nassm.com)

Sports Executive Association (sportsexec.net)

Publications

Facility Manager

International Journal of Sport Management and Marketing

International Journal of Sport Finance

Journal of Sport and Social Issues

Journal of Sports Economics

Journal of Sports Management

Sports Business Daily

Sports Business Journal

Sport Management Review

Stadium and Arena Management Magazine

Books and References

The Comprehensive Guide to Careers in Sports (2008), Glenn M. Wong

Career Opportunities in the Sports Industry, Fourth Ed. (2010), Shelly Field

A Career In Sports: Advice from Sports Business Leaders (2010), Michelle Wells, Andy Kreutzer, and Jim Kahler

Representing the Professional Athlete (2009), Peter A. Carfagna
Negotiating and Drafting Sports Venue Agreements (2010), Peter A. Carfagna

Broadcast Media
SportsBiz (CNBC)
Sportfolio (Bloomberg)
Darren Rovell (ESPN, ABC News)

Websites and Blogs
Job Resources
Game Face (gamefacesportsjobs.com)
Jobs in Sports (jobsinsports.com)
Pro Edge Sports Academy (proedgesportsacademy.com)
SportsCareers.com (sportscareers.com)
Sports Job Board (sportsjobboard.com)
SportsManagmentDegree.org (sportsmanagementdegree.org)
TeamWork Online (teamworkonline.com)
Turnkey Sports & Entertainment (turnkey.se.com)
Work in Sports (workinsports.com)

Sports Business and Information Resources
The Business of Sports (thebusinessofsports.com)
International Journal of Sport Finance (ijsf.wordpress.com)
The Sports Economist (thesportseconomist.com)
The Sports Business Exchange (thesportsbusinessexchange.com)
The Sports Info Business (sportsinfo101.com)
Sports Marketing and PR Roundup (joefavorito.com)
Sports Networker (sportsnetworker.com)
ESPN Playbook: Dollars Blog with Darren Rovell (espn.go.com/darren-rovell)
SportsBusiness Journal/Daily (sportsbusinessdaily.com)
SportsBlog Nation (sbnation.com)

Mobile and Web Apps for Events
BlinkMobile (blinkmobile.com.au)
Bloodhound (getbloodhound.com)
Cvent (cvent.com)
CrowdCompass (crowdcompass.com)
DoubleDutch (doubledutch.me)
Eventbird (eventbird.com)
Eventmobi (eventmobi.com)

EventBoard (www.eventboardmobile.com)
GenieMobile (geniemobile.com)
Guidebook (guidebook.com)
QuickMobile (quickmobile.com)
SwiftMobile (swiftmobile.com)
Zerista (zerista.com)
Zwoor Events (zwoor.com)

INDEX